KNOW BRITAIN

THE HERITAGE AND INSTITUTIONS OF AN OFFSHORE ISLAND

Lincoln Cathedral, built between 1072 and 1280. Although much of the original building was destroyed in an earthquake in 1185, some of the original Norman building survives at the west end of the present building which is in Gothic style

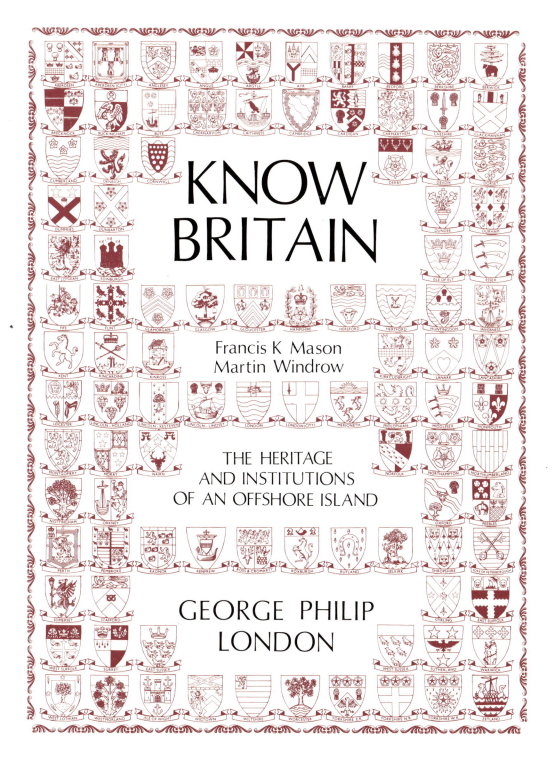

KNOW
BRITAIN

Francis K Mason
Martin Windrow

THE HERITAGE
AND INSTITUTIONS
OF AN OFFSHORE ISLAND

GEORGE PHILIP
LONDON

This book was designed and produced by
Alban Book Services Limited,
147 London Road, St. Albans, Herts, England

ISBN 0 540 00956 3

Published in Great Britain by
GEORGE PHILIP & SON LIMITED
12–14 Long Acre, London W.C.2

Filmset in 8/9 pt. Times New Roman 327
Printed in Great Britain on 118 gsm B.20 paper by
W. S. COWELL LIMITED
at the Butter Market, Ipswich, England

List of Contents

ACKNOWLEDGEMENTS

The sources consulted, and the individuals who assisted during the compilation of this book are too numerous to list here. The compilers wish to record their gratitude for all the help and co-operation which they enjoyed: and to mention that many of the figures quoted in the text, particularly in Chapters 3 and 4, are drawn from official tables published by the following departments of H.M. Government: Meteorological Office; Department of the Environment; Home Office; Ministry of Agriculture, Fisheries and Food; Department of Education and Science; Department of Health and Social Security; Central Statistical Office; Office of Population Censuses and Surveys; Department of Employment; Department of Trade and Industry; Ministry of Defence.

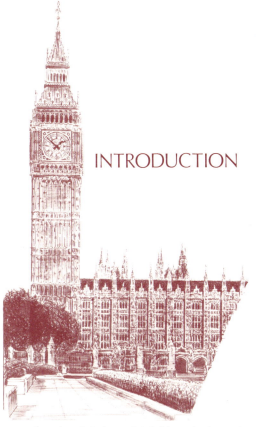

INTRODUCTION

For the sake of clarity and definition, the first point which must be made in this book is that strictly speaking there exists no geographical or political entity correctly named "Britain".

Several distinct but overlapping geographical and political units of identity exist simultaneously; their titles, both officially recognised and perpetuated by popular usage, reflect a chequered history of invasion, immigration, absorption and fragmentation over the past 2,000 years.

The British Isles is a geographical term referring to the group of approximately 920 islands which lie off the north-west coast of the European continental land-mass. In political terms these islands are divided into four parts, namely:

The United Kingdom of Great Britain and Northern Ireland
The Crown Dependency of the Isle of Man
The Crown Dependency of the Channel Islands
The Republic of Ireland

The last-named was previously known as The Irish Free State (January 1922 until December 1937) and as *Éire*. The Gaelic name for Ireland continues in general popular use. Simultaneously with the adoption of the new title, the Republic severed the last formal ties with the British Commonwealth. The use of the term "British Isles" in any political context is thus incorrect.

The United Kingdom of Great Britain and Northern Ireland, correctly abbreviated to "United Kingdom" but not to "Great Britain", is a political entity, the sovereign state loosely referred to as "Britain". Since 13th May 1927 the Parliament at Westminster has adopted as its style and title "The Parliament of the United Kingdom and Northern Ireland". Her Majesty Queen Elizabeth II, on her accession to the Crown on 6th February 1952, acceded to the style "By the Grace of God, of Great Britain, Ireland, and of the British Dominions beyond the Seas, Queen, Defender of the Faith". On 29th May 1953, shortly before her Coronation, the Royal style was brought into conformity with that of Parliament with regard to Ireland, becoming "By the Grace of God, of the United Kingdom of Great Britain and Northern Ireland and of Her other Realms and Territories, Queen, Head of the Commonwealth, Defender of the Faith".

Great Britain comprises the mainland of England, Scotland and the Principality of Wales, and the various off-shore islands administered as counties or as parts of mainland counties of Great Britain. The term was unofficially adopted on 24th March 1603 by King James VI of Scotland when, as James I, he succeeded to the English Crown, thereby bringing about a union of the kingdoms. The Principality of Wales had already been incorporated by Act of Parliament in 1536. Government of Great Britain is established centrally in Parliament at Westminster in London, although numerous administrative differences exist for Scotland and, to a lesser extent, for Wales.

Northern Ireland, now loosely referred to as Ulster (which was in fact formerly a larger province) comprises the six counties which became an integral part of the United Kingdom when the partition of Ireland took place in 1922. Northern Ireland sends a fixed number of twelve Members to the Westminster Parliament, and has, in addition, its own legislature and executive (the Stormont Parliament) to deal with domestic affairs. However, under the present conditions of civil unrest and wide-spread loss of life the Stormont Parliament was temporarily suspended in 1972 (statutorily for one year) and direct rule from Westminster restored. The Ireland Act 1949 provides that Northern Ireland cannot cease to be an integral part of the United Kingdom without the consent of Parliament at Westminster.

The Crown Dependency of the Isle of Man is situated in the Irish Sea, thirty miles from the nearest point in England (St. Bees Head in the county of Cumberland). A Lieutenant-Governor is appointed by the monarch, and the government is undertaken by the Tynwald, a very ancient assembly currently comprising the Legislative Council and the House of Keys. The current form of home-rule dates from 1866.

The Crown Dependency of the Channel Isles, although situated at their nearest point only ten miles from the coast of France, have a long-established history of loyalty to the Crown. The link dates effectively from 1106, when Henry I of England defeated Robert, Duke of Normandy at Tenchbrai and acquired Normandy, annexing the Islands to the English Crown. The two largest islands are Jersey and Guernsey; much smaller are the islands of Alderney, Sark, Herm, Brechou, Jethou, Lihou and about a dozen uninhabited islets. Administratively the islands are divided between the Bailiwicks of Jersey and Guernsey, the latter administering as dependencies all the smaller islands. Each Bailiwick has an ancient assembly (the States) which legislates on domestic matters, and a Lieutenant-Governor appointed by the monarch.

PHYSICAL FEATURES

The British Isles have a total area of about 121,650 square miles (314,940 sq. km.). The largest islands are Great Britain and Ireland; off the English south coast lies the Isle of Wight, and Anglesey lies off North Wales. The Isles of Scilly lie some distance off the extreme south-west of England. Western Scotland is fringed by numerous islands of all sizes, both inhabited and uninhabited; and the important groups of the Orkneys and Shetlands lie far to the North.

A detailed break-down of land-areas, excluding inland water, is as follows:

United Kingdom of Great Britain and Northern Ireland	93,027 square miles (240,940 sq. km.)
England	50,056 square miles (129,645 sq. km.)
Scotland	29,798 square miles (77,177 sq. km.)
Wales, including Monmouthshire	7,967 square miles (20,635 sq. km.)
Northern Ireland	5,206 square miles (13,484 sq. km.)

This apparently simple table illustrates the care which must be taken when evaluating British physical statistics. The figures above exclude inland water, as stated. The English figures exclude the border county of Monmouthshire, which occupies an ambiguous position, being included sometimes under English statistics and sometimes under Welsh. The Scottish figures include the 186 inhabited islands. The United Kingdom figures exclude the Crown Dependencies. (The Isle of Man has an area of 227·05 square miles, and the Channel Islands a total land area of approximately 75·13 square miles. Jersey and Guernsey, with 44·87 and 24·46 square miles respectively, make up the great bulk of this total.)

The total area of the British Isles thus represents roughly *one-fifth of one per cent* of the world's total land area.

England is divided into 39 geographical, or 46 administrative counties; Wales, including Monmouthshire, has 13 counties[1]; Scotland has 33 counties; and Northern Ireland, as stated above, has six.

The most northerly point of the island of Great Britain is Easter Head, on Dunnet Head, Caithness (Lat. 58° 40′ 25″ North); the most southerly is Lizard Point, Cornwall (Lat. 49° 57′ 33″ North). The most westerly point is Garbhlach Mhor, Argyllshire (long. 6° 14′ 12″ West); the prime meridian of 0° passes through the old Observatory of Greenwich, London, and the most easterly point is Lowestoft Ness, Suffolk (Long. 1° 46′ 20″ East). It is just under 600 miles (966 km.) as the crow flies from the extreme south to the extreme north of Great Britain, and just over 300 miles (483 km.) from east to west at the widest part. The coastline is so rich in bays, estuaries and inlets that no point in the British Isles is as much as 75 miles (121 km.) from tidal water.

The shores of the British Isles are washed by the Atlantic Ocean on their western seaboard, by the North Sea (approximately 222,000 square miles) on the north and east, and by the English Channel (approximately 38,000 square miles) to the south. The principal expanse of water separating Great Britain from Ireland is the Irish Sea (approximately 31,000 square miles including St. George's Channel in the south and the North Channel in the north).

Because the British Isles lie on the continental shelf, the seas surrounding them are consistently shallow; in most areas depths of less than 50 fathoms (300 feet, 91 metres) are recorded. To the north-west the edge of the shelf causes an abrupt drop from 600 to 3,000 feet (914 metres). The shallow waters have a characteristically violent tidal action. They are warmed by the North Atlantic Current, and are rich in marine life.

CLIMATE AND WEATHER

The British climate is temperate and generally mild, notable for frequent changes but few extremes. It is mainly controlled by a series of depressions from the Atlantic which move across or pass near the British Isles due to the prevailing south-westerly winds. During the summer months, owing to the extended influence of the Azores high pressure system, these depressions may pass to the north of Britain. During the winter an occasional period of cold, dry continental weather may persist with easterly winds.

Near sea level in the western areas of the British Isles the mean annual temperature ranges from 8°C (47°F) in the extreme north to 11°C (52°F) in the extreme south. At comparable latitudes the eastern part of the country is rather colder. The average monthly temperature in the winter months ranges from 4°C (39°F) in the Shetlands, to 5°C (41°F) in the extreme south. In summer, averages of 12°C (54°F) and 16°C (61°F) are recorded in these areas.

---

[1] Notwithstanding this division, Monmouthshire is described in Chapter 1 under English counties for the reason given on page 32.

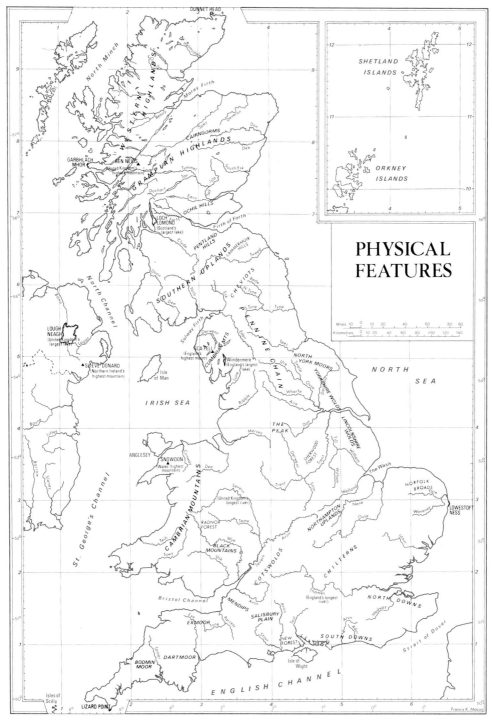

PHYSICAL
FEATURES

DUNNET HEAD

North Minch

WESTERN HIGHLANDS

Moray Firth

Beauly Spey Deveron

CAIRNGORMS

Don

Dee

GARBHLACH MHOR

BEN NEVIS
(United Kingdom's
highest mountain)

GRAMPIAN HIGHLANDS

Tummel South Esk

Dochart Tay Isla

Earn

OCHIL HILLS

LOCH LOMOND
(Scotland's
largest lake)

Forth Firth of Forth

Clyde PENTLAND HILLS LAMMERMUIR HILLS

SOUTHERN UPLANDS

Tweed

Doon Nith Esk CHEVIOTS Rede

North Channel

Bann

Dee Solway Firth Liddel North Tyne

Tyne Tyne

LOUGH NEAGH
(United Kingdom's
largest lake)

Lagan

SLIEVE DONARD
(Northern Ireland's
highest mountain)

Derwent SCA FELL
(England's
highest mount) CUMBRIAN MTS Windermere
(England's largest
lake)

PENNINE CHAIN

Tees

NORTH YORK MOORS

NORTH SEA

Ure YORKSHIRE WOLDS

Wharfe

Aire Ouse

Boyne

Isle
of Man

IRISH SEA

Ribble

Liffey

Barrow Slaney

St. George's Channel

Mersey

THE PEAK

Dove LINCOLNSHIRE WOLDS

ANGLESEY Conway Dee

SNOWDON
(Wales' highest
mountain)

Derwent SHERWOOD FOREST Trent

Soar Witham

The Wash

Welland NORFOLK BROADS Yare

LOWESTOFT NESS

Waveney

CAMBRIAN MOUNTAINS

Severn
(United Kingdom's
longest river)

Teifi RADNOR FOREST Teme Trent Nene Ouse Stour

Towy Wye BLACK MOUNTAINS

Severn COTSWOLDS Avon

NORTHAMPTON UPLANDS

CHILTERNS

Bristol Channel MENDIPS Avon Thames
(England's longest
river)

NORTH DOWNS

EXMOOR Exe Tone Parrett SALISBURY PLAIN Avon Stour Arun Medway Strait of Dover

NEW FOREST WEALD SOUTH DOWNS

Tamar DARTMOOR

BODMIN MOOR

Isle of
Wight

Isles of
Scilly

LIZARD POINT

ENGLISH CHANNEL

SHETLAND
ISLANDS

ORKNEY
ISLANDS

Miles 10 0 10 20 40 60 80 90
Kilometres 0 10 20 40 60 80 100 120 140

Francis K. Mason

9

The average range of temperature between winter and summer over the country as a whole is from 7°C to 12°C (15°F to 23°F), being greatest in easterly inland areas. During the course of a normal summer, temperatures above 27°C (80°F) are occasionally recorded in the south, but temperatures of 32°C (90°F) are very infrequent. Minimum temperatures are largely governed by local conditions, figures of −18°C(0°F) are not uncommon during still, clear winter weather, but −23°C (−10°F) is rare.[1]

RAINFALL

Rainfall is much higher in the mountainous west and north than in the low-lying south and east. The British Isles as a whole have an average annual rainfall of more than 40 inches (102 cm.), and England has about 34 inches (86 cm.).[2] While in an average year the highest areas of Scotland and Wales record rainfalls between 150 and 200 inches, some areas in the south-east of England may have less than 20 inches.[3] Rainfall is highest between October and January, and lowest between March and June, although the variation is not great and rainfall is relatively even throughout the year. A period of as long as three weeks without rain is most unusual.[4]

SUN AND WIND

Sunshine is naturally more frequent in the south than in the north; near sea level rather than at altitude; and on the coasts rather than inland. During the spring and early summer the mean daily duration of sunshine ranges from about five hours in the north of Scotland to about eight hours on the English south coast. During the periods of shortest daylight – November, December and January – sunshine averages only half an hour per day in the Scottish Highlands and the Peak District, and two hours per day in Southern England.

The prevailing winds are south-westerly. Wind speed is generally higher on the coasts than inland, in the west than the east. Predictably the north-west coast is the stormiest area of the British Isles, with an average of over 30 gales recorded every year. South-East England and the Midlands are at the opposite extreme, with winds of gale force only occurring on about two days in any

year inland, and on between 15 and 20 days on the Channel coast. Average wind speeds in the Shetlands vary from about 14 m.p.h. (23 km./hr.) in August, to about 19 m.p.h. (31 km./hr.) in January. In the London area the averages range between 7 m.p.h. (11 km./hr.) in August and 10 m.p.h. (16 km./hr.) in January.

GEOLOGY

Geologically Great Britain may be roughly divided into two main areas – the uplands which rise on the west of a line drawn between Tynemouth, Northumberland, and Exmouth, Devonshire; and the lowlands found to the east of this line.

The uplands, comprising Scotland, the Lake District, the Pennine Range, Wales and the south-western peninsula of Devon and Cornwall, consist in the main of outcrops of very ancient archaean and palaeozoic rock interspersed with plains and valleys of which the surface strata are generally of carboniferous age. The latter areas have been the main sources of Britain's mineral wealth, and the extensive coal deposits played an important part in the industrial and commercial expansion of the country in the 19th and 20th centuries.

During the great Ice Age the whole of Great Britain north of a line between the Severn and Thames estuaries was covered with ice. The ice caps and sheets swept from the uplands all previously formed soil and much rock debris, depositing it, in the form of clays, sands and gravels, over the lower ground when the ice retreated. The ice also interfered with natural drainage, and its disappearance left large waterlogged areas whose gradual drying has, again, left very fertile soil on low ground. The uplands, on the other hand, are barren and rocky; where they have not remained pared down to the naked rock, they mainly consist of bleak stretches of moorland with only thin, poor soil. The valleys which fall within these areas of geological upland are, however, rich and fertile for the reasons explained above; the West Country provides a prime example.

In the lowlands, the newer and softer rock strata have been gradually eroded into a fertile, rolling plain, interspersed with ranges of limestone hills which only rarely reach a height of 1,000 feet above sea level, covering the whole of the southern and eastern portion of the island. The mild climate, very ancient and complex geological features, and varied soils which characterise the British Isles have led to a richly diverse scenery and a wide pattern of vegetation, both natural and cultivated.

The coastline ranges from the rugged cliffs of the north and west to the low-lying fenland of East Anglia, where dykes and drainage systems have been necessary to keep the sea at bay since the earliest times. The estuaries of the rivers are thoroughly scoured by the vigorous tidal movements around the British coast, providing many natural harbours. Inland, almost the whole of the lowland area of the island has been cultivated. The more

---

[1] The lowest screen temperature recorded in the United Kingdom was −27°F (−17°C) at Braemar, Aberdeenshire, Scotland, on 11th February 1895. The highest shade temperature ever recorded was 38°C (100·5°F) at Tonbridge, Kent, on 22nd July 1868.

[2] The greatest rainfall recorded in one year in the United Kingdom was 257·0 inches (652·8 cm.) at Sprinkling Tarn, Cumberland, in 1954.

[3] The driest place in the United Kingdom is Great Wakering in Essex which recorded a mean annual rainfall of 19·2 inches during the period 1916–1950.

[4] The longest drought recorded in the United Kingdom was 73 days between 4th March and 15th May 1893, recorded at Mile End, London.

sparsely inhabited highlands remain rich in softwood forests; at one time the whole island was probably covered in forest, oak in the lowlands and pine in the uplands, but only about seven per cent of the country is currently occupied by woodlands. Largescale re-forestation programmes have been established during the past half-century. Quite large areas of hardwood forest – mainly oak, ash, beech and elm – survive in certain parts of south-east England. Everywhere in lowland Britain hedgerows, small woods and copses, and individual trees abound. In the uplands the treeless areas of exposed moor are often covered with heather and gorse.

WILDLIFE IN BRITAIN

The natural wildlife of the British Isles is described in some detail in Chapter 5. Generally speaking the British fauna is similar to that of Northern Europe as a whole, although the circumstance that Great Britain is an island has hastened the extinction of some of the larger species which are still to be found in refuges on the continental landmass, such as wolf, bear, boar and certain types of elk and deer. Red, fallow and roe deer are the largest wild animals to be found in the British Isles, generally in the thinly inhabited regions of Scotland and the West Country – but to some extent in the rural south-east. Wild ponies inhabit several areas of moorland and southern woodland. Foxes abound, and otters, badgers, and small numbers of wildcats represent the only other indigenous species of relatively large carnivores.

Grey and common seals are to be encountered in many areas of the British coastline. Fish and bird life is very numerous and varied, and is largely protected by law. Reptiles are few, and the only indigenous creature which is seriously venomous is the adder; grave illness or fatalities from snakebite are extremely rare.

There are more than 21,000 types of insect in the British Isles, most of them small; among the largest are the swallowtail butterfly, with a three to four inch wing span, and the stag beetle, which grows to about two and a half inches long. Damage and disease spread by insects is very unusual in Britain.

BRITAIN IN THE WORLD SCALES OF MAGNITUDE

British natural features do not figure significantly in compilations of the world's superlatives. Great Britain and Ireland occupy the eighth and twentieth positions respectively in the list of the world's largest islands, excluding continental landmasses:

Name of Island	Area in square miles	Location
1. Greenland	approx. 840,000	Arctic Ocean
2. New Guinea	approx. 317,000	Western Pacific
3. Borneo	approx. 287,400	Indian Ocean
4. Malagasy Republic	approx. 227,800	Indian Ocean
5. Baffin Island	183,810	Arctic Ocean
6. Sumatra	182,860	Indian Ocean
7. Honshū	88,031	Northwest Pacific
8. Great Britain	84,186	North Atlantic
9. Ellesmere Island	82,119	Arctic Ocean
10. Victoria Island	81,930	Arctic Ocean
11. Celebes	72,987	Western Pacific
12. South Island, New Zealand	58,093	Southwest Pacific
13. Java	48,763	Indian Ocean
14. Luzon	46,636	Western Pacific
15. North Island, New Zealand	44,281	Southwest Pacific
16. Newfoundland	42,734	North Atlantic
17. Cuba	41,634	Western Atlantic
18. Iceland	39,698	North Atlantic
19. Mindanao	39,191	Western Pacific
20. Ireland (incl. Northern Ireland and Republic of Ireland)	31,839	North Atlantic

A proper moderation also seems to govern the dimensions of Britain's mountains, lakes and caverns, in keeping with the traditional reserve of the inhabitants. Apart from its eighth position in the above list of islands, none of the geographical features of the British Isles features significantly among those of the world as a whole. In relation to those of the great land masses, the mountains, lakes and rivers are diminutive to say the least.

The Highest Mountains
– In the World: Mount Everest, Tibet/Nepal
29,028 feet
– In Europe: El'brus (West peak), Caucasus
18,481 feet
– In Scotland: Ben Nevis, Inverness-shire
4,406 feet
– In Wales: Snowdon, Caernarvonshire
3,560 feet
– In England: Scafell, Cumberland
3,210 feet
– In Northern Ireland: Slieve Donard, County Down
2,796 feet

The Longest Rivers
– In the World: Amazon River, South America
4,195 miles
– In Great Britain: River Severn   220 miles
– Wholly in England: River Thames   215 miles

The Largest Lakes
- In the World: Caspian Sea   143,550 square miles
- In Northern Ireland: Lough Neagh   147 square miles
- In Scotland: Loch Lomond   33 square miles
- In England: Lake Windermere   5·7 square miles

(At its normal discharge rate of approximately 4·2 million cubic feet per second, the Amazon River would fill Great Britain's largest lake, Loch Lomond, in slightly under twelve hours.)

The Highest Waterfalls
- In the World: Angel Falls, Venezuela
     3,212 feet (total drop)
- In Great Britain: Eddrachillis, Sutherland, Scotland
     658 feet (total drop)

The Deepest Caves
- In the World: Gouffre de la Pierre Saint-Martin,
     Pyrenees   4,300 feet below entrance
- In Wales: Ogof Ffynnon Du, Breconshire   800 feet
- In England: Oxlow Cavern, Derbyshire   653 feet

Population
World population, estimated in 1971:   3,570,000,000
United Kingdom of Great Britain and Northern Ireland
     (approximate 1971 figure):   55,000,000
     – or approximately 1·54% of the world's population.

CHAPTER 1
☙ Physical and Political Geography ❧

The United Kingdom of Great Britain and Northern Ireland is divided into a total of 91 geographical counties (see the following page). Of the 40 English geographical counties, 35 are also "administrative counties"; that is to say that each wholly represents a single administrative entity. The other five geographical counties are further sub-divided into twelve administrative counties as follows:

Lincolnshire: Parts of Holland; Parts of Kesteven; Parts of Lindsey
Hampshire: Hampshire (mainland); Isle of Wight
Suffolk: East Suffolk; West Suffolk
Sussex: East Sussex; West Sussex
Yorkshire: East Riding; North Riding; West Riding.

All the geographical counties in Scotland, Wales and Northern Ireland are also administrative counties, so there is a total of 98 administrative counties in the United Kingdom.

In the following summary of counties the areas, population and population density refer to those of the geographical counties as defined. The populations and areas of the administrative counties are defined as those of the geographical counties *less* those of any County Boroughs in the county. The population figures quoted from the 1801 Decennial Census refer to the geographical county boundaries as defined in that year.

In addition to the English administrative units of County and Municipal Boroughs, and Urban and Rural Districts, certain cities within the geographical boundaries of counties are classified as "Counties of a City" and "Counties of a Town" for jurisdictional purposes. Although this classification does not influence the administrative division of the geographical counties, they are listed here so as not to complicate the body of this Chapter:

Counties of a City

City of Bristol	City of Lichfield
City of Canterbury	City of Lincoln
City of Cheshire	City of Newcastle-upon-Tyne
City of Exeter	City of Norwich
City of Gloucester	City of Worcester
Kingston-upon-Hull	City of York

Counties of Towns

Berwick-on-Tweed	City of Nottingham
Carmarthen	Poole
Haverfordwest	City of Southampton

Lord Lieutenants

Each county in the United Kingdom has a Lord Lieutenant (in Scotland he is generally referred to as the Lieutenant of the County), his title being correctly styled "Her Majesty's Lieutenant for (the relative county)". In addition there is a Lord Lieutenant for the Tower of London, and in Northern Ireland, Lord Lieutenants for the City of Belfast and the City of Londonderry.

County Worthies (by birth)

Among the famous men and women quoted, there are a number whose worthiness is controversial to say the least; the noun is applied to embrace simple notoriety.

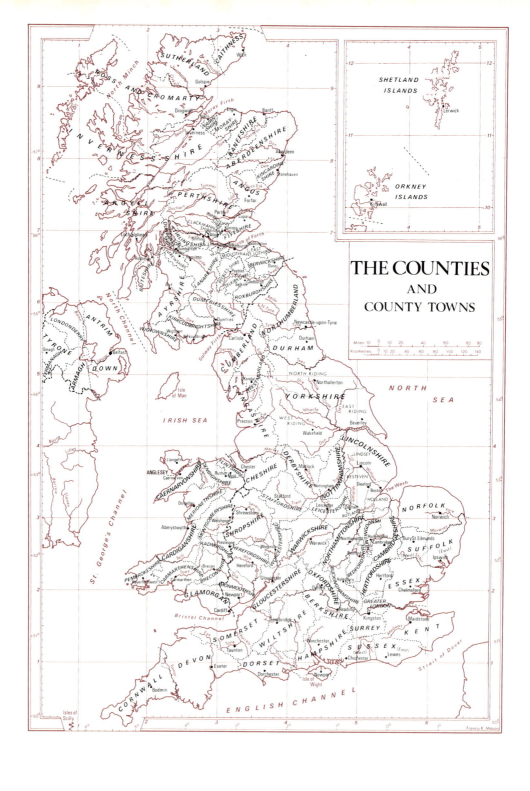

THE COUNTIES
AND
COUNTY TOWNS

Francis K. Mason

THE GEOGRAPHICAL COUNTIES OF GREAT BRITAIN

ENGLAND

1. BEDFORDSHIRE

Statutory name of administrative county: County of Bedford

Derivation and first recorded use of name: Bedcanforda, Bedanforda, Bedeford (Beda's ford), first mentioned in A.D. 571 when Cuthwulf defeated the Britons there

Population in 1801: 63,393

Population in 1971: 451,670

Area: 305,056 acres

Population density per acre in 1971: 1·48

County Town and River: Bedford, on the Great Ouse

Motto of County Council: "Constant Be"

County Borough (and population): Luton (161, 410)

Municipal Boroughs (and population): Bedford (69,170); Dunstable (30,000)

Urban Districts (and population): Ampthill (5,180); Biggleswade (9,140); Kempston (12,410); Leighton-Linslade (20,140); Sandy (5,540)

Rural Districts (and population): Ampthill (32,940); Bedford (36,840); Biggleswade (33,410); Luton (35,490); St. Neots (9,790)

Lord-Lieutenant of County: Major S. Whitbread

Principal Industries: Agriculture (mainly wheat, livestock and root crops) and market gardening; chalk quarrying; manufacture of hats, ball bearings, electrical and other precision equipment; motor vehicle manufacture; glass and brick manufacture; printing

Tourist attractions and places of interest: Luton (Church of St. Mary; Museum and Art Gallery); Luton Hoo; Totternhoe (fort and Church of St. Giles); Woburn Abbey; Houghton Regis (Church of All Saints); Leighton Buzzard (Church of All Saints); Harlington Manor; Wrest Park; Ampthill (Park House and Avenue House); Old Warden (Shuttleworth Aeronautical Collection and Museum); Bedford (Cecil Higgins Art Gallery, Museum and Public Library); Elstow (Moot Hall and Church of SS Mary and Helen); Clapham (Church of St. Thomas of Canterbury); Stevington windmill; Hinwick House; Whipsnade Park Zoo

Principal county worthies (by birth): John Bunyan (1628–1688, born at Elstow); Thomas Tompion (the famous clockmaker, born at Northill; 1639–1713); Sir Joseph Paxton (the architect, born at Milton Bryant in 1801)

Highest point above Sea Level: Dunstable Downs, 802 feet

2. BERKSHIRE

Statutory name of administrative county: Royal County of Berkshire

Derivation and first recorded use of name: Traditionally ascribed to a derivation of Bearruc, a wooded hill district, circa A.D. 860

Population in 1801: 110,752

Population in 1971: 631,080

Area: 463,830 acres

Population density per acre in 1971: 1·39

County Town and River: Reading on the River Thames

County Borough (and population): Reading (127,310)

Municipal Boroughs (and population): Abingdon (18,570); Maidenhead (46,930); Newbury (22,310); New Windsor (31,180); Wallingford (6,190); Wokingham (20,210)

Urban Districts (and population): Wantage (8,030)

Rural Districts: Abingdon, Bradfield, Cookham, Easthampstead, Faringdon, Hungerford, Newbury, Wallingford, Wantage, Windsor, Wokingham

Lord-Lieutenant of County: Hon. D. J. Smith, C.B.E.

Principal Industries: Agriculture and manufacture of agricultural machinery; seed propagation; biscuit manufacture; fruit growing; boatbuilding and light engineering; carpet manufacture; nuclear research establishments

Tourist attractions and places of interest: Windsor Castle; Abingdon (Abbey; Bridge; Church of St. Helen; Borough Museum and Town Hall); Milton Manor; Great Coxwell Tithe Barn and Coleshill Park; Uffington Castle and White Horse; Wayland Smith's Cave; Alfred's Castle (hill fort near Ashdown House); Sandleford Priory and Gardens; Newbury Borough Museum; Reading (Museum and Art Gallery; Museum of English Rural Life; Museum of Greek Archaeology); Blewbury (Church of St. Michael and All Angels); Aldworth (Church of St. Mary)

Principal county worthies (by birth): King Alfred the Great (born at Wantage; A.D. 849–899)

3. BUCKINGHAMSHIRE

Statutory name of administrative county: County of Buckingham

Derivation and first recorded use of name: Originally *hamm,* the meadow of the people of Bucca; created County Town by Alfred the Great in A.D. 886

Population in 1801: 107,900

Population in 1971: 585,560

Area: 477,750 acres

Population density per acre in 1971: 1·23

County Town: Aylesbury (previously Buckingham on the River Ouse)

Motto of County Council: Vestigia nulla retrorsum = No backward step

Municipal Boroughs (and population): Aylesbury (36,920); Buckingham (4,960); High Wycombe (57,770); Slough (93,570)

Urban Districts (and population): Beaconsfield (11,880); Bletchley (30,290); Chesham (21,140); Eton (5,280); Marlow (11,250); Newport Pagnell (6,070); Wolverton (13,520)

Rural Districts: Amersham, Aylesbury, Buckingham, Eton, Newport Pagnell, Wing, Winslow, Wycombe

Lord-Lieutenant of County: Major J. D. Young

Principal Industries: Agriculture (mainly dairy cattle); papermaking and printing; light engineering and woodworking (furniture making); railway workshops etc.

Tourist attractions and places of interest: Aylesbury County Museum; Boarstall Tower; Chequers; Claydon House; Denham Place; Edlesborough (Church of St. Mary); Haddenham (Church of St. Mary); Hartwell (Church of St. Mary the Virgin); High Wycombe Museum; Hughenden Manor; Iver Grove; Long Crendon Court House; Marlow Place; Medmenham Abbey; Nether Winchendon House; Princes Risborough Manor House; Stewkley (Church of St. Michael and All Angels); Stowe; Waddesdon Manor; West Wycombe Park

Principal county worthies (by birth): Edmund Waller (1606–1687, the writer, born at Coleshill); Sir John Herschel (1792–1871); 7th Earl of Cardigan (1797–1868)

Highest point above Sea Level: Unnamed point one mile west of Dunsmore in the Chilterns, 856 feet

4. CAMBRIDGESHIRE

Statutory name of administrative county: County of Cambridgeshire and Isle of Ely

Derivation and first recorded use of name: Corruption of the name *Grantabrycgscir*, the Shire of the bridge over the River Granta (known variously as the Granta, the Cam and the Rhee), *ante* 1006

Population in 1801: 89,346 *Population in 1971:* 304,680

Area: 531,578 acres *Population density per acre in 1971:* 0·57

County Town: City of Cambridge on the River Cam

Motto of County Council: "*Sapientes Simus*"

Municipal Boroughs (and population): City of Cambridge (100,010); Wisbech (17,480)

Urban Districts (and population): Chatteris (5,520); Ely (10,030); March (14,080); Whittlesley (11,200)

Rural Districts: Chesterton, Ely, North Witchford, Newmarket, South Cambridgeshire, Wisbech

Lord-Lieutenant of County: Col. G. T. Hurrell, O.B.E.

Principal Industries: Agriculture (mainly cereals and root crops); market gardening; light engineering

and scientific research; manufacture of electrical equipment and electronics; manufacture of chemicals; tourism (in City of Cambridge)

Tourist attractions and places of interest: City of Cambridge (the colleges of the University, Arts Council Gallery, Fitzwilliam Museum, Scott Polar Research Institute, Senate House, Whipple Museum of the History of Science); Ely Cathedral; Madingley Hall; Sawston Hall; Shepreth (Docwra's Manor); Wimpole (Hall and Church of St. Andrew); Wisbech (Pechover House)

Principal county worthies (by birth): Orlando Gibbons (1583–1625); Lord Keynes (1883–1946)

Highest point above Sea Level: Point on the B1039 road at the county boundary with Essex near Great Chishill, 479 feet

5. CHESHIRE

Statutory name of administrative county: County of Chester

Derivation and first recorded use of name: Corruption of Latin *castra* (=camp of the legions, further corrupted from *Legeceasterscir*; first recorded use probably in Charter grants of land by Edgar, king of Mercia, to the *familia* of St. Werburgh, Chester, A.D. 858

Population in 1801: 192,305 *Population in 1971:* 1,078,380

Area: 649,525 acres *Population density per acre in 1971:* 1·95

County Town and River: The City of Chester on the River Dee

Motto of County Council: "*Jure et dignitate gladii*" = By the right and dignity of the sword

County Boroughs (and population): Birkenhead (141,410); City of Chester (61,490); Stockport (139,330); Wallasey (100,470)

Municipal Boroughs (and population): Altrincham (40,710); Bebington (57,540); Congleton (19,870); Crewe (51,600); Dukinfield (17,340); Ellesmere Port (58,180); Hyde (38,240); Macclesfield (41,870); Sale (55,200); Stalybridge (21,810)

Urban Districts: Alderley Edge, Alsager, Bollington, Bowdon, Bredbury and Romiley, Cheadle and Gatley, Hale, Hazel Grove and Bramhall, Hoylake, Knutsford, Longdendale, Lymm, Marple, Middlewich, Nantwich, Neston, Northwich, Runcorn, Sandbach, Wilmslow, Winsford, Wirral

Rural Districts: Bucklow, Chester, Congleton, Disley, Macclesfield, Nantwich, Northwich, Runcorn, Tarvin, Tintwistle

Lord-Lieutenant of County: Viscount Leverhulme, T.D.

Principal Industries: Dairy farming and cheese; shipbuilding; petroleum refining and production of petroleum by-products; textiles; light engineering

Tourist attractions and places of interest: Altrincham (Art Gallery and Museum); Adlington Hall; Birkenhead (Williamson Art Gallery and Museum); Bramall Hall; Capesthorne; Chester (Castle; Cathedral; Church of St. John the Baptist; Grosvenor Museum); Dorfold Hall; Gawsworth Hall; Lyme Park; Maiden Castle; Nantwich (Churche's Mansion); Shotwick (Church of St. Michael); Tatton Park

Principal county worthies (by birth): John Speed (1552–1629, the eminent cartographer, born at Fardon); John Bradshaw (1602–1659); Emma, Lady Hamilton (c. 1765–1815); 1st Earl Beatty (1871–1936, the naval commander); 1st Earl of Birkenhead (1872–1930); Charles Dodgson (1838–1898, the author famous as Lewis Carroll, born at Daresbury); George Mallory (the Everest climber, born at Mobberley)

Highest point above Sea Level: Black Hill, on county border with Derbyshire near Disley, 1,906 feet

6. CORNWALL
(Including the Isles of Scilly)

Statutory name of administrative county: County of Cornwall

Derivation and first recorded use of name: Probably from *Cornubia* (A.D. 884), and *Cornwalum* (the land of the Cornovii, A.D. 960, in the Charter land grant by King Edgar to Eanulf, his *minister*)

Population in 1801: 192,281   *Population in 1971:* 361,930

Area: 881,894 acres   *Population density per acre in 1971:* 0·41

County Town and River: Bodmin   *Administrative centre:* City of Truro on the Truro River at the confluence of the Rivers Allen and Kenwyn

Motto of County Council: "*One and All*"

Municipal Boroughs (and population): Bodmin (8,400); Falmouth (17,360); Helston (10,190); Launceston (4,700); Liskeard (4,900); Penryn (5,200); Penzance (18,770); St. Austell with Fowey (29,830); St. Ives (8,850); Saltash (9,280); City of Truro (14,560)

Urban Districts (and population): Bude-Stratton (5,300); Camborne-Redruth (38,770); Looe (4,030); Newquay (12,480); St. Just (3,450); Torpoint (6,230); *Rural Borough:* Lostwithiel

Rural Districts: Camelford, Kerrier, Launceston, Liskeard, St. Austell, St. Germans, Isles of Scilly, Stratton, Truro, Wadebridge and Padstow, W. Penwith

Lord-Lieutenant of County: Col. Sir John Carew Pole, Bt., D.S.O., T.D.

Principal Industries: Agriculture (mainly dairy farming); market gardening; quarrying and mining; china clay; general engineering; boatbuilding and small ship repair; fishing; tourism and the holiday trade

Tourist attractions and places of interest: Altarnum (Church of St. Nonna); Antony House; Chysauster Iron Age Village; Cotehele House; Crantock (Church of St. Carantoc); Forrabury Common (Celtic stitchmeal); Glendurgan Gardens; Godolphin House; Harlyn Bay Museum; Helston (Borough Museum; Church of St. Michael); Kilkhampton (Church of St. James); Land's End; Lanyon and Zennor Quoits; Launceston (Church of St. Mary Magdalene); The Lizard; Lostwithiel (Church of St. Bartholomew); Morwenstowe (Church of St. Morwenna); Pendennis Castle; Penfound Manor; Penzance Natural

Gawsworth Hall, Cheshire, the 16th-century Elizabethan manor house, once the home of Mary Fitton (widely thought to have been Shakespeare's "Dark Lady of the Sonnets")

History Museum; St. Endellion (Church of St. Endelienta); St. Mawes Castle; St. Michael's Mount; Tintagel; Trencom Hill Fort; Trerice Manor House; Truro Cathedral

Principal county worthies (by birth): Dr. Borlase (the Cornish antiquary, born in 1696 at Pendeen); Samuel Foote (1720–1777); John Opie (1761–1807, the painter, born at St. Agnes); Captain Bligh (of the "*Bounty*", born at St. Tudy); Richard Trevithick (1771–1838, the pioneer locomotive engineer); Sir Humphrey Davy (1778–1829); Bob Fitzsimmons (the only British world heavyweight boxing champion, born in 1863 at Helston); Sir Arthur Quiller Couch (1863–1944)

Highest point above Sea Level: Brown Willy, on Bodmin Moor, 1,375 feet

ISLES OF SCILLY

The Isles of Scilly are uniquely administered (by a provision of Section 292 of the 1933 Local Government Act) by a Council comprising a Chairman, four Aldermen and 21 Councillors; for parliamentary representation the islands form part of the St. Ives electoral division. The five populated islands are Bryher (population in 1971, 56), St. Agnes (57), St. Martin's (102), St. Mary's (1,597) and Tresco (183), making a total population of 1,995. The total area of the islands is 4,040 acres.

7. CUMBERLAND

Statutory name of administrative county: County of Cumberland

Derivation and first recorded use of name: Cumbra Land (land of the Cumbrians, the Britons), c. A.D. 945

Population in 1801: 117,230

Population in 1971: 294,450

Area: 973,147 acres

Population density per acre in 1971: 0·31

County Town and River: City of Carlisle on the River Eden (at the confluence of the Rivers Petterill and Caldew)

Motto of County Council: "*Prefero*" = I carry through

County Borough (and population): City of Carlisle (71,410)

Municipal Boroughs (and population): Whitehaven (26,460); Workington (29,460)

Urban Districts (and population): Cockermouth (6,450); Keswick (4,490); Maryport (11,920); Penrith (11,140)

Rural Districts: Alton with Garrigill, Border, Cockermouth, Ennerdale, Millom, Penrith, Wigton

Lord-Lieutenant of County: J. C. Wade, O.B.E., J.P.

Principal Industries: Sheep-farming; coal-mining; iron and steel industries; nuclear power station; light engineering; forestry and timber mills; tourism

Tourist attractions and places of interest: Calder Abbey (ruins of); Carlisle (Castle; Cathedral; Tullie House; Market Place); Carrock Fell hill fort;

Hardwick Hall, Derbyshire.

Castlerigg stone circle; Cockermouth (ruins of castle; Wordsworth House); Crosscanonby (Church of St. John the Evangelist); Great Salkeld (Church of St. Cuthbert); Hadrian's Wall; Holme Cultram Abbey; Isel (Church of St. Michael); the lakes of the Lake District; Lanercost Priory; Long Meg and her Daughters (stone circle); Muncaster Castle; Naworth Castle; Over Denton Church; Penrith (Church of St. Cuthbert); St. Bees (Church of SS Mary and Bega); Wetheral (Church of the Holy Trinity; Castle Corby; St. Constantine's Cell); Whitehaven

Principal county worthies (by birth): Fletcher Christian (leader of the mutineers of the "*Bounty*", born at Eaglesfield in c. 1753); John Dalton (1766–1844); William Wordsworth (the poet, born at Cockermouth, 1770–1850); William H. Bragg (1862–1942)

Highest point above Sea Level: Scafell Pike, 3,210 feet

8. DERBYSHIRE

Statutory name of administrative county: County of Derby

Derivation and first recorded use of name: Deorbyscir, the place of the deer park; probably first recorded in a Charter of King Edmund in A.D. 942

Population in 1801: 161,567

Population in 1971: 891,670

Area: 635,456 acres

Population density per acre in 1971: 1·40

County Town and River: Matlock on the River Derwent

Motto of County Council: "Bene Consulendo" = By good Counsel

County Borough (and population): Derby (220,130)

Municipal Boroughs (and population): Buxton (20,000); Chesterfield (70,000); Glossop (23,750); Ilkeston (35,170)

Urban Districts: Alfreton, Ashbourne, Bakewell, Belper, Bolsover, Clay Cross, Dronfield, Heanor, Long Eaton, Matlock, New Mills, Ripley, Staveley, Swadlincote, Whaley Bridge, Wirksworth

Rural Districts: Ashbourne, Bakewell, Belper, Blackwell, Chapel-en-le-Frith, Chesterfield, Clowne, Repton, South-East Derbyshire

Lord-Lieutenant of County: Lt.-Col. Sir Ian Walker-Okeover, Bt., D.S.O., T.D.

Principal Industries: Coal mining; heavy engineering; motor car and aero-engine manufacture; sheep farming and market gardening; iron smelting; limestone quarrying; textiles; pottery and porcelain making

Tourist attractions and places of interest: Ashbourne (Church of St. Oswald); Ashover (Church of All Saints); Bakewell (Church of All Saints); Bolsover Castle; Buxton (the Old Hall; Museum); Chatsworth (House and Gardens); Chesterfield (Church of St. Mary and All Saints); Cromford Old Mill (and Willersley Castle); Derby (Cathedral; Museum and Art Gallery); Haddon Hall; Hardwick Hall; Kedleston Hall; Mam Tor hill fort; Melbourne Hall; Morley (Church of St. Matthew); the Peak District; Repton (Church of St. Wystan; school); Stanton Moor Bronze Age monuments; Wirksworth (Church of St. Mary); Youlgreave (Church of All Saints)

Principal county worthies (by birth): Elizabeth Shrewsbury ("Bess of Hardwick", born 1520, built H. Hall); John Flamsteed (the first Astronomer Royal, born at Denby in 1646); Samuel Richardson (the novelist, born at Smalley; 1689–1761); James Brindley (the famous canal builder, born at Tunstead in 1716); John Gerard (the Jesuit priest, born at Etwall); Joseph Wright (the painter, born at Derby); Thomas Cook (the pioneer of popular travel, born at Melbourne, 1808–1892); Herbert Spenser (the writer, born at Derby; 1820–1903); George Nathaniel Curzon (Marquess Curzon of Kedleston, born at Kedleston Hall; 1859–1925)

Highest point above Sea Level: Kinder Scout (The Peak), 2,088 feet

9. DEVON

Statutory name of administrative county: County of Devon

Derivation and first recorded use of name: Defenascir, the territory of the Dumnonii, a tribal name adopted by the Saxons; probably first formally used in an A.D. 739 Charter by Aethelheard, king of Wessex, to Bishop Forthere

Population in 1801:	*Population in 1971:*
340,720	885,990

Area: 1,657,920 acres   *Population density per acre in 1971:* 0·54

County Town and River: City of Exeter on the River Exe

Motto of County Council: "Auxilio Divino" = By Divine Assistance

County Boroughs (and population): City of Exeter (93,340); City of Plymouth (256,600); Torbay (104,000)

Municipal Boroughs (and population): Barnstaple (16,920); Bideford (11,500); Dartmouth (7,130); Great Torrington (3,200); Honiton (6,080); Okehampton (3,900); Tiverton (15,140); Totnes (5,700) *Rural Borough:* South Molton

Urban Districts: Ashburton, Buckfastleigh, Budleigh Salterton, Crediton, Dawlish, Exmouth, Ilfracombe, Kingsbridge, Lynton, Newton Abbot, Northam, Ottery St. Mary, Salcombe, Seaton, Sidmouth, Teignmouth

Rural Districts: Axminster, Barnstaple, Bideford, Crediton, Holsworthy, Honiton, Kingsbridge, Newton Abbot, Okehampton, Plympton St. Mary, St. Thomas, South Molton, Tavistock, Tiverton, Torrington, Totnes

Lord-Lieutenant of County: The Lord Roborough

Principal Industries: Dairy-farming; beef cattle; sheep-rearing; cereal crops; cider apple growing; clay working; dockyard at Devonport; tourism and the holiday trade

Tourist attractions and places of Interest: Atherington (Church of St. Mary); Berry Pomeroy Castle; Bideford; Blackbury Castle (Iron Age fort); Buckland Abbey; Chittlehampton (Church of St. Urith); Collacombe Manor; Compton Castle; Crediton (Church of Holy Cross); Dartmouth (castles; Borough Museum; Butterwalk); Dunsland House; Exeter (Cathedral; ruins of castle; Guildhall; museum of the Devonshire Regiment); Hembury hill fort; Holcombe Court; Ilfracombe chapel lighthouse; Legis Tor (Bronze Age settlement); Okehampton Castle (ruins of); Powderham Castle; Saltram House; South Molton (Borough Museum); Sydenham House; Tavistock (Church of St. Eustace); Totnes (Church of St. Mary; Dartington Hall); Trowlesworthy Warren (Bronze Age moorland settlement); Wortham Manor

Principal county worthies (by birth): Saint Boniface (the 7th century Bishop of Mainz, born at Crediton); Sir John Hawkins (the sea captain, born at Plymouth; 1532–1595); Sir Francis Drake (the sea captain, born near Tavistock; c. 1540–1596); Sir Walter Raleigh (the sea captain, born at East

Budleigh; 1552–1618); George Monk (1st Duke of Albermarle, 1608–1670); 1st Duke of Marlborough (the statesman and military commander, 1650–1722); Thomas Newcomen (the steam engineer, born at Dartmouth; 1663–1729); Samuel Taylor Coleridge (the poet, born at Ottery St. Mary; 1772–1834); Joanna Southcott (born at Gittisham); Sir Joshua Reynolds (the great painter, 1723–1792); John Walcott ("Peter Pindar", the satirist, born at Kingsbridge in 1738); Nicholas Stone (the sculptor, born at Woodbury); James Anthony Froude (the famous historian, born at Dartington; 1819–1894); Charles Kingsley (the writer, born at Holne; 1819–1875); Capt. Robert Falcon Scott (the explorer, born at Devonport; 1868–1912); William Temple (1881–1944)

Highest point above Sea Level: High Willhays, 3·5 miles south of Okehampton, 2,039 feet

Iwerne Minster (Church of St. Mary); Lyme Regis (Philpot Museum); Maiden Castle (Iron Age fort); Milton Abbey; Moignes Court; Portland lighthouse; Sandford Orcas Manor; Shaftesbury (Abbey ruins and museum); Sherborne (Abbey church and castles); Tolpuddle (Martyrs' tree); Wimborne Minster (Church of St. Cuthberga); Yetminster (Church of St. Andrew)

Principal county worthies (by birth): 1st Earl of Shaftesbury (1621–1683); Sir Thomas Thornhill (the painter, born at Weymouth); Vice-Admiral Sir Thomas Masterman Hardy (Flag Captain in Nelson's "*Victory*", born at Winterborne Abbas; 1769–1839); William Barnes (1801–1886); Thomas Hardy (the great novelist, born at Upper Brockhampton; 1840–1928); Sir Frederick Treves (1853–1923)

Highest point above Sea Level: Minterne Magna, 3 miles north of Cerne Abbas, 836 feet

10. DORSET

Statutory name of administrative county: County of Dorset

Derivation and first recorded use of name: A contraction of *Dorn-gweir* (place of fist-play), *saete* (dwellers), and thus of Dorseteschire; Charters given by King Athelstan between A.D. 932 and 940 (e.g. to Shaftesbury Abbey in A.D. 932)

Population in 1801: 114,452   *Population in 1971:* 357,370

Area: 623,740 acres   *Population density per acre in 1971:* 0·57

County Town and River: Dorchester on the River Frome

Motto of County Council: "Who's Afear'd"

Municipal Boroughs (and population): Blandford Forum (3,670); Bridport (6,580); Dorchester (13,760); Lyme Regis (3,330); Poole (104,640); Shaftesbury (3,600); Wareham (4,180); Weymouth and Melcombe Regis (42,580)

Urban Districts (and population): Portland (13,270); Sherborne (8,580); Swanage (8,190); Wimborne Minster (4,590)

Rural Districts: Beaminster, Blandford, Bridport, Dorchester, Shaftesbury, Sherborne, Sturminster, Wareham and Purbeck, Wimborne and Cranborne

Lord-Lieutenant of County: Col. J. W. Weld, O.B.E., T.D.

Principal Industries: Dairy and sheep farming; cereal crops; quarrying and cement manufacture; sand and gravel; holiday trade

Tourist attractions and places of interest: Abbotsbury (Benedictine Abbey); Athelhampton Hall; Blandford Forum; Bridport (Museum and Art Gallery); Corfe Castle; Dorchester; Dorset Cursus Neolithic site); Eggardon (Iron Age hill fort); Hambledon Hill (fort); Hod Hill (Iron Age fort);

11. DURHAM

Statutory name of administrative county: County Durham

Derivation and first recorded use of name: cf. Dunholm (*dun*, Old English, = hill; *holm*, Norse, = islet in a river); referred to in Anglo-Saxon charters, *ante* A.D. 1000

Population in 1801: 149,384   *Population in 1971:* 1,486,790

Area: 649,439 acres   *Population density per acre in 1971:* 2·41

County Town and River: City of Durham on the River Wear

County Boroughs (and population): Darlington (84,340); Gateshead (100,060); South Shields (104,600); Sunderland (221,000); Hartlepool (98,080);

Municipal Boroughs (and population): City of Durham (25,750); Jarrow (29,240)

Urban Districts: Barnard Castle, Bishop Auckland, Blaydon, Boldon, Brandon and Byshottles, Chester le Street, Consett, Crook and Willington, Felling, Hebburn, Hetton, Houghton le Spring, Ryton, Seaham, Shildon, Spennymoor, Stanley, Tow Law, Washington, Whickham

Rural Districts: Barnard Castle, Chester le Street, Darlington, Durham, Easington, Lanchester, Sedgefield, Stockton, Weardale

Lord-Lieutenant of County: The Lord Barnard, T.D.

Principal Industries: Coal mining; iron and steel; heavy engineering and shipbuilding industries; hill farming; dairy farming; root crops

Tourist attractions and places of interest: Barnard Castle; Bishop Auckland (Church of St. Andrew); Darlington (Church of St. Cuthbert); Durham (Cathedral and Castle; Grammar School; Bishop Cosin's Hall); Finchale Priory; Hartlepool (Church of St. Hilda); Haughton-le-Skerne

The Old Siege House, Colchester, Essex

(Church of St. Andrew); Jarrow (Church of St. Paul); Lumley Castle; Monkwearmouth monastery; Pittington (Church of St. Lawrence); Raby Castle; Seaham (Church of St. Mary); Staindrop (Church of St. Mary); Sunderland (Museum and Art Gallery); Washington (Old Hall)

Principal county worthies (by birth): The Venerable Bede (A.D. 673–735); Jack Crawford (who "nailed the flag to the mast at Camperdown" in 1797, born at Sunderland); Thomas Sheraton (the furniture-maker, born at Stockton-on-Tees; 1751–1806); William Wouldhave (the inventor of the lifeboat, born at South Shields in 1789); Elizabeth Barrett Browning (the writer, born at Coxhoe; 1806–1861); Sir Henry Havelock (who relieved Lucknow in 1857, born at Sunderland); the Earl of Avon (born 1897)

Highest point above Sea Level: Burnhope Seat, on county border with Cumberland, 2,452 feet

12. ESSEX

Statutory name of administrative county: County of Essex

Derivation and first recorded use of name: East Seaxe, land of the East Saxons. First referred to in the charter grant of land at Tillingham by King Aethelberht of the English to Bishop Mellitus in A.D. 604

Population in 1801:
227,682
Area: 907,846 acres

Population in 1971:
1,343,500
Population density per acre in 1971: 1·48

County Town and River: Chelmsford at the confluence of the Rivers Chelmer and Cann

County Borough (and population): Southend-on-Sea (164,770)

Municipal Boroughs (and population): Chelmsford (57,840); Colchester (76,970); Harwich (15,050); Maldon (13,260); Saffron Walden (10,190)

Urban Districts: Basildon, Benfleet, Braintree and Bocking, Brentwood, Brightlingsea, Burnham on Crouch, Canvey Island, Chigwell, Clacton, Epping, Frinton and Walton, Halstead, Harlow, Rayleigh, Thurrock, Waltham Holy Cross, West Mersea, Witham, Wivenhoe

Rural Districts: Braintree, Chelmsford, Dunmow, Epping and Ongar, Halstead, Lexden and Winstree, Maldon, Rochford, Saffron Walden, Tendring

Lord-Lieutenant of County: Col. Sir John Ruggles-Brise, Bt., C.B., O.B.E., T.D., J.P.

Principal Industries: Cereal and fruit-growing; pigs, poultry and dairy-farming; sugar beet; general and light engineering (ship repairs and electrical component manufacture); cement manufacture; tourism

Tourist attractions and places of interest: Arkesden Wood Hall; Audley End; Beeleigh Abbey; Bradwell-on-Sea (Church of St. Peter's-on-the-Wall); Castle Hedingham; Chelmsford Cathedral; Colchester (castle keep and museum; Church of the Holy Trinity); Copford church; Cressing Temple; Dedham (Castle House); Finchingfield village; Greensted juxta Ongar (Church of St.

Early 17th century cottages of Arlington Row, Bibury, Gloucestershire

Andrew); Hatfield Broad Oak (Church of St. Mary the Virgin); Horham Hall; Ingatestone Hall; Layer Marney Towers; Little Dunmow and the Dunmow Flitch; Maldon (Church of All Saints; Moot Hall; Blue Boar Inn); Newport village; North End (Black Chapel); St. Clere's Hall; Saffron Walden; Southend-on-Sea (Prittle-well Priory museum); Tiptofts Manor; Tewes manor house; Tilbury (Thurrock Museum); Waltham Abbey

Principal county worthies (by birth): Samuel Purchas (the early topographer, born at Thaxted, *c.* 1575); Christopher Jones (Captain of the "*Mayflower*", born at Harwich); Dick Turpin (the highwayman, born at Hempstead in *c.* 1705); Sir Rowland Hill (1795–1879); George Shillibeer (the founder of London omnibuses, born at Chigwell in 1797); the First Lord Lister (the great surgeon, born at West Ham; 1827–1912); Charles Spurgeon (the famous preacher, born at Kelvedon Hatch in 1834)

Highest point above Sea Level: One mile south-east of Elmdon, near Saffron Walden, 482 feet

13. GLOUCESTERSHIRE

Statutory name of administrative county: County of Gloucester

Derivation and first recorded use of name: Gloiu-ceaster (*gloiu*, Old Welsh = the proud place; *ceaster* = in the vale of, or at the foot of); the name is referred to in charters granted by King Aethelred between A.D. 990 and 1016; it may have been referred to as early as *c.* A.D. 682 in charters granted by King Caedwalla of Essex to the Church

Population in 1801: 250,723

Population in 1971: 1,080,530

Area: 804,932 acres   *Population density per acre in 1971:* 1·34

County Town and River: City of Gloucester on the River Severn

Motto of County Council: "Prorsum Semper"

County Boroughs (and population): City of Bristol (426,370); City of Gloucester (90,110)

Municipal Boroughs (and population): Cheltenham (75,720); Tewkesbury (8,920)

Urban Districts: Charlton Kings, Cirencester, Kingswood, Mangotsfield, Nailsworth, Stroud

Rural Districts: Cheltenham, Cirencester, Dursley, East Dean, Gloucester, Lydney, Newent, North Cotswold, Northleach, Sodbury, Stroud, Tetbury, Thornbury, Warmley, West Dean

Lord-Lieutenant of County: His Grace the Duke of Beaufort, K.G., P.C., G.C.V.O.

Principal Industries: Dairy cattle and sheep farming; fruit-growing (apples and plums); manufacture of agricultural machinery; manufacture of aircraft, aero-engines and aircraft instruments and components; holiday and tourist trade (in Cotswolds)

Tourist attractions and places of interest: The Cotswold villages; Ampney Crucis (Church of the Holy Rood); Ashleworth (tithe barn); Badminton House; Berkeley Castle; Bibury (Church of St. Mary); Bishop's Cleeve (Church of St. Michael and All Angels); Chedworth Roman Villa; Chipping Campden (Church of St. James; market hall); Cirencester (Church of St. John the Baptist; Corinium museum); Cleeve Cloud (Iron Age fort); Deerhurst (Church of St. Mary); Dodington House; Gloucester Cathedral; Horton Court; Leckhampton Iron Age fort; Little Sodbury Manor; Newland (Church of All Saints); Northleach (Church of SS Peter and Paul); Offa's Dyke; Quenington (Church of St. Swithin); St. Briavels Castle; Sapperton (Daneway House); Severn Bridge; Severn Wildfowl Trust; Sudeley Castle; Tewkesbury (Abbey church of St. Mary the Virgin; also many inns and timbered houses); Westonbirt Arboretum; Woodchester and Woolaston Roman Villas

Principal county worthies (by birth): Sir Edward Coke (the Lord Chief Justice who opposed King James I, 1552-1634); Sir Richard Whittington (Dick Whittington, the famous Lord Mayor of London, born at Newent); John Kyrle (the "Man of Ross", born at Dymock in 1634); Edward Jenner (1749-1823); John Keble (the writer, born at Fairford; 1792-1866); W. G. Grace (the famous cricketer, born at Downend; 1848-1915); Gustav Holst (the composer, born at Cheltenham in 1874); Dr. Ralph Vaughan Williams (the composer, born at Down Ampney)

Highest point above Sea Level: Unnamed point four miles east of Cheltenham on South Cleeve Common, 1,083 feet

14. HAMPSHIRE AND THE ISLE OF WIGHT

Hampshire (excluding the Isle of Wight)

Statutory name of administrative county: Hampshire

Derivation and first recorded use of name: cf. *Hamtunscir* (*ham*, a meadow; *tun*, a homestead; *scir*, shire); first known use in A.D. 755, although it was almost certainly referred to in Church territorial grants made by Charter in A.D. 701-705 by Ine, king of the West Saxons

Population in 1801: 197,073   *Population in 1971:* 1,561,600

Area: 962,190 acres   *Population density per acre in 1971:* 1·62

County Town and River: Winchester on the River Itchen

County Boroughs (and population): Bournemouth (147,540); Portsmouth (211,790); City of Southampton (209,660)

Municipal Boroughs (and population): Aldershot (39,500); Andover (25,680); Basingstoke (44,300); Christchurch (32,010); Eastleigh (45,700); Gosport (76,600); Lymington (33,790); Romsey (9,060); City of Winchester (31,380)

Urban Districts: Alton, Fareham, Farnborough, Fleet, Havant and Waterloo, Petersfield

Rural Districts: Alton, Andover, Basingstoke, Droxford, Hartley Wintney, Kingsclere and Whitchurch, New Forest, Petersfield, Ringwood and Fordingbridge, Romsey and Stockbridge, Winchester

Lord-Lieutenant of County: The Lord Ashburton, K.G., K.C.V.O.

Principal Industries: Cattle and sheep farming; cereal crops; market gardening; general engineering, aircraft manufacture and boatbuilding; Southampton international port; large petroleum refinery at Fawley; yachting, holiday trade and tourism

Tourist attractions and places of interest: Alton (Curtis museum); Basing House (ruins of); Beaulieu (village, abbey and Montagu Motor Museum); Bournemouth (Rothesay and Russell-Cotes museums); Breamore House (and Church of St. Mary); Bucklers Hard (maritime museum); Butser Hill Fort; Chawton (Jane Austen's home); Fareham (old High Street); Hambledon (site of first game of cricket); Ladle Hill (half-completed Iron Age fort); Netley Abbey (ruins of); the New Forest; Odiham (main street; ruins of King John's Castle; Church of All Saints); Portchester (castle remains and Church of St. Mary); Portsmouth (Southsea Castle; Round Tower; Nelson's

The King Aelfred statue, Winchester, Hampshire

"*Victory*" and Victory Museum; dockyard); Rockbourne village; Romsey (abbey church; King John's House); Silchester (Calleva museum); Southampton (Bargate Guildhall; God's House Tower; Tudor House; Wool House); The Vyne (Tudor mansion); Winchester (Cathedral; Guildhall; City Museum; Church of St. Cross; Pilgrim's Hall; the regimental museums of the Royal Green Jackets and the Royal Hampshire Regiment; Winchester College)

Principal county worthies (by birth): King Henry III (born at Winchester; 1207-1272); William of Wykeham (founder of Winchester College, 1324–1404, born at Wickham); Gilbert White (the naturalist, born at Selborne; 1720-1793); Edward Gibbon (the 18th-century historian, born at Buriton; 1737-1794); Jane Austen (the authoress, born at Steventon; 1775-1817); Viscount Palmerston (the statesman, born at Romsey; 1784-1865); Isambard Kingdom Brunel (the great engineer, born at Portsmouth; 1806-1859); Charles Dickens (the great novelist, born at Portsmouth; 1812-1870); George Meredith (the writer, born at Portsmouth, 1828-1909)

Highest point above Sea Level: Pilot Hill, on county border with Berkshire near East Woodhay, 937 feet

The Isle of Wight

Statutory name of administrative county: County of the Isle of Wight

Derivation and first recorded use of name: Possibly from *Vectis* = that which rises from the sea; hence presumably first used shortly after the arrival of the Romans. Earliest known Anglo-Saxon charter to include land on the Isle was granted by Egbert, king of England, in A.D. 826

Population in 1801:   *Population in 1971:*
   22,097   104,800

Area: 94,140 acres   *Population density per acre in 1971:* 1·11

County Town and River: Newport on the River Medina

Motto of County Council: "All this beauty is of God"

Municipal Boroughs (and population): Newport (22,170); Ryde (22,690)

Urban Districts: Cowes, Sandown-Shanklin, Ventnor

Rural District: Isle of Wight

Principal Industries: Light aircraft manufacture; boatbuilding; catering; holiday trade

Tourist attractions and places of interest: Arreton Manor; Bembridge (Ruskin Galleries); Brading (Roman) Villa; Carisbrooke (Church of St. Mary; castle); Cowes (Royal Yacht Squadron); Osborne House; Shorwell village

Principal county worthies (by birth): Sir Thomas Fleming (1544-1613); Dr. Thomas James (1570-1629); Dr. Thomas Arnold (the writer, born at Cowes; 1795-1842)

Highest point above Sea Level: St. Boniface Down, above Bonchurch, 787 feet

15. HEREFORDSHIRE

Statutory name of administrative county: County of Hereford

Derivation and first recorded use of name: Here(paeth)ford = River-crossing for a military roadway; the subject of charter leases by Cuthbert, bishop of Hereford, between A.D. 840 and 852

Population in 1801:   *Population in 1971:*
   87,927   141,620

Area: 539,165 acres   *Population density per acre in 1971:* 0·26

County Town and River: City of Hereford on the River Wye

Motto of County Council: "Pulchra terra Dei donum" = This fair land is the gift of God

Municipal Boroughs (and population): City of Hereford (46,640); Leominster (6,940)

Urban Districts: Kington, Ross-on-Wye

Rural Districts: Bromyard, Dore and Bredwardine, Hereford, Kington, Ledbury, Leominster and Wigmore, Ross and Whitchurch, Weobley

Lord-Lieutenant of County: J. F. Mclean, J.P.

Principal Industries: Cattle farming; cider-apple and hop growing; light engineering

Tourist attractions and places of interest: Abbey Dore; Aconbury Iron Age camp; Berrington Hall; Bishopstone (Church of St. Lawrence); Bosbury (Church of the Holy Trinity); Canon Pyon (Church of St. Lawrence); Croft Castle (and Croft Ambrey hill fort); Dinedor Hill Roman camp; Dinmore Manor; Dorstone barrow; Eastnor Castle; Eye Manor; Garway (Church of St. Michael and All Angels); Goodrich Castle; Hereford (Cathedral; City Museum and Art Gallery); Kentchurch Court; Kilpeck (Church of SS Mary and David); King Arthur's Cave (extinct animal remains); Leominster (Church of SS Peter and Paul); Lower Brockhampton House; Madley; Offa's Dyke; Pembridge Castle; Ross-on-Wye (Church of St. Mary the Virgin; Weston Hall); Weobley (village and ruins of fortified manor house); Wharton Court

Principal county worthies (by birth): Richard Hakluyt (the writer, c. 1550–1572); David Garrick (1717–1779)

Highest point above Sea Level: Unnamed point two miles south of Hay Bluff on the Black Mountain on the county border with Breconshire, 2,302 feet

gardening; aircraft manufacture and avionics; brewing; printing and papermaking; quarrying; brickmaking; pharmaceuticals

Tourist attractions and places of interest: Anstey (Church of St. George); Ashwell (village and Chantrey House); Ayot St. Lawrence (Shaw's Corner); Benington (ruins of castle; The Lordship); Berkhamsted (earthwork remains of Norman castle); Bishop's Stortford (Church of St. Michael); Flamstead (Church of St. Leonard); Great Wymondley (village and Delamere House); Hatfield House; Hertford (castle; Fore Street; Lombard House; museum); Hitchin (Church of St. Mary); Knebworth House; Little Gaddesden; Little Wymondley (Wymondley Hall and Priory); Much Hadham (village; Church of St. Andrew; Palace); Ravensburgh Castle (hill fort); St. Albans (Abbey; Roman *municipium* of Verulamium; Church of St. Michael; Clock Tower; Fishpool Street); Therfield Heath (Neolithic barrow); Tyttenhanger Park; Ware Priory (remains of)

Principal county worthies (by birth): Nicholas Breakspear (Pope Adrian IV, England's only Pope, born at Abbot's Langley; 1110–1159); Sarah,

16. HERTFORDSHIRE

Statutory name of administrative county: County of Hertford

Derivation and first recorded use of name: Heortford, the river-crossing of the harts (stags); the charter grant of land at Aldenham (in the Shire) by Offa, king of Mercia, to St. Peter's, Westminster, in A.D. 785

Population in 1801:
97,393

Area: 403,804 acres

Population in 1971:
912,000

Population density per acre in 1971: 2·25

County Town and River: Hertford on the River Lea

Motto of County Council: Trust and Fear Not

Municipal Boroughs (and population): Hemel Hempstead (67,000); Hertford (19,310); City of St. Albans (52,750); Watford (76,740)

Urban Districts: Baldock, Berkhamsted, Bishop's Stortford, Bushey, Cheshunt, Chorleywood, Harpenden, Hitchin, Hoddesdon, Letchworth, Potters Bar, Rickmansworth, Royston, Sawbridgeworth, Stevenage, Tring, Ware, Welwyn Garden City

Rural Districts: Berkhamsted, Braughing, Elstree, Hatfield, Hemel Hempstead, Hertford, Hitchin, St. Albans, Ware, Watford, Welwyn

Lord-Lieutenant of County: Major-General Sir George Burns, K.C.V.O., C.B., D.S.O., O.B.E., M.C.

Principal Industries: Cereals and root crops; market

St. Albans, Hertfordshire: The Clock Tower, built between 1403 and 1412 at the centre of the medieval city

Duchess of Marlborough (born near Wheat-hampstead); Bishop Ken (born at Little Berk-hampstead; *c.* 1660-1711); William Cowper (the poet and hymn-writer, born at Berkhamsted; 1731-1800); Henry Manning (1808-1892); Sir Henry Bessemer (the pioneer of steel production; 1813-1898); 3rd Marquess of Salisbury (1830-1903); Cecil Rhodes (the colonial administrator; 1853-1902); H.M. Queen Elizabeth, the Queen Mother (born in 1900)

Highest point above Sea Level: Unnamed point between Hastoe village and the county border with Buckinghamshire in the Chilterns, 806 feet

17. HUNTINGDON AND PETERBOROUGH

Statutory name of administrative county: Huntingdon and Peterborough

Derivation and first recorded use of name: cf. *hunta-dun*, the huntsman's hill. Numerous tracts of land were subject of a charter grant by Edgar, king of Mercia, to Thorney Abbey, Cambridgeshire, in A.D. 973

Population in 1801:
47,725

Population in 1971:
199,040

Area: 310,857 acres

Population density per acre in 1971: 0·64

County Town and River: Huntingdon on the River Ouse

Motto of County Council: "*Cor Unum*" = One Heart

Municipal Boroughs (*and population*): Huntingdon and Godmanchester (15,730); City of Peterborough (66,870); Saint Ives (6,150)

Urban Districts: Old Fletton, Ramsey, St. Neots

Rural Districts: Barnack, Huntingdon, Norman Cross, Peterborough, Saint Ives, Thorney

Lord-Lieutenant of County: Lord Hemingford

Principal Industries: Cereal crops; fruit farming and market gardening; light and general engineering; brick-making; rubber processing

Tourist attractions and places of interest: Bodsey House; Brampton (Pepys's House); Fenstanton (home of Capability Brown); Godmanchester (Church of St. Mary the Virgin); Hartford village; Hunting-don (Hinchinbrooke); Kimbolton Castle; Offord Darcy (Manor House); Orton Waterville church; Peterborough (Cathedral; museum and Maxwell art gallery); Ramsey Abbey gatehouse; Ripping-ton Hall; St. Ives (priory remains and bridge); St. Neots market town; Toseland Hall

Principal county worthies (*by birth*): Oliver Cromwell (1599-1658); Sir Frederick Henry Royce (the great car and aero-engine industrialist, born at Alwalton; 1863-1933)

Highest point above Sea Level: Two miles west of Wittering, on the county border with Northamptonshire, 272 feet

18. KENT

Statutory name of administrative county: County of Kent

Derivation and first recorded use of name: From *canto*, a Celtic word for a river estuary. In use before Roman occupation, perhaps as early as 300 B.C. Anglo-Saxon land charters concern territory in Kent from the earliest period, i.e. those by

Burghley House, Huntingdonshire. Begun in 1552 by Sir William Cecil, it was completed in 1587. It contains woodwork by Grinling Gibbons

Aethelbehrt, king of Kent, A.D. 604–605.

Population in 1801: 258,973

Population in 1971: 1,394,340

Area: 921,630 acres

Population density per acre in 1971: 1·51

County Town and River: Maidstone on the River Medway

Motto of County Council: "*Invicta*" = Unconquered

County Borough (and population): City of Canterbury (33,150)

Municipal Boroughs (and population): Chatham (56,560); Dartford (46,260); Deal (27,250); Dover (35,390); Faversham (14,710); Folkestone (43,610); Gillingham (90,900); Gravesend (54,490); Hythe (11,860); Lydd (4,380); Maidstone (67,770); Margate (48,550); New Romney (3,640); Queenborough-in-Sheppey (28,860); Ramsgate (38,900); City of Rochester (56,230); Royal Tunbridge Wells (45,800); Sandwich (4,540); Tenterden (5,890)

Urban Districts: Ashford, Broadstairs and St. Peters, Herne Bay, Northfleet, Sevenoaks, Sittingbourne and Milton, Southborough, Swanscombe, Tonbridge, Whitstable

Rural Districts: Bridge-Blean, Cranbrook, Dartford, Dover, East Ashford, Eastry, Elham, Hollingbourne, Maidstone, Malling, Romney Marsh, Sevenoaks, Strood, Swale, Tenterden, Tonbridge, West Ashford

Lord-Lieutenant of County: The Lord Cornwallis, K.C.V.O., K.B.E., M.C.

Principal Industries: Cereal crops and sheep farming; fruit and hop growing; coal-mining; paper mills; quarrying; general and light engineering; naval dockyards and establishments; holiday trade

Tourist attractions and places of interest: Allington Castle; Aylesford priory; Biddenden village; Boughton Monchelsea Place; Broadstairs (Bleak House); Canterbury (Cathedral; Roman pavement; St. Augustine's Abbey; Royal Museum; West Gate Museum); Chartwell; Chiddingstone village; Chilham Castle; Cobham Hall; Deal Castle; Dover (Castle; Roman lighthouse); Faversham (Arden's House; Freemason's Hall); Glassenbury Park; Godinton Park; Hever Castle; Hythe; Ightham Mote; Kit's Coty House (Neolithic remains); Knole; Luddesdown Court; Lullingstone (Castle; Villa; manor house); Lympne Castle (and Lemanis fort); Maidstone (Old Palace; Chillington Manor; Old College); Minster (Church of SS Mary and Sexburga); Penshurst Place; Reculver (fort; Church of St. Mary); Rochester (Cathedral; castle; King's School); Royal Tunbridge Wells; Sissinghurst Castle; Sittingbourne (Court Hall museum); Sundridge Old Hall; Sutton-at-Hone (St. John's Jerusalem); Walmer Castle; Westerham (Squerryes Court)

Principal county worthies (by birth): Sir Philip Sidney (the soldier, poet, statesman, born at Penshurst Place; 1554–1586); Christopher Marlow (the writer, born at Canterbury; 1564–1593); Sir William Harvey (1578–1657); John Tradescant (the botanist, born at Meopham in 1608); General James Wolfe (the victor at Quebec, born at Westerham; 1727–1759); Edward Hasted (the Kentish historian, born at Eastling in 1732); William Pitt the Younger (born at Hayes; 1759–1806); William Hazlitt (the writer, born at Maidstone; 1778–1830); Sir William Jenner (1815–1898); Robert Bridges (1844–1930); Frank Woolley (the great cricketer, born at Tonbridge in 1887)

Highest point above Sea Level: Point south of Westerham Hill on county border with Surrey, 809 feet (exact location disputed)

19. LANCASHIRE

Statutory name of administrative county: County of Lancaster

Derivation and first recorded use of name: cf. *Lunecastrum*, the camp on the River Lune. Mentioned in the will of Wulfric, abbot of St. Augustine's, bequeathing land at Burton Abbey, in A.D. 1004, and confirmed by King Aethelred

Population in 1801: 673,486

Population in 1971: 5,191,330

Area: 1,201,850 acres

Population density per acre in 1971: 4·32

County Town and River: Preston on the River Ribble

Motto of County Council: "*In Concilio Consilium*" = In Council is Wisdom

County Boroughs (and population): Barrow-in-Furness (63,510); Blackburn (100,010); Blackpool (150,000); Bolton (152,010); Bootle (79,780); Burnley (76,610); Bury (67,880); City of Liverpool (667,000); City of Manchester (590,000); Oldham (108,080 Preston (100,140); Rochdale (87,720); St. Helens (102,900); City of Salford (135,530); Southport (83,000); Warrington (70,300); Wigan (79,300)

Municipal Boroughs (and population): Accrington (36,070); Ashton-under-Lyne (47,880); Bacup (16,220); Chorley (30,780); Clitheroe (12,920); Colne (18,790); Crosby (58,200); Darwen (28,300); Eccles (39,430); Farnworth (26,430); Fleetwood (28,910); Haslingden (14,550); Heywood (30,400); City of Lancaster (48,500); Leigh (46,130); Lytham St. Anne's (36,890); Middleton (56,950); Morecombe and Heysham (40,200); Mossley (9,790); Nelson (30,800); Prestwich (32,660); Radcliffe (28,710); Rawenstall (21,370); Stretford (58,380); Swinton and Pendlebury (40,400); Widnes (55,730)

Urban Districts: Abram, Adlington, Ashton-in-Makerfield, Aspull, Atherton, Audenshaw, Barrowford,

Billinge and Winstanley, Blackrod, Brierfield, Carnforth, Chadderton, Church, Clayton-le-Moors, Crompton, Dalton-in-Furness, Denton, Droylesden, Failsworth, Formby, Fullwood, Golborne, Grange, Great Harwood, Haydock, Hindley, Horwich, Huyton-with-Roby, Ince-in-Makerfield, Irlam, Kearsley, Kirkby, Lees, Leyland, Litherland, Littleborough, Little Lever, Longridge, Milnrow, Newton-le-Willows, Ormskirk, Orrell, Oswaldtwistle, Padiham, Poutton-le-Fylde, Preesall, Prescot, Rainford, Ramsbottom, Rishton, Royton, Skelmersdale and Holland, Standish with Langtree, Thornton Cleveleys, Tottington, Trawden, Turton, Tyldesley, Ulverston, Urmston, Walton-le-dale, Wardle, Westhoughton, Whitefield, Whitworth, Withnell, Worsley

Rural Districts: Blackburn, Burnley, Chorley, Clitheroe, Fylde, Garstang, Lancaster, Lunesdale, North Lonsdale, Preston, Warrington, West Lancashire, Whiston, Wigan

Lord-Lieutenant of County: Rt. Hon. The Lord Rhodes, P.C., D.F.C.

Principal Industries: Textiles (cotton) and clothing manufacture; heavy engineering; coal-mining; can-manufacture; cattle, sheep and poultry farming; dockyards and ports; glass manufacture; rubber processing; aircraft manufacture; holiday trade (Blackpool, etc.)

Tourist attractions and places of interest: Blackburn (Museum and Art Gallery); Blackpool Tower; Blackstone Edge Roman Road; Bootle (Art Gallery and Museum); Borwich Hall; Burnley (Towneley Hall); Chorley (Astley Hall); Coniston (John Ruskin Museum); Furness Abbey; Gawthorpe Hall; Hall-I'-Th'-Wood; Halsall (Church of St. Cuthbert); Hawkshead (Hall and Ann Tyson's cottage); Heysham (Church of St. Peter); Hill Top (Beatrix Potter's house); Hoghton Tower; Hornby Castle; Lancaster (Castle; City Museum); Liverpool (Roman Catholic and Anglican Cathedrals; Bluecoat Chambers; City Museum; Picton, Hornby and Brown Libraries; St. George's Hall; Speke Hall; Walker Art Gallery); Manchester (Cathedral; City Art Gallery; Chetham's Library; Heaton Hall; Liverpool Road Station; Town Hall; Whitworth Art Gallery); Manchester Ship Canal; Ribchester (remains of Roman fort; museum of Roman antiquities); Rufford (Old Hall); St. Helens (Pilkington Glass Museum); Scarisbrick Hall; Smithills Hall; Southport (Atkinson Art Gallery); Turton Tower; Whalley (Church of St. Mary).

Principal county worthies (by birth): John Byrom (the hymnologist, born in Manchester in 1692); Sir Richard Arkwright (the inventor of the spinning frame, born at Preston; 1732–1792); George Romney (born in Dalton-in-Furness; 1734–1802); Thomas de Quincey (born in Manchester in 1785); Sir Robert Peel (the statesman, born at Chamber Hall, near Bury; 1788–1850); Felicia Hemans (the writer, born at Liverpool; 1793–1835); 14th Earl of Derby (the statesman, born at Knowsley; 1799–1869); William Ewart Gladstone (the statesman, born at Liverpool; 1809–1898); Henry Tate (of sugar fame, and founder of the Tate Gallery, born at Chorley in 1819); 1st Earl Lloyd-George of Dwyfor (the statesman, born at Manchester; 1863–1945)

Highest point above Sea Level: The Old Man of Coniston, in the Lake District; 2,633 feet

20. LEICESTERSHIRE

Statutory name of administrative county: Leicester

Derivation and first recorded use of name: Laegreceastre, Legra-castra, the Camp by the River Legra (now the River Soar). The latter form probably used in Charters granted by King Edgar, *c.* A.D. 967

Population in 1801: 130,082

Population in 1971: 745,740

Area: 533,543 acres

Population density per acre in 1971: 1·39

County Town and River: City of Leicester on the River Soar

Motto of County Council: "For'ard, for'ard"

County Borough (and population): City of Leicester (276,690)

Municipal Borough (and population): Loughborough (40,560)

Urban Districts: Ashby-de-la-Zouch, Ashby Woulds, Coalville, Hinckley, Market Harborough, Melton Mowbray, Oadby, Shepshed, Wigston

Rural Districts: Ashby-de-la-Zouch, Barrow upon Soar, Billesdon, Blaby, Castle Donington, Lutterworth, Market Bosworth, Market Harborough, Melton and Belvoir

Lord-Lieutenant of County: Col. R. A. St. G. Martin, O.B.E.

Principal Industries: Cattle and sheep farming; quarrying and coal-mining; clothing manufacture; general and light engineering; food processing

Tourist attractions and places of Interest: Appleby Magna (Church of St. Michael); Ashby-de-la-Zouch castle; Belvoir Castle; Breedon on the Hill (Church of SS Mary and Hardulph); Burrough Hill (Iron Age fort); Hallaton (Church of St. Michael); Kirby Muxloe Castle; Leicester Cathedral; Church of St. Margaret; Guildhall; Jewry Wall; Newarke Houses Museum); Market Harborough (Church of St. Dionysius); Melton Mowbray (Church of St. Mary); Stanford Hall;

Belvoir Castle, Leicestershire, built by the Duchess of Rutland in the early 19th century

Stapleford Park; Staunton Harold (church and hall)

Principal county worthies (by birth): Hugh Latimer (bishop under Henry VIII, born at Thurcaston; 1470–1555); Queen Jane (born at Bradgate Park; 1537–1554); George Fox (founder of the Quakers, born at Fenny Drayton; 1624–1691); Lord Macaulay (the poet, born at Rothley; 1800–1859)

Highest point above Sea Level: Unnamed point in Charnwood Forest, 2 miles east of Coalville, 910 feet

21. LINCOLNSHIRE

Statutory names of administrative counties: (a) Lincoln, Parts of Holland. (b) Lincoln, Parts of Lindsey. (c) Lincoln, Parts of Kesteven. See below

Derivation and first recorded use of name: Lincolnshire, cf. Lincolnescir, and a derivation from the Roman name of LINDVM (*lindum* = the widening of a river). The name Lincolnescir probably dates from A.D. *c.* 664 when numerous parcels of land were granted by Wulfhere, king of Mercia.

Area of geographical county: 1,704,025 acres

Lord-Lieutenant of County: The Earl of Ancaster, T.D.

Principal Industries: Cereal crops, potatoes and sugar beet; livestock (cattle and pigs); market gardening and flower bulbs; general engineering; iron and steel industries; the holiday trade

Highest point above Sea Level: Normanby le Wold, four miles north of Market Rasen (Lindsey), 548 feet

(a) Lincoln, Parts of Holland

Statutory name of administrative county: Lincoln, Parts of Holland

Derivation and first recorded use of name: cf. *Hōh-land*, (Old English (= land near a *hōh*, = a slight rise of ground, i.e. near Spalding). Probably first used formally in *c.* 1150

Population in 1801: 36,399

Population in 1971: 105,090

Area: 267,845 acres

Population density per acre in 1971: 0·39

County Town and River: Boston on the River Witham

Motto of County Council: "*Labor ipse merces*"

Municipal Borough (and population): Boston (25,410)

Urban District: Spalding

Rural Districts: Boston, East Elloe, Spalding

Tourist attractions and places of interest: Boston (Church of St. Botolph; the "Stump"; Fydell House; Guildhall); Holbeach (Church of All Saints); Lond Sutton (Church of St. Mary); Spalding (Ayscoughfee Hall; White Horse Inn)

Principal county worthies (by birth): Hereward the Wake (the Anglo-Saxon rebel, fl. 1071, probably born in north Holland); John Foxe (1516–1587); 1st Lord Burghley (1520–1598); Capt. Matthew Flinders (the explorer, born at Donington in 1774)

(b) Lincoln, Parts of Lindsey

Statutory name of administrative county: Lincoln, Parts

of Lindsey

Derivation and first recorded use of name: Probably a contraction of the Roman name LINDVM for the city of Lincoln (although it has been suggested that the name is derived from the Welsh *llyn*, an undrained fen). Probably first formally used in charters granted in A.D. *c.* 680 by Aethelred, king of Mercia, to the Church

Population in 1801:	*Population in 1971:*
115,210	541,520
Area: 974,438 acres	*Population density per acre in 1971:* 0·55

County Town and River: City of Lincoln on the River Witham

Motto of County Council: "Service Links All"

County Boroughs (and population): Grimsby (96,020); City of Lincoln (74,760)

Municipal Boroughs (and population): Cleethorpes (35,980); Louth (11,460); Scunthorpe (69,660)

Urban Districts: Alford, Barton-upon-Humber, Brigg, Gainsborough, Horncastle, Mablethorpe and Sutton, Market Rasen, Skegness, Woodhall Spa

Rural Districts: Caistor, Gainsborough, Glanford Brigg, Grimsby, Horncastle, Isle of Axholme, Louth, Spilsby, Welton

Tourist attractions and places of interest: Barton-upon-Humber (churches of St. Mary and St. Peter); Caistor (excavations of walled town); Epworth (Old Rectory); Gainsborough (Old Hall); Gunby Hall; Ingoldmells (Church of SS Peter and Paul); Kirton-in-Lindsey (Church of St. Andrew); Lincoln (Cathedral; castle remains; City and County Museum; Roman Town gate; Jew's House; Stonebow and Guildhall; Usher Art Gallery); Louth (remains of abbey; Church of St. James); Tattersall Castle; Thornton Abbey

Principal county worthies (by birth): William of Waynflete (the founder of Magdalen College, Oxford, born at Wainfleet); King Henry IV (1366–1413, born at Old Bolingbroke, Spilsby); Charles Wesley (the founder of Methodism, born at Epworth; 1703–1791); Sir John Franklin (the explorer, born at Spilsby; 1768–1847); Alfred, 1st Lord Tennyson (the great poet, born at Somersby; 1809–1892)

(c) Lincoln, Parts of Kesteven

Statutory name of administrative county: Lincoln, Parts of Kesteven

Derivation and first recorded use of name: Contraction of Welsh *coed* (= a wood) and Norse *stefna* (= a location or area), becoming *coeftefne*, and probably first formally used prior to A.D. 1000

Population in 1801:	*Population in 1971:*
57,016	146,850
Area: 463,490 acres	*Population density per acre in 1971:* 0·32

County Town and River: Sleaford on the River Slea

Motto of County Council: "*Perseverentia vincit*" = Perseverance succeeds

Municipal Boroughs (and population): Grantham (26,660); Stamford (14,110)

Urban Districts: Bourne, Sleaford

Rural Districts: North, East, South and West Kesteven

Tourist attractions and Places of Interest: Belton House; Bourne (town and castle remains); Brant Broughton (Church of St. Helen); Doddington Hall; Grantham (Church of St. Wulfram; Angel and Royal Hotel); Grimsthorpe Castle; Honington Camp (Iron Age fort); Cranwell (Royal Air Force College); Sleaford (Church of St. Denys); Woolsthorpe Manor (Sir Isaac Newton's house)

Principal county worthies (by birth): Sir Isaac Newton (originator of the universal law of gravitation, born at Woolsthorpe Manor; 1642–1727)

22. GREATER LONDON

Statutory name of administrative area: Greater London (N.B. The former administrative county of Middlesex was abolished under the 1963 London Government Act on 1st April 1965. It is however still used for postal purposes)

Derivation and first recorded use of name: Roman name of LONDINIVM, probably first used about A.D. 40, possibly derived from a tribal leader, Londin (cf. *londo* = a bold one, Old Irish)

Population in 1801:	*Population in 1971:*
959,310	7,612,280
Area: 393,809 acres	*Population density per acre in 1971:* 19·33

River: River Thames

Boroughs (and population; Registrar General's figures for mid-1970):

Barking	166,060	Kensington	
Barnet	313,080	and Chelsea	203,730
Bexley	215,480	Kingston-	
Brent	278,500	upon-Thames	142,690
Bromley	301,820	Lambeth	321,260
Camden	223,150	Lewisham	279,350
Croydon	327,810	Merton	181,460
Ealing	294,820	Newham	247,170
Enfield	262,690	Redbridge	242,840
Greenwich	226,130	Richmond-	
Hackney	233,490	upon-Thames	174,550
Hammersmith	187,980	Southwark	284,690
Haringey	238,410	Sutton	166,480
Harrow	206,060	Tower Hamlets	182,260
Havering	252,130	Waltham	
Hillingdon	235,780	Forest	235,040
Hounslow	204,380	Wandsworth	317,410
Islington	227,340	City of	
		Westminster	234,430

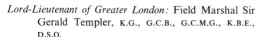

Lord-Lieutenant of Greater London: Field Marshal Sir Gerald Templer, K.G., G.C.B., G.C.M.G., K.B.E., D.S.O.

Principal Industries: Centre of commerce, banking, insurance, national government and industrial administration; warehousing, packing and shipping; centre of professions (legal, medical and other consultancies); centre of wholesale and retail distribution (foodstuffs, textiles, furnishings, etc.); general engineering, printing, etc.; tourism

Tourist attractions and places of interest: Abbeys, cathedrals and churches. All Hallows By-the-Tower (E.C.3); All Saints (W.1); All Souls (W.1); Chapel Royal, St. James's Palace (S.W.1); The Brompton Oratory (S.W.7); Queen's Chapel of the Savoy, Strand (W.C.2); St. Albans, Holborn (E.C.1); St. Bartholomew-the-Great (E.C.1); St. Bride, Fleet Street (E.C.4); St. Clement Danes, Strand (W.C.2); St. George's, Hanover Square (W.1); St. George's, Southwark (S.E.1); St. Margaret's, Westminster (S.W.1); St. Martin-in-the-Fields, Trafalgar Square (W.C.2); St. Mary-le-Bow, Cheapside (E.C.2); St. Paul's Cathedral (E.C.4); Southwark Cathedral; Temple Church, Fleet Street (E.C.4); Westminster Abbey (S.W.1); Westminster Cathedral, Victoria Street (S.W.1)

Art Galleries and Museums: Royal Academy, Piccadilly (W.1); British Museum (W.C.1); British Transport Museum, Clapham (S.W.4); Dickens House, 48 Doughty Street (W.C.1); Geological Museum (S.W.7); Hampton Court Palace; Imperial War Museum, Lambeth Road (S.E.1); Iveagh Bequest, Kenwood, Hampstead Heath (N.W.3); Keats' Museum, Hampstead (N.W.3); Lancaster House (S.W.1); London Museum, Kensington Gardens (W.8); National Gallery, Trafalgar Square (W.C.2); National Maritime Museum, Greenwich (S.E.10); National Portrait Gallery, Trafalgar Square (W.C.2); Natural History Museum, Cromwell Road (S.W.7); Science Museum, Exhibition Road (S.W.7); Tate Gallery (S.W.1); Victoria and Albert Museum, South Kensington (S.W.7); Wallace Collection, Manchester Square (W.1); Wellington Museum, Apsley House, Hyde Park Corner (W.1); Whitechapel Art Gallery (E.1)

Memorials, Monuments and Palaces: Buckingham Palace (S.W.1); Clarence House (S.W.1); Kensington Palace (W.8); St. James's Palace (S.W.1); Admiralty Arch, The Mall; Albert Memorial; Artillery Memorial, Hyde Park Corner; Cenotaph; Cleopatra's Needle; Eros Statue, Piccadilly Circus; Marble Arch; Nelson's Column in Trafalgar Square; Roosevelt Memorial, Grosvenor Square

Other places of interest: The Tower of London; Tower Bridge; Houses of Parliament and Parliament Square

Principal worthies of Greater London (by birth): Kings and Queens: King Edward I (1239-1307; born at Westminster); King Edward V (1470-1483; born at Westminster); King Henry VIII (1491-1547; born at Greenwich); King Edward VI (1537-1553; born at Hampton Court); Queen Elizabeth I (1533-1603; born at Greenwich); Queen Mary I (1516-1558; born at Greenwich); King Charles II (1630-1685; born at St. James's Palace); King James II (1633-1701; born at St. James's Palace); Queen Mary II (1662-1694; born at St. James's Palace); Queen Anne (1665-1714; born at St. James's Palace); King George III (1738-1820; born at Norfolk House); King George IV (1762-1830; born at St. James's Palace); King William IV (1765-1837; born at Buckingham Palace); King Edward VII (1841-1910; born at Buckingham Palace); Queen Victoria (1819-1901; born at Kensington Palace); King George V (1865-1936; born at Marlborough House); Queen Elizabeth II (born 1926 at 17 Bruton Street, W.1)

Statesmen: 1st Earl of Chatham (William Pitt the Elder, 1708-1778; born at St. James's Westminster); 3rd Duke of Grafton (1735-1811; born at St. Marylebone); Lord North (1732-1792; born at Albemarle Street, Piccadilly); Spencer Perceval (1762-1812; born at Audley Square); Viscount Goderich (1782-1859); 3rd Viscount Melbourne (Sir William Lamb, 1779-1848; born at Melbourne House, Piccadilly); 1st Earl Russell 1792-1878; born at Hertford Street, Mayfair); Earl of Beaconsfield (Benjamin Disraeli, 1804-1881; believed born at the Adelphi, Westminster); 5th Earl of Rosebery (1847-1929; born at Charles Street, Berkeley Square); 1st Earl Attlee (1883-1967; born at Putney); Harold Macmillan (born in 1894 at 54 Cadogan Place); Sir Alexander Douglas-Home (born in 1903 at 28 South Street)

Other worthies: Thomas à Beckett (1118-1170); Sir Thomas More (1478-1535, the humanist, born in Milk Street); Edmund Spenser (1552-1599, the poet; traditionally thought to have been born in East Smithfield); Ben Johnson (1572-1637); Inigo Jones (the architect, 1573-1652); Thomas Wentworth, Earl of Strafford (1593-1641); Sir Thomas Browne (1605-1682); John Milton (the writer and poet, 1608-1674; born at Bread Street, Cheapside); Edmond Halley (the astronomer, 1656-1742); Daniel Defoe (the writer, 1660-1731); Alexander Pope (the poet and satirist, 1688-1744, born at Lombard Street); Thomas Gray (the writer, 1716-1771); Earl Howe (victor of the Battle of the First of June, 1726-1799); John Nash (the architect, 1752-1835); Joseph Turner (the Romantic landscape painter, 1775-

Her Majesty the Queen's London residence, Buckingham Palace, which was built by the Duke of Buckingham and Chandos, and bought by King George III in 1761

1851); Sir Charles Napier (1782–1853; the British commander in India); Viscount Stratford de Redcliffe (the British diplomat, 1786–1880); Michael Faraday (1791–1867); Thomas Hood (1799–1855); Charles Lamb (1775–1834, born at Crown Office Row, Temple); Robert Browning (1812–1889); Anthony Trollope (1815–1882); George F. Watts (the painter and sculptor, 1817–1904); John Ruskin (the writer, critic and artist, 1819–1900; born in Bloomsbury); Dante Gabriel Rossetti (the poet and painter; 1828–1882); Sir William Gilbert (the writer and poet, 1836–1911); Algernon Charles Swinburne (the poet and critic, 1837–1909); Sir Arthur Sullivan (the composer, 1842–1900); Lord Baden-Powell (the founder of the Scout movement, 1857–1941); John Stuart Mill (the philosopher and economist, 1806–1873; born at Pentonville); Sir Max Beerbohm (the author and caricaturist; 1872–1956); Gilbert Keith Chesterton (the journalist and poet, 1874–1936); the Hon. Charles Stewart Rolls (the pioneer motorist and aviator, 1877–1910); Francis Osbert Sitwell (the poet and satirist, 1892–1969)

23. MONMOUTHSHIRE

Note: Not only is the County of Monmouth popularly regarded as part of the Principality of Wales, it is also largely administered as part thereof, and is occupied by many people who speak Welsh. Constitutionally the County is English however, being contained in the List of English (and not Welsh) Counties in the First Schedule of the Local Government Act, 1933. By Statute the boundary between England and Wales may not be altered by the processes of local administration; this does not apply to the boundary between Wales and the County of Monmouth, hence the provision for its administration as part of the Principality. See motto

Statutory name of administrative county: County of Monmouth

Derivation and first recorded use of name: cf. Aper Mynuy, early Welsh for "mouth of the Monnow river", and hence its translation to Monomude, formally recorded in 1086. The Monnow river was recognised as such as early as the 7th century

Population in 1801:   *Population in 1971:*
45,568   464,560

Area: 346,762 acres   *Population density per acre in 1971:* 1·34

County Town and River: Newport (Welsh, *Casnewydd*) on the River Usk

Motto of County Council: "*Utrique fidelis*" = Faithful to Both

County Borough (and population): Newport (111,780)

Municipal Boroughs (and population): Abergavenny (9,520); Monmouth (6,360)

Urban Districts: Abercarn, Abertillery, Bedwas and Machen, Bedwellty, Blaeravon, Caerleon, Chepstow, Cwmbran, Ebbw Vale, Mynyddislwyn, Nantyglo and Blaina, Pontypool, Rhymney, Risca, Tredegare, Usk

Rural Districts: Abergavenny, Chepstow, Magor and

St. Mellons, Monmouth, Pontypool

Lord-Lieutenant of County: Colonel E. R. Hill, D.S.O.

Principal Industries: Coal-mining; iron and steel; general engineering; chemical industries; dairy cattle farming

Tourist attractions and places of interest: Abergavenny (Priory Church; district museum); Bettws Newydd church; Caerleon Roman amphitheatre; Caerwent (remains of the Roman city of Venta Silurum); The Kymin; Llanthony Priory; Llanvihangel Crucorney (Llanvihangel Court); Monmouth (Monnow bridge gatehouse; Shire Hall; Great Castle House; Nelson Museum); Newport (Cathedral of St. Woolos; Museum and Art Gallery); Raglan Castle; Skenfrith Castle; Tintern Abbey; Treowen manor house; Usk (Priory Church of St. Mary)

Principal county worthies (by birth): King Henry V (born in Monmouth Castle; 1387-1422); Robert Owen (the "father" of the co-operative movement, born at Newtown; 1771-1858); W. H. Davies ("The Tramp Poet", born at Newport; 1871-1940); Aneurin Bevan (the politician, 1897-1960)

Highest point above Sea Level: Chwarel-y-Fan, 2,228 feet

24. NORFOLK

Statutory name of administrative county: County of Norfolk

Derivation and first recorded use of name: cf. *nor-folk,* the northern folk of East Anglia. Featured in grants of privileges and fish renders made by King Cnut between 1018 and 1023

Population in 1801: 273,479

Population in 1971: 617,380

Area: 1,314,341 acres

Population density per acre in 1971: 0·47

County Town and River: The City of Norwich on the River Wensum

County Boroughs (and population): Great Yarmouth (50,180); City of Norwich (120,140)

Municipal Boroughs (and population): King's Lynn (30,720); Thetford (12,800)

Urban Districts: Cromer, Diss, Downham Market, East Dereham, Hunstanton, North Walsham, Sheringham, Swaffham, Wells, Wymondham

Rural Districts: Blofield and Flegg, Depwade, Docking, Downham, Erpingham, Forehoe and Henstead, Freebridge Lynn, Loddon, Marshland, Mitford and Launditch, St. Faiths and Aylsham, Smallburgh, Swaffham, Walsingham, Wayland

Lord-Lieutenant of County: Lieut.-Col. Sir Edmund Bacon, Bt., K.B.E., T.D.

Principal Industries: Cereal and root crops; poultry farming (turkeys); market gardening (vegetables); general engineering and manufacture of agricultural machinery; motor-car manufacture; fores-

try; confectionery; tourism and the holiday trade (seaside and the Broads)

Tourist attractions and places of interest: Aylsham (Old Hall); Binham Priory; Blakeney (Church of St. Nicholas; Red House); Blickling Hall; Breckles Hall; Caister Castle ruins; Caistor St. Edmund; Castle Acre (castle and priory remains; Church of St. James); Castle Rising (the castle; Bede House); Gowthorpe Manor; Great Cressingham Priory; Grimes's Graves (Neolithic mine shafts); Holkham Camp (Iron Age fort) and Holkham Hall; King's Lynn (Guildhall; Hampton Court; Museum and Art Gallery; King Street; Custom House; Church of St. Nicholas; South Gate); North Runcton (Church of All Saints); Norwich (Cathedral; Castle; Elm Hill; Church of St. Peter Mancroft; City Hall; Priory; Maddermarket; Royal Norfolk Regiment Museum); Oxburgh Hall; Potter Heigham (Church of St. Nicholas); Ranworth (Church of St. Helen); Raynham Hall; St. Benet's Abbey; Sandringham House and gardens; Scole (White Hart Inn); Thetford (Castle Hill; Bell Hotel; Ancient House; Museum; King's House; Cage and Stocks); Walsingham Priory ruins; Warham Camp (Iron Age fort); West Acre Priory remains; West Walton (Church of St. Mary); Wymondham (Church of SS Mary and Thomas of Canterbury; abbey ruins)

Principal county worthies (by birth): Sir Edward Coke (Lord Chief Justice in James I's reign, born at Mileham; 1552-1634); 2nd Viscount Townshend (born at Raynham; 1675-1738); Sir Robert Walpole (1676-1745); Thomas Paine (the writer and father of socialism, born at Thetford; 1737-1809); Fanny Burney (the writer, born at King's Lynn; 1752-1840); 1st Viscount (Horatio) Nelson (born at Burnham Thorpe; 1758-1805); Mrs. Elizabeth Fry (the Quaker preacher, born at Norwich; 1780-1845); George Borrow (the writer, born at Dumpling Green, Dereham; 1803-1881); 1st Earl of Cromer (1841-1917); Edith Cavell (the nurse, executed by the Germans, born at Swardeston; 1865-1915); H.M. King George VI (born at Sandringham; 1895-1952)

Highest point above Sea Level: At the site of the Roman signal station ("Roman Camp"), one mile south of West Runton, Sheringham; 345 feet

25. NORTHAMPTONSHIRE

Statutory name of administrative county: County of Northampton

Derivation and first recorded use of name: North *Hamtunscir,* the northern people's shire (*scir*) around the homestead (*tun*) and meadow (*ham*); almost certainly used formally as early as A.D. 833 in Charter grants of land and privileges by King

Wiglaf of Mercia to Siward, abbot of Crowland

Population in 1801: 121,600

Population in 1971: 461,410

Area: 585,149 acres†

Population density per acre in 1971: 0·79

County Town and River: Northampton on the River Nene

Motto of County Council: "*Rosa concordiae signum*" = A Rose, the Symbol of Harmony

County Borough (and population): Northampton (122,790)

Municipal Boroughs (and population): Brackley (5,520); Daventry (11,940); Higham Ferrers (4,760); Kettering (40,260)

Urban Districts: Burton Latimer, Corby, Desborough, Irthlingborough, Oundle, Raunds, Rothwell, Rushden, Wellingborough

Rural Districts: Brackley, Brixworth, Daventry, Kettering, Northampton, Oundle and Thrapston, Towcester, Wellingborough

Lord-Lieutenant of County: Lieut.-Col. J. Chandos-Pole, O.B.E., J.P.

Principal Industries: Beef and dairy cattle farming; sheep farming; cereal and root crops; steel works; paper mills; manufacture of clothing and footwear; general and light engineering

Tourist attractions and places of interest: Aldwincle (Church of St. Peter); Althorp mansion; Aynho Park mansion; Brixworth (Church of All Saints); Brockhall manor house; Castle Ashby mansion; Church Stowe (Church of SS Peter and Paul); Cotterstock Hall; Deen Park; Delapre Abbey; Earls Barton (Church of All Saints); Easton Neston House; Gayton Manor; Hardingstone (Church of St. Edmund); Lowick (Church of St. Peter; Northampton (Church of the Holy Sepulchre; Church of All Saints; Church of St. Peter; Central Museum and Art Gallery; Northamptonshire Regiment Museum); Rainsborough Camp (hill fort); Rockingham Castle and Hall; Rushton Hall; Stoke Park Pavilions; Sulgrave Manor (the ancestral home of George Washington)

Principal county worthies (by birth): King Richard III (born at Fotheringhay Castle; 1452-1485); Sir Christopher Hatton (Elizabeth I's Lord Chancellor, born at Holdenby; 1540-1591); John Dryden (born at Oundle, 1631-1700); William Law (the religious writer, born at King's Cliffe in 1686)

Highest point above Sea Level: West Haddon, 609 feet

† Excluding the Soke of Peterborough

26. NORTHUMBERLAND

Statutory name of administrative county: County of Northumberland

Derivation and first recorded use of name: cf. *Norohymbraland* (and Northumbria), the land north of the River Humber. Known in use in A.D. 895; may date much earlier, perhaps to A.D. 664, as recognised by Wulfhere, king of Mercia, and used in some North Country land grants

Population in 1801: 168,078

Population in 1971: 821,010

Area: 1,292,040 acres

Population density per acre in 1971: 0·63

County Town and River: City of Newcastle upon Tyne, on the River Tyne

County Boroughs (and population): City of Newcastle upon Tyne (236,730); Tynemouth (71,680)

Municipal Boroughs (and population): Berwick-upon-Tweed (11,440); Blyth (35,320); Morpeth (14,700); Wallsend (46,940); Whitley Bay (37,910)

Urban Districts: Alnwick, Amble, Ashington, Bedlingtonshire, Gosforth, Hexham, Longbenton, Newbiggin-by-the-Sea, Newburn, Prudhoe, Seaton Valley

Rural Districts: Alnwick, Belford, Bellingham, Castle Ward, Glendale, Haltwhistle, Hexham, Morpeth, Norham and Islandshires, Rothbury

Lord-Lieutenant of County: His Grace The Duke of Northumberland, K.G., T.D.

Principal Industries: Sheep and cattle farming; coalmining; heavy engineering and shipbuilding; general and light engineering

Tourist attractions and places of interest: Alnwick Castle; Berwick-upon-Tweed (castle remains; town wall and gates; river bridges); Bolam (Church of St. Andrew); Brinkburn Priory; Dunstanburgh Castle (remains); Greaves Ash (Iron Age settlement units); Hadrian's Wall; Hexham and Hexham Abbey; Kirkwhelpington (Church of St. Bartholomew); Lindisfarne Priory and Castle; Newcastle upon Tyne (Cathedral; Hancock Museum; High-level Bridge; Laing Art Gallery; Royal Northumberland Fusiliers Regimental Museum); Old Bewick hill fort; Seaton Deleval Hall; Tynemouth (Priory Church remains); Warkworth Castle; Yeavering Bell fort

Principal county worthies (by birth): Lancelot "Capability" Brown (the great landscape gardener, born at Kirkharle; 1715-1783); Admiral Lord Collingwood (1750-1810); 2nd Earl Grey (1764-1845); George Stephenson (the railway and locomotive. pioneer, born at Wylam; 1781-1848); John Dobson (the architect, born at North Shields in 1787); Grace Darling (the famous rescuer of survivors from the "*Forfarshire*" in 1838, born at Bamburgh; 1815-1842)

Highest point above Sea Level: The Cheviot, 2,676 feet

27. NOTTINGHAMSHIRE

Statutory name of administrative county: County of Nottingham

Blenheim Palace, Oxfordshire – Queen Anne's gift in gratitude to John Churchill, Duke of Marlborough. It was also the birthplace of Sir Winston Churchill

Derivation and first recorded use of name: cf. *Snotinga-ham,* the homestead (*ham*) of the followers of Snot, a Norseman. Probably first formally used in King Eadwig's Charter grants of land to Bishop Oscytel in *c.* 960

Population in 1801:   *Population in 1971:*
140,350   970,310

Area: 539,313 acres   *Population density per acre in 1971:* 1·79

County Town and River: City of Nottingham on the River Trent

County Borough (and population): City of Nottingham (300,580)

Municipal Boroughs (and population): East Retford (18,810); Mansfield (55,860); Newark-on-Trent (24,580); Worksop (35,600)

Urban Districts: Arnold, Beeston and Stapleford, Carlton, Eastwood, Hucknall, Kirkby-in-Ashfield, Mansfield Woodhouse, Sutton-in-Ashfield, Warsop, West Bridgford

Rural Districts: Basford, Bingham, East Retford, Newark, Southwell, Worksop

Lord-Lieutenant of County: Rear-Admiral R. St. V. Sherbrooke, v.c., c.b., d.s.o., r.n.

Principal Industries: Dairy and sheep farming; cereal and root crops; horticulture and market gardening; coal-mining and stone quarrying; general engineering; textiles

Tourist attractions and places of interest: East Markham (Church of St. John the Baptist); Hawton (Church of All Saints); Newark-on-Trent (Church of St. Mary Magdalene; town museum); Newstead Abbey; Nottingham (castle ruins; Church of St. Mary); Sherwood Forest; Southwell Minster; Thoresby Hall; Thumpton Hall; Wollaton Hall; Worksop Priory

Principal county worthies (by birth): Thomas Cranmer (Henry VIII's Primate, 1489-1556); Edmund Cartwright (1743-1823); General William Booth (founder of the Salvation Army, born at Nottingham; 1829-1912); Samuel Butler (1835-1902); Viscount Allenby (born at Southwell in 1871); D. H. Lawrence (the writer, born at Eastwood; 1885-1930)

Highest point above Sea Level: Unnamed point on south of Stanton Hill, east of Sutton-in-Ashfield; 660 feet

28. OXFORDSHIRE

Statutory name of administrative county: County of Oxford

Derivation and first recorded use of name: cf. Oxenfordscir, the shire of Oxenford, the river ford for oxen. The town name of Oxnaforda was first recorded in A.D. 912, and featured in King Athelstan's charters shortly afterwards.

Population in 1801:   *Population in 1971:*
111,977   379,860

Area: 479,178 acres   *Population density per acre in 1971:* 0·79

The High Street, Oxford

County Town and River: City of Oxford on the River Isis (River Thames at Oxford)

Motto of County Council: "*Sapere Aude*" = Dare to be Wise

County Borough (and population): City of Oxford (109,330)

Municipal Boroughs (and population): Banbury (28,650); Chipping Norton (4,700); Henley-on-Thames (10,710); Woodstock (2,300)

Urban Districts: Bicester, Thame, Witney

Rural Districts: Banbury, Bullingdon, Chipping Norton, Henley, Ploughley, Witney

Lord-Lieutenant of County: Lieut.-Col. John Thomson, T.D.

Principal Industries: Dairy farming and cereal crops; motor-car manufacture; car accessories; associated metal sheet processing; light engineering; paper mills and printing; clothing manufacture; blanket manufacture (Witney); tourism (Oxford and neighbourhood)

Tourist attractions and places of interest: Oxford (colleges and buildings of the University; the Cathedral; Bodleian Library; Ashmolean Library; Church of St. Mary the Virgin; Church of St. Michael; Martyrs' Memorial); Bampton (Manor and town); Banbury (town and Cross); Blenheim Palace; Bloxham (Church of Our Lady); Broughton Castle; Burford (Tolsey Museum); Church Hanborough (Church of SS Peter and Paul); Ditchley Park; Dorchester Abbey; Ewelme (Church of St. Mary the Virgin; Grammar School and Almshouse); Iffley (Church of St. Mary); Mapledurham House; Minster Lovell (and Hall ruins); North Leigh Roman Villa; Rousham House; Stanton Harcourt (Church of St. Michael); Stonor Park; Witney (Church of St. Mary the Virgin; Blanket Hall; Butter Cross); Woodstock; Wroxton Abbey

Principal county worthies (by birth): King Richard I (born at Oxford; 1157–1199); King John (born at Beaumont Palace, Oxford; 1167–1216); the Black Prince (born at Woodstock); John White (chief founder of Massachusetts, U.S.A., born at Stanton St. John; 1575–1648); Sir William D'Avenant (the Poet Laureate, baptised at Oxford; 1606–1668); Warren Hastings (the first Governor-General of India, born at Churchill; 1732–1818); Sir John Soane (the architect, born at Whitchurch; 1753–1837); Maria Edgeworth (the authoress, born at Black Bourton in 1767); William Smith (the famous geologist, born at Churchill; 1769–1839); Charles Reade (the author, born at Ipsden; 1814–1884); Lord Randolph Churchill (born at Blenheim Palace, 1849–1895); Sir Winston Churchill (born at Blenheim Palace, 1874–1965)

Highest point above Sea Level: Unnamed point two miles east of Watlington, in the Chilterns; 837 feet

29. RUTLAND

Statutory name of administrative county: County of Rutland

Derivation and first recorded use of name: cf. *Roteland, rota* (Old English *rot*, the happy person); first used in A.D. 863 (and a more modern form used in the Charter grant by Edward the Confessor to Westminster Abbey, *c.* 1053

Population in 1801: 16,300

Population in 1971: 30,070

Area: 97,273 acres

Population density per acre in 1971: 0·31

County Town: Oakham

Motto of County Council: "*Multum in Parvo*" = Much in Little

Urban District (and population): Oakham (6,940)

Rural Districts (and population): Ketton (3,980); Oakham (12,540); Uppingham (6,610)

Lord-Lieutenant of County: Capt. T. C. S. Haywood, O.B.E.

Principal Industries: Sheep and cattle farming; cereal crops; quarrying; manufacture of agricultural machinery; pre-casting of concrete structures; light engineering

Tourist attractions and places of interest: Clipsham (Church of St. Mary); Ketton (Church of St. Mary); Langham (Church of SS Peter and Paul); Liddington Bede House; Oakham (Castle and town; Church of All Saints); Ryhall (Church of St. John the Evangelist); Tickencote (Church of St. Peter); Tixover Church; Whissendine (Church of St. Andrew); Uppingham School

Principal county worthies (by birth): Sir Everard Digby (of Gunpowder Plot fame, born at Stoke Dry in 1578); Titus Oates (the renegade Anglican priest, born at Oakham; 1648–1705)

Highest point above Sea Level: Unnamed point, one mile north-west of Langham; 645 feet

30. SHROPSHIRE

Statutory name of administrative county: County of Salop

Derivation and first recorded use of name: cf. *Scrobbesbyrigscir* and hence *Scrobbesburgscir*, the fortified place (*burg*) of the gruff man (*scrobb*) within the shire (*scir*). Pre-A.D. 1000; referred to in the Wills of Wulfgeat of Donington, and Wulfric (*c.* 1000–1004)

Population in 1801: 169,757

Population in 1971: 335,520

Area: 862,485 acres

Population density per acre in 1971: 0·39

County Town and River: Shrewsbury (Welsh *Amwythig*) on the River Severn

Motto of County Council: "*Floreat Salopia*" = Let Salop Flourish

Municipal Borough (and population): Shrewsbury (54,310)

Urban Districts: Dawley, Newport, Oakengates, Wellington

Rural Districts: Atcham, Bridgnorth, Clun and Bisops Castle, Ludlow, Market Drayton, North Shropshire, Oswestry, Shifnal, Wellington

Rural Boroughs: Bishops Castle, Bridgnorth, Ludlow, Much Wenlock, Oswestry

Lord-Lieutenant of County: Lieut.-Col. Arthur Heywood-Lonsdale, C.B.E., M.C., J.P.

Principal Industries: Beef and dairy cattle farming; market gardening and root crops; quarrying; heavy engineering and iron-working; light service industries

Tourist attractions and places of interest: Acton Burnell (Church of St. Mary); Acton Round Hall; Attingham Hall; Boscobel House; Bridgnorth (Church of St. Leonard; Bishop Percy's House); Buildwas Abbey ruins; Claverley (Church of All Saints); Clun (Church of St. George); Coalbrookdale (Museum of Ironfounding); Condover Hall; Haughmond Abbey ruins; Lilleshall Abbey ruins; Ludlow (Castle; Church of St. Laurence); Morville (Church of St. Gregory) and Morville Hall; Much Wenlock (Church of the Holy Trinity and ruins of Wenlock Priory); Munslow Aston (the White House); Offa's Dyke; Old Oswestry (hill fort); Pitchford Hall; Quatt (Church of St. Andrew); Shifnal (Church of St. Andrew); Shrewsbury (Abbey Church of the Holy Cross; Church of St. Mary; Art Gallery; Rowley's House Museum); Stokesay Castle; Tong (Church of St. Bartholomew); Whitchurch (town and old buildings); Whitton Court; Wilderhope Manor; Wroxeter (Church of St. Andrew; remains of Roman town)

Principal county worthies (by birth): William Wycherley (the playwright, born at Preston Brockhurst; 1640–1715); Lord Clive of Plassey (the colonial administrator, 1725–1774); Thomas Percy (later Bishop of Dromore in Ireland, born at Bridgnorth in 1729); Charles Darwin (born at Shrewsbury; 1809–1882); Captain Matthew Webb (1848–1883); Sir Edward German (the composer, born at Whitchurch; 1862–1936)

Highest point above Sea Level: Brown Clee Hill (near Ditton Priors); 1,790 feet

31. SOMERSET

Statutory name of administrative county: County of Somerset

Derivation and first recorded use of name: cf. *Sumaersaeton*, the territory of the people (*Saete*), dependent on *Sumerton* (a summer settlement): in common use in 1015; also referred to earlier, possibly by King Edgar in his renewal of liberty of Taunton, *c.* 970

Population in 1801: 273,577

Population in 1971: 670,140

Area: 1,032,325 acres

Population density per acre in 1971: 0·65

County Town and River: Taunton on the River Tone

Motto of County Council: "*Defendamus*" = We Defend

County Borough (and population): City of Bath (84,810)

Municipal Boroughs (and population): Bridgwater (26,820); Chard (7,230); Glastonbury (6,350); Taunton (37,410); City of Wells (8,380); Weston-super-Mare (48,000); Yeovil (26,150)

Urban Districts: Burnham-on-Sea, Clevedon, Crewkerne, Frome, Ilminster, Keynsham, Minehead, Norton Radstock, Portishead, Shepton Mallet, Street, Watchet, Wellington

Rural Districts: Axbridge, Bathavon, Bridgwater, Chard, Clutton, Dulverton, Frome, Langport, Long Ashton, Shepton Mallet, Taunton, Wellington, Wells, Williton, Wincanton, Yeovil

Lord-Lieutenant of County: Colonel C. T. Mitford-Slade

Principal Industries: Dairy-farming (including Cheddar cheese); market gardening (including cider apples); aircraft manufacture (Yeovil); textiles, clothing and leather goods; tourism and the holiday trade

Tourist attractions and places of interest: Barrington Court; Bath (Abbey; Roman Baths; Holburne of Menstrie Museum; numerous Georgian houses; Victoria Art Gallery; Museum of Costume); Bridgwater (Castle Street Georgian houses; Admiral Blake museum); Cadbury Castle (Iron Age fort and important excavations); Cheddar (Gough's Cave); Claverton Manor (the American Museum in Britain); Cleeve Abbey (remains); Clevedon Court; Coleridge Cottage (the one-time home of Samuel Taylor Coleridge); Congresbury Vicarage; Cothay Manor; Croscombe (Church of St. Mary); Dunster Castle; East Lambrook Manor; Farleigh Castle (ruins); Frome (town of Saxon origins); Glastonbury (Abbey remains; Lake Village museum); Lytes Cary manor house; Montacute House; Muchelney Abbey (ruins); Sandford Orcas Manor; Taunton (castle with important county museum); Tintinhull House; Wansdyke earth defences; Washford Abbey; Wellow (Church of St. Julian); Wells (Cathedral; Church of St. Cuthbert); Weston-zoyland; Wookey Hole caves; Yatton (Church of St. Mary); Yeovil (Church of St. John the Baptist; Henford Manor House with Borough museum); Yeovilton (Fleet Air Arm museum)

Principal county worthies (by birth): Saint Dunstan (A.D. 924–988); Roger Bacon (c. 1212–1294); Sir Edward Dyer (the Elizabethan poet, born at Sharpham); Dr. John Bull ·the traditional composer of the National Anthem, born at Wellow in 1562); Tom Coryate (the poet and traveller, born at Odcombe; 1577–1617); John Pym (the statesman, born at Brymore; 1583–1643); Robert Blake (the Admiral under Oliver Cromwell, born at Bridgwater; 1599–1657); John Locke (the philosopher, born at Wrington, near Bristol; 1632–1704); William Dampier (the explorer, born at East Coker; 1652–1715); Henry Fielding (the writer, born at Sharpham; 1707–1754); Hartley Coleridge (the writer, born at Clevedon; 1796–1849); Sir Henry Irving (the famous actor, born at Keinton Mandeville; 1838–1905); Ernest Bevin (the great trades unionist and politician; 1881–1951)

Highest point above Sea Level: Dunkery Beacon in Exmoor Forest, 1,707 feet

32. STAFFORDSHIRE

Statutory name of administrative county: County of Stafford

Derivation and first recorded use of name: cf. *Staethford-scir* hence *Staeffordscir,* the shire about a ford (crossing place) on a river with a landing place (*staeth*); probably first mentioned in the Will of Wulfric (c. 1002), King Edmund's minister

Population in 1801: 242,693   *Population in 1971:* 1,856,550

Area: 740,971 acres   *Population density per acre in 1971:* 2·51

County Town and River: Stafford on the River Sow

Motto of County Council: "The Knot Unites"

County Boroughs (and population): Burton-upon-Trent (50,600); City of Stoke-on-Trent (270,800); Walsall (184,430); West Bromwich (173,010); Wolverhampton (263,580)

Municipal Boroughs (and population): City of Lichfield (23,156); Newcastle-under-Lyme (76,590); Stafford (54,740); Tamworth (39,090)

Urban Districts: Aldridge-Brownhills, Biddulph, Cannock, Kidsgrove, Leek, Rugeley, Stone, Uttoxeter

Rural Districts: Cannock, Cheadle, Leek, Lichfield, Newcastle-under-Lyme, Seisdon, Stafford, Stone, Tutbury, Uttoxeter

Lord-Lieutenant of County: Arthur Bryan, Esquire

Principal Industries: Dairy farming; coal-mining; potteries; iron and steel works; general engineering; clothing and textile industries

Tourist attractions and places of interest: Blithfield (Hall and Museum of Childhood and Costume); Bradley (Church of All Saints); Brewood (Church of St. Mary the Virgin); Cannock (fort); Caverswall Castle; Checkley (Church of St. Mary and All Saints); Chillington Hall; Church Eaton (Church of St. Editha); Croxden (Abbey remains); Eccleshall (Church of the Holy Trinity); Gnoshall (Church of St. Laurence); Ingestre (Church of St. Mary); Lichfield (Cathedral; Tudor houses; Milley's Hospital; Samuel Johnson's house; Staffordshire Regimental Museum); Moseley Old Hall; Sandon Hall; Shugborough; Stafford (Church of St. Chad); Stoke-on-Trent (City Museum with pottery collection); Tamworth Castle (and museum); Tutbury (Church of St.

The Guildhall, Lavenham, Suffolk, built in about 1530

Mary); Wall (Letocetum Roman fort remains and museum); Walsall (Flint Art Gallery); West Bromwich (Oak House); Weston Park; Wightwick Manor (art collection and gardens); Wootton Lodge

Principal county worthies (*by birth*): Isaak Walton (the writer, born at Stafford; 1593–1683); Joseph Addison (the essayist and statesman, born at Lichfield; 1672–1719); Dr. Samuel Johnson (the great lexicographer, born at Lichfield; 1709–1784); David Garrick (the actor, born at Lichfield; 1717–1779); Josiah Wedgwood (the great pottery designer, born at Burslem; 1730–1795); Admiral Earl St. Vincent ·the famous naval commander, born at Shugborough Park; 1735–1823); Jerome K. Jerome (author of *Three Men in a Boat*, born at Walsall; 1859–1927); Arnold Bennett (the novelist, born at Hanley; 1867–1931)

Highest point above Sea Level: Bareleg Hill, four miles west of Longnor; 1,534 feet

33. SUFFOLK

Statutory names of administrative counties: Suffolk, East, and Suffolk, West

Derivation and first recorded use of name: cf. *Suthfolchi*, the folk of the southern territory of East Anglia; first known mention in Charter grant of land by Alfred, king of the Saxons, in A.D. 895, to Burhric, bishop of Rochester (land at Freckenham)

Lord-Lieutenant of County: Commander The Earl of Stradbroke, R–N. (Retd.)

(a) Suffolk, East

Population in 1801:   *Population in 1971:*
   133,601   385,540
Area: 557,354 acres   *Population density per acre in*
                          1971: 0·71

County Town and River: Ipswich on the River Orwell

Motto of County Council: "*Opus Nostrum Dirige*" = Direct Our Work

County Borough (*and population*): Ipswich (121,930)

Municipal Boroughs (*and population*): Aldeburgh (3,250); Beccles (8,280); Eye (1,650); Lowestoft (50,000); Southwold (2,090)

Urban Districts: Bungay, Felixstowe, Halesworth, Leiston-cum-Sizewell, Saxmundham, Stowmarket, Woodbridge

Rural Districts: Blyth, Deben, Gipping, Hartismere, Lothingland, Samford, Wainford

Principal Industries: Cereal crops and sugar beet; shire and racehorse breeding; manufacture of agricultural machinery; fertilizers; fishing; tourism and the holiday trade

Tourist attractions and places of interest: Aldeburgh (Moot Hall); Bacton (Church of St. Faith); Beccles (Old Town Hall; Rose Hall); Bedingfield (Flemings Hall); Bungay (castle remains; Butter Cross); Butley Priory gatehouse; Erwarton House); Flatford Mill and Willy Lott's cottage; Framlingham (Castle; Church of St. Michael); Freston Tower; Helmingham Hall; Heveningham Hall; Hintlesham Hall; Ipswich (Christchurch Mansion; Wolsey's Gateway; Ancient House; Museum); Leiston (Abbey remains);

39

Mendlesham (Church of St. Mary); Moat Hall; Needham Market (Church of St. John the Baptist); Orford Castle; Otley Hall; Parham Hall; Saxted Green Mill; Somerleyton Hall; Southwold (Church of St. Edmund, King and Martyr); Woodbridge (Seckford shire hall; town houses)

Principal county worthies (by birth): Bishop Grosseteste (born at Stradbroke at the beginning of the 13th century); Cardinal Thomas Wolsey (born at Ipswich, 1473–1530); Sir John Downing (after whom Downing Street was named; born at Dunwich); John Constable (the great landscape painter, born at East Bergholt; 1776–1837); Edward Fitzgerald (translator of Omar Khayyám, born at Bredfield; 1809–1883); Sir Joseph Hooker (the famous botanist, born at Halesworth; 1817–1911)

Highest point above Sea Level: Unnamed point, five miles south of Stowmarket, 300 feet

(b) Suffolk, West

Population in 1801:
80,803

Population in 1971:
166,830

Area: 390,916 acres

Population density per acre in 1971: 0·43

County Town and River: Bury St. Edmunds on the River Lark

Municipal Boroughs (and population): Bury St. Edmunds (25,150); Sudbury (7,960)

Urban Districts: Hadleigh, Haverhill, Newmarket

Rural Districts: Clare, Cosford, Melford, Mildenhall, Thedwastre, Thingoe

Principal Industries: Cereal crops and sugar beet; racehorse breeding (Newmarket area); fruit growing; manufacture of agricultural machinery

Tourist attractions and places of interest: Bury St. Edmunds (Abbey; Church of St. Mary; Hengrave Hall; Moyses Hall museum; Suffolk Regimental Museum); Cavendish (Hall and village); Clare (Church of SS Peter and Paul; the Ancient House; other village buildings); Gedding Hall; Hadleigh (Church of St. Mary; Deanery; Guildhall); Ickworth mansion; Ixworth Abbey and Roman Camp; Kedington (Church of SS Peter and Paul); Lavenham (Church of SS Peter and Paul; Guildhall and other magnificent wood-framed houses); Long Melford (Church of the Holy Trinity; Melford Hall; Kentwell Hall; Bull Inn; the main street); Mildenhall (Church of SS Mary and Andrew); Pakenham windmill; Sudbury (Church of St. Gregory; Moot Hall; Gainsborough's House); Wattisfield Potteries; West Stow Hall; Wickhambrook (Gifford's Hall)

Principal county worthies (by birth): John Lidgate (the poet, born at Lidgate in 1375); Thomas Gainsborough (the great painter, born at Sudbury;

Orford Castle, of which only the keep survives, was built by Henry II between 1165 and 1173

1727–1788); Robert Bloomfield (the poet, born at Honington; 1766–1823)

Highest point above Sea Level: Unnamed point near the hamlet of Rede, seven miles south-west of Bury St. Edmunds, 422 feet

34. SURREY

Statutory name of administrative county: County of Surrey

Derivation and first recorded use of name: cf. Suthrige, derived from *suther-gé*, Old English for Southern District; probably as early as A.D. 688 in charter grants of land by Caedwalla, king of the West Saxons, to churchmen for foundation of a minster in the area of Farnham

Population in 1801:
105,857

Population in 1971:
1,005,790

Area: 418,291 acres

Population density per acre in 1971: 2·40

County Town and River: Kingston-upon-Thames on the River Thames

Municipal Boroughs (and populations): Epsom and Ewell (71,700); Godalming (18,360); Guildford (56,850); Reigate (57,820)

Urban Districts: Banstead, Caterham and Warlingham, Chertsey, Dorking, Egham, Esher, Farnham, Frimley and Camberley, Haslemere, Leatherhead, Staines, Sunbury-on-Thames, Walton and Weybridge, Woking

Rural Districts: Bagshot, Dorking and Horley, Godstone, Guildford, Hambledon

Lord-Lieutenant of County: The Earl of Munster, P.C., K.B.E.

Principal Industries: General engineering (aircraft and component manufacture); general agriculture (mainly dairy farming and cereals)

Tourist attractions and places of interest: Albury Park; Bletchingley (village and houses); Charterhouse school; Chipstead (Church of St. Margaret); Clandon Park; Farnham (Castle; Willmer House museum; West Street and Castle Street); Godalming (Borough museum); Great Bookham (Church of St. Nicholas); Guildford (Cathedral; castle remains; High Street); Loseley House; Ockham (Church of All Saints); Polesden Lacy; Puttenden Manor; Stoke d'Abernon (Church of St. Mary, and brasses therein); Waverley Abbey (ruins); Wisley (Royal Horticultural Society's gardens)

Principal county worthies (by birth): Augustus Toplady (the author-poet, born at Farnham; 1740–1778); William Cobbett (born at Farnham; 1762–1835); Thomas Malthus (the economist and demographer, born near Dorking; 1766–1834); John Galsworthy (the novelist and playwright, born at Kingston Hill; 1867–1933); the Duke of Windsor (King Edward VIII, born 1894); Aldous Huxley (the writer; 1894–1936)

Highest point above Sea Level: Leith Hill, near Dorking; 965 feet. The tower (built in 1766 thereon) rises to 1,029 feet

35. SUSSEX

Statutory names of administrative counties: Sussex, East, and Sussex, West

Derivation and first recorded use of name: cf. *Suth Seaxe,* the territories of the *suth seaxa,* the South Saxons. The Charter grants of land and privileges by Nunna, king of Sussex, in *c.* 714–720, were probably the first formal use of these or similar names

Population of geographical county in 1971: 1,228,390

Area of geographical county: 932,559 acres

Lord-Lieutenant of the counties: The Most Noble The Duke of Norfolk, K.G., P.C., G.C.V.O., G.B.E., T.D.

(a) Sussex, East

Population in 1801:   *Population in 1971:*
    91,198   716,960

Area: 530,210 acres   *Population density per acre in 1971:* 1·35

County Town and River: Lewes on the River Ouse

County Boroughs (and population): Brighton (162,070); Eastbourne (70,130); Hastings (74,000)

Municipal Boroughs (and population): Bexhill (33,900); Hove (70,760); Lewes (14,180); Rye (4,570)

Urban Districts: Burgess Hill, Cuckfield, East Grinstead, Newhaven, Portslade-by-Sea, Seaford

Rural Districts: Battle, Chailey, Cuckfield, Hailsham, Uckfield

Principal Industries: Cattle and poultry farming; market gardening; tourism and the holiday trade

Tourist attractions and places of interest: Alfriston (Church of St. Andrew; Clergy House; Ship Inn); Bateman's (Rudyard Kipling's home); Battle (Abbey and gatehouse; the Deanery and Church of St. Mary); Bodiam Castle; Brede Place; Brighton (Royal Pavilion; Preston Manor; Museum and Art Gallery; Motor Museum); The Caburn (Iron Age and Roman defences); Camber Castle remains; Charlestone Manor; Eastbourne (Towner Art Gallery); Firle Place; Glynde Place; Great Dixter manor house; Hastings (Pelham Crescent); Hollingbury (Iron Age fort remains); Holtye (Roman road excavations); Hurstmonceux Castle (the Royal Observatory); Lewes (Castle; Barbican House; Anne of Cleves House); Michelham Priory; Newtimber Place; Pevensey (Church of St. Nicholas; castle and Roman fort remains); Rotherfield (Church of St. Denys); Rye (Church of St. Mary; Mermaid Street; Ypres Tower; Gun Garden; Lamb House); Wilmington Long Man (chalk hill carving); Worth (Church of St. Nicholas)

Principal county worthies (by birth): John Fletcher (1579–1625)

Highest point above Sea Level: Ditchling Beacon, 813 feet

(b) Sussex, West

Population in 1801:   *Population in 1971:*
    68,273   481,330

Area: 405,349 acres   *Population density per acre in 1971:* 1·18

County Town: City of Chichester

Municipal Boroughs (and population): Arundel (3,030); City of Chichester (21,170); Worthing (84,130)

Urban Districts: Bognor Regis, Crawley, Horsham, Littlehampton, Shoreham-by-Sea, Southwick

Rural Districts: Chanctonbury, Chichester, Horsham, Midhurst, Petworth, Worthing

Principal Industries: General agriculture; electrical component manufacture; tourism and the holiday trade

Tourist attractions and places of interest: Amberley (castle ruins and church); Arundel Castle; Bosham (Church of the Holy Trinity); Boxgrove (Church of SS Mary and Blaise, and Priory); Bramber Castle remains; Chanctonbury Ring (hill fort and remains of Roman temple); Chantry Green House; Chichester (Cathedral; Market Cross; Guildhall Museum; Corps of Royal Military Police Museum); Christ's Hospital (Blue Coat School); Cowdray Park (mansion remains); Goodwood House; Highdown Hill (site of Bronze Age settlement and Iron Age hill fort); New Shoreham (Church of St. Mary de

Haura); North Marden (Church of St. Mary); Parham mansion; Petworth (Petworth House and gateway; Somerset Lodge; New Grove House; market place and streets); Shipley (the reliquary in the Church of St. Mary); Shoreham-by-Sea (Marlipins Museum); Sompting (Church of St. Mary the Virgin); Steyning (Church of St. Andrew); Stopham medieval river bridge; The Trundle (Iron Age fort and Neolithic ditch); Uppark House; West Chiltington (Church of St. Mary)

Principal county worthies (by birth): John Selden (the 17th century lawyer, 1584–1654); William Collins (1721–1759); Percy Bysshe Shelley (the poet, born at Field House, near Horsham; 1792–1822); Richard Cobden (the exponent of free trade, born at Heyshott; 1804–1865)

Highest point above Sea Level: Blackdown Hill, near Fernhurst, 918 feet

36. WARWICKSHIRE

Statutory name of administrative county: County of Warwick

Derivation and first recorded use of name: Referred to as Waerincwicscir by Bishop Leofsige in his Charter lease of land at Bishopton to his minister Godric in 1016; name possibly derived from old English *wering* (a weir) and *wick* (a livestock holding)

Population in 1801: 206,798

Population in 1971: 2,155,930

Area: 623,938 acres

Population density per acre in 1971: 3·46

County Town and River: Warwick on the River Avon

Motto of County Council: "*Non sanz droict*" = Not Without Right

County Boroughs (and population): City of Birmingham (1,084,180); City of Coventry (335,230); Solihull (111,050)

Municipal Boroughs (and population): Royal Leamington Spa (46,140); Nuneaton (64,860); Rugby (57,840); Stratford-upon-Avon (19,320); Sutton Coldfield (82,010); Warwick (18,440)

Urban Districts: Bedworth, Kenilworth

Rural Districts: Alcester, Atherstone, Meriden, Rugby, Shipston-on-Stour, Southam, Stratford-upon-Avon, Warwick

Lord-Lieutenant of County: C. M. T. Smith-Ryland, Esquire

Compton Wynyates, Warwickshire, the home of the Marquess of Northampton

Principal Industries: Heavy and general engineering (machine tools, aircraft and motor vehicles); dairy farming, market gardening, fruit and cereal crops; cement works; synthetic yarn manufacture; rubber processing; food canning; trade administration

Tourist attractions and places of interest: Alcester (medieval houses); Arbury Hall; Berkswell (Church of St. John the Baptist); Birmingham (Cathedral Church of St. Philip; Roman Catholic Cathedral of St. Chad; City Museum and Art Gallery; Assay Office; Aston Hall; Barber Institute; Museum of Science and Industry); Brailes (Church of St. George); Castle Bromwich Hall; Charlecote Park; Clopton House; Compton Wynyates; Coughton Court; Coventry (old and new cathedrals); Kenilworth Castle (ruins); Lapworth (Church of St. Mary); Maxstoke Castle (and Church of St. Michael); Merevale (Church of St. Mary); Packwood House; Ragley Hall; Royal Leamington Spa (Art Gallery and Museum); Stoneleigh Abbey; Stratford-upon-Avon (Royal Shakespeare Theatre; Town Hall; Harvard House; Guild Chapel; Church of the Holy Trinity; Clopton Bridge); Upton House; Warwick (Castle; Church of St. Mary; County Museum; Court House; Queen's Own Hussars Regimental Museum); Wootten Wawen (Church of St. Peter)

Principal county worthies (by birth): John Shakespeare (the great playwright's father, born at Snitterfield); Mary Arden (William Shakespeare's mother, born at Wilmcote); Anne Hathaway (Shakespeare's wife, born at Shottery in 1556); William Shakespeare (born at Stratford-upon-Avon; 1564–1616); Michael Drayton (the poet, born at Hartshill Green; 1563–1631); Sir William Dugdale (the famous antiquary, born at Shustoke; 1605–1686); The Earl of Wilmington (the statesman, 1673–1743); Walter Savage Landor (the writer, born at Warwick; 1775–1864); Richard Congreve (the philosopher, born at Leamington Spa; 1818–1899); George Eliot (Mary Ann Cross, the Victorian woman novelist, born on the Arbury estate; 1819–1880); Dame Ellen Terry (the actress, born at Coventry; 1847–1928); Neville Chamberlain (the statesman, born at Edgbaston; 1869–1940); Rupert Brooke (the poet, born at Rugby; 1887–1915)

Highest point above Sea Level: Ilmington Down, 854 feet

37. WESTMORLAND

Statutory name of administrative county: County of Westmorland

Derivation and first recorded use of name: cf. Westmoringaland, the land west of the moors (the Yorkshire moors); said to have been traced back to A.D. 966

Population in 1801:	*Population in 1971:*
40,805	72,700
Area: 504,917 acres	*Population density per acre in 1971:* 0·14

County Town and River: Kendal on the River Kent

Municipal Boroughs (and population): Appleby (1,980); Kendal (20,480)

Urban Districts (and population): The Lakes (5,280); Windermere (7,740)

Rural Districts (and population): North Westmorland (15,780); South Westmorland (21,440)

Lord-Lieutenant of County: Lieut.-Cdr. P. N. Wilson, O.B.E., D.S.C., J.P.

Principal Industries: Sheep and dairy farming; quarrying of granite, limestone and slate; lead mines; shoe manufacture; paper mills; blankets; carpet making

Tourist attractions and places of interest: Bolton (Church of All Saints); Crosby Garrett settlement group; Grasmere (Dove Cottage, home of William Wordsworth); Kendal (castle ruins; town hall; Abbot Hall art gallery; Borough Museum); Levens Hall; Middleton Hall; Sizergh Castle

Principal county worthies (by birth): Catherine Parr (Sixth and last wife of Henry VIII, born in Kendal Castle, *c.* 1512–1548); George Whitehead (founder of the Society of Friends; born at Orton in 1636)

Highest point above Sea Level: Helvellyn, on the county border with Cumberland; 3,118 feet

38. WILTSHIRE

Statutory name of administrative county: County of Wiltshire

Derivation and first recorded use of name: cf. Wiltunscir, the shire around Wiltun, the town (*tun*) on the River Wiley. Earliest formal mention was probably in the Will of King Alfred in the Charter bequests to his children and the Church (A.D. 873–888)

Population in 1801:	*Population in 1971:*
183,665	500,400
Area: 860,099 acres	*Population density per acre in 1971:* 0·58

County Town and River: Trowbridge on the River Biss

Municipal Boroughs (and population): Calne (9,880); Chippenham (18,930); Devizes (10,300); Malmesbury (2,660); Marlborough (6,110); City of Salisbury (36,270); Swindon (98,110); Wilton (3,900)

Urban Districts: Bradford-on-Avon, Melksham, Trowbridge, Warminster, Westbury

Rural Districts: Amesbury, Bradford and Melksham, Calne and Chippenham, Cricklade and Wootton

Bassett, Devizes, Highworth, Malmesbury, Marlborough and Ramsbury, Mere and Tisbury, Pewsey, Salisbury and Wilton, Warminster and Westbury

Lord-Lieutenant of County: Lord Margadale, T.D., J.P.

Principal Industries: Sheep and dairy farming; cereal crops; railway and general engineering (Swindon); carpet manufacture (Wilton); tobacco, rubber and leather processing

Tourist attractions and places of interest: Aldbourne (Church of St. Michael); Avebury (henge monument; Alexander Keiller Museum; Avebury Manor); Battlesbury Hill (Iron Age hill fort); Bradford-on-Avon (Anglo-Saxon Church of St. Laurence; Church of the Holy Trinity; Town Bridge and Gudgeon); Bratton Castle hill fort and Westbury White Horse; Britford (Church of St. Peta); Castle Combe village; Chippenham (town hall, bridge and town houses); Corsham Court; Cricklade (Saxon burh); Devizes (Museum; Wiltshire Regimental Museum); Great Chalfield Manor; Heytesbury (Church of SS Peter and Paul); Knap Hill (Neolithic camp); Lacock Abbey and village; Littlecote manor house; Longford Castle; Longleat House; Lydiard Mansion; Normanton Down (barrow group); Old Sarum (Iron Age defences and Roman Serviodunum); Potterne (Church of St. Mary); Salisbury Cathedral; Silbury Hill; Stonehenge Bronze Age sanctuary; Stourhead (gardens and lake); Swindon (Great Western Railway museum); Urchfont (Church of St. Michael); Wansdyke earthworks; Wardour Castle; West Kennet (Neolithic long barrow); Westwood Manor; Wilton House; Woodhenge (Neolithic monument)

Principal county worthies (by birth): 1st Duke of Somerset (*c.* 1500-1552); Thomas Hobbes (the philosopher, born at Malmesbury; 1588-1679); 1st Earl of Clarendon (1609-1674); Sir Christopher Wren (the great architect and scientist, born at East Knoyle; 1632-1723); Joseph Addison (the parliamentarian, 1672-1719); William Fox Talbot (the pioneer photographer, born at Lacock; 1800-1877); Sir Isaac Pitman (the originator of shorthand, born at Trowbridge; 1813-1897); Richard Jefferies (the writer, born at Coate; 1848-1887)

Highest point above Sea Level: Milk Hill (between Marlborough and Devizes), 964 feet

39. WORCESTERSHIRE

Statutory name of administrative county: County of Worcester

Derivation and first recorded use of name: cf. Wirecestrescir, probably contracted from the Shire (*scir*) around the fort (*ceastre*) or camp in the Wyre Forest. Almost certainly dates from Charter grants of land by Cenwulf, king of Mercia, to his bishop, Deneberht, of Worcester, *c.* 814-820

Population in 1801: 146,441

Population in 1971: 688,370

Area: 450,376 acres

Population density per acre in 1971: 1·53

County Town and River: City of Worcester on the River Severn

County Boroughs (and population): Dudley (182,420); Warley (166,790); Worcester (71,920)

Municipal Boroughs (and population): Bewdley (7,250); Droitwich (11,650); Evesham (13,190); Halesowen (52,320); Kidderminster (47,000); Stourbridge (52,210)

Urban Districts: Bromsgrove, Malvern, Redditch, Stourport-on-Severn

Rural Districts: Bromsgrove, Droitwich, Evesham, Kidderminster, Martley, Pershore, Tenbury, Upton-on-Severn

Lord-Lieutenant of County: The Viscount Cobham, K.G., P.C., G.C.M.G., T.D.

Principal Industries: Beef and dairy cattle farming; orchard farming (apples, plums and hops); iron and steel foundries; pottery and porcelain; light engineering (radio and electrical components); carpet manufacture (Kidderminster); chemical industry

Tourist attractions and places of interest: Bewdley (Tickenhill House); Birtsmorton Court; Bredon (Church of St. Giles); Bredon Hill (Iron Age hill fort); Broadway village; Burford House Gardens; Croome d'Abitot (Church of St. Mary Magdalene); Dowles Manor; Evesham (Abbey remains); Great Malvern (Priory Church of SS Mary and Michael); Hartlebury Castle; Harvington Hall; Holt Castle; Little Malvern (Church of St. Giles); Ombersley village; Pershore Abbey; Stoke Prior (Church of St. Michael); Worcester (Cathedral; Dyson Perrins Museum and ceramics collection; Assembly Room; Guildhall; Shire Hall; Edgar Tower; Nash House)

Principal county worthies (by birth): Samuel Butler (the writer, born at Strensham; 1612-1680); Abraham Darby (the pioneer iron processer, born at Dudley in 1677); Sir Rowland Hill ("father" of the uniform Penny Post in 1840, born at Kidderminster; 1795-1879); Sir Edward Elgar (the composer and Master of the King's Musick to King George V, born at Worcester; 1857-1934); Alfred Edward Housman (the writer, born at Fockbury; 1859-1936); Stanley Baldwin (the statesman and Prime Minister, born at Bewdley; 1867-1947)

Highest point above Sea Level: Worcester Beacon in the Malvern Hills, 1,395 feet

40. YORKSHIRE

Statutory name of administrative counties: County of

The magnificent cathedral of Salisbury, Wiltshire, with its 404-foot spire, the tallest in England. Building commenced in 1220

York; East, North and West Ridings (see below)
Derivation and first recorded use of name: cf. a remote contraction of *Eoferwiscir*, a territory ruled by Eburos; the word Riding is a development of "thirding", hence the three divisions. The first formal use of a recognisable contraction of the name was probably used in Charter grants of land (*c.* 1033) by King Cnut to Aelfric, his archbishop of York
Population of geographical county: 5,088,250
Area of geographical county: 3,917,889 acres

(a) Yorkshire, East Riding

Population in 1801:   *Population in 1971:*
   110,614   545,680
Area: 750,231 acres   *Population density per acre in 1971:* 0·73
County Town and River: Beverley on the Hull
County Borough (and population): City of Kingston-upon-Hull (290,270)
Municipal Boroughs (and population): Beverley (17,220); Bridlington (26,420); Hedon (2,600)

Urban Districts: Driffield, Filey, Haltemprice, Hornsea, Norton, Withernsea
Rural Districts: Beverley, Bridlington, Derwent, Driffield, Holderness, Howden, Norton, Pocklington
Lord-Lieutenant of County: The Earl of Halifax
Principal Industries: General agriculture (crops and livestock); sea ports, docks and warehousing; cattle cake manufacture
Tourist attractions and places of interest: Beverley (Minster; Church of St. Mary); Boynton Hall; Bridlington (Art Gallery and Museum, with Amy Johnson collection; Bayle Museum); Burton Agnes Hall; Burton Constable; Eastrington (Church of St. Michael); Goodmanham (Church of All Saints); Hemingbrough (Church of St. Mary); Howden (Church of St. Mary); Kingston-upon-Hull (Church of the Holy Trinity; Maritime Museum; Hull Trinity House; Wilberforce House); Patrington (Church of St. Patrick); Sledmere House; Swine (Church of St. Mary)
Principal county worthies (by birth): Andrew Marvell (the poet, born at Winestead; 1621–1678); Wil-

liam Wilberforce (the philanthropist and slavery abolitionist, born at Kingston-upon-Hull; 1759–1833); Amy Johnson (the famous woman pilot, born at Kingston-upon-Hull; 1903–1941)

Highest point above Sea Level: Garrowby Hill, five miles north of Pocklington, 808 feet

(b) Yorkshire, North Riding

Population in 1801:
    158,013
Area: 1,376,629 acres

Population in 1971:
    743,120
Population density per acre in 1971: 0·54

County Town and River: Northallerton on the Sun Bec (a tributary of the River Wiske)

County Borough (and population): Teesside (411,200)

Municipal Boroughs (and population): Richmond (7,570); Scarborough (42,080)

Urban Districts: Guisborough, Loftus, Malton, Northallerton, Pickering, Saltburn and Marske-by-the-Sea, Scalby, Skelton and Brotton, Whitby

Rural Districts: Aysgarth, Bedale, Croft, Easingwold, Flaxton, Helmsley, Kirkbymoorside, Leyburn, Malton Masham, Northallerton, Pickering, Reeth, Richmond, Scarborough, Startforth, Thirsk, Wath, Whitby

Lord-Lieutenant of County: The Most Hon. The Marquis of Normanby, M.B.E.

Principal Industries: General agriculture; iron and steel; heavy engineering (and ship-building); natural gas; oil and byproducts

Tourist attractions and places of interest: Beningbrough Hall; Byland Abbey remains; Castle Howard; Coxwold (Church of St. Michael); Easby (Church of St. Agatha and abbey ruins); Gilling Castle; Hackness (Church of St. Peter); Jervaulx Abbey ruins; Middlesbrough (Dorman Memorial Museum and Municipal Art Gallery); Mount Grace Priory (remains); Nunnington Hall; Richmond (Castle; Green Howards' Regimental Museum); Rievaulx Abbey; Scarborough (Castle; Roman Signal Station); Thirsk (Church of St. Mary); Whitby (Abbey and Church of St. Mary)

Principal county worthies (by birth): John Wycliffe (the theologian, traditionally born at Hipswell; *c.* 1330–1384); Roger Ascham (1515–1568); Captain James Cook (the explorer, 1728–1779); Thomas Lord (of Lords cricket ground fame, born at Thirsk in 1755); Lord Baltimore (founder of the American state of Maryland, born near Scorton); Frederick, Lord Leighton (1830–1878); Edith Sitwell (the authoress, born at Scarborough; 1887–1964); Richard and Cherry Kearton (the pioneers of wild-life photography, born at Thwaite)

Highest point above Sea Level: Micklefell, above the Lune Forest, 2,591 feet

(c) Yorkshire, West Riding

Population in 1801:
    590,506
Area: 1,791,029 acres

Population in 1971:
    3,799,450
Population density per acre in 1971: 2·12

County Town and River: City of Wakefield on the River Calder

Motto of County Council: "*Audi Consilium*" = Take Heed of Counsel

County Boroughs (and population): Barnsley (74,470); City of Bradford (291,960); Dewsbury (51,840); Doncaster (83,590); Halifax (93,220); Huddersfield (129,840); City of Leeds (502,320); Rotherham (86,360); City of Sheffield (525,230); City of Wakefield (59,450); City of York (107,150)

Municipal Boroughs (and population): Batley (41,680); Brighouse (32,990); Castleford (38,990); Goole (18,320); Harrogate (62,810); Keighley (55,160); Morley (44,090); Ossett (17,350); Pontefract (31,140); Pudsey (37,740); City of Ripon (11,880); Spenborough (38,980); Todmorden (15,130)

Urban Districts: Adwick-le-Street, Aireborough, Baildon, Barnoldswick, Bentley with Arksey, Bingley, Colne Valley, Conisbrough, Cudworth, Darfield, Darton, Dearne, Denby Dale, Denholme, Dodworth, Earby, Elland, Featherstone, Garford, Hebden Royd, Heckmondwike, Hemsworth, Holmfirth, Horbury, Horsforth, Hoyland Nether, Ilkley, Kirkburton, Knaresborough, Knottingley, Maltby, Meltham, Mexborough, Mirfield, Normanton, Otley, Penistone, Queensbury and Shelf, Rawmarsh, Ripponden, Rothwell, Royston, Saddleworth, Selby, Shipley, Silsden, Skipton, Sowerby Bridge, Stanley, Stocksbridge, Swinton, Tickhill, Wath-upon-Dearne, Wombwell, Worsbrough

Rural Districts: Bowland, Doncaster, Goole, Hemsworth, Hepton, Kiveton Park, Nidderdale, Osgoldcross, Penistone, Ripon and Pateley Bridge, Rotherham, Sedbergh, Selby, Settle, Skipton, Tadcaster, Thorne, Wakefield, Wetherby, Wharfedale, Wortley

Lord-Lieutenant of County: Brigadier Kenneth Hargreaves, C.B.E., T.D.

Principal Industries: Coal mining; wool; steel (and stainless steel cutlery); dairy farming and cereal crops

Tourist attractions and places of interest: Batley (Bagshaw Museum); Bolton Priory ruins; Bradford (Cathedral; Bolling Hall; City Art Gallery and Museum); Bramham Park mansion; Browsholme Hall; Cannon Hall; Conisbrough Castle; East Riddlesham Hall; Fountains Hall; Halifax (Church of St. John; Shibden Hall); Harewood House; Ilkley (manor house); Ilkley Moor (Bronze Age carvings); Leeds (Abbey House Museum; City Museum); Markenfield Hall;

Nostell Priory; Pontefract (Castle museum; King's Own Yorkshire Light Infantry Regimental Museum); Ripley Castle; Ripon Cathedral; Rotherham (Church of All Saints); Rudding Park; Saxton (Church of All Saints); Sheffield (Cathedral Church of SS Peter and Paul; Beauchief Abbey remains; City Museum; York and Lancaster Regimental Museum); Skipton (Castle; Church of the Holy Trinity); Snaith (Church of St. Laurence); Spofforth Castle ruins; Studley Royal and Fountains Abbey Gardens; Temple Newsam House; Tickhill (Church of St. Mary); Victoria Cave; Wakefield (Cathedral; Bridge Chapel); York (Minster and old city)

Principal county worthies (by birth): King Henry I (born at Selby; 1068–1135); Lord Darnley (husband of Mary Queen of Scots, born at Leeds in 1545); Guy Fawkes (of Gunpowder Plot fame; 1570–1606); Thomas Fairfax (the Cromwellian commander, 1612–1671); William Congreve (1670–1729); Thomas Chippendale (the great furniture designer, born at Otley; 1718–1779); Joseph Priestley (the scientist and philosopher, born at Birstall, near Leeds; 1733–1804); Sir Francis Chantrey (born at Norton in 1781); Adam Sedgwick (the geologist, born at Dent; 1785–1873); the Brontë Sisters (the famous novelists; Charlotte, 1816–1855; Emily, 1818–1848; Anne, 1820–1849; all born at Thornton, near Bradford); William Stubbs (the historian and Bishop of Oxford, born at Knaresborough; 1825–1901); Sir William Harcourt (the statesman, born at York; 1827–1904); the Earl of Oxford and Asquith (Herbert Asquith, the statesman, born at Morley; 1852–1928); George Gissing (the writer, born at Wakefield; 1857–1903); Herbert Sutcliffe and Sir Leonard Hutton (the great cricketers, both born at Pudsey)

Highest point above Sea Level: Whernside, near the county borders with Lancashire and Westmorland, 2,414 feet

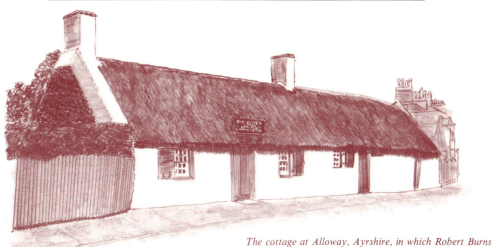

The cottage at Alloway, Ayrshire, in which Robert Burns was born in 1759

SCOTLAND

1. ABERDEENSHIRE

Statutory name of administrative county: County of Aberdeen

Derivation and first recorded use of name: "Aber", at the mouth of; the river Dee or Don; known to have been used before 1100

Population in 1801: 121,065

Population in 1971: 318,820

Area: 1,246,585 acres

Population density per acre in 1971: 0·26

County Town and River: City of Aberdeen on the River Dee

Large Burghs (and population): City of Aberdeen (181,751)

Small Burghs (and population): Ballater (1,063); Ellon (2,021); Fraserburgh (10,987); Huntly (3,889); Inverurie (5,376); Kintore (796); Old Meldrum (1,132); Peterhead (13,536); Rosehearty (1,135); Turriff (2,813)

District Councils: Aberdeen, Alford, Deer, Deeside, Ellon, Garioch, Huntly, Turriff

Lieutenant of County: Sir Robert I. A. Forbes Leith of Fyvie, Bt., M.B.E.

Principal Industries: Agriculture (beef cattle, barley, oats and root crops); engineering; papermaking; quarrying and·granite-working; ship-building; fishing; textiles

Tourist attractions and places of interest: Barmekin of Echt hill fort; Balmoral Castle, Craithie; Braemar Castle; Barra Castle; Drum Castle; Cullerlie stone circle; Craigievar Castle; Kildrummy Castle; Broomend of Crichie; Inverurie Museum; Pitcaple Castle; Haddo House; Leith Hall; Druminnor House; Huntly Castle; Delgatie Castle; Picardy and Maiden Stones; Midmar Castle; Pitmedden gardens; Peterhead Arbuthnot Museum; Dyce (Church of St. Fergus). *In Aberdeen:* Art Gallery; Cathedral; Marischal College; Mercat Cross; Music Hall; Medieval Aberdeen; the houses of Provost Ross and Provost Skene; Robert Gordon's College; University Anthropological Museum

Principal county worthies (by birth): John Barbour (c. 1316–1395)

2. ANGUS

Statutory name of administrative county: County of Angus

Derivation and first recorded use of name: Disputed

Population in 1801:	*Population in 1971:*
99,053	276,728

Area: 546,861 acres

Population density per acre in 1971: 0·51

County Town and River: Forfar

Motto of County Council: "*Lippen on Angus*" = Depend on Angus

Large Burghs (and population): Royal City of Dundee (181,508); Arbroath (21,724)

Small Burghs (and population): Brechin (6,735); Carnoustie (5,753); Forfar (10,066); Kirriemuir (4,107); Monifieth (5,541); Montrose (10,117)

District Councils: Brechin, Carnoustie, Forfar, Kirriemuir, Monifieth, Montrose

Lieutenant of County: The Rt. Hon. the Earl of Dalhousie, G.B.E., M.C., LL.D.

Principal Industries: Agriculture (cereals and root crops); beef cattle and sheep rearing; shipbuilding; flax, jute and brick factories; canning and confectionery; preserves; fishing

Tourist attractions and places of interest: Affleck Castle; Airlie Castle; Arbroath Abbey (remains of); Brechin Cathedral and Round Tower; Bridge of Dun; Caterthun hill forts; Claypott Castle; Eassie Stone; Edzell Castle; Forfar Meffan Institute Museum; Fowlis Easter Church; Glamis Castle and gardens; Glenesk folk museum; Montrose Old Church

Principal county worthies (by birth): Sir James Barrie (1860–1937); H.R.H. The Princess Margaret (b. 1930 at Glamis Castle)

Highest point above Sea Level: Glas Maol, 3,502 feet, on County boundary with Aberdeenshire

Glamis Castle, Angus; a castle in the so-called Scottish baronial style

3. ARGYLL

Statutory name of administrative county: County of Argyll

Derivation and first recorded use of name: Gaelic word *Earraghaidheal* meaning "coastline of the Gael", probably *ante* A.D. 970

Population in 1801: 81,277

Population in 1971: 58,424

Area: 1,990,510 acres

Population density per acre in 1971: 0·029

County Town and River: Lochgilphead (main county administrative offices); county offices also at Dunoon, Oban and Campbeltown

Motto of County Council: Gaelic, *"Seas ar coir"* = Maintain our right

Small Burghs (and population): Campbeltown (6,285); Dunoon (9,122); Inverary (467); Lochgilphead (1,251); Oban (6,715); Tobermoray (634)

District Councils: Ardnamurchan, Cowal, Islay, Jura and Colonsay, North Lorn, South Lorn, Kintyre, Mid-Argyll, Mull, Tiree and Coll

Lieutenant of County: The Rt. Hon. the Lord Maclean of Duart and Morvaren, K.T., K.B.E.

Principal Industries: Beef cattle farming and sheep-rearing: forestry and timber-working for paper pulp; sand-working for optical glass-making; quarrying; tourism

Tourist attractions and places of interest: Carnasserie Castle (remains of); Crarae Lodge gardens; Dunadd hill fort; Dunaverty Castle (ruins of); Dunstaffnage Castle; Dunlossit gardens, Islay; Duntrune Castle (ruins of); Fingal's Cave (Island of Staffa); Glencoe (location of 1692 Massacre); Inveraray Castle; Iona (landing place of St. Colomba in A.D. 563); Kilchurn Castle (ruins of)

Principal county worthies (by birth): Colin MacLaurin (1698-1746); James Chalmers (1841-1901)

Highest point above Sea Level: Bidean nam Bian, 3,766 feet, near Glencoe

4. AYRSHIRE

Statutory name of administrative county: County of Ayr

Derivation and first recorded use of name: From Gaelic river name *Ar*, signifying clear or rapid, *ante* A.D. 958

Population in 1801: 84,207

Population in 1971: 356,581

Area: 724,234 acres

Population density per acre in 1971: 0·49

County Town and River: Ayr on the River Ayr

Motto of County Council: "God Schaw the Richt" = God favours the Righteous

Large Burghs (and population): Ayr (47,873); Kilmarnock (47,794)

Small Burghs (and population): Ardrossan (10,150); Cumnock and Holmhead (5,962); Darvel (3,180);

Galston (4,094); Girvan (6,990); Irvine (21,833); Kilwinning (8,205); Largs (8,858); Maybole (4,521); Newmilns and Greenholm (3,534); Prestwick (13,787); Saltcoats (14,392); Stevenston (11,563); Stewarton (4,169); Troon (11,038)

District Councils: Girvan, Maybole, Ayr, Dalmellington, Cumnock, Kilmarnock, Irvine, Kilbirnie, West Kilbride

Lieutenant of County: Sir James Fergusson of Kilberran, Bt., LL.D.

Principal Industries: Dairy farming; beef cattle; poultry; pigs; oats, turnips and potatoes; vegetable canning; petroleum refining; whisky blending; coalmining; iron and steel; shipbuilding; textiles; chemical industries; boot and shoe manufacture; furniture-making; quarrying; fishing

Tourist attractions and places of interest: Alloway (Burns Cottage, birthplace of Robert Burns); Ayr (Carnegie Library, Museum and Art Gallery; also Town Hall); Glenapp Castle; Killochan Castle; Culzean Castle; Maybole Castle; Saltcoats Museum; Millport (Isle of Cumbrae; the Robertson Natural History Museum)

Principal county worthies (by birth): Robert Burns (1759-1796, born at Alloway); John Boyd Dunlop (1840-1921); Sir Alexander Fleming (1881-1955); John Galt (Novelist; 1779-1839); John Loudon McAdam (1756-1836); William Murdoch (discoverer of coal gas

Highest point above Sea Level: Kirriereoch Hill (on the county border with Kirkcudbrightshire), 2,565 feet

5. BANFFSHIRE

Statutory name of administrative county: County of Banff

Derivation and first recorded use of name: Suggested as being a derivation of Queen Banba, *ante* A.D. 1064

Population in 1801: 37,216

Population in 1971: 43,372

Area: 403,084

Population density per acre in 1971: 0·11

County Town and River: Banff on the River Deveron

Small Burghs (and population): Aberchirder (861); Aberlour (798); Banff (3,568); Buckie (7,742); Cullen (1,243); Dufftown (1,511); Findochty (1,227); Keith (4,089); Macduff (3,471); Portnockie (1,110); Portsoy (1,699)

District Councils: Aberchirder, Banff, Buckie, Cullen, Dufftown, Keith

Lieutenant of County: Colonel Thomas R. Gordon-Duff of Drummuir, M.C.

Principal Industries: Agriculture (beef cattle, dairy farming, cereals and root crops); boat-building; limestone quarrying; whisky distilling; timber mills; textiles; fisheries (cod and herring)

Tourist attractions and places of interest: Balvenie Castle, Dufftown (ruins of); Castle and Duff House at Banff; Cullen House; the Spey Bridge at Craigellachie

Principal county worthies (by birth): James Gordon Bennet, Snr., 1795–1872; Sir James Clark (1788–1870); James Ferguson (1710–1776); James Sharp 1618–1679)

Highest point above Sea Level: Ben Macdhui (on the county boundary with Aberdeenshire), 4,296 feet

6. BERWICKSHIRE

Statutory name of administrative county: County of Berwick

Derivation and first recorded use of name: Old English *bere*, bare, and *wic*, place; probably first used *c.* 1080–1098

Population in 1801:	Population in 1971:
30,206	20,285
Area: 292,535 acres	Population density per acre in 1971: 0·07

County Town: Duns

Small Burghs (and population): Coldstream (1,242); Duns (1,885); Eyemouth (2,320); Lauder (573)

District Councils (and population): East (5,638); Middle (4,669); West (3,958)

Lieutenant of County: Lieut.-Col. W. B. Swan, C.B.E., T.D.

Principal Industries: Agriculture (cereals and sheeprearing); fishing; tweed and hosiery mills; quarrying; sawmills and joinery; fertilizers

Tourist attractions and places of interest: Thirlstane Castle; Duns Castle and Edin's Hall; Coldstream Bridge over the Tweed, and Coldstream Market Place; Fouldon Tithe Barn; Hume Castle (ruins of); Mellerstain; Dryburgh Abbey; Addinston and Longcroft hill forts; Earn's Heugh hill forts

Principal county worthy (by birth): Thomas Baston (1677–1732)

Highest point above Sea Level: Meikle Says Law, 1,750 feet (on county boundary with East Lothian)

7. BUTE

Statutory name of administrative county: County of Bute

Derivation and first recorded use of name: Variously ascribed as follows: From the Erse word *both*, meaning a group or cell (referring to St. Brendan's 6th century foundation); from the Gaelic *Ey Bhiod*, meaning "the island of corn"; or from the Old Irish *bòt*, a beacon or signal fire. *c.* 1090

Population in 1801:	Population in 1971:
11,791	12,263
Area: 139,711 acres	Population density per acre in 1971: 0·087

County Town: Rothesay (administrative centre)

Small Burghs (and population): Millport (1,234); Rothesay (6,119)

District Councils (and population): Arran (3,189); Bute (1,674); Cumbrae (47)

Lieutenant of County: The Most Honourable the Marquess of Bute

Principal Industries: Agriculture (cereals and root crops); fishing; tourism and the holiday trade

Tourist attractions and places of interest: Auchagallon, Isle of Arran (stone circle); Brodick Castle; Dunagoil; Kames Castle; Kyles of Bute; Millport (Robertson Museum and Aquarium); Rothesay (ruins of castle)

Principal county worthies (by birth): Sir William McEwen (1848–1924); J. W. Mackail (1859–1945); Professor Hugh Black (1868–1938)

Highest point above Sea Level: Goat Fell, Isle of Arran, 2,867 feet

. 8. CAITHNESS

Statutory name of administrative county: County of Caithness

Derivation and first recorded use of name: cf. *cait* (cat) and *ness* (cape) hence a province or cape of the Cats; *c.* A.D. 970

Population in 1801:	Population in 1971:
22,609	28,078
Area: 438,833 acres	Population density per acre in 1971: 0·064

County Town and River: Wick on the River Wick

Motto of County Council: "Commit thy work to God"

Small Burghs (and population): Thurso (9,118¶); Wick (7,358)

District Councils (and population): Central Caithness (1,778); Eastern Caithness (3,040); Northern Caithness (1,421); Southern Caithness (2,005); Wester Caithness (3,358)

Lieutenant of County: John Sinclair, Esquire, M.B.E.

Principal Industries: Sheep farming; root crops and cereals; dairy farming and cheese making; distilleries; glass-making; clothing; fishing

Tourist attractions and places of interest: Camster (Grey Cairns); Dounreay atomic energy breeder-reactor plant; Dunbeath Castle; Forse (settlement complex); Langwell (homestead)

Principal county worthies (by birth): General Arthur St. Clair (1734–1818); Alexander Bain (1810–1877)

Highest point above Sea Level: Morven, 2,313 feet

¶ Only 1970 population figure available

9. CLACKMANNANSHIRE

Statutory name of administrative county: County of Clackmannan

Derivation and first recorded use of name: Clackmannan, the Stone of Manau, *c.* 1133

Population in 1801:	Population in 1971:
10,858	44,935

Area: 34,937 acres   *Population density per acre in 1971:* 1·29

County Town and River: Alloa on the Forth

Motto of County Council: "Look about you" (or "Look aboot ye")

Small Burghs (and population): Alloa (14,296); Alva (4,118); Dollar (2,254¶); Tillicoultry (4,099)

District Councils (and population); Alloa (16,814); Hillfoots (3,371)

Lieutenant of County: Col. The Rt. Hon. The Earl of Mar and Kellie

Principal Industries: Sheep and dairy farming; general and light engineering; coal mining; distilleries; paper mills; textiles; glass manufacture

Tourist attractions and places of interest: Alloa Tower; Clackmannan Tower; Castle Campbell; Dollar Academy; Menstrie Castle; Sauchie Tower

Principal county worthies (by birth): Sir William Alexander, Earl of Stirling (1577–1640); General Sir Ralph Abercrombie (victor at Battle of Aboukir, in which he was killed; 1734–1801)

Highest point above Sea Level: Ben Cleugh in the Ochil Hills, 2,363 feet

¶ Only 1970 population figure available

10. DUMFRIES-SHIRE

Statutory name of administrative county: County of Dumfries

Derivation and first recorded use of name: cf. Fort Dum, and *prys* (= copse); *c.* 1183

Population in 1801:   *Population in 1971:*
54,597   86,816

Area: 682,960 acres   *Population density per acre in 1971:* 0·13

County Town and River: Dumfries on the River Nith

Large Burgh (and population): Dumfries (28,194)

Small Burghs (and population): Annan (5,990); Langholm (2,367); Lochmaben (1,250¶); Lockerbie (2,904); Moffat (1,837); Sanquhar (2,086)

District Councils (and population): Annan (5,723); Dumfries (13,515); Gretna (5,161); Langholm (2,085); Lockerbie (3,735); Moffat (1,350); Thornhill (6,124); Upper Nithsdale (4,495)

Lieutenant of County: Kenneth M. McCall, Esquire

Principal Industries: Beef cattle farming and root crops; coal-mining; forestry; limestone and sandstone quarrying; chemical processing (rubber and plastics); fishing

Tourist attractions and places of interest: Barr's Hill (hill fort); Burnswark (Roman defences and hill fort); Caerlaverock Castle ruins; Craigdarroch; Drumlanrig Castle; Dumfries (Old Bridge House Museum; Burgh museum; Devorgilla Bridge; Mid Steeple); Durisdeer Church; Ecclefechan (Carlyle's House); Lincluden Abbey remains; Ruthwell Church (Saxon cross)

Principal county worthies (by birth): Thomas Telford (the great bridge builder and road engineer; 1757–1834); Thomas Carlyle (the essayist and historian, born at Ecclefechan; 1795–1881)

Highest point above Sea Level: White Coomb, ten miles north-east of Moffat, 2,695 feet

¶ Only 1970 population figure available

Tantallon Castle, East Lothian, overlooking the Firth of Forth. Chief stronghold of the Douglas Earls of Angus, it withstood sieges in 1491 and 1528, but later fell to Commonwealth forces under General Monk in 1651 after a bombardment lasting 12 days

The castle at Braemar, Aberdeenshire; nearby in 1715 the Earl of Mar raised his standard in support of the Old Pretender

11. DUNBARTON

Statutory name of administrative county: County of Dunbarton

Derivation and first recorded use of name: cf. *dun Breatuin,* for the Britons (of Strathclyde); probably *c.* 1180

Population in 1801:	*Population in 1971:*
20,710	231,597

Area: 154,432 acres   *Population density per acre in 1971:* 1·50

County Town and River: Dumbarton on the River Clyde

Motto of County Council: "*Levenax*" (the old name for Lennox)

Large Burghs (and population): Clydebank (49,386); Dumbarton (25,213)

Small Burghs (and population): Bearsden (23,645); Cove and Kilcreggan (1,286); Cumbernauld (29,853); Helensburgh (13,798); Kirkintilloch (24,880); Milngavie (10,125)

District Councils: Helensburgh, Kirkintilloch, Old Kilpatrick, Vale of Leven

Lieutenant of County: Robert Arbuthnott, Esquire, M.B.E., T.D.

Principal Industries: Cattle and sheep farming and cereal crops; shipbuilding and heavy engineering; coal-mining and quarrying; light engineering; textiles; whisky distilleries

Tourist attractions and places of interest: Antonine Wall remains; Dumbarton Rock and Castle; Knockderry Castle; Loch Lomond

Principal county worthies (by birth): John Logie Baird (first to give public demonstration of television (27th January 1926), 1888–1946); Tobias Smollet (the Scottish novelist, born at Cardross; 1721–1771)

Highest point above Sea Level: Ben Vorlich, 3,088 feet

12. EAST LOTHIAN

Statutory name of administrative county: County of East Lothian

Derivation and first recorded use of name: Lothian is believed to have been a man's name (according to legend, King Loth); earliest recorded use, *c.* 970

Population in 1801:	*Population in 1971:*
29,986	55,142

Area: 170,971 acres   *Population density per acre in 1971:* 0·32

County Town and River: Haddington on the River Tyne

Small Burghs (and population): Cockenzie and Port Seton (3,565¶); Dunbar (4,421); East Linton (834); Haddington (6,819); North Berwick (4,116); Prestonpans (3,207); Tranent (6,988¶)

District Councils: Dunbar, Haddington, North Berwick, Prestonpans, Tranent

Lieutenant of County: The Rt. Hon. The Earl of Wemyss and March, K.T.

Principal Industries: Root crops, cereals and sheep farming; coal-mining and quarrying; fishing

Tourist attractions and places of interest: Aberlady bird sanctuary; Dirleton Castle; Dunbar (Town House); Gifford (Yester House and Yester Castle ruins); Haddington Church; Hailes Castle remains; The Hopes (hill fort); Lennoxlove mansion; Prestonpans (Hamilton House); Traprain Law (hill fort); Winton House

Principal county worthies (by birth): John Knox (founder of the Presbyterian Church, born at Haddington; *c.* 1513–1572); Mrs. Jane Welsh Carlyle (1801–1866); Arthur James Balfour (the 1st Earl of Balfour, the Conservative Prime Minister; 1848–1930; born at Whittingehame)

Highest point above Sea Level: Meikle Says Law, on the county border with Berwickshire, 1,750 feet

¶ Only 1970 population figure available

13. FIFE

Statutory name of administrative county: County of Fife

Derivation and first recorded use of name: Traditionally said to be derived from *Fibh,* possibly one of the seven sons of the British patriot, Criuthne; *c.* 590

Population in 1801:	*Population in 1971:*
93,743	327,816

Area: 322,878 acres   *Population density per acre in 1971:* 1·02

County Town: Cupar

Motto of County Council: "*Virtute et Opera*" = By Virtue and Industry

Large Burghs (and population): Dunfermline (50,572); Kirkcaldy (52,075)

Small Burghs (and population): Auchtermuchty (1,270); Buckhaven and Methil (18,900); Burntisland

(5,451¶); Cowdenbeath (10,400); Crail (945); Culross (491); Cupar (6,655); Elie and Earlsferry (744); Falkland (941); Inverkeithing (5,424); Kilrenny with Anstruther Easter and Anstruther Wester (2,799); Kinghorn (2,088); Ladybank (1,135); Leslie (3,300); Leven (9,060); Lochgelly (8,016); Markinch (2,317); Newburgh (2,089); Newport-on-Tay (3,464); Pittenweem (1,435); St. Andrews (10,803¶); St. Monance (1,206); Tayport (2,963)

District Councils: Cupar, Dunfermline, Glenrothes, Kirkcaldy, Lochgelly, St. Andrews, Wemyss

Lieutenant of County: Sir John McWilliam

Principal Industries: Dairy and beef cattle, and sheep farming; cereals and root crops; coalmining and quarrying of sandstone and limestone; shipbuilding and general engineering; distilleries; linoleum and fabrics; paper mills; fishing; tourism and the holiday trade

Tourist attractions and places of interest: Aberdour; Anstruther (Manse); Balcaskie House; Balmerino Abbey ruins; Culross (Palace; The Study; Town House; Church of St. Andrew); Dunfermline Abbey; Elie Castle; Inchcolm Abbey ruins; Isle of May lighthouse; Kirkcaldy (Ravenscraig Castle ruins; Museum and Art Gallery); Lindores Abbey ruins; Lower Largo ("Robinson Crusoe" statue); St. Andrews (Cathedral; Martyrs' Graves); Scotstarvit Tower; Tarvit House

Principal county worthies (by birth): King Charles I (born at Dunfermline; 1600–1649); Alexander Selkirk (Defoe's Robinson Crusoe, born at Lower Largo; 1676–1721); Adam Smith (the political economist, born at Kirkcaldy; 1723–1790); the Adams brothers (the great architects, Robert 1728–1792, and James 1730–1794); Sir David Wilkie (1785–1841); Andrew Carnegie (1835–1918)

Highest point above Sea Level: West Lomond, 1,713 feet

¶ Only 1970 population figure available

14. INVERNESS-SHIRE

Statutory name of administrative county: County of Inverness

Derivation and first recorded use of name: Origin unknown, probably 13th century

Population in 1801:	*Population in 1971:*
72,672	85,116
Area: 2,695,094 acres	*Population density per acre in 1971:* 0·029

County Town: Inverness

Motto of County Council: "*Air son math na siorrachd*" = For the Good of the County

Large Burgh (and population): Inverness (32,625)

   Small Burghs (and population): Fort William (4,006¶); Kingussie (1,006)

District Councils: Aird, Bedenoch, Barra, Harris, Inverness, Lochaber, North Uist, Skye, South Uist

Lieutenant of County: Colonel D. H. Cameron of Lochiel, C.V.O., T.D., J.P.

Principal Industries: Beef cattle farming; distilleries; fishing; tourism

Tourist attractions and places of interest: Balnuarin of Clava (Druidical ring cairn); Beauly Priory ruins; Culloden (battle memorial cairns); Dunvegan Castle; Fort Augustus; Fort George (Regimental Museums of the Queen's Own Highlanders, the Queen's Own Cameron Highlanders, and the Seaforth Highlanders); Fort William ruins; Glenfinnan Monument (memorial to the raising of the Prince Charles Stewart Standard); Inverness (Abertarf House and other town houses); Kilpheder round-house; Kingussie (Highland folk museum); Kisimul Castle (Isle of Barra); Spean Bridge (Commando Memorial)

Principal county worthies (by birth): Duncan Forbes 1685–1746); Flora Macdonald (the Young Pretender's supporter, born at Milton, South Uist; 1720–1790)

Highest point above Sea Level: Ben Nevis, 4,406 feet

¶ Only 1970 population figure available

15. KINCARDINESHIRE

Statutory name of administrative county: County of Kincardine

Derivation and first recorded use of name: cf. *Cinnchàrdin,* Pict Gaelic for "at the head of the woods"– 1295

Population in 1801:	*Population in 1971:*
26,349	25,336
Area: 242,460 acres	*Population density per acre in 1971:* 0·10

County Town and River: Stonehaven on the River Carron

Motto of County Council: "*Laus Deo*" = Praise be to God

Small Burghs (and population): Banchory (2,168); Inverbervie (881¶); Laurencekirk (1,340); Stonehaven (4,572)

District Councils: Laurencekirk, Lower Deeside, St. Cyrus, Stonehaven, Upper Deeside

Lieutenant of County: George A. M. Saunders, Esquire

Principal Industries: Cereals and root crops; distilleries; manufacture of woollen garments; fishing

Tourist attractions and places of interest: Arbuthnott (Church of St. Ternan); Crathes Castle; Dunnottar Castle ruins; Fettercairn (Kincardine Tower Cross); Kinneff church; Muchalls Castle

Highest Point above Sea Level: Mount Battock, 2,555 feet

¶ Only 1970 population figure available

16. KINROSS-SHIRE

Statutory name of administrative county: County of Kinross

Derivation and first recorded use of name: cf. *kin-ros*, at the head of the moor (*ros*, Celtic), *c.* 1140

Population in 1801: 6,725

Population in 1971: 6,270

Area: 52,025 acres

Population density per acre in 1971: 0·12

County Town: Kinross

Motto of County Council: "For All Time"

Small Burgh (and population): Kinross (2,348)

Lieutenant of County: Lieut.-Col. Robert Christie Stewart, T.D.

Principal Industries: Cereals and root crops; beef and dairy cattle farming; textiles

Tourist attractions and places of interest: Burleigh Castle ruins; Kinross House and gardens; Loch Leven castle remains; Rumblingbridge (old and new bridges)

Highest point above Sea Level: Bishop Hill, 1,492 feet

17. KIRKCUDBRIGHTSHIRE

Statutory name of administrative county: County of Kirkcudbright

Derivation and first recorded use of name: cf. Church (kirk) of Saint Cudberct of Melrose in Roxburghshire, *c.* 1273, probably by Devorgilla, wife of John Balliol of Barnard Castle

Population in 1801: 29,211

Population in 1971: 27,645

Area: 574,024 acres

Population density per acre in 1971: 0·05

County Town: Kirkcudbright

Small Burghs (and population): Castle Douglas (3,292); Dalbeattie (3,304); Gatehouse of Fleet (810); Kirkcudbright (2,733); New Galloway (342)

District Councils: Castle Douglas, Western, Dalbeattie, Eastern, Glenkens, Kirkcudbright

Lieutenant of County: Lieut.-Col. The Rt. Hon. The Earl of Galloway

Principal Industries: Cattle and sheep farming; dairy produce; sandstone and granite quarrying

Tourist attractions and places of interest: Cardoness Castle (ruins); Cauldside (cairns); Dundrennan Abbey (ruined Cistercian abbey); Dungarry and Suie Hill (hill forts); Gatehouse of Fleet; Glenquicken (stone circle); Sweetheart Cistercian Abbey; Threave Castle (ruined 14th century castle of the Lords of Galloway); Trusty's Hill (vitrified fort)

Highest point above Sea Level: Merrick, 2,764 feet, to the west of the Rhinns of Kells

18. LANARKSHIRE

Statutory name of administrative county: County of Lanark

Derivation and first recorded use of name: Possibly from the Welsh, *Llanerch*, a forest glade, *c.* 1110

Population in 1801: 147,492

Population in 1971: 1,527,363

Area: 535,605 acres

Population density per acre in 1971: 2·85

County Town (administrative centre): Hamilton

County of City (and population): City of Glasgow (907,672)

Large Burghs (and population): Airdrie (36,773); Coatbridge (52,827); East Kilbride (65,452); Hamilton (46,457); Motherwell and Wishaw (74,453); Rutherglen (25,100)

Small Burghs (and population): Biggar (1,636); Bishopsbriggs (20,428); Lanark (8,684)

District Councils: First, Second, Third, Fourth, Sixth, Seventh, Eighth, Ninth

Lieutenant of County: Lord Clydesmuir, C.B., M.B.E., T.D.

Principal Industries: Agriculture (livestock) and horticulture (market gardening, vegetables and soft fruits); iron and steel industries; heavy and general engineering industries; aircraft and aero-engine manufacture; textiles

Tourist attractions and places of interest: Part of the Antonine Wall; Arbory Hill (hill fort); Barncluith House; Blantyre (David Livingstone's house); Cadzow Castle (ruins); Chatelherault Lodge; Cow Castle (ruins of "Tillietudlem Castle" of Scott's *Old Mortality*); Glasgow (St. Mungo's Cathedral; University of Glasgow buildings and Hunterian Museum; St. Vincent Street Church; Caledonia Street Church; Tolbooth Steeple; City Art Gallery and Museum; Hutcheson's Hospital; Provand's Lordship; School of Art; New Lanark (Robert Owen's model village); Pollokshaws (Pollok House)

Principal county worthies (by birth): Sir John Moore (the great Peninsular War commander, 1761–1809); Sir Henry Campbell-Bannerman (the Liberal prime minister, born at Kelvinside House, Glasgow; 1836–1908); David Livingstone (the explorer and missionary, born at Blantyre; 1813–1873)

Highest point above Sea Level: Culter Fell, 2,454 feet

19. MIDLOTHIAN

Statutory name of administrative county: County of Midlothian

Derivation and first recorded use of name: Lothian was almost certainly the name of an unknown man, being applied to the area sometime before A.D. 1000

Population in 1801: 122,597

Population in 1971: 599,692

The Palace of Holyroodhouse, Edinburgh, is the official residence in Scotland of the reigning monarch; begun by James IV of Scotland in 1501, it suffered at the hands of Cromwell's troops but restoration was undertaken at the end of the seventeenth century

Area: 201,046 acres   *Population density per acre in 1971:* 2·98

County Town: City of Edinburgh

County of City (and population): City of Edinburgh (464,764)

Small Burghs (and population): Bonnyrigg and Lasswade (7,004), Dalkeith (9,459), Loanhead (5,931), Musselburgh (17,186), Penicuik (9,913)

District Councils: Currie, East Calder, Gala Water, Lasswade, Musselburgh, Newbattle, Penicuik, West Calder

Lieutenant of County: Sir Maxwell I. H. Inglis of Glencorse, Bt.

Principal Industries: Agriculture (cereals, root crops, sheep-rearing and market-gardening) coal-mining; heavy, general and light engineering; textiles; carpet manufacture; paper making; printing and bookbinding; brewing and distilling; tourist trade

Tourist attractions and places of interest: Borthwick Castle; Cakemuir Castle; Craigmillar Castle; Chrichton Castle; Dalhousie Castle; Dalkeith Palace; Edinburgh (Castle; Cathedral Church of St. Giles; Palace of Holyroodhouse; Holyrood Abbey remains; National Gallery of Scotland; National Library of Scotland; Scottish United Services Museum; Regimental Museum of the Royal Scots; numerous other churches and buildings); Glencorse (Castle Law fort excavations); Pinkie House; Roslin Castle ruins

Principal county worthies (by birth): King James I and VI (born in Edinburgh Castle; 1566–1625); John Napier (the great mathematician and inventor of logarithms, born in Edinburgh; 1560–1617); David Hume (1711–1776); 3rd Earl of Bute (the Tory prime minister, born at Parliament Square, Edinburgh; 1713–1792); Sir Walter Scott (the novelist and poet, born in Edinburgh; 1771–1832); Lord Francis Jeffrey (the judge and literary critic, born in Edinburgh; 1773–1850); 1st Earl Brougham and Vaux (the Lord Chancellor and law reformer, born in Edinburgh; 1778–1868); 4th Earl of Aberdeen (1784–1860); David Roberts 1796–1864); David Moir (the author, born at Musselburgh; 1798–1851); Sir Alexander Mackenzie (the composer, born in Edinburgh; 1847–1935); Kenneth Grahame (the essayist and storyteller, born in Edinburgh; 1859–1932); Robert Louis Stevenson (1850–1894); Sir Arthur Conan Doyle (1859–1930); 1st Earl Haig (the British army commander of the First World War, born in Edinburgh; 1861–1928)

Highest point above Sea Level: Blackhope Scar, 2,136 feet

20. MORAYSHIRE

Statutory name of administrative county: County of Moray

Derivation and first recorded use of name: Suggested as being derived from the Gaelic for "among the seagoing men". First use not known

Population in 1801: 27,760   *Population in 1971:* 52,191

Area: 304,931 acres   *Population density per acre in 1971:* 0·17

County Town and River: City of Elgin on the River Lossie
Motto of County Council: "Sub Spe" = In Hope
City (and population): City of Elgin (16,529)
Small Burghs (and population): Burghead (1,369); Forres (4,585); Grantown-on-Spey (1,581); Lossiemouth and Branderburgh (6,379); Rothes (1,096)
District Councils: Cromdale, Duffus and Drainie, Elgin, Fochabers, Forres, Rothes and Knockando
Lieutenant of County: Captain Iain Mark Tennant
Principal Industries: Agriculture (livestock and cereals); whisky distilling; sandstone quarrying; manufacture of woollen goods; forestry; fishing and tourism
Tourist attractions and places of interest: Elgin (Cathedral ruins; Anderson's Institution; Gray's Hospital); Spynie Palace
Principal county worthies (by birth): Lord Strathcona (the financier and statesman, born at Forres; 1820–1914); James Ramsay MacDonald (the first Labour prime minister, born at Lossiemouth; 1866–1937)
Highest point above Sea Level: Cäm a' Chille Chearr, 2,329 feet

21. NAIRNSHIRE

Statutory name of administrative county: County of Nairn
Derivation and first recorded use of name: The origins are pre-Celtic, probably before the 4th century B.C.; first used in the modern form in the 12th century A.D.

Population in 1801:
8,322

Population in 1971:
7,901

Area: 104,251 acres

Population density per acre in 1971: 0·08

County Town: Nairn
Motto of County Council: "Unite and be Mindful"

Small Burgh (and population): Nairn (5,206)
District Council (and population): Nairn (2,695)
Lieutenant of County: The Rt. Hon. The Earl of Leven and Melville
Principal Industries: Agriculture (beef and dairy cattle, cereals and root crops, and sheep rearing); granite quarrying; whisky distilling; fertilizer manufacture
Tourist attractions and places of interest: Auldearn Boath dove-cot and site of Auldearn Castle); Cawdor Castle; Dulsie Bridge; Fort George
Highest point above Sea Level: Carn-Glas-Choire, 2,162 feet

22. ORKNEY (ISLANDS)

Statutory name of administrative county: County of Orkney
Derivation and first recorded use of name: cf. Ork (Norse, = a sea monster), and ay (Old Norse, = an island). Like many of the islands in the county, which also use the -ay derivation, the name-form is very old, probably dating back to the 2nd century B.C.

Population in 1801:
24,445

Population in 1971:
16,925

Area: 240,848 acres

Population density per acre in 1971: 0·07

County Town: Kirkwall (on Mainland)
Motto of County Council: "Boreas domus, mar amicus" = The North our home, the Sea our friend
Small Burghs (and population): Kirkwall (4,688¶); Stromness (1,518)
District Councils (and population): Eday (172¶); Hoy and Walls (536¶); Mainland (6,488); North Ronaldsay (124); Rousay (258¶); Sanday (566¶); Shapinsay (357¶); South Ronaldsay and Burray (1,036); Stronsay (427); Westray and Papa Westray (823¶)
Lieutenant of County: Colonel H. W. Scarth of Breckness

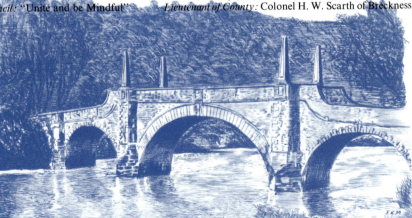

General Wade's Bridge, Aberfeldy, Perthshire, designed by William Adam, and built in 1733

Principal Industries: Agriculture (beef and dairy cattle, pigs, cereals and root crops); sandstone quarrying; whisky distilling; tourism

Tourist attractions and places of interest: Blackhamar (cairn on Rousay); Cuween (chambered cairn on Mainland); Dwarfie Stane (rock-cut tomb on Hoy); Egilsay (ruins); Kirkwall (Cathedral of St. Magnus); Knowe of Laird (cairn on Rousay); Skara Brae (Neolithic settlement); Stenness stone rings; Taversoe Tuack (two-storied cairns); Unstan cairn; Wideford Hill cairn

Highest point above Sea Level: Ward Hill, Hoy, 1,565 feet

¶Only 1970 population figure available

23. PEEBLESSHIRE

Statutory name of administrative county: County of Peebles

Derivation and first recorded use of name: Probably from *pebyll* (Welsh, = tent(s)), *c.* 1116

Population in 1801:   *Population in 1971:*
8,735   13,242

Area: 222,242 acres   *Population density per acre in 1971:* 0·06

County Town and River: Peebles on the River Tweed

Motto of County Council: "Onward Tweeddale" (Tweeddale was the old county name)

Small Burghs (and population): Innerleithen (2,233); Peebles (5,600)

District Councils (and population): Broughton (996); Innerleithen (1,418); Linton (1,837); Peebles (1,158)

Lieutenant of County: Sir Robert Heatlie Scott, G.C.M.G., C.B.E.

Principal Industries: Agriculture (sheep and dairy farming, and cereals); manufacture of Tweed and woollen goods

Tourist attractions and places of interest: Cademuir Hill (hill forts); Neidpath Castle; Stobo church; Traquair House

Principal county worthies (by birth): 4th Duke of Queensberry ("Old Q", born at Peebles; 1725–1810); the Chambers brothers (authors and publishers; Robert, 1802–71, and William, 1800–83, born at Peebles); Professor Veitch (born at Peebles, 1829–94)

Highest point above Sea Level: Broad Law, 2,755 feet

24. PERTHSHIRE

Statutory name of administrative county: County of Perth

Derivation and first recorded use of name: Traditionally from the Welsh *perth* (= thicket), *c.* 1130

Population in 1801:   *Population in 1971:*
125,583   123,375

Area: 1,595,804 acres   *Population density per acre in 1971:* 0·077

County Town and River: City of Perth on the River Tay

Motto of County Council: "Pro lege et liberate" = For Law and Liberty

City (and population): City of Perth (41,623)

Small Burghs (and population): Aberfeldy (1,555): Abernethy (772¶); Auchterarder (2,417); Aylth (1,680); Blairgowrie and Rattray (5,229); Callander (1,814); Coupar Angus (1,951); Crieff (5,522); Doune (738); Dunblane (4,086); Pitlochry (2,438)

District Councils: Central, Eastern, Highland, Kinross, Perth, Western

Lieutenant of County: The Rt. Hon. The Earl of Mansfield and Mansfield

Principal Industries: Agriculture (beef cattle, cereals and root crops); whisky distilling; fishing and tourism

Tourist attractions and places of interest: Aberfeldy (General Wade's Bridge); Ardoch Roman Camp; Blair Castle; Doune Castle; Drummond Castle gardens; Dunblane Cathedral; Dunkeld Cathedral; Dunsinane fort; Finlarig Castle ruins; Meikleour House (the great beech hedge); Ossian's Hall; Perth; Scone Palace

Principal county worthies (by birth): Lord Mansfield (William Murray, born at Perth; 1705–1793); Robert Sandeman (who spread the Glassite doctrines, born at Perth; 1723–1771); Lord Lynedoch (the victor at Barrosa, 1811, born at Balgowan House; 1748–1843); John Buchan 1st Lord Tweedsmuir (1875–1940); William Soutar (the vernacular poet, 1898–1943, born at Perth)

Highest point above Sea Level: Ben Lawers, 3,984 feet

¶ Only 1970 population figure available

25. RENFREWSHIRE

Statutory name of administrative county: County of Renfrew

Derivation and first recorded use of name: cf. Welsh *rhen frui* (= flowing river); *c.* 1130

Population in 1801:   *Population in 1971:*
78,501   361,263

Area: 143,829 acres   *Population density per acre in 1971:* 2·51

County Town: Paisley

Motto of County Council: "Avito viret honore" = He flourishes with ancient honour

Large Burghs (and population): Greenock (69,620); Paisley (95,434); Port Glasgow (22,220)

Small Burghs (and population): Barrhead (17,752); Gourock (10,773); Johnstone (23,443); Renfrew (19,109)

District Councils: First, Second, Third, Fourth, Fifth

Lieutenant of County: The Rt. Hon. The Viscount Muirshiel, C.H., C.M.G.

Principal Industries: Agriculture (dairy and beef cattle, cereals and root crops); shipbuilding; heavy, general and light engineering; textiles and carpet manufacture; quarrying

Tourist attractions and places of interest: Eaglesham village; Greenock (McLean Museum); Kilbarchan (weaver's cottage); Paisley Abbey, Port Glasgow (Newark Castle)

Principal county worthies (by birth): William Wallace (the national hero and inspiration of Scottish resistance to King Edward I, *c.* 1270–1305; traditionally born at Elderslie); Captain William Kidd (the pirate, born at Renfrew; *c.* 1645–1701); James Watt (the engineer and inventor, born at Greenock; 1736–1819); Alexander Wilson (the poet and American ornithologist, born at Paisley; 1766–1813); Robert Tannahill (the weaver-poet, born at Paisley; 1774–1810); Professor John Wilson (the writer, born at Paisley, 1785–1854); the Caird brothers (the scholars, John, 1820–1898, and Edward, 1835–1908, born at Paisley); John Davidson (the poet, born at Barrhead; 1857–1909); Sir James Guthrie (the painter, born at Greenock; 1859–1930); Hamish MacCunn (the composer, born at Renfrew; 1868–1916)

Highest point above Sea Level: Hill of Stake, 1,713 feet

26. ROSS AND CROMARTY

Statutory name of administrative county: County of Ross and Cromarty

Derivation and first recorded use of name: cf. Celtic *ros* (= a moor) or Old Gaelic *ros* (= a peninsula); and Gaelic *crom badh* (= a crooked bay). The form *Crumbathyn* dates from 1257

Population in 1801:	*Population in 1971:*
56,318	57,184

Area: 1,977,254 acres *Population density per acre in 1971:* 0·029

County Town: Dingwall on the Firth of Cromarty

Motto of County Council: "Dread God and Do Well"

Small Burghs (and population): Cromarty (587¶); Dingwall (4,171); Fortrose (1,037); Invergordon (2,583); Stornoway (5,282); Tain (1,770)

District Councils: Avoch, Dingwall, Fearn, Fortrose, Gairloch, Invergordon, Lewis, Lochbroom, Lochcarron, Muir-of-Ord, South West, Tain

Lieutenant of County: Captain Alexander F. Matheson, R.N.(Retd.)

Principal Industries: Agriculture (cattle, sheep, cereal crops and potatoes); Harris tweed; whisky distilling; forestry; fishing and tourism

Tourist attractions and places of interest: Callanish, Lewis (stone circle and cairn); Castle Leod; Cromarty (town and harbour buildings; Hugh Miller's cottage); Eilean Donan Castle; Garynahine, Lewis (stone circle); Inverewe Gardens; Stein-a-Cleit cairn; Strome Castle ruins

Principal county worthies (by birth): Sir Alexander MacKenzie (*c.* 1775–1820); Sir Roderick Murchison (the geologist, born at Taradale House, near Fortrose; 1792–1871); Hugh Miller (the geologist, stone-mason, accountant and author, born at Cromarty; 1802–56); General Sir Hector Macdonald (born at Urquhart, near Dingwall; 1853–1903)

Highest point above Sea Level: Càrn Eige, 3,877 feet

¶ Only 1970 population figure available

27. ROXBURGHSHIRE

Statutory name of administrative county: County of Roxburgh

Derivation and first recorded use of name: cf. Castle of Hroc (Old English, = the rock), and Rook Barugh, North Yorkshire. *Sic* in 1158, but *Rokisburc* in 1127

Population in 1801:	*Population in 1971:*
33,721	42,806

Area: 425,564 acres (incl. 2,800 of water) *Population density per acre in 1971:* 0·10

County Town and River: Jedburgh on Jed Water; administrative headquarters, Newton St. Boswells on the River Tweed

Motto of County Council: "Ne cede malis sed contra audientor ito" = Yield not to adversity, but oppose it more boldly

Small Burghs (and population): Hawick (16,760); Jedburgh (3,785); Kelso (4,579); Melrose (2,236)

District Councils: Hawick, Jedburgh, Kelso, Melrose

Lieutenant of County: His Grace The Duke of Buccleuch and Queensberry, K.T., G.C.V.O., T.D., LL.D.

Principal Industries: Sheep farming, tweed, fishing and tourism

Tourist attractions and places of interest: Abbotsford House; Eildon Hills (Iron Age fort and Roman signal station); Floors Castle; Hermitage Castle; Jedburgh Abbey; Kelso Abbey remains; Melrose Abbey; Woden Law (fort and Roman siege works)

Principal county worthies (by birth): James Thomson (1700–1748); Dr. John Leyden (the poet, born at Denholm; 1775–1811); Mrs. Somerville (Mary Fairfax, the mathematician, born at Jedburgh; 1780–1872); Sir David Brewster (born at Jedburgh; 1781–1868); Henry F. Lyte (author of *Abide with Me,* born near Kelso; 1793–1847); John Scott (the botanist, born at Denholm; 1836–1880); Sir James Murray (compiler of the Oxford English Dictionary, born at Denholm; 1837–1915)

Melrose Abbey, Roxburghshire, founded by Cistercian monks in 1136

Highest point above Sea Level: Unnamed point on the border with England, between Auchope Cairn (in Roxburghshire) and the Cheviot (in Northumberland); 2,422 feet.

28. SELKIRKSHIRE

Statutory name of administrative county: County of Selkirk

Derivation and first recorded use of name: Probably cf. church (kirk or *kyrke*) in the house (Old English *sæl* or *sele*). Sic in 1306, but similar in 1113.

Population in 1801:   *Population in 1971:*
5,388   20,415

Area: 171,209 acres   *Population density per acre in 1971:* 0·12

County Town and River: Selkirk on the River Ettrick

Small Burghs (and population): Galashiels (12,218); Selkirk (5,564)

District Councils: North, South

Lieutenant of County: Vice-Admiral Sir Edward Michael Conolly Abel Smith, G.C.V.O., C.B.

Principal Industries: Sheep and cattle farming; manufacture of wollen goods

Tourist attractions and places of interest: Newark Castle

Principal county worthies (by birth): James Hogg (1770–1835); Mungo Park (1771–1806); Andrew Lang (born at Selkirk; 1844–1912); Anne Redpath (the first woman painter admitted to the Royal Scottish Academy, born at Galashiels; 1895–1965)

Highest point above Sea Level: Broad Law, on county border with Peeblesshire; 2,755 feet

29. SHETLAND (ISLANDS)

Statutory name of administrative county: County of Zetland

Derivation and first recorded use of name: cf. Hjaltland (the old Norse name of which the origin is now generally accepted as inexplicable), in use in 1289; by 1403 the name Zetlandie had gained currency

Population in 1801:   *Population in 1971:*
22,379   17,032

Area: 352,337 acres   *Population density per acre in 1971:* 0·049

County Town: Lerwick on the island of Mainland

Motto of County Council: "*Med lögum Skal Land Byggja*" = By Law is the Land Built

Small Burgh (and population): Lerwick (5,933)

District Councils (and population): Bressay (241); Burra (608); Delting (679); Dunrossness (2,006); Fetlar (94); Gulberwick and Quarff (177); Nesting and Lunnasting (352¶); Northmavine (724); Sandsting and Aithsting (891¶); Tingwall (1,596); Unst (1,175); Walls and Sandness (607); Whalsay and Skerries (915); Yell (1,031)

Lieutenant of County: Robert Hunter Wingate Bruce of Sumburgh, C.B.E.

Principal Industries: Sheep farming and wool-working; fishing

Tourist Attractions and Places of Interest: Broch of Clickimin; Broch of Mousa; Lerwick (Shetland County Museum); St. Ninian's Isle; Scalloway Castle

Principal county worthies (by birth): Arthur Anderson (1792–1868); Sir Robert Stout (1844–1930)

Highest point above Sea Level: Ronas Hill, 1,475 feet

¶ Only 1970 population figure available

30. STIRLINGSHIRE

Statutory name of administrative county: County of Stirling

Derivation and first recorded use of name: Though Gaelic explanations are considered unreliable, two origins are suggested; either cf. *Struthlinn,* literally "a river pool", in use 1100; or cf. *Strevelyn,* the dwelling of Velyn, in use before 1127

Population in 1801:
50,825

Population in 1971:
205,767

Area: 288,349 acres

Population density per acre in 1971: 0·71

County Town and River: Stirling on the Forth

Large Burghs (and population): Falkirk (38,559); Stirling (29,205)

Small Burghs (and population): Bridge of Allan (4,281); Denny and Dunipace (8,951); Grangemouth (23,255); Kilsyth (9,855)

District Councils: Central 1, Central 2, Eastern 1, Eastern 2, Eastern 3, Western 1, Western 2, Western 3

Lieutenant of County: Colonel The Viscount Younger of Leckie, O.B.E., T.D.

Principal Industries: Dairy-cattle farming; heavy engineering, shipbuilding and general engineering; coalmining; brewing and whisky distilling; timber and forestry; chemical industries; manufacture of cotton goods

Tourist Attractions and Places of Interest: Antonine Wall; Bannockburn (1314 battle site); Castlecary (Roman fort and remains of Castle Cary); Duntreath Castle; Falkirk (Rough Castle; Hamilton's Steeple); Loch Lomond; Stirling (Castle; Wallace Memorial; Church of the Holy Rood; Smith Art Gallery and Museum)

Principal county worthies (by birth): King James III (born at Stirling, 1451); King James IV (believed born at Stirling in 1472); Prince Henry, son of James VI (born in Stirling Castle in 1594)

Highest point above Sea Level: Ben Lomond, 3,192 feet

Scone Palace, Perthshire. Home of the Earl of Mansfield, the palace was largely rebuilt in 1803, but earlier palaces on the site housed the Stone of Destiny until 1296, and were the scene of many Scottish coronations before the accession of Charles II in 1651

31. SUTHERLAND

Statutory name of administrative county: County of Sutherland

Derivation of first recorded use of name: Name developed from *Sudreys* (Norse name for the Hebrides); hence *Sudrland* (*c.* 1040, the southern land), to *Suthernelande* (i.e. south of the Orkneys, *c.* 1250)

Population in 1801: 23,117

Population in 1971: 13,040

Area: 1,297,914 acres

Population density per acre in 1971: 0·010

County Town (Administrative Headquarters): Golspie

Motto of County Council: "*Dluth lean do dhuthchas le durachd*" = Cling to thy Heritage with Diligence

Small Burgh (and population): Dornoch (929)

District Councils (and population): Assynt (867); Dornoch and Creich (2,129); Eddrachillis and Durness (1,013); Golspie, Rogart and Lairg (3,177); Kildonan, Loth and Clyne (3,123); Tongue and Farr (1,786)

Lieutenant of County: The Hon. Lord Migdale

Principal Industries: Sheep farming; coalmining; forestry; fishing and tourism

Tourist Attractions and Places of Interest: Cape Wrath; Dunrobin Castle; Kilpheder; Learable Hill (stone-rows and cairns); Reay Forest

Principal county worthies (by birth): Hugh Mackay (1640-1692); Robert Mackay ("Rob Donn", the Reay Forest Bard, born in West Sutherland; 1740-1778)

Highest point above Sea Level: Ben More Assynt, 3,273 feet

32. WEST LOTHIAN

Statutory name of administrative county: County of West Lothian

Derivation and first recorded use of name: Probably from *Loth*, an unknown man in *c.* 970; various variations were in use between 1091 and 1200, e.g. *Louthion, c.* 1200

Population in 1801: 17,844

Population in 1971: 108,235

Area: 78,860 acres

Population density per acre in 1971: 1·37

County Town and Rivers: Linlithgow on the Rivers Avon and Almond

Small Burghs (and population): Armadale (7,165); Bathgate (14,763); Bo'ness (or Borrowstounness; 13,636); Linlithgow (5,572); South Queensferry (4,709); Whitburn (9,640)

District Councils: Bo'ness and Carriden; Kirkliston and Winchburgh; Linlithgow; Torphichen and Bathgate; Uphall; Whitburn and Livingston

Lieutenant of County: The Most Hon. The Marquess of Linlithgow, M.C.

Principal Industries: Cattle farming; coalmining; iron and steel industries; motor car manufacture; light engineering and electronics

Tourist Attractions and Places of Interest: The Binns mansion; Bo'ness (end of the Antonine Wall; Kinneil House and home of James Watt); Bowden Hill and Cockleroy (hill walls and forts); Cairnpapple (Neolithic and Iron Age remains); Dalmeny church; the Forth Railway Bridge; Hopetoun House; Linlithgow (Palace; Church of St. Michael); Niddry Castle ruins; Queensferry (Plewlands House)

Principal county worthies (by birth): King James V (born at Linlithgow Palace in 1512); his daughter Mary, Queen of Scots (born at Linlithgow Palace in 1542); Henry Bell (the pioneer of steamboat travel, born at Torphichen; 1767-1830); Sir James Y. Simpson (who introduced the use of chloroform in 1847; believed born at Bathgate; 1811-1870); Principal Shairp (born at Houston; 1819-1885)

Highest point above Sea Level: The Knock, 1,023 feet

33. WIGTOWNSHIRE

Statutory name of administrative county: County of Wigtown

Derivation and first recorded use of name: cf. *Wyggeton*, village (*ton*) of Wig or Wiga, cf. *vig-r*, Old Norse for "a spear"; *c.* 1283

Population in 1801: 22,918

Population in 1971: 27,340

Area: 311,984 acres

Population density per acre in 1971: 0·087

County Town: Wigtown. Stranraer on Loch Ryan is the county administrative centre.

Small Burghs (and population): Newton-Stewart (1,791); Stranraer (9,511); Whithorn (911); Wigtown (1,127)

District Councils (and population): Machars (5,187); Rhins (8,733)

Lieutenant of County: The Rt. Hon. The Earl of Stair, C.V.O., M.B.E.

Principal Industries: Cattle and sheep farming; dairy products; fishing and tourism

Tourist Attractions and Places of Interests: Castle of Park; Dunskey Castle; Castle Kennedy ruins; Glenluce Abbey ruins; Lochinch Castle; Logan Gardens; St. Ninian's Cave and Whithorn Priory; Stranraer (Castle; Wigtown County Museum); Torhouse Standing Stones (Bronze Age circle)

Principal county worthies (by birth): John Dalrymple, 1st Earl of Stair (1646-1695); Sir John Ross (the Arctic explorer, born at Balsarroch, near Stranraer; 1777-1856); Sir Herbert Maxwell (1845-1937)

Highest point above Sea Level: Craigairie Fell, 1,051 feet

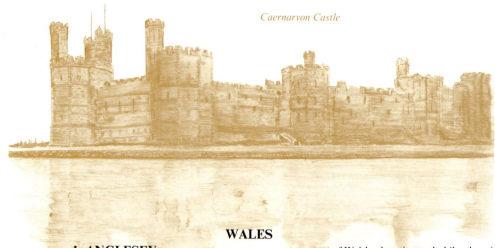

Caernarvon Castle

WALES

1. ANGLESEY

Statutory name of administrative county: County of
Anglesey

Derivation and first recorded use of name: Anglesey
(= isle of the Angles) was probably first used in
the Saxon period (*c.* 1100); the Welsh name for
Anglesey, *Môn*, was referred to by Tacitus in
A.D. 98.

Population in 1801:	*Population in 1971:*
33,806	60,000*
Area: 176,676 acres	*Population density per acre in*
	1971: 0·34¶

County Town and River: Llangefni on the Cefni

Motto of County Council: "*Môn Mam Cymru*" = Mona
Mother of Wales

Municipal Borough (*with population*): Beaumaris (2,080)

Urban Districts: Amlwch, Holyhead, Llangefni, Menai
Bridge

Rural Districts: Aethwy, Twrcelyn, Valley

Lord Lieutenant: Sir Richard Williams-Bulkeley, BT.,
T.D., J.P.

Principal Industries: Agriculture (livestock); light engineering; boatbuilding; chemical manufacture;
fishing; quarrying.

Tourist Attractions and Places of Interest: Beaumaris
Castle, Church and Courthouse; Bryn Celli Ddu
(cairn); Bryn Yr Hen Bobl (burial chamber); Din
Lligwy (native settlement); Hafotty (medieval
house); Penmon Priory; South Stack lighthouse;
Trefignath (megalithic cairn); Llanfair P.G.§

Principal County worthies (*by birth*): Lewis Morris (poet,
philologist and antiquary, born at Tyddyn Melus;
1700-1765); Goronwy Owen (the poet; born at
Rhos Fawr; 1723-1769); Sir Hugh Owen (the

promoter of Welsh education and philanthropist,
born near Talyfoel Ferry; 1804-1881)

* *Registrar General's estimate at 30th June 1970*
¶ *Based on the 1970 population estimate by the Registrar
General*
§ *The celebrated* "*longest place-name*", *viz:*
Llanfairpwllgwyngyllgogerychwyrndrobwllllantysiliogo-
gogoch = The Church of St. Mary in a hollow of white
hazel near to a rapid whirlpool and to St. Tysilio's
Church near to a red cave.

2. BRECONSHIRE

Statutory name of administrative county: County of
Brecknock

Derivation and first recorded use of name: Name derived
from Brychan, Prince of Regulus, ruled A.D.
400–*c.* 450; first recorded use in A.D. 916

Population in 1801:	*Population in 1971:*
32,325	54,690
Area: 469,281	*Population density per acre in*
	1971: 0·12

County Town and River: Brecon on the River Usk

Motto of County Council: "*Undeb Hedd Llwyddiant*"
= Unity, Peace, Prosperity

Municipal Borough (*and population*): Brecon (6,480)

Urban Districts (*and population*): Brynmawr (6,470);
Builth Wells (1,550); Hay (1,320); Llantwryd
(510)

Rural Districts: Brecon, Builth, Crickhowell, Hay,
Vaynor and Pendery, Ystradgynlais

Lord Lieutenant: Capt. N. G. Garnons Williams, M.B.E.,
R.N. (Retd.)

Principal Industries: Agriculture (beef cattle and sheep); quarrying; mining

Tourist Attractions and Places of Interest: Brecon (Cathedral; South Wales Borderers Regimental Museum); Brecon Gaer native hill fort; Castell Coch; Tretower Court fortified manor house

County Worthies (by birth): Sarah Siddons (the actress; born at the Shoulder of Mutton public house, Brecon; 1755–1831); Sir George Everest (the military engineer after whom Mount Everest was named; born at Gwernvale; 1790–1866)

Highest point above Sea Level: Pen-y-Fan (or Cader Arthur), 2,907 feet

3. CAERNARVONSHIRE

Statutory name of administrative county: County of Caernarvon

Derivation and first recorded use of name: cf. *caer 'n arfon* (Old Welsh, = "fort opposite *mona*" or Anglesea); hence *Kaerarvon* (*c.* 1196), and *Carnaruan*, (1307)

Population in 1801:	*Population in 1971:*
41,521	121,500
Area: 364,108 acres	*Population density per acre in 1971:* 0·34

County Town and River: Caernarvon, lying between the Cadnant and Seiont Rivers

Motto of County Council: "*Cadernid Gwynedd*" = The Strength of Gwynnedd

Municipal Boroughs (and population): City of Bangor (15,190); Caernarvon Royal (9,150); Conway (12,080); Pwllheli (3,880)

Urban Districts: Bethesda, Betws-y-Coed, Criccieth, Llandudno, Llanfairfechan, Penmaenmawr, Portmadoc

Rural Districts: Gwyfrai, Lleyn, Nant Conway, Ogwen

Lord Lieutenant of County: Sir Michael Duff, BT.

Principal Industries: Sheep and dairy farming; horse-breeding; weaving; tourism

Tourist Attractions and Places of Interest: Bangor Cathedral; Bodwrdda house; Caernarvon (Castle; Roman fort at Segontium); Clynnog-fawr (Church of St. Beuno); Cochwillan House; Conway (Castle; Plas Mawr; Aberconway); Dolwyddelan Castle; Garn Bodfean (Iron Age hill fort); Glynllifon mansion; Gwydir Castle; Llandegai village; Llanengan church; Llanystumdwy (Lloyd George Memorial and Museum); Menai Suspension Bridge; Penrhyn Castle; Plas-yn-Rhiw; Tre'r Ceri (Iron Age hill fort); Snowdonia

Principal county worthies (by birth): King Edward II (born at Caernarvon Castle, 1284–1327); Bishop William Morgan (the first to translate the Old Testament into Welsh, born at Ty Mawr; 1540–1604); John Gibson (the sculptor, born near Conway; 1790–1866); T. E. Lawrence (1888–1935)

Highest point above Sea Level: Snowdon (*Y Wyddfa*), 3,560 feet

4. CARDIGANSHIRE

Statutory name of administrative county: County of Cardigan

Derivation and first recorded use of name: Said to derive from the Welsh prince Caredig, hence *Caredigion*, *c.* 991, written in 1298 as *Cardygan*

Population in 1801:	*Population in 1971:*
42,956	53,180
Area: 443,189 acres	*Population density per acre in 1971:* 0·12

County Town and River: Aberystwyth at the mouth of the Rheidol and Ystwyth Rivers

Motto of County Council: "*Golud gwlad rhyddid*" = The Wealth of the Land is Freedom

Municipal Boroughs (and population): Aberystwyth (10,400); Cardigan (3,790); Lampeter (2,120)

Urban Districts: Aberaeron, New Quay

Rural Districts: Aberaeron, Aberystwyth, Teifside, Tregaron

Lord Lieutenant of County: Captain J. H. Lewes, O.B.E., R.N. (Retd.)

Principal Industries: Cattle and sheep farming; stone and slate quarrying; ship-building, general and light engineering; manufacture of woollen goods; tourism and the holiday trade

Tourist Attractions and Places of Interest: Aberaeron village port; Aberystwyth (University College; National Library of Wales); Cardigan Castle ruins; Crosswood house; Devil's Bridge; Lampeter (St. David's College); Nanteos Mansion; Pen Dinas (Iron Age hill fort); Strata Florida Norman abbey remains)

Principal county worthies (by birth): Dafydd ap Gwilym (the 14th century poet, born near Aberystwyth); Isaac Williams (the poet and leader of the Oxford Movement, born at Cwm Cynfelyn; 1802–1865); Henry Richard (the politician, born at Tregaron; 1812–1888); Sir John Rhys (1840–1915)

Highest point above Sea Level: Plynlimon, 2,468 feet

5. CARMARTHENSHIRE

Statutory name of administrative county: County of Carmarthen

Derivation and first recorded use of name: Possibly originated in the Greek (*c.* 150) Μαριδύνον, hence *Cair-merdin* (*c.* 800), = the fort of Merlin, and *Kaermerdin*, 1242.

Population in 1801:	*Population in 1971:*
67,317	164,300
Area: 588,472 acres	*Population density per acre in 1971:* 0·28

County Town and River: Carmarthen on the River Towy

Motto of County Council: "*Rhyddid Gwerin Ffyniant Gwlad*" = The Freedom of the People is the Prosperity of the Land

Municipal Boroughs (and population): Carmarthen (13,090); Kidwelly (2,950¶); Llandovery (2,140); Llanelli (27,940)

Urban Districts: Ammanford, Burry Port, Cwmamman, Llandeilo, Newcastle Emlyn

Rural Districts: Carmarthen, Llandeilo, Llanelli, Newcastle Emlyn

Lord Lieutenant of County: Colonel C. W. Nevill, O.B.E., T.D.

Principal Industries: Anthracite mining; dairy farming; iron and steel industries; tinplating; motor car and accessory manufacture; tourism

Tourist Attractions and Places of Interest: Carreg-Cennen Castle ruins; Dryslwyn Castle ruins; Dynevor Castle (Norman castle remains and modern castle); Kidwelly Castle; Meini Gwyr stone circle; Pumpsaint (Roman gold mines); Taliaris Park; Talley (12th century abbey remains); Y Gaer Fawr (hill fort)

Principal County Worthies (by birth): Griffith Jones of Llanddowror (the great clergyman and founder of Welsh charity schools; born at Cilrhedyn; 1683–1761); Rhys Prichard (the theologian and author, born at Llandovery; 1579–1644); John Dyer (the poet, probably born at Aberglasney; *c.* 1700–1758); William Williams (the revivalist and hymn writer, born at Cefncoed near Llandovery; 1717–1791); General Sir William Knott (victor of the First Afghan War, born at Carmarthen; 1782–1845); Sir Lewis Morris (the poet, born at Carmarthen; 1833–1907); E. W. Tristram (best known for his work in preserving medieval wall paintings, born at Carmarthen; 1882–1952)

Highest point above Sea Level: Carmarthen Van, 2,632 feet (on county border with Breconshire)

¶ Only 1970 population figure available

6. DENBIGHSHIRE

Statutory name of administrative county: County of Denbigh

Derivation and first recorded use of name: cf. Welsh *din-bach* (= the little hill). Charts of *c.* 1350 indicate *Dynbiegh*.

Population in 1801:	*Population in 1971:*
60,299	182,860
Area: 427,977 acres	*Population density per acre in 1971:* 0·43

County Town and River: Ruthin on the River Clwyd

Motto of County Council: "*Duw A Digon*" = With God, Enough

Municipal Boroughs (and population): Colwyn Bay (25,100); Denbigh (8,360); Ruthin (4,180¶); Wrexham (37,770)

Urban Districts: Abergele, Llangollen, Llanrwst

Rural Districts: Aled, Ceirog, Hiraethog, Ruthin, Wrexham

Lord Lieutenant of County: Colonel Sir Watkin Williams-Wynn, Bt., O.B.E.

Principal Industries: Cereal crops; dairy and sheep farming; mining and limestone quarrying; steel manufacture; tourism and the holiday trade

Tourist Attractions and Places of Interest: Bodnant Gardens; Capel Garmon cairn; Chirk Castle; Garthewin mansion; Gloddaeth Hall; Llangollen (Plas Newydd and town houses); Parc-y-Meirch (Dinorben fort); Pen-y-Corddyn (Iron Age hill fort); Pont Cysyllte (Telford aqueduct); Ruthin (Church of St. Peter; Lordship court house; Exmewe Hall; Nantclwyd House); Sycharth (motte and bailey castle remains); Trevalyn Hall; Valle Crucis Abbey; Wrexham (Church of St. Giles); Wynnstay Hall

Principal County Worthies (by birth): William Salesbury (lexicographer and first translator of the New Testament into Welsh, born at Llansannan; *c.* 1520–*c.* 1620); Humphrey Llwyd (the great physician and antiquary, born at Denbigh; 1527–1568); Gabriel Goodman (later Dean of Westminster, born at Ruthin; *c.* 1540–1601); Sir Hugh Myddelton (engineer, politician and projector of the New River canal to London, born at Hênllan; 1560–1631); Daniel Williams (the nonconformist divine and benefactor, born at or near Wrexham; *c.* 1643–1716); Thomas Gee (the printer, publisher and nonconformist preacher and leader of Welsh thought, born at Denbigh; 1815–1898); Sir Henry M. Stanley (John Rowlands, the explorer and the "discoverer" of Livingstone; born near Denbigh Castle; 1841–1904)

Highest point above Sea Level: Moel Sych, at the junction of the county borders of Denbighshire, Montgomeryshire and Merionethshire; 2,713 feet

¶ Only 1970 population figures available

7. FLINTSHIRE

Statutory name of administrative county: County of Flint

Derivation and first recorded use of name: cf. *flint* or *flynt*, Old English, a flint or rock; the form in 1277 was Flynt or Fflint. Note: This derivation is strongly denied by some authorities, but alternative suggestions are not offered.

Population in 1801:	*Population in 1971:*
39,469	173,070
Area: 163,707 acres	*Population density per acre in 1971:* 1·06

County Town and River: Mold on the River Alyn

Motto of County Council: "Gorau Tarian Cyfiawnder" = The Best Shield is Justice

Municipal Borough (and population): Flint (14,830)

Urban Districts: Buckley, Connah's Quay, Holywell, Mold, Prestatyn, Rhyl

Rural Districts: Hawarden, Holywell, Maelor (detached enclave), St. Asaph

Lord Lieutenant of County: Brigadier H. S. K. Mainwaring, C.B., C.B.E., D.S.O., T.D.

Principal Industries: Cereal crops; stock rearing and dairy farming, poultry and pigs; iron and steel industries; cement and brickmaking; chemicals and man-made fibres; paper-making; woollen goods; tourism and the holiday trade

Tourist Attractions and Places of Interest: Basingwerk Abbey ruins; Bodrhyddan Hall; Ewloe Castle; Faenol Fawr; Flint Castle ruins; Gop Cairn (prehistoric cairn); Holywell (St. Winifred's Chapel); Mold (Church of St. Mary); Plas Teg mansion; Rhuddlan Castle ruins; St. Asaph Cathedral

Principal County Worthies (by birth): Thomas Pennant (antiquarian and local historian, born near Mostyn; 1726–1798)

Highest point above Sea Level: Moel Famma, on county border with Denbighshire; 1,820 feet

8. GLAMORGAN

Statutory name of administrative county: County of Glamorgan

Derivation and first recorded use of name: cf. Morganwg, Old Welsh name for the dominion of Morgan, a 10th century Welsh prince; hence Clamorgan (1242) and Glomorgan (1250)

Population in 1801: 70,879

Population in 1971: 1,259,200

Area: 523,244 acres

Population density per acre in 1971: 2·41

County Town (administrative headquarters) and River: City of Cardiff on the River Taff

Motto of County Council: "A ddioddefws a orfu" = He that Endureth Overcometh

County Boroughs (and population): City of Cardiff (284,010); Merthyr Tydfil (56,130); City of Swansea (170,870)

Municipal Boroughs (and population): Barry (42,370); Cowbridge (1,500); Neath (29,470); Port Talbot (51,000); Rhondda (94,000)

Urban Districts: Aberdare; Bridgend; Caerphilly; Geligaer; Glyncorwg; Llwchwr; Maesteg; Mountain Ash; Ogmore and Gawr; Penarth; Pontypridd; Porthcawl

Rural Districts: Cardiff; Cowbridge; Gower; Llantrisant and Llantwitfardre; Neath; Penybont; Pontardawe

Lord Lieutenant of County: Colonel Sir Cennydd Traherne, T.D.

Principal Industries: Coalmining; steel manufacture; sheep farming and dairy cattle; forestry; fishing; market gardening

Tourist Attractions and Places of Interest: Beaupre (Elizabethan mansion); Caerphilly Castle; Cardiff (Castle; Roman fort; National Museum of Wales; Welch Regiment Regimental Museum); Coity Castle; Ewenny Priory; Margam Abbey; Merthyrmawr village; Merthyr Tydfil (Cyfarthfa Castle and museum); Parc Cwm (Neolithic cairn); Paviland (Goat's Hole Cave); Penrice Castle ruins; Pontypridd bridge; Neath Abbey ruins; Reynoldston (Arthur's Stone); St. Donat's Castle; St. Fagan's Castle (Welsh Folk Museum); Swansea (Industrial Museum of South Wales)

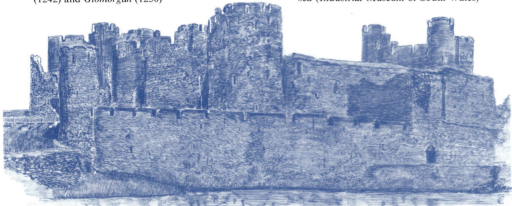

Second only in size among British castles to Windsor, Caerphilly Castle, Glamorgan, was commenced in 1271

Principal County Worthies (*by birth*): Bishop Gower of St. David's (born near Swansea; died in 1347); Philip Jones (the Parliamentarian, born at Swansea; 1618–1674); Count Albert de Belleroche (the painter, born at Swansea; 1864–1944); Beau (Richard) Nash (the lawyer, wit and dandy, born at Swansea; 1674–1762); Joseph Parry (the composer, born at Merthyr Tydfil; 1841–1903); Dylan Marlais Thomas (the poet and essayist, born at Swansea; 1914–1953)

Highest point above Sea Level: Craig-y-Llyn, 1,969 feet

9. MERIONETHSHIRE

Statutory name of administrative county: County of Merioneth

Derivation and first recorded use of name: Named after *Merion,* grandson of Cunedda Wledig, *c.* 420–440; later *Merionydd* (*c.* 1100)

Population in 1801: 29,506	*Population in 1971:* 37,510
Area: 422,372 acres	*Population density per acre in 1971:* 0·089

County Town and River: Dolgellau on the Rivers Wnion and Aran

Motto of County Council: "Tra Mor Tra Meirion" = While the Sea Lasts so shall Merioneth

Urban Districts (*and population*): Bala (1,600); Barmouth (2,320); Dolgellau (2,690); Ffestiniog (6,350); Tywyn (4,540)

Rural Districts (*and population*): Dendraeth (6,930); Dolgellau (6,560); Edeyrnion (4,120); Penllyn (2,490)

Lord Lieutenant of County: Colonel J. F. Williams-Wynne, D.S.O.

Principal Industries: Sheep farming, dairy cattle and poultry; slate quarrying; forestry; nuclear and hydro-electric power sources; tourism

Tourist Attractions and Places of Interest: Castell-y-Bere (castle ruins); Ffestiniog railway; Glyn Cywarch (county house); Harlech Castle; Portmeirion (architecture and landscaping); Rug Chapel; Tomen-y-Mur (Roman fort); Towyn (narrow-gauge railway museum); Trawsfynydd Nuclear Power Station

Principal County Worthies (*by birth*): Thomas Ellis (the famous Member of Parliament for Merionethshire, born at Cynlas, near Bala; 1859–1899)

Highest point above Sea Level: Aran Fawddwy, ten miles north-east of Dolgellau; 2,970 feet

10. MONTGOMERYSHIRE

Statutory name of administrative county: County of Montgomery

Derivation and first recorded use of name: cf. *Mons* (Latin, the mountain), of *Gomeric* (a Norman); reference is made pre-1100 to *Castellium de*

The Norman keep of Cardiff Castle, Glamorgan

Montgomerie. The Welsh name, *Trefaldwyn*, house of Baldwin, its Norman founder; in 1806 the castle was taken by Roger Montgomery, thereafter called thus.

Population in 1801: 48,184	*Population in 1971:* 43,270
Area: 510,110 acres	*Population density per acre in 1971:* 0·084

County Town and River: Welshpool on the River Severn

Motto of County Council: "Powys Paradwys Cymru" = Powys, Paradise of Wales

Municipal Boroughs (*and population*): Llanfyllin (1,080); Llanidloes (2,330); Montgomery (1,020); Welshpool (7,010)

Urban Districts: Machynlleth; Newton and Llanllwchaiarn

Rural Districts: Forden; Llanfyllin; Machynlleth; Newtown and Llanidloes

Lord Lieutenant of County: Colonel J. L. Corbett-Winder, O.B.E., M.C.

Principal Industries: Sheep and cattle farming; cereal crops; forestry; leather works; light engineering

Tourist Attractions and Places of Interest: The Breiddin (Iron Age hill-fort); Gregynog Hall; Montgomery Castle; Newtown (Robert Owen Memorial Museum); Welshpool (Powis Castle); Maesmawr Hall

Principal County Worthies (*by birth*): George Herbert (the poet, born at Montgomery Castle; 1593–1633); Richard Wilson (the landscape painter, born at Penegoes; 1714–1782); Robert Owen (the pioneer socialist, born at Newtown; 1771–1858); Ann Griffiths (the Welsh hymn-writer, born at Llanfihangel yn Ngwynfa, near Llanfyllin; 1780–1805)

Highest point above Sea Level: Moel Sych, at the junction of the county borders of Denbighshire, Montgomeryshire and Merionethshire; 2,713 feet

11. PEMBROKESHIRE

Statutory name of administrative county: County of Pembroke

Derivation and first recorded use of name: cf. *pen broc* (Old Welsh, = head of the sea land); hence *Pembrochia* (c. 1180), *Pembrok* (1350) and *Pembroke* (1450)

Population in 1801:
56,280

Area: 393,007 acres

Population in 1971:
101,200

Population density per acre in 1971: 0·26

County Town and River: Haverfordwest on the River Cleddau

Motto of County Council: "*Ex Unitate Vires*" = Strength from Unity

Municipal Boroughs (and population): Haverfordwest (10,630); Pembroke (14,390); Tenby (4,500)

Urban Districts: Fishguard and Goodwick; Milford Haven; Narbeth; Neyland

Rural Districts: Cemaes; Haverfordwest; Narbeth; Pembroke

Lord Lieutenant of County: Hon. Richard Hanning Philipps, M.B.E.

Principal Industries: Sheep and dairy farming; root crops; oil refining; fishing

Tourist Attractions and Places of Interest: Angle Hall; Carew Castle ruins; Carew Cheriton church; Cilgerran Castle ruins; Manorbier Castle; Milford Haven (Church of St. Katherine; natural harbour); Pembroke Castle; Prescelly Hills (Iron Age hill fort of Moel Trigarn; "bluestones"); St. David's (Cathedral of St. David; Bishop's Palace); St. David's Head (promontory fort); Tenby (Church of St. Mary; Plantagenet House; castle remains and museum)

Principal County Worthies (by birth): Bishop Asser (of Sherborne, and author of the *Life of Aelfred the Great;* died c. 909); Giraldus Cambrensis (Giraldus de Barri, the theologian, born at Manorbier Castle; c. 1146–c. 1220); King Henry VII (born at Pembroke Castle; 1457–1509); Robert Recorde (the great mathematician, born at Tenby; c. 1510–1558); Lieut.-Gen. Sir Thomas Picton (the army commander who served in the West Indies and the Peninsula, etc., and who fell at Waterloo, born at Poyston, near Haverfordwest; 1758–1815); Augustus John (the painter, born at Tenby; 1887–1961)

Highest point above Sea Level: Prescelly Top, 1,760 feet

12. RADNORSHIRE

Statutory name of administrative county: County of Radnor

Derivation and first recorded use of name: cf. *raden ora* (Old English, = edge of the road; a Roman road ran from Wroxeter to Abergavenny and Cæleon);

an alternative origin may lie in *rade-nore* (Old English, = land of mountain tracks); probably *ante*-1100.

Population in 1801:
19,135

Area: 301,165 acres

Population in 1971:
18,590

Population density per acre in 1971: 0·061

County Town: Presteigne on the River Lugg; the county administrative headquarters are at Llandrindod Wells on the River Ithon

Motto of County Council: "*Ewch yn uwch*" = Go Higher

Urban Districts (and population): Knighton (2,200); Llandrindod Wells (3,250); Presteigne (1,310)

Rural Districts (and population): Colwyn (1,630); Knighton (2,540); New Radnor (1,980); Painscastle (1,570); Rhayader (4,120)

Lord Lieutenant of County: Brigadier Sir Michael Venables-Llewelyn, Bt., M.V.O.

Principal Industries: Sheep farming and cereal crops; quarrying; forestry; tourism

Tourist Attractions and Places of Interest: Llananno church; Llandegeley (the Pales Quaker Meeting House); Llandrindod Wells; Maesyronen Chapel; Painscastle

Principal County Worthies (by birth): John Dee (the mathematician and astrologer, 1527–1608; asserted to have been born near Knighton); Thomas Jones (the painter, born at Aberedw; 1743–1803); David Lloyd (the divine and poet, born at Croscunnon Llanbister; 1752–1838)

Highest point above Sea Level: Great Rhôs in Radnor Forest, 2,166 feet

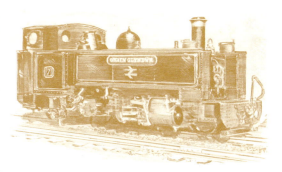

British Rail's last scheduled steam train service operates in Cardigan's Rheidol Valley. "Owain Glyndŵr", shown here, is the oldest of the three locomotives used and was built in 1902

67

NORTHERN IRELAND

1. ANTRIM

Statutory name of administrative county: County of Antrim

Derivation and first recorded use of name: Probably a contraction of the name Aentrebh, a 5th century monastry

Population in 1821: 270,883

Population in 1971: 333,800 (excl. Belfast)

Area: 718,257 acres

Population density per acre in 1971: 0·46

County Borough (and population): City of Belfast (383,600)

Municipal Boroughs (and population): Ballymena (16,950); Carrickfergus (15,034); Larne (18,100); Lisburn (25,800)

Urban Districts: Ballycastle, Ballyclare, Ballymoney, Newtownabbey, Portrush, Whitehead

Rural Districts: Antrim, Ballycastle, Ballymena, Ballymoney, Larne, Lisburn

Lord Lieutenant: Capt. R. A. F. Dobbs

Principal Industries: Shipbuilding and container trade; general engineering; linen and other textiles; tobacco; poultry processing; cement manufacture; shoe manufacture; tyre manufacture; furniture making; agriculture (principally cereals, root crops and flax); fishing; tourism

Tourist Attractions and Places of Interest: Belfast (the Castle; Church of St. George; St. Malachy's Catholic Church; Old Museum; Ulster Museum); Castle Upton; Castle Dobbs; Carrickfergus Castle; Dunluce Castle; Ballycastle; Ballygally Manor House; Ballinderry Middle Church

Principal County worthies (by birth): James Bryce (1838–1922)

Highest point above sea level: Trostán, 1,817 feet

2. ARMAGH

Statutory name of administrative county: County of Armagh

Derivation and first recorded use of name: Name probably derived from Queen Macha, fl. *c.* 300 B.C.

Population in 1821: 197,427

Population in 1971: 130,000

Area: 312,767 acres

Population density per acre in 1971: 0·41

Municipal Boroughs (and population): Lurgan (20,900); Portadown (21,606)

Urban Districts (and population): Armagh (12,300); Craigavon (12,000); Keady (2,250); Tandragee (1,700)

Rural Districts (and population): Armagh (28,000); Newry No. 2 (27,998); Tandragee (3,020)

Lord Lieutenant: Capt. the Rt. Hon. Sir Norman Stronge, Bt., M.C., M.P.

Principal Industries: Agriculture; fruit growing; linen, lace; carpets; pottery; manufacture of metal cans; electrical equipment; river fishing; tourism; quarrying; miscellaneous light engineering

Tourist Attractions and Places of Interest: Navan hill fort (traditionally the seat of the Kings of Ulster); Armagh cathedral; Gosford Castle; Tynan Abbey; Killeavy "castle"; Richhill Manor House

Principal County worthies (by birth): Francis Johnston (Founder of the Royal Hibernian Academy (b. Armagh; 1761–1829).

Highest point above sea level: Slieve Gullion, 1,894 feet

3. DOWN

Statutory name of administrative county: County Down

Derivation and first recorded use of name: cf. *dun*, a

fortress, i.e. St. Patrick's fort. Date of original use not known

Population in 1821:
325,410

Population in 1971:
302,835

Area: 609,439 acres

Population density per acre in 1971: 0·49

Municipal Boroughs (and population): Bangor (30,600); Newtownards (14,500)

Urban Districts (and population): Banbridge (6,700); Donaghadee (3,740); Downpatrick (7,500); Dromore (2,204); Holywood (8,900); Kilkeel (2,600); Newcastle (4,800); Newry (12,010¶); Warrenpoint (3,269¶)

Rural Districts (and population): Banbridge (19,320¶); Castlereagh (53,460); East Down (32,000); Hillsborough (34,992); Moira (8,670); Newry No. 1 (14,230); North Down (31,840); South Down (13,500)

Lord Lieutenant of County: The Rt. Hon., The Earl of Clanwilliam

Principal Industries: Cereal crops and dairy farming; poultry; flax growing and linen industry; light engineering; leather goods, clothing and hosiery

Tourist Attractions and Places of Interest: Arglass (Ardglass Castle; Jordan's Castle); Ballynahinch (Echo Hall); Ballynoe (stone circle); Carrowdore Castle; Castleward House; Castlewellan (town houses and castle); Cultra Manor (Ulster Folk Museum); Downpatrick (St. Patrick's Cathedral; town houses); Dundonald (Anglo-Norman fort); Dundrum Castle; Gill Hall House; Grey Abbey; Kilclief (tower-house); Kirkistown Castle; Legananny dolmen; Moira church; Mount Stewart Gardens; Newry (St. Patrick's Church; town houses); Newtownards town hall; Rowallane Garden; Stormont (Parliament House); Strangford Castle

Principal county worthies (by birth): Sir Hans Sloane (founder of the British Museum, born at Killyleagh; 1660–1753); General Ross of Bladensburg (captor of Washington in 1814, born at Rostrevor; 1766–1814); Viscount Castlereagh (the statesman, born at Newtownards; 1769–1822); Rev. Patrick Brontë (father of the Brontë sisters, born at Emdale; 1777–1861); 3rd Marquess of Downshire (born at Hillsborough, 1788–1845); Captain Francis Crozier (Sir John Franklin's second-in-command on his last voyage in search of the North-West Passage; born at Banbridge; 1796–1848); John Mitchel (the Irish patriot and author, born at Newry; 1815–1875); Mayne Reid (the novelist, born at Ballyroney; 1818–1883); Lord Russell of Killowen (born at Newry; 1832–1900)

Highest point above Sea Level: Slieve Donard, 2,796 feet

¶ Only 1970 population figures available

4. FERMANAGH

Statutory name of administrative county: County of Fermanagh

Derivation and first recorded use of name: So-called after the tribe of *Fir-Monach*, originally a Leinster tribe named after their ancestor, *Monach*, fifth in descent from Cahirmore, monarch of Ireland from A.D. 120–123

Population in 1821:
130,997

Population in 1971:
49,876

Area: 457,376 acres

Population density per acre in 1971: 0·108

Note: Under the Local Government Act (Northern Ireland) 1966, the Enniskillen Borough Council and the Rural District Councils of Enniskillen, Lisnaskea and Irvinestown were amalgamated with Fermanagh County Electoral Division with effect from 2nd June 1967

Principal Industries: General agriculture; man-made fibres: linen manufacture; hydro-electric power; pottery

Tourist Attractions and Places of Interest: Caldragh churchyard; Castlecoole house; Crom Castle; Devenish Island (Round Tower); Enniskillen (Cathedral; Maguire Castle remains); Killadeas (graveyard with carved stones); Monea (Plantation castle); Tully Plantation Castle; White Island (carved stone figures)

County worthy: General Sir Galbraith Lowry Cole (fought in the Peninsular War and later became Governor of Cape Colony; believed to have been born at Enniskillen; 1772–1842)

Highest point above Sea Level: Cuilcagh, on the border with Cavan in the Republic of Ireland, 2,188 feet

5. LONDONDERRY (Co. Derry)

Statutory name of administrative county: County of Londonderry

Derivation and first recorded use of name: Derry, cf. *diore*, Celtic word for an oak grove. The prefix "London" dates from 1613 when James I granted Charters to the Livery Companies of the City of London for land development in Ireland.

Population in 1821:
193,869

Population in 1971:
178,900

Area: 520,851 acres

Population density per acre in 1971: 0·34

County Town: City of Londonderry

Motto of County Council: "*Auxilium a Domino*" = Help from the Lord

County Borough (and population): City of Londonderry (56,000)

Municipal Borough (and population): Coleraine (14,340)

Urban Districts (and population): Limavady (5,250); Portstewart (4,800)

Rural Districts (and population): Coleraine (18,400);

Limavady (19,070); Londonderry (26,700); Magherafelt (34,340)

Lord Lieutenant of County: Senator John Cherry Drennan, C.B.E.

Lord Lieutenant of the City of Londonderry: Colonel Sir Basil McFarland, Bt., C.B.E., E.R.D.

Principal Industries: General agriculture and dairy farming; synthetic fibres and textiles; fishing and tourism

Tourist Attractions and Places of Interest: Boom Hall; Derry (St. Colomb's Catholic Cathedral; Protestant Cathedral; Walker Monument; Bishop Street and city walls); Downhill Castle remains; Dungiven (Church of the Augustinian friary); Maghera church ruins; Mount Sandel (ring fort)

Principal County Worthies (by birth): George Farquhar (the playwright, born in the town of Londonderry; 1678–1707); Charles Thompson (as Secretary of the United States Congress prepared the manuscript of the American Declaration of Independence; born at Maghera; 1730–1824); George Canning (the British statesman and prime minister, widely believed to have been born at Garvagh; 1770–1827); General Sir George White (the defender of Ladysmith; born at Low Rock Castle, Portstewart, in 1835); William Ferguson Massey (later prime minister of New Zealand, born at Limavady; 1856–1925)

Highest point above Sea Level: Sawel Mountain, 2,240 feet

6. TYRONE

Statutory name of administrative county: County of Tyrone

Derivation and first recorded use of name: cf. *Tir-Eoghain* (Owen), meaning the descendants of Eoghan (Owen), son of Niall of the Nine Hostages, hence Tir-Owen. Earliest use not known

Population in 1821:	*Population in 1971:*
261,865	139,239

Area: 806,918 acres   *Population density per acre in 1971:* 0·17

County Town and River: Omagh on the River Strule

Urban Districts (and population): Cookstown (6,500); Dungannon (8,009); Omagh (10,700); Strabane (10,000)

Rural Districts (and population): Castlederg (8,379); Clogher (9,600); Cookstown (14,411); Dungannon (26,330); Omagh (28,310); Strabane (17,000)

Lord Lieutenant of County: His Grace The Duke of Abercorn

Principal Industries: Sheep farming; linen manufacture; natural and man-made fibres; pottery; brick manufacture

Tourist Attractions and Places of Interest: Arboe (High Cross); Benburb fort; Castlecaulfeild House (ruins); Clogher (Cathedral of St. Macartan); Donaghmore (High Cross); Dungannon (Royal School); Killymoon Castle; Knockmany cairn; Newtownstewart (town with Plantation castle)

Principal County Worthies (by birth): Guy Carleton, Lord Dorchester (Governor of Quebec, 1766–1796, born at Strabane); William Carleton (the novelist, born at Prolusk, near Clogher; 1794–1869); General James Shields ("the only man to beat Stonewall Jackson"; later Governor of Oregon, born at Altmore; 1806–1879); Sir William McArthur (1809–1887); Dr. George Sigerson (the poet and Professor of Biology at Dublin, born at Strabane; 1838–1925); Earl Alexander of Tunis (the famous desert commander of the Second World War, born 1891)

Highest point above Sea Level: Sawel Mountain, on county border with Londonderry, 2,240 feet

THE CROWN DEPENDENCIES
1. THE ISLE OF MAN

Origin of name and brief history: The origin of the island's name is controversial, although opinion favours the Old Celtic *man* (meaning "a place"). The name *Monapia* occurs in Roman records, and reference is made to Μοναρίνα (island of Mona) in the Greek. By about 1110 the name Insula Man was current. The island has been continuously inhabited since at least 6,000 B.C., and by about A.D. 450 the island was occupied by Gaelic-speaking inhabitants. Norsemen settled from the 9th century onwards, of whom Godred was the most prominent chieftain – conquering the island in 1079 and ruling until 1095. Man remained a Norse kingdom until, by the Treaty of Perth of 2nd July 1266, the title was sold to Alexander III of Scotland. Edward I of England took the island in 1290, but his son Edward II lost it to Bruce; later it was retaken by Edward III. Kingship was granted to the 1st Earl of Salisbury, and later to the Stanley family. The Stanleys (Earls of Derby after 1485) ruled as "Lords of Mann" until Elizabeth I took over the island in 1594. It was returned to the Derbys in 1609 and in 1736 the Duchess of Atholl, daughter of the 10th Earl, succeeded. After Parliament purchased the manorial rights in 1828, agitation by the islanders brought about a return to a modified form of home rule in 1866.

Administration: The island is covered by the Legislature, consisting of the House of Keys (name probably cf. Norse *keise* = chosen), one of the most ancient legislative assemblies in the world, and

70

La Corbière lighthouse, Jersey, Channel Islands

the Legislative Council which comprises:

(1) *The Lieutenant-Governor:* His Excellency Sir Peter Hyla Gawne Stallard, K.C.M.G., C.V.O., M.B.E.

(2) The Bishop of Sodor and Man.

(3) The First Deemster (a judge of the high court).

(4) The Attorney General, and

(5) Seven members appointed by the House of Keys.

Area: 141,063 acres   *Population (1966 figures):* 50,423 (23,226 males, 27,197 females)

Borough (Municipal Borough equivalent): Douglas (population, 19,517)

Towns (Town Commissioners, and population): Castletown (2,378); Peel (2,739); Ramsey (3,880; approximately 4,850 in 1972 due to boundary extensions)

Villages (Village Commissioners, and population): Laxey (1,132); Michael (378); Onchan (4,000); Port Erin (1,640); Port St. Mary (1,409)

Parish Authorities: Andreas, Arbory, Ballaugh, Braddan, Bride, German, Jurby, Lezayre, Lonan, Malew, Marown, Michael, Maughold, Onchan, Patrick, Rushen, Santon

Principal Industries: Tourism and the holiday trade; agriculture (mainly oats and barley, cattle, sheep and potatoes)

2. THE CHANNEL ISLANDS

Brief history: After inhabitation by Acheulian and Neanderthal man (prior to about 100,000 B.C.) and by Iverian settlers since *c.* 2000 B.C., the Channel Islands were occupied by Gauls and Romans, and were visited by Christian missionaries between the 6th and 9th centuries A.D. Towards the end of this period Viking raids resulted in the establishment of the duchy of Normandy by Rollo in A.D. 911. By 1106 all the islands had been annexed by the British crown, and when Normandy was conquered by the French and King John declared to have forfeited his title to the duchy, the islanders remained loyal to the British crown, as they have ever since. The islands were occupied by German forces between 30th June and 1st July 1940 until relieved by Allied forces on 9th May 1945.

Administration: Administration of the Islands is divided between two Bailiwicks, the States of Jersey and the States of Guernsey, each having a Lieutenant-Governor and Commander-in-Chief appointed by and personal representative to the Monarch and the means of communication between H.M. Government and the Island administrations. Also appointed by the Crown are the Bailiffs (Presidents of the Assembly of the States and of the Royal Court). The States of Guernsey include councillors, people's deputies, representatives of the parish councils and representatives of Alderney. The States of Jersey include elected senators and deputies. All the smaller islands are administered as Dependencies of Guernsey.

Areas and Populations: Jersey (28,717 acres; population 75,532); Guernsey (15,654 acres; population 45,072); Alderney (1,962 acres; population 1,472);

Great Sark (1,035 acres; population, with that of Little Sark, 550); Little Sark (239 acres); Herm (320 acres; uninhabited); Brechou (74 acres; uninhabited). Jethou (44 acres; uninhabited); Lihou (38 acres; uninhabited). Other uninhabited islands include Ortach, Burhou, the Casquets, Les Minquiers and the Ecrehou Islands.

Administrative Towns: St. Helier, Jersey; St. Peter Port, Guernsey

Principal Industries: Agriculture (cattle, tomatoes, fruit and flowers); tourism and the holiday trade

Island worthies (by birth): Philip D'Auvergne (later admiral and Duke D'Auvergne and Bouillon, born on Jersey; 1754-1816); Edward D'Auvergne (military historian, born on Jersey; 1660-1737); James Saumarez, Vice-Admiral Lord de Saumarez (commanded under Lord Howe, etc., born at St. Peter Port; 1757-1836); Lily Langtry (the actress, born at St. Saviour's Rectory; died in 1929).

CHAPTER 2
⚘ History and Constitution ⚘

The United Kingdom of Great Britain and Northern Ireland is a monarchical State, the origins and customs of which are seen in the history of its components. As will be seen in the following Chronology, England was unified under the Saxon King Egbert in the ninth century; Wales and Ireland were joined to it by the end of the thirteenth century; while the English and Scottish crowns were dynastically joined in the person of James I and VI in 1603.

A BRITISH CHRONOLOGY

55 B.C.   26th August. First landings by the Romans under Julius Caesar at Pevensey, Sussex.

54 B.C.   Second expedition to Britain by the Romans.

A.D. 43   Claudian invasion and conquest of the East and South by four legions under Aulus Plautius. Defeat of Caractacus and capture of Camulodunum (Colchester, Essex). Campaigns in the West (*Legio II Augusta* under Vespasian), in the Midlands (*XX Valeria Victrix* and *XIV Gemina*) and in the East (*IX Hispana*).

47   The governor, Ostorius Scapula, establishes a frontier across the country from the Severn to the Trent.

49–50   *Colonia Victricensis* is founded at Camulodunum. Scapula invades South Wales. Legionary fortresses are established at Glevum (Gloucester) and Lindum (Lincoln).

51   Caractacus is defeated by Scapula at Caer Caradoc, and flees to Queen Cartimandua of the Brigantes but is surrendered to the Romans.

53   Death of Ostorius Scapula.

c. 55   The new governor, Didius Gallus, supports Queen Cartimandua in a civil war among the Brigantes.

61   A new governor, Suetonius Paulinus, successfully attacks centre of druidic cult on Anglesey. Rebellion by the Iceni under Boudicca (Boadicea); Paulinus crushes the revolt after the sack of Camulodunum, Londinium (London) and Verulamium (St. Albans).

62	Boudicca commits suicide.
66	One Roman legion (*XIV Gemina*) is withdrawn from Britain.
68	The governor, Trebellius Maximus, fails to gain the support of the Army in Britain in the revolt against Galba, and the following year fails to prevent the defection of the Brigantes.
71–74	The new governor, Petilius Cerealis, crushes the Brigantes with a fresh legion (*II Adiutrix*). A legionary fortress is established at Eburacum (York).
74–78	The governor, Sextus Julius Frontinus, completes the subjugation of Wales and establishes garrisons, and legionary fortresses at Deva (Chester) and Isca (Caerleon, Monmouth). In A.D. 78 Julius Agricola completes the conquest of Anglesey and North Wales, and the following year sets the seal on the subjugation of the Brigantes.
81–84	Agricola advances northwards, builds a line of fortresses between the Forth and Clyde to contain the Picts, and defeats the Caledonians at the battle of Mons Graupius. A Roman fleet circumnavigates Britain. A legionary fortress is established at Inchtuthil.
85	Agricola is recalled by Domitian, and the following year one Roman legion (*II Adiutrix*) is withdrawn from Britain.
90–96	The fortress at Inchtuthil is evacuated; *Lindum Colonia* is founded at Lincoln.
96–98	*Colonia Nervia Glevensis* is founded at Gloucester.
99–100	Most of the Scottish forts are evacuated, and the legionary fortresses at Isca and elsewhere are rebuilt in stone. During the following ten years the fortresses at Deva and Eburacum are also rebuilt in stone.
c. 117	A revolt breaks out in north Britain.
120–122	*Legio IX Hispana* replaced by *VI Victrix*. Hadrian visits Britain and initiates the construction of "Hadrian's Wall" from the Solway to the Tyne; building commenced by Aulus Platorius Nepos.
139–142	Lollius Urbicus, Antoninus Pius' governor, advances north and commences building the Antonine Wall along the line of the old Forth-Clyde forts.
155–158	Julius Verus crushes a rebellion in the North, but temporarily evacuates the Antonine Wall. During the following six years Calpurnius Agricola rebuilds the fortresses.
180	Ulpius Marcellus suppresses a further revolt in the North, but again the Antonine Wall is broken.
196	Following intrigues in Rome, garrison troops are withdrawn by Clodius Albinus for use in his fight for emperorship, but are defeated by Severus.
197	The Maeatae overrun Hadrian's Wall, destroy the fortress of Eburacum and many other forts. Virius Lupus regains control and commences to rebuild the forts.
205–208	Alfenus Senecio commences to rebuild Hadrian's Wall. In 208 Severus, Geta and Caracalla arrive in Britain from Rome and make preparations to conduct campaigns in the North, and the following year achieve the surrender of the Caledonians.
211	Severus dies at Eburacum. Roman forces withdrawn to Hadrian's Wall. Southern Scotland administered as a Roman protectorate. In the following year Caracalla divides Britain into two provinces and extends Roman citizenship to all free provincials.
259–c. 274	Britain forms part of the Gallic Empire under Postumus and his successors.
287	The commander of the British fleet, Carausius, usurps the Empire of Britain and northern Gaul. In 293 Constantius, as Caesar, recaptures the continental territories for Rome. In the following year Carausius is murdered in Britain by Allectus, who succeeds him.
296	Constantius lands in Britain, and defeats and kills Allectus, restoring Britain to Rome. Against constant inroads by the northern barbarians, the fortresses at Deva and Eburacum are rebuilt. Britain is again reorganised by further subdivision into four provinces, while the military administration is separated from the civil government.
306	After campaigning in Scotland, Emperor Constantius dies at Eburacum.
313–314	Following the grant of toleration by the Edict of Milan for the Christian Church, three bishops from Britain attend the Council of Arles.
343–360	Period of attempted pacification of the Picts and Scots. Lupicinus is sent north to repel raids in 360. By 364 raids on Britain were being carried out by Picts, Scots, Attacotti and Saxons.
367	Substantial invasion by Picts, Scots and Attacotti, together with Saxon pirates; Franks make a simultaneous attack on Gaul. The Count of the Saxon Shore, Nectaridus, is killed, and the Duke of Britain, Fullofaudes, is defeated.
369	Valentinian I sends Count Theodosius to clear Britain of the invading tribes and to restore Hadrian's Wall. Theodosius restores

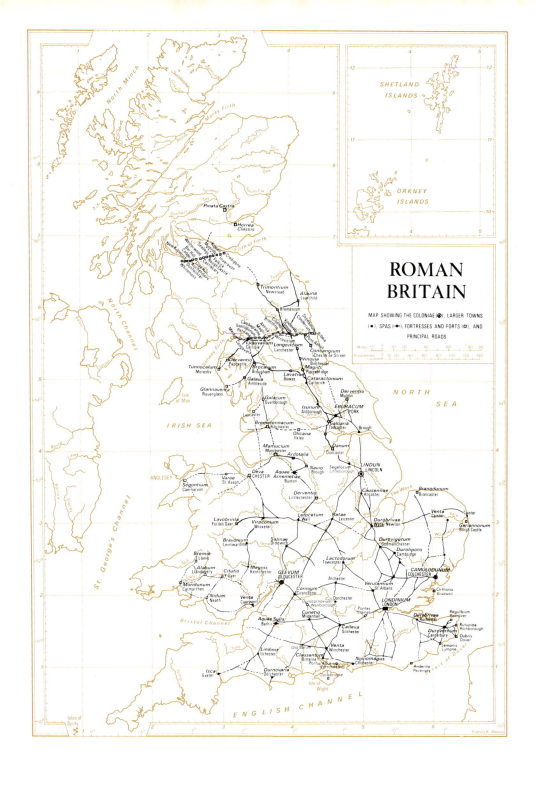

ROMAN BRITAIN

MAP SHOWING THE COLONIAE (◉), LARGER TOWNS (●), SPAS (★), FORTRESSES AND FORTS (□), AND PRINCIPAL ROADS

Francis K. Moxon

the administration in Britain, and builds signal stations on the east coast.

383–388   Period of revolt by Magnus Maximus, a military commander in Britain, who conquers Gaul and Spain from Gratian. Hadrian's Wall is overcome by invading tribes, and is never rebuilt again. In 388 Maximus is defeated by Count Theodosius.

406–410   Britain is stripped of Roman forces by the usurper, Constantine III, for his reconquest of Spain and Gaul; the country is left at the mercy of the Picts, and Honorius warns the British *civitates* to look to their own defences.

446   The British *civitates* make a final appeal to the Romans for their protection against marauding tribes.

449   Landing of Hengist and Horsa. Jutes, Saxons and Angles land in Britain, 449–450. Hengist and Horsa establish a Jutish kingdom in Kent.

c. 460–480   Ambrosius Aurelianus, a Romano-British leader, confines the Anglo-Saxon settlements to the south and east by constant warfare.

c. 490   Major westward advance by Saxons decisively defeated at Mount Badon (Badbury?) by British army under Arthur, supreme Romano-British military leader. Anglo-Saxon expansion checked for half a century.

c. 511   Arthur killed in battle at Camlann during factional warfare.

552   The West Saxons storm the British stronghold at Old Sarum, Wiltshire.

577   After a further victory at Deorham, the West Saxons isolate the British in Wales from those in Cornwall.

591   The West Saxon king, Caewlin, is defeated at Wansborough, and progress by the West Saxons is halted for two centuries.

591   Augustine, a Roman monk, introduces orthodox Christianity into Kent.

616   Aethelfrith of Northumbria isolates the British in Wales from those in the North at the Battle of Chester.

617   Edwine is acknowledged king of Northumbria.

627   Edwine is converted and becomes a champion of Christianity.

633   Penda of Mercia, champion of paganism, defeats Edwine at Hatfield (Heathfield).

635   Oswald, Edwine's successor, crushes the British at Heavensfield.

642–652   Oswald is defeated and killed at Maserfield; Oswy succeeds him and reunites Northumbria.

655   Oswy defeats and kills Penda at Winwaed; Christianity is accepted by Mercia.

664   Synod of Whitby. Conformity with Rome is declared by Oswy. Theodore becomes Primate and reorganises the Church.

670   Death of Oswy.

757–796   Offa, the great king and lawgiver, rules Mercia.

787   First appearance of the Danes in a raid at Weymouth.

802–839   Egbert rules as king of Wessex.

815   Conquest of the British in the South-West is completed by the West Saxons under Egbert.

826   Kent, Sussex, Essex and East Anglia submit to Egbert.

828   Mercia is overrun by the West Saxons under Egbert.

835   Revolt by Cornishmen against the West Saxons is crushed at Hengistdun by Egbert who is then acknowledged as "King of the English".

851   Organised invasion attempt by 350 Danish ships. London and Canterbury sacked. Defeated at Aclea (Ockley, Surrey) by Aethelwulf.

871   The Danes are routed at Ashdown by Aethelred and his brother, Alfred.

877   The Danes, under Guthrum, are driven from Exeter by Alfred.

878   The Danes are completely routed at Ethandun by Alfred. Guthrum accepts Christianity by the Peace of Wedmore; the Danes are confined to the Danelaw.

884   Renewal of the Danish invasion in the South-East. The Danes are driven from London and Rochester.

893–894   Further Danish invasion of Kent and Essex.

895   Danes defeated on the River Lea by Alfred.

899   Death of Alfred, who is succeeded two years later by his son, Edward the Elder (the "Unconquered"); Edward reigns until 925.

919   Aethelflaed, "Lady of the Mercians" and sister of Edward, captures the boroughs of Derby, Leicester and York from the Danes.

924   Edward is acknowledged "King of All Britain", although the Danish kingdom of York was not finally eliminated until 954.

925–940   Athelstan, son of Edward the Elder, rules.

937   League of Scots, British and Danes is defeated by Athelstan at Brunanburgh.

940–946   Athelstan is succeeded by his brother Edmund who conquers Strathclyde and gives it in fief to Malcolm I of Scotland.

946   Edmund is murdered, and is succeeded by Eadred, last grandchild of Alfred, elected by English, Welsh and Danes.

| 946–955 | Reign of Eadred. Dunstan, Abbot of Glastonbury, is chief adviser. | | Eadred. |
| 947 | Northmen, led by Archbishop Wulfstan of York, rise in revolt but are suppressed by | 955 | Death of Eadred with title of "Caesar of the Whole of Britain". |

SUMMARY OF BRITISH RULERS AFTER THE END OF THE ROMAN OCCUPATION

Setting aside tradition and legend, an accurate chronology is now regarded as to some extent speculative for the period of the nine kingdoms which flourished (sic) between A.D. 410 and 1066, and exact dates of reigns are seldom positively recorded, much dependence being laid on surviving charter grants of land, often confirmed by the contemporary rulers, underkings, ealdormen and churchmen.

1. THE KINGS OF KENT (c. 455 until conquered by the West Saxons in 825)

c. 600–c. 616	King Aethelberht I	c. 730–	King Aethelberht II
c. 616–	King Eadbald	–c. 761	King Eadberht
–c. 680	King Hlothhere	762–	King Sigered
c. 680–c. 689	King Eadric	765– 779	King Egbert
c. 690	King Swaefheard (Suabhardus)	c. 783–	King Ealhmund
690–c. 693	King Oswine	c. 805–	King Cuthred
c. 693–	King Wihtred		

2. THE KINGS OF SUSSEX (The South Saxons; A.D. 477 until absorbed by Wessex, c. 786)

fl. 688	King Nothhelm	c. 762–	King Osmund
fl. 714–725	King Nunna	fl. 770	King Ealdwulf
c. 733–	King Aethelberht of Kent		

3. THE KINGS OF WESSEX (The West Saxons; A.D. 519–954 on assumption of authority over All England.)

fl. 519	Kings Cerdic and Cynric	c. 758–c. 760	King Cynewulf
fl. 591	King Ceawlin	died 762	King Aethelberht of Kent
c. 666–c. 675	King Cenwalh	c. 785–	King Beorhtric
c. 680–	King Baldred	802– 839	King Egbert
c. 682	King Centwine	839–	King Aethelwulf
c. 688–c. 720	King Ine	fl. 855	King Aethelbald
c. 725–c. 740	King Aethelheard	c. 860–c. 870	King Aethelred
c. 741– 745	King Cuthred of the Gewisse	871– 899	King Alfred
745–c. 755	King Cuthred of Wessex	[899– 925	King Edward the Elder]

4. THE KINGS OF BERNICIA (A.D. 547–670, when annexed by Northumbria)

fl. 547	King Ida	c. 642– 670	King Oswy

5. THE KINGS OF NORTHUMBRIA (A.D. 588–876, when defeated by the Danish Kingdom of York)

– 617	King Aethelfrith	c. 652– 670	King Oswy of Bernicia
617– 633	King Edwine	fl. 685	King Ecgfrith
633–c. 638	King Oswald	fl. 738	King Edbert

6. THE KINGS OF MERCIA (c. 580–880)

fl. 660– 655	Chief Ealdorman, Penda	828–c. 838	King Wiglaf
fl. 664– 666	King Wulfhere	c. 838–c. 852	King Berhtwulf
c. 671–c. 699	King Aethelred	c. 852–c. 869	King Burgred
c. 705–c. 709	King Cenred	c. 870–	King Ceolwulf (II?)
710–c. 714	King Ceolred	c. 880– 883	Aethelred (dux et patricia)
c. 715–c. 750	King Aethelbald	883– 884	Aethelred (ealdorman of Mercia)
757– 796	King Offa	c. 885–c. 895	Aethelred (procurator of Mercia)
796	King Ecgfrith	post 895	Aethelred and Aethelflaed (Lady of the Mercians), Rulers.
c. 797– 821	King Cenwulf		
c. 822–c. 828	King Ceolwulf (I?)		

7. THE KINGS OF DEIRA (A.D. 599–654, when annexed by Bernicia)

8. THE KINGS OF EAST ANGLIA (The East Angles; c. 600–870 when conquered by the Danes)

9. THE RULERS OF ESSEX (The East Saxons; c. 600–825 on submission to the West Saxons)

fl. 700	King Offa of Mercia, recte	c. 702	King Swaefred

Where the Roman and Norman invaders landed. The ruins of Pevensey Castle, Sussex

955–959	Reign of Eadwig, who creates a new ealdormanry of Mercia which declares for his brother, Edgar. Dunstan is forced to flee.
959–975	Edgar ("The Peaceful") reigns as sole king.
959	Recall of Dunstan, who is made Primate and reforms the Church.
975–979	Edward II ("The Martyr") reigns, but is murdered after a stormy reign.
979–1016	Aethelred II (Unraed or "The Unredig") reigns.
988	Death of Dunstan; he had brought Crown and Church into close harmony.
1001	The Danish land-tax, *Danegeld*, of £24,000 is paid.
1002	Aethelred orders a great massacre of the Danes on 13th November, St. Brice's Day; among the murdered is the sister of Swegn, King of Denmark.
1003–1013	Swegn (King Swegn Forkbeard of Denmark) ravages the country in revenge, and is acknowledged King in 1013. Aethelred escapes to Normandy.
1014	Swegn dies and Aethelred returns, but Cnut is proclaimed king by the Danes.
1016	Aethelred dies and is succeeded by Edmund Ironside, who is elected by the people. In support of their king, the Danes defeat the English at Assandun. Peace is declared at Olney, Buckinghamshire. Edmund Ironside dies or is murdered.
1016–1035	Cnut, aged 22, becomes King of All England, and adopts an English policy.
1025	Cnut makes a pilgrimage to Rome.

1031	King Malcolm II of Scotland swears allegiance to Cnut.
1035	Cnut dies and leaves the throne to Harthacnut (Hardicanute) by will.
1035–1040	Harthacnut rules in the South, and Harald "Harefoot" in the North.
1040	Harald dies and Harthacnut becomes the sole king.
1042–1066	Edward III ("The Confessor"), remaining son of Aethelred, succeeds to the throne after the death of Harthacnut. Godwine, opposed to the Norman influence, is outlawed and flees to Flanders.
1053	Godwine dies and his son, Harold, becomes Earl of Wessex.
1066	On Edward's death Harold Godwineson becomes king by popular acclaim. A Norwegian invasion in the north, engineered by his brother Tostig, is defeated at Stamford Bridge; Tostig and the famous King Harold Hardrada of Norway are killed. William the Bastard, Duke of Normandy, lands at Pevensey on 28th September and joins battle with Harold on Saturday 14th October. Harold is defeated and slain at Senlac (the Battle of Hastings).

THE REIGN OF WILLIAM THE CONQUEROR, 1066–1087

1067	William returns to Normandy. The English rise against the oppression of Bishop Odo of Bayeux, and FitzOsbern.
1068	William returns to crush the revolt in the

South-West, and forces Edgar and Morkere to submit in the North.

1069   Edgar again rises in the North. William crushes the revolt and lays waste to Yorkshire.

1070   Archbishop Stigand, Primate since 1052 and aloof from military matters, is deposed and succeeded by Lanfranc, who remodels the Church and founds the Spiritual Courts.

1070–1071   Hereward "the Wake" and Morkere, with an English army, make their last stand on the Isle of Ely, but are defeated after Morkere and the Ely monks turn traitor.

1074   Waltheof, Earl of Northamptonshire and Huntingdonshire (and the last great English noble), conspires with other nobles against William, but is arrested and executed in 1076.

1083   A *Danegeld* of 72 pennies on each hide of land is levied; to assist the collection of this a general survey of the country is ordered, and the result of this is the compilation of the Domesday Book (1085–1086).

1087   War breaks out with France. William is fatally injured when his horse stumbles during the destruction of Mantes. The feudal system had been regularised in England by the Salisbury Decree (1086) which declared every freeman as the king's, as well as his immediate lord's "man".

THE REIGN OF WILLIAM II, 1087–1100

1087   William II, "Rufus", elected king by the Great Council with the assistance of Lanfranc.

1089   Lanfranc dies, and Ralf Flambard, Bishop of Durham, comes to power.

1091   The Treaty of Caen is concluded by William and Robert, Duke of Normandy, by which, on the death of one, the survivor succeeds to the dominion of both.

1093   Malcolm III of Scotland, after several years of raiding the North of England, is defeated and killed. Archbishop Anselm becomes Primate after four years' vacancy since the death of Lanfranc.

1096   Normandy is pledged to William for 10,000 marks by Robert who then sets out on the First Crusade to the Holy Land. William invades Wales and builds a line of forts to restrain the Welsh. He then takes possession of all Normandy.

1097   Anselm receives the pallium in Rome.

1100   2nd August. William is killed by an unknown bowman while hunting in the New Forest.

THE REIGN OF HENRY I, 1100–1135

1100   Henry ("The Lion of Justice"), younger brother of William Rufus, secures his election as king by the nobles at Winchester, and gains the goodwill of the English by his Great Charter, and by marrying Edith, an English princess. Flambard is imprisoned. Robert and the Barons return and claim England (by the terms of the Treaty of Caen), but are resisted by Henry who is supported by the English and the Church.

1104   Henry invades Normandy and in 1106 defeats Robert at Tenchebrai. Normandy is acquired for the second time, and Henry imprisons Robert for the remaining 28 years of his life.

1109   Anselm dies, and the See of Canterbury remains vacant for five years.

1111–1121   While Scotland remains peaceful throughout the reign, Henry continues to make progress in his conquest of Wales.

1113   Henry compels King Louis ("The Fat") of France, by the Peace of Gisors, to cede him the overlordship of Brittany and Maine.

1119   King Louis of France, supporting a revolt against Henry, is defeated by him at Noyon, or Brenneville. Queen Edith dies.

1120   Henry's only legitimate son and heir, William, is drowned during a shipwreck in the English Channel.

1127   The wars in France come to an end.

1128   After his son's death, in the absence of a male heir, Henry constrains the Great Council to swear allegiance to his daughter, Empress Matilda, widow of Emperor Henry V of Germany, as his heir. Matilda then marries Geoffrey Plantagenet of Anjou.

1135   Henry dies of a fever contracted while hunting in Normandy, on 1st December. His body is brought to England and buried at Reading.

THE REIGN OF STEPHEN, 1135–1154

1135   Despite the oath to Matilda, Stephen (grandson of William I) is elected king by the Great Council and crowned on 22nd December. David of Scotland remains faithful to his oath.

1137   David invades England on behalf of Matilda, and secures peace by the cession of Cumberland to Scotland. Dissatisfied, he renews his invasion the following year but is defeated by Archbishop Thurstan of York at the Battle of the Standard.

1139   Matilda, with Robert of Gloucester (surviving illegitimate son of Henry I), lands in

England having conquered Normandy. Civil war, lasting eight years, breaks out.

1141 Stephen, having been deserted by his mercenaries, is defeated and taken prisoner (2nd February) at the great Battle of Lincoln.

1147 Matilda returns to Normandy after having lost the support of her followers, and in 1148 Earl Robert dies.

1152 Henry, Matilda's son by her second marriage, is knighted by David of Scotland at the age of nineteen. In the same year he marries Eleanor, the divorced wife of Louis VII of France, thereby adding Aquitaine to Brittany, of which he is overlord.

1153 Peace is negotiated by Stephen at Wallingford on 6th November. Henry is adopted as heir to the throne. Stephen dies of a heart attack at Dover on 25th October 1154.

THE DOWNFALL OF FEUDALISM

THE REIGN OF HENRY II, 1154–1189

1154 19th December, Henry II is crowned and appoints Thomas of London his chancellor. Nicholas Breakspear, as Adrian IV, becomes the only English pope.

1155 Adrian IV commissions Henry to reduce Ireland.

1158–1161 Henry wages war against France, seizes Nantes and masters Brittany, Toulouse and the Vexin. He introduces a scutage of forty shillings on knights' fees in lieu of personal service. Louis is forced to sue for peace.

1162 Becket becomes Primate and resigns the chancellorship; he upholds the authority of the Church. Dispute of the "benefit of clergy".

1164 The Constitutions of Clarendon are made law, and Becket is forced by Henry to uphold them. Becket escapes from England and the Pope condemns the Constitutions.

1166 Becket is made papal legate for England. The grand jury system is extended by the Assize of Clarendon to include criminal cases.

1170 Henry summarily dismisses the Sheriffs and questions their conduct. Prince Henry is crowned by the Archbishop of York. Becket is allowed to return but is murdered on 29th December by four of Henry's court at the altar of Canterbury cathedral.

1171 Henry lands at Waterford in Ireland with 4,000 men. Within three weeks all the bishops acknowledge obedience to Rome, and most of the native kings pay him homage.

1173 The Barons of England, Brittany, Normandy and Aquitaine rise in revolt, but Henry, with the support of the native English, puts down the rising. A renewal of the trouble occurs the following year, and William the Lion of Scotland is taken prisoner. Again Henry quickly crushes the revolt and a general peace is signed at Falaise.

1178 A court of appeal is established at Westminster with the appointment of five judges; this constituted the origin of the Courts of King's Bench and Common Pleas. A period of relative peace ensues.

1188 Following news of the fall of Jerusalem to the Saracens, Henry imposes the Saladin tithe of one-tenth of all property.

1189 Philip Augustus of France, in alliance with Richard of Aquitaine, Henry's son, brings about the downfall of Henry, who escapes to Anjou but contracts a fatal fever and dies on 6th July, aged 56, at the Castle of Chinon, near Tours. He is buried at Fontévraud.

THE DOMINIONS OF HENRY II

ENGLAND Inherited by the terms of the Peace of Wallingford in 1153 through his mother as the daughter of Henry I.

NORMANDY AND BRITTANY Inherited from his mother.

ANJOU, MAINE AND TOURAINE Inherited from his father, Geoffrey of Anjou, on his death in 1151.

AQUITAINE Secured by his marriage with Eleanor, Duchesse of Aquitaine.

TOULOUSE Secured by conquest.

ENGLISH POSSESSIONS IN FRANCE ~1188~

NORMANDY
BRITTANY MAINE
ANJOU
TOURAINE
AQUITAINE
TOULOUSE

THE REIGN OF RICHARD I, 1189–1199

1189   The Coronation of Richard "Lion-Heart" (*Coeur de Lion*) is the occasion of a massacre of Jews. He sets out for the Holy Land and the Third Crusade, appointing Hugh of Durham and the Chancellor William of Longchamp as his justiciars. Of his ten-year reign only ten months are spent in England.

1191   Richard captures Cyprus, and marries Berengaria of Navarre. Philip of France returns home and plots with John, youngest son of Henry II, against Richard. John drives Longchamp from the country.

1192   Richard is captured during his return home near Vienna by Leopold of Austria, and the following year is ransomed for £100,000.

1194   Richard returns to England, but retires to Normandy leaving Hubert Walter in control. The Grand Jury system is greatly extended by Hubert.

1195   The modern Justices of the Peace take their origin from an edict that everyone over fifteen years should swear before a knight of the shire that he would aid in keeping the king's peace.

1198   The bishops and barons refuse to furnish knights for foreign service. Permanent landtax, called Carucage, imposed.

1199   During a minor action against Philip in France (at the Castle of Châlus in the Limousine) Richard is mortally wounded by an arrow and dies on 6th April, aged 41.

THE REIGN OF JOHN, 1199–1216

1199   John ("Lackland") becomes king by election, not by inheritance. Arthur, son of John's elder brother Geoffrey, and a minor, is acknowledged in Anjou, Main and Touraine, prompting Philip to attack John in Normandy.

1201   The English tenants-in-chief refuse to support John in Normandy.

1203   Arthur falls into John's hands and is never seen alive again. John is sentenced to death as a murderer in Paris (*in absentia*).

1204   John loses Normandy, retaining only Aquitaine overseas.

1208   England is laid under an interdict by the Pope following John's refusal to accept Stephen Langton as Primate. John's excommunication follows in 1209.

1213   John is reconciled with the Pope. The Barons summon the reeve and four representatives of every town to St. Albans.

1214   John is defeated by Philip at Bouvines. The Barons meet at Bury St. Edmunds to formulate their demands.

1215   *Magna Carta* is signed by John at Runnymede, a meadow between Staines and Windsor, on 15th June. It is annulled by the Pope and civil war breaks out. John ravages Yorkshire.

1216   The Barons offer the crown to Louis, son of Philip of France, and Louis sails up the Thames. John gains ascendancy and support, but dies of dysentery at Newark Castle on 19th October after naming his son Henry, aged 10, his heir.

THE REIGN OF HENRY III, 1216–1272

1216   Henry III, son of John, is crowned king on 28th October. Louis is defeated at Lincoln (the "Fair of Lincoln") on 19th May 1217 and is allowed to leave England. William, Earl of Pembroke, is made regent and guardian of the king.

1217   The Great Charter is issued in its final form in November.

1219   Pembroke dies and Hubert de Burgh assumes control of the administration in opposition to the foreign influences of Peter des Roches.

1226   The Great Council decrees that English law does not sanction payment of extortionate Papal demands.

1232   Peter des Roches influences Henry to dismiss Hubert de Burgh, who is imprisoned in Devizes Castle, but who escapes the following year to join the Barons rising in revolt against Peter and the king. Peter secures the murder of Hubert but loses favour and is dismissed. Peace is restored in 1234.

1238   Simon de Montfort becomes Earl of Leicester and marries Eleanor, Henry's sister.

1242   An English expedition to Poitu, undertaken to recover the empire of Henry II, is defeated at Taillebourg. Through want of leadership and under severe extortions by Rome, the English people become discontented, resulting in a council of Barons, which in 1244 demands a responsible ministry and promises the provision of a treasury subject to its use under their supervision.

1254   The Great Council of Westminster is attended by four knights of each Shire elected by the county court.

1258   The "Mad Parliament" meets at Oxford on 11th June. Under the Provisions of Oxford the influence of the executive passes from

1264	the King to the Barons.
	War breaks out following Louis' annullment of the baronial reforms, and at the Battle of Lewes on 14th May the Barons under Simon defeat the royal forces. The Mise of Lewes binds the King to keep the Charter and to live moderately. Simon is made protector.
1265	Simon summons Parliament with representatives of cities and boroughs, as well as Shires. The royal forces join battle under Prince Edward, defeating Simon's forces at Kenilworth on 1st August, and at Evesham four days later. Simon de Montfort is killed.
1266	Simon's forces surrender after six months' siege at Kenilworth, and the Dictum de Kenilworth sets the pattern for the Statute of Marlborough (of November 1267) which grants all the principal demands of the "Mad Parliament"; thereby *Magna Carta* becomes recognised as the law of the land, and the Crown retains executive power. Edward sets sail with a number of Barons for the Holy Land where he hears of his father's death on 16th November 1272 (aged 65).

THE REIGN OF EDWARD I, 1272–1307

1274	After a leisurely return from the Holy Land, Edward I is crowned in August. At his coronation Alexander III of Scotland, his brother-in-law, and John of Brittany do homage.
1275	In return for the issue of the First Statute of Westminster Edward receives from Parliament a permanent grant of the customs of England's staple products – wool, leather and skins.
1277	Llewellyn, a reigning prince in Wales who had not attended Edward's coronation, ravages the border countryside, but is forced to submit to Edward by the end of the year.
1278	The Statute of Gloucester requires the nobles to declare by what right (*quo warranto* = by what warrant) they hold their land and titles.
1279	The Statute de Religiosis forbids the holding of land in *mortmain* (= deadhand) in the future.
1282	Llewellyn, and his brother David, again rise in revolt and capture Flint and Rhuddlan castles, but after laying waste the land as far as Chester they are defeated by Edward's forces and Llewellyn is killed. David is captured the following year, brought to Shrewsbury for trial by his peers

	and executed as a traitor. Edward finally subjugates Wales.
1284	25th April. Edward's wife, Eleanor of Castille, gives birth to a son at Caernarvon Castle, who in 1301 receives the title Prince of Wales – henceforth borne by the king's eldest son.
1285	The writ of *Circumspecte Agatis* limits the jurisdiction of the Church to spiritual matters only. The Second Statute of Westminster institutes the law of entail. Edward relinquishes all claim to Normandy.
1286	During an absence by Edward in France the Barons refuse to pay grants; the Earls of Gloucester and Hereford make war on each other, and the Welsh rise in revolt. Alexander III of Scotland dies leaving no male heir.
1289	Margaret (the "Maid of Norway"), granddaughter of Alexander III, dies, and the direct line of William the Lion becomes extinct. Robert Bruce of Annandale, John Baliol and John Hastings are claimants to the Scottish crown. Edward hurries home to restore peace.
1290	The Jews are banished by Edward and do not return for four centuries. The Third Statute of Westminster is decreed.
1291	Baliol, through the English feudal custom, is supported by Edward in his claim to the Scottish throne and is crowned at Scone; does homage for Scotland in 1292 (see Page 95 for the Scottish kings).
1293	Following continuous sea warfare between English sailors of the Cinque Ports and the French, a battle off St. Mahé between a fleet of English, Dutch, Gascon and Irish ships and those of France, Flanders and Genoa, results in the total destruction of the latter. Philip, in revenge, takes possession of Guienne.
1295	Guienne is recovered by the English and Edward suppresses a further revolt by the Welsh. But Philip recaptures Bordeaux and supports a rising by the Scots. Alliance between Philip and Baliol. The "Model Parliament" is summoned, representing barons, prelates, knights and burghers.
1296	27th April. Edward inflicts a crushing defeat on the Scots at Dunbar and forces the surrender of Edinburgh, Perth and Stirling. Baliol gives up the crown and is sent to the Tower. John Warenne, Earl of Surrey, is made governor of Scotland, and Edward carries off the Coronation Stone of Scone. He enters conflict with Pope Boniface VIII over the papal bull, *Clericis*

The ruins of Kidwelly Castle, Carmarthenshire, built by Edward I at the end of the 13th century

Laicos, which had forbidden payment of taxes upon Church property. Edward coerces the clergy and strips recalcitrants, which include the Primate.

1297 William Wallace leads the Scots in revolt and defeats the English under Warenne and Hugh Cressingham at Stirling on 11th September.

1298 Edward makes peace abroad and returns to force Wallace to battle at Falkirk on 22nd July. English archers first come to prominence and contribute to a massacre of 15,000. Wallace escapes to France.

1300 Edward confirms the Charters in Parliament by the *Articuli super Cartas*.

1301 The Barons reject paper claims at the Parliament of Lincoln.

1303 By the terms of the marriage of Prince Edward to Isabella of France in 1299 Guienne is restored by Philip. Wallace returns to Scotland, captures Stirling and destroys an English force at Roslyn. Edward marches north.

1304 Stirling falls to Edward, and in 1305 Wallace is betrayed, captured and brought for trial at Westminster Hall. He is executed, his head placed on London Bridge and quarters sent to Newcastle, Berwick, Perth and Aberdeen.

1306 The Scots rise under Robert Bruce, grandson of Bruce of Annandale, and drive the English over the border. Bruce is crowned at Scone on 25th March by the Bishops of Glasgow and St. Andrews. Pembroke de-feats Bruce at Methven on 26th June. Bruce escapes to Ireland.

1307 Bruce returns and drives Lord Clifford out of Carrick Castle. Edward marches north but dies of dysentery on 6th July at Burgh-on-Sands, three miles short of the border.

THE REIGN OF EDWARD II, 1307–1327

1307 Edward II, elder son of Edward I by his marriage to Eleanor of Castille, succeeds to the throne and recalls his foster brother, Piers Gaveston (previously banished by his father). Gaveston is made Earl of Cornwall.

1308 Gaveston offends the Barons who compel Edward to dismiss him.

1309 Edward recalls Gaveston, and the Barons refuse to attend Parliament, and in 1311 once again force banishment of the King's favourite. Edward again recalls him and takes him on a campaign against Scotland. Gaveston is captured by Pembroke at Scarborough Castle, is condemned by the Barons and executed near Warwick on 19th June 1312.

1314 Following a successful campaign by Robert Bruce in Scotland, Stirling is beseiged. Edward marches north with 100,000 men but is disastrously defeated on 23rd–24th June at Bannockburn. Stirling surrenders to Bruce and Scotland wins her independence, formally recognised in 1328.

1316 Bannockburn leaves Edward impotent before the Barons. Lancaster becomes President of the Council. The crops fail, disease

One of the great border castles, Alnwick Castle, Northumberland, was the home of the family from 1309, and was restored by the 1st and 4th Dukes of Northumberland in the 17th and 18th centuries

	and hunger sweep the country. Lancaster fails to check the ravages by the Scots.
1322	Edward moves against Lancaster who offends the Barons. Pembroke and the Earls of Norfolk and Kent join Edward who marches north and captures Lancaster at Boroughbridge; he is then executed. Edward forces Parliament to repeal the Ordinances, thereby recovering the executive power of the Crown.
1323	Edward undertakes another unsuccessful campaign against Scotland, thereby reviving the Barons' contempt. Roger Mortimer, previously imprisoned for his support of Lancaster, escapes from the Tower to France. Charles IV of France demands forfeiture of Gascony. Edward sends his wife Isabella, sister of Charles, to France to intercede on his behalf.
1326	Isabella conspires with Mortimer, is joined by Prince Edward (Edward II's son), and lands at Harwich on 24th September with a large force. This force is joined by large numbers of Barons, by the Primate and by other prelates. The Queen enters London and Edward tries in vain to escape to Ireland. The Earl of Winchester is brutally executed, and Edward surrenders.
1327	24th January. Parliament proclaims Prince Edward king, and his father is deposed, being imprisoned in various castles. He is murdered (traditionally by anal impalement with a red-hot iron) at Berkeley Castle on 21st September and buried at St. Peter's, Gloucester. Henry of Lancaster becomes nominal guardian of the King, and Mortimer is created Earl of March.

REIGN OF EDWARD III, 1327–1377

1328	25th January. Edward III marries Philippa of Hainault. The Scottish campaign is ended by the Peace of Norham on 1st March. Independence of Scotland under King Robert Bruce is acknowledged. Isabella's daughter Joanna marries David Bruce, Robert's son.
1329	7th June. Robert Bruce dies.
1330	Edward determines to rid himself of Mortimer's influence, and during the Parliament of Nottingham seizes him at the castle. He is brought to trial; no defence is allowed and he is hung on the common gallows at Tyburn on 29th November. Isabella is permitted to retire to Rising.
1332	Edward Baliol, son of John Baliol, invades the Scottish coast of Fife but is driven south over the border. Edward comes to his aid, routs the Scots at Halidon Hill, near Berwick on 18th July 1333, and demands that Baliol be recognised as king by the Scottish parliament. In 1341 David Bruce returns and Baliol is again driven out. The following year Edward makes peace.
1338	The beginning of the Hundred Years War with France. The three causes of this long conflict were the continued French aid to Scotland, the danger of Gascony, and the protection of England's vital wool trade with Flanders. Parliament gives to Edward half the wool in the realm; the King exercises pre-emption and sells it to Flanders. He uses its protection as an excuse to land at Antwerp in July to support his claim to the French crown.

1339	Edward fails in his siege of Cambrai, but assumes the title King of France with the motto *Dieu et mon Droit*, and quarters the French lilies with the English lions in the English Royal Arms.
1340	Edward again sails to Flanders, now assisted by the great Flemish towns. Philip prepares a large fleet at Sluys but is defeated by Edward on 24th June with the loss of almost all his ships and 28,000 men. For thirty years England commands the seas. Parliament sets down the responsibility of ministers.
1341	War with France is resumed over a disputed succession in Brittany. Hostilities continue until 1343.
1345	Edward loses Flemish support but sends Lancaster with an expedition to take Gascony. The following year Philip moves a large army against him and Edward prepares to go to his aid. Changing his plans at the last moment, Edward lands 40,000 men on the undefended Normandy coast. Battle of Crécy, 26th August; complete ascendancy of English bowmen, and total defeat of French with huge losses. Blockade of Calais results.
1346	David Bruce, David II, is defeated by the Archbishop of York and the great Barons of the North at the Battle of Neville's Cross on 17th October. Bruce is taken prisoner and remains captive until 1359.
1347	Surrender of Calais, 4th August, provides port at which English exports can be sold.
1348–1350	The Black Death, bubonic plague, which had followed the western course of commerce from Asia, ravages the country and costs the lives of 800,000 in Britain.
1349	The Statute of Labourers obliges labourers to work at the rates of wages that existed in 1347.
1350	Edward acquires the title "King of the Seas" after his destruction of the Spanish fleet between Sluys and Sandwich in the Battle of "*L'Espagnols sur Mer*".
1351	Following a drain on England's resources, the Statute of Provisors is passed to forbid the collection of papal dues from the people.
1352	The Statute of Treasons defines the crimes of treason.
1353	The First Statute of Praemunire is passed to outlaw and punish all who sued in foreign courts for matters for which the King was answerable.
1355	The Black Prince (Edward, Prince of Wales) sails for Guienne and devastates France

	from Bordeaux to the Mediterranean, returning laden with spoil. Edward himself has to abandon his operations in France, hastens north to relieve Berwick from fresh inroads by the Scots, is crowned King of Scotland at Bamborough and, in February 1356, utterly devastates the Lothians ("Burnt Candlemas").
1356	The Black Prince, after a victorious campaign from the Dordogne to the Loire, falls back towards Bordeaux with 8,000 men, but turns to fight King John with 50,000 at Poitiers on Monday 19th September. The Prince of Wales wins a great victory and captures the French king and his son Philip. France is humiliated, demoralised and impoverished. Civil war in Paris is followed by the "*Jacquerie*", an appalling revolt by famished peasants.
1360	Treaty of Brétigny is signed with France to establish peace, and Aquitaine, Montreuilt, Ponthieu, Calais and Guisnes are ceded to Edward who in turn gives up his claim to the French crown. The Black Prince takes over the government of Aquitaine.
1362	It is ordered that the English language will henceforth be used for the proceedings in law courts. Edward consents to lay no taxes on wool without prior consent of Parliament and gives up the right of purveyance.
1365	Praemunire is repeated in stronger terms.
1367	In Spain the atrocities of Pedro the Cruel prompt Henry of Trastamare to drive him from the throne of Castille. Pedro had been in alliance with Edward III, so the Black Prince leads 10,000 men across the Pyrenees to defeat Henry's much larger army at Navarette on 3rd April. The Prince's army is swept by disease and retires to Bordeaux.
1369	Henry defeats Pedro in Spain, kills him and ascends the throne to found a new dynasty. Charles V of France renews the War by declaration in May. The Black Prince captures Limoges in 1370.
1372	An English fleet under the Earl of Pembroke is defeated at sea by the Spanish in June.
1373	The French overrun Brittany.
1375	27th June. A truce for one year is agreed at Bruges. Following the failure and wastage of an army under John of Ghent ("Gaunt"), the English lose all but Bayonne, Brest, Bordeaux, Calais and Cherbourg.
1376	The "Good Parliament", encouraged by the Black Prince, seeks to limit the influence of John of Ghent who opposed popular privileges. The Black Prince dies on 8th

June. The "Good Parliament" is dissolved and the authority of John is re-affirmed.

1377 John Wycliffe, a reforming politician and theologian, is summoned before the convocation of St. Paul's for heresy but is supported by John of Ghent. Edward III, aged 64, dies peacefully at Sheen on 21st June. Geoffrey Chaucer publishes *The Canterbury Tales*.

TABLE ILLUSTRATING EDWARD III's CLAIM TO THE FRENCH CROWN

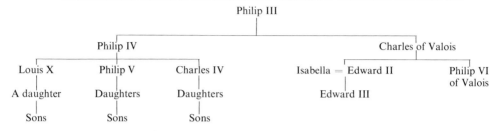

(*Salic law prevented females from inheriting the French crown. On the death of Charles IV, Philip VI succeeded as male heir, but Edward III claimed the throne on the ground that although females could not inherit they could transmit a claim to their descendants; his claim was therefore invalidated as the surviving grandsons of Louis X, Philip V and Charles IV had prior claim by transmission of claim through their daughters.*)

THE REIGN OF RICHARD II, 1377–1399

1377 Richard II, son of the Black Prince by his marriage to Joan of Kent, becomes king. Parliament grants finance under the direction of two treasurers, and insists that during the king's minority it shall have the right to appoint the Great Officers of State.

1380 To meet the vast expense of war, Parliament imposes an ungraduated poll-tax of one shilling on everyone over fifteen. An attempt to raise this was the signal for the Peasants' Revolt the following year.

1381 The people rise in Essex when in May Thomas the Baker of Fobbings drives out the judge and kills the jury called to assess the poll-tax. On 10th June the people of Kent under Wat the Tiler (*i.e.* bricklayer) take Canterbury and march on London. Wat is struck dead by the Lord Mayor, Walworth. The young king promises to meet the mob's demands and the people disperse. Before the end of the year, however, the nobles take revenge and 8,000 die in fight or on the gallows. The Bible is translated into English by Wycliffe, who dies in 1384; his followers, called Lollards, increase rapidly.

1382 Parliament guarantees loans to the Crown for the first time.

1385 Edmund and Thomas, the king's uncles, are created Dukes of York and Gloucester. John of Ghent fails to prosecute the English claim upon the crown of Castille.

1386 Thomas of Gloucester and Henry of Derby reform the baronial party, and imprison Suffolk, the king's Chancellor. Gloucester is appointed to head a Commission of Regency, but Richard's Council of Nottingham declares the Commission illegal.

1387 Gloucester, Warwick and Arundel march on London, and Richard submits. The Duke of Ireland raises an army in support of the king but is defeated by Henry of Derby at Radcot Bridge on the Thames.

1388 Arundel, Derby, Gloucester, Nottingham and Warwick (the "Appellants") accuse the king's advisers of treason, and they are impeached. Arundel wins a great sea battle over the combined fleets of the French, Flemish and Spanish. On 9th August the Battle of Otterburn is fought between Henry Percy (Hotspur) and Lord James Douglas; Hotspur is made prisoner in Scotland and Douglas is killed.

1389 May 3rd. Richard assumes the government; this is the third failure to divest the crown of authority to rule. Constitutional rule continues for almost six years.

1394 Anne of Bohemia, Richard's queen, dies childless, and the king's mood changes. The "Appellants" renew their quarrels with the king.

1396 Richard marries Isabella, the child daughter of the French king.

1398 The packed Parliament of Shrewsbury,

favouring the King's authority, repeals the Commission of Regency; the Earl of Arundel is comdemned and executed; Warwick, Norfolk and Henry of Derby are banished; Gloucester is secretly murdered.

1399   John of Ghent dies and Richard seizes his Lancastrian estates, then sails to Ireland where Roger, Earl of March, the recognised heir, has just been killed. Henry, now Duke of Lancaster, returns with considerable support; Richard is deserted and captured, taken to the Tower and forced to abdicate on 30th September.

THE REIGN OF HENRY IV, 1399–1413

1399   Henry IV becomes king by Parliamentary grant on 30th September. The provisions of the "Merciless Parliament" of 1388 are re-affirmed.

1400   Realising the weakness of Henry's claim to the throne, Richard's followers conspire, but the conspiracy is betrayed and Richard himself dies at Pontefract Castle, Yorkshire, aged 33, c. 14th February, a sufferer from neurasthenia.

1401   The Church forces Henry to pledge suppression of heresy, and the first persecuting statute, *De Heretico Comburendo*, is passed. The first English martyr, William Sawtré of King's Lynn, is burnt at Smithfield.

1402   Henry invades Wales three times but is forestalled by weather and poverty. Owain Glyndŵr defeats the English, capturing Sir Edmund Mortimer, uncle of Edmund, heir to the throne. The Percys, however, defeat the invading Scots at Hambledon Hill, near Wooler, on 4th September through the prowess of the English archers. Douglas is taken prisoner.

1403   Discontent among the Percys leads to revolt, and they join forces with Owain Glyndŵr, but are intercepted and defeated by Henry and the Prince of Wales at the Battle of Shrewsbury on 21st July; Hotspur is killed; Douglas Worcester and Northumberland captured. Worcester is beheaded, Northumberland pardoned.

1404   The "Unlearned Parliament" – so called owing to its exclusion of all lawyers – meets and expresses its desire to seize Church property.

1405   The Percys again revolt and Henry hurries north. Mowbray, son of the Duke of Norfolk, and Scrope, Archbishop of York, are executed without trial, in violation of Henry's own Ordinance of 1399, thereby

alienating the clergy. James, heir to the Scottish throne, is captured at sea.

1406   Public audit of Government accounts is demanded by Parliament, the principle thus being established that the Commons are the source of all public grants.

1408   Third and final revolt of the Percys under Northumberland, who is defeated and killed at Bramham Moor, near Tadcaster.

1410   The anti-clerical factions, being strong in the Commons, propose to confiscate the lands of the bishops and religious corporations.

1411–1413   The Prince of Wales assumes an increasing burden of government as Henry's health fails. From 12th June 1411 the King remains in Westminster Palace, and eventually dies after an epileptic fit on 20th March 1413 brought on by pustulated eczema and gout. He is buried in Canterbury Cathedral.

THE REIGN OF HENRY V, 1413–1422

1413   Having successfully filled successive appointments (*i.e.* Constable of Dover, Warden of the Cinque Ports, and Governor of Calais), Henry of Monmouth succeeds to the throne with substantial Parliamentary confidence, displayed by the grant of four years' wool revenue. His avowed aims are to win the French crown and to finally suppress heresy.

1414   The Lollards assemble on 4th January in St. Giles's Fields, thereby provoking their renewed persecution.

1415   Henry prepares a large army against France, but while assembling at Southampton he learns of the exposure of a conspiracy among his relatives in support of the Earl of March. The offenders are tried and Richard, Earl of Cambridge, Sir Thomas Grey of Heton, and Lord Scrope of Masham are executed. Henry renews Edward III's claim to the French throne, sails for France, captures Harfleur (then France's principal sea port), and wins a great victory against the French at the Battle of Agincourt on 25th October, the Feast of St. Crispin and St. Crispian.

1416   The French blockade Harfleur by land and sea; on 15th August a British fleet gains a resounding victory over the investing fleet.

1417   Henry conquers most of Normandy. At home the leader of the Lollards, Sir John Oldcastle, is executed for heresy.

1419   Henry completes his conquest of Normandy with the capture of Rouen in

January. After attempted negotiations with Isabella, Henry renews the war, and captures Pontoise.

1420   The Dauphin is driven south and on 21st May the Treaty of Troyes is concluded which acknowledges Charles VI as King during his lifetime, and Henry as heir; meanwhile Henry is Regent, and marries Catherine, Charles' daughter. He enters Paris on 1st December.

1421   In deference to home wishes Henry returns to England but is recalled to France after his brother Clarence is defeated and killed on 23rd March at Beaugè. Henry recovers all lost ground in ten weeks.

1422   Henry moves against the Dauphin who still holds central France, but is struck down by dysentry at Vincennes and dies on 31st August, aged 34.

THE REIGN OF HENRY VI, 1422–1461

1422   The Duke of Bedford becomes Regent in France, and Humphrey of Gloucester is Protector in England during the minority of Henry VI. The infant King succeeds at the age of eight months on 1st September with the title and style *Dei Gratia Rex Angliae et Franciae et Dominus Hiberniae.*

1423–1424   The Dauphin is decisively beaten by the English at the Battles of Crévant and Verneuil, despite a substantial contingent of Scots – who are killed almost to a man. The latter battle represented the peak of English success in France.

1428   As part of the English determination to drive Charles VII beyond the Loire, Orléans is besieged.

1429   Jeanne D'Arc raises the siege and Charles VII is crowned King in Orléans. The following year the "Maid of Orléans" attempts to relieve Compeigne but is captured by the English and burnt at the stake on 30th May 1431 in the marketplace of Rouen following a trial marked by cruelty and treachery.

1432   Bedford's Burgundian alliance, resulting from his marriage to the sister of the Duke of Burgundy, fails following his wife's death.

1435   Bedford dies in September. His successor as Regent of France is Richard, Duke of York, who recovers much of the lost territory.

1441   Richard checks Charles' ambition in Guienne, and in 1444 negotiates a two-year truce, which is later extended.

1445   Henry VI marries Margaret of Anjou in April, a peace expedient put forward by William de la Pole, Earl of Suffolk. The plan had been opposed by the Duke of Gloucester, leader of those who favoured continued war with France.

1447   Gloucester is arrested at the instigation of Suffolk and dies in prison within a few days. Suffolk is created a duke the following year.

1448   Charles breaks the truce and the French quickly occupy much of Normandy. The English army, in an attempt to relieve Caen, is heavily defeated at Formigny, and in April 1450 the English garrison at Cherbourg surrenders. Normandy is lost forever.

1449   Parliament, in the midst of disorders, mutinies, and a war between the Percys and the Nevilles in the North, meets and demands redress of grievances before supply.

1450   Suffolk is impeached, banished and murdered on 2nd May. Cade's rebellion and the march on London demonstrates the need for firm government. With the death of Suffolk the King's nearest relatives, Somerset (representing the house of Lancaster, after Henry VI) and Richard (direct heir to the throne through the dukedom of York) are the opposing claimants to power. Herein lie the seeds of the Wars of the Roses.

1451   Charles VII conquers Gascony and Guienne with scarcely a blow. Only Calais remains English. Two years later, despite efforts by Talbot, Earl of Shrewsbury, Gascony and Guienne are lost forever.

1453   Henry's son, Edward, Prince of Wales, is born. The King suffers mental illness and Richard becomes Protector.

1455   The Wars of the Roses begin. In May Richard, Salisbury and Warwick march to a council at Leicester with 3,000 men, but meet Somerset and the King at St. Albans, and defeat them in a street battle. Somerset, Northumberland and Stafford are killed.

1458   A formal reconciliation between Yorkists and Lancastrians is attempted in February, and peace lasts for a year.

1459   The country is restless and no parliaments are held. Margaret's hatred of the Yorkists prompts her to renew the War but she is defeated at Bloreheath by Salisbury on 23rd September. Henry with 30,000 men forces the dispersal of the Yorkists, who are attainted for treason.

1460   The King is defeated and taken prisoner at Northampton on 10th July by Edward, Salisbury and Warwick. Margaret escapes to Scotland and rallies the North. On 30th December a large force defeats the Yorkists in the Battle of Wakefield, and Richard of York is killed.

1461 Edward, son of Richard, defeats the Lancastrians under the King's half-brother, Jasper Tudor, Earl of Pembroke, at Mortimer's Cross on 2nd February. Margaret defeats Warwick at the second Battle of St. Albans on 17th February and regains possession of the King. Henry VI is deposed and Edward is elected and proclaimed King on 4th March.

THE REIGN OF EDWARD IV, 1461–1483

1461 Edward heavily defeats the Lancastrians at the Battle of Towton on 29th–30th March; more than 28,000 are killed. Henry and Margaret escape to Scotland. Parliament confirms the claim of Edward who is crowned on 28th June. An act of attainder is passed against the Lancastrian party. Only Wales stands in support of Henry.

1464 The Lancastrians are defeated by Montague on 25th April at Hedgeley Moor, and on 14th May at Hexham.

1465 Henry is captured and imprisoned in the Tower; Somerset is captured and executed. Montague is created Earl of Northumberland.

1469 The Lancastrians again revolt and defeat the royalists at Edgecote, near Banbury. Shortly afterwards Warwick captures Edward, but releases him in return for pardons.

1470 Sir Robert Welles raises Lincolnshire for Henry VI, but the rebels under Warwick are defeated by Edward at Erpingham in Rutland. Warwick escapes and with French aid invades England and restores Henry VI. Edward in turn escapes to Flanders.

1471 On 14th March Edward returns to England and defeats the army of Warwick and Montague at the Battle of Barnet on Easter Sunday, 14th April; Warwick is killed. On this day Margaret lands at Weymouth and marches north, but is defeated on 4th May by Edward at the Battle of Tewkesbury. Henry is again taken prisoner and is stabbed to death in the Tower on 21st May. Henry Tudor, Earl of Richmond, is now sole Lancastrian claimant.

1475 By levying huge taxes on the defeated Lancastrians, Edward raises a large army and sails for France in June. Louis XI makes peace for seven years at the Treaty of Pecquigny, paying Edward a substantial pension.

1477 Caxton sets up the first press in England,

his first book, *The Dictes of the Philosophers*, being printed in this year.

1480 Louis' intrigues with Scotland bring about war. Gloucester marches against Edinburgh, securing peace in 1482 with the restoration of Berwick to England.

1483 Edward dies suddenly from pneumonia on 9th April at Westminster, aged 40.

EDWARD V, 1483

1483 9th April–25th June. The young prince Edward, elder son of Edward IV, succeeds to the throne, but is placed in the Tower by Gloucester, with his brother Richard. Richard III, brother of Edward IV, is declared Protector. Declaring the illegitimacy of Edward IV's children, Buckingham (Henry Stafford) claims the throne for Richard III who, on 26th June, is informally elected King.

THE REIGN OF RICHARD III, 1483–1485

1483 The young princes are said to be murdered in the Tower.* Buckingham leads a revolt in Wales, expecting support from Henry Tudor, but is betrayed into Richard's hands and put to death.

1484 Parliament confirms Richard's claims to the throne.

1485 Henry Tudor, determined to marry Elizabeth, daughter of Edward IV – thereby ending dynastic rivalries – lands with a small army at Milford Haven on 7th August. Henry marches north with 5,000 men, meets and defeats Richard with twice as many at Bosworth on 22nd August. Richard is killed, his body being taken and buried without honour at Grey Friars in Leicester.

THE TUDORS

THE REIGN OF HENRY VII, 1485–1509

1485 Henry claims the throne, and Parliament confers the crown upon him and his rightful heirs. The Commons grant the new King tonnage and poundage, together with customs on leather for life. The Yorkists favour Edward, Earl of Warwick, as heir to the throne, but he is imprisoned in the Tower. The "Yeomen of the Guard" are formed for the protection of the King.

---

* Despite constant doubts expressed down the years as to the truth of the reports of the murders, a body of the stature and dentition of a twelve-year-old boy was discovered at the Tower on 6th July 1933.

1486	Henry marries Elizabeth in January, thereby uniting the houses of York and Lancaster so long as no heir is born. Thus the birth of Arthur in September is the signal for fresh Yorkist risings.
1487	Lambert Simnel, impersonating the Earl of Warwick, lands from Ireland with 2,000 men and is joined by other Yorkists. Henry utterly routs them at the Battle of Stoke (near Newark) on 16th June. To conciliate the Yorkists, Elizabeth is publicly crowned. Henry obtains the establishment of the Court of Star Chamber, which comes to cover almost every crime and to represent the epitome of tyranny and extortion.
1488	Parliament persuades Henry to give active assistance to Duchesse Anne of Britanny against Charles VIII who seeks to incorporate the province with his kingdom. Grants are made but Henry does practically nothing. The following year Charles gains his objective by a forced marriage with Anne.
1491	Perkin Warbeck, affecting to be Richard, Duke of York, one of the supposedly murdered sons of Edward IV, gains Yorkist support in Ireland and France, joining Margaret, Dowager Duchess of Burgundy, sister of Edward IV. Caxton dies.
1492	Henry invades France with an army of more than 25,000 men, the first regularly-paid and fully disciplined English army. Peace is made with Charles by the Treaty of Etaples. [Columbus discovers the West Indies.]
1494	After the relative successes of the two pretenders in Ireland (Lambert Simnel and Perkins Warbeck), Sir Edward Poynings is appointed Deputy in place of Kildare. Poynings causes an act to be passed that no law can be submitted to the Irish parliament until it has been sanctioned by the King. Poynings' law remained in force for three centuries.
1495	Parliament passes a law by which the King *de facto* is also King *de jure*.
1496	Warbeck makes a vain attempt to besiege Waterford in Ireland, then crosses to Scotland where he is welcomed by James IV, who gives his relative, Catherine Gordon, in marriage. Freedom of trade between England and Flanders is established by the *Intercursus Magnus*.
1497	Henry levies new taxes and 16,000 Cornish miners under Lord Audley and Thomas Flammock march in revolt to Kent. They are met at Blackheath by royal forces and

dispersed with the loss of 2,000 dead; the leaders are executed. James and Warbeck ravage the North, and Warbeck sails to Cornwall, raises 6,000 men and attempts to take Exeter. On the eve of the Battle of Taunton with Henry, Warbeck abandons his cause and surrenders himself (and is executed after two years in the Tower on 16th November 1499). Cabot, under Henry's protection and sailing from Bristol, reaches America.

1499–1504	Henry rules without a parliament, and the Tudor despotism emerges.
1501	Henry VII's son, Prince Arthur, is married to Catherine of Aragon, thereby uniting England with Spain.
1502	Arthur dies and his widow is contracted to his younger brother, Henry (later Henry VIII).
1503	James IV of Scotland is married to Margaret, Henry's eldest daughter, and the English King continues to amass wealth by flagrant extortion, the chief agents for which are two Barons of the Exchequer, Sir Richard Empson and Edmund Dudley. By the time of his death in 1509 he had accumulated the sum of £1·8 million. Henry VII dies on 21st April 1509, aged 52, at Richmond, from rheumatoid arthritis and gout, and is buried at Westminster.

THE REIGN OF HENRY VIII, 1509–1547

1509	Henry VIII, younger son of Henry VII, ascends the throne at the age of eighteen on 22nd April. He arrests Empson and Dudley, who are attainted and executed the following year for conspiracy. Henry marries Catherine of Aragon in June.
1511	Henry joins the Holy League against Louis XII.
1513	Henry lands with 25,000 men at Calais and defeats the French on 22nd August at Guinnegatte (the Battle of the Spurs), capturing Tournai. James IV, in alliance with France, invades England from the North with 100,000 men, but is met by the Earl of Surrey and defeated at the Battle of Flodden with the loss of 10,000 killed. James IV is slain, as are almost all the Scottish peerage. Surrey is made Duke of Norfolk.
1514	Peace is made with France after Maximilian and Ferdinand refuse to continue the War, and Louis XII marries Mary, the sixteen-year-old sister of Henry. The following January Louis dies and Mary marries Brandon, Duke of Suffolk.

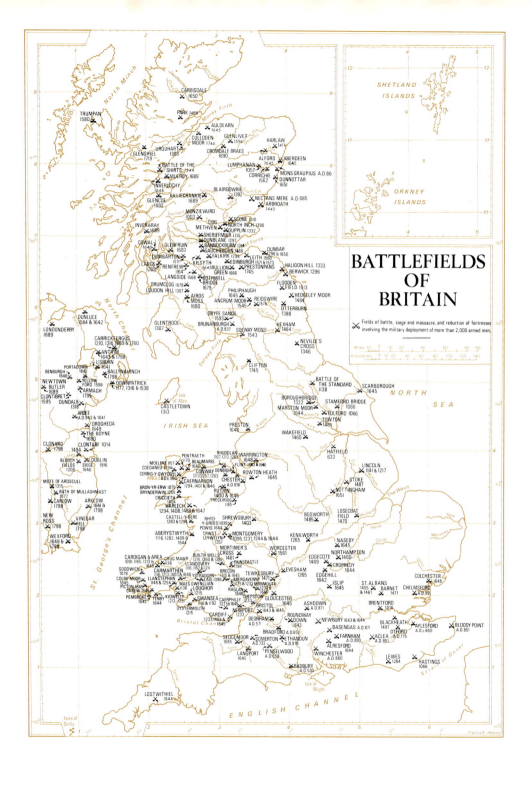

1515	Wolsey, Archbishop of York and an advocate of peaceful preservation of the balance of power, is made a cardinal and becomes Henry's Chancellor.
1517	Luther makes his great "protest" against the corruptions and extortions of Rome.
1519	By the deaths of Ferdinand and Emperor Maximilian, Charles becomes master of Austria, Germany, Spain and her colonies. He becomes Emperor and seeks Henry's alliance at a meeting near Calais – the Field of the Cloth of Gold.
1521	Henry tires of his wife Catherine and secures a divorce, thereby engendering difficulties with Rome. He seeks to marry Anne Boleyn, granddaughter of Thomas Howard, Duke of Norfolk. The Duke of Buckingham, heir to the throne after Mary, is executed. Henry, as a result of his stand against Luther's protestation, is named "Defender of the Faith" by the Pope.
1529	Wolsey and Carpeggio, in their Legatine Court, try the case of Catherine, whose marriage with Henry had been proclaimed by Wolsey as against Levitical law. Wolsey falls from favour.
1530	In exasperation at delay, Henry consults the European universities on the legality of his marriage to Catherine. Wolsey is restored to his archbishopric, but is arrested and dies in November.
1531	On the threats of writs of praemunire against the whole clergy, convocation acknowledges Henry as the supreme head of the Church in England, and abolishes appeals and payments of Annates to Rome.
1533	Thomas Cranmer, an advocate of divorce, is made Primate. Henry secretly marries Anne Boleyn, a marriage declared valid by Cranmer's court at Dunstable. The Pope reverses Cranmer's decision thereby aggravating the rift between Rome and the "protestants".
1534	The Act of Supremacy declares the King to be "the only supreme head on earth of the Church of England". Appointment of bishops is transferred from Rome to a *congé d'élire* from the King. In the absence of a male heir, an Act of Succession declares Elizabeth, Henry's daughter by Anne Boleyn, heir to the throne.
1535	Thomas Cromwell, previously an agent of Wolsey, becomes Vicar General in ecclesiastical matters. At this time the separation from Rome is evidenced by a change in allegiance rather than doctrine. The monks of Charterhouse, with their prior, Haughton, suffer death as traitors for refusing the oath of succession – the work of Cromwell.
1536	Dissolution of the smaller monasteries. Henry tires of Anne, who had born him no son; she is tried before a packed court on charges of adultery, incest and conspiracy, and is beheaded on 19th May. Cranmer declares Henry's marriage to Anne void and on the following day Henry marries Jane Seymour. Wales is legally joined to England.
1537	Jane Seymour gives birth to a son (later Edward VI) but dies a few days later. Cromwell causes the suppression of the larger monasteries, and these are followed by the friaries in the next year.
1539	Henry makes parliament impose the "Six Articles" – the complete negation of Protestanism. Parliament gives the force of law to the King's proclamations.
1540	Cromwell urges Henry to marry Anne, sister of the powerful Protestant Duke of Cleves; this would have united France and the German princes against Charles V. The marriage takes place on 6th January. Cromwell is arrested and executed for conspiracy on 28th July. Henry divorces Anne by Act of Parliament and marries Catherine Howard, cousin of Anne Boleyn, in August.
1542	12th February, Catherine Howard is beheaded on (probably false) charges of adultery.
1543	12th July, Henry marries Catherine Parr, who survives him.
1544	Henry lands in France with 40,000 men and captures Boulogne in a campaign undertaken with Charles V to divide France.
1547	Peace is made with France. The Earl of Surrey is executed, and the execution of his father, the Duke of Norfolk, is only avoided by the death of Henry on 28th January (at the Palace of Westminster, aged 55, from chronic sinusitis and periostitis of the leg).

THE REIGN OF EDWARD VI, 1547–1553

1547	Edward VI, Henry VIII's only son, succeeds to the throne, not by election but by an act of parliament passed before his accession. The "Six Articles" are repealed by Parliament, thereby giving the force of law to royal proclamations. Somerset invades Scotland with 20,000 men (many of whom are well-armed mercenaries) and routs the Scots at Pinkiecleugh on 10th September.
1549	Cranmer publishes the Catechism and *Book*

of Common Prayer, their use being enforced by the Act of Uniformity. Mercenary forces are used to put down Ket's rising in Norfolk, and another in Devon. Dudley, Earl of Warwick (later Duke of Northumberland) forces the retirement of Somerset, and takes his place in power.

1550 Warwick, now Duke of Northumberland, negotiates peace with France – surrendering Boulogne – and with Scotland.

1552 The Second Prayer Book is issued, accompanied by a new Act of Uniformity. The Church is empowered to make parish collections (by churchwardens) to support their poor. Somerset is charged with conspiring to kill Northumberland and executed.

1553 Cranmer publishes the Forty-two Articles of Religion. Northumberland induces Edward VI to annul Henry VIII's will settling the succession on Mary and Elizabeth, in favour of Jane Gray who had married his son, Guildford Dudley. Edward VI dies on 6th July of pulmonary tuberculosis, aged 15, and is buried in Westminster Abbey.

LADY JANE GRAY, 1553

1553 Northumberland secures the Tower and causes his daughter-in-law, Lady Jane Gray, to be proclaimed on 6th July. He quickly loses support and himself proclaims Mary at Cambridge, but is arrested. Jane is thus deposed on 19th July.

THE REIGN OF MARY I, 1553–1558

1553 Mary, daughter of Henry VIII and Catherine of Aragon, is proclaimed Queen on 19th July. Northumberland, his son Warwick, and Northampton are brought to trial; Northumberland and Warwick are executed. Mary restores the Mass, but not the Church lands, nor Papal supremacy.

1554 Widespread revolts in support of Protestantism. Failure of Sir Thomas Wyatt and the rising by the Kentish men. Execution of Lady Jane Gray and her husband Lord Guildford Dudley. Mary marries Philip of Spain, son of Charles V, and permits Cardinal Pole, the Papal legate, to land in England. Parliament votes to reunite with Rome and receives absolution.

1555 4th January, Parliament's Grand Bill restores the Catholic situation in existence prior to 1529, but studiously preserves the rights of Elizabeth. Massive persecution of the Protestants; deprived churchmen are executed, and Ridley and Latimer are burnt at the stake in Oxford. Cranmer is convicted of heresy and burnt on 21st March 1556.

1557 War is renewed between France and Spain. 7,000 English are sent to join Philip (now Philip II of Spain). The Scots invade England but are dispersed. The French are routed at St. Quentin on 10th August.

1558 Calais (having been in British hands since 1347) is taken by the French. Mary, worn out and dispirited, dies from endemic influenza on 17th November. Shortly afterwards Cardinal Pole also dies.

Queen Elizabeth I, the daughter of Henry VIII by his marriage to Anne Boleyn

THE REIGN OF ELIZABETH I, 1558–1603

1559 By the Second Act of Supremacy all beneficed clergy and crown officials are bound to swear an oath against papal authority on penalty of death. Acceptance of a new prayer book, which represents a religious compromise, is ordered by the Second Act of Uniformity.

1560 Peace is negotiated at the Treaty of Edinburgh between Francis II of France, the Scottish nobles and Elizabeth. Francis II dies in December.

1561 Mary, widow of Francis II, lands in Scotland.

1564 William Shakespeare is born.

1565 Mary marries her cousin, Lord Darnley, Henry Stuart, in July.

1566 Mary gives birth to a son, James, on 27th

May, later to become James VI of Scotland (see below), and James I of England.

1567 Darnley is murdered (9th February); Mary is compelled to marry James Hepburn, Earl of Bothwell, who had been suspected of Darnley's murder, but Bothwell is driven out of Scotland. Mary is forced to abdicate and is confined in Lochleven Castle. James Stuart, Earl of Murray, is made regent for the infant James VI.

1568 Mary escapes from Lochleven but is defeated in the Battle of Langside, 13th May; she flees to England to seek Elizabeth's help against the rebels, but is confined in Tutbury Castle in Staffordshire.

1569 Murray is assassinated in Linlithgow.

1570 The Pope excommunicates Elizabeth and absolves her subjects from allegiance.

1571 The Protestant retort is to pass harsh acts against Mary (depriving her of the right to succeed to the English throne), against the Pope and Catholic refugees.

1572 Norfolk and Northumberland are tried and executed. On 24th August, St. Bartholomew's Day, tens of thousands of Huguenots are massacred in France, and the Protestant outcry in England forces Elizabeth to openly head the English Protestant cause.

1575 Elizabeth insists that Parliament stops interfering in religious matters.

1577 Following the pacification of Ghent (1576) the Netherland states form themselves into a confederate republic whose aim is to expel the Spaniards. 5,000 English volunteers go to the aid of the Netherlands, assisting William of Orange to form the seven northern provinces into the Protestant Union of Utrecht.

1577–1580 Sir Francis Drake circumnavigates the world.

1580 Philip of Spain conquers Portugal. The Jesuits, Campion and Parsons, arrive in England.

1581 The Recusancy Acts are passed against the Jesuits.

1583 Whitgift is made Primate. The High Commission Court is formed.

1584 William of Orange is murdered. A conspiracy to murder Elizabeth and make Mary Queen is foiled. Further repressive acts are passed against Catholics.

1585 Elizabeth sends Leicester with 6,000 men to assist the Dutch but he is defeated at the Battle of Zutphen (1586), in which Sir Philip Sidney is killed. Drake sails with twenty-five ships and destroys San Domingo and Carthagena, raiding the coasts of Cuba

and Florida, in retaliation for the seizure of British shipping by Philip of Spain.

1587 A further plot to assassinate Elizabeth is discovered and is followed by the execution of Mary Queen of Scots at Fotheringay on 8th February. Drake destroys fifty Spanish store ships in Cadiz harbour in March ("the singeing of the Spanish king's beard"), ravages the Portuguese coast and captures the great East Indies treasure ship.

1588 The Armada sails on 30th May against England under the Duke of Medina-Sidonia. The English Catholics remain loyal to Elizabeth; the Armada is defeated and shattered by storms. Only fifty-three vessels out of the original 130 manage to return to Spain.

1589 Henry III of France is assassinated. Henry IV of Navarre accepts Catholicism and becomes King of France.

1590 English verse, dormant since Chaucer, is seen again in Edmund Spenser's *Faerie Queen*.

1596 Calais falls to Philip of Spain. A combined English and French expedition, under Lord Howard of Effingham and Robert Devereux, Earl of Essex, sacks Cadiz and destroys Spanish ships in the harbour.

1597 Essex sets sail to intercept the Spanish West Indies fleet.

1599 Essex is sent to put down a rebellion in Ireland under O'Neale, Earl of Tyrone, but fails. He returns and is prosecuted before the Star Chamber; he is deprived of all offices and dismissed the Court.

1600 Essex, believing that he holds the support of the masses, marches on London calling on the people to rise. He is arrested, tried and executed on 25th February 1601.

1601 Elizabeth is forced to yield to the Commons' demand for the surrender of monopolies, which had been conferred upon her favourites. Depressed at the death of Essex, Elizabeth falls ill and dies on 24th March 1603, aged 69, naming James her successor.

SUMMARY OF THE KINGS OF SCOTLAND, 1005–1603

With the succession of James VI of Scotland to the throne of England as James I in 1603, it is convenient here to summarise the rulers of the Kingdom of Scotland. During the years A.D. 944–945 King Edmund ("King of All Britain") overran Strathclyde, including the Lake District, and gave it to the Alban King Malcolm I, then reigning; this territory was subsequently lost to the English and then annexed to the new Kingdom of Scotland in 1015.

Malcolm II (1005–1034). Formed the Kingdom of Scotland, *c.* 1015, but swore allegiance for Northumbria to King Cnut in 1031.

Duncan I (1034–1040). Son of Bethoc, daughter of Malcolm II.

Macbeth (1040–1057). Son of Donada, daughter of Malcolm II.

Lulach (1057–1058). Stepson of Macbeth, and son of his wife Gruoch.

Malcolm III (1058–1093). Son of Duncan I and brother-in-law of William Rufus.

Donald Bane (1093–1094, deposed, and 1094–1097, deposed). Son of Duncan I, and the last of the pure Scottish line of Kings.

Duncan II (1094). Son of Malcolm III.

Edgar (1097–1107). Elder son of Malcolm III and Margaret, and half-brother of Duncan II.

Alexander I (1107–1124). Younger son of Malcolm III, and brother of Edgar.

David I (1124–1153). Youngest son of Malcolm III, and brother of Edgar.

Malcolm IV (1153–1165). Grandson of David I, and son of Henry, Earl of Huntingdon.

William I (1165–1214). Elder brother of Malcolm IV;
(The Lion) was forced to swear homage to King of England, who was acknowledged overlord, 1174–1189.

Alexander II (1214–1249). Son of William I; married Joan, daughter of John of England.

Alexander III (1249–1286). Son of Alexander II.

Margaret "*Maid of Norway*". Granddaughter of Alexander III, and daughter of Margaret by marriage to King Eric II of Norway. Died on only voyage to Scotland, aged seven.

FIRST INTERREGNUM, 1290–1292

John Baliol (1292–1296). Son of Devorguil, great-great-granddaughter of David I through his youngest grandson David. Forced to abandon his throne by Edward I of England.

SECOND INTERREGNUM, 1296–1306

Robert I (1306–1329). Great-great-great-grandson of David I, whose great-granddaughter Isabella married a Bruce.

David II (1329–1371). As son of Robert I, acceded in infancy.

Robert II (1371–1390). Son of Walter the Stewart and Marjorie Bruce; founded the Stewart dynasty.

Robert III (1390–1406). Natural (declared legitimate) son of Robert II.

James I (1406–1437). Son of Robert III; is captured in 1405 by the English at sea, and kept prisoner until 1424. Marries Jane Beaufort, granddaughter of John of Ghent.

James II (1437–1466). Son of James I.

James III (1466–1488). Son of James II.

James IV (1488–1513). Son of James III and Margaret of Denmark; marries Margaret Tudor, elder daughter of Henry VII.

James V (1513–1542). Son of James IV and Margaret Tudor; marries Margaret of Guise.

Mary (Queen of Scots) (1542–1567). Daughter of James V and Margaret of Guise. Acceded as an infant. Succeeded by James VI, her son by her marriage to Henry Stuart, Lord Darnley. Executed at Fotheringay, 8th February 1587.

James VI (1567–1625). Son of Mary and Lord Darnley. Succeeded to the English throne as James I in 1603, thereby uniting the two kingdoms.

THE REIGN OF JAMES I, 1603–1625

1603   James confirms Robert Cecil, second son of Lord Burghley, as secretary of state. Cecil opposes James's favour of Catholicism, resulting in the Catholic "Bye" plot, and afterwards in the Protestant "Main" plot. Raleigh is implicated and imprisoned for thirteen years in the Tower.

1604   The Hampton Court Conference is summoned, its only achievement being the new issue of the Bible in 1611. The canons issued by the Conference fail to gain support from James's first Parliament. The "Apology" of the Commons is presented to define Parliament's relationship with the King. Peace is made with Spain on favourable terms.

1604–1605   The Gunpowder Plot by Catholic malcontents is hatched to destroy the King, Lords and Commons. Its discovery leads to substantial persecution of the Catholics.

1606   By royal charter granted to Judge Popham, colonies are founded in Virginia.

1607   The two great Earls of Ulster, Tyrone and Tyrconnel, flee to the Continent under suspicion of treason, and the English seize the opportunity to commence "plantation" with Protestant colonies.

1610   James negotiates and secures a twelve-year truce between the Dutch and the Spanish. The Great Contract between King and Parliament is attempted but is abandoned; James in frustration dissolves Parliament (1611). He partially re-establishes Episcopacy in Scotland.

1612   Henry, the King's eldest son, dies suddenly. Cecil also dies, and the rule of favourites

	begins. The King's first favourite is Robert Carr whom James creates Viscount Rochester, and later Earl of Somerset.
1613	James's daughter, Princess Elizabeth, marries the Protestant Elector Palatine, grandson of William of Orange.
1614	James meets Parliament, which earns the name "Addled", undertaking no legislation and only seeking to consider grievances. It is angrily dissolved by the King, who then rules for seven years without a parliament.
1615	Somerset falls from royal favour, his place being taken by George Villiers, later Duke of Buckingham.
1617	Sir Francis Bacon is made Keeper of the Seals, and the following year Lord Chancellor with the title Baron Verulam. Raleigh is conditionally released at Buckingham's instigation to sail to Guiana; he disobeys the King's orders to avoid provoking the Spanish, and is executed on his return in 1618.
1618	James in Scotland forces the General Assembly of the Kirk to accept the Five Articles of Perth. On return to England he issues the Declaration of Sport, permitting "lawful recreation" after divine service on Sunday. The religious Thirty Years' War (1618–1648) breaks out in Bohemia.
1620	The *Mayflower*, 180 tons, with 102 "Pilgrim Fathers" sets sail for America on 6th September, making landfall on the coast of Massachusetts on 11th December. Their point of arrival is named New Plymouth. Frederick, James's son-in-law, is driven from his Palatinate by Austrian and Spanish forces.
1621	Parliament meets and attacks monopolies, reviving the right of impeachment. Bacon, Lord Chancellor, is impeached for receiving bribes, imprisoned and deprived of office. Displaying increasing Protestantism, Parliament is anxious to assist Frederick, and to see James's younger son, Prince Charles, marry a Protestant.
1622	James, angered by the Commons' participation in affairs of state, dissolves parliament.
1623	James permits Catholics to worship in private houses. Charles, accompanied by Buckingham, visits Madrid to arrange a marriage of the Prince to the Infanta of Spain; the match is broken off, to the delight of the English people.
1624	Buckingham urges war with Spain at the meeting of a new parliament. A treaty is signed for the marriage of Charles to Henrietta Maria, daughter of Henry IV of

France, but before the marriage is concluded James falls to Bright's disease and dies, aged 58, on 27th March 1625.

THE REIGN OF CHARLES I, 1625–1649

1625	Charles' first parliament is dissolved after constant disputes over supply. The King levies tonnage and poundage on his own authority and thereby secures an expedition against Cadiz – which meets with failure.
1626	Sir John Eliot, a protagonist of "control by Parliament", leads the opposition in Charles' second parliament. Buckingham is impeached; Charles dissolves parliament to reverse the impeachment, and commits Eliot to prison.
1628	Eliot and Sir Thomas Wentworth lead the opposition in Charles' third parliament. The Petition of Rights gains royal assent, forbids unparliamentary taxation, arbitrary arrest and detention, and the billetting of soldiers in private houses. The Puritans, being gradually driven from the Church, join the opposition in parliament. Wentworth quarrels with Eliot and joins the King. Buckingham is murdered.
1629	A violent scene in the Commons results in the King's dismissal of the third parliament. Eliot is imprisoned in the Tower and dies in 1632. For eleven years the nation is governed without a parliament.
1633–1640	Wentworth becomes Lord Deputy in Ireland and pursues a policy of reform, suppressing piracy, disciplining the army, repairing and garrisoning the fortresses, developing commerce and industry, and substantially improving the exchequer.
1633	Laud becomes Primate and embarks on a substantial reformation of the Church, in particular advocating utmost leniency towards Catholics. He accompanies Charles to Scotland where the King is crowned with full ritual.
1634	The attorney-general, Noy recommends the revival of ship-money (taxation of the maritime counties for the maintenance of the fleet). Noy dies, and the following year Chief Justice Finch extends ship-money to include all counties.
1637	The King is supported by the judges in levying ship-money, but is opposed by John Hampden. A riot breaks out in St. Giles's Church, Edinburgh, following an attempt to introduce a new Prayer Book.
1638	Formation of the National Covenant against the Prayer Book and Episcopacy.

1639   Charles marches north to Berwick against Scotland with 20,000 men but, faced by an equal force under Alexander Leslie, negotiates peace at the Treaty of Berwick on 17th June. Wentworth becomes Earl of Strafford.

1640   John Pym leads the opposition in the "Short Parliament", which Charles dissolves peremptorily on 5th May. This antagonises the people who are supported by the Scots. Leslie crosses the Tweed with 26,000 men, and Charles is forced to summon a new Parliament – "The Long Parliament" – wherein new, severe measures are passed against the Catholics.

1641   The Triennial Bill is passed limiting parliamentary sessions to three years. Strafford is impeached and abandoned by the king; but, fearing acquittal by the Lords, the Commons substitute attainder and secure his execution. The army is disbanded, and the Courts of Star Chamber and High Commission abolished. A revolt breaks out in Ireland. The Grand Remonstrance is presented to Charles. The Commons determine to impeach the Queen.

1642   Charles attempts to arrest Pym, Hampden, Hazelrig, Holles and Strode in the Commons, but they escape into the City. He refuses to give assent to the Militia Bill, but fails to secure Hull where the military provisions for the war against Scotland are stored. The royal standard is raised at Nottingham.

THE CIVIL WARS, 1642–1649

1642   Episcopacy is abolished. Charles wins a narrow victory over the Earl of Essex at Edgehill on 23rd October.

1643   The royalist forces gain further successes at Stratton, Exeter, Roundway Down, Taunton, Bridgwater, Bristol and Adwalton Moor. Prince Rupert, Charles' nephew, sweeps the country, and Hampden is killed at Chalgrove Field, near Oxford, on 18th June. The Assembly of Divines meets at Westminster to decide on the acceptance and form of Puritanism. Parliament seeks help from the Scots, resulting in the "Solemn League and Covenant" between the two kingdoms. Gloucester, under siege by the king, is relieved by Essex. The first Battle of Newbury is fought without result. Oliver Cromwell, cousin of Hampden, achieves prominence as a military com-

The Lord Protector, Oliver Cromwell

mander of the parliamentary forces, and raises the siege of Hull.

1644   The king's fortunes turn when the Scots cross the Tweed to assist Parliament, and the royalists are heavily defeated at Marston Moor on 2nd July, largely as a result of Cromwell's generalship. The Marquis of Montrose temporarily revives the royalist cause in the Highlands. A second Battle of Newbury is fought, again with doubtful issue.

1645   Archbishop Laud is attainted and executed. Cromwell introduces "The New Model", a standing parliamentary army of 21,000 men under regular pay. The Self-denying Ordinance is passed to rid the army of Presbyterian generals; Fairfax becomes lord-general, Skippon major-general, and Cromwell is placed in command of cavalry. Charles' defeat at the Battle of Naseby on 14th June virtually ends the war in England, but Montrose continues his successes in the Highlands.

1646   Charles attempts to negotiate an alliance with the Scots in Newcastle, but following his refusal to support the abolishing of Episcopacy he is surrendered to parliament.

1647   The king is lodged in Holmby House, Northamptonshire, but escapes to Carisbrooke Castle in the Isle of Wight, where he remains effectively a prisoner of the parliamentary factions with his children, Prince Henry and Princess Elizabeth. He signs an "engagement" with the Scottish Commissioners.

1648   A second Civil War breaks out, caused by a reaction in the king's favour. The Presbyterian party is temporarily supreme in parliament. Hamilton, as a result of the "engagement" of 1647, marches south to aid the royal cause, but is defeated at Preston. The army turns on parliament, presenting the Grand Army Remonstrance, and removes Charles to Hurst Castle in Hampshire, thence to Windsor. The Remonstrance is rejected by parliament; the Commons are purged by Colonel Pride, the Independent remainder being termed the Rump. On 23rd December the Rump votes for the trial of Charles.

1649 Charles, arraigned as "tyrant, traitor, murderer, public and implacable enemy of the commonwealth of England", is condemned, and is executed on 30th January outside the banqueting hall of Whitehall.

THE COMMONWEALTH, 1649–1660

1649 The monarchy and the House of Lords are abolished. Cromwell crosses to Ireland and storms Drogheda and Wexford. Charles II is acknowledged in Scotland.

1650 Montrose is defeated on 17th April by Strachan at Corbiesdale in Ross-shire. Charles lands in Scotland. Cromwell moves against the Scots and defeats David Leslie at the Battle of Dunbar on 3rd September. Charles is crowned at Scone, marches south but is defeated at the Battle of Worcester by Cromwell exactly one year later, on 3rd September 1651.

1651 Charles escapes to France. The Navigation Act, designed to stimulate the shipping enterprises of England and crush those of Holland, is passed, and war with the Dutch ensues.

1652 Robert Blake, previously a successful Parliamentarian commander, takes command of the English navy, but is defeated by the Dutch under Van Tromp.

1653 Blake decisively defeats Van Tromp three times thereby destroying the Dutch capacity to continue the war. Cromwell dissolves the "Rump", and summons the "Barebone" Parliament, so-called after one of Cromwell's nominees, a leatherseller named Barebone. Cromwell is made Lord Protector under the Instrument of Government.

1654 The Dutch negotiate peace terms. "Triers" and "Ejectors" are elected to secure suitable ministers in parliament which meets but violates the Instrument of Government, and is promptly dissolved by Cromwell.

1655 A state of siege exists in England which is governed by "major-generals". War breaks out with Spain and an English squadron captures Jamaica, thus establishing British power in the West Indies. A commercial treaty is concluded with France.

1656 Parliament is recalled and The Petition and Advice, presented to Cromwell, becomes law. The kingship is offered to, but refused by Cromwell.

1657 Cromwell concludes an offensive alliance with France to forestall a Franco-Spanish attack on England. Blake destroys the Spanish ships and forts at Teneriffe, and dies shortly afterwards at Plymouth.

1658 Cromwell's Ironsides, serving in Turenne's French army, capture Dunkirk and Gravelines from Spanish forces. Parliament, proving refractory, is dissolved. Oliver Cromwell dies on 3rd September, anniversary of Dunbar and Worcester, after nominating his son, Richard, as his successor. The army demands a republic and independence of the civil power.

1659 The Rump is restored by the army, and Richard Cromwell is content to resign. General Lambert rejects the Rump, but his troops revolt and it is restored again.

1660 George Monk (Duke of Albemarle) marches from Scotland and enters London; the members expelled by Pride's Purge of 1648 are restored, and the Long Parliament is finally dissolved. A royalist parliament is returned. Charles II signs the Declaration of Breda and lands at Dover.

THE REIGN OF CHARLES II, 1660–1685

(1660–1667. The administration of Edward Hyde, Earl of Clarendon, Lord Chancellor.)

1660 The "Convention" parliament is dissolved, and the "Cavalier" parliament reverses the acts of the Long Parliament. The Coldstream Guards are retained as the nucleus of a standing army. A fixed revenue of £1,200,000 from tonnage and poundage and excise is granted for life.

1661 The first of a series of persecuting statutes against Dissenters is passed, the Corporation Act.

1662 2,000 nonconforming clergy resign their livings rather than take the oath, following the passing of the Act of Uniformity; many of them accepted poverty or exile, and henceforth Presbyterianism became the creed of a dissenting sect. Thus had the English church adopted its final shape. Charles marries Catherine of Braganza, the

King Charles II (1630–1685). Reigned de jure 1649–1685

Infanta of Portugal, whose dowry includes Bombay and Tangiers. Dunkirk is sold to Louis XIV of France for £200,000.

1665   Despite the peace terms negotiated with the Dutch in 1654, hostilities had continued in America, Africa and Asia, and are renewed in Europe in 1665. The English fleet severely defeats the Dutch off Lowestoft on 3rd June. The Great Plague breaks out and sweeps the country; by September 1,000 deaths are being recorded daily in London alone.

1666   Parliament demands the appointment of Commissioners to examine national expenditure. On 1st June the Dutch fleet under Ruyter and Tromp heavily defeat the English under Monk and Rupert off the Dunes, but two months later fortunes are reversed when the English destroy 150 Dutch ships by use of fireships at the mouth of the Texel. The Great Fire of London breaks out on 2nd September and lays most of the City in ruins within a week.

1667   The Covenanters revolt in Scotland but are suppressed. On 7th June a Dutch fleet under De Witt sails up the Thames, capturing and burning British ships at Rochester and Sheerness. The Treaty of Breda, by which each nation retains its conquests, ends the first Dutch War. Clarendon is impeached but escapes to France, where he dies in 1674. Milton's *Paradise Lost* is completed and published.

(1667–1673.   The "Cabal" Administration.)

1668   England, Holland and Sweden form the Triple Alliance; in consequence Louis XIV makes peace with Spain at Aix-la-Chapelle.

1670   Charles concludes a secret treaty with Louis (the Treaty of Dover) and publishes a sham one. The right of juries to find verdicts against the crown is established.

1672   Charles' debts force him into a fraudulent bankruptcy, called the "Stop of the Exchequer"; interest on loans are halved, bankers are made to forego repayments of loans, and great hardship is forced upon private persons. Charles issues a Declaration of Indulgence, suspending the penal laws. The second Dutch War breaks out.

1673   A new parliament is summoned which compels Charles to revoke the Declaration of Indulgence, and passes the Test Act. Parliament refuses supplies and opposes the Cabal administration.

1674   Deprived of financial support, Charles is forced to negotiate the Peace of Westminster, ending the second Dutch War; by it, England acquires St. Helena.

(1674–1679.   The administration of the Earl of Danby (Sir Thomas Osborne), and a return to the policies of Clarendon.)

1675   Parliament is divided between the "courtiers", led by Danby, and the "country" party, led by Shaftesbury. Bribed by Louis, Charles prorogues parliament for fifteen months.

1677   Parliament reassembles and the country party is defeated; their leaders are imprisoned. James's eldest daughter, Mary, marries William of Orange, prompting Louis into alliance with the opposition.

1678   The Peace of Nijmegen ends the Franco-Dutch war. Another secret treaty is agreed between Charles and Louis. A widespread dread of the Catholics is fanned by the pretended disclosures of Titus Oates, a previously-discredited informer who had been expelled from the church, the Dissenters and the Jesuits.

1679   The Commons impeach Danby, but his life is saved when Charles dissolves parliament. Archbishop Sharp is murdered in Scotland. The Covenanters defeat the royal forces under Claverhouse, but meet defeat at Bothwell Brig. Shaftesbury heads a new parliament which passes the Habeas Corpus Act, but which is dissolved almost immediately.

1680   Charles throws over the country party and dismisses Shaftesbury; he places the administration in the hands of the "Chits": Sunderland, Lawrence Hyde (son of Clarendon), and Sydney Godolphin, who is particularly skilled as a financier. Charles' third parliament is summoned but, following the failure of the Exclusion Bill to pass through the Lords, is again dissolved.

1681   Charles' fourth and last parliament is summoned; it again proposes an Exclusion Bill, rejects a Regency Bill, and is dissolved.

(1681–1685.   Government without a parliament by the aid of pensions from Louis. A "Tory" reaction emerges against the "Whigs" (the exclusionists), and Shaftesbury escapes to Holland, where he dies in 1683.)

1683   Using writs of *Quo warranto?* judges order many charters to be forfeited, and the municipalities are made subservient, driving the Whigs to despair. The Rye House Plot to assassinate Charles is discovered, and the participants suffer death or banishment. Charles becomes absolute.

1685   On 5th February Charles dies of apoplexy, aged fifty-five, having secretly received the last rites of the Catholic church.

THE REIGN OF JAMES II, 1685–1689

1685   James II, younger son of Charles I, and a Catholic advocate, succeeds to the throne. The Penal Laws are suspended by Royal Proclamation. James obtains £2,000,000 for life from a subservient parliament in which the "Chits" retain principal power. The Duke of Argyle lands in Scotland from Holland and heads a rebellion, but is captured and executed. Monmouth leads a revolt in the West Country but is defeated by Lord Feversham at the Battle of Sedgemoor, is captured and executed. The insurgents, as well as many innocents, are judicially murdered or deported as slaves as sentenced by the "Bloody Assize", presided over by the brutal Lord Chief Justice, Jeffreys (who is rewarded by James with the appointment of Lord Chancellor).

1687   The Declaration of Indulgence proclaims liberty of conscience. The Universities are forced to admit Catholics, and the fellows of Magdalen College, Oxford, are expelled for having refused to admit one of James's nominees.

688   Sancroft, the Primate, and six bishops are committed to the Tower for refusing to read the Declaration. They are tried for sedition by the King's Bench but acquitted – amidst popular rejoicing. A son, James (later called the Old Pretender) is born to James II by his second wife, Mary of Modena – two daughters, Mary and Anne, having been born from his first marriage, to Anne Hyde. William of Orange, Protestant husband of James's daughter Mary, is invited to England by Danby, Shrewsbury, Compton bishop of London, and others. James, faced with a Protestant revolution and now deserted by his children, attempts to escape and is received by Louis in France.

1689   A convention parliament is summoned which declares the throne vacant. The crown is offered to William of Orange and Mary upon conditions set down in the Declaration of Right. The First Act of Settlement provides for a Protestant succession.

THE PROVISIONS OF THE ACT OF SETTLEMENT

1. The Crown would be held by William and Mary for their joint and separate lives;
2. It would then fall to Mary's children;
3. Next to Anne and her children;
4. Lastly to the children of William by any other wife.
5. A Catholic, or one who should marry a Catholic, should forfeit the right to the succession, and the next Protestant heir should succeed.

THE NEW MONARCHY

THE REIGN OF WILLIAM III, 1689–1702 (IN CONJUNCTION WITH MARY II, 1689–1694)

1689   William straightway faces hostility from church, parliament and the army. Sancroft, six bishops and four hundred clergy resign their livings rather than take the oath of allegiance. The Mutiny Act is passed, followed by the Toleration Act which suspended penal laws against all but Catholics and Unitarians. In Scotland James Grahame of Claverhouse (Viscount Dundee), with a commission from James II, defeats the royal troops at the Battle of Killiecrankie, 27th July. In Ireland the siege of Londonderry is raised and James's troops are defeated at Newtown Butler.

1690   The Corporation Bill is passed restoring the charter of London (forfeited under *Quo warranto?* in 1683), and parliament is dissolved. A new parliament grants the king a "civil list" of £800,000. William lands in Ireland and defeats James in the Battle of the Boyne on 1st July, going on to occupy

Dublin and Waterford. Returning to England, he sends John Churchill, Earl of Marlborough, to capture Cork, a task accomplished in six weeks.

1691 The Dutch commander Ginkell defeats St. Ruth, a French general commanding James II's troops in Ireland, at Aughrim in Galway on 11th July, and captures Limerick on 1st October. The war is ended by the Treaty of Limerick.

1692 Massacre of the Macdonalds at Glencoe on 13th February. An English fleet of ninety vessels under Admiral Russell defeats the French off La Hogue on 19th May, and soon afterwards destroys six warships in Cherbourg under the very eyes of James. William, however, with an Anglo-Dutch army is badly defeated by the French under Marshal Luxembourg at Steinkirk.

1693 Continuation of the war against France demands increased revenue, and Montague, a commissioner of the Treasury, proposes the raising of a new loan, thereby originating the National Debt. William again takes the field and is again defeated by Luxembourg, now at Landen.

1694 Mary II dies from smallpox and pneumonia at Kensington on 28th December. Further loan proposals by Montague result in the formation of the Bank of England. An English expedition against Brest ends in failure.

1695 Following the death of Marshal Luxembourg, the fortunes of war begin to turn in England's favour. On 1st September William recaptures Namur.

1696 A Jacobite plot to assassinate William is uncovered and the leaders are executed. The Treason Act is passed, furnishing the rights of an accused person. The national coinage, being hammered and therefore vulnerable to clipping, is reformed under the Coinage Act; the new coinage, carefully milled, is issued under the direction of Sir Isaac Newton, the great philosopher, who becomes Master of the Mint.

1697 On 10th September peace terms with France are negotiated at Ryswick by England, Spain and Holland.

1698 The possible sudden death of Charles II of Spain without male heir creates a European crisis owing to belligerent competition for the Spanish empire. Among the claimants to the Spanish crown are the French Dauphin, the Emperor Leopold of Austria and the Electoral Prince Joseph of Bavaria; the succession is settled upon the latter, with the support of France in return for the transfer of Guipuscoa, Naples and Sicily to the Dauphin. This is the First Partition Treaty. In England, a new Tory party is returned in parliament which, while maintaining the navy at strength, severely reduces the army.

1699 The Electoral Prince of Bavaria dies, necessitating a new partition treaty; agreement is reached between France and England that Archduke Charles shall be heir to Spain and the Spanish colonies, while fresh cessions would be made to Louis, in addition to those of the first treaty. Such unilateral disposals anger Spain, especially as she holds considerable grievances against England. The Commons meet in November and the following year annul the Irish grants (ensuring its passage through the Lords by "tacking" it to the Land Bill); thus William is forced to consent, albeit angrily, and promptly prorogues parliament.

1700 Following the death of the Electoral Prince, and that of Charles II of Spain in November, the Second Partition Treaty is invoked.

1701 A Second Act of Settlement is rendered necessary by the death of the young Duke of Gloucester, the last of Anne's children. The provisions of this Act are so fundamental constitutionally that they are set down fairly fully, as follows:

1. *The sovereign must be a member of the Church of England.*
2. *Should the crown fall to anyone not a native of England (such as the Electress of Hanover), the consent of parliament is necessary before the nation engages in war for the defence of any land not belonging to the crown of England.*
3. *The Sovereign may not leave the country (as William had) without parliament's consent.*
4. *The whole privy council must be consulted and must sign resolutions adopted.*
5. *No foreigners (such as Dutchmen) may hold civil or military posts.*
6. *No one holding a crown office or pension may sit in parliament.*
7. *Judges are to be deprived of office only upon an address from both houses.*
8. *No pardon under the Great Seal may henceforth be claimed in bar of a parliamentary impeachment.*
These conditions would take effect on the accession of the House of Hanover (in fact, with the accession of George I in 1714).

Despite England's acquiescence to the Second Partition Treaty, it was not generally popular owing to the great advantages conferred on France. Nevertheless when Louis

XIV seizes the "Barrier Towns", thereby threatening the Dutch, there is popular clamour for war against France. The Grand Alliance is thus formed between England, Holland and Austria (and shortly joined by Prussia).

1702   William dies of pleuro-pneumonia following a fracture of his collar-bone suffered while riding; his death at 51 occurred on 8th March at Kensington.

THE REIGN OF ANNE, 1702–1714

1702   The succession of Anne, only surviving daughter of James II and Anne Hyde, satisfies Tory sentiment of hereditary right and that of the Whigs of parliamentary election. A Tory ministry is returned which favours peace, but the influence of Marlborough predominates; war – the War of Spanish Succession – is declared on 4th May. Marlborough captures Liége, receives the thanks of parliament and is created a duke by Anne. An English fleet sacks Port St. Mary, near Cadiz.

1703   Marlborough gains successes on the Rhine and captures Bonn, in spite of the sluggishness of the Dutch.

1704   Some anti-war Tories are dismissed and Marlborough's influence secures the appointment of Harley as secretary of state, and Henry St. John as secretary at war; Lord Godolphin remains as lord high treasurer. By his great victory at Blenheim on 13th August, Marlborough saves Austria from destruction, and checks French aggression for a century; he receives as reward the royal manor of Woodstock, near Oxford, on which is built, at public expense, the palace of Blenheim. Admirals Rooke and Cloudesley Shovel capture Gibraltar.

1705   Parliament is dissolved and a new Whig ministry is returned. Barcelona is taken by the Earl of Peterborough.

1706   Marlborough forces the French line of defences constructed from Antwerp to Namur, and decisively beats the French under Marshal Villeroi in the Battle of Ramillies on 23rd May. He reduces the French garrisons and drives them from the Netherlands. Peterborough enters Madrid, but the Spanish enterprise ends in failure and he withdraws to Italy. Louis XIV offers peace, but it is refused by Marlborough.

1707   The Act of Union between England and Scotland is passed in the Scottish parlia-

ment in January, and in that of England in February, receiving the royal assent the following month. The Allied army of Galway and Las Minas suffer defeat from the Duke of Berwick in the Battle of Almanza on 25th April. A Tory attack on Marlborough's influence fails, although Robert Walpole replaces Henry St. John as secretary at war.

1708   Marlborough and Prince Eugene defeat Marshal Vendôme in the Battle of Oudenarde on 11th July, and go on to capture Lille, Ghent and Bruges, General Stanhope seizes Sardinia and Minorca, the latter becoming an English possession by the terms of The Peace of Utrecht (see 1713).

1709   Louis XIV again seeks peace terms, but refuses the conditions imposed. Marlborough and Prince Eugene defeat Marshal Villars in the Battle of Malplaquet, but suffer 20,000 casualties, and go on to capture Mons.

1710   The trial of Henry Sacheverell, rector of St. Saviour's, Southwark (who had angered the Whigs with two High Church sermons), brings about the fall of the Whig party; parliament is dissolved and a strong Tory majority is returned. After a series of failures in Spain, the English under Stanhope are forced to surrender at Brihuega, leaving Philip V master of Spain. Harley becomes Earl of Oxford. Property qualifications are imposed on members of parliament, and remain in force until 1858.

1711   Following the death of Joseph I, Charles VI becomes emperor, and England is no longer interested in supporting his succession to the Spanish throne. Marlborough is accused of corruption and is dismissed.

1712   An armistice is proclaimed on 6th June between France and England, a measure which meets with the disapproval of England's allies, and of her own army. To suggest that it was carried out with the queen's approval, St. John becomes Viscount Bolingbroke and the Earl of Oxford receives the Garter.

1713   No longer opposed by English forces, Marshal Villars gains ground so rapidly that the Allies are forced to negotiate peace. and on 31st March are signed the various treaties which constitute The Peace of Utrecht.

1714   Bolingbroke ensures the passage of the Schism Bill to retain the support of the church. The Earl of Oxford is dismissed, leaving Bolingbroke supreme. Following

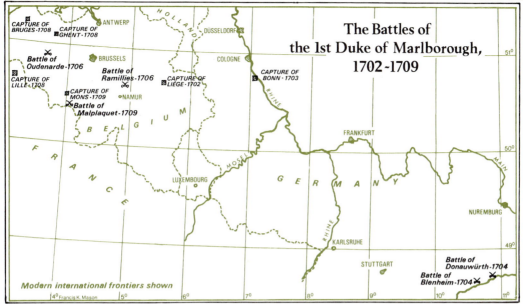

The Battles of
the 1st Duke of Marlborough,
1702-1709

CAPTURE OF BRUGES-1708
CAPTURE OF GHENT-1708
ANTWERP
HOLLAND
DUSSELDORF
Battle of Oudenarde-1706
BRUSSELS
COLOGNE
CAPTURE OF LILLE-1708
Battle of Ramillies-1706
CAPTURE OF LIEGE-1702
CAPTURE OF BONN-1703
CAPTURE OF MONS-1709
NAMUR
Battle of Malplaquet-1709
BELGIUM
FRANCE
RHINE
MOSEL
LUXEMBOURG
GERMANY
FRANKFURT
51°
50°
RHINE
NUREMBURG
49°
KARLSRUHE
MAIN
STUTTGART
Battle of Donauwürth-1704
Battle of Blenheim-1704

Modern international frontiers shown

Francis K. Mason   4°   5°   6°   7°   8°   9°   10°   11°

an apoplectic fit on 30th July, Anne dies on 1st August of a cerebral haemorrhage, aged 49, at Kensington. The Whigs promptly seize power and the Tories are driven out of government.

THE HOUSE OF HANOVER
THE REIGN OF GEORGE I, 1714–1727

1714   As the son of the marriage between Sophia and the Elector of Hanover, and great-grandson of James I, George I accedes to the throne at a moment of Whig supremacy. Government by party – the Whigs – commences with men of such calibre as Townshend, Stanhope (both secretaries of state), Walpole, Sunderland, Halifax, Cowper and Wharton; only one Tory, Nottingham, is included in the ministry.

1715   Bolingbroke is attainted, and the Earl of Oxford is committed to the Tower. The Riot Act is passed. Although deprived of support by the death of Louis XIV, the Old Pretender (son of James II by his marriage to Mary of Modena) lands in Scotland where the Earl of Mar is already in revolt; 3,000 rebels under Forster march south as far as Preston on 9th November but are obliged to surrender. A further revolt in Scotland collapses when, after the indecisive Battle of Sheriffmuir on 13th November, the rebel forces disperse.

1716   Lord Derwentwater, an architect of the rebellion, and others are executed. The Old Pretender and the Earl of Mar leave the shores of Scotland. Parliament passes the Septennial Act (fixing the parliamentary session at a maximum of seven years). The Schism Act is repealed.

1717   A treaty between France and England (reached in 1716) is now joined by Holland. This leads to a split in the Whig party, resulting in Townshend and Walpole leaving the ministry.

1718   With the participation of the emperor the Quadruple Alliance, thus formed between England, France and Holland, is intended to check the aggressiveness of Spain being revived under Cardinal Alberoni. Alberoni overruns Sicily and lays siege to Messina, but Admiral Byng, who had sailed to the Mediterranean with twenty-ships, appears off Cape Passaro on 11th August and so utterly destroys the Spanish fleet that Alberoni abandons his invasion plans.

1719   Alberoni seeks peace terms but England insists on his banishment; Philip V then joins the Quadruple Alliance. Townshend and Walpole rejoin the ministry. An act is passed to enable the English parliament to make laws in Ireland.

1720   The South Sea Bubble (so called after the South Sea Company, an enterprise formed by Harley) originates in a scheme for the reduction of the National Debt, but fails and results in widespread financial ruin.

(1721–1742. The administration of The Rt. Hon., Sir Robert Walpole, K.G., K.B.)

1721   Walpole is called in to rectify the mischief caused by the South Sea Bubble, becoming First Lord of the Treasury, and the first "Prime Minister". Under his guidance the Whigs become the party of peace and diplomacy. A Jacobite conspiracy, encouraged by the birth of Charles Edward, the Young Pretender, is detected and suppressed.

1725   Disturbances break out in Scotland following repeal of the Malt Tax (which had been widely evaded) and the substitution of a duty of 3d. on every barrel of ale. Bolingbroke, by means of substantial bribes to the royal mistresses, secures his pardon and the restoration of his estates; he returns and with political sympathisers (the "Patriots") expresses opposition to Walpole in his political newspaper, the *Craftsman*. Spain forms an alliance by the Treaty of Vienna with the emperor against England, and guarantees the Pragmatic Sanctions. As a counter-alliance, England, France and Prussia sign the Treaty of Hanover, and this is later joined by Sweden and Holland.

1727   Spain fails to capture Gibraltar after a siege during which the English fleet had kept the garrison supplied with provisions. Peace is signed in Paris on 31st May. George I dies suddenly of coronary thrombosis while travelling near Osnabrück at the age of 67 on 11th June, and is buried at Hanover.

THE REIGN OF GEORGE II, 1727–1760

1727   George II, only son of George I and Sophia Dorothea, succeeds to the throne on the death of his father. Using his influence with the new queen, Caroline of Brandenburg-Anspach, Walpole retains power.

1729   England, Spain and France enter a defensive alliance in the Treaty of Seville.

1731   Walpole secretly enters into the Second Treaty of Vienna and guarantees the Pragmatic Sanction.

1733   An Excise Bill is proposed by Walpole in an effort to check smuggling; but dislike of the Excisemen and his reluctance to use troops to support tax collection compels him to withdraw it.

1735   William Pitt (the Elder), later the 1st Earl of Chatham, first enters parliament as Whig member for Old Sarum at the age of 27,

and quickly establishes himself as the foremost of Walpole's opponents.

1736   An instance of Walpole's practice of avoiding active opposition is the occasion of the Porteous Riots in Edinburgh. An officer so named is sentenced to death for firing on a mob but reprieved; Porteous is lynched by the mob, prompting parliament to introduce a bill that would have destroyed the liberties of the city. Although opposed in both houses it is passed but subsequently withdrawn in favour of a milder bill.

1737   Queen Caroline dies on 20th November and Walpole finds himself beset by popular opposition, with little influence by which to safeguard his position.

1739   In consequence of "Jenkin's ear" (an uncorroborated charge by a British sea captain that he had been tortured by the Spanish during an illegal interception and search on the high seas), and other alleged outrages, Walpole is forced to declare war against Spain – the War of Jenkin's Ear. An English naval squadron under Commodore Anson sails against Spanish America and harasses the coast of Peru; another, under Admiral Vernon, captures Porto Bello.

1740   Charles VI dies and Maria Theresa succeeds to the Austrian dominions, but France and Spain repudiate the Pragmatic Sanction which is upheld by England and Holland.

1741   A new parliament is summoned in which Walpole has a substantially reduced majority. Maria Theresa is defeated by Frederick at Molwitz.

1742   Walpole resigns and is created Earl of Orford (of the second creation). The Elector of Bavaria becomes emperor as Charles VII. The parliamentary administration passes to the Earl of Wilmington, although Cartaret is effectively prime minister; Cartaret gives aid to Maria Theresa who cedes Silesia to Frederick and drives the French out of Bohemia.

1743   40,000 English, Hanoverians and Dutch under George II defeat 60,000 French troops under Marshal Noailles in the great Battle of Dettingen on 27th June – the last occasion on which a British king personally takes the field of battle. The Earl of Wilmington resigns and dies shortly after; Henry Pelham becomes Prime Minister. A French invasion attempt in support of the Young Pretender is frustrated by a storm.

1744   An indecisive battle is fought between the English and French fleets on 22nd February off Toulon. The following month France formally declares war on England. Commodore Anson returns from a remarkable voyage round the world with Spanish treasure amounting to £1,500,000. William Pitt, as paymaster of the forces, joins the government – now known as the "Broad Bottom" ministry.

1745   Emperor Charles VII dies and the Austrian succession is settled on Francis, Maria Theresa's husband, who is acknowledged by Frederick the Great. By the Treaty of Dresden, Maria Theresa allows Frederick to retain Silesia. The island of Cape Breton, which commands the entrance to the St. Laurence river, is taken from the French after an attack by New England volunteers and royal troops. The Young Pretender, Charles Edward, leads a rebellion in Scotland, defeats Sir John Cope at Preston Pans and marches south as far as Derby where he is halted and forced to retreat.

1746   The Young Pretender defeats General Hawley at Falkirk on 17th January, but is immediately forced to continue his retreat before the forces of the Duke of Cumberland. Charles turns to fight on Culloden Moor on 16th February, but the disciplined troops of Cumberland withstand the Highlanders' charge and an unsparing slaughter ensues. Charles escapes to France where he dies in 1788.

1747   The French invade Holland and defeat forces under the Duke of Cumberland and the Prince of Orange at Lauffeld, near Maastricht; but at sea Anson destroys a French squadron off Cape Finisterre, and Hawke wins another victory at Belleisle. No fewer than 644 prizes are captured during the year.

1748   The Peace of Aix-la-Chapelle brings the war to an end.

1750   Joseph François Dupleix, the French Governor in India – always awaiting an opportunity to sweep the sub-continent free of British influence (which existed in the three presidencies of the East India Company, Bombay, Madras (Carnatic) and Fort William on the Hooghly River) – begins the process of building up French power and influence in Madras. (Dupleix had captured Madras in 1746, but two years later, by the terms of the Treaty of Aix-la-Chapelle, it was handed back to Britain.)

1751   George's elder son, Frederick, Prince of Wales and heir to the throne, dies, but leaves a twelve-year-old son, the future George III. Chesterfield, with the help of the Earl of Macclesfield and Bradley the mathematician, reforms the calendar, a reform by which the legislative year henceforth begins on 1st January rather than 25th March. Robert Clive, a young captain employed by the East India Company, commanding a small English force, beats off his besiegers at Arcot, relieves Trichinopoly, defeats Dupleix, and returns to England.

1754   The Prime Minister Pelham dies on 6th March and the administration passes to the Duke of Newcastle-upon-Tyne ten days later. Dupleix is superseded and sent home to France.

1755   Henry Fox, a political adventurer of great ability, enters the Newcastle cabinet without office. General Braddock, who had been sent out to America in consequence of the French establishment of Fort Duquesne on the Ohio, is defeated by the French and Indians. War is declared against France.

1756   Minorca, an English possession under the terms of the Peace of Utrecht, falls to the French after a spirited action by its commander, Blakeney, with 2,800 men. Admiral Byng (son of the victor of Passaro) fails in the island's relief and suffers disgrace; he is executed the following year. Faced by growing French strength, England enters an alliance with Frederick the Great against Louis XV. Clive returns as governor of Fort St. David; Surajah Dowlah incarcerates 145 Europeans in the "Black Hole of Calcutta", and only twenty-three survive. The Duke of Newcastle (and Henry Fox) resigns, and the 4th Duke of Devonshire heads the new administration (in which Pitt was really, though not nominally, prime minister). The Highland regiments are enrolled and the militia reorganised.

1757   Admiral Byng is executed and William Pitt, who had advocated his pardon, is dismissed. Clive recaptures Calcutta and Chandernagore, defeats Surajah Dowlah in the great Battle of Plassey on 23rd June, and becomes governor of Bengal.

(1757–1762.   The second administration of the Duke of Devonshire, formed as a coalition of Newcastle and Pitt; Fox becomes paymaster.)

1758   Pitt repudiates the Closterseven treaty (a humiliating convention agreed by Cumberland in 1757) and pays £670,000 to Frederick. In America, Fort Duquesne is captured and its name changed to Pittsburg.

1759   Rodney bombards Le Havre and destroys a French force preparing to invade England. Boscawen destroys the Toulon fleet, Hawke blockades Brest and later in the year defeats a French fleet off Quiberon. Hopson and Moore capture Guadaloupe in the West Indies. Pitt sends three expeditions to conquer Canada. The first defeats Fort Niagara, thereby preventing Canada and Louisiana joining forces. The second drives the French out of Ticonderoga. The third, under General Wolfe, storms the Heights of Abraham and attacks the French army under Montcalm, capturing Quebec on 18th September. Both Wolfe and Montcalm die from wounds. In India Clive greatly expands English territory and reduces Masulipatam; he then returns home a rich man, receives an Irish peerage and enters parliament. Ferdinand of Brunswick, with 12,000 British troops wins the great Battle of Minden on 1st August.

1760   After Clive's return from India, Colonel Eyre Coote arrives with reinforcements from England and defeats the French at Wandewash. Montreal is taken and all Canada becomes English. George II dies, aged 76, on 25th October of coronary thrombosis at the Palace of Westminster. He is succeeded by his grandson, George William Frederick – his son Frederick Lewis, Prince of Wales, having previously died in 1751.

THE REIGN OF GEORGE III, 1760–1820

1760   George III succeeds to the throne at the age of 22.

1761   Pitt determines to declare war on Spain, but is opposed by the government, and resigns from office. In India, Coote captures Pondicherry in the Carnatic on 16th January, thereby finally destroying French power in the sub-continent.

1762–1763   Tory administration under the 3rd Earl of Bute, the first of eleven Eton-educated Tory prime ministers. The continuing aggressive tone of Spain forces Bute to declare war. France loses her West Indian islands, while Havannah and the Philippines are taken from the Spanish together with fifteen warships with treasure valued at £3,000,000. A British force drives Spanish troops out of Portugal.

1763   The Peace of Paris, signed on 10th February, ends the war; France gives up all North America except Louisiana, Senegal, Grenada, St. Vincent, Dominica and Tobago; Pondicherry is restored to her on conditions of no military occupation. Spain gives up Florida and loses her fishing rights off Newfoundland. Bute, never popular with the people, resigns in April.

(1763–1765.   The administration of George Grenville, Whig prime minister.)

1763   The affair of John Wilkes, M.P. for Aylesbury: A newspaper, *North Briton* (*issue No. 45*) is published in which Wilkes attacks the speech from the throne and comes close to questioning the king's honesty. Despite his parliamentary privilege, Wilkes is arrested on a "general warrant" and thrown into the Tower. Chief Justice Pratt (later Lord Camden) declares general warrants illegal.

1764   The Commons, bowing to popular feeling, decides that parliamentary privilege does not extend to seditious libel and on 19th January Wilkes is expelled and later outlawed.

1765   The king, unplaced by Grenville's handling of the Wilkes affair, appeals to the old Duke of Newcastle to advise on a new administration. In July the 2nd Marquess of Rockingham becomes prime minister (Edmund Burke, his private secretary, is the famous political philosopher). Before the change in the administration however, Grenville's Stamp Act, by which the colonies are taxed directly from London to alleviate the National Debt (now at £140 million), is passed through both houses.

1765–1766   Though shortlived, the Rockingham administration achieves good work; "general warrants" are condemned; commerce with Russia firmly established; and, following riots in the American colonies and sanctions against trade with England, the repeal of Grenville's Stamp Act. However, despite the latter, the government passes the Declaratory Act, affirming parliament's right to pass laws binding the colonies in all cases – the very right which the colonists denied. Almost immediately the Rockingham ministry resigns.

(1766–1770.   William Pitt's administration until 1768, after which that of the 3rd Duke of Grafton).

1766   Despite failing health, Pitt agrees to lead a new ministry but loses popularity as a great commoner when he accepts a peerage as Earl of Chatham.

1767   Pitt's continuing ill health leaves the Duke of Grafton in charge of the ministry. The government in confusion. France is allowed to purchase Corsica from Genoa and thereby recovers her presence in the Mediterranean. Charles Townshend, Grafton's chancellor of the exchequer, pledges himself to raise revenue from the American colonies to support the troops, and passes an act imposing duties upon tea, glass and paper. Townshend dies almost immediately afterwards and is succeeded as chancellor by Lord North, son of the Earl of Guildford.

1768   John Wilkes returns from France and is elected M.P. for Middlesex, thereby infuriating the king. In India Hyder Ali invades the Carnatic. Chatham resigns and the Duke of Grafton formally takes office as prime minister.

1769   On 2nd February Wilkes is expelled again from parliament; he is again elected and then declared incapable of sitting in the present parliament; a third successful election is declared void, and on a fourth occasion his opponent, Colonel Luttrell, is seated in the house with a marked minority vote. Throughout all elections Wilkes remains in prison.

1770   Wilkes is released from prison amid popular celebration, and in turn is elected alderman, sheriff and lord mayor of the City of London, eventually receiving £4,000 in damages against Lord Halifax (who had issued the "general warrant"). The Duke of Grafton resigns.

(1770–1782.   The sixth prime minister in ten years, Lord North leads a Tory administration and, principally because of a disarrayed opposition, survives in office for twelve years.)

1770   North repeals all taxation legislation on the American colonists, except that on tea.

1771   North's government concedes the right to print reports on parliamentary debates; Wilkes' growing influence results in confirmation of this right, resulting in the effective birth of politically-orientated London newspapers. Within six years seventeen newspapers, presenting political controversy, are being published in London.

1772   The Royal Marriage Act is passed by which no English descendant of George II may marry before the age of 25 without royal consent, and after this age they must give twelve months' notice to the Privy Council.

1773   The seeds of the American War of Independence are sown. On 16th December a consignment of tea from India arrives in Boston harbour; a party of men disguised as Mohawks board the ships and throw the tea into the water, in protest against the tax on tea. The London government peremptorily threatens to ruin Boston by removing the customs house to Salem. Lord North relieves the East India Company with a loan, but reorganises the company's constitution; Warren Hastings is made the first Governor-General.

1774   Acts are passed in parliament partly revoking the charter of Massachusetts (thereby increasing ties with the English crown), and giving toleration to the large French Catholic population in Canada (thereby offending the New England Puritanism). In the face of continuing unrest in the Colonies, General Gage occupies Boston with six regiments. The colonists hold a congress at Philadelphia, demand the repeal of all recent parliamentary legislation and threaten sanctions on all English trade. A second congress is held in October at Massachusetts at which the colonists propose to collect arms, train a militia and seek assistance from the Indian tribes.

1775   The parliamentary elections return Lord North with increased majority and he is encouraged to reject any compromise with the American colonists. The first blood is shed in a skirmish between the militia and some of Gage's troops at Lexington on 19th April. Thereafter Gage is besieged in Boston. The colonists capture Ticonderoga and Crown Point on 10th May, and George Washington is appointed commander-in-chief of the militia drawn from all the colonies. Gage, however, with reinforcements under Burgoyne, Clinton, Hall and Howe, defeats the Americans at the Battle of Bunker's Hill on 17th June, but loses a thousand men. The following day the colonists send a petition (the "Olive Branch") but are rebuffed by the king. An attempt to invade Canada by the Americans fails.

1776   General Howe, Gage's successor, evacuates Boston and captures New York, while his brother, Admiral Lord Howe, enters the harbour with an English fleet. Despite defeats by Clinton and Lord Cornwallis, the Americans under Washington continue to harass the English, and on 4th July the thirteen colonies issue the Declaration of Independence, declaring themselves thereby "Free and Independent States".

1777   Washington and Cornwallis fight an indecisive engagement at Princeton on 13th January. Howe defeats Washington at Brandywine and captures Philadelphia on

26th June. Burgoyne recaptures Ticonderoga, but is beaten at Bennington and Stillwater, and retires upon Saratoga where, on 17th October, he capitulates to General Gates with his army of 6,000 men. France thereupon acknowledges the independence of America and negotiates an alliance.

1778 On 7th April the Duke of Richmond proposes to make peace, and recall the English troops the better to face France; the aged Chatham, rising to answer, suffers a stroke and dies on 11th May. In India Warren Hastings takes Chandernagore and Pondicherry from the French.

1779 The war in America languishes while England's attention is distracted and the American States are bankrupt; Washington's army lies in great distress at Valley Forge. Spain now declares war. Paul Jones, sailing with an American commission, inflicts serious damage on British commerce and in September intercepts a Baltic convoy, defeats the escorting squadron, and sails the English merchantmen to Holland. In July Spain lays siege to Gibraltar.

1780 Denmark, Russia, Sweden and Holland join in an "armed neutrality" against Britain, and shortly afterwards Holland joins the war against her. Following the passage of the Catholic Relief Bill (passed in 1778 to grant rights of greater freedom of worship by Catholics in England), "No Popery" riots break out in Scotland and England under the weak-headed Lord George Gordon, second son of the Duke of Gordon; London is the scene of four days' pillage and rioting before the troops can be assembled. 200 rioters are shot dead and 250 wounded. Admiral Rodney, after a great victory off Cape St. Vincent, brings relief to Gibraltar, although the siege is not finally lifted until 1782.

1781 Following a serious defeat of the English at the Cowpens in January, Cornwallis achieves a partial redemption by a victory at Guildford in March, and then goes on to drive the enemy forces out of North Carolina. However, despite limited successes by Lord Rawdon at Camden and elsewhere, limited resources in a hostile country force Cornwallis to fall back and, closely blockaded by a French fleet behind him, he is defeated and forced to surrender to Washington at Yorktown on 18th October. Thus the war is virtually over. The Dutch are driven out of India and Eyre Coote defeats Hyder Ali at Porto Novo.

1782 Spain and France make a supreme effort to capture Gibraltar using 40,000 troops with 186 guns, and 47 ships of the line and 212 floating batteries. The 7,000 men of the garrison under the veteran governor Eliott withstand the attack on 9th September, destroy the entire force of floating batteries, and inflict 2,000 casualties for the loss of but ninety men, and the seaborne blockade is raised. In the West Indies France captures everything but Jamaica, Barbados and Antigua. An expedition against the Dutch at the Cape of Good Hope fails, and Minorca is surrendered to the Spanish (more on account of disease than war).

On 20th March Lord North resigns, and the Marquess of Rockingham again becomes prime minister. The legislative independence of Ireland is secured by the repeal of the 1719 Act; 60,000 Revenue officers are disfranchised, and Burke's proposal for economic reform is carried. Rodney defeats the French fleet in the West Indies by cutting the enemy line of ships in two, and captures the great ship *Ville de Paris*. This victory and the failure to capture Gibraltar prompt France and Spain to seek peace, but the death of Rockingham causes delay. The administration is now led by the 2nd Earl of Shelburne, a Whig, with William Pitt, son of the Earl of Chatham, as chancellor of the exchequer.

1783 Peace is made with America by the Shelburne ministry, and on 20th January is signed the Treaty of Versailles bringing peace between Britain, France and Spain. Although Britain emerged from the war with a diminished empire and an augmented National Debt, her fleet was supreme and her hold on India strengthened, while the war had left America, France and Spain bankrupt. Peace is also made with Holland. A coalition ministry is formed by Fox and North under the premiership of the 3rd Duke of Portland. Fox attempts to introduce his India Bill, but this is defeated in the Lords, and the ministry is dismissed. William Pitt (the Younger) leads a Tory administration.

1784 Parliament is dissolved, and the elections return Pitt with an immense majority; thus the king finally triumphs over the Whigs. Pitt carries through sweeping economic reforms and establishes a sinking fund. His India Bill passes through parliament and remains in force until 1858.

1785 Pitt tries to reform parliament but the bill

1786   is thrown out; his ministry's attempts to carry out reforms in Ireland are also abandoned.

1786   Warren Hastings, who had returned from India in 1785, is accused by Burke and Sheridan who move that he should be impeached on numerous charges before the Lords (these include the Rohilla War, the Benares case, the outrage upon the Begums of Oude, the Mahratta War, and the receipt of presents). Although the trial before the Lords lasts for six years, Hastings is impeached in 1788.

1788   The slave trade agitation begins, progressively attaining its objects in 1807 and 1833. King George III becomes insane and Fox maintains (in opposition to Pitt) that the Prince of Wales can assume the regency by constitutional right.

1789   The king recovers his mental health. In France the age-old and continuing repression of the peasants finally results in the French Revolution; on 5th May the States-General (three chambers representing the *noblesse*, the church and the *Tiers État* – the common people) are summoned for the first time since 1614. The people call for equal representation at a National Assembly, but the king calls in troops to overawe the members and Paris rises in revolt. The Bastille is stormed on 14th July. The French king and queen are brought to Paris.

1791   The French king and queen attempt to escape from the country, but are brought back to Paris in June.

1792   The French Legislative Assembly, which had succeeded the National Assembly, declares the nobles traitors, conscripts an army, and on 20th April declares war on Austria and Prussia. A second revolution follows an invasion of France by Austria and Prussia; Louis XVI is deposed and a republic is proclaimed.

1793   England, Holland and Spain join Austria and Prussia in the First Coalition against France. The French revolutionary "Convention" guillotines Louis XVI and declares war on England. Pitt passes an Alien Act to impose control of all foreigners in the country, granting rights for their deportation if necessary. All trading with France is forbidden. France defies all Europe on land, but is beaten by the English at sea.

1794   On 1st June Howe severely beats the French fleet off Brest, but the new Republic, with over a million men under arms, drives the

Admiral Lord Horatio Nelson (1st Viscount Nelson), 1758–1805

British out of Holland and invades Germany.

1795   Spain and Prussia are forced into alliance with France, followed shortly afterwards by Holland. A British expedition to assist royalist insurgents in Brittany fails. England takes the Cape of Good Hope, Ceylon, Java and the Malaccas from the Dutch.

1796   French attempts to invade Britain fail with their expeditions to Bantry Bay in Ireland, and to Pembrokeshire in Wales.

1797   On 14th February an English fleet of eighteen ships under Admirals Jervis and Parker, and Commodore Horatio Nelson, defeats a Spanish fleet of twenty-seven ships of the line and ten frigates off Cape St. Vincent, a victory which prevents the Spanish fleet from joining the French in Brest and the Dutch in the Texel. On 11th October Admiral Duncan destroys a Dutch fleet off Camperdown as it is sailing for an attempted invasion of Ireland. Trinidad is taken from Spain, and thousands of merchant ships are taken as prizes by English fleets. The Bank of England suspends cash payments. Conditions in the Royal Navy lead to mutinies at Spithead and at the Nore.

1798   An abortive rising takes place in Ireland but the insurgents are dispersed at Vinegar

Hill by Lake. In August, following visits to France by Wolfe Tone, Lord Edward Fitzgerald and Arthur O'Connor, French troops land in Mayo but, although they gain a small success at "the Castlebar Races", are soon forced to surrender. Napoleon captures Malta and lands in Egypt at Alexandria on 1st July. Nelson's fleet finds the French at anchor in Aboukir Bay and, in the Battle of the Nile on 1st–2nd August, captures or destroys the entire enemy fleet of line-of-battle ships. By this victory France is rendered powerless at sea, India is saved, Napoleon is isolated in Egypt, the hopes of Europe revived and a new coalition against France is encouraged.

1799   The coalition against France is formed between England, Austria and Russia, but the French under Marshal Masséna defeat the allies at Zurich. Napoleon invades Syria from Egypt; Acre is successfully defended by the Turks assisted by Sir Sydney Smith. Napoleon returns to France, overthrows the "Directory" and assumes office as First Consul. The French defeat the Austrians at Hohenlinden. In India the English, under General Harris, storm Hyder Ali's capital, Seringapatam; Sir Arthur Wellesley defeats the Mahrattas at Assaye and Argaum.

1800   Napoleon defeats the Austrians at Marengo on 14th June. The Act of Union between England and Ireland is passed. The Northern League is revived by Russia, Denmark and Sweden, who thereby resist the right to search ships at sea claimed by England.

1801   Austria makes peace with France at Lunéville on 9th February, thereby leaving Britain to fight on single-handed; she had however recaptured Malta and destroyed the French squadron sent to its relief. When George III refuses to grant Catholic relief, William Pitt resigns. Henry Addington, a Tory and later 1st Viscount Sidmouth, becomes prime minister on 1st March. In Egypt, General Abercrombie defeats a French army at Aboukir (but is killed); Cairo is recaptured and the French troops are returned to France in English ships. On 2nd April Admiral Parker, with Nelson second in command, sails into Copenhagen harbour and destroys the Danish fleet; Denmark sues for peace and the Northern League is broken up. Nelson then sails to Revel, and Russia, thus threatened, also makes peace and restores all captured ships and prisoners on 17th June.

Nelson's flagship, H.M.S. Victory

1802   Both England and France are ready to negotiate peace; England can do nothing on land and France nothing at sea. The Peace of Amiens, signed on 28th March, ends the war.

1803   Notwithstanding the Peace of Amiens, Napoleon annexes Elba and Piedmont, and occupies Parma and Placentia; because of these ambitions, England refuses to give up Malta, as required by the Treaty, and war is again declared on 18th May. Napoleon invades Hanover.

1804   A French army of over 100,000 veteran troops is assembled at Boulogne as preparations are made for the invasion of Britain. Such a crisis demands the return of Pitt; Addington resigns on 10th May. Pitt's ministry abandons Catholic emancipation. Napoleon is proclaimed Emperor.

1805   Pitt works for a new coalition against France, and is immediately assisted by Russia; when Napoleon has himself crowned King of Italy and annexes Genoa and Lucca, Austria and Sweden join the allied coalition. Napoleon promptly abandons his plans to invade Britain and marches his army against Austria, completely outmanoeuvring the opposing force of 30,000 men under Mack on 19th October and forcing their surrender at Ulm – thereby opening the road to Vienna. Two days later Nelson and Collingwood with thirty-one ships encounter Villeneuve and Gravina with forty-one ships off Trafalgar. A great victory is won by Nelson, twenty of the enemy ships are sunk or taken, Villeneuve captured and Gravina killed, and France and Spain effectively deprived of their sea power for the remainder of the war. Nelson is struck by a musket ball and dies in the moment of victory. Napoleon occupies Munich and Vienna without firing a shot, and on 2nd December ruinously defeats the Emperors of Austria and Russia at the Battle of Austerlitz. Austria makes peace at Presburg, ceding the Tyrol and Venice to France.

1806   William Pitt dies on 23rd January and is buried in Westminster Abbey. He is succeeded by the 1st Baron Grenville, son of George Grenville (prime minister 1763–1765), while Charles Fox becomes foreign minister. Prussia, which had held aloof from the coalition against France, now reaps the fruits of her selfishness and is ruthlessly crushed by Napoleon in October in the Battles of Jena and Auerstadt. He issues the Berlin Decrees, declaring a total blockade of all British ports, a ban on all trade with England and threatening to take in prize any vessel caught attempting to run the blockade.

1807   The Grenville ministry passes an Act for the abolition of slavery. In the continuing war between France and Russia, Napoleon narrowly escapes defeat at Eylau, but in the fearful battle of Friedland he gains a crushing victory, resulting in the Peace of Tilsit signed on 25th June. In answer to the Berlin Decrees, the British government issues the "Orders in Council" prohibiting all trade (even by neutral nations) with France and ports in French possession; unlike the Berlin Decrees, this was no empty threat owing to Britain's command of the sea. Following quarrels over the Catholic question, the Grenville ministry is dismissed and an anti-Catholic ministry under the Duke of Portland is formed. George Canning becomes foreign secretary. Secret clauses in the Peace of Tilsit (involving the surrender of the Danish fleet to Napoleon) are suspected by Canning, and an English army and fleet descends on Copenhagen which is bombarded from land and sea, and shamefully plundered after capitulation; thereafter the entire Danish fleet, with all store vessels, are taken captive to England. Secure in the East, Napoleon invades Spain, and a French army under Marshal Junot enters Lisbon on 30th November; thus starts the Peninsular War.

1808   The Bourbons of Spain, Charles IV and his son Ferdinand, are forced to abdicate in favour of Napoleon's brother Joseph. On 1st March a new French army under Marshal Murat enters Spain and occupies Madrid on the 23rd. The Spanish rise and everywhere attack the invaders; an army of 23,000 troops under Dupont is forced to surrender at Baylen. Joseph is deposed and the French retreat behind the Ebro, leaving Junot with 30,000 men in Portugal. Sir Arthur Wellesley lands with an army from England at the mouth of the Mondego on 1st August, joins a division of 12,000 men under General Spenser, and defeats the French at Rolica and Vimiero. Junot signs the Convention of Cintra by which he agrees to evacuate Portugal. Wellesley returns home and is made secretary for Ireland. Napoleon however invades Spain with a large army, defeats the Spanish armies and enters Madrid in triumph on 4th December. Meanwhile Sir John Moore takes command of the British troops at Lisbon and advances on Salamanca, but, hearing of Napoleon's threat to his rear with 40,000 men, marches north to Benevente at the end of December.

1809   On 1st January Napoleon is recalled to France and leaves Marshal Soult in command to press the pursuit of Moore's army which reaches Corunna on 11th January with 14,000 men. While awaiting the arrival of transports to evacuate his army, Moore gives battle and wins a great victory on the

16th, but is killed at the moment of victory. His troops are then embarked and brought home, leaving Joseph Bonaparte king of Spain and 300,000 of Napoleon's troops under the best French generals supreme in the Peninsula. The war between France and Austria is renewed; Napoleon repairs a defeat at Aspern by a victory at Wagram on 5th-6th July. Peace is again made with Austria at Vienna, leaving Napoleon free to return to Spain. Meanwhile Wellesley has returned to Portugal, entering the Tagus on 22nd April. He crosses the Douro, drives Soult out of Oporto, and defeats Victor in the Battle of Talavera on 28th May, but is then forced to retreat. His victories have nevertheless destroyed the prestige of his enemies and he is now made Baron Douro of Wellesley and created Viscount Wellington of Talavera. Nearer home, an expedition under Lord Chatham (William Pitt's elder brother) is sent against Antwerp but fails to progress beyond Walcheren and returns home with the loss of 2,000 men. Canning and Lord Castlereagh (secretary at war) quarrel over the failure, and this leads to the resignation of the ministry. Spencer Perceval thereupon becomes Tory prime minister, and Wellington henceforth receives improved support from home through the appointment of his brother, the Marquis of Wellesley, as foreign secretary.

1810 Wellington retires upon Lisbon where his engineers had been preparing a triple line of fortifications – the Lines of Torres Vedras, but turns once against Marshal Masséna, beating him heavily at Busaco. On 8th October Wellington reaches the safety of the Lines. At home George III becomes permanently insane and on 11th February the following year the Prince of Wales is made regent.

1811 Marshal Masséna, unable to support his army, retires from Torres Vedras in March, and, after losing 30,000 men, abandons Portugal, pursued by Wellington. Wellington defeats Masséna at Fuentes d'Onoro on 5th May and captures Almeida. Napoleon takes over command from Masséna who goes into retirement. Marshal Soult is defeated by General Beresford on 16th May at the Battle of Albuera – the bloodiest battle of the war – which was saved by the famous bayonet charge of the British infantry. Wellington invests Badajoz, but retreats northwards on the advance of Soult in force.

1812 Wellington storms Ciudad Rodrigo on 12th January, a victory disgraced by the excesses of the troops. (Wellington is created an earl, and lavishly honoured by Spain and Portugal.) He returns to Badajoz and invests it on 17th March, and on 6th April storms the town. Again, maddened by the conditions of slaughter, the troops wreak their passions on the wretched inhabitants. At home, the prime minister, Spencer Perceval, is murdered in the lobby of the House on 11th May, and is succeeded by the 2nd Earl of Liverpool; his ministry included Robert Peel and Lord Palmerston. Napoleon resolves to invade Russia, crosses the Vistula with 450,000 men, and after fighting the Battle of Borodino, enters Moscow. Enormous casualties and desperate privations force the French to retreat, starting back with 100,000 men on 19th October; these are reduced to 65,000 by 9th November when he reaches Smolensk – when the Russian winter sets in. Harried relentlessly by Cossacks, only 20,000 French troops recross the Vistula. In the Peninsula Wellington defeats Marmont at the Battle of Salamanca on 22nd July, enters Madrid on 12th August, but fails in the siege of Burgos, successfully entering winter quarters in the face of increasing French strength. War breaks out between Britain and the American States over the terms of the 1807 "Orders in Council"; this maritime conflict lasts until 1814.

1813 Napoleon defeats the Prussians at Lutzen and Bautzen and then grants an armistice; he goes on to defeat the Austrians at Dresden on 26th-27th August, but is heavily beaten by the united allied armies on 16th-19th October at Leipzig and forced to cross the Rhine. Wellington utterly defeats Joseph Bonaparte on 21st June at Vittoria, storms San Sebastian on 8th September after a costly siege lasting seventy-three days.

1814 A small British force is sent to Holland but fails in an attempt to take Bergen-op-Zoom. Wellington, who has crossed the Pyrenees into France, defeats Marshal Soult at Orthez on 27th February (and is slightly wounded), and again shortly afterwards at Toulouse, the last battle of the war. On 12th April Napoleon abdicates, the allies enter Paris and he is banished to Elba. The restored Bourbon, Louis XVIII, signs the First Peace of Paris with the allies on 20th May; by this treaty, at which Wellington represents England, Great Britain restores to France the colonies (except Mauritius) taken from her; France is allowed to retain most of the art treasures which Napoleon had despoiled; Switzerland is declared independent, as are the various states of Germany (albeit united by a federal tie).

1815 Parliament passes the 1815 Corn Law which prohibits the import of corn into England until the price of wheat should reach eighty shillings a quarter; this was intended as much as a protection for the nation's farming industry as to curb the drain on the economy (for the wars had increased the National Debt to almost £300 million). Napoleon, having escaped from Elba, returns to Paris, raises an army of 200,000 men and places himself at their head on 12th June. Marshal Ney attacks Wellington at Quatre Bras on 16th June but the battle is indecisive. Napoleon attacks Blücher at Ligny at the same time, and after a battle in which 30,000 men die, Blücher is forced to give way – but disengages skilfully. Wellington, expecting to be joined by Blücher, falls back on the village of Waterloo with 70,000 men, including 12,000 cavalry, and 156 guns. Against him Napoleon has 72,000 men, including 15,000 cavalry, and 240 guns. The greatest battle of the age is fought near Mont St. Jean on 18th June. Between mid-morning and sunset, some 45,000 men fall dead or seriously wounded as the Emperor's brilliant army is battered to pieces against the stoic British infantry. Wellington's last and greatest victory is confirmed by the arrival of the Prussians at sunset. Napoleon flees to Paris but on 3rd July the city surrenders; he abdicates and is sent to St. Helena where he dies in 1821. Russia, Austria, Prussia, France and Spain join in the Holy Alliance, directed against popular movements. The Second Treaty of Paris restores peace to Europe, and at the negotiations Great Britain demands the abolition of slavery. (In the previous two years Sweden and Holland had yielded to British pressure, while Portugal had agreed to abolish the trade north of the equator.) France now agrees to maintain the abolition, but Spain steadfastly refuses.

1816 Lord Exmouth, commanding the English fleet in the Mediterranean, is charged with the reduction of pirate and slaving bases in the Barbary States on the north coast of Africa. He demands an end of piracy and slaving by the Beys of Tunis and Tripoli, and sails against the Dey of Algiers, entering the harbour and destroying the town. The Dey accedes to all demands and Exmouth secures the Mediterranean for peaceful commerce. In Britain the harvest fails, and the price of bread rises owing to the operation of the 1815 Corn Law. Unemployment figures, already high, are swelled by the disbanded armies; farms are burnt by discontented labourers, and a huge mob meets in December in Spa Fields and marches on the City – a crisis averted only by the firmness of the lord mayor and the City constables.

1817 The Habeas Corpus Act is suspended in February for the last time in England. The Seditious Meetings Bill is passed, making death the penalty for refusing to disperse when called upon. Fortunately the 1817 harvest is abundant, conditions improve and trade increases rapidly. Savings' Banks are established to encourage thrift among the workers. With the return of prosperity, national discontent subsides.

1818 Notwithstanding a national economic recovery, industrial strife increases. The first organised strike (in which the strikers are regularly maintained by those still at work) takes place among Lancashire cotton-spinners and lasts from July to September. It is ended by a compromise in which the strikers gain their principal demands.

1819 The depression returns, workers in the coal mines and in the weaving industry are among the worst sufferers – with long working hours, cruel conditions and wholly inadequate earnings. While parliamentary reform is being planned, a huge assembly meets at St. Peter's Fields in Manchester. The magistrates become alarmed and the yeomanry are ordered to the spot; by sheer mismanagement, the troops are allowed to charge the crowd killing many people; others are arrested and imprisoned for a seditious meeting. This, the "Peterloo massacre", prompts Castlereagh and Lord Sidmouth to introduce the Six Acts – further strengthening the magistrates and generally increasing repression by the authorities.

1820 Blind, deaf, insane and unaware of the discontent and oppression surrounding him, King George III dies of senility on 29th January at Windsor, aged 81 years and 239 days. He is succeeded by his eldest son, George Augustus Frederick.

THE AGE OF REFORM

THE REIGN OF GEORGE IV, 1820–1830

1820	George IV, eldest son of George III and Charlotte Sophia (1744–1818), succeeds to the throne, aged 57, on 29th January. His wife and first cousin, Caroline Amelia Elizabeth, dies the following year after suffering humiliation at the king's coronation. The Cato Street conspiracy is uncovered (in which a body of anarchists led by an ex-officer, Arthur Thistlewood, had planned to assassinate the entire cabinet) and the conspirators are arrested, and executed on 1st May.
1821	A bill for the entire abolition of Catholic disabilities passes through the Commons, but is defeated in the Lords. The funeral of the queen is the occasion of a riot in London in which a number of people are killed by the military escort. Great distress is manifest among agricultural workers and is caused by ever-decreasing prices for wheat, following over-production after the 1815 Corn Law and the gluts of 1817 and 1820. This encourages the conservative class of landlords and tenants to join the radicals in pressing for sweeping reforms.
1822	Lord Londonderry (Castlereagh), one of the chief opponents of reform, commits suicide on 12th August); his place is taken by his old rival, George Canning.
1823	The first major reform of the Criminal Code is undertaken by Sir Robert Peel, who reduces by one hundred the number of crimes punishable by death. This is almost the first time that a Tory ministry passes a popular measure. The Navigation Act (which had been passed in 1651 and which, by placing the world's trade in English ships, had been a leading cause of England's supremacy at sea) is partially repealed, and various other acts are passed to encourage free trade. Daniel O'Connell founds the Catholic Association. Canning recognises the independence of the Spanish colonies.
1824	Certain acts prejudicial to the Spitalfields silk weavers (by which the law required the same wages to be paid to skilled and unskilled workers, thereby discouraging the development of efficient machinery) are repealed. The Combination Acts, which had made it illegal for workers to meet to discuss their wages, are also repealed.
1825	The First Burmese War results in the annexation of Assam, Arakan and Tenasserim by

the East India Company. At home, a prosecution of O'Connell for treasonable language has to be abandoned, and an Act for the supression of the Catholic Association is passed, but easily evaded. Increasing prosperity leads to widespread investment in foreign mines, shipbuilding and other industries; this continues until, in April, the drain on small banks (caused by an unchecked issue of small banknotes and a calling-up by numerous companies of their unpaid shares) leads to commercial panic. An act is then passed to prevent the issue of small banknotes. The Stockton and Darlington railway is opened – this is the first practical application of steam locomotive power and marks the first step in the massive development of railways in Britain.

1827	Lord Liverpool is struck down with apoplexy having been nominal prime minister since 1812. He resigns and his place is taken by George Canning, on 10th April, who forms an alliance with Russia and France. An English, French and Russian naval squadron, under Admiral Sir Edward Codrington, destroys a Turkish fleet at Navarino on 18th October thereby preventing an attack upon the Ionian Islands. Canning dies on 8th August, and is succeeded by his follower, John Robinson (now Lord Goderich).
1828	Lord Goderich resigns on 8th January, and is followed as prime minister by the Duke of Wellington (who had taken his seat in the Lords on 28th June 1814 as Viscount, Earl, Marquess and Duke). The Test and Corporation Acts are repealed by Lord John Russell.
1829	The Duke of Wellington's Tory ministry passes the Catholic Relief Bill, but at the same time the freehold qualification in Ireland is raised from forty shillings to ten pounds.
1830	The unpopular king, George IV, dies suddenly on 26th June following rupture of the stomach blood vessels, and of alcoholic cirrhosis. He is succeeded by his elder surviving brother, William Henry (his only child, Princess Charlotte, having died in child-birth on 6th November 1817).

THE REIGN OF WILLIAM IV, 1830–1837

1830	Wellington, who had favoured a strong Turkey facing Russia and spoken in opposition to the fleet action at Navarino in 1827, resigns as prime minister in the face of

popular support for Greece in her struggle against Turkey. Following a revolution in Paris, Louise Philippe becomes king in place of Charles X. Belgium secures its independence. The 2nd Earl Grey becomes prime minister of a Whig administration, opposed by Sir Robert Peel. The government's first task is to restore order in the Southern counties which are being terrorised by rioting farm workers; they are crushed and more than a thousand rioters are tried by a special commission.

1831   The first Reform Bill, seeking a sweeping reform of the franchise and representation, is introduced by Lord John Russell but fails in passage, and parliament is dissolved. In the new parliament the Whigs are returned with an immense majority. A second Reform Bill passes through the Commons but is rejected in the Lords. Popular indignation is accompanied by dangerous rioting, especially in Bristol. The third Reform Bill is introduced.

1832   The constant opposition and resistance to reform by the Lords prompts Earl Grey to resign, but he is recalled by Wellington who fails to form a ministry. The opposition peers yield to the intervention by the king and the Reform Bill passes through the Lords.

1833   The reformed parliament meets. O'Connell, "the uncrowned king of Ireland", still agitates for the repeal of the Union; a strong Coercion Act is consequently passed, followed by a Church Act which severely reduces the number of Irish archbishoprics and bishoprics. Owing to the inability of the Irish Protestant clergy to collect tithes from the Catholics, the government assumes responsibility for collection and pays £1,000,000 of arrears. On 14th May Edward Stanley, secretary for the colonies, introduces his Act for the Abolition of Slavery, by which all slaves in British colonies would be nominally free after 1st August 1834, and £20,000,000 would be paid in compensation to the planters. The first education grant is made, and Althorpe's Factory Act passed, limiting the employment of children in factories.

1834   The Poor Law Amendment Act is passed, forcing mothers to support their illegitimate children and greatly increasing the number of workhouses. Grey's ministry resigns on the question of renewing the Coercion Act for Ireland. The 3rd Viscount Melbourne becomes prime minister on 16th

July, but is dismissed in November. Sir Robert Peel leads a Tory ministry, but when Lord John Russell carries a bill to apply the Irish church revenues to lay purposes, the Peel administration resigns on 8th April 1835.

(1835–1841. The administration of Lord Melbourne. Lord John Russell is home secretary, and Lord Palmerston foreign secretary.)

1835   Lord John Russell introduces the Municipal Reform Act, by which each council is elected by ratepayers of three years' standing, one-third to retire annually. It becomes law in September, and is extended to Ireland in 1840.

1836   The Reform of the Marriage Law is passed, enabling persons to be married in chapel as well as church, after due notice given to a registrar. The Tithe Commutation Act is passed. "Taxes on knowledge", that is, the Newspaper Tax and Paper Excise, are reduced.

1837   William IV dies on 20th June, aged 71, at Windsor of pleuro-pneumonia and alcoholic cirrhosis. As Salic law does not permit the Hanover crown to pass to a female, it passes to his brother, Ernest, Duke of Cumberland. The English crown passes to his niece, Alexandrina Victoria, only child of Edward, Duke of Kent and Stratheam, fourth son of George III.

THE REIGN OF VICTORIA, 1837–1901

1837   Victoria comes to the throne at the age of 18 years and 27 days. In Canada a revolt by the French population against English "packing" of parliamentary seats is suppressed. Popular protest against the provisions of the Poor Law is manifest in two distinct forms, Socialism (whose aim had been to give comfort to the poor man) and Chartism (to give the poor man political power). The points demanded by the "Chartists" are embodied in the People's Charter.

1838   The Anti-Corn-Law League, led by Richard Cobden and John Bright, is established.

1839   Following the troubles in Canada, Lord Durham is sent out as governor, but his despotic measures rouse a storm in Parliament. However Melbourne is not strong enough to support his subordinate and, realising that faced with so many pressing problems his ministry cannot continue to exist simply on sufferance, he resigns. Peel is invited to form a government, but when his insistence that the queen should part with the influential Whig ladies of the bedchamber is refused by the queen, the Melbourne cabinet returns.

1840   Rowland Hill's postal reform bill, passed in 1839, comes into force in 1840, introducing a prepaid charge of one penny (by postage stamp), instead of fourpence gathered on delivery. Victoria marries her first cousin, Prince Albert (Francis Albert Augustus Charles Emanuel) of Saxe-Coburg-Gotha on 10th February. The First Chinese War results from the British insistence on introducing opium into China (contrary to Chinese laws); Hong Kong is occupied in 1841 and ceded in 1842.

1841   Upper and Lower Canada are united. The first Afghan War breaks out when the Afghans rise against the British at Kabul and massacre almost the entire garrison; one man out of 15,000 reaches Jellalabad. At home, Lord Melbourne resigns in August. Sir Robert Peel leads a Tory reform administration which survives until 1846.

1842   Sir Robert Sale defends Jellalabad against Akbar Khan from January until relieved by General Pollock who had forced the Khyber Pass. The British are finally victorious in Afghanistan and evacuate the country having restored Dost Mohammed as ruler. Peel imposes an income tax of 7d. for three years, but remits some duties thereby initiating Free Trade.

1843   Despite exemption from Peel's income tax, Ireland is wracked by poverty; demands for the repeal of the Union result in the arrest of Daniel O'Connell and his conviction for sedition. A great schism in Scotland leads to the establishment of the Free Kirk of Scotland. In India Sir Charles Napier annexes Scinde.

1845   The Irish potato crop fails causing a severe famine. Peel proposes a progressive abolition of the Corn Duties but receives no Cabinet support; he therefore resigns. However Lord John Russell fails to form a ministry and Peel returns to the premiership.

1846   Peel succeeds in passing a bill for the progressive abolition of the Corn Laws, to be completed by 1849. British victories in India at Moodkee and Ferozeshah in 1845 had been the first stages of the First Sikh War for the annexation of the Punjab. Further victories at Aliwal and Sobraon in 1846 bring this war to an end. A Coercion Bill for Ireland is defeated in parliament, and Peel resigns.

(1846–1852. Lord John Russell's Whig administration.)

1846   A further potato failure in Ireland causes an appalling famine, and almost a quarter-million Irish die from sheer starvation.

1847   Growth of industry demands a rapid growth of the railway system, in which investment and speculation reaches new heights. No less than £700 million is sought in loans; then comes a sudden crash and very few banks survive the run made on them.

1848   A revolution in France, which removes Louis Philippe from the throne, encourages Irish nationalists towards revolt. Fresh coercive laws have to be passed to meet the crisis. The Second Sikh War opens in India.

1849   A savage faction fight breaks out on 12th July at Dolly's Brae in County Down, Ireland, but later in the year Queen Victoria pays a visit to the country and is received with enthusiastic loyalty – after which a period of relative tranquillity ensues. General Gough retrieves a partial defeat in India at Chillianwalla by his victory at Gujerat on 21st February. The entire Punjab is annexed and the Second Sikh War ends. The Navigation Act of 1651 (see also 1823) is totally repealed.

1850   Sir Robert Peel dies on 2nd July, aged 72, after a fall from his horse.

1851   The Great Exhibition opens at the Crystal Palace. Following the re-establishment by Pope Pius IX of Roman Catholic dioceses in 1850, the government secures the passage of The Ecclesiastical Titles Bill which forbids the assumption of territorial titles by Roman Catholic prelates. Lord Palmerston is dismissed as foreign secretary after expressing approval of the *coup d'état* by which Napoleon made himself President for life.

1852   Palmerston defeats the government on a bill to strengthen the country against France, and Lord John Russell resigns in February; the 14th Earl of Derby (previously Edward Stanley) becomes prime minister. The capture of Rangoon and the annexation of Pegu ends the Second Burmese War. The Duke of Wellington dies at Walmer Castle on 14th September, aged 83. Napoleon III is proclaimed emperor. The government is defeated over Disraeli's free trade budget in December and resigns. The 4th Earl of Aberdeen (previously George Gordon) becomes prime minister, leading an essentially Peelite administration.

1853   War breaks out between Turkey and Russia when Turkish troops under Omar Pasha cross the Danube, and the Russian Black Sea fleet attacks and destroys the Turkish squadron at Sinope on 30th November.

1854   An ultimatum is sent by Britain to Russia but is contemptuously rejected by the Tsar. Rather than cripple Russian trade by blockade it is decided to destroy the great arsenal and dockyard of Sebastopol in the Crimea and an Anglo-French army (under Lord Raglan and Marshal St. Arnaud) lands north of the port on 13th September. The British win a great victory on the River Alma on 20th September, a partial victory at Balaclava on 25th October, and undisputed ascendancy at Inkerman on 4th November.

1855   The Russian winter brings appalling hardship on the allied armies in the Crimea, made worse by disease and inadequate hospital facilities. Severe criticism is levelled at Aberdeen's government and its mismanagement of the Crimean operations, and the administration resigns on 5th February; so begins the first ministry of the 3rd Viscount Palmerston. Tsar Nicholas dies and in September the French capture the Malakoff redoubt overlooking Sebastopol; after a year's siege the port is taken.

1856   Peace is made with Russia, and the results of the War are summarised in the Declaration of Paris. Oude is annexed and this virtually completes the occupation of India. The Second Chinese War breaks out, ostensibly over the seizure of a smuggling ship flying the British flag. Canton is taken, and by 1858 treaty ports are opened for European trade.

1857   Continuing unrest in India is fanned by the alleged use of rifle ammunition greased with the fat of pigs and cows (the one hateful to Mohammedans, the other sacred to Hindoos). In May a serious revolt takes place at Meerut, near Delhi; the *3rd Native Cavalry* mutiny and march on Delhi. The Mahratta Nan Sahib invests Cawnpore and on 27th June orders the massacre of English women and children. The British relief force under Major Nicholson retakes Delhi by storm on 20th September, and Lucknow is relieved by three regiments under Colonel Neill on 25th September. "Clemency Canning", the governor-general, tries to check the ferocious vengeance of the British.

1858   Sir Colin Campbell eventually suppresses the Indian Mutiny. Following an attempt to murder Napoleon III in France, Lord Palmerston introduces, but fails to pass a

Queen Victoria

bill to punish similar conspiracies (the plot had been hatched in London). Palmerston resigns, and Lord Derby becomes prime minister for the second time. The property qualifications imposed on members of parliament in 1710 are abolished. Following the Indian Mutiny, the government of India is transferred from the East India Company to the crown.

1859   Disraeli, chancellor of the exchequer, introduces a bill to extend the franchise, but it fails in passage and Lord Derby's ministry resigns.

(1859-1865. Lord Palmerston's second administration.)

1860   A Free Trade Treaty is negotiated with France by Richard Cobden. The Lords interfere in a finance bill for the last time on the occasion of a proposed repeal of the paper duty put forward by Palmerston. The Second Maori War breaks out in New Zealand and continues until 1872.

1861   In America, South Carolina repudiates the authority of the Union; Civil War breaks out between the Northern States ("free" and strong in manufacturing industries) and the South (slave-owning and largely agricultural). Being politically commited against slave-owning, Britain, while maintaining a formal neutrality, is steadfastly sympathetic with the North, and in thus being deprived of the cotton imports from the South, suffers a considerable industrial crisis in the cotton-working industry of Lan-

1864 — cashire. The Prince Consort dies on 11th December, aged 41.

1864 — The American Civil War ends in victory for the Northern States. The loss of 800,000 jobs in the Lancashire cotton industry prompts a rapid development of cotton-growing in India. Lord Palmerston dies on 18th October 1865 in office. Lord John Russell becomes prime minister for the second time, with William Gladstone as chancellor of the exchequer.

1866 — In March attempts to introduce a reform bill are opposed by a new Liberal party – the self-styled "Adullamites" – and Lord Russell resigns. For the third time Lord Derby heads a Tory government. The Austro-Prussian war breaks out, lasts six weeks and results in a total victory for Prussia.

1867 — Disraeli introduces the Second Reform Bill, a substantially Tory paper; rather than face further rebuffs, he accepts widespread Liberal manipulations and alteration, and it is finally passed as a notably democratic measure. Fenian outrages are committed in England, and there is an abortive rising in Ireland.

1868 — Lord Derby resigns and Disraeli becomes prime minister on 27th February. Gladstone's bill for the abolition of compulsory church rates is passed. An expedition sent to Abyssinia in 1867 under Sir Robert Napier to secure the release of British subjects imprisoned by King Theodore reaches Magdala in April 1868; the town is stormed without the loss of a British life, and the king commits suicide. Gladstone carries against the government a resolution to dis-establish and dis-endow the Irish church. Disraeli resigns, and the general election returns a Liberal majority. William Gladstone becomes prime minister for the first time.

1869 — Gladstone finally carries the Irish Church Bill. Transportation to the colonies is at last abolished.

1870 — The Irish Land Act, giving facilities for Irish tenants to purchase their holdings, is secured by Gladstone. Also passed is the Elementary Education Act, ordering the formation of school boards to build and manage rate-supported schools where there was no adequate alternative accommodation; it also established the parliamentary grant to such schools. The Franco-Prussian War breaks out in August.

1871 — The purchase of commissions in the Army is abolished, although certain regiments retained the "privilege" for a few more years. Religious tests at the universities of Oxford and Cambridge are abolished. The Ballot Act, proposing secrecy of voting to discourage bribery and intimidation, fails in passage. The war in France ends in victory for Prussia.

1872 — The Ballot Act is carried.

1873 — A Supreme Court is established for the hearing of appeals. Gladstone's Education Bill for Ireland is defeated, but he retains office until the General Election of February 1874.

1874 — The General Election discloses a strong Conservative reaction and Benjamin Disraeli becomes prime minister for the second time. The Ashanti War (in the Gold Coast) is concluded by Sir Garnet Wolseley by the burning of the capital town, Kumasi. The Public Worship Regulation Act is passed.

1876 — An insurrection in Bulgaria is suppressed by Turkey with atrocities which arouse indignation among the British public, and Disraeli loses popularity when he dismisses them with apparent levity. Queen Victoria is proclaimed Empress of India, this title being incorporated in the royal style.

1877 — Russia invades Turkey and the fall of Pleven leaves the road open to Constantinople.

1878 — Lord Beaconsfield (previously Disraeli) orders the British fleet to the Dardanelles and obtains a war vote of £6,000,000. Russia signs a treaty with Turkey at San Stephano, but some of the treaty conditions are unacceptable to Beaconsfield who then orders a large contingent of Indian troops to Malta. Such warlike policies are distasteful to Lord Derby and Lord Caernarvon who now resign; Lord Salisbury becomes foreign minister. Russian designs are once more in evidence in Afghanistan, and an armed mission is sent to check them by occupation of Kabul and Kandahar.

1879 — Cavagnari, the head of the mission to Afghanistan, is murdered, and a fresh invasion of the country follows. In Africa, Dutch settlers (the Boers) in the Transvaal quarrel with the Zulu chiefs; to prevent the native tribes from overrunning the territory, Britain annexes the Transvaal. War breaks out against the Zulus under Cetewayo; the British are badly beaten on 22nd January at Isandhlwana, but the situation is alleviated by the defence of Rorke's Drift and a victory at Ulundi by Lord Chelmsford. Cetewayo is captured and imprisoned.

1880	The nation tires of Beaconsfield's spirited foreign policies and in March he dissolves Parliament. Following the "Midlothian campaign", Gladstone rouses a substantial Liberal vote and his party returns with a majority of 106 seats.
1881	Lord Beaconsfield dies on 19th April, leadership of the Conservatives being assumed by the 3rd Marquess of Salisbury. Gladstone carries The Irish Land Act which establishes a commission to fix rents for fifteen years in advance, thereby effectively reducing them, but continued agitation in Ireland necessitates a fresh Coercion Act. In Africa, the continued annexation of the Transvaal leads to war with the Boers who inflict a severe defeat on British troops under General Colley at Majuba Hill; this leads to the evacuation of the Transvaal. Afghanistan is also evacuated.
1882	Lord Frederick Cavendish, secretary for Ireland, is murdered in Phoenix Park and a more stringent Coercion Act is passed. In Egypt, Arabi Pasha heads a rebellion against the Khedive; an English fleet bombards Alexandria, and a British force under Sir Garnet Wolseley defeats Arabi at Tel-el-Kebir.
1883	A revolt breaks out in the Sudan under the Mahdi, and an Egyptian army under General Hicks, sent to restore order, is cut to pieces.
1884	The franchise is extended to include agricultural labourers. General Gordon is sent to the Sudan to hold Khartoum.
1885	Death of General Gordon as a result of the late arrival of a relief column sent to Khartoum. Gladstone is defeated on the budget and resigns on 12th June. Salisbury returns to the premiership but remains in office for only seven months. The Third Burmese War ends with the deposition of King Theebaw and the annexation of Upper Burma.
1886	Lord Salisbury resigns on 28th January and Gladstone returns for the third time. The Home Rule Bill splits the Liberal party; it provides for an Irish parliament in Dublin without authority over foreign affairs, the army or navy – but proposes that Ireland should contribute to imperial expenses. Gladstone resigns once more on 20th July, and once more Salisbury returns with the aid of the Liberal Unionists.
1887	The year of Queen Victoria's Jubilee.
1888	The Local Government Act is passed giving the people of each county greater control of their own affairs; it is welcomed by all parties.
1889	A Charter granted to the British South Africa Company brings into British imperial influence a tract of land, now named Rhodesia, inhabited by the mild Mashona tribe and the fierce Matabeles.
1893	The Matabeles invade the territory of the Mashona and clash with the Chartered and Imperial police. A punitive expedition is sent in and captures Bulawayo, the capital.
1894	Advancing age compels Gladstone to resign, his place in office (though scarcely in power) is taken by the Liberal 5th Earl of Rosebery.
1895	The Liberal government possesses such a slender majority in the Commons (and in the Lords is such a puny minority) that effective legislation is impossible and parliament is dissolved on 21st June. The election is a triumph for the Conservatives who, with heavy support from the Liberal "Unionists", secure a majority of 150 seats. Lord Salisbury's cabinet includes Joseph Chamberlain, the Duke of Devonshire, Lord Henry James and the Marquis of Lansdowne, all of whom had been followers of Galdstone ten years previously. The Jameson Raid into Transvaal in December.
1897	The year of Queen Victoria's Diamond Jubilee.
1898	After the death of the Mahdi in the Sudan, another despot, the Khalifa had threatened to invade Egypt. General Sir Herbert Kitchener is made Sirdar and entrusted with the restoration of order in the Sudan. In September he inflicts a crushing defeat at the Battle of Omdurman, leaving 27,000 dead or wounded tribesmen. Khartoum is captured and the Khalifa killed soon after.
1899	Bitter discontent in South Africa increases between the Uitlanders (predominantly Anglo-Celtic) and the Boers (predominantly Dutch). The former complained of cruel and discriminatory government by the Boer Raad. In April the British Uitlanders petition for protection from Westminster, and as a result of constant reports of arms being supplied to the Boers (payment for which was made with Transvaal gold – almost exclusively handled by the Boers), an ultimatum is sent by the British cabinet on 8th September. On 3rd October a train shipment of British gold is taken by the Boers, and war is declared at 5 p.m. on Wednesday 11th October. Thus starts the South African War. On 20th October is

fought the indecisive Battle of Talana Hill, a tactical victory but a strategic defeat for the British. Sir George White narrowly escapes disaster in the Battle of Ladysmith. Lord Methuen suffers defeat at the Battle of Magersfontein on 11th December, and General Gatacre at the Battle of Stormberg. General Sir Redvers Buller is defeated in Battle of Colenso on 15th December. Plans are made to send Lord Roberts and Lord Kitchener out to South Africa with 30,000 men.

1900 General Buller's forces are defeated at Spion Kop on 22nd January. On 3rd March Buller finally relieves Ladysmith having lost over 5,000 men – more than a fifth of his army. Kimberley, under siege since the start of the War, is relieved by General French on 15th February. Lord Roberts marches on Bloemfontein and enters the town on 13th March. The siege of Mafeking, commenced on 13th October 1899, contines until 17th May when the defence, under Colonel Baden-Powell, is relieved by Colonel Plumer. Roberts continues his march north and enters Pretoria, the Boer capital, on 5th June. This terminates the first phase of the war, but there now follows a lengthy period of guerilla warfare under various Boer commanders, and a second invasion of Cape Colony by de Wet.

1901 On 22nd January Queen Victoria dies of senility, aged 81 and 243 days, at Osborne in the Isle of Wight. She is succeeded by her elder surviving son, Albert Edward.

THE REIGN OF EDWARD VII, 1901–1910

1901 Edward VII comes to the throne aged 59, the royal style being "By the Grace of God, of the United Kingdom of Great Britain and Ireland and of the British Dominions beyond the Seas, King, Defender of the Faith, Emperor of India." At the time of his accession there is a Conservative government under Lord Salisbury.

1902 Peace is signed at Pretoria on 31st May, ending the South African War. James Balfour becomes prime minister of a Conservative government on 12th July.

1905 Sir Henry Campbell-Bannerman is returned as prime minister of a Liberal government on 5th December.

1906 The Liberal administration loses ground to the Conservatives in the face of the German "menace" – the threat to British naval superiority. The main Liberal policies are Free Trade, Home Rule for Ireland, and Humanitarianism.

1908 Henry Herbert Asquith assumes the premiership a fortnight before Campbell-Bannerman's death on 22nd April. The Liberals adopt a policy of Lords and Commons reform, advocating abolition of the Lords' power of veto over certified Money Bills, a delaying power of only three sessions over other Bills, and a reduction from seven to five years' parliamentary life.

1909 On 25th July a Frenchman, Louis Blériot, completes the first aeroplane crossing of the English Channel, flying from Barraques, near Calais, to Dover.

1910 The Liberals go to the country on their Lords reform policies but are returned with 125 fewer seats. On 6th May Edward VII dies of bronchitis at Buckingham Palace; he is succeeded by his only surviving son, George Frederick Ernest Albert.

THE REIGN OF GEORGE V, 1910–1936

1910 George V succeeds to the throne at the age of 44. He insists on a second appeal to the nation by the Liberals before promising to create a number of Liberal peers necessary to carry through the Parliamentary Bill. The election is held in December, both Liberals and Conservatives being returned with 272 seats – the Liberals remaining in office under Asquith.

1914 Following the assassination of the Archduke Franz Ferdinand at Sarajevo on 28th June, Britain declares war on Germany on 4th August when Germany refuses to guarantee the neutrality of Belgium. The Battle of Mons opens on 23rd August, and the Battle of the Marne on 6th September. From 5th November a state of war exists between Britain and Turkey.

1915 A general attack in March on the Dardenelles by the British fleet fails, principally owing to enemy minefields. British landings commence at Gallipoli on 25th April. Britain declares war on Bulgaria on 15th September.

1916 The Commons pass the first military service bill. The Battle of Verdun opens on 21st February. Easter Rising, and unilateral declaration of Irish independence, April. The Battle of Jutland, 31st May. The Battle of the Somme begins on 1st July. A coalition government is formed in December under the Liberal prime minister David Lloyd-George.

1917	In January Germany announces the start of unrestricted submarine warfare. America declares war on Germany on 6th April. 162 people are killed in the first heavy raid by aeroplanes on London. The Battle of Cambrai opens on 20th November.
1918	On 21st March a heavy German offensive begins on the Western Front, but is halted on 14th June. A British advance opens in Flanders on 18th August. The Hindenburg Line is captured by the Allies during October. An Armistice is signed with Turkey on 30th October. The First World War is ended by the signing of an Armistice with Germany on 11th November. On 14th December Lloyd-George goes to the country and continues to head a coalition government with a substantial Conservative majority (383 Conservatives, 161 Liberals, 73 Labour, 90 other seats); in this election women over thirty were first granted the franchise.
1919	First meeting of the Peace Conference in Paris in January. First non-stop air crossing of the Atlantic by Alcock and Brown on 14th-15th June. Versailles Treaty of Peace signed on 28th June.
1922	The Royal Air Force assumes military control in Iraq thereby assuring the new Service's continued existence. Partition of Ireland into Irish Free State and British province of Ulster. Lloyd-George's Coalition loses Conservative confidence owing to the prime minister's vacillating foreign policy (the lack of firmness during the Chanak Crisis in Turkey almost results in war). The election of 15th November returns the Conservatives with a majority of 75 over all other parties, and Labour overtake the Liberals thereby becoming the official Opposition for the first time. Lloyd-George resigns and Bonar Law becomes prime minister – advocating "tranquillity".
1923	Bonar Law retires owing to illness and dies shortly after. Stanley Baldwin takes his place, facing severe problems of unemployment. Baldwin favours protective tariffs and puts the question to the electorate; the Conservatives are returned on 6th December but with a substantially reduced vote.
1924	The Conservatives inevitably fall to a Labour-Liberal alliance, and Ramsay MacDonald (Labour) becomes premier on 22nd January. He lacks talented ministers and is defeated by the Conservatives and Liberals over the sedition charges brought against a journalist, J. R. Campbell. At the 29th October election the Conservatives win 419, Labour 151; Baldwin again becomes prime minister, remaining until 1929.
1925	The Locarno Pact, a treaty of mutual guarantee, is signed on 16th October between Britain, Belgium, France, Germany and Italy.
1926	The General Strike is called by the Trades Union Congress (T.U.C.) in support of the Miners' Federation, lasting from 4th-12th May; 1,580,000 people are involved and $14\frac{1}{2}$ million working days lost. The Locarno Treaty is ratified on 14th September.
1929	The general election of 30th May returns Labour on its triple policy of world peace, disarmament, and reduction of unemployment. MacDonald again assumes the premiership.
1931	Despite election policies, Labour commits itself to increased expenditure, but unemployment rises rapidly. In the pattern of world trade depression, a crisis follows loss of confidence in the Pound. MacDonald tries to secure economies, including a reduction in unemployment benefits – sternly opposed by the Labour party and T.U.C. The Labour government resigns (24th August) and MacDonald forms a National Government and goes to the polls on 27th October. A National Government (basically Conservative) wins 521 seats, Labour only 52. Ramsay MacDonald remains in office until 1935.
1932	The German July elections return the National Socialists as the strongest party; on 30th January 1933 Adolf Hitler becomes German Chancellor.
1933	Japan leaves the League of Nations when it refuses to recognise the puppet state of Manchukuo on 27th March. Germany withdraws from the League of Nations and the International Disarmament Conference with the determination by the invigilating Powers to maintain their own military superiority.
1934	The German military threat reappears with the Nazi party under Hitler. The recovery of British industry after the Depression is assisted by announcement of limited steps towards re-armament.
1935	Ramsay MacDonald (National Labour) resigns as premier on 7th June and is followed by Baldwin (Conservative) who holds a snap election on 14th November. Labour's policy is to attack the "Means Test" as the qualification for unemploy-

ment assistance. The National Government is returned with a large majority (432 seats, the majority Conservative) over Labour (154 seats). Hitler repudiates the military clauses in the Versailles Peace Treaty on 21st May. Italy declares war on Abyssinia on 3rd October. Further steps are taken to expand British forces.

1936   King George V dies of bronchitis at Sandringham House, Norfolk, on 20th January at the age of 70. He is succeeded by his eldest son, Edward Albert Christian George Andrew Patrick David.

REIGN OF EDWARD VII 1936

1936   Edward VIII succeeds to the throne on 20th January, aged 41. A constitutional crisis follows the king's announcement of his intention to marry a commoner, Mrs. Simpson. He abdicates for himself and his heirs, and is succeeded by his eldest brother Albert Frederick Arthur George on 11th December.

REIGN OF GEORGE VI, 1936–1952

1936   George VI comes to the throne on 11th December, three days before his 41st birthday. In Spain General Franco leads a right-wing revolt against the left-wing Republican government on 18th July.

1937   Neville Chamberlain, chancellor of the exchequer, proposes on 11th February that the government will assume powers to raise loans of up to £400 million during the next five years to support the National Government's re-armament plans. Air power is used devastatingly in the Spanish Civil War. Stanley Baldwin resigns as prime minister on 28th May, and is followed by Neville Chamberlain.

1938   Hitler annexes Austria on 13th March. The Munich Crisis: Chamberlain signs an agreement (on 30th September) with Germany, France and Italy allowing Germany to occupy mainly German Sudeten territories in Czechoslovakia. Chamberlain returns and makes his famous "peace in our time" speech. Nevertheless Britain accelerates her military expansion programmes.

1939   Britain recognises General Franco's administration on 27th March as the legal government of Spain, and Madrid surrenders on 28th March. On 14th March Hitler states that Czechoslovakia has become a German protectorate and on the next day German troops occupy the coun-

try. Italy occupies Albania in April. Germany attacks Poland on 1st September and her failure to accede to a British ultimatum to withdraw the forces results in the declaration of war on 3rd September. Warsaw falls to German forces and Poland is partitioned between Germany and Russia. A British Expeditionary Force (with air force elements) is sent to France to defend her northern sectors. Russia attacks Finland on 30th November.

1940   Finland is forced to accept Russian armistice terms on 13th March. German forces overrun Denmark on 9th April and attack Norway the same day. Britain sends forces to assist Norway but the country is lost. Chamberlain resigns on 10th May, and Winston Churchill becomes prime minister. On the same day Germany invades Holland, Belgium and Luxembourg, thus outflanking the French Maginot Line. The famous evacuation of Dunkirk of 30th May–4th June, recovers the greater part of the British Army. Hostilities end in France on 25th June. Italy declares war on the Allies on 10th June. German forces occupy the Channel Islands on 1st July. The air Battle of Britain rages throughout July, August, September and October, resulting in an unqualified defeat of the German *Luftwaffe*, and thus of Hitler's plans to invade Britain. The heavy daylight attacks reach their peak on 15th September but are crushed by R.A.F. Fighter Command under Lord Dowding. The daylight raids give way to the night *blitz* which continues against British cities throughout the winter months.

1941   Heavy night raids on British cities continue until May and sporadically thereafter. Britain and her Commonwealth stand alone against the Axis powers. Germany invades Jugoslavia and Greece on 6th April, and Greece and Crete are lost during April and May. British forces put down an Axis-inspired revolt in Iraq on 30th May and occupy Syria early in June. On 22nd June Germany attacks Russia, and Churchill pledges support for Russia. German armies make steady progress towards Moscow but are finally defeated by the Russian winter. Japan enters the War with a devastating surprise air attack on Pearl Harbour on 7th December and invades Malaya. Hong Kong falls to the Japanese on Christmas Day. America declares war on Japan on 8th December, and on Germany and Italy on the 11th.

Field Marshal Viscount Montgomery of Alamein and Hindhead, K.G., G.C.B., D.S.O.

1942   Singapore falls to the Japanese on 15th February; Japan makes considerable gains in the Philippines and Burma by extensive use of naval air power. British bombers are used in increasing stength in night raids on German cities. The decisive desert battle at El Alamein, Egypt – a great victory for the 8th Army – is followed by an advance along the North African coast towards Tunisia. On 8th November British and American forces land in Algeria and eventually link up with Montgomery's 8th Army (April 1943), clearing North Africa of German and Italian forces.

1943   The tide of war turns in the Allies' favour. Russia raises the siege of Leningrad on 18th January. The Japanese in the Far East are checked by American and British Commonwealth forces. The German forces at Stalingrad are destroyed during January. Churchill confers with his allies at Casablanca in January, at Washington in May, and Quebec in August. The invasion of Sicily begins on 9th–10th July, and of Italy on 3rd September. Italy surrenders unconditionally on 8th September, and the following day the Allies land at Salerno. Italy declares war on Germany on 13th October. Churchill, Roosevelt and Stalin confer at Tehe-

ran, 27th November–1st December.

1944   Round-the-clock bombing of Germany and German-held territory increases throughout the year. Progress is made against the Japanese, by the Russians on the Eastern Front, and by the British and American forces in Italy. Rome falls on 4th–5th June. Massive British and American forces land on the Normandy coast on 6th June to commence the reconquest of Europe under the command of General Dwight D. Eisenhower. The German flying-bomb attack opens on London and South-East England. Paris falls on 24th August. Russian forces enter Bucharest on 31st August. The German V-2 rocket attack on England begins on 8th September. British airborne forces are defeated at Arnhem, Holland, between 17th and 25th September. Churchill confers with Stalin in Moscow on 9th October. A last German offensive against the Americans in the Ardennes opens on 16th December but is defeated after three weeks' hard fighting.

1945   Warsaw falls to the Russians on 17th January. Churchill, Roosevelt and Stalin confer at Yalta in the Crimea on 2nd February. Berlin is encircled by the Russians on 25th April, and Hitler kills himself on 29th April. Collapse and surrender of German forces begin on 4th May, ending with the surrender of German forces at Dunkirk on 11th May. Churchill tenders the resignation of the Coalition government on 23rd May, forming a caretaker Conservative government (including Liberal Nationalists and Independents). A general election is held, resulting in a landslide victory for Labour with 393 seats. Clement Attlee becomes prime minister. The war against Japan continues (Mandalay having fallen to Commonwealth forces on 20th March). Atom bombs are dropped by American aircraft on Hiroshima (6th August) and Nagasaki (9th August); Japan surrenders unconditionally on 14th–15th August, and the War is ended formally on 2nd September. The Charter of the United Nations is approved on 25th June.

1946   The National Health Service Act establishes a comprehensive public health service for all persons in England and Wales (in Scotland, 1947, and Northern Ireland, 1948) by national funds subscribed from the central exchequer.

1947   As part of the Labour Government's policy of nationalisation, the Transport Act 1947 brings the railways under public ownership as a single enterprise – British Railways. The coal mines also pass into public ownership by the Coal Industry Nationalisation Act 1946 which sets up the National Coal Board to manage the industry. H.R.H. Princess Elizabeth, heir to the throne, marries her third cousin, Philip, son of Prince Andrea of Greece and Princess Alice (great-grand-daughter of Queen Victoria) on 20th November.

1948   Ernest Bevin, Foreign Secretary, proposes the Western Union of European nations, culminating in the 50-year military, economic and social Treaty of Brussels (on 17th March) between Britain, France, Belgium, the Netherlands and Luxembourg. British mandate for Palestine ends on 14th May; the new state of Israel is attacked by Egypt, Syria and Lebanon, but a truce is supervised through the United Nations (11th June). Communist-inspired violence breaks out in Malaya during May. The Russians stop all surface transport entering Berlin from the West; the Berlin Air Lift commences on 26th June. The Israeli-Egyptian war is resumed in October.

1949   The North Atlantic Treaty is signed on 4th April in Washington by Belgium, Britain, Canada, Denmark, France, Holland, Iceland, Italy, Luxembourg, Norway, Portugal and the United States. Formal ties between the Republic of Ireland and the British Commonwealth are ended on 18th April. The Berlin blockade is ended on 12th May, although the Air Lift continues until 6th October. An autumn balance of payments crisis compels the Labour Government to devalue the pound against the dollar.

1950   Britain accords *de jure* recognition to the Communist Government in China (4th January). A general election of 23rd February returns Attlee and the Labour Government with an overall majority of only six seats. On 25th June North Korean forces invade South Korea; two days later the U.N. Security Council calls on U.N. member nations to give assistance to South Korea. The Korean War substantially influences Western defence expenditure for the next three years. British military, naval and air forces are sent to aid South Korea, as are strong forces from the Commonwealth.

1951   The British Government accelerates its rearmament programme in January. A new Persian government seizes all foreign oil installations, including the Anglo-Iranian Oil Company on 28th April. Anti-British

rioting in Egypt in October. A general election (resulting from constant pressure against Labour's slender majority), held on 25th October introduces a Conservative administration under Winston Churchill with a majority of 17 seats.

1952   More anti-British mob violence breaks out in Egypt during January. King George VI dies on 6th February at Sandringham at the age of 57. His eldest daughter, Princess Elizabeth, at this time on a visit to East Africa with her husband, the Duke of Edinburgh, succeeds to the throne.

THE REIGN OF QUEEN ELIZABETH II (since 1952)

1952   Churchill as prime minister relinquishes the post of Minister of Defence to Field Marshal Earl Alexander of Tunis. The first test explosion of a British atomic bomb takes place off the north-west coast of Australia on 3rd October.

1953   The war in Korea ends with the signing of an armistice at Panmunjom on 27th July.

1954   Negotiations are completed on 23rd October for the termination of the occupation regime in Western Germany and for that nation's entry into the North Atlantic Treaty Organisation.

1955   Sir Winston Churchill resigns as prime minister on 7th April and his place at the head of the Conservative Government is taken by Sir Anthony Eden. The general election on 26th May returns the Conservatives with an overall majority of 58. EOKA campaign of terrorism in Cyprus intensifies throughout year.

1956   Egypt seizes control of the Suez Canal in November; strong British and French forces are sent to restore the situation, but although considerable military success attends the operation, political pressures against Britain by other nations force abandonment of the venture so that unilateral control of the Canal inevitably passes to Egypt.

1957   Following the strains imposed during the Suez Crisis of the previous months, Sir Anthony Eden resigns the premiership, his place being taken by Harold Macmillan. The Government suffers considerable unpopularity following passage of the 1957 Rent Act which provides a large measure of de-control of housing rents. Zurich agreement of November 1958 leads to reduction in Cyprus hostilities. End of Malayan Emergency.

1959   Following a visit to Russia by Harold Macmillan and a reduction in income tax, and in an atmosphere of domestic euphoria, the Conservatives are returned at the general election (8th October) with their overall majority increased to 100 seats. Labour, under Hugh Gaitskell, runs into trouble with promises of no higher taxes, yet with expensive projects.

1960   The "Cold War" with the Communist Bloc reaches a new intensity with the destruction of an American U-2 spy aircraft over Russian territory on 1st May. This incident severely affects efforts to reduce tensions between East and West. The dominion of Ghana (previously the Gold Coast) becomes a republic on 1st July. Cyprus gains its independence on 16th August, and is admitted as a republic to the Commonwealth on 13th March the following year.

1962   Revolt in Brunei begins "confrontation" between Malaysia and Indonesia. British troops aid Malaysian Federal forces.

1963   Fighting breaks out in Cyprus in December between the Greek and Turkish communities following proposals to alter the constitution by President Makarios. British troops assume responsibility for maintaining law and order until a U.N. peace-keeping force is established on 27th March 1964. Kenya achieves full internal self-government on 1st June. The Federation of Rhodesia and Nyasaland is dissolved on 31st December, the latter gaining independence as Malawi on 6th June 1964. Harold Macmillan resigns owing to ill health, the premiership being assumed by Sir Alexander Douglas-Home.

1964   Conservative fortunes are adversely affected by party wrangling over methods of choosing the parliamentary leadership, and by the Profumo scandal. Although the nation clearly wants a change of government at the general election on 15th October, the Conservatives are defeated not so much by Labour (whose vote was lower than in 1959) but by a rise in the Liberal vote from 5·9% to 11·2%. Labour is thus returned with an overall majority of only 4 seats. The Gambia achieves independence on 18th February, followed by Malta on 21st September.

1965   Sir Winston Churchill dies on 24th January at Hyde Park Gate, London, aged 90, and is buried at Bladon in Oxfordshire. Rhodesia makes a Unilateral Declaration of Independence.

1966   After a tenuous period of twenty months in office, prime minister Harold Wilson goes to the country on a slogan "You Know Labour Government Works" and is returned at the 31st March general election with a Labour majority increased to 97 seats. The Conservatives fail to convince the electorate with their proposals to enter the European Common Market and for reforms of the Trade Unions. Success of Anglo-Malaysian operations leads to end of "confrontation" and fall of Soekarno regime in Indonesia.

1967   Britain makes her second application (the first had been in 1961) to join the European Common Market. The Wilson government passes new legislation to control immigration into the United Kingdom. After months of terrorism, British forces withdraw from Aden. Gibraltar votes to remain British in spite of pressures by Spain. The Government devalues the Pound by 14·3%, and Britain borrows $1,400m abroad.

1968   In October negotiations between the British government and the Rhodesian Smith regime, aimed at ending the illegal form of unilateral constitution, end in deadlock, and sanctions against Rhodesia remain in being.

1969   Harold Wilson abandons legislation intended to control trades unions. In August violence in support of civil rights erupts in Ulster, and British troops are called in. British exports rise by 14%.

1970   The Conservatives gain a surprise victory in the June general election, the new government being led by Edward Heath. A third application is made to join the European Common Market, and progress is made towards agreement. There is further violence in Ulster during June and July. Iain Macleod, the Chancellor of the Exchequer, dies in July and is succeeded by Anthony Barber. A Conservative pledge to resume supply of arms to South Africa angers black members of the Commonwealth.

1971   Decimal currency is introduced. Brian Faulkner replaces Major Chichester-Clark as prime minister in Northern Ireland. Finally, the Stormont government is suspended in favour of direct rule from London, and internment without trial is introduced for suspected terrorist activists. Casualties mount as the Irish Republican Army terrorists intensify their campaign of attacks on the commercial and public life of the province. Following massive increases in technical development costs of the RB-211 aero-engine, the great company of Rolls-Royce collapses, and in order to safeguard numerous defence contracts the Government takes over the aviation side of the company. Terms for Britain's entry into the Common Market are finally agreed, and the Government commences the process of introducing legislation to enable Britain to assume membership. The nation's unemployment figure, at more than one million, is the highest since the 1930's.

THE MONARCHY AND THE CONSTITUTION

THE ORDER OF SUCCESSION

As the oldest secular institution in the United Kingdom, the monarchy's continuity has only been broken once in over a thousand years. Her Majesty Queen Elizabeth II is a descendant of the Saxon King Egbert and of King Malcolm II of Scotland.

Succession to the Crown is derived from the 1701 Act of Settlement (see page 101) and its inheritance is governed by rules of descent providing that the sons of the Sovereign are in Order of Succession to the Throne according to their seniority; in the absence of sons, the daughters succeed in order of their seniority. The consort of a king takes the rank and style of her husband, but the converse does not apply and the constitution has never attached any special rank to the husband of a Queen-Regnant.

No interregnum exists between the death of one Sovereign and the accession of the heir; the new Sovereign is immediately proclaimed at an Accession Council to which all Privy Councillors are summoned.

The Sovereign's coronation follows the accession after a period of about a year, the ceremony in Westminster Abbey having remained much the same as that of King Edgar's coronation at Bath in 973, although detailed changes have been introduced to conform with contemporary customs. Invited to the Coronation ceremony are representatives of the Lords, the Commons and the leading public interests, as well as leading members of Commonwealth and foreign states.

THE CONSTITUTION

The Queen is the personification of the State. She is the head of the executive, and of the judiciary in England and Wales, Scotland and Northern Ireland, the commander-in-chief of all the armed forces of the Crown and the temporal head of the established Church of England. However, as the result of the long evolutionary constitutional processes, the absolute power of the monarchy has been reduced so that the Queen acts on the advice of her ministers which she cannot constitutionally ignore. Therefore she reigns – but does not rule. Her Majesty's Government governs in the name of the Queen.

The United Kingdom's supreme legislative authority is the Queen in Parliament – the Queen and the two Houses of Parliament, the House of Lords and the elected House of Commons. As a law-making organ of the State, Parliament is a corporate body which cannot legislate without concurrence by all its parts (except under the Parliament Acts of 1911 and 1949). Representative of all the member countries of the United Kingdom, the Parliament at Westminster retains supreme authority and in theory there is nothing that it cannot legally do.

Under the 1911 Parliament Act the life of a Westminster Parliament is fixed at a maximum of five years (although it may be dissolved for a general election before the expiry of the legal term). During its life it may make or unmake any law, and even legalise past illegalities – thereby reversing the decision of the courts.

Nevertheless, despite this absolute supremacy, Parliament does not exercise its power in this way. The elected members cannot ignore the common law which has evolved through the centuries, and although the validity of Acts of Parliament cannot be contested in the law courts, no Parliament would introduce any Act which might receive no public support. Thus the system of government by political party ensures that Parliament legislates only with electoral responsibility foremost in mind.

Her Majesty the Queen summons, prorogues and dissolves Parliament, opening a new session with a speech from the throne. Any Bill which has passed all its stages in both Houses must gain the Royal Assent before it becomes a legal enactment.

The Queen confers titles, honours and appointments to all important State offices, and her consent and approval are required before a minister can assume office; and by reason of her pre-eminent position as Head of State has the power to conclude treaties, to declare war and to make peace.

THE PEERAGE, TITLES AND HONOURS

The British peerage is divided between the spiritual and temporal ranks, the former established in extent, the latter variable. The seniority of members, being inter-related, is thus best shown in a single table as follows:

Peers of the Blood Royal	– temporal
Archbishops (of Canterbury and of York)	– spiritual
Dukes	– temporal
Marquesses	– temporal
Earls	– temporal
Countesses in their own right	– temporal
Viscounts	– temporal
Bishops (by seniority*)	– spiritual
Barons (hereditary)	– temporal

Continued on page 128

THE ORDER OF SUCCESSION TO THE CROWN

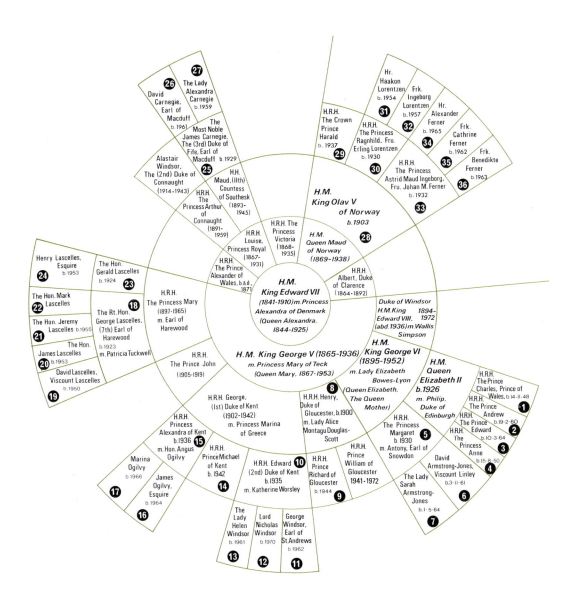

Continued from page 126

> Baronesses in their own right (*hereditary*) – *temporal*
> Lords of Appeal in Ordinary   – *temporal*
> Life Peers (*Barons*)   – *temporal*
> Life Peeresses (*Baronesses*)   – *temporal*
> (* *24 Bishops, always including the Bishops of London, Durham and Winchester, and always excluding the Bishop of Sodor and Man.*)

As stated above all honours and titles are conferred by the Queen, although most are conferred on the advice or recommendation of the Prime Minister. A few (the Order of Merit, the Royal Victorian Order, the Most Noble Order of the Garter, and the Most Noble and Most Ancient Order of the Thistle) are the Sovereign's personal gift.

ORDERS, DECORATIONS AND MEDALS

Strict orders of precedence exist in the award and wearing of Orders, Decorations and Medals conferred by the Sovereign, just as strict conventions are observed in the correct sequence of authorised post-nominal abbreviations. Pre-eminent in this convention is the absolute precedence vested in the two supreme awards for valour in the face of the enemy, the Victoria Cross and the George Cross. The full list of Orders, Decorations and Medals, their authorised post-nominal letters and their order of wearing is as follows:

1. Victoria Cross (**V.C.**)
2. George Cross (**G.C.**)
3. Order of the Garter (*K.G.*)
4. Order of the Thistle (*K.T.*)
5. Order of St. Patrick (*K.P.*)
6. Order of the Bath (*G.C.B., K.C.B., and D.C.B., and C.B.*)
7. Order of Merit (*O.M.; ranks next after G.C.B.*)
8. Order of the Star of India (*G.C.S.I., K.C.S.I. and C.S.I.*)
9. Order of St. Michael and St. George (*G.C.M.G., K.C.M.G. and D.C.M.G., and C.M.G.*)
10. Order of the Indian Empire (*G.C.I.E., K.C.I.E. and C.I.E.*)
11. Order of the Crown of India (*C.I.*)
12. Royal Victorian Order (*G.C.V.O., K.C.V.O. and D.C.V.O., and C.V.O.*)
13. Order of the British Empire (*G.B.E., K.B.E. and D.B.E., and C.B.E.*)
14. Order of the Companion of Honour (*C.H.; ranks next after G.B.E.*)
15. Distinguished Service Order (*D.S.O.*)
16. Royal Victorian Order (*M.V.O, Class IV*)
17. Order of the British Empire (*O.B.E.*)
18. Imperial Service Order (*I.S.O.*)
19. Royal Victorian Order (*M.V.O., Class IV*)
20. Order of the British Empire (*M.B.E.*)
21. Indian Order of Merit (*I.O.M.*) – *Military*
22. Order of Burma (*for Gallantry*) (*O.B.*)
23. Royal Red Cross (*R.R.C.*)
24. Distinguished (*previously Conspicuous*) Service Cross (*D.S.C.*)
25. Military Cross (*M.C.*)
26. Distinguished Flying Cross (*D.F.C.*)
27. Air Force Cross (*A.F.C.*)
28. Royal Red Cross (*A.R.R.C., Class II*)
29. Order of British India (*O.B.I.*)
30. Kaisar-i-Hind Medal
31. Order of Burma (*For Good Service*) (*O.B.*)
32. Order of St. John
33. Albert Medal (*A.M.*)
34. Union of South Africa King's (*Queen's*) Medal for Bravery, in Gold
35. Distinguished Conduct Medal (*D.C.M.*)
36. Conspicuous Gallantry Medal (*C.G.M.*)
37. George Medal (*G.M.*)
38. King's (*Queen's*) Police Medal, for Gallantry (*K.P.M., K.P.F.S.M., Q.P.M.*)
39. Queen's Fire Service Medal, for Gallantry (*Q.F.S.M.*)
40. Edward Medal (*E.M.*)
41. Royal West African Frontier Force Distinguished Conduct Medal (*D.C.M.*)
42. King's African Rifles Distinguished Conduct Medal (*D.C.M.*)
43. Indian Distinguished Service Medal (*I.D.S.M.*)
44. Burma Gallantry Medal (*B.G.M.*)
45. Union of South Africa King's (*Queen's*) Medal for Bravery, in Silver
46. Distinguished Service Medal (*D.S.M.*)
47. Military Medal (*M.M.*)
48. Distinguished Flying Medal (*D.F.M.*)
49. Air Force Medal (*A.F.M.*)
50. Constabulary Medal (*Ireland*)
51. Board of Trade Medal for Saving Life at Sea (*S.G.M.*)
52. Indian Order of Merit (*Civil*) (*I.O.M.*)
53. Empire Gallantry Medal (*E.G.M.*)
54. Indian Police Medal for Gallantry
55. Burma Police Medal for Gallantry
56. Ceylon Police Medal for Gallantry
57. Sierra Leone Police Medal for Gallantry
58. Sierra Leone Fire Brigades Medal for Gallantry
59. Colonial Police Medal for Gallantry
60. Uganda Services Medal (*if awarded for Gallantry*)
61. British Empire Medal (*B.E.M.*)
62. Canada Medal (*C.M. or M. du C.*)
63. Life Saving Medal of the Order of St. John
64. King's (*Queen's*) Police Medal for Distinguished Service (*K.P.M., K.P.F.S.M., Q.P.M.*)
65. Queen's Fire Service Medal for Distinguished Service (*Q.F.S.M.*)
66. Queen's Medal for Chiefs
67. War Medals (*in order of dates of campaigns*)

68. *Polar Medals (in order of dates)*
69. *Royal Victorian Medal*
70. *Imperial Service Medal*
71. *Police Medals for Meritorious Service*
72. *Uganda Services Medal (if awarded for meritorious service)*
73. *Badge of Honour*
74. *Jubilee, Coronation and Durbar Medals*
75. *King George V Long and Faithful Service Medal*
76. *King George VI Long and Faithful Service Medal*
77. *Queen Elizabeth II Long and Faithful Service Medal*
78. *Efficiency and Long Service Decorations and Medals, Medals for Champion Shots, Independence, etc., Medals*
79. *Other Commonwealth Orders, Decorations and Medals (instituted since 1949, other than by the Sovereign), and awards by the States of Malaysia and the State of Brunei)*
    Foreign Orders (in order of the date of award)
    Foreign Decorations (in order of date of award)
    Foreign Medals (in order of date of award)

LAW AND ORDER

Britain has no complete written code of law. The systems enforced by the courts of England and Wales, Scotland, and Northern Ireland (subject to certain regional differences of procedure) are drawn from two sources – legislation and common law. Legislative law consists of some 3,000 Acts of Parliament; Parliament is the supreme source of law, and its enactments are absolutely binding on all courts. Common law is the body of precedent built up on past decisions of the courts, based on the ancient customs of the realm and the principles of natural justice. It would be impossible in a review of this extent to detail the many and complex provisions laid down for the trial of the different types of offence, or the entire range of courts and tribunals which sit in Britain. Some of the main types of court are as follows.

CRIMINAL COURTS

In Britain a distinction is maintained between criminal law – covering offences against the community as a whole – and civil law, covering the obligations and rights which exist between one citizen and another. In rising order of gravity, criminal cases are heard by:
Magistrates' courts, presided over by a bench of between two and seven lay magistrates or justices of the peace, without a jury. Justices are appointed on a local basis, from among persons of local standing, who are chosen by criteria of personal integrity rather than legal knowledge. They are appointed by the Lord Chancellor, on the advice of the Lord Lieutenant of the County. They undergo a period of basic instruction, and qualified legal advisers are available to them at all times. Magistrates hear about 98 per cent of all criminal cases; the types of offence which they may try, and the range of penalties which they may impose, are strictly controlled. In some of the more serious types of case the accused has the right to choose trial by the magistrates or trial by jury in a superior court.
Courts of Quarter Sessions sit in each county at least four times a year, and try the bulk of the more serious offences, Additionally some 94 boroughs are entitled to hold their own courts, which are presided over by a judge known as a Recorder. A Quarter Sessions bench usually comprises a number of lay magistrates with a legally qualified chairman. Trial is by a jury of twelve. The gravest and most difficult cases are tried by
Courts of Assize, which sit in a number of major towns and cities throughout the country. These are branches of the High Court, presided over by a High Court judge "on circuit", and sit at least three times a year. Greater London's assize court is the Central Criminal Court, which sits in continuous session at the Old Bailey. Trial is by a jury of twelve.

CIVIL COURTS

The main civil courts are the County Courts and the High Court, although magistrates' courts have limited jurisdiction over certain types of cases. There are some 400 county courts, presided over by some 106 county court judges, each having a circuit. The judge usually sits alone, although under some circumstances a jury of eight may be empanelled.

The High Court of Justice is divided into the Chancery Division, Queen's Bench Division, and the Probate, Divorce and Admiralty Division. The High Court is staffed by 68 judges, and in the first instance they usually hear cases sitting singly.

THE JUDICIARY

The only judge who is engaged in political life in any way is the Lord Chancellor, the head of the judiciary and a high officer of the current government. The highest positions in the judiciary – the Lord Chief Justice, the Master of the Rolls, the Lords of Appeal in Ordinary, the Lords Justices who sit in the Courts of Appeal, and so forth – are filled by the Sovereign on advice from the Prime Minister. All other judges and magistrates are appointed by the Lord Chancellor, on advice from various relevant authorities.

Judges are appointed from among practising barristers, advocates or solicitors, and their training and careers are not subject to State interference in any way. Judges can only be removed from their positions under certain stringently enforced conditions – for instance, proven misconduct or incapacity – and the complete independence of the judiciary from the executive branch of government is a central foundation of the British system.

The professional standards and progress of a solicitor or barrister are governed at every stage by the Law Society and the General Council of the Bar – professional bodies unconnected with the executive branch of government.

Juries are summoned from among British subjects, men and women alike, between the ages of 21 and 60, subject to certain qualifications designed to ensure that persons of insufficient mentality, and persons with criminal records, are excluded. The issue of guilt or innocence in all relevant types of case is entirely the decision of the jury, and they are afforded considerable legal protection from interference or improper influence, exercised by the court or anyone else.

THE POLICE AND THE PRISON SERVICE

There are 67 regular police forces in Britain, linked with local government authorities but subject to the ultimate control of the Home Secretary (in England and Wales), the Secretary of State for Scotland, and the Minister for Home Affairs in Northern Ireland (although at the time of writing the Royal Ulster Constabularly is under the direct control of the Home Secretary).

The authorised establishment of the regular police forces in England and Wales as at December 1970 was 108,400; the actual strength was 92,800. The Scottish establishment was 11,100; actual strength was 10,400. The actual strength of the R.U.C. was 3,800.

Each force is maintained by a local government committee made up of councillors and justices, who fix the establishment and appoint the Chief Constable, the Deputy Chief Constable and the Assistant Chief Constable – subject to the approval of the Home Secretary. Under the Home Secretary the local police authorities are responsible for providing an efficient and adequately equipped force for their area. At all levels there is close co-operation between forces.

There are currently 58 men's prisons in England and Wales. Figures for 1970 give an average daily prison population in England and Wales of 39,028. At one stage in 1971 the total rose to 40,470. The 1971 average women's prison population was 1,035. This figure breaks down into some 35,535 convicted prisoners, of whom 17,224 were serving sentences of less than three years, and 3,493 civil prisoners and untried prisoners on remand. The daily average prison population in Scotland in the same period was just over 5,000. During 1970 there were a total of 140,997 receptions in prisons in England and Wales, and 20,351 in Scotland. (Note: These figures refer to prisons, detention centres, and Borstal institutions for young offenders together.)

Crime figures are subject to so many different methods of interpretation that it is difficult to provide examples which are both brief and reliable. However, figures have been published from government sources covering certain 1970 statistics which may be of interest. In England and Wales during 1970 "indictable offences known to the police" totalled about 1,556,000; in connection with these, 350,700 persons were proceeded against, of whom 322,900 were convicted. Of these 322,900 persons found guilty, about 176,500 were convicted of theft, and 70,700 of the allied but distinct crimes of burglary or robbery. Some 23,490 of the convictions were for violence against the person, some 22,700 for handling stolen goods, and about 12,300 for fraud. There were 6,700 convictions for sexual offences.

In 1970 in England and Wales approximately 1,351,200 people were convicted of non-indictable offences. Of these the vast majority, some 991,200, were found guilty of motoring offences. About 86,800 were convicted under the laws governing intoxicating liquor, and about 91,400 under the revenue laws. There were 19,800 convictions for malicious damage, and about 40,300 under the Wireless Telegraphy Acts – it may be presumed that the vast majority of these latter were in connection with television licenses.

THE FORTY-EIGHT PRIME MINISTERS OF GREAT BRITAIN AND THE UNITED KINGDOM

Name	Ministries	Dates of birth and death	Education	Parliamentary career
1. The Rt. Hon. Sir Robert WALPOLE, K.G., K.B., P.C. (created 1st Earl of Orford on retirement)	3–4–1721 to 8–2–1742 (Whig)	b. 26–8–1676 at Houghton, Norfolk d. 18–3–1745 at 5 Arlington Street, Piccadilly, London	Eton and King's Cambridge	Castle Rising, 1701–1702 (Whig); King's Lynn, 1702–1742 (Whig)
2. The 1st Earl of WILMINGTON, K.G., K.B., P.C. (previously The Rt. Hon., the Hon. Sir Spencer Compton)	16–2–1742 to 2–7–1743 (Whig)	b. 1673 d. 2–7–1743	St. Paul's School, London, and Trinity, Oxford	Eye, Suffolk, 1698–1710 (Tory then Whig); East Grinstead, 1713–1715 (Whig); Sussex, 1715–1728 (Whig); Speaker, 1715–1727

Name	Ministries	Dates of birth and death	Education	Parliamentary career
3. The Rt. Hon., the Hon. Henry PELHAM, P.C.	27–8–1743 to 6–3–1754 (Whig)	b. 1695 (?) d. 6–3–1754 at Arlington Street, London	Westminster School and Hart Hall, Oxford	Seaford, 1717–1722 (Whig); Sussex, 1722–1754 (Whig)
4. His Grace the 1st Duke of NEWCASTLE-upon-Tyne and 1st Duke of Newcastle-under-Lyne (previously the Rt. Hon., the Hon. Sir Thomas Pelham-Holles, Bt., K.G., P.C.)	(1) 16–3–1754 to 26–10–1756 (Whig) (2) 2–7–1757 to 25–10–1760 (Whig) (3) 25–10–1760 to 25–5–1762 (Whig)	b. 21–7–1693 d. 17–11–1768 at Lincoln's Inn Field, London	Westminster School and Claire Hall, Cambridge	—
5. His Grace the 4th Duke of DEVONSHIRE (previously Sir William Cavendish, K.G., Lord Cavendish of Hardwick (until 1729) and Marquess of Hartington (until 1755))	16–11–1756 to 5–1757 (Whig)	b. 1720 d. 2–10–1764 at Spa, Germany	Educated privately	Derby county, 1741–1751 (Whig); summoned to the Lords in father's barony, Cavendish of Hardwick
6. The 2nd Earl WALDEGRAVE of WALDEGRAVE, P.C. (previously James Waldegrave)	8–6–1757 to 12–6–1757 (Whig Interministerium)	b. 14–3–1715 d. 28–5–1763	Eton	Succeeded to the peerage on the death of his father in 1741
7. The 3rd Earl of BUTE (previously The Rt. Hon., the Hon. Sir John Stuart, K.G., K.T., P.C.)	26–5–1762 to 8–4–1763 (Tory)	b. 25–5–1713 at Parliament Square, Edinburgh d. 10–3–1792 at Grosvenor Square, London	Eton	—
8. The Rt. Hon., the Hon. George GRENVILLE, P.C.	16–4–1763 to 10–7–1765 (Whig)	b. 14–10–1712 d. 13–11–1770 at Bolton Street, London	Eton and Christ Church, Oxford	Buckingham, 1741–1770 (Whig)
9. The Most Hon. The 2nd Marquess of ROCKINGHAM, K.G., P.C. (previously The Rt. Hon. Lord Charles Watson-Wentworth)	(1) 13–7–1765 to 7–1766 (Whig) (2) 27–3–1782 to 1–7–1782 (Whig)	b. 13–5–1730 d. 1–7–1782	Westminster School	Took his seat in the Lords on 21–5–1751
10. The 1st Earl of CHATHAM, P.C. (previously The Rt. Hon. William PITT)	30–7–1766 to 14–10–1768 (Tory)	b. 15–11–1708 at St. James's, Westminster d. 11–5–1778 at Hayes, Kent	Eton, Trinity (Oxford) and Utrecht	Old Sarum, 1735–1747 (Whig); Seaford, 1747–54 (Tory); Aldeburgh, 1754–1756 (Tory); Buckingham, 1756 (Tory); Okehampton 1756–57 (Tory); Bath, 1757–66 (Tory)
11. His Grace the 3rd Duke of GRAFTON, K.G., P.C. (previously The Rt. Hon., Sir Augustus Henry FitzRoy; and the Earl of Euston)	14–10–1768 to 28–1–1770 (Whig)	b. 28–9–1735 at Marylebone, London d. 14–3–1811 at Euston Hall, Suffolk	Westminster School and Peterhouse, Cambridge	Bury St. Edmunds, 1756–57 (Whig); succeeded to dukedom in 1757
12. Lord NORTH, K.G., P.C. (previously The Rt. Hon., the Hon. Sir Frederick North, and the 2nd Earl of Guildford)	28–1–1770 to 20–3–1782 (Tory)	b. 13–4–1732 Albermarle Street, London d. 5–8–1792 at Lower Grosvenor Street, London	Eton; Trinity, Oxford; Leipzig	Banbury, 1754–90 (Tory); took his seat in the Lords, 25–11–1790

Name	Ministries	Dates of birth and death	Education	Parliamentary career
13. The 2nd Earl of SHELBURNE, K.G., P.C. (previously William Fitz-Maurice (until 1751); Rt. Hon., the Hon. Sir William Petty (until 1753); Viscount Fitz-Maurice (until 1761); created 1st Marquess of Lansdowne, 6–12–1784)	4–7–1782 to 24–2–1783 (Whig)	b. 20–5–1737 at Dublin, Ireland d. 7–5–1805 at Berkeley Square, London	Privately and Christ Church, Oxford	Chipping Wycombe, 1760–61 (Whig); took seat in Lords as Baron Wycombe, 3–11–1761
14. His Grace the 3rd Duke of PORTLAND, K.G., P.C. (previously The Most Noble Sir William Henry Cavendish Bentinck, Marquess of Titchfield, until 1–5–1762)	(1) 2–4–1783 to 12–1783 (Coalition) (2) 31–3–1807 to 10–1809 (Tory)	b. 14–4–1738 d. 30–10–1809 at Bulstrode, Bucks	Eton and Christ Church, Oxford	Wembley, 1761–62 (Whig)
15. The Rt. Hon., the Hon. William PITT, P.C.	(1) 19–12–1783 to 14–3–1801 (Tory) (2) 10–5–1804 to 23–1–1806 (Tory)	b. 28–5–1759 at Hayes, Kent d. 23–1–1806 at Putney,	Privately and Pembroke Hall, Cambridge	Appleby, c. 1770–1806 (Tory)
16. The Rt. Hon., Henry ADDINGTON, P.C. (created 1st Viscount Sidmouth in 1805)	17–3–1801 to 30–4–1804 (Tory)	b. 30–5–1757 at Bedford Row, London d. 15–2–1844 at Richmond Park, Surrey	Winchester and Brasenose College, Oxford	Devizes, 1783–1805 (Tory); Speaker,
17. The Rt. Hon. the 1st Baron GRENVILLE of Wotton-under-Bernewood, P.C. (previously William Wyndham Grenville, until 1790)	10–2–1806 to 3–1807 (Tory)	b. 25–10–1759 d. 12–1–1834 at Dropmore Lodge, Bucks	Eton and Christ Church, Oxford	Buckingham, 1782–1784 (Tory); Buckinghamshire, 1784–1790 (Tory); Speaker, 1789
18. The Rt. Hon., the Hon. Spencer PERCEVAL, P.C., K.C.	4–10–1809 to 11–5–1812 (Tory)	b. 1–11–1762 at Audley Square, London d. 11–5–1812, murdered in lobby of House	Harrow and Trinity, Cambridge	Northampton, 1796 and 1797 (Tory)
19. The Rt. Hon. the 2nd Earl of LIVERPOOL (previously Sir Robert Banks Jenkinson, K.G., P.C., until 1796; Lord Hawkesbury, until 1808)	(1) 8–6–1812 to 29–1–1820 (Tory) (2) 29–1–1820 to 17–2–1827 (Tory)	b. 7–6–1770 d. 4–12–1828 at Coombe Wood, Surrey	Charterhouse and Christ Church, Oxford	Rye, 1796–1803 (Tory); summoned to Lords in father's barony of Hawkesbury, 15–11–1803
20. The Rt. Hon. George CANNING, P.C.	10–4–1827 to 8–8–1827 (Tory)	b. 11–4–1770 in London d. 8–8–1827 at Chiswick Villa	Eton and Christ Church, Oxford	Newton, I.o.W., 1793–96; Wendover, 1796–1802; Tralee, 1802–06; Newton, 1806–07; Hastings, 1807–12; Liverpool, 1812–23; Harwich, 1823–26; Newport, 1826–27; Seaford, 1827 (all Tory)
21. The Viscount GODERICH (previously Rt. Hon., the Hon. Frederick John Robinson, P.C., until 1833; Earl of Ripon)	31–8–1827 to 8–1–1828 (Tory)	b. 1–11–1782 in London d. 28–1–1859 at Putney Heath	Harrow and St. John's College, Cambridge	Carlow, 1806–07 (Tory); Ripon, 1807–27 (Tory)
22. His Grace The 1st Duke of WELLINGTON, K.G., G.C.B., G.C.H., P.C. (previously The Hon. Arthur Wellesley, until 1804; The Hon. Sir Arthur Wellesley, K.B., until 1809; The Viscount Wellington, created Earl of Wellington, 2–1812; Marquess of Wellington, 10–1812; and Duke, 5–1814)	(1) 22–1–1828 to 26–6–1830 (Tory) (2) 26–6–1830 to 21–11–1830 (Tory) (3) 17–11–1834 to 9–12–1834 (Tory)	b. 1–5–1769 in Dublin d. 14–9–1852 at Walmer Castle, Kent	Eton; Brussels; and The Academy at Angiers	Rye, 1806 (Tory); St. Michael, 1807 (Tory); Newport, I.o.W., 1807–09; took seat in the Lords, 28–6–1814 as Viscount, Earl, Marquess and Duke

Name	Ministries	Dates of birth and death	Education	Parliamentary career
23. The 2nd Earl GREY (previously The Rt. Hon., the Hon. Sir Charles Grey, Bt., K.G., P.C., Viscount Howick, 1806–07)	22–11–1830 to 7–1834 (Whig)	b. 13–3–1764 at Fallodon, Northumb. d. 17–7–1845	Eton and Trinity, Cambridge	Northumberland, 1786–1807 (Whig); Appleby, 1807 (Whig); Tavistock, 1807 (Whig)
24. The 3rd Viscount MELBOURNE (previously The Rt. Hon., the Hon. Sir William Lamb, Bt., P.C.)	(1) 16–7–1834 to 11–1834 (Whig) (2) 18–4–1835 to 20–6–1837 (Whig) (3) 20–6–1837 to 8–1841 (Whig)	b. 15–3–1779 at Piccadilly, London d. 24–11–1848	Eton and Trinity College, Cambridge	Leominster, 1806; Haddington Borough, 1806–07; Portarlington, 1807–12; Peterborough, 1816–19; Herts, 1819–26; Newport, 1827; Bletchingley, 1827–28; took his seat in the Lords, 1–2–1829
25. The Rt. Hon. Sir Robert PEEL, Bt., P.C. (previously Robert Peel, Esq., M.P. until 5–1830 when he succeeded as 2nd Baronet)	(1) 10–12–1834 to 8–4–1835 (Tory) (2) 30–8–1841 to 29–6–1846 (Conservative)	b. 5–2–1788 near Bury, Lancs d. 2–7–1850 after fall from horse	Harrow and Christ Church, Oxford	Cashel, 1809–12; Chippenham, 1812–17; University of Oxford, 1817–29; Westbury, 1829–30; Tamworth, 1830–50; (all Tory)
26. The Rt. Hon. Lord John RUSSELL, P.C., and after 30–7–1861, the 1st Earl RUSSELL, K.G., G.C.M.G., P.C.	(1) 30–6–1846 to 2–1852 (Whig) (2) 29–10–1865 to 6–1866 (Liberal)	b. 18–8–1792 at Hertford Street, London d. 28–5–1878 at Richmond, Surrey	Westminster School and Edinburgh University	Tavistock, 1813–17, 1818–20, 1830–31; Hunts, 1820–26; Bandon, 1826–30; Devon, 1831–32; S. Devon, 1832–35; Stroud, 1835–41; City of London, 1841–61; took seat in Lords, 30–7–1861
27. The 14th Earl of DERBY, K.G., G.C.M.G., P.C. (previously Rt. Hon. Sir Edward Geoffrey Smith-Stanley, and Lord Stanley, M.P. until 1844)	(1) 23–2–1852 to 18–12–1852 (Conservative) (2) 20–2–1858 to 11–6–1859 (Conservative) (3) 28–6–1866 to 26–2–1868 (Conservative)	b. 19–3–1799 at Knowsley, Lancs d. 23–10–1869	Eton and Christ Church, Oxford	Stockbridge, 1822–26 (Whig); Preston, 1826–30 (Whig); Windsor, 1831–32 (Whig); North Lancs 1832–44 (Whig); but changed to Tory in 1835; summoned to Lords as Lord Stanley, 1844; succeeded to Earldom, 1851
28. The Rt. Hon. Sir George Hamilton Gordon, Bt., 4th Earl of ABERDEEN, K.G., K.T., P.C. (previously known as Lord Haddo, until 1801)	19–12–1852 to 5–2–1855 (Peelite-Conservative)	b. 28–1–1784 at Edinburgh d. 14–12–1860 at St. James's, London	Harrow and St. John's, Cambridge	Took seat in Lords, 1814
29. The Rt. Hon. Sir Henry John Temple, 3rd Viscount PALMERSTON, K.G., G.C.B., P.C.	(1) 6–2–1855 to 19–2–1858 (Liberal) (2) 12–6–1859 to 18–10–1865 (Liberal)	b. 20–10–1784 d. 18–10–1865 at Brocket Hall, Herts	Harrow; University of Edinburgh and St. John's, Cambridge	Newport, 1807–11 (Tory); Cambridge University, 1811–31 (Tory, then Whig after 1829); Bletchingley, 1831–32 (Whig); S. Hants, 1832–34 (Whig); Tiverton, 1835–65 (Whig, then Liberal)

Name	Ministries	Dates of birth and death	Education	Parliamentary career
30. The Rt. Hon. Benjamin DISRAELI, 1st Earl of BEACONSFIELD, K.G., P.C. (until 1838 known as Benjamin D'Israeli)	(1) 27–2–1868 to 11–1868 (Conservative) (2) 20–2–1874 to 4–1880 (Conservative)	b. 21–12–1804 in London d. 19–4–1881 at 19 Curzon Street, London	Lincoln's Inn	Maidstone, 1837–41; Shrewsbury, 1841–47; Buckinghamshire, 1847–76 (all Conservative); took his seat in the Lords, 1876
31. The Rt. Hon. William Ewart GLADSTONE, P.C.	(1) 3–12–1868 to 2–1874 (2) 23–4–1880 to 12–6–1885 (3) 1–2–1886 to 20–7–1886 (4) 15–8–1892 to 3–3–1894 (All Liberal)	b. 29–12–1809 in Liverpool d. 19–5–1898 at Hawarden Castle, Wales	Eton and Christ Church, Oxford	Newark, 1832–45 (Tory); University of Oxford, 1847–65 (Peelite until 1859, Liberal afterwards); S. Lancs, 1865–68 (Liberal); Greenwich 1868–80 (Liberal); Midlothian, 1880–95 (Liberal)
32. The Rt. Hon. Robert Arthur Talbot Gascoyne-Cecil, the 3rd Marquess of SALISBURY, K.G., G.C.V.O., P.C. (known as Lord Robert Cecil until 1865, and Viscount Cranbourne, M.P. until 1868)	(1) 23–6–1885 to 28–1–1886 (2) 25–7–1886 to 8–1892 (3) 25–6–1895 to 22–1–1901 (4) 23–1–1901 to 11–7–1902 (All Conservative)	b. 3–2–1830 at Hatfield House d. 22–8–1903 at Hatfield House, Herts	Eton and Christ Church, Oxford	Stamford, 1853–68 (Conservative)
33. The Rt. Hon. Sir Archibald Philip Primrose, Bt., 5th Earl of ROSEBERY, K.G., K.T., V.D., P.C. (known as Lord Dalmeny from 1851 to 1868)	5–3–1894 to 21–6–1895 (Liberal)	b. 7–5–1847 in London d. 21–5–1929 at Epsom, Surrey	Eton and Christ Church, Oxford	—
34. The Rt. Hon. Arthur James BALFOUR, P.C. (later, 1922, the 1st Earl of Balfour, K.G., O.M., P.C.)	12–7–1902 to 4–12–1905 (Conservative)	b. 25–7–1848 in East Lothian d. 19–3–1930 at Woking, Surrey	Eton and Trinity College, Cambridge	Hertford, 1874–85; East Manchester, 1885–1906; City of London, 1906–22 (all Conservative)
35. The Rt. Hon. Sir Henry CAMPBELL-BANNERMAN, G.C.B., P.C. (known as Henry Campbell, Esq., until 1872)	5–12–1905 to 5–4–1908 (Liberal)	b. 7–9–1836 at Glasgow d. 22–4–1908 at 10 Downing Street	Glasgow High School; Glasgow University and Trinity, Cambridge	Stirling District, 1868–1908 (Liberal)
36. The Rt. Hon. Herbert Henry ASQUITH, P.C., and from 1925, 1st Earl of OXFORD AND ASQUITH, K.G.	(1) 7–4–1908 to 7–5–1910 (Liberal) (2) 8–5–1910 to 5–12–1916 (Liberal)	b. 12–9–1852 at Morley, Yorks d. 15–2–1928 at Sutton Courtney, Berks	City of London School, and Balliol, Oxford	East Fife, 1886–1918 (Liberal); Paisley, 1920–24 (Liberal)
37. The Rt. Hon. David Lloyd GEORGE, O.M., P.C. (later, from 1945, 1st Earl LLOYD-GEORGE of Dwyfor)	7–12–1916 to 19–10–1922 (Coalition)	b. 17–1–1863 in Manchester d. 26–3–1945 Ty Newydd, Wales	Educated privately	Caernarvon Boroughs, 1890–1945 (Liberal, 1890–1931 and 1935–45; Independent Liberal, 1931–35)
38. The Rt. Hon. Andrew Bonar LAW, P.C.	23–10–1922 to 20–5–1923 (Conservative)	b. 16–9–1858 at Kingston, New Brunswick, Canada d. 30–10–1923 in London	In New Brunswick and at Glasgow High School	Blackfriars Divn. of Glasgow, 1900–06; Dulwich Divn. of Camberwell, 1906–10; Bootle Divn. of Lancs, 1911–18; Central Divn. of Glasgow, 1918–23 (all Conservative)

Name	Ministries	Dates of birth and death	Education	Parliamentary career
39. The Rt. Hon. Stanley BALDWIN, P.C. (later, from 1937, 1st Earl Baldwin of Bewdley, K.G.)	(1) 22–5–1923 to 22–1–1924 (Conservative) (2) 4–11–1924 to 4–6–1929 (Conservative) (3) 7–6–1935 to 20–1–1936 (National) (4) 21–1–1936 to 11–12–1936 (National) (5) 12–12–1936 to 28–5–1937 (National)	b. 3–8–1867 at Bewdley, Worcs. d. 14–12–1947	Harrow and Trinity, Cambridge	Bewdley Divn. of Worcestershire, 1908–37 (Conservative)
40. The Rt. Hon. James Ramsay MacDONALD, P.C.	(1) 22–1–1924 to 4–11–1924 (Labour) (2) 5–6–1929 to 7–6–1935 (Labour, and National Coalition from 1931)	b. 12–10–1866 at Lossiemouth d. 9–11–1937 at sea, Atlantic	Drainie Parish Board School	Leicester, 1906–18 (Labour); Aberavon, 1922–29 (Labour); Seaham Divn. of Co. Durham, 1929–31 (Labour), 1931–35 (Nat. Labour); Scottish Universities, 1936–37
41. The Rt. Hon. Arthur Neville CHAMBERLAIN, P.C.	28–5–1937 to 10–5–1940 (National)	b. 18–3–1869 at Edgbaston d. 9–11–1940 at Hickfield, Reading	Rugby School and Mason College	Ladywood Divn. of Birmingham, 1918–29; Edgbaston Divn. of Birmingham, 1929–40 (both Conservative)
42. The Rt. Hon. Sir Winston Leonard Spencer(-)CHURCHILL, K.G., O.M., C.H., T.D., P.C.	(1) 10–5–1940 to 26–7–1945 (Coalition, and Conservative from 23–5–1945) (2) 26–10–1951 to 6–2–1952 (Conservative) (3) 7–2–1952 to 5–4–1955 (Conservative)	b. 30–11–1874 at Blenheim Palace d. 24–1–1965 at Hyde Park Gate, London	Harrow and Royal Military College	Oldham, 1900–06 (Conservative until 1904, then Liberal); N.W. Manchester, 1906–08 (Liberal); Dundee, 1908–18 (Liberal), and 1918–22 (Coalition Liberal); Epping, 1924–45 (Conservative); Woodford, 1945–64 (Conservative)

(*Continued overleaf*)

Name	Ministries	Dates of birth and death	Education	Parliamentary career
43. The Rt. Hon. Clement Richard ATTLEE, C.H., P.C. (created 1st Earl Attlee, K.G., O.M., in 1955)	26–7–1945 to 25–10–1951 (Labour)	b. 3–1–1883 at Putney, London d. 8–10–1967 in London	Haileybury and University College, Oxford	Limehouse Divn. of Stepney, 1922–50 (Labour); West Walthamstow, 1950–55 (Labour)
44. The Rt. Hon. Sir Robert Anthony EDEN, K.G., M.C., P.C. (created, 1961, 1st Earl of Avon)	6–4–1955 to 9–1–1957 (Conservative)	b. 12–6–1897 at Windlestone, Durham	Eton, and Christ Church, Oxford	Warwick and Leamington, 1923–57 (Conservative)
45. The Rt. Hon. Maurice Harold MACMILLAN, P.C.	10–1–1957 to 18–10–1963 (Conservative)	b. 10–2–1894 at 52 Cadogan Place, London	Eton, and Balliol, Oxford	Stockton-on-Tees, 1924–29 (Conservative); Bromley, 1945–64 (Conservative)
46. The Rt. Hon. Sir Alexander Frederick DOUGLAS-HOME, K.T., P.C. (previously, until 1918, the Hon. A. F. Douglas-Home; then until 11–7–1963, Lord Dunglass; then until disclaimer of 23–10–1963, 14th Earl of Home)	19–10–1963 to 16–10–1964 (Conservative)	b. 2–7–1903 at 28 South Street, London	Eton, and Christ Church, Oxford	South Lanark, 1931–45 (Conservative); Lanark, 1950–51 (Conservative); Kinross and West Perthshire, 1963 to date (Conservative)
47. The Rt. Hon. James Harold WILSON, O.B.E., P.C.	16–10–1964 to –6–1970 (Labour)	b. 11–3–1916	Wirral Grammar School and Jesus College, Oxford	Ormskirk, 1945–50 (Labour); Huyton, 1950 to date (Labour)
48. The Rt. Hon. Edward Richard George HEATH, M.B.E., P.C.	–6–1970 to date (Conservative)	b. 9–7–1916 at Broadstairs, Kent	Chatham House School, Ramsgate; Balliol, Oxford	Bexley, 1950 to date (Conservative)

CHAPTER 3

Economy, Industry and Trade

In 1969 Britain's gross national product at factor cost was around £38,601,000,000 – an increase in real terms of about 35% since 1959. Roughly one-third of this figure was contributed by the manufacturing industries. Financial, health, educational, professional and personal services accounted for some 21%. Gas, electricity and water contributed some 3·6%; agriculture, forestry and fishery, some 3%; the distributive trades about 11%; communications 8%; and mining 2%. (These figures, like most of those that follow, are based on published 1969 Government analyses.)

ECONOMIC BACKGROUND

In international terms, Britain ranks ninth in national income per head of population, below the U.S.A., Canada, Australia, New Zealand, Sweden, Switzerland, France and Federal Germany. Ranking 75th nation in physical size, Britain comes tenth in the population league, with less than 2% of the world's inhabitants.

Fourth in population density, Britain takes roughly one-fifth of the world's exports of primary products, and provides some 8% of the world's exports of manufactured products. Britain has few natural resources apart from coal, natural gas and iron ore, and can grow only about half the food needed to feed the population; the country is therefore, inevitably, among the world's leading importers of grain, meat, certain dairy products, fruit, tobacco, timber, and so on. Against this dependence must be set Britain's position as a leading exporter of motor vehicles, electrical and other machinery, textiles, chemicals etc. This clear commitment to a manufacturing economy is borne out by the fact that no other developed country has such a small proportion of the working population engaged in agriculture.

As the financial centre of the sterling area, an economic grouping which includes about one quarter of the population of the world, Britain is also one of the world's major banking nations, and about one-third of world trade is carried out in pounds sterling. This situation brings much "invisible wealth" into Britain.

Britain's 19th century position as the world's leading manufacturer, banker, merchant and carrier was brought to an end by the two World Wars. While competition from the United States and other European nations grew steadily in the years between about 1890 and 1914, Britain's clear lead in industrial expansion, and the rise in world trade generally, enabled her to maintain her high level of economic achievement. After the First World War, however, the longer established industries such as coal, iron and steel, and textiles met increasing competition from abroad, and the world-wide depression of the inter-War years caused great distress in certain areas of the economy. At the same time Britain failed to secure as strong a position as she might have in the newer areas of trade, such as certain aspects of engineering. The world slump of the early 1930s was to some extent offset in its effects on Britain by relatively cheap imports of necessities, such as food, and by the income from invisible earnings. Production, employment and investment improved as the 1930s progressed, and the general revival of world trade combined with re-armament to underwrite a marked expansion in such fields as chemicals, aviation, electrical products and vehicles. The construction industry also enjoyed a sharp upsurge, and by the years immediately before the Second World War average income per head has risen, in real terms, by some 14% over the 1929–30 figures.

There can be few clearer examples in recorded history of a nation winning a cataclysmic war but crippling itself in the process, than that provided by Britain in the 1939–45 period. The War reduced British domestic capital by about £3,000,000,000 through a variety of causes including massive bomb damage and shipping losses. By 1944 British exports had, inevitably, plunged to between one-quarter and one-third of their 1938 level. The massive liquidation of overseas investments, in order to pay for the daily progress of Britain's greatest military effort of all time, could never be made good; some £1,000,000,000 worth of investments were sold, nearly half of them in the U.S.A., and additional overseas debts of some £3,000,000,000 were incurred.

The nation's economic recovery since the War has been a slow and wavering process. The rationing of a wide range of consumer necessities, and other forms of central control, persisted for years after the end of hostilities. It was to be 1958 before regulations covering international financial dealings were returned to normality. Gradually production, trade and living standards recovered, and despite repeated balance of payments difficulties the overall picture has been one of slow growth, increasingly high living standards, and relatively low unemployment. The volatile nature of the movements of world capital render an up-to-date analysis of Britain's current balance of payments position unreliable; suffice it to note, however, that since the 1967 devalua-

tion of the pound sterling to a figure of $2.40, and the simultaneous imposition of certain other fiscal measures, a reorientation of the economy has been gradually achieved. Exports and invisible overseas earnings increased roughly four times as fast as the gross domestic product between 1967 and 1970. The balance of payments improved rapidly, and at the beginning of 1970 the surplus on current transactions stood at an annual figure in excess of £500,000,000.

PUBLIC FINANCE

Funds administered by central government and local authorities are made up of various monies. The main funds of the central government are raised by taxation, and are paid into and out of the Consolidated Fund in accordance with government proposals approved by Parliament. There are also funds administered for specific purposes by central government departments, and maintained by revenue which does not pass through the Consolidated Fund – such as the National Insurance Fund used for the payment of various benefits under the welfare system, and administered by the Secretary of State for Social Services. Local government authorities receive their revenue partly in the form of rates – local taxes on property – and partly in the form of various central government grants.

Central government expenditure falls under certain major headings, as follows:

Supply Services. The main section of government expenditure, authorised by Parliament through annual Appropriation Acts, and covering such areas as defence, social services and the general administration of the nation.

Standing Services. Expenditure specifically authorised by Acts of Parliament other than the annual Appropriation Acts. These direct charges on the Consolidated Fund include the residual cost of servicing the National Debt, financial provision for members of the Royal Family, and salaries and pensions for judges and other high officers. This group also includes expenditure from the various special funds.

Lending and Debt. All government domestic lending to the nationalised industries, local authorities and public corporations, and principal repayments and servicing of the National Debt, passes through the National Loans Fund.

The following figures outline central government receipts, and central government expenditure, broken down under various headings, as estimated for the year ending 31st March 1971, and published by Her Majesty's Stationery Office during 1971. This set of figures, rather than more up-to-date statistics, has been chosen for presentation here because of the relatively complete details of the proportions of the totals contributed by the various subsidiary headings. It is felt that information on the proportional contribution of the various areas will be more valuable to the reader seeking a general idea of the British economy, than would be up-to-date figures for which detailed breakdowns are not yet available. A "typical set of yearly accounts" then, is as follows:

A. TAXATION AND MISCELLANEOUS RECEIPTS, 1970–1971

TAXATION: Inland Revenue

	£
Income Tax	5,653,000,000
Surtax	277,000,000
Corporation Tax	1,900,000,000
Capital Gains Tax	150,000,000
Death Duties	371,000,000
Stamp Duties	119,000,000
Special Charges	4,000,000
Other	1,000,000
TOTAL INLAND REVENUE	**£8,475,000,000**

Customs and Excise

Tobacco	1,160,000,000
Purchase Tax	1,260,000,000
Oil	1,380,000,000
Spirits, beer and wine	905,000,000
Betting and Gaming	120,000,000
Other Revenue Duties	10,000,000
Protective Duties	230,000,000
Less Import Deposits	−425,000,000
Less Export Rebates	−5,000,000
TOTAL CUSTOMS AND EXCISE	**£4,635,000,000**

Motor Vehicle Duties, less rebates	430,000,000
Selective Employment Tax, gross	2,042,000,000
TOTAL TAXATION	**£15,582,000,000**

Miscellaneous Receipts

Broadcast Receiving Licences	102,000,000
Interest and Dividends	100,000,000
Other	340,000,000
TOTAL RECEIPTS	**£16,124,000,000**

N.B. It should be noted that the current administration is engaged in a wide-ranging study for the reform of the taxation structure in Britain. Certain changes have already come into operation, and a major reorientation is due to be implemented during 1973–74. The single most important measure is the proposed substitution of a Value Added Tax for the present Purchase Tax system.

B. EXPENDITURE: GENERAL FUNCTIONAL ANALYSIS OF 1970–1971 ESTIMATES

(These figures are not directly comparable with figures for government expenditure on specific areas quoted elsewhere in this book. There are inconsistencies of defini-tion, due to the complex series of direct and indirect grants, the part played by local authorities, and so on.)

	£
Defence budget	2,280,000,000
Other military expenditure	95,000,000
Overseas aid	218,000,000
Other overseas services	135,000,000
Technological services	184,000,000
Other assistance to employment and industry	975,000,000
Research councils, etc.	110,000,000
Agriculture, forestry and fishery	383,000,000
Roads and public lighting	373,000,000
Transport	165,000,000
Housing	250,000,000
Local environment services	49,000,000
Law and Order	294,000,000
Arts	21,000,000
Education	378,000,000
Health and Welfare	1,554,000,000
Social Security	1,432,000,000
Financial administration	272,000,000
Common services	258,000,000
Miscellaneous services	50,000,000
Selective Employment Tax refunds	1,151,000,000
Non-specific grants to local authorities	2,164,000,000
TOTAL EXPENDITURE	**£12,791,000,000**

(*This excludes a supplementary provision of £141,000,000*)

After allowing for budget changes and for certain supplementary provisions totalling £141,000,000, the total expenditure from central funds for the year ending 31st March 1971 was estimated at £13,526,000,000. This included £12,933,000,000 for Supply Services, and £593,000,000 for Standing Services. Estimated total revenue of £16,124,000,000 included £15,582,000,000 in receipts from taxation. An estimated surplus of £2,598,000,000 was thus available for transfer to the National Loans Fund. Net lending from this Fund in the year was estimated at £1,544,000,000; thus, after special transactions, it was estimated that net repayment of debts amounting to some £1,054,000,000 would be made by central government.

EXTERNAL TRADE: IMPORTS

The expansion of domestic agricultural productivity has reduced the proportion of foodstuffs in the total import volume to some 23%. Basic raw materials have also dropped to some 15% of total imports, due to the growing use of synthetics. Imports of crude fuels and lubricants still represent by far the biggest single item by value – about 11% of the total value of imports during the past ten years. There has been a sharp rise – in Britain, as in other developed nations – in the proportion of imports of finished manufactured goods and semi-manufactured goods.

An approximate breakdown of imports into categories, by value and by percentage of total imports, is as follows, based on 1970 figures:

	£	
Total Imports	*9,037,000,000*	*100%*
Food, drinks, tobacco	2,047,000,000	23%
Basic materials	1,362,000,000	15%
Mineral fuels, lubricants	945,000,000	11%
Semi-manufactured goods	2,500,000,000	28%
Finished manufactured goods	2,072,000,000	22%
Miscellaneous	111,000,000	1%

These broad categories include 399,000 tons of butter, valued at £126,000,000; 4,843,000 tons of grain (£140,000,000); 1,800,000 tons of sugar (£95,000,000); 249,000 tons of tea (£105,000,000); £1,653,000 standards of coniferous timber (£183,000,000); 3,038,000 tons of wood pulp (£195,000,000); 101,349,000 tons of crude and semi-refined petroleum (£712,000,000); 20,268,000 tons of petroleum products (£213,000,000); and 442,000 tons of copper, valued at £272,000,000.

SOURCES OF SUPPLY

The main sources of imports to Britain, broken down by value of imports (and also based on 1970 figures) are as follows; the individual national totals are calculated on 1969 figures.

	£	
Total Imports	*9,037,000,000*	*100%*
Sterling area	Approx. 2,457,000,000	29%
Non-sterling area	Approx. 6,561,000,000	71%
North America	1,856,000,000	
Latin America	326,000,000	
European Economic Community	1,822,000,000	
European Free Trade Association	1,405,000,000	
Soviet Union, Eastern Europe	354,000,000	
Remainder of world, total	798,000,000	
U.S.A.	1,130,900,000	
Canada	506,400,000	
Federal Germany	466,800,000	
Netherlands	409,200,000	
Sweden	332,900,000	
France	324,500,000	
South Africa	302,400,000	
Irish Republic	296,300,000	
Denmark	246,200,000	
Australia	237,500,000	
Italy	223,000,000	
New Zealand	216,200,000	

EXTERNAL TRADE: EXPORTS

More than 80% of Britain's exports consist of manufactured goods, of which by far the most important group are engineering products. Rapidly increasing exports of many types of machinery, electrical equipment, chemical products, road and agricultural vehicles and scientific instruments have been noted in recent years. Metals and textiles have tended to drop – the latter represented more than 18% of total exports in 1948 and only 5% in 1969, a clear indication of the changing patterns of world trade.

An approximate breakdown of exports into categories, by value, based on 1970 figures, is as follows:

	£
Total Exports	*8,061,000,000*
Food, drinks, tobacco	514,000,000
Basic materials	273,000,000
Mineral fuels, lubricants	207,000,000
Metals	959,000,000
Engineering products	3,510,000,000
Textiles	396,000,000
Miscellaneous	1,941,000,000

These broad categories include 70,000,000 proof gallons of potable spirits (mainly Scotch whisky), valued at £211,000,000; 3,900,000 tons of finished steel (£322,000,000); 115,000 tractors (£120,000,000); aircraft, aircraft engines and spares valued at £247,000,000; 23,000 tons of office machinery (£152,000,000); 83,000 tons of textile machinery (£123,000,000); 118,000 tons of electric power machinery and switchgear (£130,000,000); and 895,000 cars, commercial vehicles and chassis, valued at £524,000,000.

MARKETS

Britain's main overseas markets, calculated on 1970 figures, are as follows. The individual national totals are calculated on 1969 figures:

	£	
Total Exports	*8,061,000,000*	*100%*
Sterling area	Approx. 2,216,000,000	27%
Non-sterling area	Approx. 5,808,000,000	73%
North America	1,232,000,000	
Latin America	284,000,000	
European Economic Community	1,753,000,000	
European Free Trade Association	1,277,000,000	
Soviet Union, Eastern Europe	259,000,000	
Remainder of world, total	1,004,000,000	
U.S.A.	912,000,000	
Federal Germany	415,000,000	
Irish Republic	337,400,000	
Australia	323,000,000	
France	313,000,000	
Canada	310,900,000	
Sweden	302,000,000	
Netherlands	295,700,000	
South Africa	292,800,000	
Belgium and Luxembourg	290,500,000	

| Italy | 210,400,000 |
| Denmark | 197,900,000 |

INVISIBLE EARNINGS

For nearly two hundred years Britain's balance of payments has been enormously aided by her earnings from "invisible" overseas transactions – that is, business which has no tangible end product in the sense of an imported or exported object, but which produces earnings. The main areas of invisible earnings are government services; transport and travel; other services (covering such items as royalties, sales of TV and film rights, financial services, and so on); interest, profits and dividends; and private transfers, such as migrants' funds and legacies. The figures for both debits and credits in all these categories are given below, for the years 1965 and 1970, to demonstrate the considerable growth in British earnings from these sources over the five-year period:

Invisible transactions	1965	1970
	£	£
Government services	46,000,000	51,000,000
Shipping	749,000,000	1,371,000,000
Civil aviation	162,000,000	316,000,000
Travel	193,000,000	433,000,000
Other services	592,000,000	1,126,000,000
Interest, profits and dividends		
Private sector	947,000,000	1,313,000,000
Public sector	45,000,000	68,000,000
Private transfers	135,000,000	182,000,000
TOTAL CREDITS	£2,869,000,000	£4,860,000,000
TOTAL DEBITS	£2,684,000,000	£4,284,000,000
INVISIBLE CREDIT BALANCE	£185,000,000	£576,000,000

INTERNAL TRADE: WHOLESALE

Internal trade falls into two sections: trade in raw materials, unfinished products and components, and capital goods; and the trade in consumer products. Most of the following statistics are necessarily drawn from the figures relating to the 1965 wholesale trades census and the 1966 retail and service trades census, adjusted in accordance with 1969 figures in some areas. The date of origin of any information is quoted.

The census of 1965 showed that there were just over 41,000 "business units" engaged in the wholesale trade in Great Britain, of which some 23,650 were directly engaged in wholesale distribution of goods. Of this latter category some 2,000 businesses, with a turnover of just under £2,000,000,000, dealt in groceries and provisions, employing full- and part-time staff totalling about 67,000. Concerns dealing solely with vegetable and fruit distribution totalled another 2,630, with a turnover of nearly £470,000,000, and 38,000 male and female full- and part-

time employees. Clothing, footwear and textile distributors numbered 3,435, with a turnover of about £495,000,000, and some 42,500 staff. Hardware and electrical goods were distributed on a wholesale basis by some 2,400 firms, with a combined turnover of £385,000,000 and 40,000 employees.

Another sub-category of the wholesale trade was the group of firms dealing in coal, builders' material, grain and agricultural supplies, on a mixed wholesale and retail basis. These businesses returned figures indicating about 4,290 coal merchants, 2,308 builders' merchants, and 1,683 agricultural dealers, giving a total of 8,280-odd, with a total turnover of some £2,308,000,000, and about 148,000 employees. In addition, some 9,117 firms were dealers in various industrial materials and machinery, with a total turnover of some £3,235,000,000 and about 164,000 employees. Finally there were seven Marketing Boards, with turnovers totalling £457,000,000 and 4,000 employees.

Taking all these categories together, the wholesale trades in Great Britain had, in 1965, a total turnover of about £14,770,000,000, and employed some 779,000 men and women.

Methods of distribution vary from trade to trade. London's major wholesale markets handle great quantities of foodstuffs each year; Covent Garden, soon to be rehoused, handled about 1,200,000 tons of fruit and vegetables in 1970, and Smithfield handles more than 340,000 tons of meat and poultry each year. The centre of wholesale fish dealing is Billingsgate market, where port wholesalers who have purchased catches on the quayside, as it were, sell to inland wholesalers (although there is an increasing movement towards direct contract sales to fryers and processors). Fruit, vegetables and other agricultural products, some of which are regulated by statutory marketing boards, are sold either direct from grower to wholesaler, or by grower to commission agent, to wholesaler and retailer. The Co-operative Wholesale Society Ltd. and the Scottish equivalent supply retail co-operative societies, and recorded a combined turnover in excess of £600,000,000 in 1969.

RETAIL

This area of trade also breaks down into three basic categories for statistical purposes – multiples, co-operative societies, and independents. The multiples are those businesses other than co-operatives which have ten or more branches. In 1966 some 73,900 establishments owned by multiples – including multiple department stores – recorded a turnover totalling £3,837,000,000. The increasing number of multiple-owned stores, and the increasing share of the total retail sales market which these establishments are capturing, is a feature of all recently-published figures. The 1966 census, for instance, indicated that multiples then commanded some 34% of total retail sales, as against some 29% five years earlier. There is no reason to suppose that this trend has slackened significantly since.

The retail co-operative societies, voluntary organisations controlled by their members which distribute the trading surplus to their members in various ways (foodstuff price reductions, redeemable stamps, etc.), slipped from 11% to 9% of the total retail sales in the period 1961–1966. This was a less marked setback than that suffered by most independent retailers in the face of the challenge from the multiples, and the 1969 figures show that the co-operatives have increased their turnover slightly, although the number of establishments had decreased. Total receipts from sales and services by the retail co-operatives in 1969 were of the order of £1,130,000,000, compared with some £1,016,000,000 three years earlier. Co-operative retail establishments totalled 26,684 in 1966, operated (in 1969) by some 469 societies. The largest single society in Great Britain is the London Co-operative Society, with 1,150,000 members and a 1969 turnover of £81,000,000.

Independent shops have certainly been losing ground in the retail trade, but still account for the vast majority of British retail establishments – in 1966 there were 403,876 businesses out of a total of 504,412 retailers of all kinds. Turnover by independents in 1966 totalled about £6,279,000,000; this represented an 18% increase, while the number of independent businesses had dropped by 9% in the period 1961–1966.

In 1966 there were 760 department stores in the United Kingdom, with a total turnover of about £653,000,000 – representing some 6% of the total turnover of retail traders. Of this total number, 308 were owned by independents, 238 by co-operatives and 218 by multiples.

1961 figures indicated that there were then ten shops in Great Britain whose takings averaged more than £2,000 each hour – giving an annual turnover in excess of £5,000,000.

In 1961 there were some 9,500 shops operating wholly or partly on the "self-service" principle. At the end of 1969 there were more than 23,000. Of these more than 3,300 are supermarkets (defined as self-service shops with at least 2,000 square feet of selling space), which handled about 25% of Britain's total retail grocery trade. In 1961 there were only about 870, and at that time 524 were owned by multiples, 308 by co-operatives and 38 by independents.

The following is a breakdown of the retail trades into certain major categories of business, with numbers of establishments and turnover figures from the 1966 census:

Trade	Establishments	Turnover
Grocers, provision dealers	123,385	£2,908,000,000
Other food retailers	104,359	£2,081,000,000
Confectioners, tobacconists, and newsagents	63,333	£1,046,000,000
Clothing, footwear shops	83,199	£1,741,000,000
Household goods shops	69,761	£1,327,000,000
General stores	2,835	£1,041,000,000
Other (non-food) retailers	57,540	£ 988,000,000

A category of retail traders usually dealt with separately in all figures are gas and electricity showrooms. In 1966 there were 3,012 of these establishments, with a total turnover of £186,000,000; of this total some £29,000,000 represented receipts from maintenance, repairs and installations.

Another category which is usually statistically isolated is that of mail order houses. This has been an increasingly widespread method of selling over the past ten years; between 1961 and 1966 retail mail order business soared from £227,000,000 to £429,000,000, and turnover has continued to rise steadily ever since. In 1966 there were about 500 businesses engaged in this form of selling.

The total value of retail sales in Great Britain, including the above two categories of trading, rose between 1961 and 1966 from £9,250,000,000 to £11,747,000,000. The fastest growth was in the sector of radio and television sales and hire, mail order business, gas and electricity showroom sales of durable goods, leisure and sporting items, and photographic goods. Food and clothing did not make any dramatic advances. The number of persons engaged in the retail trades, excluding the showrooms, rose from 2,524,000 in 1961 to 2,556,000 in 1966.

The Northern Ireland census of the retail trades, carried out in 1965, showed 22,000 establishments with a total turnover of about £385,000,000. Trade is believed to have increased by some 14% between 1965 and 1969.

SERVICE TRADES

The catering trade recorded some detailed figures of trading in 1964, the most recent available. There were then some 150,900 establishments primarily concerned with catering (that is, hotels and restaurants, cafés, public houses, canteens, etc.), with a turnover totalling some £2,036,000,000. In addition there were about 22,000 registered clubs, taking a total of about £203,000,000. Of the other main categories of business, there were about 8,900 licensed hotels and holiday camps, with a total turnover of some £286,000,000 (exclusive of about £120,000,000 in takings by unlicensed hotels); 68,900 public houses and hotels under brewery management, with takings of about £1,033,000,000; some 32,500 cafés, restaurants and snack bars, with a total turnover of about £413,000,000; and, splendid to relate, no less than 17,200 fish-and-chip shops with a total turnover of some £101,000,000. Nearly half the total catering trade turnover is from sales of alcoholic drink.

The motor trade recorded the following figures for trading in 1967, since when turnover is estimated to have risen by about 11%:

Total businesses	43,000
Total establishments	51,500
Total turnover	£4,198,000,000

Types and numbers of Establishments	Turnover
	£
13,600 new vehicle dealers	2,907,000,000
4,600 secondhand vehicle dealers	200,000,000
1,800 motorcycle dealers	43,000,000
11,100 general repairers	270,000,000
3,400 specialist repairers	54,000,000
2,100 motor accessory dealers	52,000,000
2,200 tyre dealers	124,000,000
11,300 petrol stations	413,000,000
1,100 wholesalers of accessories, etc.	105,000,000
400 caravan dealers	30,000,000

The 1966 census revealed about 5,600 commercial laundry, launderette and dry cleaning establishments in Great Britain, with a total turnover of about £172,000,000. Between 1961 and 1966 this worked out at a growth of 53%, but this trend was not maintained, and apart from increased takings by coin-operated self-service establishments, turnover changed little during the late 1960s.

Hairdressing establishments displayed the same general picture. Between 1950 and 1961 turnover as a whole rose from around £38,000,000 to around £97,000,000, and between 1961 and 1966 it rose further to around £136,000,000. Since 1966 however takings have risen by around 4% only. In that year there were about 48,000 hairdressing salons trading in Great Britain.

It is estimated that Great Britain has some 15,800 licensed betting offices, more than 3,500 funeral undertaking businesses, and around 4,000 television rental establishments.

Instalment Sales

At the end of 1970 the instalment credit debt outstanding in Great Britain to the major hire purchase organisations was some £1,384,000,000. About two-thirds of this total was owed to finance companies, and the remainder to durable goods shops and department stores. Hire purchase debts outstanding in Northern Ireland, directly financed by the major finance companies operating from Ulster premises, totalled about £19,500,000 in 1969.

Advertising

During 1969 it is estimated that a total of some £530,000,000 was spent on all types of advertising in Great Britain. Government analyses show that there has been no significant change in the proportion of the gross national product (1·4%) and of consumer expenditure (1·9%) represented by advertising over the past ten years or so. The Press still commands the major portion of the advertising budget, accounting for about £360,000,000 of the 1969 total, with television taking another £130,000,000 worth.

Packaging

Current annual expenditure on packaging in the United Kingdom is estimated at about £850,000,000. The materials mainly used are paper of various types (turnover about £380,000,000 annually); tinplate (£130,000,000); glass (£65,000,000); and plastics (£70,000,000).

BANKING, INVESTMENT AND INSURANCE

The British banking system comprises the central bank, the Bank of England, established as a corporate body by Act of Parliament and Royal Charter in 1694; commercial banks which conduct the usual banking services; and various special institutions such as merchant banks, London offices of overseas banks, and so on.

The entire stock capital of the Bank of England passed to the Government in 1946. The Bank acts as the Government's banker, and provides services for overseas central banks and British commercial banks. It is the note-issuing authority, and the registrar for about 200 government, local authority, public board and nationalised industry stocks. As agent for the Government it manages the Exchange Equalisation Account, comprising the nation's gold and foreign exchange reserves, and advises the current administration on the shaping and execution of financial policy. The Bank is the usual channel of communication between the Government of the day and the various commercial banks and other financial institutions collectively referred to as "the City". While the Bank has the sole right to issue notes in England and Wales, commercial banks in Scotland and Northern Ireland have limited rights to issue their own notes, subject to certain strict central controls. All coin for circulation is issued by the Royal Mint.

The principal commercial banks comprise four major groups (Barclays, Lloyds, Midland and National Westminster) based in London, with branches throughout the country; several small but long-established London bankers, which do not have widespread networks of branches but which provide normal deposit facilities as well as more specialised services; two main Scottish banks; and two Northern Ireland banks owned by London clearing banks.

At the close of 1969 current and deposit accounts with the deposit banks operating in the United Kingdom totalled about £11,800,000,000, representing rather less than half the total deposits in British and foreign currency of the banking sector as a whole. The London Clearing House, comprising the deposit banks and the Bank of England, passed a monthly average of £58,266,000,000 in cheques, drafts and bills during 1969. Average monthly value of the credit transfer clearing during the same period was £1,137,000,000. The London clearing banks generally maintain a ratio between cash reserves and total deposits of about 8%, and at least 28% of deposits are normally held in liquid assets.

Apart from the London clearing banks, there are about 36 British overseas and Commonwealth banks with branches or headquarters in London; about 32 United

States banks, 13 Japanese banks, and about 80 other foreign banks are also represented in the capital.

The London Stock Exchange is one of the world's two foremost markets, but it is only one of eight stock exchanges which operate in the United Kingdom. It is however incomparably the most important; about 9,000 securities are quoted on the London exchange, with a total market value (as at 31st March 1970) of £120,040,000,000.

At the end of 1970 there were about 2,400,000 unit holdings in more than 200 unit trusts catering to British investors, with a total value of some £1,315,500,000. This represents a doubling of funds invested in these trusts since 1966.

In 1970 there were 481 building societies registered in Britain, with total assets of £10,818,800,000. However, eight of the largest societies, each with assets exceeding £250,000,000, represent more than half the total funds. Together the societies represent more than 10,265,000 share investors.

There are currently some 570 insurance companies incorporated in the United Kingdom. The bulk of the business is in the hands of about 100 companies, however. There are also some 170 foreign companies which carry on business in Britain. The total funds of British insurance companies and collecting societies in 1968 stood at around £14,830,000,000, most of it in respect of life assurance policies. The figures below indicate the funds in the hands of the British companies at the end of 1969, broken down roughly into the various categories of business:

	£
Life assurance, ordinary business	9,751,000,000
Life assurance, industrial business	1,897,000,000
Motor vehicle insurance business	200,000,000
Fire insurance business	231,000,000
Marine, aviation, transit insurance business	206,000,000

Lloyds
Named after a late 17th century coffee-house which became the favoured meeting place for London's maritime merchants, Lloyd's is an incorporated society of private insurers, a market for insurance where business is transacted by about 6,000 underwriters grouped into some 280 competitive syndicates. Originally devoted to maritime business, and famous for its worldwide shipping intelligence system, Lloyd's has also become the market for many other types of insurance. It is regulated by a series of Acts of Parliament, and membership is subject to the most stringent financial requirements. Only elected underwriting members may do business at Lloyd's, and insurance may only be placed through Lloyd's brokers, who negotiate in their turn with the underwriters.

THE CIVIC ADMINISTRATION AND THE LIVERY COMPANIES OF THE CITY OF LONDON

"A Town of the Highest Repute and a busy Emporium for Trade and Traders"

In such terms was Londinium described early in the period of Roman occupation of Britain between A.D. 43 and early in the fifth century, becoming the centre of the road system and the financial headquarters of the Roman province of Britain. During the occupation the Romans also constructed substantial protective walls around the town on the north bank of the River Thames.

In A.D. 604 the first Saxon bishop of London, Bishop Mellitus, was appointed and a church dedicated to St. Paul, London's patron saint, was built on the hill overlooking Ludgate shortly afterwards. In 886 Alfred the Great appointed his son-in-law, Aethelred (who at the time was *procurator* of Mercia) to be Governor of London; thus was the city's municipal system established, together with the county status which still survives. City Sheriffs (cf. *shire-reeves*, magistrates of the Shire) had jurisdiction over Middlesex as well as London, and the office of Sheriff of Middlesex continued until 1888 to be filled by Sheriffs of the City.

The first City Sheriffs were "Portreeves", officers of the principal trading communities – literally "magistrates of a trading town", as the City of London was acknowledged as an independent kingdom making and upholding its own laws: these laws, relating to trade, later became embodied in the whole English legal system. The City came to be divided into Wards, the majority of which still exist, each governed by an Alderman (cf. *ealdor-man*, the older man) who presided over the Wardmotes, or meetings and elections of the Wards. A "folkmoot" of all London citizens used to meet in the shadow of old St. Paul's.

So influential had London become by the time of the Norman conquest that William the Conqueror had to come to terms with the City, granting the citizens a Charter which is still preserved at Guildhall; this Charter ratified the many rights and privileges of the citizens. Despite the existence of these rights the City owed allegiance to the Crown, the citizens being bound to support the King's Household and the Royal Exchequer.

Successive English monarchs confirmed the ancient rights, and further immunities were from time to time obtained from the Crown, being embodied in the various Royal Charters; for example the City has up to the present day continued to enjoy the right to appoint its own justices.

Among the provisions of the Great Charter (*Magna Carta*) granted by King John in 1215 was endorsement and confirmation of the rights, privileges and free customs of London's citizens. Among the officials appointed to ensure that the terms of the Charter were upheld was the Mayor of London. The City of London's Common

Council, whose existence was endorsed in 1322 when Edward II undertook his consolidation of democratic government, is unique among British local authorities in retaining the power to pass its own Acts and governing its own constitution.

The City's boundaries have remained virtually unchanged since the time of the Norman conquest, enclosing an area of 677 acres – comprising the 325 acres inside the old Roman walls, and the "suburbs and liberties without the walls" which came to be incorporated in Saxon times.

The civic administration of the City has remained basically unchanged to this day, the administrative body comprising the Lord Mayor, twenty-five other Aldermen, and the Common Councilmen. The Aldermen and Councilmen are elected by the qualified residents and ratepayers of the Wards, and there are no party politics in the civic government of the City. The Aldermen are elected for life, but Members of the Common Council stand for re-election at the wardmotes held every St. Thomas's Day, 21st December.

The two City Sheriffs have since 1199 been elected annually, their elections being held on Midsummer Day each year since 1585. The citizens had however obtained the right by a much earlier Royal Charter to elect Sheriffs from among their own number. They are elected by the City's livery – the members of the City livery companies – and take office on 28th September, on the Vigil of St. Michael the Archangel; they hold office for one year and are not eligible for a second term of office. Each Sheriff appoints his own deputy (or Under Sheriff), and by custom one of the two City Sheriffs is normally a member of the Court of Aldermen.

THE LORD MAYOR

The City's mayoralty is a tradition unbroken since 1189 when Henry Fitz Aylwyn became the first Mayor of London. The title "Lord Mayor" evolved, but has never been conferred or confirmed by Charter or otherwise.

All Aldermen who have served in the office of Sheriff are automatically among those nominated for the election of Lord Mayor each year. The deciding factor is usually seniority in service as Alderman, but the City liverymen have the right to nominate in Common Hall two qualified Aldermen for the election of one of them by the Court of Aldermen on 29th September.

After the Lord Mayor's election has gained the monarch's approval, and the Lord Mayor-elect has been received by the Lord Chancellor in the House of Lords, he travels through the City streets in procession on the second Saturday in November to take the oath of office before the Judges of the King's Bench Division. This is the occasion of the celebrated "Lord Mayor's Show". He is the Chief Magistrate of the City, and the head of the City Lieutenancy; within the City boundaries he takes precedence over every subject, taking his place immedi-

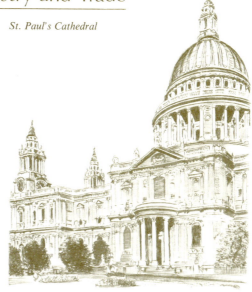

St. Paul's Cathedral

ately after the Sovereign. No troops may pass through the City without his permission.

THE CITY LIVERY COMPANIES

The origins of the Craft Guilds of the City of London, of which no fewer than 82 flourish today, are almost obscured in the mists of antiquity. They were originally voluntary fraternities whose objects were religious and social, and came into existence towards the close of the Dark Ages, becoming fairly commonplace throughout Europe in the eleventh and twelfth centuries among towns which were struggling into existence. Their associations with specific crafts were almost accidental – but probably inevitable since exponents of a craft tended to collect and live within the same neighbourhood.

Such craft fraternities certainly existed in and around London in Saxon times, but although Charters were granted by Crown and Church during this period (bestowing grants of privileges and land), none exists today to indicate the formality and authority of any surviving "guild". Nevertheless it is known, by tradition if nothing more, that the Worshipful Company of Mercers – the senior of the twelve great Companies – has origins which took root long before the Norman conquest.

Bearing in mind the substantial religious structure of Britain's society in the Middle Ages, it was to be expected that regularly-established fraternities would adopt the outward trappings of, and associations with, the Church; and it was also therefore natural that their meetings would be conducted in nearby churches or monasteries, whose patron saint would be adopted. Therein lies the strong element of religious influence which has survived up to modern times. Often the fraternities would adopt the uniform robes and gowns of their associated church – in much the same way that uniform liveries were adopted by the armed retainers of the great households of the Middle Ages; this distinctive "uniform" gave rise to the term Livery Companies.

Notwithstanding this religious element, the Livery Companies were primarily, and have remained essentially, Craft Guilds. Acquiring considerable authority by reason of their establishment within the great trading City of London, the various Guilds came to exercise unmatched influence in the trading activities of the nation as a whole, with the result that, one by one, they achieved formal status in the grant of Charters by the ruling monarch, defining their powers and privileges. Their authority became extraordinary and, within the social structure and limitations imposed by inadequate legislation that existed during the period from the fourteenth to eighteenth centuries, this authority provided an essential measure of respectability, which became integral with the respect frequently enjoyed by Britain in her trading relations during these six hundred years. It would be no exaggeration to find the seeds of labour protection and the trades unions, as well as consumer protection organisations within the motivations expressed by the Charters of the Livery Companies, long before the huge influential bodies of today ever came into being.

Another characteristic that was bound to find expression in the Livery Companies was the encouragement of good fellowship and hospitality, both within their own membership and towards the community at large. As England gained prosperity in the fifteenth and sixteenth centuries, measurably enhanced by the efforts of the Guilds themselves, so they prospered, and during this period they established great halls in the City wherein their members could meet and feast, gatherings for which the Companies were, and still are, famous. Alas, these great Halls suffered tragically in the Fire of London in 1666, and again in the night bombing raids of 1940–41. Of the 33 Halls that were standing in 1939, only 15 survived the War, and of these only two were undamaged. Many have now been restored or re-built and about thirty are in normal use today.

Despite the fact that the Guilds can no longer make the same sort of contribution to their respective crafts and ancient mysteries in modern times, it is probably true that there has never in their long history been a greater interest than there is now in the Livery Companies and what they represent. Not only are there a number of organisations awaiting the opportunity to petition the Court of Aldermen for the grant of a livery, but the ancient Companies have never been so active in their contributions to the community as they are today. These contributions range from substantial financial grants for education and the maintenance of schools and scholarships at all levels, to the provision, staffing and maintenance of hospitals and homes for old people. A measure of the enthusiasm with which the Companies pursue their great works may be gained from the size of their collective liveries, which today stands at no fewer than 14,000 liverymen.

THE TWELVE GREAT COMPANIES OF THE CITY OF LONDON (in order of seniority)

The Worshipful Company of Mercers
    Hall: Ironmonger Lane, London E.C.2
The Worshipful Company of Grocers
    Hall: Princes Street, London E.C.2
The Worshipful Company of Drapers
    Hall: Throgmorton Street, London E.C.2
The Worshipful Company of Fishmongers
    Hall: Adelaide Place, London Bridge, E.C.4
The Worshipful Company of Goldsmiths
    Hall: Foster Lane, London E.C.2
The Worshipful Company of Merchant Taylors
    Hall: Threadneedle Street, London E.C.2
The Worshipful Company of Skinners
    Hall: Dowgate Hill, London E.C.4
The Worshipful Company of Haberdashers
    Hall: Staining Lane, Gresham Street, E.C.2
The Worshipful Company of Salters
    Office: 36 Portland Place, London W.1
The Worshipful Company of Ironmongers
    Hall: Shaftesbury Place, Aldersgate, E.C.1
The Worshipful Company of Vintners
    Hall: Upper Thames Street, London E.C.4
The Worshipful Company of Clothworkers
    Hall: Dunster Court, London E.C.3

INDUSTRY

The United Kingdom's industry presents an extremely varied pattern of control and organisation; the first nation in the world to become highly industrialised, Britain has evolved the present structure over nearly three centuries. Like all entities which evolve slowly rather than spring into life as part of a deliberate and co-ordinated plan, British industry defies any attempt at neat labelling and categorisation. Businesses range from the thousands of tiny workshops with one, two or half a dozen employees, to giant enterprises such as Imperial Chemical Industries Ltd., which employs 145,000 men and women in the United Kingdom. Private enterprise, publicly owned industries, co-operatives and self-employed individuals all play their part in the pattern.

MANUFACTURING INDUSTRIES

Most of the manufacturing enterprises in Britain are privately owned. Exceptions include the nationalised British Steel Corporation, the manufacture of fissile materials and isotopes by the Atomic Energy Authority, a 49% government holding in British Petroleum Ltd., and certain other controlling interests.

Total output of the manufacturing industries (in 1968 valued at £36,893,000,000) has increased by almost half since 1958; the 1969 figures were 3·3% up on 1968. Output per head was up 2·3% in 1969, making an aggregate increase of 25·3% since 1963. It is calculated that the manufacturing industries employ 8,600,000 people in the United Kingdom, or some 37% of the total number of employees (1969 figure).

Iron and Steel. Britain is the world's fifth largest producer of steel. At the end of 1970 there were 71 blast furnaces in the United Kingdom. Pig iron production in 1970 totalled 17,393,000 tons. There were 622 steel furnaces, and in that year crude steel production reached 27,869,000 ingot tons. Imports totalled 2,749,000 ingot tons. Actual deliveries totalled 3,721,000 tons of steel for export and 18,288,000 tons for home use. The main overseas customers were the United States, Spain and Sweden (1969 figures: £48,800,000, £17,300,000 and £16,100,000 respectively from a total export value of £285,000,000).

The main producing areas are Wales, with 29% of the total crude steel output; Yorkshire and Humberside, with 26%; the North, with 18%; and Scotland, with 12%. Wales produces mostly flat products such as tinplate and sheet steel, while the North-East and Scotland concentrate mainly on heavy steel products. Sheffield is the centre of alloy steel production. The iron and steel industry employs some 280,000 men and women.

Iron castings. About 900 firms employ around 110,000 men and women in the iron founding industry; output in 1969 stood at 3,760,000 tons – more than 5% up on 1968.

Non-ferrous metals. Among Western nations Britain is second only to the U.S.A. as a consumer of aluminium, copper and lead, and her non-ferrous metal industry is the largest in Europe. 1969 aluminium output totalled 33,000 long tons of virgin metal and 223,500 tons of unwrought alloys. In the same year output of refined copper was 49,000 tons of virgin metal and 147,000 tons of secondary metal. The output of lead was 139,000 tons of secondary metal refined from scrap and 117,000 tons of virgin metal refined from imported bullion. Zinc production reached 149,000 tons of slab metal. Exports of non-ferrous base metals in 1969 totalled £312,000,000, including copper and copper alloys (£109,700,000), nickel and nickel alloys (£37,900,000), and aluminium and its alloys (£23,900,000). Major overseas markets included Federal Germany (£52,400,000), the United States (£34,600,000) and China (£28,000,000).

About half the industry is situated in the Midlands, and important plants are also to be found in South Wales, London, Tyneside and Avonmouth. Britain is also a major producer of the new, specialised metals used in the fields of aircraft manufacture, electronics and atomic energy.

ENGINEERING PRODUCTS

Metal-working machine tools. 70,000 employees, mainly in the Midlands, Yorkshire and Lancashire. 1969 deliveries valued at £169,000,000, including exports of £71,300,000. 1970 deliveries valued at £198,700,000.

Industrial engines. 35,000 employees. 1969 deliveries valued at £135,000,000, including exports of £39,600,000; additional exported parts valued at £28,800,000.

Textile machinery. 48,000 employees, mainly with small firms in Lancashire, Yorkshire, Northern Ireland, Dundee, Leicester and Nottingham. 1969 exports valued at £105,700,000, including sales of over £9,000,000 each to the United States, Federal Germany and Pakistan. 1970 total deliveries were valued at £144,500,000.

Mechanical handling equipment. 60,000 employees scattered among many small firms. 1969 deliveries valued at £200,000,000; exports, £69,500,000. 1970 deliveries valued at £245,000,000.

Contractors' plant and quarrying machinery. 41,000 employees. 1969 deliveries valued at £232,000,000 including exports of £123,000,000 to France, Australia, Federal Germany and Ireland. 1970 deliveries valued at £232,100,000.

Office machinery. 57,000 employees. 1969 deliveries valued at £103,000,000, including £56,100,000 for export.

Engineers' small tools and gauges. 74,000 employees. 1969 deliveries valued at £110,000,000 including £20,000,000 for export.

Industrial plant and steelwork. 182,000 employees. 1969 deliveries totalled £611,500,000.

Other important non-electrical engineering products include boilers and boilerhouse plant (1969 deliveries, £142,000,000); chemical plant and oil refining plant (1968 deliveries, £129,000,000); and miscellaneous machinery products such as mining, printing, refrigeration, pumping, and food, drink and tobacco processing plant – which employ a total labour force of around 366,000 men and women and which recorded deliveries valued at around £635,000,000 in 1969.

Scientific and industrial instruments. Manufacture of these occupied about 132,000 people and accounted for £199,000,000 in deliveries during 1969, including £72,200,000 in exports. *Photographic equipment* deliveries in 1969 totalled £120,000,000.

The *electrical engineering industry* employs about 905,000 people. It is engaged in the production of every type of generating, transmission and distribution equipment, telecommunications apparatus, domestic appliances, and specialised equipment. The total value of production in 1969 was estimated at £2,100,000,000. Exports of electrical machinery and apparatus in that year reached £466,000,000.

The industries engaged in the *manufacture of vehicles, ships and aircraft* employ well over a million workers and contributed in 1969 total exports valued at £1,071,000,000, or about 14% of Britain's total exports for that year.

Motor vehicles represent the largest part of this industry, employing about 507,000 men and women. From its original locations in the London and Midlands areas

The best-selling British car, the British Leyland Motor Corporation 1100/1300

the industry has spread into Merseyside, Wales and Scotland. Car and freight vehicle production is dominated by four large firms: British Leyland Motor Corporation, Ford, Chrysler United Kingdom (Rootes), and Vauxhall. Between them these giants account for over 95% of total vehicle production; the remaining 5% or so is made up of small specialist firms producing sports cars, coaches and luxury cars. Total car output in 1969 was 1,720,000; exports totalled 772,000 valued at £341,000,000. Production of commercial vehicles and chassis reached 466,000 in 1969, of which 181,000 were exported at a value of £168,500,000.

(1970 total deliveries: cars, 1,641,000; commercial vehicles, 458,000.)

Rail vehicles are produced for export and for British Rail use by private suppliers, and British Rail workshops also produce large numbers of vehicles both for their own use and for sale. The manufacture of railway locomotives and rolling stock occupies about 55,000 employees, and in 1969 some £13,500,000 worth of stock was exported.

Aircraft manufacture and repair occupies some 238,000 British workers, concentrated in two large airframe manufacturers (British Aircraft Corporation, and the Hawker Siddeley Group, which have gradually swallowed up all the smaller firms whose names were once famous in British aviation), one helicopter company, and a few important smaller companies. In 1969 the aerospace industry as a whole recorded exports totalling £305,000,000, and aero-engines and parts provided a further £117,000,000 in exports during that year. Twelve types of British jet engines power more than thirty aircraft types currently in production overseas.

Shipbuilding and marine engineering industries are concentrated in four main areas of the country – the Clyde, Belfast, and North-East and North-West England – with a total labour force of around 188,000. Numerous

smaller yards around the British coasts produce fishing vessels, yachts, harbour craft and pleasure craft. Between 1955 and 1964 there was a fall in tonnage launched from British yards, but this has since been halted; in 1969 launchings totalled 1,040,000 gross tons, the fourth highest figure in the world. Launchings in that year included seventeen oil tankers, 22 bulk carriers, and 24 cargo vessels. At the end of 1970 there were 136 ships under construction in British yards, including 31 for export (1,612,000 and 403,000 gross tons respectively). A further 200 vessels totalling 3,282,000 gross tons were on the order books, of which 49 (798,000 tons were destined for export. Vessels completed in 1970 totalled 144 (1,297,000 gross tons) including 25 (260,000 gross tons) for export.

CHEMICAL PRODUCTS

The British chemical industry has a total labour force of around 480,000. The industry may be broken down into the following categories: general chemicals (147,000 employees), pharmaceutical chemicals and preparations (70,000 employees), toilet preparations (26,000 employees), paints, dyestuffs and pigments (60,000 employees), soaps and detergents (25,000 employees), synthetic resins, plastics and rubber (59,000 employees), fertilisers (14,000 employees), and other chemical products (78,000 employees). The export of chemical elements and compounds in 1969 amounted to £166,500,000. Plastics exports in the same year totalled 480,000 tons, valued at £124,800,000. Synthetic rubber and latex exports totalled 98,000 tons. Exports of paints (£44,000,000), fertiliser (£5,400,000), medicinal and pharmaceutical products (£117,700,000), and of toilet, soap and cosmetic preparations (£60,700,000) all contributed to the chemical industry's record export total of around £745,000,000 in 1969, representing about 10% of Britain's total exports for that year.

TEXTILES

Despite their decreasing importance in terms of percentage of total exports over the past two decades, due to many different factors, textiles are still a major area of British industry. In the summer of 1969 the industry had a total labour force of about 756,000 people, half of them women. The production of textiles rose by 16% between 1958 and 1968, and by 3·5% between 1968 and 1969. The industry has survived by a painstaking and sometimes painful reorientation into directions best favoured by the special skills and characteristics of British mills and materials. The bulk of the spinning and warp knitting activities carried out in Britain are controlled by four multi-fibre, multi-process groups, with a degree of technical co-operation and research co-ordination through the Textile Council, a body financed by the industry.

In 1969 the total value of textile exports was of the order of £347,000,000. The labour force was distributed roughly as follows: 53,000 on production of man-made fibres; 75,000 in spinning and doubling cotton, flax, and man-made fibres; 66,800 in weaving cotton, linen and man-made fibres; 159,000 in the woollen and worsted industry; 66,000 in textile finishing; 140,000 in knitted goods and hosiery; and about 45,000 in the carpet trade.

The basic figures for 1970 production were as follows:

Raw cotton imports	436,000,000 lb.
Cotton yarn production	447,000,000 lb.
Cotton cloth production	686,000,000 lin. yds.
Man-made fibre production	1,321,000,000 lb.
Spun man-made fibre and mixture yard	171,000,000 lb.
Man-made fibre and mixture cloth	530,000,000 lin. yds.
Virgin wool imports	314,000,000 lb.
Virgin wool production	68,000,000 lb.
Deliveries of worsted yarn	215,000,000 lb.
Deliveries of woven fabrics	286,000,000 sq. yds.
Weft knitted fabric sales	94,000,000 lb.
Warp knitted fabric sales	£72,000,000
Garment and hosiery sales	£304,000,000
Carpet and rug sales	143,000,000 sq. yds.

The *cotton* industry is mainly concentrated in Lancashire, with the weaving trade largely in the north-east of the county, and the spinning trade in the south-east. The trade's commercial centre is Manchester, with Liverpool as the main port of entry for raw cotton imports. *Wool* is largely the province of small or medium-sized firms, with only a few giant enterprises. The most important area is the West Riding of Yorkshire, with specialist centres in Scotland and the West. *Man-made fibres* are, not unnaturally, produced by several very large organisations spread over the country. The *hosiery and knitwear* trades are widely distributed, with a large number of small firms engaged, but Scotland and the eastern Midlands are important centres. Northern Ireland is the traditional centre of the *linen* trade, and heavier materials of this type are also produced in Scotland. Dundee is the centre of the *jute* trade.

CLOTHING, FOOTWEAR AND LEATHER

Britain has the largest *clothing* industry in Europe, with some 390,000 employees. Exports of clothes other than knitted goods totalled £61,600,000 in 1969. The bulk of the industry is made up of some 200 relatively small firms, although there are one or two mass-production giants. The centres are London, Leeds and Manchester.

Britain has the third largest *footwear* industry in the world, with factories spread throughout the country. In 1969 manufacturers sold 194,000,000 pairs of shoes and other types of footwear; of these, some £33,500,000-worth went in export sales. The industry employs about 105,000 workers, and certain areas are traditionally engaged in certain types of production – most women's shoes are made in Leicester and in the Norwich area.

Leather tanning, the production of leather goods, and fur manufacture provide work for about 60,000 people in Britain, with concentrations in Lancashire, Yorkshire, Cheshire, the northern Midlands and London. Exports of all types of leathers were valued at £31,200,000 in 1969.

CONSUMABLES

Altogether more than 850,000 people work in the British food, drink, tobacco and confectionery industries. The value of exports in all sectors of this industry totalled £387,000,000 in 1969.

There are upwards of 200,000 employees in the *grain-milling, bread and flour* confectionery industry, and some 83,000 in the *chocolate and sugar confectionery* trade. As indicated in Chapter 5, consumption of chocolate and sugar confectionery is higher in Britain than in any other country in the world. Britain is also the largest exporter in the world in this field, accounting for about a third of the total world export trade.

Fruit and vegetable products – conserves, sauces, etc. – occupy the services of some 74,000 workers. *Canned vegetables and fruits* are produced in large quantities; total

Output of *canned meat* and meat products rose to plus 103,000 tons of canned and bottled fruit and 286,000 tons of canned soup. The most popular canned foods are peas (277,000 tons) and baked beans in tomato sauce (250,000 tons). The *frozen food* industry is steadily increasing its sales in Britain, and 190,000 tons of vegetables and fruit were processed in this way in 1969.

Output of *canned meat* and meat products rose to 130,000 tons in 1969, and *bacon and ham curing* to 234,000 tons. About 96,000 tons of *frozen fish* were produced, and a much smaller amount of canned fish – only some 8,000 tons. Exports of meat, fish, and meat and fish products and preparations totalled some £30,000,000 in the year.

More than 155,000 workers are employed by the beer, spirits, wine and soft drinks industries, the majority of them – well over 90,000 – being employed by the *brewing and malting* trades. In 1969 33,000,000 bulk barrels of beer were produced in Britain, and consumers in the home market are estimated to have spent £1,058,000,000 on beer. In the same year some 52,000,000 proof gallons of *whisky* were exported, valued at £168,000,000. During the year 126,000,000 proof gallons were produced and laid down for sale later. Stocks of whisky amount to the staggering total of 700,000,000 proof gallons. *Soft drink* output in 1969 amounted to about 66,000,000 gallons of concentrated liquid ("squash") and about 262,000,000 gallons of unconcentrated drinks. About twenty firms are active in this field, although two dominate the market.

Some 40,000 people are employed by the *tobacco* industry in Britain, which is based around Bristol, Liverpool, London, Manchester, Newcastle, Nottingham, Glasgow and Belfast. The industry used, in 1969, about 306,000,000 pounds of unmanufactured tobacco – all of it imported – the main sources being the U.S.A., Canada and India. Consumer expenditure on tobacco products in that year totalled about £1,690,000,000, and some 125,000,000,000 cigarettes were smoked, 75% of them filter tipped. Tobacco industry exports – mainly to Germany, Hong Kong and Kuwait – were worth £34,900,000 in 1969.

PRINTING, PUBLISHING AND PAPER

Altogether this area of British industry employs about 635,000 workers. A vast range of products stems from the *printing and publishing* trades – everything from greetings cards to books – and in this sector there are some 405,000 workers, including about 143,000 engaged in newspaper and periodical publishing. British consumers spend more on newspapers per head of population than any other nationality in the world, and total expenditure on books, papers, journals and periodicals was nearly £400,000,000 in 1968. Publishers recorded a combined turnover of £138,000,000, of which exports of books represented some £42,600,000. The *paper and board* trades employ some 92,000 workers, in the largest industry of its kind in Europe. More than 4,900,000 tons of paper and boards of all types were produced in 1969, with exports valued at £78,600,000. Sales of cardboard *boxes and cartons* amounted to £129,000,000 in 1969, and those of fibre board packing cases to £126,000,000. This section of the industry employs some 64,000 people.

BUILDING MATERIALS

Cement production occupies some 17,000 employees, mainly around the Medway towns of Kent. Output in 1969 totalled more than 17,000,000 tons. The *timber* trade employs about 110,000 people, and although imports of timber stood at £218,000,000 in 1969, the output of home-grown timber and home-grown pitwood from British mills reached 65,000,000 cubic feet. There

are about 60,000 employees in the *brick*, *tile*, *fireclay* and allied material industry, mainly in the Bedford and Peterborough areas. In 1969 building brick production totalled 6,734,000,000.

POTTERY AND GLASS

Britain imports little *pottery*, as home production supplies virtually all domestic and industrial needs. The industry has been well established for more than 200 years, and specialist British firms are household names in the industry all over the world. The industry is largely concentrated around Stoke-on-Trent in Staffordshire. Raw materials are transported from Devon and Cornwall. Domestic pottery sales in 1969 were valued at £58,000,000, and exports at £25,900,000. Some 60,000 workers are employed in the pottery trade.

The British *glass* industry is the third largest in the world, with 83,000 employees and 1969 exports valued at £39,400,000.

RUBBER

More than half the output of the British rubber industry is taken up by tyres and tubes, and in 1969 this sector used 249,000 tons of rubber. The industry's total consumption that year was 178,000 tons of natural, 235,800 tons of synthetic, and 24,400 tons of reclaimed rubber. Direct exports of all rubber goods were valued at £72,400,000.

FURNITURE

Deliveries of domestic furniture in 1969 were valued at £177,000,000; exports of all categories reached £23,200,000. A total labour force of about 90,000 is engaged in the industry, which is centred around London.

FUEL AND POWER

The main sources of energy currently used in Britain are coal, petroleum products, nuclear energy, natural gas, and water power. More than half the primary energy needs are still met by the consumption of coal mined within Britain, but this proportion is dropping. The use of oil fuels, virtually all imported, has been increasing in proportion.

The energy consumption figures for 1970, on a heat supplied basis, have been published as follows:

	therms
Gross consumption of primary fuels:	83,481,000,000
Coal	39,284,000,000
Petroleum	36,931,000,000
Nuclear, hydro-electric and natural gas	7,266,000,000
Total consumption by final users (after export, stock conversion, consumption by fuel suppliers, etc.)	57,963,000,000

Class of consumer:

Domestic	14,680,000,000
Transport	11,186,000,000
Iron and steel industry	7,198,000,000
Other industries	17,473,000,000
Other final consumers	7,426,000,000

With the exception of the petroleum industry the fuel and power industries are publicly owned. Responsibility is vested in the Minister of Technology. Altogether the fuel and power industries employ about 770,000 people, or 3% of the total working population. Their net output is some 5% of the gross national product, their annual turnover is in the region of £4,000,000,000, and their capital investment in 1971 was about £700,000,000, or about 16% of total investment.

The main areas of *coal-mining* are the Yorkshire, Nottinghamshire and Derbyshire fields, producing nearly half the country's total output; the Durham and Northumberland fields; the South Wales field; and the Scottish field. As they have been worked for 700 years the best coal seams are partly exhausted, but adequate resources survive to satisfy domestic demand well into the 21st century. At the same time production has been deliberately contracted over the past twenty years, to keep pace with falling consumption and demand. The average figures for the period 1955–1959, with the 1969 figures:

	1955–1959	1969
Total output	217,800,000 tons	150,600,000 tons
Total consumption	215,700,000 tons	164,700,000 tons
Total labour force	690,200	311,100
Overall output per man-shift	1·3 tons	2·2 tons
Percentage of output mechanically loaded	22%	92%

National Coal Board figures for 1970–71 show a further drop of total output to 133,354,000 tons, and a further increase in output per man-shift to 2·4 tons. These figures may be compared with the peak year of 1913, when British mines produced 287,000,000 tons of which 94,000,000 tons were exported, and employed over a million workers.

At 31st March 1970 there were 299 collieries in operation in the United Kingdom.

The supply of *electricity* in Great Britain is in the hands of the Central Electricity Generating Board, through twelve Area Boards; in Scotland there are two regionally organised public corporations, and in Northern Ireland the Belfast and Londonderry Corporations supplement the activities of the publicly owned board. The co-ordinating body of the whole industry is the Electricity Council. Total employment currently runs at about 223,000 workers.

Most electricity is supplied by coal-fired steam generating stations. Oil fuels, natural gas and nuclear energy are all destined for much more widespread use in the electricity generating industry, but conversions of power stations are being controlled to avoid further problems in the coal industry. The electricity authorities currently take about half the British consumption of coal and about 24% of fuel oil consumption. Hydroelectric generation is not a prominent feature of the British system – only small areas of Wales and Scotland are physically suitable for this method. Nuclear power stations provided about 12% of Britain's public supply electricity generation in 1969, and the proportion is expected to rise to about 25% within the next three years. At the present rate Britain accounts for about a third of the world's total nuclear generation.

Generating figures for 1970 totalled around 246,000,000,000 kWh, higher than any other country, except the United States of America, for which figures were available (thus excluding the U.S.S.R. and China).

The main electricity transmission lines – the "national grid" – totalled about 23,200 miles (37,200 km.) in Great Britain in March 1969. Direct cross-Channel links enable Britain and France to take mutual advantage of the difference in the times of peak loading in the two countries; this system has been in operation since 1961. The British grid system is the largest integrated power network in the world.

Gas supply is co-ordinated by the Gas Council, through twelve Area Boards. (In Northern Ireland the industry remains in the hands of a number of municipal organisations and other suppliers.) The main single source of gas in 1972 is natural gas, the use of which has increased very rapidly in recent years. In 1969 it represented only some 36% of the gas available; the following year the figure was around 50%. A massive programme of conversion of appliances from manufactured to natural gas is underway. Natural gas in liquid form has been supplied by a national high pressure pipeline system since 1964, but by 1970 only some 1,500 miles of the required 2,500 miles had been completed. It is estimated that gas demand will increase by some 20% annually for the next five years; the development of the recently tapped resources of North Sea gas fields is therefore of the first importance. The first pipeline from this source was opened in 1967; by 1969–70 the daily abstraction rate was around 960,000,000 cubic feet, and it is expected to rise to some 3,000,000,000 cubic feet by 1975.

Total gas sales in 1970 were around 5,803,000,000 therms. Of these, domestic demand accounted for 3,583,000,000 therms; industrial demand accounted for 1,466,000,000 therms and commercial demand for 683,000,000 therms.

In 1969 the deliveries of *petroleum products* for inland consumption totalled about 89,000,000 tons; fuel oil represented some 37·5% of the total. About 13,000,000 tons of motor spirit were sold. The steel industry accounted for about 14% of fuel oil consumption, the electricity generating industry about 24%, and non-industrial central heating for a further 12%. Crude oil is the largest single item among British imports, and in 1969 some 93,000,000 tons valued at £671,000,000 were imported. There are 22 oil refineries in operation in the United Kingdom, with a total capacity at the end of 1969 of around 106,000,000 tons per year. The output of refined petroleum products had risen to 84,000,000 tons in 1969 (not counting the refineries' own consumption). Exports of refined products were valued at £147,000,000 in 1969, as against imports of £237,000,000. British or partially British oil companies produce more than one third of all oil entering international trade, and the British tanker fleet represents about a quarter of the world's total tanker tonnage if chartered vessels are included.

TRANSPORT AND COMMUNICATIONS

In June 1969 it was calculated that nearly 7% of the total labour force in Great Britain was employed in some capacity by the agencies of transport and communications. These aspects of national activity contribute around 9% of the gross national product. Of the 1,500,000-odd transport and communications workers, some 30% were engaged in postal and telecommunications services, some 32% in road passenger transport and road haulage work, 17% in rail transport, 5% in sea transport and 4% in air transport.

In Great Britain in 1970 about 2,001,000,000 tons of freight of all kinds were transported in one way or another. Road transport carried about 1,695,000,000 tons; rail about 205,000,000 tons; inland waterways, about 6,000,000 tons; and coastal shipping, around 48,000,000 tons. Included in the total figure were movements of liquids – but not gases – by pipeline; this category accounted for about 47,000,000 tons. (Internal movement of freight by air did not contribute significant figures to this total – in a country the size of Britain air freight is only a realistic economic proposition in the case of small quantities of specialised cargo which have to be moved with great urgency.)

In the same year it is calculated that passengers travelled a total of about 253,700,000,000 passenger miles. The vast majority of this total – approximately 196,200,000,000 passenger miles – was contributed by private road transport. Some 34,100,000,000 passenger miles were recorded by public service road transport agencies; about 22,200,000,000 by rail authorities; and some 1,200,000,000 by domestic airline operators.

ROAD TRANSPORT

It is estimated that at the end of 1970 Great Britain had about 207,900 miles of public roads. Some 700 miles of this total were Motorways – multi-lane high-fluency highways between major cities. "Trunk" roads – major internal routes not built to Motorway standard –

accounted for another 8,300 miles. "Principal" roads totalled 20,200 miles, and the remaining 178,700 miles (about 86% of the total) were "other than principal" or "unclassified".

At the end of March 1970 there were estimated to be 14,109 miles of public road in Northern Ireland, comprising 379 miles of "trunk" roads; 1,012 miles of Class I roads; 1,733 miles of Class II roads; 2,876 miles of Class III roads; and 8,109 miles of unclassified roads.

Expenditure of public funds on roads in 1969 totalled £663,500,000. Major improvements and new construction, most of it devoted to Motorways and trunk roads, took around £391,700,000 of this. Another £142,900,000 went on maintenance and minor improvements; and cleaning, watering, snow clearing and administration took a further £86,600,000.

During September 1970 – an arbitrary control date – there was a total of 14,950,000 vehicles with current licences on the road in Great Britain. The number of unlicensed vehicles is, obviously, unknown but probably raises the total beyond the 15,000,000 mark. During 1970 a total of 1,524,800 new vehicles were registered.

Of the total number of licensed vehicles, 11,515,000 were private cars. (This figure gives Great Britain a rate of 203 cars per 1,000 population; comparable rates abroad are 414 in the U.S.A., 302 in New Zealand, 297 in Canada, 286 in Australia; 230 in France; 202 in Sweden, 195 in Germany, 188 in Belgium, 153 in the Netherlands, 155 in Italy; 12 in Poland, 1 in India.)

There were 1,622,000 goods vehicles registered in Great Britain in September 1970. Buses, coaches and taxis totalled 103,000, and there were 1,141,000 motor-cycles and three-wheeled vehicles.

Estimated traffic on British roads in 1970 presented the following picture; the units are "thousand million vehicle miles":

Vehicle Class	All roads	Motor-ways	Urban trunk and principal roads	Rural trunk and principal roads
All classes	128·40	5·98	49·72	49·92
Cars, taxis	100·25	4·26	39·54	38·49
Buses, coaches	2·25	0·06	1·11	0·73
Light vans	11·73	0·33	4·10	4·61
Other freight vehicles	11·76	1·31	3·96	5·38
Motorcycles	2·41	0·01	1·01	0·72

(*Department of the Environment*)

Despite having one of the highest densities of road traffic in the world, Britain's road fatality figures are better than those in many other Western countries. The major legal steps taken to reduce road casualties are in the fields of speed limits, technical requirements, and sanctions against the drinking driver. In built-up areas there are legal speed limits of 30 and 40 m.p.h. (48 and 64 km./hr.) and limits of 50 m.p.h. and 70 m.p.h. (80

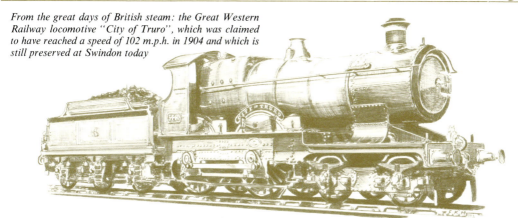

From the great days of British steam: the Great Western Railway locomotive "City of Truro", which was claimed to have reached a speed of 102 m.p.h. in 1904 and which is still preserved at Swindon today

km./hr. and 112 km./hr.) are applied on certain important trunk roads, and on all otherwise unrestricted roads, respectively. The mechanical condition of vehicles is scrutinised regularly, through the application of the legal requirement to have all private cars and light goods vehicles over three years old tested and certificated annually at approved garages. Heavy freight vehicles are tested annually, regardless of age. Any vehicle may be stopped and examined by the police at any time, and strict requirements are laid down to ensure that such components as tyres, lights, and so forth are not defective. Drivers of all classes of vehicle are required to pass a strict test of fitness to drive and skill on the road, imposed by government examiners, before being granted a driving licence. Driving without a valid licence, third party insurance, or an up-to-date vehicle test certificate are all serious offences. The police have had the right, since 1967, to examine drivers whom they suspect of having more than a legal maximum of 80 milligrammes of alcohol per 100 millilitres in their bloodstream. (The amount of actual alcohol consumed to produce this level varies considerably from individual to individual and from occasion to occasion, but a rough average is three tots of spirits or three pints of strong beer.) It is an absolute offence to drive with more than this level of alcohol in the blood, and one of the offences for which a driver may be banned from driving for periods of a year and upwards.

The following are some comparative road casualty figures for the United Kingdom and other major countries for the year 1969:

Country	Population (millions)	Road traffic deaths	Road traffic injuries
United Kingdom	55·3	7,620	352,935
France	49·9	14,264	312,398
Federal Germany	58·0	16,646	472,387
Italy	52·8	9,891	230,809
U.S.A.	201·2	55,500	*Not available*

RAIL TRANSPORT

Britain was the pioneer of rail transport, and the opening of the first rail links in the 1820s and 1830s began a century of rapid railway building. During the 1914–1918 war the railways were brought under government direction, for the sake of co-ordinating the war effort; and the Railways Act of 1921 amalgamated about 130 private railway companies into four large regional groups. The Transport Act of 1947 brought the railways under public ownership as a single enterprise titled British Railways, and since 1962 the running of the country's railways has been directed by the British Railways Board, appointed by the Minister of Transport.

Two major features of Britain's railway system should be mentioned. One is the contraction of the services offered, due to the apparently irreconcilable requirements of (a) profitability, and (b) the provision of an adequate service to the public. In 1968 the Transport Act signalled a new approach. The government wrote off large capital debts, and a system of grants was instituted for the upkeep of passenger services which are uneconomical but socially necessary. Restrictions on some of the Board's fringe activities were removed, and the railways are now expected to pay their way. Total receipts in 1969 were of the order of £533,000,000, and following interest payments a profit of about £15,000,000 was recorded.

The other feature of railway operations in the past 15 years has been the rapid modernisation of rolling stock. In 1955 there were some 18,000 steam locomotives in service, with 71 electric and only 71 diesel locomotives. By the end of 1969 steam locomotives had effectively disappeared from scheduled British Rail services; there were 328 electric locomotives and 4,183 diesels.

Other rail statistics for 1970, with comparable 1960 figures in parentheses, are as follows (*Department of the Environment data*):

Permanent route open for traffic	11,800 miles (18,400)
Stations open	2,868 (7,283)
Total locomotives	4,449 (15,961)
Passenger carriages	18,700 (40,100)
Freight vehicles	371,000 (962,000)
Total passenger seats	1,155,000 (2,331,000)
Total freight tonnage capacity	6,420,000 (14,339,000)
Passenger receipts	£227,800,000 (£151,300,000)
Freight receipts	£270 600,000 (£316,900,000)

Apart from railway services as such, there are the subsidiary British Transport Hotels Ltd., which owns 34 hotels; the cross-Channel service operated by British Rail Hovercraft Ltd., with its two *SRN-4* 165-ton hovercraft; the 100 or so passenger and freight vessels plying between Britain, the Continent and the Republic of Ireland and on coastal routes, owned by the Railways Board and various shipping subsidiaries; and the subsidiary British Engineering Ltd., which has 37,000 employees in its fourteen main workshops. Altogether the Railways Board employs some 225,500 people.

During 1970, in accidents involving trains, 19 people died and about 350 were injured. The majority of these were railways staff. There were an estimated 824,000,000 passenger journeys in Britain that year.

TRANSPORT IN LONDON

With New York and Tokyo, London is one of the world's largest cities. Approximately 7,700,000 people live within 15 miles of Charing Cross, and many hundreds of thousands more flood into the area to work each day.

The unique problems of transportation caused by this circumstance are now, since 1969, the responsibility of the Greater London Council, to whom the Ministry of Transport handed over in that year. The former London Transport Board was replaced by the financially independent London Transport Executive as the planning and operating authority for London's internal transport. The L.T.E. operates all road and rail passenger transport within the Greater London area, with the exception of the London lines of British Rail and the 7,600-odd taxi cabs, which latter are privately operated but subject to licensing by the Metropolitan Police. London Transport employs a staff of about 60,000. It has responsibility for 254 miles of railway track, some 100 of which are underground. There are 276 stations served by London Transport trains, and rolling stock includes more than 4,300 railway cars. Some 6,570 buses and coaches serve road routes totalling 1,699 miles.

SHIPPING

Shipping comes under the responsibility of the Board of Trade, which administers many regulations concerned with marine safety and welfare. Among other activities the Board of Trade administers the Coastguard Service, with its 550 full-time and 7,000 part-time coastguards. The coastguards operate in close liaison with the Royal National Lifeboat Institution; an entirely voluntary body supported by public subscription, the Institution operates lifeboats and inshore rescue craft all round Britain's shores, and is reported to have saved 1,035 lives in 2,373 launchings during 1969. The lighthouse authority and chief pilotage authority for England and Wales, and the Channel Islands, is the Corporation of Trinity House; Trinity House received its first Royal Charter in the 16th century. Together with the authorities for Scotland and Ireland (the Commissioners of Northern Lighthouses and the Commissioners of Irish Lights), Trinity House administers more than 190 lighthouses, many minor markers and several lightships. Of the 1,600-odd licensed pilots in Britain, Trinity House licenses about 700; the remainder come under the responsibility of various harbour authorities and local councils.

The Merchant Navy currently employs some 85,000 United Kingdom personnel, and a smaller number of foreign nationals. Officers and seamen of United Kingdom registered vessels must hold various certificates of competency in the respective ratings, awarded after Board of Trade examinations. Wages, conditions of employment and so on are negotiated by the National Maritime Board, whose members are drawn from the shipowners' associations and the seamen's unions.

In 1970 there were estimated to be 1,977 United Kingdom registered merchant vessels of 500 gross tons or over in service, with a tonnage of 24,061,000 gross tons. Of these totals 129 vessels (1,230,000 gross tons) held passenger certificates; a further 1,362 vessels (10,982,000 gross tons) were dry cargo ships; and 486 (11,849,000 gross tons) were tankers. The gross tonnage of new ships delivered to British owners in 1969 amounted to 2,400,000. Foreign trade arrivals and departures at principal British ports during 1970 amounted to 180,500,000 net tons and 180,400,000 net tons respectively; London, Southampton and Liverpool had the greatest departure tonnages with 35,200,000, 19,400,000 and 15,500,000 tons respectively. The total coasting trade departures in the year were around 79,900,000 net tons; Belfast, London and Southampton were the most active ports in this trade, with departures of 7,400,000, 6,900,000 and 6,300,000 net tons respectively.

INLAND WATERWAYS

Britain's canals, which played an important part in the industrial and commercial expansion of the country in the late 18th and 19th centuries, have naturally been of decreasing importance since the growth of the railways. There are still about 2,500 miles of navigable inland waterways in Great Britain, however. Some 2,000 miles are owned by the British Waterways Board, and the remainder by local authorities or private companies. Traffic on the Board's waterways (of which some 340 miles are commercial waterways) amounted in 1969 to about 6,700,000 tons, made up of 2,600,000 tons of coal, 2,700,000 tons of general cargo, and about 1,400,000 tons of bulk liquids. Most of the traffic is handled by independent carriers, although the Board is the largest single carrying operator. The Board owned, in that year, about 575 freight-carrying craft.

AIR TRANSPORT

The Board of Trade has general responsibility for civil aviation matters in the United Kingdom. It appoints the boards of the publicly-owned corporations, and has certain powers over their operations. It appoints the Air Transport Licensing Authority, which considers the applications for licences to operate scheduled and charter services advanced by both the public corporations and independent operators.

There were, at the beginning of 1970, 46 licensed independent air transport operators in the United Kingdom. In addition there are the publicly-owned British Overseas Airways Corporation, and British European Airways. BOAC provides long-haul international services, and BEA operates a network of services within Britain and Europe, the Middle East and North Africa. The independents are generally involved in domestic passenger and cargo services, ferry services of a specialist nature and low-cost foreign travel services. They compete with BEA on several routes, and in 1969 carried some 8,000,000 passengers.

BOAC operates a fleet of (June 1970 figures): eighteen Boeing 707-436, seventeen B.A.C. Super VC-10, eleven VC-10, eight Boeing 707-336 and three Boeing 747s. Aircraft on order at that time included two Boeing 707-336 and nine Boeing 747; since that time firm orders for the Anglo-French supersonic *Concorde* have been placed.

BOAC's gross traffic revenue in the year 1969-70 amounted to £198,000,000, with an operating surplus of £31,000,000 and net profits of £19,000,000. In the year ended March 1970 the corporation's capacity on scheduled services reached 1,856,000,000 capacity-ton-miles.

BEA enjoyed a gross revenue of £126,000,000 in the same year, of which £6,500,000 was net profit. It carried 8,500,000 passengers in that year. Its fleet in March 1970 consisted of twenty B.A.C. Viscount 802, eighteen B.A.C. One-Eleven, fourteen Hawker Siddeley Trident 2, twenty-one Trident 1, ten B.A.C. Vanguard 935, seven B.A.C. Viscount 806, five Vanguard 951, four Hawker Siddeley Comet 4B, four Hawker Siddeley Argosy and two Hawker Siddeley Heron. At that time twenty-six Trident 3 were on order.

The proportion of international passenger traffic and international trade traffic handled by air rather than sea is increasing steadily. In all, British airlines offered a capacity of 3,375,000,000 capacity-ton-miles in 1969. In that year 18,500,000 passengers arrived in or left Britain by air, compared with 10,500,000 by sea. The 1955 figures had been 2,500,000 to 5,700,000. While in 1956

only 1·7% of imports and 2·9% of exports, calculated by value, were carried by air, the 1969 figures were 13·3% and 13% respectively. The value of all imports, exports and re-exports by air that year was £2,063,000,000.

The following data are drawn from published Department of Trade and Industry figures, and refer in all cases to the year 1970 (* indicates 1966–70 total):

Activity by all U.K. airlines

Total aircraft in service	378
Passengers carried on scheduled and charter services	20,499,000
Passenger-miles flown	17,936,000,000
Passengers killed*	220
Passengers seriously injured*	3
Passengers carried per passenger(s) killed*	289,400
Passenger-miles flown per passenger killed*	212,400,000

Activity at civil airports

Civil aircraft movements		1,388,000
(London/Heathrow	270,000	
London/Gatwick	92,000)	
Passengers handled		32,411,000
Freight handled		580,043 metric tons
Mail handled		49,079 metric tons

THE POST OFFICE

The Post Office is a public corporation headed by a chairman and board appointed by and responsible to the Minister of Posts and Telecommunications. It employs a total labour force of about 420,000 men and women, and has some 25,000 post offices throughout the country.

The inland postal services carry about 11,600,000,000 items of mail each year. Overseas mail in 1969-1970 amounted to about 575,000,000 items, of which 68% were carried by air. About 7,500 tons of internal mail are carried by air annually. Besides the collection and delivery of mail, the Post Office provides numerous services to the public. At the post office counter the British citizen can buy licences for his car, dog, radio and television; deposit or draw money from a wide range of savings and investment schemes (including the National Savings Bank and the Premium Bond national lottery scheme); buy national insurance stamps; draw his pension and family allowance; send a telegram; or transmit money in a number of ways. The post office is also the owner and operator of the telephone service in Britain.

The following figures apply to Post Office activities in 1970:

Total number of letters posted	11,400,000,000
Total number of parcels posted	203,000,000
Postal orders issued	472,000,000
Telegrams sent through the P.O.	29,000,000
Length of telephone wire in use	67,000,000 miles
Private telephone subscribers	13,769,000

Public telephone installations	75,000
Telephone exchanges	6,138
Subscriber Trunk Dialling exchanges	2,738¶
Telex stations	29,147

¶ *On 31st March 1970, serving 86% of all subscribers.*

AGRICULTURE, FORESTRY AND FISHERY

Of the 60,000,000 acres of land in Great Britain, no less than 46,500,000 acres are in agricultural use. In Ulster 2,700,000 of the 3,300,000 available acres are in agricultural use. Some 706,000 people in Great Britain are professionally engaged in agriculture, that is some 3% of the total working population. Agriculture contributes about 3% of the gross national product. In Ulster the proportions are 9% and 10% respectively. About one-sixth of agricultural land in England and Wales is classified as "rough grazing", suitable for sheep but little else; the proportions in Northern Ireland and Scotland are one-quarter and three-quarters.

There are today about 340,000 farms in Britain – the term is used here to cover every type of holding from very small one-man units farmed part-time by owners with another means of livelihood, to farm businesses occupying three or four men full time. The average size of full-time English and Welsh farms is 160 acres, of Scottish farms, 170 acres. There are about 190,000 full-time farm businesses in Britain, including about 22,300 in Scotland and 18,000 in Northern Ireland, where the average size is only 40 to 70 acres. More than half the farms in Great Britain are owner-occupied.

Most British farms accomplish a variety of produce. Dairy farming is widespread throughout the country. Arable crops are mainly found in the eastern part of the country, in the East Riding of Yorkshire, Lincolnshire, Kent and East Anglia. South Lincolnshire and Cambridgeshire – the Fen country – is rich in potato and vegetable crops generally, as are the Thames and Humber valleys and southern Lancashire. Beef cattle and sheep are extensively raised in hill areas throughout the country.

Wheat growing is mainly restricted to East Anglia; about half the crop goes for flour milling, the remainder mainly for animal foodstuffs. Barley yield has improved dramatically in the past ten years; the bulk of the crop goes for animal foodstuffs, but about one-sixth is taken by the distilling and brewing industries. Sugar beet is grown, largely in Lincolnshire and East Anglia, under contract to the British Sugar Corporation which takes the whole crop.

Milk is primarily produced for liquid consumption in Great Britain, although Ulster uses the majority of the milk yield in the production of butter and cheese. The average yield of a dairy cow is well over 800 gallons per year; advances in breeding, hygiene and management have improved British herds to the extent that British livestock generally is in continual demand by overseas breeders. Britain is rich in sheep pasture, and the adequate grazing and severe winters, combined with veterinary advances, have produced more than thirty breeds of hardy and fertile beasts. In the south and east of the country pig breeding is important, although it is generally widespread throughout the islands. About 30% of pig meat is used for bacon curing, the remainder for sale as fresh pork and in manufactured foods.

Intensive breeding techniques are in use over the whole range of British livestock farming, but nowhere more so than in the field of poultry farming. About 80% of laying birds are in flocks of 1,000 and upwards, and there are several flocks of over 100,000. Egg yield per bird is well over 200 a year on average, and for several years Britain has filled her egg requirements from home production. In 1969 about 285,000,000 broilers and other table chickens were produced.

Horticultural crops, which occupy only about 2½% of the area under crops and grass, contribute high returns per acre, and receipts from this type of crop represented more than 10% of the output from all agricultural holdings in Britain in 1969–70.

The following figures refer to the year ended June 1970, and are quoted from published statistics of the Ministry of Agriculture, Fisheries and Food:

Use of land in the United Kingdom	*Acres*
Total agricultural	46,543,000
Arable	17,788,000
Permanent grass	12,217,000
Rough grazing	16,537,000
Use of arable land	
Wheat	2,495,000
Barley	5,542,000
Oats	929,000
Other cereals	208,000
Potatoes	669,000
Sugar beet	463,000
Fodder crops	725,000
Hops	17,000
Mustard	16,000
Vegetables	510,000
Fruit	204,000
Flowers and nursery stock	37,000
Other	32,000
Bare fallow	241,000
Temporary grass	5,700,000

The following figures of farming output in the United Kingdom refer to the year June 1970–May 1971:

Farm crops	£458,000,000
Livestock and livestock products	£1,587,000,000
Horticulture	£286,000,000
Sundry outputs, receipts	£53,000,000
Production grants	£112,000,000
Total receipts	£2,496,000,000
Total expenditure	£1,388,000,000

Net income after adjustment for
depreciations, rent, labour, interest £589,000,000

The following data refer to crops harvested in the United Kingdom in the year 1970–71, with average yield per acre in parentheses:

Wheat	4,169,000 tons	(33·4 cwt.)
Barley	7,410,000 tons	(26·7 cwt.)
Oats	1,198,000 tons	(25·9 cwt.)
Potatoes	7,364,000 tons	(11·0 tons)
Sugar beet	6,311,000 tons	(13·7 tons)
Turnips and swedes	5,561,000 tons	(22·4 tons)
Mangolds	571,000 tons	(23·8 tons)
Hay from temporary grassland	4,219,000 tons	(34·5 cwt.)
Hay from permanent grassland	3,645,000 tons	(28·2 cwt.)

The following are the reported figures for livestock on United Kingdom agricultural holdings for the year 1970:

Total cattle	12,581,000
of which cows, heifers in milk	3,946,000
cows in calf, not in milk	597,000
heifers in calf, first calf	863,000
bulls, bull calves for service	92,000
other cattle	7,083,000
Total sheep	26,080,000
of which ewes for breeding	10,544,000
rams for service	302,000
other sheep	15,235,000
Total pigs	8,088,000
of which sows for breeding	953,000
boars for service	45,000
other pigs	7,090,000
Total poultry	143,430,000
of which fowls	137,207,000
ducks	1,256,000
geese	174,000
turkeys	4,793,000

The Ministry of Agriculture, Fisheries and Food estimates that in the year 1969–70 British agriculture and fisheries provided 52·1% of all food products consumed in Britain, as against 47·9% imports. Of those foods indigenous to the United Kingdom, home resources provided 65·5% as aginst 34·5% imports.

FORESTRY

The total area of woodland in the United Kingdom is estimated at 4,711,000 acres, or about 7·75% of the land area of the country; of this total 4,578,000 acres lie in Great Britain, and 133,000 in Northern Ireland. Not all this woodland is productive, however – that is, currently under active management for economic gain. The proportion of productive woodland is about 3,280,000 acres in Great Britain, and about 99,000 acres in Ulster.

The national forestry authority, which owns a large acreage of productive forest land and manages its resources for economic gain, and which also provides advisory, training, research and marketing facilities for private owners of woodland, is the Forestry Commission. This body owns some 2,110,000 acres of forest land, of which about 1,800,000 acres are currently under trees, in 380 forests scattered throughout England, Scotland and Wales. The planting in these forests is almost entirely coniferous, and is largely made up of Norway spruce, Sitka spruce, Scots pine and Lodgepole pine. These softwoods are the class of timber in most demand by industry – some 90% and more of total demand falls into this category. In private woodlands and natural forest allowed to grow without economic management, the commonest broadleaved trees in Britain are the oak, beech, elm and birch; larches grow widely in natural coniferous forests.

In Forestry Commission forests, a total of about 500 acres was lost to fire in the year ended 30th September 1970. In Northern Ireland – where forestry is managed by the Ministry of Agriculture – the loss was 10 acres.

FISHERIES

The sea fishing industry is an important employer in coastal areas of Great Britain, and makes up a vital sector of Scottish industry in particular. Of the total of 5,680 fishing vessels registered in British ports on 31st December 1970, no less than 2,617 hailed from Scottish ports.

The industry breaks down into several sectors. The three basic divisions concern the fishing of whitefish (e.g. cod, turbot, haddock, sole, plaice, mackerel, pilchard, sprats); herring; and shellfish (e.g. lobster, crab, escallops, mussels, cockles, oysters). Whitefish represents about 82% of the total catch. The whitefish industry includes distant water fishery (Icelandic waters, the west Atlantic, Greenland, Bear Island, the Barents Sea); near and middle water fishery (North Sea, Irish Sea, the Faroes); and inshore fishery. The herring fishery is almost entirely in Scottish waters, and the inshore fishery areas yield the bulk of the shellfish catch.

There are about 18,000 fishermen in regular employment from Great Britain's ports, and another 4,000 or so in part-time employment. There are about 500 regular fishermen sailing from Northern Ireland.

Hull, Grimsby and Fleetwood are the main distant water fishing ports, and at the end of 1969 a total of some 160 distant water trawlers were operating from these three towns. These vessels are generally more than 140 feet in length; accompanied by freezer trawlers and factory ships – which have enabled them to fish off Labrador and Newfoundland in recent years – they spend about 17 to 23 days at sea at a time. At the end of 1969 near and middle water trawlers numbered about 375. Some of the larger vessels in this class make voyages to the Faroes, but most, in the 80 to 140-foot class, make voyages of between three or four days and two weeks at a time. The inshore ships are generally under 80 feet

157

Fishing vessels at Mevagissey, Cornwall

long, and make daily landings – as do the herring boats. An exception are the seiners, of which there are some 550 operating from Scottish and Ulster ports, and 170 from English ports. The chief whitefish ports, apart from those mentioned above, are Milford Haven, Lowestoft and North Shields, and in Scotland Aberdeen, Granton, Fraserburgh, the Moray Firth and the Shetlands. The herring fishery is based on Fraserburgh, Ullapool, Mallaig, Oban, Ayr and the Shetlands. The main fishing ports in Ulster are Ardglass, Portavogie and Kilkeel.

The following figures published by the M.A.F.F. refer to 1970:

Landings and value of fish of British taking:

Whitefish	756,800 tons	£64,654,000
of which cod	338,700 tons	£32,308,000
haddock	173,400 tons	£13,605,000
Herring	139,000 tons	£4,553,000
Shellfish	52,200 tons	£6,279,000

INDUSTRIAL ASSOCIATIONS

In almost every industry in Britain there are employers' associations; in all, some 1,400 organisations are federated to about 85 national organisations. The central co-ordinating body, to which most of these national employers' associations, most nationalised industries and many individual firms are affiliated, is the Confederation of British Industry.

In December 1970 there were 481 trades unions, with a total membership of about 11,000,000 made up of around 8,296,000 male workers and 2,704,000 female. Of this total, however, the vast majority – some 70 % – belonged to the 19 or 20 largest unions, and more than 50 % were members of the nine unions which each have more than 250,000 members. There were at that time 23 British unions with memberships over 100,000, and 256 unions with memberships under 1,000. The central body of the trades union movement is the Trades Union Congress.

THE DEVELOPMENT AND CURRENCY OF BRITISH COINAGE

The earliest coins found in Britain were probably made in Gaul and were extensively circulated in these islands as the result of the migration of Belgic peoples. These and other early coins were derivatives of gold staters of King Philip II of Macedonia (359–336 B.C.).

With the arrival of the Romans in the 1st century the currency of the Roman Empire became the only coinage of Britain, and this coinage existed in four fundamental categories:

(a) Roman Emperors' coins and those of Emperors who counted Britannia as a Roman possession,
(b) Roman coins relating to the conquest of Britannia,
(c) Roman coins struck in Britain, and
(d) British imitations of Roman coins.

After the departure of the Romans, gold and silver coins continued to be minted throughout the country for the Kings of East Anglia, Kent, Mercia and Northumbria, as well as for the Archbishops of York and Canterbury. Numerous mints were established throughout the country up to the time of the Norman invasion when there were no fewer than 102 mints. Up to the reign of Edward I the currency was largely based upon the silver penny (the *denarius* or "d" of £.s.d.), but in 1278 was introduced the farthing, the halfpenny and the groat (4d.). The groat however was not issued between about 1282 and 1351.

Following two unsuccessful attempts to re-introduce gold coinage, the currency was reformed in 1351 with gold Nobles, Half-Nobles and Quarter-Nobles minted in London and Calais; these were accompanied by silver groats, pennies, halfpennies and farthings minted in London, York, Canterbury, Durham, Berwick, Bury St. Edmunds and Reading. A Halfgroat was also introduced in 1351.

This pattern of currency continued in being until in 1464-65, during the reign of Edward IV, to increase the supply of bullion to the mint the weight of the penny was reduced, and the value of the Noble raised to 8s. 4d. A ten-shilling coin, the Ryal or "Rose-Noble" was introduced in gold; also introduced was the Angel which, at 6s. 8d. valuation, replaced the Noble at its old value. To assist with the re-coinage (which now comprised the Noble, Quarter-Noble, Ryal, Half-Ryal, Quarter-Ryal, Angel, Groat, Half-Groat, penny, halfpenny and farthing), mints were opened for a short time at Bristol, Coventry and Norwich, as well as the Royal Mints at York and Canterbury.

By 1470 the Noble gold had been discontinued and in that year the Ryal was also abandoned, only Angel gold being issued, including the Half-Angel. The farthing also temporarily disappeared in 1470.

DEVELOPMENT OF THE TUDOR-RENAISSANCE STYLE

The reign of Henry VII (1485-1509) witnessed not only the introduction of new denominations (with the appearance of the gold sovereign and the testoon or shilling), but also a marked improvement in the quality of coinage through the skills of the German die-sinker, Alexander Bruchsal.

Sovereigns appeared before the close of the fifteenth century (even double- and treble-sovereigns are known to have existed), while the Ryal (10s.), Angel (6s. 8d.), Half-Angel or angelet (3s. 4d.) continued in gold. The silver groat, half-groat, penny and halfpenny were joined by the testoon (1s.).

The constant calls on the exchequer by Henry VIII resulted in a lowering in the fineness of the coinage, commencing in 1526 with the manufacture of some coins in 22 carat, and in 1543 this was followed by the debasement of the silver, at first to five parts fine to one of alloy, and ultimately to only one-third silver. Later the gold was reduced to 20 carat. Also introduced to the gold coinage was the George-Noble (6s. 8d.) and the Half-George-Noble (3s. 4d.).

The Crown coinage also appeared during the period

1526-1544, with the Crown of the Rose (4s. 6d.), Crown of the Double Rose (5s.), and the Halfcrown (2s. 6d.).

A partial restoration of the coinage was undertaken during the reign of Edward VI with a return of the gold coinage to 22 carat, and the "silver" to 50%. The gold coins included sovereigns (20s.), half-sovereigns (10s.), crowns (5s.), halfcrowns (2s. 6d.), Angels (10s.) and Half-Angels (5s.), and "fine" sovereigns (30s.), while double-sovereigns were also known. Towards the end of Edward VI's reign the crown and halfcrown were minted in silver, and were joined by the sixpence and threepence coins.

The introduction of the horse-drawn mill by the French engraver, Eloye Mestrelle, resulted in a substantial increase in the number of variations in coins during the reign of Elizabeth I (1558-1603). In hammered gold there were the "fine" sovereign (30s.), the Ryal (15s.), the pound (20s.), half-pound (10s.), crown (5s.) and half-crown (2s. 6d.), while the last three were also minted as milled coins. Silver coins proliferated during this reign, crowns, halfcrowns, shillings, sixpences, groats, threepences, halfgroats, threehalfpences, pennies, three-farthings and halfpennies being hammered in response to the public's clamour for more coins of small denomination.

Following the accession of James I in 1603 the weight of the gold pound was reduced and a new coin, the Unite, was introduced, as was a new four-shilling coin, the Thistle Crown (both with obvious associations with Scotland and the union of kingdoms). In 1612 the value of gold coins was raised by 10% and the Unite was replaced by a new, lighter 20s. coin, the Laurel; there were also Half-Laurels and Quarter-Laurels, all in gold.

THE APPEARANCE OF COPPER COINS

Continuing demand for low value denominations resulted in James I granting to Lord Harrington a licence to coin farthings in copper, commencing in 1613 and continuing during the reign of Charles I, until revoked in 1644. Copper farthings reappeared during the Commonwealth with the head of Cromwell thereon, and continued in 1672 during the reign of Charles II – being joined in that year by copper halfpennies. The Civil Wars caused disruption to the supply of coinage, and coins were struck in towns under Royalist control (among them Carlisle, Newark, Oxford, Pontefract, Scarborough and Shrewsbury). In 1637 a mint was established at Aberystwyth to strike coins from silver mined in Wales.

The Restoration brought about concerted efforts to rationalise the coinage, and in 1662 hand-hammering of coins was abandoned in favour of improved mill and screw presses. The gold coins of Charles II's reign came to be called "guineas", from the gold imported from Guinea by the Africa Company; at first this term was applied to coins of 100s., 40s., 20s. and 10s. currency (Five Guineas, Two Guineas, Guineas and Half-Guineas respectively), and it was not until late in George

III's reign that the Guinea's value was increased to 21s., being replaced by the 20s. gold sovereign. Hammered gold was ultimately demonetised in 1733.

Rationalisation of the coinage was virtually complete by the time James II came to the throne in 1685 (although in an effort to assist the depressed tin industry in Cornwall halfpennies and farthings were minted in tin, with copper plugs, between 1684 and 1692), and this king's accession is a convenient point at which to tabulate the modern currency of British coinage. It is of interest to note that, despite the recent change to decimal currency, at the time of writing (in 1972) the oldest coin which is still technically legal tender is the 1816 sixpence (tendered as 2½ "new pence").

CURRENCY OF BRITISH COINS SINCE 1685

Gold

Five Guineas 1686–1688, 1691–1694, 1699–1701, 1703, 1705, 1706, 1709, 1711, 1713, 1714, 1716, 1720, 1726, 1729, 1731, 1735, 1738, 1741, 1746, 1748, 1753, 1770*, 1773*, 1777*

Five Pounds 1820*, 1826†, 1839†, 1887, 1893, 1902, 1911†, 1937†, 1953†

Two Guineas 1687, 1688, 1691, 1693, 1694, 1701, 1709, 1711, 1713, 1714, 1717, 1720, 1726, 1734, 1735, 1738–1740, 1748, 1753, 1768*, 1773*, 1777*

Two Pounds 1820*, 1823, 1826†, 1831†, 1887, 1893, 1902, 1911†, 1937†, 1953†

Guinea 1689–1703, 1705–1741, 1743, 1745–1753, 1755, 1756, 1758–1761, 1763–1779, 1781–1799, 1813 (the Military Guinea)

Sovereign 1817–1833, 1835–1839, 1841–1866, 1868–1932, 1937†, 1953†, 1958, 1959, 1962–1968

Half-Guinea 1686–1703, 1705, 1707–1715, 1717–1740, 1743, 1745–1753, 1755, 1756, 1758–1760, 1762–1766, 1768, 1769, 1772–1779, 1781, 1783–1798, 1800–1804, 1806, 1808–1811, 1813

Half-Sovereign 1817, 1818, 1820, 1821, 1823–1828, 1835–1838, 1839†, 1841–1867, 1869†1887, 1889–1916, 1918, 1923†, 1925, 1926, 1937†, 1953†

Third-Guinea 1797–1804, 1806, 1808–1811, 1813

Quarter-Guinea 1718, 1762

Silver

Crown 1686–1688, 1691–1692, 1695–1697, 1700, 1703, 1705–1708, 1713, 1716, 1718, 1720, 1723, 1726, 1732, 1734–1736, 1739, 1741, 1743, 1746, 1750, 1751, 1818–1822, 1826†, 1831†, 1839†, 1844, 1845, 1847, 1887–1900, 1902, 1927–1937, 1951§, 1953§, 1960§, 1965§

Dollar (Bank of England issue, current for 5s.) 1804

Dollar (Emergency issue, Spanish American 8 reales countermarked, current for 4s. 9d.) c. 1781–c. 1800

A gold Double-Noble of Elizabeth I

Double-florin (4s.) 1887–1890

Three shillings 1811–1816

Half-dollar (Emergency issue countermarked; current for 2s. 10d.?) c. 1781–c. 1800

Halfcrown 1685–1693, 1696–1701, 1703–1710, 1712–1715, 1717, 1720, 1723, 1726, 1731, 1732, 1734–1736, 1739, 1741, 1743, 1745, 1746, 1750, 1751, 1816–1821, 1823–1826, 1828, 1829, 1831†, 1834–1837, 1839–1846, 1848–1850, 1874–1946; 1947–1967 (cupro-nickel)

Florin (2s.) 1848†, 1849, 1851–1860, 1862–1881, 1883–1933, 1935–1946; 1947–1951§, 1953–1967§

Eighteen pence 1811–1816

Shilling 1685–1688, 1692, 1693, 1695–1705, 1707–1729, 1731, 1732, 1734–1737, 1739, 1741, 1743, 1745–1747, 1750, 1751, 1758, 1763 (the "Northumberland" shilling), 1787, 1798 (the "Dorrien and Magens" shilling), 1816–1821, 1823–1827, 1829, 1834–1846, 1848–1946; 1947–1951§, 1953–1966§. (Note: During the reigns of King George VI and Queen Elizabeth II Scottish shillings were also in currency, viz: 1937–1946, 1947–1951§, 1953–1966§)

Ninepence 1812*

Sixpence 1686–1688, 1693–1701, 1703, 1705, 1707–1714, 1717, 1720, 1723, 1726, 1728, 1731, 1732, 1734–1736, 1739, 1741, 1743, 1745, 1746, 1750, 1751, 1757, 1758, 1787, 1816–1821, 1824–1829, 1831, 1834–1846, 1848, 1850–1860, 1862–1946; 1947–1967§

Groat (4d.) 1686–1694, 1697–1706, 1708–1710, 1713, 1717, 1721, 1723, 1727, 1729, 1731, 1732, 1737, 1739, 1740, 1743, 1746, 1760, 1763, 1765, 1770, 1772, 1776, 1780, 1784, 1786, 1792, 1795, 1800

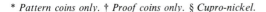

* *Pattern coins only.* † *Proof coins only.* § *Cupro-nickel.*

* *Pattern coins only.* † *Proof coins only.* § *Cupro-nickel.*

Threepence (3d.) *1685-1694, 1698-1701, 1703-1710,*
1713, 1717, 1721, 1723, 1727, 1729, 1731, 1732,
1737, 1739, 1740, 1743, 1746, 1760, 1762, 1763,
1765, 1766, 1770, 1772, 1780, 1784, 1786, 1792,
1795, 1800, 1817, 1818, 1820, 1822-1830, 1834-
1846, 1849-1851, 1853-1922, 1925-1926, 1927†,
1928, 1930-1944

Twopence (2d.) *1689, 1691-1694, 1698-1701, 1703-*
1710, 1713, 1717, 1721, 1723, 1726, 1727, 1729,
1731, 1732, 1735, 1739, 1740, 1743, 1746, 1756,
1759, 1760, 1763, 1765, 1766, 1772, 1776, 1780,
1784, 1786, 1792, 1795, 1800

Penny (1d.) *1689-1694, 1698-1701, 1703, 1705, 1706,*
1708-1710, 1713, 1716, 1718, 1720, 1723, 1725-
1727, 1729, 1731, 1732, 1735, 1737, 1739, 1740,
1743, 1746, 1750, 1752-1760, 1763, 1765, 1766,
1770, 1772, 1776, 1779-1781, 1784, 1786, 1792,
1795, 1800

Maundy Sets (silver 4d., 3d., 2d., 1d.) *1686-1689, 1691-*
1694, 1698-1701, 1703, 1705, 1706, 1708-1710,
1713, 1723, 1727, 1729, 1731, 1732, 1735, 1737,
1739, 1740, 1743, 1746, 1760, 1763, 1765, 1766,
1772, 1780, 1784, 1786, 1792 ("Wire money"),
1795, 1800, 1817, 1818, 1820, 1822-1971¶

Threehalfpence (for Colonial use) *1834-1843, 1860,*
1862

Tin

Halfpenny *1685-1687, 1689-1692*
Farthing *1685-1687, 1689-1692*

Copper

Twopence (Soho "Cartwheel" coinage) 1797
Penny (Soho "Cartwheel" coinage) *1797; 1806, 1807,*
1825-1827, 1831, 1834, 1837, 1839†, 1841, 1843-
1849, 1851, 1853-1860; 1860-1922‡, 1926-1940‡,
1944-1951‡, 1953‡, 1961-1967‡

Halfpenny *1694-1701, 1717-1724, 1729-1740, 1742-*
1754, 1770-1775, 1779, 1806, 1807, 1825-1827,
1831, 1834, 1837-1839, 1841, 1843-1848, 1851-
1860; 1860-1960‡, 1962-1967‡

Farthing *1694-1700, 1714, 1717, 1719-1724, 1730-*
1737, 1739, 1741, 1744, 1746, 1749, 1750, 1754,
1771, 1773-1775, 1799, 1806, 1807, 1821-1823,
1825-1831, 1834-1860; 1860-1869‡, 1872-1876‡,
1877†, 1878-1888‡, 1890-1956‡

Half-farthing *1828, 1830, 1837 (for use in Ceylon);*
1839, 1842-1844, 1847, 1851-1856; 1868 (bronze
proof and copper-nickel proof)

Third-farthing *1827, 1835, 1844 (for use in Malta);*
1866‡, 1868‡, 1876‡, 1878‡, 1881‡, 1884‡, 1885‡

Quarter-farthing (for use in Ceylon) *1839, 1851-1853;*
1868 (bronze proof and copper-nickel proof)

---

* Pattern coins only. † Proof coins only. § Cupro-nickel.
¶ Maundy coins are now the only coins struck in silver.
‡ Bronze.

Nickel Brass

Threepence (dodecagonal) *1937-1946, 1948-1967*

BRITISH ISLAND COINAGE

Jersey

Crown (cupro-nickel) *1966*
Three Shillings (silver) *1813*
Eighteenpence (silver) *1813*
1/4 Shilling (nickel brass) *1957, 1960, 1964, 1966*
1/12-Shilling (bronze) *1877, 1881, 1888, 1894, 1909,*
1911, 1913, 1923, 1926, 1931, 1933, 1935, 1937,
1945, 1946, 1947, 1957, 1960, 1964, 1966

1/13-Shilling, copper: *1841, 1844, 1851, 1858; bronze:*
1865, 1866, 1870, 1871

1/24-Shilling (bronze) *1877, 1888, 1894, 1909, 1911,*
1923, 1926, 1931, 1933, 1935, 1937, 1946, 1947

1/26-Shilling, copper: *1841, 1844, 1851, 1858; bronze:*
1861, 1866, 1870, 1871

1/48-Shilling, bronze: *1877*
1/52-Shilling, copper: 1841; bronze: 1861

Guernsey

Ten shillings (cupro-nickel) *1966*
Threepence *1956, 1959, 1966†*
Eight Doubles *1834, 1858, 1864, 1868, 1874, 1885, 1889,*
1893, 1902, 1903, 1910, 1911, 1914, 1918, 1920,
1934, 1938, 1945, 1947, 1949, 1956, 1959, 1966†

Four Doubles *1830, 1858, 1964, 1868, 1874, 1885, 1889,*
1893, 1902, 1903, 1906, 1908, 1910, 1911, 1914,
1918, 1920, 1945, 1949, 1956, 1966†

Two Doubles *1858, 1868, 1874, 1885, 1889, 1899, 1902,*
1903, 1906, 1908, 1911, 1914, 1917, 1918, 1920,
1929

Doubles *1830, 1868, 1885, 1889, 1893, 1899, 1902,*
1903, 1911, 1914, 1929, 1933, 1938

Isle of Man

Five pounds *1965† (Commemorative issue)*
Sovereign *1965† (Commemorative issue)*
Half-Sovereign *1965† (Commemorative issue)*
Penny. 10th Earl of Derby: 1709, 1733; 2nd Duke of
Atholl: 1758; George III: 1786, 1798, 1813;
Victoria: 1839, 1841, 1859

Halfpenny. 10th Earl of Derby: 1709, 1733; 2nd Duke
of Atholl: 1758; George III: 1786, 1798, 1813;
Victoria: 1839, 1841, 1860

Farthings. Victoria: 1839, 1841, 1860

Lundy

Puffin (Martin Coles Harman) 1929, 1965†
Half-Puffin (Martin Coles Harman) 1929, 1965†

---

† Proof coins only.

CHAPTER 4
ஃ The British People ஃ

Ethnically, the present inhabitants of England, Wales and Scotland are the interbred descendants of successive waves of migrants and invaders who arrived in the British Isles between roughly 1000 B.C. and 1000 A.D. It is no longer realistic to attempt to identify among the present population the relative prominence of all the different racial characteristics brought to the islands by these ancient peoples. By the accident of long isolation, or by genetic accident, physical types which may be described loosely as "pure Saxon", "pure Celt" or "pure" Norman still occur among the population, but the genetic heritage of the islanders is, by and large, a random mixture of many strains. Among these are the pre-Celtic strain of the earliest known racial types; the Celtic characteristics brought to Britain by the great migrations of the 1st Millenium B.C.; the many different racial strains introduced into the population by the inter-marriage of natives with Imperial auxiliaries and legionaries from all parts of the Roman Empire in the period between the 1st and 5th centuries A.D.; the huge Anglo-Saxon and Scandinavian element added to the melting-pot during the period between the breakdown of Romano-British culture and the Norman invasion; and finally, the great Norman-French influx of the 11th century. The Normans were themselves descendants of Scandinavian settlers on the north French coast, their name being merely another form of "Norsemen". Since the last successful invasion in 1066 various minor migrations have taken place, usually in periods of political or religious persecution on the Continent of Europe; each small group of refugees has added something to the British blood – and a few new surnames to the parish registers.

Memories of the distinct ethnic groups which have contributed to Britain's past survive as widely as do the tangible relics of their occupation, usually in the form of personal and place names, traditional myths, and certain forms of verbal usage. The English language is largely a marriage of Norman French and Anglo-Saxon, with some Celtic features and a very few words and forms which are known to survive from pre-Roman times. It has been predominant in England since the absorbtion of the Normans in early medieval times. However, in areas of natural physical refuge such as the Scottish Highlands, Wales, the Isle of Man and Cornwall – the areas to which previous cultures were naturally driven by later waves of invaders, and in whose remote and easily defended holds ancient racial memories could be handed down without disturbance – significant elements of Celtic culture have always survived. In the 1961 census some 26% of the population of the Principality of Wales claimed to speak Welsh, a form of British Celtic which is still the first language of a majority of the inhabitants of the western counties. Since 1967, in response to popular demand, the Welsh and English languages have been recognised as having equal validity in the administration of government and justice throughout the Principality. Some 81,000 people in the counties of Ross and Cromarty, Inverness, Argyll and Lanark – including the Western Isles which largely fall under the administration of Ross and Cromarty – are believed to speak the Scottish form of Gaelic, another Celtic tongue; and small numbers of people in Northern Ireland speak the Irish form, which is of course widespread in the Republic of Ireland.

Other forms of Celtic, quite widely spoken in previous times in the Isle of Man and Cornwall, are no longer effectively living languages, although Manx is still preserved in certain official and ceremonial procedures. Folk memories survive in these areas, but not to nearly such an extent as in Wales and Scotland, which have preserved their national cultures, identity, history and traditions down the centuries. In very early times, when the periodic defeats and occupations of the Celtic areas by the Norman-English brought harsh discriminatory rule, the preservation of national language and culture was often the only avenue of patriotism open to the inhabitants. In recent years, in a reflection of the general revulsion against the impersonal mass society of the 20th century, there has been a vigorous revival of Celtic national identity. In isolated and extreme cases this has seen the short-lived but violent activities of tiny national separatist movements; but in the main it is characterised by a healthy and assertive pride in regional history, identity, and cultural patterns.

In the Channel Islands English is the main language, but a unique Norman-French *patois* may still be heard, and French remains the official language of Jersey.

The various statistics which follow are, for the most part, based on 1969 figures; these are the latest to be interpreted and published in detailed form. Where earlier and later figures are quoted, the relevant dates are indicated.

POPULATION

The *de facto* or resident national population of the United Kingdom is currently about 55,711,000. The 1969 figures, by region, were as follows:

England
Males: 22,423,700   Females: 23,678,000
                                Total: 46,102,300

Wales (including Monmouthshire)
Males: 1,328,300   Females: 1,396,200
                                Total: 2,724,500

Scotland
Males: 2,493,900   Females: 2,700,800
                                Total: 5,194,700

Northern Ireland
Males: 737,800   Females: 774,700
                                Total: 1,512,500

Isle of Man
Males: 23,003   Females: 26,809
                                Total: 49,812

Jersey, Guernsey and associated Channel Islands
                                Total: 121,089

The most densely populated administrative area of the United Kingdom is the South-East of England, with some 17,316,000 inhabitants; the most sparsely inhabited mainland region is East Anglia, with some 1,673,000 (1970 figures). The overall density of population in England and Wales is 837 people per square mile. The figure for the Greater London area is 12,600 per square mile. The density over the United Kingdom as a whole is about 589 per square mile.
(*Comparative figures:* France, 236; Germany, 604; Italy, 455; U.S.A., 56)

As far as it is possible to separate the population figures for cities and towns from the figures for areas of conurbation, the twenty communities in the United Kingdom with the largest populations are listed below, with the density in persons *per acre*.

Great London	..	7,612,000	19·4
Birmingham	.. ..	1,084,000	20·6
Glasgow	..	908,000	25·2
Liverpool	..	667,000	24·9
Manchester	..	590,000	22·0
Sheffield	..	525,000	12·2
Leeds ..	..	502,000	12·4
Edinburgh	..	465,000	13·9
Bristol	..	426,000	16·0
Teesside	..	411,000	—
Belfast ..	..	384,000	24·9
Coventry	..	335,000	16·4
Nottingham	..	301,000	16·6
Bradford	..	292,000	11·4
Kingston-upon-Hull	..	290,000	20·5
Cardiff	..	284,000	16·8
Leicester	..	277,000	15·6
Stoke-on-Trent	..	271,000	11·8
Wolverhampton	..	264,000	15·4
Plymouth	..	257,000	15·2

In addition to the above, there are seventeen other cities and towns with populations in excess of 150,000.

Population growth. It is estimated that the population of Great Britain at the end of the 11th century was approximately 2,000,000. A contemporary estimate in the year 1700 put the population of England and Wales at 5,500,000 and that of Scotland at 1,000,000; in other words the total had rather more than trebled in 500 years. In the two centuries between 1700 and 1901, which saw the birth of modern medical science and the industrial revolution, the population jumped to 38,200,000. In 1961 it was 52,709,000. In 1980 it is estimated that the figure will be 58,903,000; in 1990, 62,343,000; and in 2000, 66,509,000.

Immigration. Between the years 1815 and 1931 it is estimated that more than 20,000,000 people emigrated from Britain to destinations outside Europe. In the same period large numbers of immigrants arrived in Britain from Continental Europe, but between 1871 and 1931 it is believed that the net population loss was in the region of 4,000,000. Since 1931 the trend has been steadily towards a net inflow; since 1967, however, a small net outflow has been recorded. The two main periods of inflow were between 1931 and 1941, when emigration was low, many emigrants returned home, and many thousands of refugees from Europe entered Britain; and between the early 1950s and 1967, which was the period of major immigration from the West Indies, India and Pakistan. Total net immigration in the three years 1960, 1961 and 1962 was some 388,000. During 1969 some 36,500 Commonwealth immigrants were admitted to settle, of whom about 29,500 were dependants of previous immigrants. In the same year some 30,000 persons acquired United Kingdom citizenship.

POPULATION BY AGE AND SEX

Of the total United Kingdom population of approximately 55,711,000, there are about 13,400,000 children aged fourteen years or less; 33,475,000 men between the ages of fifteen and sixty-four, and women between the ages of fifteen and fifty-nine (i.e. persons between normal school-leaving and retirement ages); and about 8,840,000 men and women above retirement age (1970 figures). The figures quoted at the beginning of this section show that there are roughly 106 women to every 100 men in the United Kingdom. In fact male live births are always about 6% higher than female live births, but mortality rates in all age groups are higher for men than women. The difference only becomes significant in age groups from about forty-five years and upwards.

BIRTH AND DEATH RATES

For much of the 19th century the annual birth rate was about 35 per 1,000 of the population, and the death rate was about 20 per 1,000. With obvious distortions to the death rate in the periods 1914–1918 and 1939–1945, the picture over the last one hundred years has been of a steadily declining birth rate and death rate. There were enormous peaks in the birth rate in the years immediately following the two World Wars. The advances of medical science, and in particular the vastly improved survival rates among infants and women in childbirth, have ensured a slowly increasing population and a steadily rising average age and life expectancy. The death rate has remained almost steady at about 12 per 1,000 annually since 1920; after reaching a peak of around 18·7 per 1,000 in 1964, the birth rate has slowly declined, and currently stands at about 16·2 per 1,000. Life expectancy for a man

and women born between 1900 and 1910 was 48 years and 52 years respectively. The comparative figures for the period 1965–67 are 68·5 and 74·6.

The 1970 figures show that eight out of every hundred live births were illegitimate. The birth rate for Northern Ireland continues to be dramatically higher than in other parts of Britain, and currently stands at about 21 per 1,000 annually.

The 1966 census showed that of 16,937,000 private households in the United Kingdom, representing some 97% of the population, about 15% consisted of one person only, about 30% of two persons, 21% of three persons, 18% of four persons, and 16% of five or more. There were approximately 13,334,000 families with one child; 3,287,000 families without children; and 312,000 families with two children. In 1971 there were 126,774 legal abortions and about 783,000 live births.

MARRIAGE AND DIVORCE

In 1938 some 42% of the population of Britain were married; in 1969 the figure was 50·7%. In the same period the proportion of the population made up of single people over the age of fifteen has dropped from about 36% to about 18%. The average age for marriage in Britain has also dropped sharply. In 1938 only just over 25% of women between the ages of 20 and 24 were married; in 1969 the figure was 57%.

In 1969 there were some 452,000 marriages in the United Kingdom. The largest age group among the husbands of these marriages was 21 to 24 years of age (206,000) and the next most numerous group were the roughly 89,000 between the ages of 25 and 29. Some 35,000 were aged 20, and only 14,000 were 18 or under. Among the wives of these marriages a different pattern emerged. Some 173,000 were between 21 and 24; about 58,000 were aged 20; about 50,000 were aged 19; and at least 62,000 were 18 or under.

In 1969, for every 1,000 married couples in England and Wales, about four divorce decrees were finalised. The incidence of divorce in marriages which took place when the wife was under the age of 20 is twice as high as in marriages which took place when the wife was aged between 20 and 24.

MORTALITY

The causes of death in the United Kingdom have altered radically over the past century, in common with all other highly developed countries. The 1970 figures are as follows:

Total deaths from natural causes	629,000
Deaths from lung cancer	34,200
Deaths from other forms of cancer	96,900
Deaths from cerebral haemorrhage, embolism	91,700
Deaths from coronary diseases	161,400
Deaths from respiratory diseases	95,400
Deaths caused by pregnancy, childbirth and abortion	200
Other natural causes	149,300

Mortality from the main acute infectious diseases of childhood is now down to less than 0·5% of the rate which prevailed in the mid-19th century, and mortality from tuberculosis is down to less than 2% of the rate recorded at that time. In the period 1900–1902 infant mortality – deaths of children under one year old per 1,000 live births – was running at 142; in 1969 this horrifying figure had dropped to 18·6. Maternal mortality has dropped from 4·7 per 1,000 live births in 1900–1902, to 0·19 per 1,000 in 1969.

Deaths from violent causes totalled 26,300 in 1970. These figures have not been authoritatively broken down at the time of writing, but the comparative figures for 1960 and 1965 are as follows, and indicate a general pattern:

	1960	1965	
Total deaths from violent causes ..	26,600	27,800	
Deaths from transport accidents	8,300	9,100	(1970: 7,900)
Deaths from domestic, industrial and other accidents	12,400	12,700	
Suicides	5,600	5,600	(1970: 4,400)
Homicides	300	400	

EMPLOYMENT AND INCOME

In June 1970 the total working population of the United Kingdom was 25,637,000. This total comprised 16,416,000 men and 9,221,000 women. Of these some 579,000 were registered as wholly unemployed; this represented a national average of 2·6% unemployment. (Regional percentages were England, 2·4%; Wales, 4%; Scotland, 4·3%; Northern Ireland, 7%.) At the time of writing the total unemployment figure had risen (spring 1972) to a fluctuating level in excess of 900,000. Regional differentials were broadly similar to the figures quoted above.

The total working population represents about 47% of the entire population. It includes about 73% of persons of normal working age – that is, men between the ages of fifteen and 64, and women between the ages of fifteen and 59. About 91% of the men of working age are engaged in or are actively seeking employment. The remaining 9% is made up of those pursuing secondary education, the disabled, and a small percentage of men with private means. Some 53% of the women of working age are engaged in or are seeking employment. Some 60% of working women are married. Apart from those of conventional working age, about 1,000,000 men and women over retirement age are still working. Some 1,700,000 people out of the total working population of more than 25 million are employers, or are self-employed.

Still quoting the June 1970 figures, it appears that taking the total numbers of employed as 100, some 25·2% are employed in the public sector (national and local government, H.M. Forces, local authorities, public

corporations, etc.) and 74·8% in the private sector.

The total numbers of employees in certain main areas of the economy in June 1970 were as follows:

Agriculture, forestry, fishing	.. ..	380,000
Mining, quarrying	.. ..	418,000
Food, drink, tobacco manufacture ..	..	891,000
Coal and petroleum product manufacture..		63,000
Chemical industries	.. ..	475,000
Metal manufacture	.. ..	592,000
Mechanical, electrical, instrument engineering	.. ..	2,283,000
Shipbuilding, marine engineering ..	..	199,000
Vehicle building	.. ..	842,000
Textile industries	.. ..	716,000
Clothing, footwear manufacture ..	..	501,000
Paper, publishing and printing ..	..	655,000
Construction	.. ..	1,591,000
Gas, electricity, water	..	391,000
Transport, communications..	..	1,591,000
Distributive trades	.. ..	2,706,000
Finance, business, professional and scientific services	..	3,851,000
National government services ..	..	573,000
Local government services	..	858,000

In June 1970 the figures for unemployment associated with specific areas of the economy included:

Manufacturing industries ..	.. ..	186,400
Construction	.. ..	102,500
Distributive trades	.. ..	54,600
Transport and communications ..	..	34,800
Insurance, banking, finance ..	..	12,900
Professional and scientific services ..	..	15,700

In October 1970 the average weekly earnings of British workers, including bonuses and overtime payments, and before deductions of tax and national insurance, were as follows:

Administrative, technical, clerical		Men	Women
Manufacturing industries..	..	£36·49	£15·44
Construction industry	..	£35·45	—
Manual			
Manufacturing industries..	..	£28·91	£13·98
Construction industry	..	£26·85	—

It is estimated that in April 1970 there were in the total British labour force some 8,300,000 men earning less than £35·00 gross weekly; some 6,700,000 earning less than £30·00; some 4,900,000 earning less than £26·00; some 1,900,000 earning less than £20·00; and some 1,100,000 earning less than £18·00 gross weekly.

In October 1969 the number of hours actually worked per week by manual workers in all areas of British industry averaged 46·5 for men, and 38·1 for women on full-time work.

EDUCATION

All aspects of education in the United Kingdom are the responsibility of the Secretary of State for Education and Science, the Secretary of State for Scotland, and, until very recently, the Minister of Education for Northern Ireland. (The recent introduction of direct rule from Westminster and the suspension of the Stormont government in Northern Ireland has complicated this aspect, and the situation may have changed once more by the time this material is published.)

Parents in Britain are required by law to see that children receive proper education on a full-time basis between the ages of five and sixteen. There are four main types of school in Britain: county schools, voluntary schools, direct-grant schools, and independent schools. The first group, by far the largest, are the main publicly-maintained schools. It is the responsibility of local education authorities to ensure that adequate primary and secondary school places are available in their areas. Education at these schools is entirely free of charge. The voluntary schools are those which were founded and maintained by some voluntary body – usually, one of the major churches – before the introduction of the relevant legislation. These have now been absorbed into the local public education system, with varying degrees of financial support from public funds. Over one-third of the 28,500-odd publicly-maintained schools in England and Wales fall into this category.

The direct-grant schools are completely independent of local education authorities, but receive government grants; a relatively small category, this includes the "grammar" schools, many of ancient foundation and high educational standard.

The last group, the independent schools, are entirely self-supporting. They are often of ancient foundation, and a high proportion provide a "boarding" – living-in – education. The fees range from about £400 to about £900 per annum. The "preparatory" schools within this category cater for the child between about eight and about thirteen years of age, and the paradoxically-named "public" schools provide a secondary education up to university entrance age. Standards of academic achievement in these schools are often very high.

All the above categories of school, whatever the nature of their relationship with the Department of Education and Science, are governed by national regulations in the areas of premises, staff, health aspects, and the efficiency of the education they offer, and are subject to inspection.

In January 1970 there were 32,900 schools in England and Wales, 3,700 in Scotland and 1,600 grant-aided schools in Northern Ireland, giving a national total of 37,940 schools of all types. The total number of children attending schools was in excess of 9,960,000. In England and Wales some 7,800,000 attended publicly-maintained schools; an additional 128,450 attended direct-grant schools; and 417,250 attended independent fee-paying schools. In Scotland about 951,000 children were attending education authority or direct-grant schools, and a further 17,000 were enrolled in independent schools. There are some 2,920 independent schools in England and Wales, and a further 111 in Scotland. Of the former,

some 1,450, attended by 72% of the total pupil enrollment of the independent schools, have been granted the status of "recognised as efficient" by the Department of Education and Science (this does not imply that the remainder are necessarily below the required standards – recognition is only considered on receipt of an application).

There were in January 1970 some 370,000 full-time teachers in England and Wales, 44,900 in Scotland and 14,200 in Northern Ireland. Statistics of that month gave an average class size in education authority schools as 27·4 children per teacher (primary) and 17·8 (secondary). Despite this average, a large majority of actual primary classes (an estimated 102,079 out of 151,084) consisted of more than thirty children. In October 1969 there were a total of 127,486 student teachers under instruction, of whom some 8,400 only were graduates.

"Further education" is the term used for all education beyond the secondary stage – i.e. beyond the age of sixteen, but excluding education at universities, colleges of education and certain advanced courses at other establishments, all of which are described as "higher education". In England and Wales these further education establishments, comprising polytechnics, national colleges, regional colleges, evening institutes, agricultural and arts colleges, etc., totalled 1,174 in the autumn of 1970. Total enrollment was 3,181,200, of whom 237,800 were full-time students. There were 1,225 establishments in Scotland, with more than 353,000 students altogether. Northern Ireland had 146 centres of technical instruction, with a total of 61,800 students. All these establishments of further education are maintained or assisted from local authority funds, or receive direct grants.

The Universities are the main organ of higher education in Britain. Admission is by examination and selection; no student is barred for reasons of finance, religion, colour or race. At the beginning of the academic year 1969–70 over 219,000 full-time students attended Britain's 44 universities, of whom over 90% were aided by grants from public or private funds. The government provides about 80% of the universities' income, working through the independent University Grants Committee, an advisory body set up by the Secretary of State for Education and Science. By means of the "buffer", state aid is distributed according to informed assessment of need, and the government has no direct control over the work or teaching of the universities.

The total number of students pursuing higher education courses in Britain in 1969–70 was some 437,000. Apart from the 44 universities, they were enrolled at colleges of education – of which there were some 180 of various types – or were taking courses of university degree standard at other establishments. Prominent among institutions where work is of university standard are the University of Manchester Institute of Science and Technology; two business schools supported jointly by

Cambridge University is second only to Oxford in seniority of date of foundation; St. John's College, founded by Lady Margaret Beaufort in 1511, is built on either side of the River Cam, its buildings being linked by the Bridge of Sighs, designed by Hutchinson in 1831

public funds and by industry – Manchester Business School and the London Graduate School of Business Studies; Cranfield Institute of Technology; and the Royal College of Art.

The following list of British universities is annotated by an asterisk to indicate universities which have received their charter since 1960. The Universities of Oxford and Cambridge date from the 12th and 13th centuries, and the Scottish Universities of St. Andrews, Glasgow, Aberdeen and Edinburgh from the 15th and 16th centuries. All the others have been founded in the last 175 years:

*Aston, Birmingham	Leicester
*Bath	Liverpool
Birmingham	London
*Bradford	*Loughborough
Bristol	Manchester
*Brunel, London	Newcastle-upon-Tyne
Cambridge	Nottingham
*City, London	Oxford
Durham	Reading
*East Anglia	*Salford
*Essex	Sheffield
Exeter	Southampton
Hull	*Surrey
Keele	*Sussex
*Kent at Canterbury	*Warwick
*Lancaster	*York
Leeds	

The federated University of Wales comprises four university colleges, the University of Wales Institute of Science and Technology, the Welsh National School of Medicine, and St. David's College, Lampeter.

The Scottish universities are:

Aberdeen	*Heriot-Watt, Edinburgh
*Dundee	St. Andrews
Edinburgh	*Stirling
Glasgow	*Strathclyde, Glasgow

In Northern Ireland there are Queen's University, Belfast, and the New University of Ulster* at Coleraine.

In 1968–69 there were about 26,070 full time university teachers in Great Britain, some 11·5% of them being professors. The overall ratio of staff to students was about one to eight – one of the most favourable in the world. A UNESCO survey has recorded the opinion that the university students of Britain come from a wider social background than those of any other western European nation.

Total government expenditure on education in the year 1969–70 was £2,365,500,000 – approximately 12% of total public expenditure for the year.

HEALTH AND SOCIAL SERVICES

The total public expenditure on social services of all kinds for the year 1970 was £8,953,000,000. The figure rises steadily, and currently the public funds are responsible for services costing about £168 for every man, woman and child in the United Kingdom.

The major breakdown items for 1970 were as follows:

Education	£2,592,000,000
National health	£2,089,000,000
Local welfare services ..	£111,000,000
Child care	£79,000,000
School meals, free milk, welfare foods	£174,000,000
Social security benefit ..	£3,908,000,000
Housing, environment ..	£2,204,000,000
Libraries, museums, arts ..	£98,000,000
Police	£371,000,000
Prisons	£65,000,000

There is no space in this book to detail the vast variety of services provided for the individual citizen by the state within the welfare system, but brief details of some of the more important aspects are as follows:

The National Health Service is available to all according to medical need, regardless of any insurance or other qualifications. With the exception of small nominal prescription charges – from which many classes of citizens are exempt, e.g. children, expectant and nursing mothers, the elderly, and several other categories of special need – the full range of medical services are entirely free.

As at 30th September 1970 the service provided 536,300 "staffed hospital beds". The average daily number of inpatients was 440,300. Total attendances by out-patients in 1970 were about 58,200,000. In England and Wales medical, dental, professional and technical staff totalled 58,480 persons. In addition there were some 189,400 full-time and 101,000 part-time nurses and mid-wives; and about 254,660 administrative and clerical staff. In Scotland, medical, dental, professional and technical personnel totalled 9,786; there were about 28,200 full-time and 14,860 part-time nurses and mid-wives, and some 36,200 administrative and clerical staff. Northern Ireland had 2,565 medical, dental, professional and technical staff, about 8,900 full-time and 1,300 part-time nurses and mid-wives, and some 10,300 administrative and clerical staff.

Within the bounds of normal variation, the following figures are accurate for the year 1970:

Numbers of general practitioners (principals) listed:
England and Wales: 20,357; Scotland: 2,608; Northern Ireland: 755.

Numbers of patients per doctor:
England and Wales: 2,460; Scotland: 2,087; Northern Ireland: 2,019.

Prescription items dispensed:
England and Wales: 266,600,000; Scotland: 28,900,000; Northern Ireland: 10,500,000.

Other major charges on the welfare system include unemployment benefit, sickness benefit, retirement pensions, widow's benefit, maternity benefit, family allowances, supplementary benefits, industrial injury benefits, and so forth. Broadly, the citizen's entitlement to these benefits is covered by a single deduction from his wage or salary, at source, the amount graduated according to his income.

As at 31st December 1970 the following numbers of people were receiving various forms of benefit:

Unemployment	327,000
Sickness	1,058,000
Retirement pension	7,568,000
Widows' benefit	572,000
Injury	71,000
Industrial disablement	211,000

HOUSING AND HOUSEHOLD GOODS, CONSUMPTION AND LEISURE

The total number of dwellings, of all types, in the United Kingdom was estimated in December 1970 at 18,731,000, of these 9,270,000, or roughly 50%, were owner occupied. Some 5,705,000 (roughly 30%) were rented from local authorities, and some 2,798,000 (roughly 15%) were privately rented. About 39% of the total were built since 1944, about 24% between 1919 and 1944, and about 37% prior to 1919. In 1970 about 362,300 permanent houses and flats were built. Of this total some 177,000 were built for local housing authorities, 11,000 for other public bodies, and about 174,300 for private owners.

Of about 16,900,000 private households recorded in Britain in the 1966 census, about 15% consisted of one person living alone, about 30% of two people, about 21% of three people, about 18% of four people, and about 16% of five or more people. About 85% of British families live in houses, and about 14% in flats. The same census recorded that about 85% of British households had exclusive use of a hot water system, and about 81% had a fixed bath. The average weekly rent on a council house (local authority-owned property) in 1970 was £3·16 in the Greater London area, and £2·18 in the rest of England and Wales. Comparative figures for privately rented unfurnished property were £5·67 and £3·29. The average monthly gross mortgage repayment for an owner-occupier (assuming 90% mortgage over 25 years on a new property) was £37·56 in June 1970. No realistic estimate of the average value of different types of property can be attempted, owing to recent unprecedentedly rapid increases in property prices.

About 35% of British households have a telephone, about 65% a washing machine, about 66% a refrigerator, and about 80% a vacuum cleaner. Regional samples returned averages of 50% for telephones (Greater London), 82% for washing machines (Yorkshire and Humberside), and 81% for refrigerators (South-East England) in 1970.

Less than one in twenty British households employ any

regular paid domestic help; less than one in 200 has a living-in servant of any kind. About one household in 750 has an "*au pair* girl".

In mid-1970 there were some 11,515,000 licensed private cars in Britain. A national sampling recorded an average of 52% of all households running one or more cars.

About 30% of all households – projected from a nation-wide sampling of about 6,400 households – have ful or partial central heating. An estimated 90% of all new houses and flats currently under construction or recently completed have at least partial central heating.

It is estimated that the "average British citizen" consumes in one year (on 1970 figures) more than 92 lb of fresh and frozen meat; 25 lb. of bacon and ham; more than 23 lb. of poultry; and 16 lb. of fish. The per-head consumption of flour (i.e. bread and other baked foods) was 145 lb; of milk in liquid form, more than 240 pints; and of butter, more than 19 lb. Average per-head consumption of eggs was 249 in the year; of cheese, nearly 12 lb.; and of potatoes, no less than 224 lb. Sugar consumption, including sugar incorporated in manufactured foods and in brewed drinks, was 103 lb. per head in 1971. 1969 figures give a per-head consumption of chocolate and other sweets of nearly 8 oz. per week. The average citizen consumes some 8 lb. of tea and 4·7 lb. of coffee over the year; 13 lb. of tomatoes; and more than 122 lb. of other fresh vegetables. He consumes 21½ lb. of fresh citrus fruit, 51 lb. of other fresh fruits, and 18 lb. of canned fruit.

In 1971 the average Briton drank 184 pints of beer. Cigarette consumption totalled nearly 125,000,000, or forty a week for every man, woman and child in the country. Nevertheless, total consumption of cigarette tobacco dropped – the trend towards smaller, cheaper cigarettes continued. Since 1959 sales of pipe tobacco have also declined, but cigar tobacco sales have tripled. In 1969 about 68% of men and 43% of women sampled declared themselves to be smokers.

LEISURE AND RECREATION

The following figures are the percentages of total leisure time spent on the quoted activity by the various population groups, according to a survey conducted in 1965–66:

MALES	School age	Single, 19–22	Married with children; 23–30	Married with children; 31–45	ALL
Watching TV	13	11	25	29	23
Reading	10	3	4	4	5
Hobbies	3	7	5	4	4
House/vehicle maintenance	1	6	10	10	8
Social activity	4	2	4	2	3
Drinking	2	6	3	3	3

MALES	School age	Single, 19–22	Married with children; 23–30	Married with children; 31–45	ALL
Physical recreation	33	27	10	10	11
Physical recreation, spectator	3	1	3	2	3
Cinema, theatre	4	4	–	–	1

From these statistics it may be inferred that the average British male is almost entirely illiterate, abstemious and unsociable, and divides the bulk of his leisure time between watching television, painting his house and servicing his car, and indulging in vigorous physical sport. The reader with any personal knowledge of the British male will draw his own conclusions on the relationship between the results of mass surveys, and real life. The corresponding figures for females in these population groups show a markedly higher incidence of all activities except house and vehicle maintenance, drinking, and watching television.

The popularity of television is backed by a figure of 16,333,000 TV licences current on 31st December 1970. Considering the number of unlicensed sets known to be in use, it may be conservatively estimated that about nine out of every ten British households have a TV set.

In February 1971 households with TV sets spent the following numbers of hours per week viewing, on average:

Social Class A (c. 5% of total population)
  Families of professionals, and senior executives in commerce and industry .. .. 14 hours
Social Class B (c. 25% of total population)
  Families of senior clerical staff, teachers, managers, small employers and other professional workers .. .. 16·8 hours
Social Class C (c. 70% of total population)
  The remainder of the population .. 19·1 hours
  (Overall average weekly hours spent viewing television .. .. 18·6 hours)

In 1970 a total of 1,529 cinemas reported about 193,000,000 admissions, with a total gross box office taking of £59,000,000.

In a survey carried out in 1965–66 the following percentages of a sample of urban males between the ages of fifteen and 70 in England and Wales claimed to take part in the following sports and games regularly – i.e. at least once a month for at least part of the year, summer or winter:

Swimming (pools)	17%	10-pin bowling	..	7%
Soccer	10%	Golf	..	6%
Table tennis	9%	Swimming (sea)	..	6%
Cricket	8%	Tennis	..	5%
Fishing	8%	Fencing/archery/ shooting	..	5%

169

(All other individual sports or games, under 5% of the sample.)

The same sample returned the following figures for games and sports watched regularly, by the same definition:

Soccer	27%	Boxing/wrestling ..	4%
Cricket	14%	Motor sports ..	4%
Rugby football ..	6%	Swimming ..	3%
Tennis	5%	Horse/dog racing..	3%

The increasing popularity of holidays abroad, and their increasing availability to a wide range of income levels, are reflected in the figures for holidaying abroad in 1970. A total of about 5,605,000 United Kingdom residents spent holidays abroad. Western Europe, including the Mediterranean countries, attracted 4,259,000 of these; 812,000 visited the Irish Republic, and about 223,000 visited other overseas destinations within the Sterling area. About 50,000 visited North America, and some 120,000 other overseas destinations outside the Sterling area.

✍ Natural History ✍

ENCROACHMENT ON THE COUNTRYSIDE

It is perhaps to be expected in a community whose stated aims include constant economic growth and improvement in the domestic amenities of its members that the overall environment of the community must undergo a gradual change. Since the age of the Industrial Revolution the change in Britain has noticeably accelerated and the last twenty years have witnessed what many people consider an alarming trend towards a loss of balance in environmental priorities.

Unquestionably a balance must be maintained and Britain is by no means alone in the world in expressing concern at recent symptoms of malady in the environment. It is difficult to equate sentiment with hard economic necessity – perhaps nowhere more difficult than in Britain whose survival must depend upon industrial efficiency.

Yet national capacity for efficiency must to a very great extent depend upon a state of contentment – perhaps a knowledge that one's environment is *not* being wholly subordinated to the arrogance of mankind. Leaving aside the disturbing trends of chemical pollution by modern industry, Britain has suffered a constant erosion of her countryside through the essential demands for urban growth to accommodate her fast growing population. To some extent successive Governments have recently recognised the dangers of uncontrolled urban growth into rural areas and have introduced limited measures to bring about some measure of control. These include the New Towns, specific connurbations in which urban development may be pursued; and the encouragement of "Green Belts", areas around particular towns and cities wherein urban development is strictly limited or even prohibited. Obviously such restrictions have tended to check encroachment on the countryside, but at the same time they have imposed a substantial and to some extent distasteful element in the living habits of large sections of the community. Housing property and land, by its confinement, has become very expensive, and a growing proportion of the urban population is seeking vertical, rather than horizontal growth – hence the large increase in high-rise dwellings.

Nevertheless these restrictions and modified life-styles are considered by many to be necessary if rural Britain is to be preserved. It is frequently the very people who, subject to the pressures of modern community life in today's connurbations, seek relaxation and pleasure in the contrast provided by rural interests. It is in all likelihood these pressures that commend the contrasting importance of the countryside, especially among the younger generations in Britain – an awareness that is strongly fostered in the schools and universities as well as through mass media such as television and the Press.

Conservation is thankfully passing from the realms of private concern into the broad national concensus, a transformation of opinion that has clearly occurred just in time. Isolated instances of Government legislation to curb pollution, as well as steps taken by local authorities have to some extent assisted in demonstrating public concern for conservation.

BRITAIN'S VANISHED WILDLIFE

Wildlife in Britain today, wide ranging though it is, is but a remnant of a once much more prolific fauna. The greater mammals which roamed Britain in the Lower Pleistocene Period (the million years before about 500,000 B.C.) have all disappeared, the Elephant, Elk, Rhinoceros and Zebra becoming extinct with the onset of the Ice Age; only the Beaver and Wolf survived until relatively recent times.

Two thousand years ago Britain was covered with large areas of forest, ranging from the thick lush tree forests of the low lying areas in the south, midlands and east, and the dense scrubland of the uplands to the desolate moorlands of the greater ranges and massifs in the west and north. In these contrasting surroundings ranged a huge variety of wildlife – much of which has survived to this day.

Before passing on to the surviving species of wildlife, it is worth listing here the indigenous species of British mammalia which have become extinct; dates against certain species indicate those whose extinction can probably be attributed to the depredations of modern man, either out of necessity for human safety or sheer ignorance.

Lower Pleistocene Period (c. 1,500,000 to c. 500,000 B.C.)

Beaver (13th century A.D.)	Southern Elephant
Elk	Wild Horse
Gazelle	Wolf (18th century A.D.)
Giant Deer	Zebra
Rhinoceros	

Middle Pleistocene Period (500,000–240,000 B.C.)

Aurocks	Hippopotamus
Bison	Irish Deer
Cave Bear	Lemming
Cave Lion	Mammoth
Giant Beaver	Wolverine

Upper Pleistocene Period (since 240,000 B.C.)

Arctic Fox	Reindeer
Brown Bear	(13th century A.D.)
(11th century A.D.)	Straight-Tusked Elephant
Hyena	Wild Boar
Lynx	(late 17th century A.D.)
Marmot	Woolly Rhinoceros
Musk Ox	

The subject of conservation is frequently misunderstood as being the preservation of yesterday's world. In fact very few of Britain's "open" areas are natural or even semi-natural; medieval destruction of forest and woodland did far more to modify the natural character of the countryside than have the demands of industrial expansion in the past 150 years. But conservation is not necessarily preservation; it is, broadly speaking, the balancing of often conflicting demands by the natural and the human worlds, so that each may survive. Nor is the human demand only manifest in urban growth; the modernisation and rationalisation of British agriculture have imposed a substantial hazard by the scientific elimination of pests – both fauna and flora – thereby imposing changes in much wider ranges of associated species.

Yet the Briton is paradoxical in his view of conservation. The same person may be an avid supporter of wildlife conservation as well as being a devotee of fox hunting – seeking, with some justification, to excuse the latter in a belief that the fox actually benefits from the controlled nature of the sport. The survival of the fox is almost certainly owed to this form of control down the centuries. On the other hand, nature's pattern would

undergo other changes – not necessarily welcome – were the number of foxes to increase materially.

TOWARDS CONSERVATION

In a country that had produced and respected many great naturalists in the 17th and 18th centuries, it was to be expected that in the wake of the Industrial Revolution would follow public concern for the natural amenities of rural Britain. The advance of this concern may best be summarised in the space available here in the following brief chronology:

1865 The Commons, Open Spaces and Footpaths Preservation Society is formed.

1889 The Society for the Protection of Birds is founded; its Royal Charter follows in 1904.

1895 The National Trust is founded.

1904 The Committee for the Study of British Vegetation is established; in 1913 this becomes the British Ecological Society.

1912 The Society for the Promotion of Nature Reserves is founded largely through the initiative of the Hon. Charles Rothschild.

1926 The Norfolk Naturalists' Trust, the first County Trust, is established.

1943 The Council for the Promotion of Field Studies is inaugurated on 10th December.

1947 Wildfowl counts are pioneered by the Wildfowl Inquiry Committee of the British Section, International Council for Bird Preservation.

1949 The Nature Conservancy is created, its first Director-General (1949–1952) being Captain Cyril Diver.

1951 The first National Nature Reserve, Beinn Eighe in Ross-shire, Scotland, is declared on 1st November.

1953 The Welsh Committee of the Conservancy is established.

1954 England's first National Nature Reserve – Scolt Head, north Norfolk, is declared in March. The Protection of Birds Act becomes law.

1958 The Council for Nature is established.

1959 The Council of the Conservation Corps is established.

Such a brief chronology can give little idea of the considerable progress in spreading awareness of the dangers which can threaten the wildlife of Britain. Today the Council of Nature, under the patronage of H.R.H. The Duke of Edinburgh, describes itself as ". . .*the national representative body of the voluntary natural history movement in the United Kingdom, acting on behalf of naturalists and others to further the study and conservation of Nature. A major part of the Council's function is to encourage among all a greater appreciation of wildlife.*"

Its corporate membership, totalling nearly 500 members, includes National and Local Societies, Naturalists'

Trusts, Museums, Universities, Colleges and Schools. Those members having a direct interest in the study and conservation of wildlife include:

Amateur Entomologists' Society
Botanical Society of the British Isles
British Bryological Society
British Ecological Society
British Lichen Society
British Ornithologists' Union
British Trust for Ornithology
Cave Research Group of Great Britain
Conchological Society of Great Britain
Council for the Protection of Rural England
Council for the Preservation of Rural Wales
Fauna Preservation Society
Field Studies Council
Freshwater Biological Association
Institute of Biology
Institute of Landscape Architects
Linnean Society of London
Mammal Society of the British Isles
Marine Biological Association of the United Kingdom
Quekett Microscopical Society
Royal Entomological Society
Royal Society for the Protection of Birds
Scottish Field Studies Association
Society for the Promotion of Nature Reserves
Soil Association
Wildfowl Trust
Wildfowlers' Association of Great Britain and Ireland
Zoological Society of London

In 1965 the Nature Conservancy surrendered its Royal Charter to become a Committee of the National Environment Research Council, continuing its work much as before through a number of specialist working and regional sub-committees.

By 1968 there were sixty-two Nature Reserves in England totalling 58,160 acres, thirty-seven in Scotland totalling 182,535 acres, and twenty-seven in Wales totalling 17,690 acres. The following is a list of the areas of Great Britain set aside for the conservation and study of the many aspects of natural history. For reasons of space zoological gardens and parks are omitted, as are various private reserves. Access to these areas is often, for obvious reasons, restricted or wholly prohibited at certain times of the year, and prior reference should always be made to the administering Trust or other body before paying visits.

The Grey Squirrel (Sciurus carolinensis), *a mammal now common in Britain but one which was introduced from America in 1876; the native Red Squirrel is however becoming increasingly rare*

CONSERVATION AREAS AND COUNTY NATURALISTS' TRUSTS
ENGLAND

BEDFORDSHIRE (Bedfordshire and Huntingdonshire Naturalists' Trust Ltd.)

Sandy Lodge	Nature Reserve of the Royal Society for the Protection of Birds (102 acres)
Knocking Hoe	National Nature Reserve since 1958 (22 acres)
Totternhoe Knolls	Local Nature Reserve of Bedfordshire and Huntingdonshire Naturalists' Trust Ltd.

BERKSHIRE (Berkshire, Buckinghamshire and Oxfordshire Naturalists' Trust Ltd.)

Cothill	National Nature Reserve since 1956 of National Trust and Nature Conservancy
Windsor Forest and Great Park	Part of the Forest (45 acres at High Standing Hill) is a Forest Nature Reserve

BUCKINGHAMSHIRE (*Berkshire, Buckinghamshire and Oxfordshire Naturalists' Trust Ltd.*)

Boarstall	Ringing Station of Wildfowlers' Association of Great Britain and Ireland
Dancer's End	Nature Reserve of the Society for the Promotion of Nature Reserves (76 acres)
Coombe Hill	Nature Reserve, in effect, of National Trust
Church Wood, Hedgerley	Nature Reserve of the Royal Society for the Protection of Birds
Cliveden	In effect a Nature Reserve of the National Trust with beautiful woodland
Burnham Beeches	City of London Nature Reserve

CAMBRIDGESHIRE (*Cambridge and Isle of Ely Naturalists' Trust Ltd.*)

Wicken Fen	Nature Reserve of the National Trust (320 acres) and a Regional Wildfowl Refuge since 1957.
Chippenham Fen	National Nature Reserve (193 acres) since 1963
Wandlebury	Iron Age hill fort and Nature Trail of Cambridge and Isle of Ely Naturalists' Trust Ltd., and Cambridge Preservation Society

CHESHIRE (*Cheshire Conservation Trust Ltd.*)

East Wood, Stalybridge	Nature Reserve of the Royal Society for the Protection of Birds (12 acres)
Hilbre Islands	Nature Reserve of the Hoylake Urban District Council
Harrock Wood, Irby	Nature Reserve of the National Trust
Rostherne Mere	National Nature Reserve since 1961 (327 acres) and a National Wildfowl Refuge
Cotterill Clough	Nature Reserve of Cheshire Conservation Trust Ltd., and Society for the Promotion of Nature Reserves (13 acres)
Weston Marsh, Runcorn	Nature Reserve of the Merseyside Nationalists' Association
Budworth Mere	Nature Reserve of the Cheshire Conservation Trust Ltd., and Society for the Promotion of Nature Reserves (6 acres)
Burton Wood	Nature Reserve of the National Trust
Wybunbury Moss	National Nature Reserve since 1955 (26 acres)

CORNWALL (*Cornwall Naturalists' Trust Ltd.*)

Peter's Wood, Boscastle	Nature Reserve of National Trust and Cornwall Naturalists' Trust Ltd.
Walmsley Sanctuary, Wadebridge	Regional Wildfowl Refuge since 1948 (42 acres). Private accessibility only
Trethias Island	Nature Reserve of the Cornwall Bird Watching and Preservation Society
Stoke Climsland	Nature Reserve of Cornwall Naturalists' Trust (19 acres)
Hawke's Wood, Wadebridge	Nature Reserve of Cornwall Naturalists' Trust (9 acres)

CUMBERLAND (*Lake District Naturalists' Trust Ltd.*)

Solway Coast	Area of Outstanding Natural Beauty, confirmed in 1965 (41 square miles)
Grune Point	Ringing station and bird migration key point
Thornthwaite Forest	State Forest of the Forestry Commission since 1920 (4,875 acres)
Thirlmere	Nature Trials of the Manchester Corporation
Hardknott	National Forest Park of the Forestry Commission
Drigg Dunes	Local Nature Reserve of the Cumberland County Council and Nature Conservancy

DERBYSHIRE (*Derbyshire Naturalists' Trust Ltd.*)

Peak District	The first National Park to be confirmed (17th April 1951), 542 square miles

DEVONSHIRE (*Devon Trust for Nature Conservation, Ltd.*)

Tamar Lake	Regional Wildfowl Refuge since 1951 (75 acres)
Woody Bay	Nature Reserve of National Trust and Exmoor Society since 1966
North Devon	Area of Outstanding Natural Beauty, confirmed in 1960 (66 square miles) with Cornish Area of Outstanding Natural Beauty and Exmoor National Park
Chapel Wood, Spreacombe	Nature Reserve of the Royal Society for the Protection of Birds, and Devon Bird Watching and Preservation Society (13 acres). Restricted entry
Arlington Court, Barnstaple	Bird Reserve of the National Trust with heronry and duck refuge
Braunton Burrows	National Nature Reserve since 1964 (560 acres)
Hartland Point	Nature Reserve of the Devon Trust for Nature Conservation since 1966
East Devon	Area of Outstanding Natural Beauty, confirmed in 1963 (103 square miles with Dorset Area of Outstanding Natural Beauty)
Dartmoor	National Park, confirmed in 1951 (365 square miles)
Axmouth-Lyme Regis	National Nature Reserve since 1955 (793 acres)
Bovey Valley	National Nature Reserve since 1963 (179 acres)
Exmouth	National Wildfowl Refuge since 1951 (1,022 acres)
Yarner Wood	National Nature Reserve since 1952 (361 acres)

Devonshire – continued

Wistman's Wood	Forest Nature Reserve of the Duchy of Cornwall and Nature Conservancy
Black Tor Copse	Forest Nature Reserve of the Duchy of Cornwall and Nature Conservancy
Dendles Wood	National Nature Reserve since 1965 (73 acres)
Buckfastleigh	Reserve of the Society for the Promotion of Nature Reserves and of the Devon Trust for Nature Conservation
South Devon	Area of Outstanding Natural Beauty, confirmed in 1960 (128 square miles)
Slapton	Field Centre of the Field Studies Council; also bird observatory of the Devon Bird Watchers' and Protection Society

DORSET (*Dorset Naturalists' Trust Ltd.*)

Dorset	Area of Outstanding Beauty, confirmed in 1959 (400 square miles)
Morden Bog	National Nature Reserve since 1956 (367 acres with bird sanctuary)
Arne	National Nature Reserve and Nature Reserve of the Royal Society for the Protection of Birds (a total of 690 acres). Entry restricted
Brownsea Island	Nature Reserve of the National Trust and Dorset Naturalists' Trust Ltd.
Hartland Moor	National Nature Reserve since 1954 (214 acres). Entry restricted
Studland Heath	National Nature Reserve since 1962 (429 acres). Danger of unexploded missiles
Furzebrook	Research Station and headquarters, Nature Conservancy, S.W. and S. England
Radipole Lake	Regional Wildfowl Refuge (70 acres) and Nature Reserve of the Weymouth Corporation
Portland Bill	Bird Observatory and Field Centre

DURHAM (*Northumberland and Durham Naturalists' Trust, Ltd.*)

Hawthorn Dene	Nature Reserve of the Northumberland and Durham Naturalists' Trust Ltd.
Black Halls Rocks	Nature Reserve of the Northumberland and Durham Naturalists' Trust Ltd.
Castle Eden Denes	Local Nature Reserve of the Durham County Council since 1954 and Nature Conservancy
Teesmouth	Bird Observatory. Nature Reserve planned for about 1,500 acres
Wynyard Forest	State Forest of the Forestry Commission

ESSEX (*Essex Naturalists' Trust, Ltd.*)

Hales Wood	National Nature Reserve since 1955 (20 acres)
Stansted	Wildlife Reserve of about 50 acres
Hatfield Forest	Nature Reserve of the National Trust
Abberton Reservoir	Duck Ringing Station
Epping Forest	Proposed as Nature Reserve owned by the Corporation of the City of London
Hainault Forest	Effectively a Nature Reserve of the Greater London Council
Hadleigh Marshes	Nature Reserve of Essex County and Benfleet Urban District Councils
Gray's Chalk Quarry	Nature Reserve of Essex Naturalists' Trust, Ltd., since 1966

GLOUCESTERSHIRE (*Gloucestershire Trust for Nature Conservation, Ltd.*)

Cotswolds	(With Worcestershire) Area of Outstanding Natural Beauty
Slimbridge	Wildfowl Trust special Zoo; founded in 1946 (35 acres)
Westonbirt	Forestry Commission arboretum (116 acres)

GREATER LONDON

Ruislip	Local Nature Reserve since 1959; administered by the local authority, Nature Conservancy, and Hertfordshire and Middlesex Trust for Nature Conservation
Inner London Parks	In effect Nature Reserves (Regent's Park, Green Park, Hyde Park and St. James's Park) administered by the Ministry of Works. The headquarters of the Nature Conservancy is at 19 Belgrave Square, S.W.1
Kew	At the Royal Botanic Gardens is the national collection of living plants, founded in 1759 (approximately 300 acres)
Richmond Park	Nature Reserve administered by the Ministry of Works
Surbiton	The Wood is the Nature Reserve of Surbiton Corporation
Lea Valley Reservoirs	Wildfowl Refuges, in effect, of the Metropolitan Water Board

HAMPSHIRE (*Mainland*) (*Hampshire and Isle of Wight Naturalists' Trust, Ltd.*)

East Hampshire	Area of Outstanding Natural Beauty, confirmed in 1962 (151 square miles)
Ludshott Common	Nature Reserve of the National Trust
Selborne Common	Nature Reserve of the National Trust
Liss	Nature Reserve of the Royal Society for the Protection of Birds
Old Winchester Hill	National Nature Reserve since 1954 (140 acres); danger of unexploded missiles
Oxenbourne Down	Nature Reserve of the Hampshire and Isle of Wight Naturalists' Trust (126 acres)
New Forest	Large area (of more than 100 square miles) including the Forest Nature Reserves of Bramshaw, Mark Ash, Matley and Denny; also the Nature Reserve of the Hampshire and Isle of Wight Naturalists' Trust, Ltd
Catherington Down	Nature Reserve of the Hampshire County Council and the Hampshire and Isle of Wight Naturalists' Trust Ltd.

Hampshire – continued

Farlington Marshes	Nature Reserve of the Hampshire and Isle of Wight Naturalists' Trust Ltd.
Stanpit Marsh	Local Nature Reserve of the Nature Conservancy, Christchurch Borough Council and the Hampshire and Isle of Wight Naturalists' Trust, Ltd.
Chichester Harbour	(With Sussex) Area of Outstanding Natural Beauty, confirmed in 1964 (29 square miles)

ISLE OF WIGHT (Hampshire and Isle of Wight Naturalists' Trust, Ltd.)

Isle of Wight	Area of Outstanding Natural Beauty (excluding towns), confirmed in 1963
Osborne	Nature Reserve administered by the Ministry of Works
St. Catherine's Point	Bird Ringing station

HEREFORDSHIRE (Herefordshire and Radnorshire Nature Trust, Ltd.)

HERTFORDSHIRE (Hertfordshire and Middlesex Trust for Nature Conservation, Ltd.)

Tring Reservoirs	National Nature Reserve and Regional Wildfowl Refuge since 1955 (49 acres); at Tring are situated the headquarters of the British Trust for Ornithology

HUNTINGDONSHIRE AND PETERBOROUGH (Bedfordshire and Huntingdonshire Naturalists' Trust, Ltd.)

Barnack Hill	Nature Reserve of the Northamptonshire Naturalists' Trust
Castor Hanglands	National Nature Reserve since 1945 (220 acres)
Holme Fen	National Nature Reserve since 1952 (640 acres)
Woodwalton Fen	National Nature Reserve of the Society for the Promotion of Nature Reserves and Nature Conservancy (514 acres)
Monks Wood	National Nature Reserve since 1953 (387 acres)
Grafham Water	Partly a Nature Reserve of the Bedfordshire and Huntingdonshire Naturalists' Trust, and the Great Ouse Water Authority, since 1966

KENT (Kent Naturalists' Trust, Ltd.)

High Halstow	National Nature Reserve of the Royal Society for the Protection of Birds, and Nature Conservancy (131 acres)
Swanscombe	National Nature Reserve since 1954 (about 5 acres)
Blean Woods	National Nature Reserve since 1953 (165 acres)
Burham	Nature Reserve of Kent Naturalists' Trust, Ltd.
Stodmarsh	National Nature Reserve since 1966 for rare plants and birds
Sandwich Bay	Bird Observatory and Nature Reserve of Kent Naturalists' Trust, Ltd.
Wye	Headquarters of the Nature Conservancy, South-East of England Region
Hothfield Common	Local Nature Reserve of Kent Naturalists' Trust, Ltd., West Ashford Rural District Council and Nature Conservancy since 1961 (143 acres)
Crundale Downs	National Nature Reserve since 1961 (123 acres)
Ham Street Woods	National Nature Reserve and Nature Reserve of Kent Naturalists' Trust, Ltd.
Benenden	Collingwood Ingram Bird Sanctuary of Kent Naturalists' Trust, Ltd.
Dungeness	Nature Reserve of the Royal Society for the Protection of Birds (1,233 acres)

LANCASHIRE (Lancashire Naturalists' Trust, Ltd.)

Blelham Bog	National Nature Reserve, and National Trust and Nature Conservancy (5 acres)
Esthwaite	National Nature Reserve since 1955 (4 acres)
Grizedale	Nature Reserve of Forestry Commission
Rusland Moss	National Nature Reserve since 1958 (58 acres)
Roudsea Wood	National Nature Reserve since 1955 (about 290 acres)
Merlewood (Grange-over-Sands)	Headquarters of the Nature Conservancy, North of England Region
Leighton Moss	Nature Reserve of the Royal Society for the Protection of Birds
Walney	Joint Nature Reserves of Lancashire Naturalists' Trust and Lake District Naturalists' Trust, Ltd.)
Wyre-Lune	National Wildfowl Refuge since 1963 (9,100 acres)
Southport	National Wildfowl Refuge since 1956 (14,500 acres)
Ainsdale	National Nature Reserve since 1965 (1,216 acres) for plants and birds
Holden Clough	Nature Reserve of Oldham Microscopical Society and Field Club
Forest of Bowland	(With Yorkshire Dales National Park) Area of Outstanding Natural Beauty (310 square miles)

LEICESTERSHIRE (Leicestershire Trust for Nature Conservation, Ltd.)

Charnwood Forest	Includes Nature Reserves of the Leicestershire County Council and the Leicestershire Trust for Nature Conservation, Ltd.

LINCOLNSHIRE (Lincolnshire Trust for Nature Conservation, Ltd.)

Stapleford Moor	Nature Reserve for the Lincolnshire Trust for Nature Conservation, Ltd.
Skegness	Local Nature Reserve of the Lincolnshire Trust for Nature Conservancy, Ltd., Lindsey County Council and Skegness Urban District Council; also Regional Wildfowl Refuge and Bird Observatory at Gibraltar Point

NORFOLK (Norfolk Naturalists' Trust, Ltd.)
Scolt Head	National Nature Reserve and Regional Wildfowl Refuge since 1954 (1,821 acres); Norfolk Naturalists' Trust, National Trust and Nature Conservancy
Blakeney Point	Nature Reserve of the National Trust and Norfolk Naturalists' Trust, Ltd.
Holme	Nature Reserve since 1955
Cley Marshes	Nature Reserve of Norfolk Naturalists' Trust, Ltd., and the National Trust
Hickling Broad	National Nature Reserve and Regional Wildfowl Refuge since 1958 (1,215 acres); Norfolk Naturalists' Trust, Ltd., and Nature Conservancy
Horsey Mere	Nature Reserve of the National Trust
Winterton Dunes	National Nature Reserve since 1956 (about 260 acres)
Bure Marshes	National Nature Reserve and Regional Wildfowl Refuge since 1958 (1,019 acres); Norfolk Naturalists' Trust, Ltd., and Nature Conservancy
Norwich	At Bishopgate. Headquarters of Nature Conservancy, East Anglia Region
Weeting Heath	National Nature Reserve since 1958 (338 acres)
Thetford Chase	(With Suffolk). State Forest of Forestry Commission since 1922 (48,360 acres)

NORTHAMPTONSHIRE (Northamptonshire Naturalists' Trust, Ltd.)
Pitsford Reservoir	Wildfowl Refuge of the Northamptonshire Naturalists' Trust, Ltd.
Buckingham Arm	Nature Reserve and Nature Trail of the Northamptonshire Naturalists' Trust, Ltd.

NORTHUMBERLAND (Northumberland and Durham Naturalists' Trust, Ltd.)
Northumberland Coast	Including Farne Islands. Area of Outstanding Natural Beauty, confirmed in 1958 (about 50 square miles)
Lindisfarne	National Nature Reserve since 1964 and National Wildfowl Refuge since 1966
Farne Islands	Nature Reserve of the National Trust and the Farne Islands Association (80 acres); the world's oldest sanctuary, first managed as such by St. Cuthbert in about A.D. 676
Northumberland	National Park, confirmed in 1956 (398 square miles)
Coom Rigg Moss	National Nature Reserve since 1960 (88 acres); Forestry Commission and Nature Conservancy

NOTTINGHAMSHIRE (Nottinghamshire Trust for Nature Conservation, Ltd.)
Attenborough Gravel Pits	Nature Reserve of Nottinghamshire Trust for Nature Conservation, Ltd.

OXFORDSHIRE (Berkshire, Buckinghamshire and Oxford Naturalists' Trust, Ltd.)
Cotswolds	(With Gloucestershire and Worcestershire) Area of Outstanding Natural Beauty
Wychwood	National Nature Reserve since 1955 (about 650 acres)
Waterperry	Forest Nature Reserve since 1954 (144 acres)
Aston Rowant area	Includes a National Nature Reserve (166 acres), a Forest Nature Reserve (13 acres) and a Nature Reserve (at Chinnor Hill) of Berkshire, Buckinghamshire and Oxfordshire Naturalists' Trust, Ltd.

SHROPSHIRE (Shropshire Conservation Trust, Ltd.)
Preston Montford	Field Centre of the Field Studies Council
Attingham Park	Headquarters of the Nature Conservancy, Midland Region of England
Shropshire Hills	Area of Outstanding Natural Beauty, confirmed in 1959 (300 square miles)
Pontsford	Nature Reserve of Shropshire Conservation Trust, Ltd., since 1965 (110 acres)

SOMERSET (Somerset Trust for Nature Conservation, Ltd.)
Rodney Stoke	National Nature Reserve since 1957 (86 acres)
Bridgwater Bay	National Nature Reserve since 1954, and National Wildfowl Refuge since 1955 (about 6,080 acres); Brean Down is National Trust property
Quantock Hills	Area of Outstanding Natural Beauty, confirmed in 1957 (38 square miles)
Shapwick Heath	National Nature Reserve since 1961 (546 acres)
Sharpham Moor	Small Nature Reserve of the Society for the Promotion of Nature Reserves
Nettlecombe Court	Field Centre of Field Studies Council, since 1967
Seven Wells Bridge	Quantock Forest Trial of Forestry Commission

STAFFORDSHIRE (West Midlands Trust for Nature Conservation, Ltd.)
Coombes Valley, Leek	Nature Reserve of the Royal Society for the Protection of Birds and the West Midlands Trust for Nature Conservation, Ltd.
Hawksmoor Wood	Nature Reserve of the National Trust
Chartley Moss	National Nature Reserve since 1963 (about 100 acres)
Cannock Chase	Area of Outstanding Natural Beauty, confirmed in 1958 (26 square miles); includes the Cannock Chase State Forest of the Forestry Commission
Wren's Nest	(With Worcestershire). National Nature Reserve since 1956 (74 acres)

SUFFOLK (Suffolk Naturalists' Trust, Ltd.)
Thetford Heath	National Nature Reserve since 1958 (243 acres). Restricted entry
Horn and Weather Heaths	Nature Reserve of the Royal Society for the Protection of Birds (320 acres)

Suffolk – continued

Cavenham Heath	National Nature Reserve since 1952 (337 acres)
Westleton Heath	National Nature Reserve since 1956 (117 acres)
Minsmere	Nature Reserve of the Royal Society for the Protection of Birds, and also a Regional Wildfowl Refuge (about 1,530 acres)
Mickfield Meadow	Nature Reserve of the Society for the Promotion of Nature Reserves (4½ acres)
Thorpness	Nature Reserve of the Royal Society for the Protection of Birds (196 acres)
Orfordness area	Includes a National Nature Reserve (since 1954) and a National Wildfowl Refuge; Royal Society for the Protection of Birds, and Nature Conservancy
Flatford Mill	Field Centre of the Field Studies Council (in the Constable country)

SURREY (Surrey Naturalists' Trust, Ltd.)

Juniper Hill	Field Centre of the Field Studies Council
Surrey Hills	Area of Outstanding Natural Beauty, confirmed in 1958 (160 square miles)
Barfold Copse	Nature Reserve of the Royal Society for the Protection of Birds (13 acres)

SUSSEX (Sussex Naturalists' Trust, Ltd.)

Sussex Downs	Area of Outstanding Natural Beauty, confirmed in 1966 (379 square miles)
Wood's Mill	Nature Reserve since 1966 (15 acres)
Kingley Vale	National Nature Reserve since 1952 (230 acres)
Lullington Heath	National Nature Reserve since 1956 (155 acres)
Hampden Park	Nature Reserve of Eastbourne College
Pagham Harbour	Local Nature Reserve of the West Sussex County Council, Sussex Naturalists' Trust, Ltd., and Nature Conservancy since 1964
Beachy Head	Nature Reserve of Eastbourne Corporation. Also Bird Observatory

WARWICKSHIRE (West Midlands Trust for Nature Conservation, Ltd.)

Tile Hill Wood	Nature Reserve of Coventry Corporation

WESTMORLAND (Lake District Naturalists' Trust, Ltd.)

Moor House	National Nature Reserve since 1952; includes Moor House Field Station of the Nature Conservancy

WILTSHIRE (Wiltshire Trust for Nature Conservation, Ltd.)

Fyfield Down	National Nature Reserve since 1956 (about 610 acres)
Blackmore Copse	Nature Reserve of the Wiltshire Trust for Nature Conservation, Ltd.
White Sheet Hill	Nature Reserve of the Wiltshire Trust for Nature Conservation, Ltd.

WORCESTERSHIRE (West Midlands Trust for Nature Conservation, Ltd.)

Malvern Hills	Area of Outstanding Natural Beauty, confirmed in 1959 (40 square miles)
Cotswolds	Area of Outstanding Natural Beauty, confirmed in 1966 (582 square miles)
Randan Wood	Nature Reserve of the West Midland Trust for Nature Conservation, Ltd.

YORKSHIRE (Yorkshire Naturalists' Trust, Ltd.)

Upper Teesdale	National Nature Reserve since 1963 (about 6,500 acres)
North Yorkshire Forests	State Forests of Hambleton (18,613 acres) and Allerston (36,717 acres)
North Yorkshire	North York Moors National Park, confirmed 1952 (553 square miles)
Yorkshire Dales	Yorkshire Dales National Park, confirmed 1954 (680 square miles)
Farndale	Local Nature Reserve of the North Riding County Council and Nature Conservancy since 1955 (2,500 acres)
Fen Bog	Nature Reserve of the Yorkshire Naturalists' Trust, Ltd.
Hayburn Wyke	Nature Reserve of the Yorkshire Naturalists' Trust, Ltd., since 1966 (34 acres)
Snever Dale area	Nature Trails of the Forestry Commission
Hutton Buscel	Field Centre of the British Young Naturalists' Association
Garbutt Wood	Nature Reserve of the Yorkshire Naturalists' Trust, Ltd., since 1966 (65 acres)
Ling Gill	National Nature Reserve since 1958 (12 acres). Within the Yorkshire Dales National Park
Colt Park Wood	National Nature Reserve (21 acres) within the Yorkshire Dales National Park
Forest of Bowland	Area of Outstanding Natural Beauty
Malham Tarn	Field Centre of Field Studies Council, within the Yorkshire Dales National Park
Strensall Common	Nature Reserve of the Yorkshire Naturalists' Trust, Ltd., since 1965 (about 50 acres)
Skelton	Nature Reserve of the Yorkshire Naturalists' Trust, Ltd. (about 18 acres)
Kipling Cotes Chalk Pit	Nature Reserve of the Yorkshire Naturalists' Trust, Ltd., since 1966
Fairburn Ings	Local Nature Reserve and Regional Wildfowl Refuge since 1957 (about 620 acres)
Spurn Point	Nature Reserve of the Yorkshire Naturalists' Trust, Ltd. (about 350 acres)
Brockdale	Nature Reserve of the Yorkshire Naturalists' Trust, Ltd., and Forestry Commission
Sandall Beat	Local Nature Reserve of the Doncaster Corporation and Nature Conservancy since 1965

Yorkshire – continued

Eccleshall Wood	Bird Sanctuary of the Sheffield Corporation
Humber Wildfowl Refuge	National Wildfowl Refuge since 1955 (3,130 acres)

WALES

ANGLESEY (North Wales Naturalists' Trust Ltd.)

Anglesey Coast	Area of Outstanding Natural Beauty, confirmed in 1966
Cemlyn	Hewitt Wild Bird Sanctuary
Newborough	National Nature Reserve since 1955 (about 1,560 acres)

BRECONSHIRE (Brecknock County Naturalists' Trust, Ltd.)

Nant Irfon	National Nature Reserve since 1962 (216 acres)
Craig Cerrig Gleisiad	National Nature Reserve since 1957 (about 700 acres)
Craig y Cilau	National Nature Reserve since 1959 (about 160 acres)
Cwn Clydach	National Nature Reserve since 1962 (50 acres)
Penmoelallt	Forest Nature Reserve since 1961 (17 acres)
Brecon Beacons	(With Carmarthen and Monmouth). National Park, confirmed in 1957 (520 square miles)

CAERNARVONSHIRE (North Wales Naturalists' Trust, Ltd.)

Coed Gorswen	National Nature Reserve since 1959 (33 acres)
Coed Dolgarrog	National Nature Reserve since 1959 (170 acres)
Cwm Glas, Crafnant	National Nature Reserve since 1960 (38 acres)
Cwm Idwal	National Nature Reserve of the National Trust and Nature Conservancy (984 acres)
Beddgelert Forest	Forestry Commission State Forest in the Snowdonia National Forest Park (3,000 acres)
Snowdon	National Nature Reserve since 1964 (2,300 acres)
Coed Tremadoc	National Nature Reserve since 1957 (about 50 acres)
Lleyn	Area of Outstanding Natural Beauty, confirmed in 1957 (60 square miles). Includes the Bardsey Bird and Field Observatory (370 acres)
Snowdonia	(With Denbighshire and Merionethshire). National Park, confirmed in 1951 (837 square miles)
Gwydr Forest	(With Denbighshire). Forestry Commission State Forest in the Snowdonia National Forest Park (19,473 acres)

CARDIGANSHIRE (West Wales Naturalists' Trust, Ltd.)

Cambrian Forests	Includes Tarenig, Ystwyth and Aeron State Forests
Borth Bog	Nature Reserve of West Wales Naturalists' Trust, Ltd.
Coed Rheidol	National Nature Reserve in the Rheidol State Forest (107 acres) since 1956
Llanddeiniol	Nature Reserves at Pen-y-graig and Tyn-y-bwlch of West Wales Naturalists' Trust, Ltd., since 1966
Cors Tregaron	National Nature Reserve and Regional Wildfowl Refuge since 1955 (1,900 acres)
Cardigan Island	Nature Reserve of West Wales Naturalists' Trust, Ltd.

CARMARTHENSHIRE (West Wales Naturalists' Trust, Ltd.)

Allt Rhyd y Groes	National Nature Reserve since 1959 (153 acres)

DENBIGHSHIRE (North Wales Naturalists' Trust, Ltd.)

Rhyd-y-Creua	Field Centre of the Field Studies Council since 1967
Cilygroeslwyd Wood	Nature Reserve of North Wales Naturalists' Trust, Ltd.

GLAMORGAN (Glamorgan County Naturalists' Trust, Ltd.)

Glamorgan Forests	Extensive State Forests of the Forestry Commission
Gower	Area of Outstanding Natural Beauty, confirmed in 1956 (73 square miles), including Nature Reserves of the Glamorgan County Naturalists' Trust, Ltd., at Llandmadoc Woods, Broad Pool and Port Eynon area
Whiteford	National Nature Reserve of the Nature Conservancy and Glamorgan County Naturalists' Trust, Ltd.
Oxwich	National Nature Reserve since 1963 (542 acres)
Pysgodlyn Mawr	Nature Reserve of Glamorgan County Naturalists' Trust, Ltd.

MERIONETHSHIRE

Coed Cymerau	National Nature Reserve since 1962 (65 acres)
Coeddyd Maentwrog	National Nature Reserve since 1966 (194 acres)
Coed Camlyn	National Nature Reserve since 1959 (about 60 acres)
Coed y Rhygen	National Nature Reserve since 1961 (about 50 acres)
Morfa Harlech	National Nature Reserve since 1958 (1,214 acres)
Deudraeth and Coed y Brenin	State Forests of the Forestry Commission since 1922 (16,840 acres)
Rhinog	National Nature Reserve since 1959 (990 acres)

Merionethshire – continued
Morfa Dyffryn	National Nature Reserve since 1962 (about 500 acres)
Coed Ganllwyd	National Nature Reserve of the National Trust and Nature Conservancy (59 acres)
Cader Idris	National Nature Reserve since 1955 (about 970 acres)

MONMOUTHSHIRE (*Monmouthshire Naturalists' Trust, Ltd.*)
Tintern Forest	State Forest of the Forestry Commission since 1920, and part of the Forest of Dean National Forest Park since 1938 (4,902 acres)
Blackcliff and Wyndcliff	Forest Nature Reserve in the Forest of Dean National Forest Park since 1959 (200 acres)
Whitewall-Magor	Nature Reserve of Monmouthshire Naturalists' Trust, Ltd., since 1966 (60 acres)
Forest of Dean	(With Herefordshire and Gloucestershire). National Forest Park of the Forestry Commission, founded in 1938 (about 35,000 acres)

PEMBROKESHIRE (*West Wales Naturalists' Trust, Ltd.*)
Pembrokeshire Coast	(Including islands). National Park, confirmed in 1952 (144,000 acres)
Ramsey	Nature Reserve of the Royal Society for the Protection of Birds (688 acres)
Grassholm	Nature Reserve of the Royal Society for the Protection of Birds (22 acres)
Skomer	National Nature Reserve since 1959 (about 760 acres)
Skokholm	Bird Observatory of the Field Studies Council (272 acres)
Dale Fort	Field Centre of the Field Studies Council
St. Margaret's Island	Nature Reserve of West Wales Naturalists' Trust, Ltd.

ISLE OF MAN

Calf of Man	Nature Reserve of the Manx National Trust and Manx Museum (616 acres); also Bird Observatory

SCOTLAND
(*Scottish Wildlife Trust, Ltd., 8 Dublin Street, Edinburgh 1*)

ABERDEEN
Sands of Forvie	National Nature Reserve and National Wildfowl Refuge since 1959 (1,774 acres)
Caenlochan	(With Perthshire and Angus), National Nature Reserve since 1961 (8,991 acres)

ARGYLLSHIRE
Arriundle Oakwood	Forest Nature Reserve of Department of Agriculture for Scotland and Nature Conservancy since 1961 (288 acres)
Doire Donn	Nature Reserve of Scottish Wildlife Trust Ltd., since 1966 (70 acres)
Argyll	Argyll National Forest Park; National Forest Park of the Forestry Commission since 1922 (57,813 acres), including the State Forests of Ardgartan, Ardgoil, Glenbranter, Loch Eck, Glenfinart and Benmore
Ben Lui	(With Perthshire). National Nature Reserve since 1961 (925 acres)

AYRSHIRE
Horse Island	Nature Reserve of the Royal Society for the Protection of Birds (5 acres)
Lady Isle	Nature Reserve of the Scottish Society for the Protection of Wild Birds
Enterkine Wood	Nature Reserve of Scottish Wildlife Trust, Ltd., since 1966 (12 acres)
Glen Trool	(With Kirkcudbrightshire). National Forest Park of the Forestry Commission, including the State Forests of Carrick and Changue (116,000 acres)

BERWICKSHIRE
Duns Castle	Nature Reserve of the Scottish Wildlife Trust, Ltd., since 1966 (190 acres)
Gordon Moss	Nature Reserve of the Scottish Wildlife Trust, Ltd., since 1966 (102 acres)

BUTESHIRE
Millport	Isle of Cumbrae. Marine Station of the Scottish Marine Biological Association
Glen Diomhan	Arran. National Nature Reserve since 1956 (24 acres)

CLACKMANNANSHIRE
Dollar Glen	Effectively a Nature Reserve of the National Trust for Scotland (60 acres)

DUMFRIES-SHIRE
Forest of Ae	State Forest of the Forestry Commission since 1919 (10,683 acres)
Tynron Wood	National Nature Reserve since 1958 (12 acres)
Castle and High-tae Lochs	Local Nature Reserve and Regional Wildfowl Refuge of Dumfries County Council
Caerlaverock	National Nature Reserve and National Wildfowl Refuge since 1957 (13,514 acres)
Border Forests	(With Roxburghshire, Cumberland and Northumberland). Border Forests and Border National Forest Park. The largest planted forest system in the country, of 186,932 acres; Forestry Commission since 1920. Includes the State Forests of Newcastleton in Roxburghshire and Dumfriesshire, and Wauchope in Roxburghshire; and of Kielder, Kidland, Harwood, Wark, Redesdale, Chillingham and Rothbury in Cumberland.

DUNBARTONSHIRE
Ardmore — Nature Reserve of the Scottish Wildlife Trust, Ltd., since 1966 (480 acres)

EAST LOTHIAN
Bass Rock — Private Nature Reserve. The oldest classic Gannetry (dating from *c.* 705 A.D.)
Lamb Island — Nature Reserve of the Royal Society for the Protection of Birds
Aberlady Bay — Local Nature Reserve and National Wildfowl Refuge since 1952 (1,439 acres)

FIFESHIRE
Tentsmuir Point — National Nature Reserve (since 1954) and National Wildfowl Refuge (since 1962), 1,249 acres
Morton Lochs — National Nature Reserve and Regional Wildfowl Refuge since 1952 (59 acres)
Isle of May — National Nature Reserve since 1956 (140 acres). Also Bird Observatory of the Midlothian Ornithological Club

INVERNESS-SHIRE (Inner Isles)
Rhum — National Nature Reserve since 1957 (26,400 acres)

INVERNESS-SHIRE (Outer Isles)
St. Kilda — National Nature Reserve of the National Trust of Scotland and Nature Conservancy since 1957 (2,107 acres). Location of largest British puffinry
Balranald Marshes — North Uist. Nature Reserve of the Royal Society for the Protection of Birds since 1966 (1,500 acres)
Monach Islands — National Nature Reserve since 1966
Loch Druidibeg — South Uist. National Nature Reserve and National Wildfowl Refuge since 1958 (4,145 acres)

INVERNESS-SHIRE (Mainland)
Loch Garten — Nature Reserve of the Royal Society for the Protection of Birds (677 acres)
Glen More — National Forest Park since 1948 (12,500 acres managed by the Forestry Commission)
Craigellachie — National Nature Reserve since 1960 (642 acres)
Cairngorms — (With Aberdeenshire). National Nature Reserve since 1954 (the largest in the country with 58,822 acres)

KINCARDINESHIRE
Crathes Castle — Nature Reserve of the National Trust for Scotland
Blackhall, Banchory — Field Station of the Nature Conservancy (and Aberdeen University)
Drumtochty — State Forest of the Forestry Commission since 1926 (9,998 acres)
St. Cyrus — (With Angus). National Nature Reserve since 1962 (227 acres)

KINROSS-SHIRE
Loch Leven — National Nature Reserve since 1964 (3,946 acres)

KIRCUDBRIGHTSHIRE
Silver Flowe — National Nature Reserve since 1956 (472 acres)
Kirkconnell Flow — National Nature Reserve since 1959 (383 acres)

LANARKSHIRE
Possil Marsh — Nature Reserve of the Scottish Society for the Protection of Wild Birds
Hamilton — Low Parks Sanctuary. Regional Wildfowl Refuge of the Hamilton Borough (336 acres)

MIDLOTHIAN
Inchmickery — Nature Reserve of the Royal Society for the Protection of Birds
Duddingston Loch — Nature Reserve (40 acres), a Royal Park Sanctuary and a Regional Wildfowl Refuge

MORAYSHIRE AND NAIRNSHIRE
Culbin Forest — State Forest of the Forestry Commission since 1921 (7,546 acres)

ORKNEY ISLANDS
Calf of Eday — Patrolled by the Royal Society for the Protection of Birds
Gairsay — Patrolled by the Royal Society for the Protection of Birds

PEEBLESSHIRE
Glentress — State Forest of the Forestry Commission since 1920 (2,349 acres)

PERTHSHIRE
Kindrogan, Strathardle — Field Centre of the Scottish Field Studies Association
Rannoch Moor — National Nature Reserve since 1958 (3,794 acres)
Garth, Glen Lyon — Field Centre of the Scottish Field Studies Association
Ben Lawers — Nature Reserve of the National Trust for Scotland and Nature Conservancy (8,000 acres)
Meall nan Tarmachan — National Nature Reserve since 1964 (1,142 acres)
Strathyre — State Forest of the Forestry Commission since 1930 (10,461 acres)
Kinnoul Hill — Deer Park of the Perth Burgh Council and British Deer Society since 1966 (30 acres)
Queen Elizabeth Forest Park — National Forest Park with State Forests of Loch Ard and Rowardennan (with Stirlingshire). Forestry Commission since 1921 (41,454 acres)

RENFREWSHIRE
    Castle Semple Loch,   Nature Reserve of Renfrew County Council (207 acres)
    Lochwinnoch
ROSS AND CROMARTY (Outer Isles)
    North Rona and   National Nature Reserve since 1956 (320 acres)
    Sula Sgeir
ROSS AND CROMARTY (Mainland)
    Inverpolly   National Nature Reserve since 1961 (26,827 acres)
    Beinn Eighe   National Nature Reserve since 1951 (10,507 acres) – the first in the country
    Rassal Ashwood   National Nature Reserve since 1956 (202 acres)
SELKIRKSHIRE
    Hare and Dunbog   Nature Reserve of the Scottish Wildlife Trust, Ltd., since 1966 (10 acres)
    Mosses
SHETLAND ISLANDS
    Hermaness, Unst   National Nature Reserve since 1955 (2,383 acres wardened by the Royal Society for the
        Protection of Birds)
    Haaf Gruney   National Nature Reserve since 1959 (44 acres)
    Ronas Hill   National Nature Reserve since 1965 (more than 7,000 acres)
    Fair Isle   In effect a Nature Reserve for the National Trust of Scotland; also Bird Observatory
STIRLINGSHIRE
    Loch Lomond   (With Dunbartonshire). National Nature Reserve since 1958, and Regional Wildfowl
        Refuge since 1960 (624 acres)
SUTHERLAND
    Invernaver   National Nature Reserve since 1960 (120 acres)
    Handa   Nature Reserve of the Royal Society for the Protection of Birds (766 acres)
    Inchnadamph   National Nature Reserve since 1956 (more than 3,200 acres)
WIGTOWNSHIRE
    Mochrum and Castle   Unofficial wildfowl refuges with Scotland's largest cormorant colony
    Lochs

BRITISH MAMMALS

INDIGENOUS LAND MAMMALS

Scottish Wild Cat (*Felis silvestris grampia*)
Pole Cat (*Mustela putorius anglicus*)
Pine Marten (*Martes martes*)
Red Deer (*Cervus elaphus scoticus*)
Common Roe Deer (*Capreolus capreolus*)
Common Badger (*Meles meles*)
Common Otter (*Lutra lutra*)
Fox (*Vulpes vulpes crucigera*)
Stoat (*Mustela erminea stabilis*)
Weasel (*Mustela nivalis*)

Brown Hare (*Lepus europaeus occidentalis*)
Blue or Mountain Hare (*Lepus timidus scoticus*)
Red Squirrel (*Sciurus vulgaris leucourus*)
Black (or Ship) Rat (*Rattus rattus*)
Yellow-necked Field Mouse (*Apodemus flavicollis wintoni*)
Field or Wood Mouse (*Apodemus sylvaticus sylvaticus*)
Harvest Mouse (*Micromys minutus soricinus*)

Dormouse (*Muscardinus avellanarius*)
Water Vole (Water Rat) (*Arvicola terrestris amphibius*)
Bank Vole (*Clethrionomys glareolus britannicus*)
Common Hedgehog (*Erinaceus europaeus*)
Common Mole (*Talpa europaea*)
Common Shrew (*Sorex anareus castaneus*)
Water Shrew (*Neomys fodiens bicolor*)

MARINE MAMMALS

Common Seal (*Phoca vitulina*)
Atlantic or Grey Seal (*Halichoerus grypus*)
Bottle-nosed Dolphin (*Tursiops truncatus*)
Common Dolphin (*Delphinus delphis*)
Euphrosyne Dolphin (*Stenella styx*)
Risso's Dolphin (*Grampus griseus*)
White-beaked Dolphin (*Lagenorhynchus albirostris*)

White-side Dolphin (*Lagenorhynchus acutus*)
Porpoise (*Phocœna phocœna*)
Narwhal (*Monodon monoceros*)
Bottle-nosed Whale (*Hyperodon ampullatus*)
Blue Whale (*Balœnoptera musculus*)
Common Rorqual or Fin Whale (*Balœnoptera physalus*)
Curvier's Beaked Whale (*Ziphius cavirostris*)

Humpback Whale (*Megaptera novœanglia*)
Lesser Rorqual or Pike Whale (*Balœnoptera acutorostrata*)
North Atlantic Right Whale (*Eubalœna glacialis*)
Killer Whale or Grampus (*Orcinus orca*)
False Killer Whale (*Pseudorca crassidens*)
Pilot Whale or Blackfish (*Globicephala melœna*)

MARINE MAMMALS (Continued)
Sei Whale (*Balænoptera borealis*)
Sperm Whale (*Physeter catodon*)

Sowerby's Whale (*Mesoplodon bidens*)

True's Whale (*Mesoplodon mirus*)
White Whale (*Delphinapterus leucas*)

FLYING MAMMALS

Bechstein's Bat (*Myotis bechsteini*)
Daubenton's (Water) Bat (*Myotis daubentoni*)
Great Horseshoe Bat (*Rhinolophus ferrum-equinum insulanis*)
Lesser Horseshoe Bat (*Rhinolophus hipposideros minutus*)

Leisler's Bat (*Nyctalus leisleri*)
Long-eared Bat (*Plecotus auritus*)
Mouse-eared Bat (*Myotis lucifugus*)
Natterer's Bat (*Myotis nattereri*)
Serotine Bat (*Eptesicus serotinus*)

Whiskered Bat (*Myotis mystacinus*)
Barbastelle (*Barbestella barbestullus*)
Noctule (*Nyctalus noctula*)
Pipistrelle (*Pipistrellus pipistrellus*)

AMPHIBIANS

Common Frog (*Rana temporaria*)
Common Toad (*Bufo bufo*)

Natterjack Toad (*Bufo calamita*)
Palmated Newt (*Triturus helvetica*)

Smooth Newt (*Triturus vulgaris*)
Warty Newt (*Triturus cristatus*)

REPTILES

Adder (*Vipera berus*)
Viviparous or Common Lizard (*Lacerta vivipara*)

Grass or Ringed Snake (*Natrix natrix*)
Sand Lizard (*Lacerta agilis*)

Slow-worm (*Abguis fragilis*)
Smooth Snake (*Coronella austriaca*)

BRITISH BIRDS

The following is an adaptation and limited revision of the British Bird List of 1878, the most recent official compilation. It includes all species which populate or visit Great Britain and Ireland; it should be noted that many of these are very rare and have not been seen for many years.

Accentor, Alpine (*Prunella collaris*)
Albatross, Black-browed (*Diomedea melanophris*)
Auk, Great (*Alca impennis*)
Auk, Little (*Plautus alle*)
Avocet (*Recurvirostra avosetta*)
Bee-eater (*Merops apiaster*)
Bittern (*Botaurus stellaris*)
Bittern, American (*Botaurus lentiginosus*)
Bittern, Little (*Ixobrychus minutus*)
Blackbird (*Turdus merula*)
Blackcap (*Sylvia atricapilla*)
Bluetail, Red-flanked (*Tarsiger cyanurus*)
Bluethroat (*Cyanosylvia svecica*)
Brambling (*Fringilla montifrigilla*)
Bullfinch (*Pyrrhula pyrrhula*)
Bunting, Black-headed (*Emberiza melanocephala*)
Bunting, Cirl (*Emberiza cirlus*)
Bunting, Corn- (*Emberiza calandra*)
Bunting, Lapland (*Calcarius lapponicus*)
Bunting, Little (*Emberiza pusilla*)
Bunting, Meadow- (*Emberiza cioides*)

Bunting, Ortolan (*Emberiza hortulana*)
Bunting, Pine- (*Emberiza leucocephalos*)
Bunting, Redheaded (*Emberiza bruniceps*)
Bunting, Reed- (*Emberiza schoeniclus*)
Bunting, Rock- (*Emberiza cia*)
Bunting, Rustic (*Emberiza rustica*)
Bunting, Snow- (*Plectrophenax nivalis*)
Bunting, Yellow-breasted (*Emberiza aureola*)
Bustard, Great (*Otis tarda*)
Bustard, Houbara (*Chlamydotis undulata*)
Bustard, Little (*Otis tetrax*)
Buzzard (*Buteo buteo*)
Buzzard, Honey- (*Pernis apivorus*)
Buzzard, Roughlegged (*Buteo lagopus*)
Capercaillie (*Tetrao urogallus*)
Chaffinch (*Fringilla coelebs*)
Chiffchaff (*Phylloscopus collybita*)
Chough (*Coracia pyrrhocorax*)
Coot (*Fulica atra*)
Cormorant (*Phalacrocorax carbo*)
Cornrake (*Crex crex*)
Courser, Cream-coloured (*Cursorius cursor*)

Crake, Baillon's (*Porzana pusilla*)
Crake, Little (*Porzana parva*)
Crake, Spotted (*Porzana porzana*)
Crane (*Megalornis grus*)
Creeper, Tree- (*Certhia familiaris*)
Creeper, Wall- (*Tichodroma murarua*)
Crossbill (*Loxia curvirostra*)
Crossbill, Parrot- (*Loxia pytyopsittacus*)
Crossbill, Two-barred (*Loxia leucoptera*)
Crow, Carrion (*Corvus corone*)
Crow, Hooded (*Corvus cornix*)
Cuckoo (*Cuculus canorus*)
Cuckoo, Black-billed (*Coccyzus erythrophthalmus*)
Cuckoo, Great Spotted (*Clamator glandarius*)
Cuckoo, Yellow-billed (*Coccyzus americanus*)
Curlew (*Numenius arquata*)
Curlew, Eskimo (*Numenius borealis*)
Curlew, Stone (*Burhinus oedicnemus*)
Dipper (*Cinclus cinclus*)
Diver, Black-Throated (*Columbus articus*)
Diver, Great Northern (*Columbus immer*)

Diver, Red-Throated (*Colymbus stellatus*)
Diver, White-Billed (*Colymbus adamsii*)
Dotterel (*Charadrius morinellus*)
Dove, Collared (*Streptopelia decaoeto*)
Dove, Eastern Turtle- (*Streptopelia orientalis*)
Dove, Rock (*Columba livia*)
Dove, Stock (*Columba oenas*)
Dove, Turtle (*Streptopelia turtur*)
Duck, Buffel-Headed (*Bucephala albeola*)
Duck, Eider- (*Somateria mollissima*)
Duck, Harlequin (*Histrionicus histrionicus*)
Duck, Long-Tailed (*Clangula hyemalis*)
Duck, Ring-Necked (*Aythya collaris*)
Duck, Ruddy Sheld- (*Casarca ferruginea*)
Duck, Sheld (*Tadorna tadorna*)
Duck, Tufted (*Aythya fuligula*)
Dunlin (*Calidris alpina*)
Eagle, Golden (*Aquila chrysaëtos*)
Eagle, Spotted (*Aquila clanga*)
Eagle, White-Tailed (*Haliaeetus albicilla*)
Egret, Cattle (*Ardeola ibis*)
Egret, Large (*Egretta alba*)
Egret, Little (*Egretta garzetta*)
Eider, King (*Somateria spectabilis*)
Falcon, Gyr (*Falco rusticolus*)
Falcon, Peregrine (*Falco peregrinus*)
Falcon, Red-Footed (*Falco vespertinus*)
Fieldfare (*Turdus pilaris*)
Finch, Citril (*Carduelis citrinella*)
Firecrest (*Regulus ignicapillus*)
Flamingo (*Phoenicopterus ruber*)
Flycatcher, Brown (*Muscicapa latirostris*)
Flycatcher, Pied (*Muscicapa hypoleuca*)
Flycatcher, Red-Breasted (*Muscicapa parva*)
Flycatcher, Spotted (*Muscicapa striata*)
Flycatcher, White-Collared (*Muscicapa albicollis*)
Gadwall (*Anas strepera*)
Gannet (*Sula bassana*)
Garganey (*Anas querquedula*)
Godwit, Bar-Tailed (*Limosa lapponica*)
Godwit, Black-Tailed (*Limosa limosa*)
Goldcrest (*Regulus regulus*)
Golden-Eye (*Bucephala clangula*)
Goldfinch (*Carduelis carduelis*)

Goosander (*Mergus merganser*)
Goose, Barnacle (*Branta leucopsis*)
Goose, Bean- (*Anser arvensis arvensis*)
Goose, Brent (*Brant bernicla*)
Goose, Canada (*Branta canadensis*)
Goose, Grey Lag- (*Anser anser*)
Goose, Lesser White-Fronted (*Anser erythropus*)
Goose, Pink-Footed (*Anser arvensis brachyrhynchus*)
Goose, Red-Breasted (*Branta ruficollis*)
Goose, Snow (*Anser hyperboreus*)
Goose, White-Fronted (*Anser albifrons*)
Goshawk (*Accipiter gentilis*)
Grebe, Black-Necked (*Podiceps caspicus*)
Grebe, Great Crested (*Podiceps cristatus*)
Grebe, Little (*Podiceps ruficollis*)
Grebe, Red-Necked (*Podiceps grisigena*)
Grebe, Slavonian (*Podiceps auritus*)
Greenfinch (*Chloris chloris*)
Greenshank (*Tringa nebularia*)
Grosbeak, Pine (*Pinicola enucleator*)
Grosbeak, Scarlet (*Carpodacus erythrinus*)
Grouse, Black (*Lyrurus tetrix*)
Grouse, Pallass's Sand (*Syrrhaptes paradoxus*)
Grouse, Red (*Lagopus scoticus*)
Guillemot (*Uria aalge*)
Guillemot, Black (*Uria grylle*)
Guillemot, Brünnich's (*Uria lomvia*)
Gull, Black-Headed (*Larus ridibundus*)
Gull, Bonaparte's (*Larus philadelphia*)
Gull, Common (*Larus canus*)
Gull, Glaucous (*Larus hyperboreus*)
Gull, Great Black-Headed (*Larus ichthyaëtus*)
Gull, Greater Black-Backed (*Larus marinus*)
Gull, Herring- (*Larus argentatus*)
Gull, Iceland (*Larus glaucoides*)
Gull, Ivory (*Pagophila eburnea*)
Gull, Lesser Black-Backed (*Larus fuscus*)
Gull, Little (*Larus minutus*)
Gull, Mediterranean Black-Headed (*Larus melanocephalus*)
Gull, Ross's (*Rhodostethia rosea*)
Gull, Sabine's (*Xema sabini*)
Hammer, Yellow (*Emberiza citrinella*)
Harrier, Hen- (*Circus cyaneus*)
Harrier, Marsh (*Circus aeruginosus*)
Harrier, Montagu's (*Circus pygargus*)

Harrier, Pallid (*Circus macrourus*)
Hawfinch (*Coccothraustes coccothraustes*)
Hawk, Night- (*Chordeiles minor*)
Hawk, Sparrow- (*Accipiter nisus*)
Heron (*Ardea cinerea*)
Heron, Night (*Nycticorex nycticorax*)
Heron, Purple (*Ardea purpurea*)
Heron, Squacco (*Ardeola ralloides*)
Hobby (*Falco subbuteo*)
Hoopoe (*Upupa epops*)
Ibis, Glossy (*Plegadis falcinellus*)
Jackdaw (*Corvus monedula*)
Jay (*Garrulus glandarius*)
Kestrel (*Falco tinnunculus*)
Kingfisher (*Alcedo atthis*)
Kite (*Milvus milvus*)
Kite, Black (*Milvus migrans*)
Kittiwake (*Rissa tridactyla*)
Knot (*Calidris canutus*)
Lapwing (*Vanellus vanellus*)
Lark, Calandra (*Melanocorypha calandra*)
Lark, Crested (*Galerida cristata*)
Lark, Shore- (*Eremophila alpestris*)
Lark, Short-Toed (*Calandrella brachydactila*)
Lark, White-Winged (*Melanocorypha leucoptera*)
Lark, Wood- (*Lullula arborea*)
Linnet (*Carduelis cannabina*)
Magpie (*Pica pica*)
Mallard (*Anas platyrhynchos*)
Martin, House- (*Delichon urbica*)
Martin, Sand- (*Riparia riparia*)
Merganser, Hooded (*Mergus cucullatus*)
Merganser, Red-Breasted (*Mergus serrator*)
Merlin (*Falco columbarius*)
Moorhen (*Gallinula chloropus*)
Nightingale (*Luscinia megarhynchos*)
Nightingale, Thrush (*Luscinia luscinia*)
Nightjar (*Caprimulgus europaeus*)
Nightjar, Egyptian (*Caprimulgus aegyptius*)
Nightjar, Red-Necked (*Caprimulgus ruficollis*)
Nutcracker (*Nucifraga caryocatactes*)
Nuthatch (*Sitta europaea*)
Oriole, Golden (*Oriolus oriolus*)
Osprey (*Pandion haliaetus*)
Ouzel, Ring- (*Turdus torquatus*)
Owl, Barn (*Tyto alba*)
Owl, Eagle- (*Bubo bubo*)
Owl, Hawk- (*Surnia ulula*)
Owl, Little (*Athene noctua*)
Owl, Long-Eared (*Asio otus*)
Owl, Scops (*Otus scops*)
Owl, Short-Eared (*Asio flammeus*)

Owl, Snowy (*Nyctea scandiaca*)
Owl, Tawny (*Strix aluco*)
Owl, Tengmalm's (*Aegolius funereus*)
Oystercatcher (*Haematopus ostralegus*)
Partridge (*Perdix perdix*)
Partridge, Red-Legged (*Alectoris rufa*)
Petrel, Black-Capped (*Bulweria hasitata*)
Petrel, Bulwer's (*Bulweria bulwerii*)
Petrel, Frigate- (*Pelagodroma marina*)
Petrel, Fulmar (*Fulmarus glacialis*)
Petrel, Kermadec (*Bulweria neglecta*)
Petrel, Leach's (*Oceanodroma leucorhoa*)
Petrel, Madeiran (*Oceanodroma castro*)
Petrel, Storm- (*Hydrobates pelagicus*)
Petrel, White-Winged (*Bulweria leucoptera*)
Petrel, Wilson's (*Oceanites oceanicus*)
Phalarope, Grey (*Phalaropus fulicarius*)
Phalarope, Red-Necked (*Phalaropus lobatus*)
Pheasant (*Phasianus cochicus*)
Pigeon, Wood- (*Columba palumbus*)
Pintail (*Anas acuta*)
Pipit, American (*Anthus spinoletta rubescens*)
Pipit, Meadow- (*Anthus pratensis*)
Pipit, Petchora (*Anthus gustavi*)
Pipit, Red-Throated (*Anthus cervinus*)
Pipit, Richard's (*Anthus richardi*)
Pipit, Rock- (*Anthus spinoletta petrosus*)
Pipit, Tawny (*Anthus campestris*)
Pipit, Tree (*Anthus trivialis*)
Pipit, Water (*Anthus spinoletta spinoletta*)
Plover, American Golden (*Charadrius dominicus*)
Plover, Caspian (*Charadrius asiaticus*)
Plover, Golden (*Charadrius apricarius*)
Plover, Grey (*Charadrius squatarola*)
Plover, Kentish (*Charadrius alexandrinus*)
Plover, Little-Ringed (*Charadrius dubius*)
Plover, Ringed (*Charadrius hiaticula*)
Plover, Sociable (*Chettusia gregaria*)

Pochard (*Aythya ferina*)
Pochard, Red-Crested (*Netta rufina*)
Pochard, White-Eyed (*Aythya nyroca*)
Pratincole, Black-Winged (*Glareola normanii*)
Pratincole, Collared (*Glareola pratincola*)
Ptarmigan (*Lagopus mutus*)
Puffin (*Fratercula*)
Quail (*Corturnix corturnix*)
Rail, Sora (*Porzana carolina*)
Rail, Water- (*Rallus aquaticus*)
Raven (*Corvus corax*)
Razorbill (*Alca torda*)
Redbreast or Robin (*Erithacus rubecula melophilus*)
Redpoll (*Carduelis flammea*)
Redpoll, Arctic (*Carduelis hornemanni*)
Redshank (*Tringa totanus*)
Redshank, Spotted (*Tringa erythropus*)
Redstart (*Phoenicurus phoenicurus*)
Redstart, Black (*Phoenicurus ochruros*)
Redwing (*Turdus musicus*)
Roller (*Coracias garrulus*)
Rook (*Corvus frugilegus*)
Ruff (*Philomachus pugnax*)
Sanderling (*Crocethia alba*)
Sandpiper, Baird's (*Calidris bairdii*)
Sandpiper, Bartram's (*Bartramia longicauda*)
Sandpiper, Bonaparte's (*Calidris fuscicollis*)
Sandpiper, Broad-Billed (*Limicola falcinellus*)
Sandpiper, Buff-Breasted (*Tryngites subruficollis*)
Sandpiper, Common (*Tringa hypoleucos*)
Sandpiper, Curlew- (*Calidris testacea*)
Sandpiper, Green (*Tringa ocropus*)
Sandpiper, Marsh (*Tringa stagnatilis*)
Sandpiper, Pectoral (*Calidris melanotus*)
Sandpiper, Purple (*Calidris maritima*)
Sandpiper, Semi-Palmated (*Calidris pusilla*)
Sandpiper, Siberian Pectoral (*Calidris acuminata*)
Sandpiper, Solitary (*Tringa solitaria*)
Sandpiper, Spotted (*Tringa macularia*)
Sandpiper, Terek (*Xenus cinerea*)
Sandpiper, Wood- (*Tringa Glareola*)
Scaup (*Aythya marila*)

Scoter, Common (*Melanitta negra*)
Scoter, Surf- (*Melanitta perspicillata*)
Scoter, Velvet (*Melanitta fusca*)
Serin (*Serinus cararius*)
Shag (*Phalacrocorax aristotelis*)
Shearwater, Audubon's (*Procellaria herminieri*)?
Shearwater, Great (*Procellaria gravis*)
Shearwater, Little (*Procellaria baroli*)
Shearwater, Manx (*Procellaria puffinus*)
Shearwater, Mediterranean (*Procellaria diomedea diomedea*)
Shearwater, North Atlantic (*Procellaria diomedea borealis*)
Shearwater, Sooty (*Procellaria grisea*)
Shoveler (*Spatula cylpeata*)
Shrike, Great Grey (*Lanius excubitor*)
Shrike, Lesser Grey (*Lanius minor*)
Shrike, Red-Backed (*Lanius collurio*)
Shrike, Woodchat- (*Lanius senator*)
Siskin (*Carduelis spinus*)
Skua, Arctic (*Stercorarius parasiticus*)

The Green Woodpecker

185

Skua, Great (*Stercorarius skua*)
Skua, Long-Tailed (*Stercorarius longicaudus*)
Skua, Pomatorhine (*Stercorarius pomarinus*)
Skylark (*Alauda arvensis*)
Smew (*Mergus albellus*)
Snipe, Common (*Capella gallinago*)
Snipe, Great (*Capella media*)
Snipe, Jack (*Lymnocryptes minimus*)
Snipe, Red-Breasted (*Limnodromus griseus*)
Sparrow, Hedge- (*Prunella modularis*)
Sparrow, House- (*Passer domesticus*)
Sparrow, Tree- (*Passer montanus*)
Spoonbill (*Platalea leucorodia*)
Starling (*Sturnus vulgaris*)
Starling, Rose-Coloured (*Sturnus roseus*)
Stilt, Black-Winged (*Himantopus himantopus*)
Stint, American (*Calidris minutilla*)
Stint, Little (*Calidris minuta*)
Stint, Temminck's (*Calidris temminckii*)
Stonechat (*Saxicola torquata*)
Stork, Black (*Ciconia nigra*)
Stork, White (*Ciconia ciconia*)
Swallow (*Hirunco rustica*)
Swallow, Red-Rumped (*Hirundo daurica*)
Swan, Bewick's (*Cygnus bewickii*)
Swan, Mute (*Cygnus olor*)
Swan, Whooper- (*Cygnus cygnus*)
Swift (*Apus apus*)
Swift, Alpine (*Apus melba*)
Swift, Needle-Tailed (*Chaetura caudacuta*)
Teal (*Anas crecca*)
Teal, Blue-Winged (*Anas discors*)
Tern, Arctic (*Sterna macrura*)
Tern, Black (*Chlidonias niger*)
Tern, Bridled (*Sterna anaethetus*)
Tern, Caspian (*Hydropxogne caspia*)
Tern, Common (*Sterna hirundo*)
Tern, Gull-Billed (*Gelochelidon nilotica*)
Tern, Little (*Sterna albifrons*)
Tern, Roseate (*Sterna dougallii*)
Tern, Sandwich (*Sterna sandvicensis*)
Tern, Sooty (*Sterna fuscata*)
Tern, Whiskered (*Chlidonias hybrida*)
Tern, White-Winged Black (*Chlidonias leucopterus*)
Thrush, Black-Throated (*Turdus ruficollis atrogularis*)
Thrush, Dusky (*Turdus eunomus*)
Thrush, Golden Mountain (*Turdus dauma*)

Thrush, Mistle- (*Turdus viscivorus*)
Thrush, Rock- (*Monticola saxatilis*)
Thrush, Song- (*Turdus ericetorum*)
Titmouse (or Tit), Bearded (*Panurus biarmicus*)
Titmouse (or Tit), Blue (*Parus caeruleus*)
Titmouse (or Tit), Coal- (*Parus ater*)
Titmouse (or Tit), Crested (*Parus cristatus*)
Titmouse (or Tit), Great (*Parus major*)
Titmouse (or Tit), Long-Tailed (*Aegithalus caudatus*)
Titmouse (or Tit), Marsh- (*Parus palustris*)
Titmouse (or Tit), Willow- (*Parus atricapillus*)
Turnstone (*Arenaria interpres*)
Twite (*Carduelis flavirostris*)
Vulture, Egyptian (*Neophron perenopterus*)
Vulture, Griffon- (*Gyps fulvus*)
Wagtail, Grey (*Motacilla cinerea*)
Wagtail, Masked (*Motacilla alba personata*)
Wagtail, Pied (*Motacilla alba yarrelli*)
Wagtail, White (*Motacilla alba alba*)
Wagtail, Yellow (*Motacilla flava*)?
Warbler, Aquatic (*Acrocephalus paludicola*)
Warbler, Arctic (*Phylloscopus borealis*)
Warbler, Barred (*Sylvia nisoria*)
Warbler, Blyth's Reed- (*Acrocephalus dumetorum*)
Warbler, Bonelli's (*Phylloscopus bonelli*)
Warbler, Booted (*Hippolais caligata*)
Warbler, Cetti's (*Cettia cetti*)
Warbler, Dartford (*Sylvia undata*)
Warbler, Dusky (*Phylloscopus fuscatus*)
Warbler, Garden- (*Sylvia borin*)
Warbler, Grasshopper- (*Locustella naevia*)
Warbler, Great Reed- (*Acrocephalus arundinaceus*)
Warbler, Greenish (*Phylloscopus trochiloides*)
Warbler, Icterine (*Hippolais icterina*)
Warbler, Marsh- (*Acrocephalus palustris*)
Warbler, Melodius (*Hippolais polyglotta*)
Warbler, Moustached (*Lusciniola melanopogon*)

Warbler, Olivaceous (*Hippolais pallida*)
Warbler, Orphean (*Sylvia hortensis*)
Warbler, Paddy-Field (*Acrocephalus agricola*)
Warbler, Pallas's (*Phylloscopus proregulus*)
Warbler, Pallas's Grasshopper (*Locustella certhiola*)
Warbler, Radde's Bush (*Phylloscopus schwarzi*)
Warbler, Reed- (*Acrocephalus scirpaceus*)
Warbler, Rufous (*Agrobates galactotes*)
Warbler, Sardinian (*Sylvia melanocephala*)
Warbler, Savi's (*Locustella luscinoides*)
Warbler, Sedge- (*Acrocephalus schoenobaenus*)
Warbler, Subalpine (*Sylvia cantillans*)
Warbler, Temminck's Grasshopper (*Locustella lanceolata*)
Warbler, Willow- (*Phylloscopus trochilus*)
Warbler, Wood- (*Phylloscopus sibilatrix*)
Warbler, Yellow-Browed (*Phylloscopus inornatus*)
Waxwing (*Bombycilla garrulus*)
Wheatear (*Oenanthe oenanthe*)
Wheatear, Black-Eared (*Oenanthe hispanica*)
Wheatear, Desert- (*Oenanthe deserti*)
Wheatear, Isabelline (*Oenanthe isabellina*)
Wheatear, Pied (*Oenanthe leucomela*)
Whimbrel (*Numenius phaeopus*)
Whinchat (*Saxicola rubetra*)
Whitethroat (*Sylvia communis*)
Whitethroat, Lesser (*Sylvia curruca*)
Wigeon (*Anas penelope*)
Wigeon, American (*Anas americana*)
Woodcock (*Scolopax rusticola*)
Woodpecker, Great Spotted (*Dendrocopos major*)
Woodpecker, Green (*Picus viridis*)
Woodpecker, Lesser Spotted (*Dendrocopos minor*)
Wren (*Troglodytes troglodytes*)
Wryneck (*Jynx torquilla*)
Yellow-Legs, Greater (*Tringa melanoleuca*)
Yellow-Legs, Lesser (*Tringa flavipes*)

CHAPTER 6
❧ The Arts ❧

The Shakespeare Memorial Theatre, Stratford-on-Avon

The arts in Britain are supported jointly by private sources, such as trusts and commercial organisations, by voluntary societies, and by government and local authority funds. Government support for all the arts has greatly increased in recent years; estimated total government expenditure in this field in the year 1970–71 was approximately £24,700,000. The arts fall into the scope of the Secretary of State for Education and Science, delegating through the Paymaster General. Government policy towards the arts has been stated to be "to support the arts so that a high level of artistic achievement can be sustained, and the best in the arts made more widely available."

THE ARTS COUNCIL

General support for the visual and performing arts, and so forth, is channelled through the Arts Council of Great Britain and the Arts Council of Northern Ireland. The former body was established by Royal Charter in 1946; members are appointed by the Secretary of State for Education and Science, in consultation with the Secretaries of State for Scotland and Wales. The function of the Council is to co-ordinate the various government, local government and other programmes; to spread information and ideas; and generally to promote the standard and availability of artistic endeavours of all kinds. In the year 1970–71 the Arts Council of Great Britain received grants totalling £9,300,000 for dispersal.

The Arts Council of Northern Ireland, with similar objectives on a local level, received a Northern Ireland Government grant of £220,000 in the same period.

OTHER GOVERNMENT SUPPORT

Other government activities include grants which largely finance most of the major national museums and galleries throughout the country; this field received grants totalling some £9,800,000 during 1970–71. Through the Ministry of Public Building and Works and the Ministry of Housing and Local Government, some £3,300,000 was allocated over the same period to the preservation and upkeep of ancient monuments and historic buildings. Further direct grants are made to a number of supported establishments and bodies concerned with the arts, such as the National Trust, the British Film Institute, the Council for Industrial Design, and so on.

LOCAL AUTHORITY SUPPORT

The Local Government Act of 1948 empowers local authorities to levy a sixpenny (2½p) rate in England and Wales for expenditure on all forms of entertainment including cultural activities. They may also spend funds on building or maintaining museums and galleries. Many towns support orchestras and theatres; a prime example is the undertaking by the Greater London Council to match all government contributions towards the costs of building the new National Theatre on the south bank of the Thames.

LITERATURE

Literature is studied in all types of educational establishments in Britain, and the study and appreciation of literature generally is a major subject in the curricula of all types of colleges and universities. There are free public libraries all over the country, in addition to many private libraries. The public libraries are administered by some 474 public library authorities at local government level. There are more than 10,000 of these libraries in Great Britain, with a stock of over 100,000,000 volumes. Nearly one-third of the population are members of a public library; in remote areas there are regular circuit visits by mobile libraries, of which there are more than 500 in service. The public library often acts as a focus of local cultural activity, with special facilities for lectures, exhibitions, adult education classes, and so on. As well as books, an increasing number of libraries now provide a loan service for gramaphone records, works of art, and other amenities.

By means of a regional system of inter-lending and co-operative subject specialisation the scope of the reference services provided by the public libraries is constantly expanded.

Many large and famous libraries are maintained by private bodies, learned societies, specialist institutions of many types, and the ancient universities. The British Museum Library is the largest in the country, with over 7,000,000 volumes. The National Libraries of Scotland and Wales each have over 2,000,000 volumes. These three libraries are the nation's "copyright" libraries, entitled by law to receive a copy of every book published in Britain; the same status is enjoyed by the Bodleian Library of Oxford University, and the Cambridge University Library. These two foundations have stocks of about 3,500,000 and 4,000,000 volumes respectively.

In 1969 British publishers issued more than 23,000 new books and an additional 9,000 reprints or revised editions. There has been a vast expansion in the number of paperback editions published in recent years, including scholarly and specialist works now brought within reach of areas of society previously denied access to material of this type through poverty, as well as fictional works of all categories. The bodies involved in British publishing include the Publishers' Association, the Booksellers' Association, the Society of Authors, and the National Book League. The promotion of British works abroad is undertaken by the Book Development Council and the British Council. There are currently more than 300 active commercial publishing houses in Britain. The largest publisher is Her Majesty's Stationery Office, the government agency.

Government support for literature, through the Arts Council of Great Britain, is given in a number of ways. There are various grants for writers, subsidies to festivals of literature and poetry, and literary prizes such as the Queen's Gold Medal for Poetry, the James Tait Black Memorial Prizes for biography and literature, the Hawthornden prize for imaginative writing, and others.

At the time of writing government action is awaited on the Public Lending Right – the right of authors to receive a royalty on their books according to the use made of copies in public libraries. This concept has been accepted in principle after long agitation, and will be of enormous benefit to the whole field of British letters.

In a book of this size no significant survey of the vast field of English literature can be attempted. However, the following selection – necessarily arbitrary – of 150 major names, drawn from the whole sweep of English writing over the past 600 years, is accompanied by the briefest details of their fields of activity, and the titles of one or two major works in each instance. The list is in chronological order, by date of birth.

BRITISH AUTHORS, POETS AND DRAMATISTS

WYCLIF(FE), John, 1329-1384: Religious reformer of liberal philosophy, who questioned the unqualified authority of the church and state hierarchy, notably in his *De Dominio Divino* (1376). Instituted first translation of the whole Bible into English, and himself translated the Gospels. Huss, and in turn Luther, were influenced by Wyclif's writing. Surprisingly, he escaped the stake and died peacefully, though his remains were later dishonoured.

LANGLAND, William, c. 1332-c. 1400: Poet, to whom is attributed *The Vision Concerning Piers Plowman*, an alliterative work in Middle English second in importance to Chaucer's *Canterbury Tales* alone. He may also have written the politically inspired *Richard the Redeless.*

CHAUCER, Geoffrey, c. 1340-1400: Father of English literature, he produced work in three distinct periods. The "French" period, 1359-72, produced *The Boke of the Duchesse* and *Romaunt of the Rose*; Italian influences between 1372 and 1386 can be detected in *The Hous of Fame* and *The Parlement of Foules, Troylus and Cryseyde* and *The Legende of Good Women.* In his maturity he wrote *The Canterbury Tales, c.* 1387, roughly 17,000 lines in heroic couplets. This rich and vivid series of pen-portraits and popular tales of the period is generally accepted as the first major work in the English language.

MALORY, Sir Thomas, d. 1471: Warwickshire knight who played an active part in the Wars of the Roses in the mid-15th century, and is believed to have written, while imprisoned, the *Morte Darthur.* Completed in *c.* 1470, this is a translation and adaptation of a contemporary French manuscript, blending traditional Arthurian myths with chivalric themes. It was printed by Caxton in 1485.

CAXTON, William, 1422-1491: A considerable translator from French into English in his own right, Caxton is chiefly famous as the first English printer. He learnt the craft in 1471-74, probably in Cologne, and is believed to have set up a press at Bruges in 1473. He established a press at

William Shakespeare

BACON, Francis, 1561–1626: Lord Chancellor of England, philosopher, historian, essayist and lawyer. Prolific in several fields, he is chiefly known for his *Essays, Maxims of the Law*, and *Advancement of Learning*.

DRAYTON, Michael, 1563–1631: Prolific poet on historical, topographical, religious and satirical themes, and author of many sonnets, odes and pastoral works. His great topographical poem on England, *Polyolbion*, appeared in 1622.

SHAKESPEARE, William, 1564–1616: A poet, playwright and actor, Shakespeare was accepted in his own lifetime as the literary giant of his time, and has since been judged by many to be the most considerable writer the English language has ever produced. His vast body of work does not admit of selection, but his play *Hamlet* is probably the best-known title to the "man in the street".

MARLOWE, Christopher, 1564–1593: Poet and playwright, contemporary and friend of Shakespeare, best known for his *Edward II, Tamburlaine* and *Tragedy of Dr. Faustus*.

DONNE, John, 1572–1631: Poet, one-time Dean of St. Paul's, noted sermonist, writer of many fine elegies, satires and miscellaneous poems.

JONSON, Benjamin, 1572–1637: Soldier, actor, playwright, author of many works including *Volpone, The Alchemist*, and many masques.

FLETCHER, John, 1579–1625: Playwright, author of at least sixteen works including *The Faithful Shepherdess*, and of others in collaboration with Francis Beaumont.

HERRICK, Robert, 1591–1674: Poet, whose work covered a wide range of styles and subjects; mainly remembered for his love-poems and pastoral pieces, he published the bulk of his work in the *Hesperides*, 1648.

WALTON, Izaak, 1593–1683: Biographer, and author of *The Compleat Angler*, 1653.

WALLER, Edmund, 1606–1687: Poet, and one of the first to employ heroic couplets, a metre which was to dominate English verse for two centuries.

MILTON, John, 1608–1674: Poet and pamphleteer, whose great works *Paradise Lost, Paradise Regained* and *Samson Agonistes* sprang from a deep intellectual involvement in his turbulent age. He also wrote many fine sonnets.

HYDE, Edward, Earl of Clarendon, 1609–1674: Lawyer, politician and author of the monumental *History of the Rebellion and Civil Wars in England*.

BUTLER, Samuel, 1612–1680: Satirist, author of *Hudibras*.

COWLEY, Abraham, 1618–1667: Poet of great precocity, and influential prose stylist.

LOVELACE, Richard, 1618–1658: Lyric poet.

EVELYN, John, 1620–1706: Wealthy dilettante writer on numerous subjects, and diarist of brilliance.

Westminster in 1476 or 1477, and by 1491 had issued nearly eighty books.

MORE, Sir Thomas, 1478–1535: Scholar, controversialist, one-time Lord Chancellor of England, eventually beheaded by Henry VIII for adherence to papal authority. More's major works in English were his *Dialogue of Comfort against Tribulation, History of Richard III, Supplycacyon of Soulys* and *Apologye*.

TYNEDALE, William, 1489–1536: Scholar and philosopher, and one of the intellectual leaders of the Reformation who paid for his convictions at the stake. Chiefly famous for his translation of the Bible into English, which appeared between 1525 and 1531.

CRANMER, Thomas, 1489–1556: Archbishop of Canterbury, author and supervisor of the Anglican liturgy, Cranmer is remembered mainly for his prayer-books of 1549 and 1552. He went to the stake in the reign of Queen Mary, with memorable courage and dignity.

FOXE, John, 1516–1587: Canon of Salisbury, religious controversialist, and author of *Actes and Monuments*; this massive history of the early church, printed in English in 1563, is popularly known as the *Book of Martyrs*.

SPENSER, Edmund, 1552–1599: Prolific writer whose major works were the epic *Faerie Queene*, which appeared in six books in 1589 and 1596, and the *Epithalamion*, published in 1595.

SIDNEY, Sir Philip, 1554–1586: Famous as the paragon of young English nobility, brave, cultured, well-born and accomplished, Sidney died of wounds at Zutphen before any of his sonnets or other poems were published. Chief among them were *Arcadia, Astrophel and Stella*, and *Apologie for Poetrie*.

VAUGHAN, Henry, 1622-1695: Religious poet, noted for his *Silex Scintillans*.

AUBREY, John, 1626-1697: Antiquary and biographical writer who left a mass of valuable and charming topical material about his life and times.

BUNYAN, John, 1628-1688: Nonconformist churchman imprisoned for his beliefs, and author of the fine allegory *The Pilgrim's Progress*.

DRYDEN, John, 1631-1700: Playwright, poet laureate, and author of a vast number of satires, criticisms, odes and other works of every description, some highly topical.

PEPYS, Samuel, 1633-1703: London trademan's son who rose to be Secretary of the Admiralty, remembered for his unique *Diary* of the period 1660-1669.

NEWTON, Sir Isaac, 1642-1731: Philosopher, mathematician and scientist.

DEFOE, Daniel, 1660-1731: Soldier, satirist and pamphleteer throughout his stormy life, he also produced much fiction and several travalogues. Immortalised by his *Robinson Crusoe*.

VANBRUGH, Sir John, 1664-1726: Dramatist and architect, best known for his comedy *The Provok'd Wife*.

SWIFT, Jonathan, 1667-1745: Irish author of numerous political, religious, and social pamphlets and letters; poet, liberal thinker, and vicious satirist. His most widely known work is *Gulliver's Travels*.

CONGREVE, William, 1670-1729: Playwright, master of the "comedy of manners", author of *The Old Bachelor*, *Love for Love*, and *The Way of the World*.

CIBBER, Colley, 1671-1757: Comedy actor, theatrical writer, and general "man of the theatre".

ADDISON, Joseph, 1672-1719: Politician and poet, playwright and journalist; contemporary and friend of Swift and Steele, Congreve and Pope.

STEELE, Sir Richard, 1672-1729: Dramatist, journalist and public figure, and one-time supervisor of the Drury Lane Theatre.

POPE, Alexander, 1688-1744: Poet, satirist, translator, and author of *The Rape of the Lock*, *The Dunciad*, and numerous shorter works.

RICHARDSON, Samuel, 1689-1761: Printer of humble origins, whose modest writings led him to enormous success with two very influential novels, *Pamela* and *Clarissa Harlowe*.

FIELDING, Henry, 1707-1754: Lawyer, author of burlesques and farces, satirist and essayist, best remembered for his novel *Tom Jones*.

JOHNSON, Dr. Samuel, 1709-1784: Journalist, biographer, and lexicographer whose reputation rests more upon the delightful personality revealed in Boswell's *Life* than upon his own literary output.

STERNE, Laurence, 1713-1768: Churchman, author of several volumes of sermons and a travelogue, but famous for his humorous novel in nine volumes, *Tristram Shandy*.

GRAY, Thomas, 1716-1771: Poet and academic, whose *Elegy in a Country Churchyard* has become one of the best known poems in the language. He produced other notable works, both prose and verse, and was an elegant and cultured correspondent.

WHITE, Gilbert, 1720-1793: Curate of Selborne, Hampshire, and author of several major early works on natural history.

SMOLLETT, Tobias George, 1721-1771: Sailor, surgeon, novelist and journalist; among his novels were *Roderick Random* and *Peregrine Pickle*.

GOLDSMITH, Oliver, 1728-1774: Biographer, poet, dramatist and unsuccessful physician – best remembered for his *Vicar of Wakefield, She Stoops to Conquer*, and *The Deserted Village*.

BURKE, Edmund, 1729-1797: Reforming and liberal parliamentarian, and man of letters.

COWPER, William, 1731-1800: Poet and man of letters, whose simple style marked a departure from the classical form of such writers as Pope.

GIBBON, Edward, 1737-1794: Author of the monumental *Decline and Fall of the Roman Empire*, published between 1776 and 1788 in six volumes.

PAINE, Thomas, 1737-1809: Pamphleteer and political radical associated during his lifetime with both the French and American revolutions. Author of *Rights of Man* and *Age of Reason*.

SHERIDAN, Richard, 1751-1816: Dramatist, author of *The Rivals, School for Scandal*, and *The Critic*. Also an active parliamentarian.

CHATTERTON, Thomas, 1752-1770: Brilliant but unstable poet whose output was tainted by his attempts to pass it as the work of a spurious historical figure. Poisoned himself at the age of 17.

BLAKE, William, 1757-1827: Mystic, poet, philosopher and artist; author of numerous works of prose and verse including *Songs of Innocence* and *Songs of Experience*.

BURNS, Robert, 1759-1796: Scots poet, song writer and satirist of humble origins, author of some hundreds of verses and ballads, many of which have passed into everyday usage.

WORDSWORTH, William, 1770-1850: Poet, one-time poet laureate, author of numerous lyric works and some political observations.

SMITH, Sydney, 1771-1845: Churchman and man of letters, whose many reviews and letters earned him a reputation as a great wit.

SCOTT, Sir Walter, 1771-1832: Scots romantic novelist and balladeer, a prolific author whose best-known works include *Ivanhoe, The Heart of Midlothian, The Talisman* and *Quentin Durward*.

COLERIDGE, Samuel Taylor, 1772-1834: Poet, critic and translator, best remembered for his poems

Kubla Khan and *The Ancient Mariner*.

SOUTHEY, Robert, 1774-1843: Poet, historian and biographer whose most enduring work was in the light and gothic styles. Poet laureate.

AUSTEN, Jane, 1775-1817: Novelist and author of *Pride and Prejudice*, *Sense and Sensibility* and four other works.

LAMB, Charles, 1775-1834: Poet, critic and contributor to numerous journals, who published popular interpretations of classic works.

HAZLITT, William, 1778-1830: Essayist and critic.

HUNT, James Henry Leigh, 1784-1859: Journalist, critic, and essayist; associate of Shelley, Keats and Byron.

BYRON, Lord George Gordon, 1788-1824: Romantic poet who scandalised society by his personal life but exerted enormous influence on writing. Among his best-known works are *Childe Harold*, *Don Juan* and *The Dream*.

SHELLEY, Percy Bysshe, 1792-1822: Lyric poet and author of *Prometheus Unbound*, and many fine works of verse and prose.

HOOD, Thomas, 1795-1845: Journalist and poet, best remembered for his humorous pieces, but also for serious work such as *The Bridge of Sighs*.

KEATS, John, 1795-1821: Poet, chiefly remembered for his odes; among his best-known pieces are *Endymion*, *On a Grecian Urn* and *La Bella Dame sans Merci*.

CARLYLE, Thomas, 1795-1881: Biographer, historian and essayist.

MACAULAY, Lord Thomas, 1800-1859: Historian, politician, poet and essayist. Major works include *Lays of Ancient Rome* and *History of England*, the latter incomplete.

DISRAELI, Benjamin, 1804-1881: Prime Minister of England, also novelist and essayist.

FITZGERALD, Edward, 1809-1883: Translator and man of letters, author of English poetic version of *Rubaiyat of Omar Khayyam*, 1859.

TENNYSON, Lord Alfred, 1809-1892: Poet laureate, best remembered for his *Idylls of the King* and *The Charge of the Light Brigade*.

DARWIN, Charles, 1809-1882: Naturalist, first propounder of the theory of evolution in his great work *On the Origin of Species by means of Natural Selection*, 1859.

THACKERAY, William, 1811-1863: Novelist, essayist and journalist, whose most famous work was *Vanity Fair*.

LEAR, Edward, 1812-1888: Writer of light "nonsense" verse.

BROWNING, Robert, 1812-1889: Poet and playwright, widely known for his romantic marriage to Elizabeth Barrett and their correspondence.

DICKENS, Charles, 1812-1870: Novelist of enormous

The First Baron, Alfred Lord Tennyson (1809-1892)

success and influence, journalist and lecturer. *David Copperfield*, *Oliver Twist*, *The Pickwick Papers* and *A Tale of Two Cities* are among his most famous works.

TROLLOPE, Anthony, 1815-1882: Prolific and successful popular novelist remembered mainly for the "Barsetshire" novels, commencing with *The Warden*, 1855, and *Barchester Towers*, 1857.

BRONTË, Charlotte, 1816-1855: Author of the famous novel *Jane Eyre*.

BRONTË, Emily Jane, 1818-1848: Sister of Charlotte, a fine poet and author of the novel *Wuthering Heights*.

RUSKIN, John, 1819-1900: Essayist and pamphleteer on a wide range of social and artistic subjects, respected authority on painting and architecture.

KINGSLEY, Charles, 1819-1875: Churchman and social reformer, poet and prose writer; among his most famous works are *Westward Ho!* and *Hereward the Wake*, and the romantic fantasy *The Water Babies*.

ARNOLD, Matthew, 1822-1888: Educationalist, poet and essayist. His verse work includes *Sohrab and Rustum*, and his most important prose publication was *Essay in Criticism*, 1865.

COLLINS, Wilkie, 1824-1889: Novelist and dramatist, and friend of Dickens; his most famous titles were *The Woman in White* and *The Moonstone*.

MEREDITH, George, 1828-1909: Journalist, poet and novelist.

ROSSETTI, Dante Gabriel, 1828-1882: Painter, poet, translator and founder of the "Pre-Raphaelite" school in art.

"*CARROLL, Lewis*" (*Charles Lutwige Dodgson*), *1832–1898:* Children's writer of *Alice's Adventures in Wonderland* and *Through The Looking Glass.*

BUTLER, Samuel, 1835–1902: Satirist, critic and travel writer; his major work was the satirical *Erewhon.*

GILBERT, Sir William, 1836–1911: Humorous verse writer and contributor of lyrics to the Gilbert and Sullivan comic operas.

SWINBURNE, Algernon Charles, 1837–1909: Poet and critic whose best work was probably *Tristram of Lyonesse,* 1882.

HARDY, Thomas, 1840–1928: Novelist and poet, chiefly remembered for his novels set in Wessex, such as *Far from the Madding Crowd* and *Tess of the D'Urbervilles.*

JAMES, Henry, 1843–1916: Novelist, writer of short stories and travel pieces. American born, he spent most of his working life in England; he lived in London and Rye for almost 40 years, and here wrote his best novels including *Portrait of a Lady, The Ambassadors* and *The Golden Bowl.*

HOPKINS, Gerard Manley, 1844–1889: Poet and scholar, whose works were unpublished during his lifetime.

STEVENSON, Robert Louis, 1850–1894: Writer of essays, short stories, and romantic novels such as *Treasure Island* (1883), *The Strange Case of Dr. Jekyll and Mr. Hyde* (1886), and *Kidnapped* (1886).

WILDE, Oscar Fingal O'Flahertie Wills, 1854–1900: Poet, playwright, aesthete, imprisoned and disgraced for homosexuality, but enormously popular for such glittering social comedies as *Lady Windermere's Fan* (1893), and *The Importance of Being Ernest* (1899).

SHAW, George Bernard, 1856–1950: Critic, journalist and dramatist of great originality and power. Major works included *Major Barbara* (1907), *Pygmalion* (1916) and *Saint Joan* (1924).

CONRAD, Joseph, 1857–1924: Polish-Ukranian immigrant, sea captain, novelist and writer of short stories; major works include *Lord Jim, The Nigger of the Narcissus* and *An Outcast of the Islands.*

DOYLE, Sir Arthur Conan, 1859–1930: Author of historical and other romances such as *Micah Clarke, The White Company,* and *The Exploits of Brigadier Gerard,* but immortal for his creation of the detective Sherlock Holmes.

HOUSMAN, Alfred Edward, 1859–1936: Classical scholar and poet, author of *A Shropshire Lad.*

BARRIE, Sir James, 1860–1937: Dramatist, author of the children's classic *Peter Pan.*

QUILLER-COUCH, Sir Arthur, 1865–1944: Poet, critic, anthologist and writer of romantic fiction.

YEATS, William Butler, 1865–1939: Irish poet and dramatist, central figure in foundation of Irish national theatre. His best known works include *Cathleen ni Houlihan, The Land of Heart's Desire* and *The Wind among the Reeds.*

KIPLING, Joseph Rudyard, 1865–1936: Journalist, novelist, poet and author of numerous short stories on a variety of themes; remembered chiefly as the chronicler of British India. Most popular works include *The Jungle Books, Kim* and *Puck of Pook's Hill.*

WELLS, Herbert George, 1866–1946: Novelist, whose imaginative works have often proved remarkably prophetic. Works include *The Time Machine, The War of the Worlds* and *The History of Mr. Polly.*

BENNETT, Enoch Arnold, 1867–1931: Novelist and theatrical journalist whose books were largely set around the potteries; major works include the "Clayhanger" books and *Riceyman Steps.*

GALSWORTHY, John, 1867–1933: Dramatist and novelist, immortalised by the success of his long cycle of novels collectively known as *The Forsyte Saga.*

BELLOC, Joseph Hilaire Pierre, 1870–1953: Essayist, novelist and critic who produced much work in a variety of disciplines, the best being *The Path to Rome,* and a quantity of children's writing.

BEERBOHM, Sir Max, 1872–1956: Critic, essayist and caricaturist; major works include *Zuleika Dobson.*

DE LA MARE, Walter, 1873–1956: Novelist and romantic poet, whose most popular pieces include *Peacock Pie* and *The Listeners.*

CHESTERTON, Gilbert Keith, 1874–1936: Novelist, poet, essayist and critic whose most popular work was the creation of the detective *Father Brown.* A quantity of verse, biography and fiction includes novels such as *The Napoleon of Notting Hill.*

CHURCHILL, Sir Winston, 1874–1965: Statesman, soldier, national war leader and author of a great quantity of history, memoir, biography and one novel. Best known is his *History of the English-Speaking Peoples.*

MAUGHAN, William Somerset, 1874–1965: Novelist, dramatist and short story writer. Major works include *Of Human Bondage, The Moon and Sixpence* and *Cakes and Ale.*

BUCHAN, John (Lord Tweedsmuir), 1875–1940: Statesman and writer of successful adventure fiction including *The Thirty-Nine Steps* and *Prester John.*

TREVELYAN, George Macaulay, 1876–1962: Historian whose major works included studies of Garibaldi, and *English Social History.*

AGATE, James, 1877–1947: Diarist, journalist and broadcaster, London's leading drama critic between the World Wars.

MASEFIELD, John, 1878–1967: Poet laureate, essayist and romantic novelist. Major works include *Salt-Water Ballads, The Everlasting Mercy* and *The Tragedy of Nan.*

Robert Graves

FORSTER, Edward Morgan, 1879-1970: Novelist, best known for *A Passage to India* and the critical *Aspects of the Novel*.

WODEHOUSE, Pelham Grenville, b. 1881: Author of vast body of highly stylised humorous fiction set in imaginary aristocratic English milieu of the 1920s, creator of the character "Jeeves", the perfect manservant.

JOYCE, James, 1882-1941: Irish novelist whose powerful and eccentrically formed *Ulysses* has been very influential. Other major works include *Portrait of the Artist as a Young Man* and *Finnegan's Wake*.

WOOLF, Virginia, 1882-1941: Novelist, essayist and critic, known for her experimental approach to the novel; author of *Mrs. Dalloway* and *The Waves*.

LAWRENCE, David Herbert, 1885-1930: Novelist and poet of great influence; author of *Sons and Lovers* and *Lady Chatterley's Lover*.

SASSOON, Siegfried, 1886-1967: Poet who made a public renunciation of the First World War after being wounded and decorated for gallantry. Major works include *Memoirs of a Fox-Hunting Man* and *Memoirs of an Infantry Officer*.

BROOKE, Rupert Chawner, 1887-1915: Poet who died on active service after publishing early work of great promise.

SITWELL, Dame Edith, 1887-1964: Poet of great originality and influence.

ELIOT, Thomas Stearns, 1888-1965: American born, British resident poet, dramatist and critic; major works include *The Waste Land* and *Murder in the Cathedral*.

LAWRENCE, Thomas Edward, 1888-1935: Arabist, guerilla leader and author of *The Seven Pillars of Wisdom*.

TOLKIEN, John Ronald Reuel, b. 1892: Scholar and philologist, critical writer and author of the unique romantic fantasy *The Lord of the Rings*, a vast work which has enjoyed worldwide success.

OWEN, Wilfred, 1893-1918: Poet whose posthumously collected and published work, inspired by the horrors of trench warfare, revealed that a poet of genuine stature had been lost when Owen was killed in action.

PRIESTLEY, John Boynton, b. 1894: Novelist and man of letters, whose major works include *Angel Pavement*, *An Inspector Calls* and *The Good Companions*.

HUXLEY, Aldous Leonard, 1894-1963: Novelist and essayist whose best known work is probably *Brave New World*.

GRAVES, Robert Ranke, b. 1895: Novelist, poet and classicist of the first importance. Major works include *Goodbye to All That*, *The White Goddess* and *I, Claudius*.

LEWIS, Clive Staples, 1898-1963: Novelist, critic and author of the much respected *The Allegory of Love* and works of fantasy fiction and religious speculation.

"ORWELL, George" (Eric Blair), 1903-1950: Novelist and political writer whose intellectual honesty isolated him from the mainstream of radical thought in the 1930s. Major works include *The Road to Wigan Pier*, *Homage to Catalonia*, the allegorical *Animal Farm*, and the visionary novel *Nineteen Eighty-Four*.

DAY LEWIS, Cecil, 1904-1972: Poet and critic, appointed poet laureate in 1968. Important verse work includes *The Magnetic Mountain* and *Overtures to Death*, and the critical *The Poetic Image* is much respected.

ISHERWOOD, Christopher, b. 1904: British born, American resident novelist and writer of film scripts, whose most widely known work is set in Berlin in the 1930s. Major titles include *Goodbye to Berlin*, *The World in the Evening* and *Down There on a Visit*.

GREENE, Graham, C.H., b. 1904: Novelist and dramatist of wide reputation, much of whose work examines the nature of morality, especially Roman Catholic morality. Major works include *Brighton Rock*, *The Power and the Glory*, *The Heart of the Matter*, and *The Quiet American*.

SNOW, Lord Charles Percy, C.B.E., b. 1905: Novelist and scientist; author of a cycle of novels whose setting links the academic and political worlds.

AUDEN, Wystan Hugh, b. 1907: Poet, radical figure of

the 1930s, friend and contemporary of Isherwood, MacNeice, Spender and Day Lewis; recognised as a major figure in 20th century poetry.

MACNEICE, Louis, 1907–1963: Poet, verse dramatist, translator and broadcaster.

FLEMING, Ian, 1908–1965: Journalist and novelist who achieved unique commercial success in the 1960s with his series of fast-paced, cynical adventure stories built around the character "James Bond".

SPENDER, Stephen, C.B.E., b. 1909: Poet, critic and novelist whose work is noted both for lyricism and acerbity.

RATTIGAN, Terence Mervyn, C.B.E., b. 1911: Dramatist whose work ranges from light farce to serious drama; his best know plays include *The Winslow Boy*, *The Deep Blue Sea*, and *Ross*.

DURRELL, Lawrence, b. 1912: Poet and novelist best known for the novels of his "Alexandria Quartet".

THOMAS, Dylan, 1914–1953: Welsh poet of wide reputation, best known for his play for broadcasting, *Under Milk Wood*.

LEE, Laurie, M.B.E., b. 1914: Poet and travel writer whose pastoral autobiography *Cider with Rosie* enjoyed great success.

OSBORNE, John James, b. 1929: Dramatist and influential commentator on the age of the "angry young man" in his play *Look Back in Anger*; other major works include *The Entertainer* and *Luther*.

PINTER, Harold, b. 1930: Dramatist of highly individual style, best known for his plays *The Caretaker* and *The Birthday Party*.

DRAMA

There are about 140 professional theatres currently in full-time use in the United Kingdom. About half of these are operated commercially. While the theatrical scene in Britain is lively, active and of high artistic reputation, acting is admitted to be an overcrowded profession. It is estimated by British Equity that at any one time more than 90 per cent of the membership is out of employment. At the time of writing Equity are agitating for an increase in the minimum rate for an actor in a West End production – from £18·00 to £30·00.

There are more than 30 important theatres in or near the West End of London, the centre of British theatrical activity, and others in the suburbs of the Greater London area. Most of these theatres are rented to producing managements for each production, on a commercial basis, but four of them are occupied by important theatrical companies receiving Arts Council subsidies. The Arts Council provided a total of more than £2,000,000 in subsidies to the theatre in 1969–70; non-profit making companies in receipt of these grants own or rent about half the theatres in Britain.

The four major subsidised companies are the National Theatre Company, the English Stage Company, the Royal Shakespeare Company and the Mermaid Theatre Company. The National Theatre Company will eventually occupy the new theatre under construction on the Thames south bank site; for the time being the company's London home is the Old Vic theatre. Formed ten years ago, the company receives its running costs jointly from the Arts Council and the Greater London Council. Presenting plays of all countries and all periods, it is large enough to mount simultaneous productions in London and on tour, either at home or overseas.

The Royal Shakespeare Company presents a season of Shakespeare each year at the Royal Shakespeare Theatre, Stratford-upon-Avon, and also a wide variety of classical and modern material at the Aldwych Theatre in London. It, too, is intended to have a new permanent home eventually in the proposed arts centre on the Barbican site in the City of London.

The large provincial cities of Britain can boast about 40 large commercial theatres, and a further 60 or so, operated by subsidised repertory companies, are scattered throughout the country. Pre- and post-London runs by the major West End productions and by specially-formed touring companies are presented in the provincial theatres. While the number of commercial theatres is declining, the repertory companies, which are supported by the Arts Council and by local authorities, are flourishing. They employ leading dramatists, actors and producers, and the artistic standard is generally very high. More than a dozen new repertory theatres have been built in the past fifteen years. Prominent among them are the Nottingham Playhouse, the Belgrade Theatre in Coventry, the Phoenix Theatre in Leicester, and the Yvonne Arnaud Theatre in Guildford. There are five major professional theatres in Northern Ireland, whose productions are entitled to support from the Arts Council; these include the Ulster Group Theatre, the Belfast Arts Theatre, and the Lyric Players Theatre.

In addition there are literally thousands of amateur dramatic groups and societies in towns and villages all over Britain, with a total active membership of more than 500,000. These receive support and encouragement through the local education authorities and other regional public bodies, and through such organisations as the British Drama League, the Standing Conference of Drama Associations, and the Scottish Community Drama Association. Most institutions of further education have dramatic societies, and an annual festival of University Theatre is held in Bristol. Such long established amateur societies as the Oxford University Dramatic Society have a high artistic reputation.

Education and training for the theatre is proved by such establishments as the Royal Academy of Dramatic Art which provides lengthy courses in all aspects of theatrical work; the Central School of Speech and Drama; the Royal Scottish Academy of Music and Drama, in Glasgow; and so on.

Youth theatre is increasingly active in Britain. A

spin-off of the National Theatre, the Young Vic, was opened in 1970, and altogether there are some dozen youth companies which tour schools and theatres all over Britain. In 1969–70 Arts Council grants in support of youth theatre activity totalled £185,000.

THE VISUAL ARTS

Painting and sculpture in Britain receive state support and encouragement in a number of ways. Direct grants are made to national institutions, supplemented indirectly by purchase grants made to local art galleries and to local authorities for other programmes. The Arts Council supports various exhibitions. In all questions of grants to art galleries and museums, the government is advised by the Royal Fine Arts Commissions for England and Wales and for Scotland, and by the Standing Commission on Museums and Galleries.

Arts patronage on a regional level, involving central and local government agencies, private foundations, individuals, industry and academic institutions, is becoming more marked with recent government encouragement; in this way a wide range of artistic endeavour can be supported and made more available to the people of the various regions, by means of periodic festivals and other exhibitions mounted through regional arts associations.

The main national art exhibiting societies are the Royal Academy, the Royal Scottish Academy, the Society of Scottish Artists, the Royal Society of British Artists, the Royal Society of Painters in Water Colours, and the Royal Society of Portrait Painters. All these are associations of professional artists. Some have their own permanent galleries, the most notable being the Burlington House gallery of the Royal Academy. The Arts Council organises a large number of touring and static provincial exhibitions, arranging loans and subsidising costs. The commercial exhibitions constantly on show in the galleries of the main London art dealers are also very numerous. Overseas British painting and sculpture, like all other branches of culture, are promoted by the British Council. Some 98 international prizes have been won by British artists over the past twenty years or so.

The main national collections of art are housed in the British Museum, the Victoria and Albert Museum, the National Gallery, the Tate Gallery, the National Portrait Gallery, and the Wallace Collection, in London. These are subsidised by the government through the Arts Council. Some are the direct responsibility of the Department of Education and Science, some are run by trustee bodies. Running costs are paid, and purchase grants in the year 1970–71 totalled about £1,937,000, divided among all the national collections including those museums which are not primarily concerned with the visual arts. Local art galleries, of which all large cities and towns have at least one, are also given direct government aid through annual grants.

The large number of private homes of ancient foundation, manors, palaces, castles and mansions which have been thrown open for public exhibition in recent years also contain a wealth of art treasures now accessible to the public. Some of the "stately homes" are administered by the National Trust, others are still in private hands.

BRITISH PAINTERS AND SCULPTORS

Although Britain's contribution to the visual arts has never been as significant as her contribution to world literature, any review of past and present figures in the field of British painting and sculpture must necessarily be cursory. The following list names, and gives the briefest details of the claims on history of one hundred British painters and sculptors – including some foreigners who spent significant periods of their working lives in this country.

HILLIARD, Nicholas, 1547?–1619: The earliest important British painter whose career is known in detail. A goldsmith turned painter, he was Limner and Goldsmith to Queen Elizabeth I, whom he painted and whose Great Seal he designed. Known for his superb miniatures.

JOHNSON, Cornelius, 1593–1661: One of the most noted portrait painters in England before the arrival of Van Dyck in London, Johnson (or Jansen) was the English-born child of Dutch immigrants.

WALKER, Robert, c. 1605–1658: Portrait painter best known for his studies of Cromwell and other Parliamentary leaders of the Civil War period.

COOPER, Samuel, 1609–1672: Miniaturist who in his day enjoyed a reputation throughout Europe and commanded great fees; his study of Cromwell is widely known. Notable for painting miniatures as conventional portraits; it is said of his work that it would still command respect if enlarged to the size of conventional portraiture.

HOSKINS, John, d. 1665: Miniaturist, Limner to Charles I; he is thought to have been influenced by Van Dyck and influential in bringing conventional portrait techniques to the field of miniatures.

DOBSON, William, 1610–1646: Perhaps a pupil of Van Dyck, Dobson enjoyed enormous popularity in his time, and became Court Painter. His work shows an Italian influence.

LELY, Sir Peter, 1618–1680: Dutch born but resident in England for many years, Lely was the most influential painter in England in the 17th century. His hundreds of portraits include studies of all prominent court figures of the period.

STREETER, Robert, 1624–1680: Sergeant-Painter to Charles II, a decorator in the florid Baroque style whose best known work was a painted ceiling in the Sheldonian Theatre, Oxford. He does not approach the quality of Thornhill.

KNELLER, Sir Godfrey, 1646–1723: German-born portrait painter who came to England in 1674 and rapidly established a great reputation. His success culminated in a baronetcy in 1715, an unprecedented honour. At his best, vigorous and original, and an important influence on English portraits for years to come, he was also capable of mechanical and derivative work; he was known for his vast conceit.

RILEY, John, 1646–1691: A leading portrait painter between the dominant periods of Lely and Kneller, known for fine studies of humble folk as well as society figures.

PEARCE, Edward, d. 1695: Wood and stone carver who produced much fine decorative work for churches and great houses, and some notable busts.

GIBBONS, Grinling, 1648–1721: One of the most brilliant wood-carvers of all time. He enjoyed Royal patronage and great success.

RICHARDSON, Jonathan, 1665–1745: A pupil of Riley, the foremost portrait painter in the period between Kneller and Hudson. He also exercised considerable influence through his writings on art.

BIRD, Francis, 1667–1731: Sculptor who produced much of the statuary on the outside of St. Paul's Cathedral. Studied in Flanders and Italy, and under Grinling Gibbons.

THORNHILL, Sir James, 1675?–1734: The only English painter to follow the grand Baroque tradition of decorating. In his day his degree of social advancement and popular status was remarkable, and did not occur again until Reynolds. His work was widespread, but fine examples may be seen in St. Paul's Cathedral, Greenwich Hospital and Hampton Court.

KENT, William, 1685–1748: Architect, decorator and furniture designer of note, whose most faithful patron was Lord Burlington; he studied painting in Rome, and received important commissions both in England and Italy.

HOGARTH, William, 1697–1764: Painter and engraver, whose main fame rests on the vast popularity of the engravings in his series of "moralities" – Rake's Progress, Election, Marriage à la Mode, etc. These "dumb shows" were pirated so widely that Hogarth was instrumental in the passing of the Copyright Act of 1735.

KNAPTON, George, 1698–1778: A pupil of Richardson, a successful and fashionable portraitist in the 1740s.

SCOTT, Samuel, 1702?–1772: An early topographical and marine painter, later in his career influenced by Canaletto.

HAYMAN, Francis, 1708–1776: Founder-member and first librarian of the Royal Academy, whose best known work was a series of pictures to decorate Vauxhall Gardens. Illustrated the novels of Samuel Richardson.

DEVIS, Arthur, 1711–1787: Painter remembered for his delicate, charming portraits and "conversation pieces", who enjoyed considerable success among wealthy middle-class patrons.

WILSON, Richard, 1713–1782: Welsh landscape painter, much influenced by classicism while studying in Italy, who deserved a greater success than he actually enjoyed.

RAMSAY, Allan, 1713–1784: The Scottish contemporary of Gainsborough and Reynolds. Trained in Italy and exhibiting a strong Continental influence in his work, he enjoyed considerable success in London and was appointed painter to George III in the 1760s.

REYNOLDS, Sir Joshua, 1723–1792: Historically, England's most important painter. He was a man of education and culture, the confidant of political, intellectual and social leaders of his day, and thus raised the status of the painter as never before. He studied the great figures of Italian art at length, and acquired a deep learning and respect for the past. His success lay in his reconciliation of classical allusion with commercial portraiture; nearly every important figure of the second half of the 18th century sat for him. He was the first President of the Royal Academy in 1768, and was a great rival of Gainsborough as a society portraitist.

STUBBS, George, 1724–1806: The supreme painter of horses, renowned for his scrupulous accuracy. He was basically an anatomist, who did much dissection and kept himself by painting while preparing volumes of comparative anatomy; nevertheless his work shows a fine pictorial imagination.

SANDBY, Paul, 1725–1809: Topographical draughtsman originally employed by the Ordnance Survey, later a fine water colour painter of landscapes.

COTES, Francis, 1726–1770: English painter, a pupil of Knapton, at one time regarded as a serious competitor to Reynolds as a portraitist.

GAINSBOROUGH, Thomas, 1727–1788: One of the three or four best known English painters of all time, a contemporary and open competitor of Reynolds. Gainsborough produced both portraits and landscapes, the latter with a distinctly Arcadian feel to them. His portraits were much influenced by Van Dyck; and his technique, the physical handling of his materials, was one of his great strengths. Among his best known works are the Blue Boy and The Watering Place.

WRIGHT, Joseph, 1734–1797: Derbyshire painter of portraits and landscapes, whose personal obsession lay in reproducing light effects. Some of his exercises in this field were of extraordinary skill.

ROMNEY, George, 1734-1802: Artistically the inferior of Reynolds and Gainsborough, Romney nevertheless acquired considerable fame; he is best known perhaps for his paintings of *Lady Hamilton*. He formed an ambition to create large historical works in his later years, and large numbers of sadly inferior drawings survive.

KETTLE, Tilly, 1735-1786: English portrait painter who sought, and found, his fortune in India.

BANKS, Thomas, 1735-1805: Earliest British sculptor to be influenced by Neoclassical style, while studying and working in Rome for several years. He also travelled to Russia. He left many fine busts and monuments.

BACON, John, 1740-1799: Considered the foremost monumental sculptor of his day, he worked on many important tombs, including monuments to Chatham and Dr. Johnson. In youth he was a modeller of porcelain figures.

BARRY, James, 1741-1806: Irish protégé of Edmund Burke and of Reynolds, who studied in Italy and later executed huge historical paintings of reported quality. A Professor of Painting at the Royal Academy, he was expelled later and died in poverty.

COSWAY, Richard, 1742-1821: A miniaturist of charm and skill, also known for being a leading Regency fop and "rake-hell" of the circle of the Prince Regent.

ALLAN, David, 1744-1796: Scots genre and portrait painter who achieved some success while in Rome.

WHEATLEY, Francis, 1747-1801: Genre painter, notable for the engraved series *Cries of London*.

COZENS, John, 1752-1797: Painter known for his soft, poetic landscapes, including many scenes of Italy and Switzerland. Very influential in his day, he was highly regarded by Constable.

BEWICK, Thomas, 1753-1828: Very skilled wood engraver, known for his white-line engraving book illustrations.

BEECHEY, Sir William, 1753-1839: Careful and restrained portrait painter, made Portrait Painter to the Queen in 1793.

FLAXMAN, John, 1755-1826: English sculptor who enjoyed great renown, both for monumental statuary and for book illustrations; his work is characterised by an extremely pure Neoclassical technique. Friend and one time protégé of Josiah Wedgwood.

RAEBURN, Sir Henry, 1756-1823: Scotland's greatest portrait painter, a self-taught artist who developed a virtuoso technique all his own. He painted many of the professional and social élite of Edinburgh's great days.

ROWLANDSON, Thomas, 1756-1827: Fine draughtsman and caricaturist of contemporary manners, who lived by producing large numbers of exuberant works after gambling away an inherited fortune.

BLAKE, William, 1757-1827: (*See Writers' list*). Engraved and water-coloured the illustrations for some of his own books. His best pictures are the series of water-colours illustrating the *Book of Job*. His visionary quality, and his constant experiments with form, show in his pictures as much as in his written work.

HOPPNER, John, 1758?-1810: Portrait Painter to the Prince of Wales in 1793, a follower of Reynolds and a rival of Lawrence.

ABBOTT, Lemuel Francis, 1760?-1803: Portrait painter, best known for his *Nelson*.

OPIE, John, 1761-1807: Cornish painter of natural genius who was launched in London in the 1780s and attracted glowing praise. His best works were studies of peasant types, old people and children; Reynolds declared him finer than Caravaggio.

MORLAND, George, 1763-1804: Influenced by Dutch and Flemish 17th century styles, Morland was popular as a painter of rustic genre pieces, but eventually died in debtor's prison. His best known works include *Industry* and *Idleness*.

CROME, John, 1768-1821: Painter and etcher noted for his Norfolk scenes; he was influenced by the Dutch 17th century style.

LAWRENCE, Sir Thomas, 1769-1830: From his earliest youth a successful and skilled portraitist, he enjoyed lucrative Royal patronage and European renown. He was President of the Royal Academy in 1820.

WARD, James, 1769-1859: Landscape and animal painter, influenced by the work of his relative George Morland. His best known painting is the large landscape of *Gordale Scar, Yorkshire*.

GIRTIN, Thomas, 1775-1802: A friend of Turner, Girtin was very influential in the field of water-colour landscape painting.

TURNER, Joseph, 1775-1851: Supported from his teens by the encouragement of the Royal Academy, he was a precocious talent and a hard-headed businessman. Originally he worked mainly on water-colour landscapes, later turning to oils. He was much criticised at one point in his career and passed out of general public favour, but visits to Italy in the 1830s and 1840s produced some brilliant work remarkable for its light effects, and the influential Ruskin went into print in his praise.

WESTMACOTT, Sir Richard, 1775-1856: Sculptor, a pupil of Canova. He enjoyed a considerable success, executing commissions for Queen Charlotte and for the Prince of Wales at Brighton Pavilion; his work is also to be seen at the British

Museum and Marble Arch, and the *Achilles* in Hyde Park is his.

CONSTABLE, *John, 1776-1837:* With Turner, the major English landscape painter of the 19th century. Enormously influential, he is best known for his lush, vivid studies of the English countryside at its most beautiful and pastoral, such as *The Hay Wain* and *View on the Stour.*

CHANTREY, *Sir Francis, 1781-1841:* Noted sculptor of portrait busts, who left a large bequest to the Royal Academy for purchases.

COTMAN, *John Sell, 1782-1842:* Painter in both watercolours and oils, noted for landscapes with a fine, restrained sense of design.

GEDDES, *Andrew, 1783-1844:* Portraitist of skill and charm, who worked in Edinburgh for some years.

DE WINT, *Peter, 1784-1849:* Painter, whose main works were wide, flat studies of Lincolnshire landscapes.

ETTY, *William, 1787-1849:* Painter who specialised in the nude and showed the influence of Titian and Rubens in some ways.

MARTIN, *"Mad John", 1789-1854:* Painter of enormous and melodramatic history paintings, briefly popular, but in retrospect vulgar.

BONINGTON, *Richard, 1801-1828:* English landscape painter who trained in France; much influenced by Gros and Delacroix.

LANDSEER, *Sir Edwin, 1802-1873:* An infant prodigy who rose to great success with sentimentalised paintings of animals. His most widely known work is the quartet of lions guarding the foot of Nelson's Column.

STEELL, *Sir John, 1804-1891:* Scottish sculptor who studied in Rome, and later returned to his native country despite invitations to settle in London; he became the foremost sculptor north of the border, and left many works in Edinburgh.

PALMER, *Samuel, 1805-1881:* Follower of Blake, and painter of some remarkable landscapes during the period 1826-1835.

MÜLLER, *William, 1812-1845:* Landscape painter of German extraction, amateur antiquarian, one of the first English artists to paint Arabian scenes.

STEVENS, *Alfred, 1817-1875:* In youth a portrait painter of promise, his poverty led him to tramp Italy picking up what work and knowledge he could. Lack of formal education robbed him of any great success, although in his later years he secured some good commissions including the Wellington monument in St. Paul's Cathedral.

WATTS, *George, 1817-1904:* Portraitist of great integrity, and painter of large, rather turgid allegories – one of the last English painters to follow this high-minded symbolical style.

RUSKIN, *John, 1819-1900, (See Writers' list):* His great influence as a critic was only one aspect of this energetic, volatile, learned figure. Among other achievements was a considerable skill as a meticulous draughtsman of architectural and plant subjects.

FRITH, *William Powell, 1819-1909:* Very successful genre painter, whose detailed studies of everyday life were most popular with Victorians.

BROWN, *Ford Madox, 1821-1893:* Painter, much influenced by the Pre-Raphaelite Brotherhood. Most widely known works include *The Last of England.*

HUNT, *William Holman, 1827-1910:* Founder, with Millais and Rossetti, of the Pre-Raphaelite Brotherhood in 1848, and most faithful adherent to its principles. Known for his Biblical scenes painted in the Middle East with accurate local settings.

ROSSETTI, *Dante Gabriel, 1828-1882, (See Writers' list):* A pupil of Ford Madox Brown and of Holman Hunt, his paintings were mostly based on a medieval dream world, and were not particularly impressive.

MILLAIS, *Sir John, 1829-1896:* Co-founder of the Pre-Raphaelite Brotherhood, later a fashionable and very skilled painter of genre works and portraits; he was President of the Royal Academy, and was created baronet.

BURNE-JONES, *Sir Edward, 1833-1898:* English painter of the circle of William Morris and Rossetti. He travelled and painted in Italy, and produced stained glass and tapestry designs for Morris.

MORRIS, *William, 1834-1896:* Painter, draughtsman, writer on artistic and social subjects. Morris was very influential in the field of design, through his firm producing fabrics, furniture, wallpaper, stained glass windows, etc., and also raised standards of book design and printing through the products of his private press. He was a friend of, and influenced by, Burne-Jones and Rossetti.

TISSOT, *James, 1836-1902:* Painter of religious scenes, and charming studies of Victorian life.

SARGENT, *John Sinder, 1856-1925:* Born in Italy of American parents, he settled in England and painted portraits of Edwardian society, in the manner of "Lawrence, crossed with Velasquez". He is also remembered for his fine water-colours.

SICKERT, *Walter, 1860-1942:* With Steer, the most important British Impressionist; his best work includes scenes of London music halls, and studies of poor quarters of London, Dieppe and Venice. He was also an etcher, and wrote widely on art.

BRANGWYN, *Sir Frank, 1867-1956:* Welsh painter who specialised in large murals.

BEARDSLEY, *Aubrey, 1872-1898:* Illustrator, best known for his work in Wilde's *Salome* and in *The*

Yellow Book; his very stylised and individual figures acquired a reputation for decadence which has persisted.

BONE, Sir Muirhead, 1876-1953: Architectural draughtsman and etcher. Among his best known works are *Demolition of St. James's Hall*, and *Ruins of London from St. Bride's*.

JOHN, Augustus, O.M., 1878-1961: Superb draughtsman and portrait painter, a passionate and splendid individualist both in his work and his life.

SMITH, Sir Matthew, 1879-1959: Much influenced by the Fauve school, Smith spent most of the period 1910-1939 in France, and his paintings show characteristic French features.

EPSTEIN, Sir Jacob, 1880-1959: Sculptor, known for the ruggedness and power of his portrait busts and imaginative work; much of his commissioned statuary caused controversy in its day. Born in the U.S.A., he lived and worked in England for more than fifty years.

GILL, Eric, 1882-1940: Engraver, sculptor, typographer and writer. Although famous for the design of typefaces which bear his name, he also left some fine carvings, including the *Stations of the Cross* in Westminster Cathedral.

LEWIS, Wyndham, 1884-1957: Controversial English painter and writer, founder of the so-called "Vorticist" school.

INNES, James Dickson, 1887-1914: Welsh landscape painter, influenced by Augustus John, who was known for his powerful design sense and strong colours.

NASH, Paul, 1889-1946: Designer, book illustrator, and Official War Artist in both World Wars. He was rather influenced by the Surrealists, and exhibited in their Paris show in 1938.

SPENCER, Sir Stanley, 1891-1959: A painter whose work was much influenced by personal religious conviction, and by his experience of the First World War; he has been compared, in the character of his work, to Blake.

NICHOLSON, Ben, O.M., b. 1894: The best known British abstract painter, first winner of the Guggenheim Award. Most of his paintings and reliefs are geometrically inspired.

MOORE, Henry, b. 1898: Most eminent British sculptor living; known for his pierced forms, and for the fierce controversy aroused by some of his work.

HEPWORTH, Barbara, b. 1903: Abstract sculptor, principally a direct carver in wood and stone rather than using modelled forms. Known for her pierced and hollowed sculptures.

SUTHERLAND, Graham, O.M., b. 1903: One of the best known of living British painters, he was originally an etcher and engraver. Most of his work centres on the mood of landscape, but he has also produced religious work and portraits; notable are the huge tapestry for Coventry Cathedral, and two crucifixions.

PASMORE, Victor, b. 1908: Originally renowned for his interiors and landscapes, of great tonal subtlety, Pasmore turned to abstraction in the late 1940s and since then has worked on constructs of various materials.

BACON, Francis, b. 1909: Self-taught painter noted for his highly individual choice of subjects and his disturbing, violent effects.

BUTLER, Reg, b. 1913: Leading British sculptor, who usually works in metal; he has been both an architect and a blacksmith in the past. Best known for his award-winning *The Unknown Political Prisoner*.

CHADWICK, Lynn, b. 1914: British abstract sculptor, at one time known mainly for mobiles. Winner of a prize at the 1956 Venice Biennale.

ARMITAGE, Kenneth, b. 1916: Sculptor currently working in modelled plaster for casting in bronze; characteristic of his style are careful movement effects in thin figures. British representative at the 1958 Venice Biennale.

CARO, Anthony, b. 1924: English sculptor, one time assistant of Moore, now working in abstract metal forms.

MUSIC, OPERA AND BALLET

London, with five full-time symphony orchestras, two opera companies, several ballet companies, and a vast range of other musical activities, could be considered the musical Mecca of Europe, if not of the world.

The *London Philharmonic Orchestra* was formed by Sir Thomas Beecham in 1932 and was run by him until 1946. Since that year there have been various conductors such as van Beinum, Sir Adrian Boult, Steinburg, Pritchard, and currently Bernard Haitink. The London Philharmonic now play each summer at the Glyndebourne Opera.

The *Royal Philharmonic Orchestra* was also formed by Sir Thomas Beecham, and run by him from its inception in 1946 until his death in 1962. Lady Beecham took on the task for two years, after which period the orchestra became a self-governing body with Rudolf Kempe as its conductor for life.

The *New Philharmonia Orchestra* was formed shortly after the Second World War by Walter Legge, the head of E.M.I.; it was originally called simply the Philharmonia, and worked only on recordings. In 1964 the orchestra was disbanded by Legge, but the members re-formed themselves as a self-governing body with Otto Klemperer as artistic director and chief conductor.

The *London Symphony Orchestra* was founded in 1904 from members of the Queen's Hall Orchestra by Henry Wood, and has always been a self-governing body. The first conductor was Hans Richter, and the list of principal

Sir Malcolm Sargent

music, but promote much modern and avant-garde music; the conductor of the BBC Symphony Orchestra is Pierre Boulez, one of the great modern composers of today.

It is naturally unusual for all five of these major orchestras to be playing in London at the same time. A normal picture would include one orchestra at the Royal Festival Hall, one in the recording studios, one touring abroad and two touring the provinces. All the orchestras do frequent tours at home and abroad.

The best known of the orchestras based outside the capital is the *Hallé Orchestra*, the magnificent Manchester-based orchestra created by the late Sir John Barbarolli, which tours the North. Another active group in the northern provinces is the *City of Birmingham Orchestra*. The *Northern Sinfonia*, a chamber orchestra, has also gained an international reputation. Two groups active in the South and South-West are the *Bournemouth Symphony Orchestra* and the *Sinfonietta*.

OPERA AND BALLET

There are two opera houses in London; the Royal Opera House, Covent Garden, and Sadler's Wells at the Coliseum. At the former the operas are sung in the language of composition, at Sadler's Wells in English. Covent Garden is one of the leading opera houses of the world and has had many famous musical directors, including Kubelik and Sir Georg Solti. The current musical director is Colin Davis. In conjunction with the opera there is the Royal Ballet company, featuring principal dancers such as Margo Fonteyn and Rudolf Nureyev. The Royal Ballet has a regular London season, tours abroad, and performs in the provinces for twelve weeks each year. There is also a smaller group of some twenty-five dancers which performs in the provinces and abroad.

The Sadler's Wells Company used to be run as part of the Old Vic and Sadler's Wells Ballet, but is now purely an opera company. For ten weeks of the year the company divides into two parts and tours the country; recent touring productions include works such as Wagner's "*Götterdämmerung*".

The Glyndebourne opera company tours the provinces for some three months of the year, and every summer assembles an international cast for an opera season at its Sussex home. Other companies include *Scottish Opera* and the *Welsh National Opera*, the *English Opera Group* and the *New Opera Company*. Apart from the ballet companies mentioned above, there are the *Festival Ballet*, which spends about three months of the year in London and the remainder "on the road"; the *Ballet Rambert*, the country's oldest company, which specialises in modern and experimental works; and, further afield, the *Northern Dance Theatre* and the *Scottish Ballet*. The former Sadler's Wells premises provide a London stage for visiting foreign opera and dance

conductors since then has included such names as Elgar, Harty, Krips, Monteux, and currently André Previn.

Concerts are given regularly in the South Bank complex, which comprises three concert halls in one: the Royal Festival Hall, for large orchestras; the Queen Elizabeth Hall, for smaller groups; and the Purcell Room, for soloists. The Wigmore Hall is another London venue, where hopeful young virtuosi come to make their artistic debuts. The world famous Royal Albert Hall is the scene of a wide range of musical events throughout the year, and concerts are also given at St. Paul's Cathedral, at Westminster Abbey and St. John's, Smith Square, at the Victoria and Albert Museum, and at many other churches and halls all over London.

The British Broadcasting Corporation plays a very active part in the British music scene. Apart from broadcast programmes of serious music, which go out almost continuously, the BBC runs a symphony orchestra, a light orchestra, and several other groups, notably including regional orchestras based in Manchester, Bristol, Cardiff and Glasgow, which perform publicly as well as broadcasting. The *BBC Symphony Orchestra* bears the brunt of the annual Sir Henry Wood Promenade Concerts, a memorial festival which is staged in the Royal Albert Hall for some six weeks each summer, with concerts each night. Orchestras from all over the country and the world come to play in the series. The "Last Night of the Proms" has become an institution, with a high-spirited audience playing a noisy part in a traditional programme of pieces. The name of the late Sir Malcolm Sargent is firmly linked to this occasion by public sentiment.

The BBC do not confine their activities to classical

companies, and other theatres left vacant by touring often see short seasons by the best of the world's companies.

CHOIRS

There is a great choral tradition in England which has been maintained since the time of the Tudor monarchs, when much of the greatest church music was written. The cathedrals all have fine choirs, and several run choir schools in order to ensure a ready supply of talent; lack of funds has unfortunately caused the closure of some of these. University colleges, such as New College and Magdalen at Oxford, and King's and St. John's at Cambridge, also run choir schools; these choirs, consisting of choral scholars and boy choristers attain remarkably high standards, and may be heard on many gramophone recordings. Outside the church there are many amateur societies, three of the best known being the *Royal Choral Society*, the *London Bach Choir*, and the *Huddersfield Choral Society*. Their annual performances of such works as Handel's "*Messiah*", Walton's "*Balshazzar's Feast*" and Mendelssohn's "*Elijah*" are great favourites with choir and public alike. The symphony orchestras have their own choirs, the best known being the *New Philharmonia Chorus*, which is trained by Hagen-Groll, the Beyreuth choir master.

MUSICAL EDUCATION

In schools many children learn to play musical instruments and have opportunities to play in youth orchestras. Each county runs an orchestra, some of which reach very high standards, and trips abroad are frequent. The best-known is the *National Youth Orchestra*, which auditions more than 2,000 candidates every year. Founded by Ruth Railton and now run by Ivy Dixon, the NYO has toured in Russia, Poland, Israel and all over Europe.

Professional training is given at colleges of music. Grant-aided colleges include the Royal Academy of Music and the Royal College of Music in London, and the Royal Scottish Academy of Music and Drama in Glasgow. Nearly 160,000 candidates annually take the examinations of the Associated Board of the Royal Schools of Music. Other leading colleges include the Trinity College of Music and the Guildhall School of Music and Drama, in London; and the Royal Manchester College of Music and the Birmingham School of Music. All these offer a three- to four-year course under Britain's finest instrumentalists and teachers. On graduating the young professional must simply persevere with auditions in the hope of a job. A really outstanding player may secure a place in a London orchestra immediately, but most try to start their careers in the provinces.

COMPOSERS, CONDUCTORS AND INSTRUMENTALISTS

Among the many people of international reputation currently active in British music the following are generally conceded to be the most prominent:

Benjamin Britten, O.M., C.H. Born 1913. He is probably England's best known composer. Among his important works are the operas "*Peter Grimes*", "*Billy Budd*", "*Turn of the Screw*" and "*Owen Wyngrave*"; his "*Young Person's Guide to the Orchestra*"; the "*War Requiem*"; the "*Serenade for Tenor, Horn and Strings*" written for Peter Pears and Dennis Brain; various concertos for piano, violin and cello, and many songs and pieces of chamber music. He runs the annual music festival at Aldeburgh.

Sir William (Turner) Walton, O.M. Born 1902. He has written two symphonies, a number of concertos, an oratorio "*Balshazzar's Feast*", and operas including "*Troilus and Cressida*" and "*The Bear*". To the public at large his best known work is probably "*Facade*", an entertainment in words and music, and his several memorable film scores, notably the music for the Laurence Olivier film productions of Shakespeare's "*Henry V*" and "*Richard III*". He has twice composed music in honour of the coronations of British monarchs: "*Crown Imperial*" (in 1937), and "*Orb and Sceptre*" in 1953.

Sir Michael (Kemp) Tippett, C.B.E. Born 1905. He has written three symphonies, a concerto, operas ("*King Priam*", "*Midsummer Marriage*" and "*The Knot Garden*"), choral works including "*A Child of Our Time*", and his latest work "*The Vision of St. Augustine*".

Other British composers include Malcolm Arnold, a prolific producer of symphonies, film scores and other types of work; and the more avant-garde school such as Alexander Goehr, Birtwhistle and Maxwell-Davis. The latter runs a group called "The Fires of London" which specialises in playing avant-garde music. Also active in this field is David Atherton of the *London Sinfonietta*.

Sir Adrian (Cedric) Boult, C.H. Born 1889. Sir Adrian is one of Britain's best known veteran conductors; he was one of the original conductors of the BBC Symphony Orchestra, and was also principal conductor of the London Philharmonic for many years. He has done much to champion the cause of English music, especially that of Elgar and Vaughan-Williams.

Other well-known British conductors are Charles Groves, musical director of the Royal Liverpool Philharmonic Orchestra; Colin Davis, musical director of the Royal Opera House; Charles Mackerras, musical director of the Sadler's Wells Opera; John Pritchard, late of the London Philharmonic Orchestra; Norman

Del Mar, who is well known for his writings about music as well as for his conducting; Meredith Davies; James Loughran of the Hallé; and Neville Marriner of the "Academy of St. Martin in the Fields".

Prominent instrumentalists include Yehudi Menhuin, world famous virtuoso violinist; Clifford Curzen, the internationally acclaimed pianist; the clarinetist Jack Brymer, the horn player Barry Tuckwell, and the trumpet player John Wilbraham. Both Julian Bream and John Williams have acquired international reputations as guitarists.

FILM

British creative and technical talents and British actors have acquired an important international reputation over the past fifteen to twenty years. London is an important centre for the making of feature films for the international market, although a large volume of British feature production is supported by United States capital. The two major British enterprises in the fields of production, distribution and exhibition are the Associated British Picture Corporation, owned by Electrical and Musical Industries Ltd. (E.M.I.), and the Rank Organisation. Most feature films are made in association with these major interests by independent producers. There are many small production companies, and the side of the industry producing documentary, short and special subjects is particularly strong in talent.

The National Film Finance Corporation lends money for feature film production. This body is appointed by the Board of Trade, with funds of some £13,000,000; at one time it financed about half the main feature films made in British studios, but its involvement had declined in recent years.

The British Film Institute, founded in 1933, and partly financed by a government grant, promotes the making, distribution and appreciation of films as an art form. It administers the National Film Archive and the National Film Theatre; this latter comprises two cinemas showing films of historical, artistic and technical interest, regardless of age, nationality or commercial considerations. The Institute is currently promoting the development of some forty regional film theatres on the same lines, and may make certain grants towards their costs. The National Film Theatre organises an annual London Film Festival.

Although cinema attendances have dropped steadily over the past twenty-five years, the public interest in, and appetite for new films remains high. In 1946 there were more than 4,700 licensed cinemas in Britain, and annual attendances totalled about 1,635,000,000. In 1969 there were some 1,600 licensed cinemas, and attendance figures had slumped to around 220,000,000; the soaring availability of television receivers is generally conceded to be the main reason. A side-effect has been a far more competitive generation of film makers in Britain, and a new tradition of mature and artistically valid films com-

manding much more respect than the "formula" products of former decades. That the public's level of informed and sophisticated interest remains high is proved by the spreading popularity of specialised film clubs and societies showing work of minority appeal, from British and overseas directors. A more discriminating demand is also indicated by the current trend for exhibitors to convert large local cinemas all over the country into smaller double or triple auditoria showing a choice of several different types of film simultaneously, to smaller individual audiences.

ARCHITECTURE

Though variously described and regarded, British classical architecture is unquestionably an expression of contemporary art-form. The following is a list of twenty-five of the more successful, influential and/or important British architects of the past, with examples of their work or locations thereof. They are arranged chronologically, by date of birth where known:

JONES, Inigo, 1573–1652: Bodrhyddan Hall, Flintshire; Castle Ashby, Northamptonshire; Chilham Castle, Kent; Cobham (Cobham Hall), Kent; Enfield (Forty Hall), Middlesex; Greenwich (Royal Naval College, Queen's House), Greater London; Kirby Hall, Northamptonshire; London (St. Paul's Cathedral; Banqueting House, Whitehall; Queen's Chapel, St. James's; Somerset House); Raynham Hall, Norfolk; Stoke Park pavilions, Northamptonshire; Syon House, Greater London; Wilton House, Wiltshire.

WEBB, John, 1611–1672: Cobham (Cobham Hall), Kent; Greenwich, Greater London (Royal Naval College Library; Pembroke College Chapel); amptonshire; London (Somerset House); Thorpe Hall, Huntingdon; Wilton House, Wiltshire.

WREN, Sir Christopher, 1632–1723: Abingdon, Berkshire (Town Hall); Ampthill, Bedfordshire; Arbury Hall, Warwickshire; Cambridge (Trinity College Library; Pembroke College Chapel; Easton Neston House, Northamptonshire; Fox's Hospital, Wiltshire; Greenwich, Greater London (Royal Naval College); London (St. Paul's Cathedral; Kensington Palace; Marlborough House; Royal Hospital; Monument; Church of St. Clement Danes; Church of St. Mary Abchurch; Church of St. Benet; Church of St. Mary Aldemary; Church of St. Mary at Hill; Church of St. Stephen Walbrook); Oxford (Christ Church College; Trinity College; Sheldonian Theatre); Salisbury, Wiltshire (Theological College); Stockton-on-Tees, Durham (Church of St. Thomas).

BRUCE, Sir William, died 1710: Drumlarig Castle, Dumfriesshire; Edinburgh (Palace of Holyroodhouse); Hopetoun House, West Lothian; Kinross House, Kinross; Thirlstane Castle, Berwickshire.

HAWKSMOOR, Nicholas, 1661-1736: Castle Howard, Yorkshire; Easton Neston House, Northamptonshire; Greenwich, Greater London (Church of St. Alfege; Royal Naval College); London (Christ Church; Church of St. Anne; Church of St. Mary Woolnoth; Westminster Abbey); Ockham, Surrey (Church of All Saints).

VANBRUGH, Sir John, 1664-1726: Audley End, Essex; Woodstock, Oxfordshire (Blenheim Palace Gardens); Castle Howard, Yorkshire; Claremont, Esher, Surrey; Dalkeith Place, Midlothian; Floors Castle, Roxburghshire; Greenwich, Greater London (Vanbrugh Castle; Royal Naval College); Grimsthorpe Castle, Lincolnshire; Iver, Buckinghamshire (Iver Grove); Kimbolton Castle, Huntingdon; Seaton Delaval Hall, Northumberland; York (Debtors' Prison).

GIBBS, James, 1682-1754: Bristol (Church of All Saints); Cambridge (Senate House); Derby Cathedral; Ditchley Park, Oxfordshire; Kirkleatham, Yorkshire (Church of St. Cuthbert); London (Church of St. Clement Danes; Church of St. Martin-in-the-Fields; Church of St. Mary-le-Strand); Oxford (Radcliffe Camera); Shrewsbury, Shropshire (Church of St. Chad).

KENT, William, 1685-1748: Badminton House, Gloucestershire; Holkham Hall, Norfolk; London (Kensington Palace; Chiswick House); Milton Abbey, Dorset; Stowe, Buckinghamshire.

BROWN, Lancelot "Capability", 1716-1783: Castle Ashby, Northamptonshire; Claremont, Esher, Surrey; Dodington House, Gloucestershire; Harewood House, Yorkshire; Longleat House, Wiltshire; Blenheim Palace, Woodstock, Oxfordshire.

CARR, John, 1723-1807: Boynton Hall, Yorkshire; Bradford, Yorkshire (Bolling Hall); Burton Constable, Yorkshire; Cannon Hall, Yorkshire; Harewood House, Yorkshire; Kendal, Westmorland (Abbot Hall Art Gallery); Rotherham, Yorkshire (Municipal Museum and Art Gallery); Thoresby Hall, Nottinghamshire.

CHAMBERS, Sir William, 1723-1796: Ampthill, Bedfordshire (Avenue House); London (Church of St. Mary, Marylebone Road; Somerset House); Milton Abbey, Dorset; Wilton House, Wiltshire.

ADAM, Robert, 1728-1792: Alnwick Castle, Northumberland; Brockhall, Northamptonshire; Burton Constable, Yorkshire; Castle Upton, Antrim; Culzean Castle, Ayrshire; Gunton, Norfolk (Church of St. Andrew); Hopetoun House, West Lothian; Kedleston Hall, Derbyshire; Kimbolton Castle, Huntingdonshire; London (Hyde Park Corner; Kenwood, Iveagh Bequest; Royal Hospital); Milton Abbas, Dorset; Newby Hall,

Yorkshire; Nostell Priory, Yorkshire; Osterley Park House, Greater London; Stowe, Buckinghamshire; Syon House, Greater London.

HOLLAND, Henry, 1745-1806: Ampthill, Bedfordshire (Avenue House); Berrington Hall, Herefordshire; Brighton, Sussex (Royal Pavilion); Claremont, Esher, Surrey; Hale Park, Hampshire; Woburn Abbey, Bedfordshire.

WYATT, James, 1746-1813: Ashridge, Hertfordshire; Belton House, Kesteven, Lincolnshire; Belvoir Castle, Leicestershire; Burton Constable, Yorkshire; Cobham Hall, Kent; Dodington House, Gloucestershire; Goodwood House, Sussex.

NASH, John, 1752-1835: Attingham Hall, Shropshire; Blaise Hamlet, Gloucestershire (Blaise Castle House); Brighton, Sussex (Royal Pavilion); Helmingham, Suffolk; Kentchurch Court, Herefordshire; London (Buckingham Palace; Trafalgar Square; Marble Arch; Royal Mews; Church of All Saints; Church of All Souls); Newport, Isle of Wight (town hall and guildhall).

SOANE, Sir John, 1753-1837: Aynhoe Park, Northamptonshire; Belfast (Academical Institution); Chillington Hall, Staffordshire; Claremont, Esher, Surrey; London (Royal Hospital; Soane Museum; Church of St. John; Church of St. Peter).

BARRY, Sir Charles, 1795-1860: Brighton, Sussex (Church of St. Peter); Cliveden, Buckinghamshire; Halifax, Yorkshire (Town Hall); Harewood House, Yorkshire; Kingston Lacy, Dorset; Leeds, Yorkshire (Town Hall); London (The Houses of Parliament; Lancaster House); Manchester (City Museum); Stand, Lancashire (Church of All Saints).

SALVIN, Anthony, 1799-1881: Alnwick Castle, Northumberland; Capesthorne, Cheshire; Greystoke, Cumberland (Church of St. Andrew); Simonburn, Northumberland (Church of St. Mungo); Thoresby Hall, Nottinghamshire; Worth, Sussex (Church of St. Nicholas).

BURTON, Decimus, 1800-1881: Kew, Greater London (Palm House, Royal Botanic Gardens); London (Hyde Park Corner; Regent's Park).

SCOTT, Sir Gilbert, 1811-1878: Alconbury, Herefordshire (Church of St. John the Baptist); Alford, Lincolnshire (Church of St. Wilfrid); Aylesbury, Buckinghamshire (Church of St. Mary); Bangor Cathedral, Caernarvonshire; Bibury, Gloucestershire (Church of St. Mary); Brecon Cathedral; Bridlington, Yorkshire (Church of St. Mary); Cambridge University Library; Chester Cathedral; Crowland Abbey, Lincolnshire; Easby, Yorkshire (Church of St. Agatha); Eastnor, Herefordshire (Church of St. John the Baptist); Hillesden, Buckinghamshire (Church of All Saints); Huddersfield, Yorkshire (Church of St. Thomas the Apostle); Leicester

(Church of St. Margaret); London (Albert Memorial; St. Pancras Station); Ludlow, Shropshire (Church of St. Laurence); Northampton (Church of the Holy Sepulchre); Oxford Cathedral; Rotherham, Yorkshire (Church of All Saints); Shifnal, Shropshire (Church of St. Andrew); Wakefield Cathedral, Yorkshire; Wirksworth, Derbyshire (Church of St. Mary).

BUTTERFIELD, William, 1814–1900: Amesbury, Wiltshire (Church of SS Mary and Melor); Baldersby, Yorkshire (Church of St. James); Berkhamsted, Hertfordshire (Church of St. Peter); Canterbury, Kent (St. Augustine's Abbey); Clyffe Pypard, Wiltshire (Church of St. Peter); Huddersfield, Yorkshire (Church of St. Thomas the Apostle); London (Church of All Saints; Church of St. Mary Woolnorth); Salisbury, Wiltshire (Theological College); Trumpington, Cambridgeshire (Church of SS Mary and Michael).

PEARSON, J. L., 1817–1897: Burley-on-the-Hill, Rutland (Church of the Holy Sepulchre); Crowland Abbey, Lincolnshire; Cullercoats, Northumberland (Church of St. George); Iwerne Minster, Dorset (Church of St. Mary); London (Church of St. Augustine); Maidstone, Kent (Church of All Saints); Shrewsbury, Shropshire (Abbey Church of the Holy Cross); Wentworth, Yorkshire (Church of the Holy Trinity); Truro Cathedral, Cornwall.

STREET, George Edmund, 1824–1881: Bloxham, Oxfordshire (Church of Our Lady); Britford, Wiltshire (Church of St. Peta); Corsham, Wiltshire (Church of St. Bartholomew); Cottesbrooke, Northamptonshire (Church of All Saints); Elford, Staffordshire (Church of St. Peter); Kempsford, Gloucestershire (Church of St. Mary the Virgin); Kingston, Dorset (Church of St. James); Leicester (Cathedral; Church of St. Margaret); Manchester (Town Hall); South Mimms, Hertfordshire (Church of St. Giles); Stewkley, Buckinghamshire (Church of St. Michael and All Angels); Thirsk, Yorkshire (Church of St. Mary); Thornhill, Yorkshire (Church of St. Michael and All Angels); Toddington, Gloucestershire (Church of St. Andrew); Warfield, Berkshire (Church of St. Michael); Weaverthorpe, Yorkshire (Church of St. Andrew).

BODLEY, G. F., 1827–1907: Brant Broughton, Lincolnshire (Church of St. Helen); Cuckfield, Sussex (Church of the Holy Trinity); Leicester Cathedral; London (Church of St. John); North Stoneham, Hampshire (Church of St. Nicholas); Scarborough, Yorkshire (Church of St. Martin); Weston-super-Mare, Somerset (Church of All Saints); Whitkirk, Yorkshire (Church of St. Mary).

LUTYENS, Sir Edwin, 1869–1944: Ashwell, Hertfordshire; Breckles Hall, Norfolk; Lindisfarne Castle, Holy Island, Northumberland; London (The Cenotaph).

CHAPTER 7

☙ Sport ❧

Although the Government is not directly concerned with the promotion of sport in Britain, it is provided with the means to encourage the pursuit of sport through a Minister who has a special responsibility in this area. The Sports Council, composed of voluntary members appointed for their wide experience in sport and recreation, advises the Government on matters relating to the development of amateur sport and physical recreation. In 1969–70 direct government expenditure on sport in Great Britain amounted to £2·54 million; this covered sporting facilities, coaching and participation in international events. Grants totalling a further £540,000 were made in the same period in Northern Ireland.

SPORTING FACILITIES

The Government ministers responsible for Education in the United Kingdom require that all publicly-maintained schools shall be equipped to provide physical education of their pupils, and schools in the national systems must have the use of a playing field; and the increase in school sports amenities is a constant process. Local authorities are also providing a fast improving range of facilities, including playing fields, gymnasia, tennis courts, golf courses, boating lakes, swimming baths and athletics centres. Similarly many of the larger industrial and commercial undertakings provide substantial sports facilities for their employees.

One of the leading organisations concerned with the promotion of increased sporting facilities is the National Playing Fields Association which, since its inception in 1925, has distributed about £1·9 million in the form of grants for playing fields and facilities.

There are six National Sports Centres in Britain, of which that at Crystal Palace in London, covering 36 acres, is the most important. A National Sailing Centre is situated at Cowes, Isle of Wight, while a national rowing and canoeing regatta centre is being built at Holme Pierrepont in Nottinghamshire. There are also national mountaineering centres in Wales and Scotland.

OUTDOOR SPORTS PLAYED IN BRITAIN

Association Football
This form of football, in which only the feet are used, was adopted formally at Cambridge in 1848. The controlling body of this game is the Football Association, formed in 1863. Over 360 clubs are registered with the FA. The principal professional matches in England and Wales are controlled by the Football League which comprises 92 professional clubs, and in Scotland by the Scottish Football League with 37 clubs. Northern Ireland also has its own League.

The annual competition for the FA Cup is organised on a knock-out basis, the Cup Final always being played at Wembley Stadium near London. The Scottish Cup Final is played at Hampden Park, Glasgow.

Athletics

Governed by the Amateur Athletic Association, founded in 1880, athletics (which include road, track and cross-country running, relay racing, jumping, hurdling, throwing and race-walking) have commanded a wide interest and participation in Britain, with national championships for men and women, frequent international matches, area and county championships, and matches between the universities, Services, business houses and schools.

Scotland and Northern Ireland have their own amateur athletic associations, while selection of teams representing the United Kingdom is dealt with by the British Amateur Athletic Board.

Teams representing Britain compete in the Olympic Games, and separate teams represent England, Scotland, Wales and Northern Ireland in the Commonwealth Games, held at four-yearly intervals between the Olympic Games.

Bowls

The game of bowls has been played in Britain since the thirteenth century, and is today regulated by the International Bowling Board (founded in 1905), and in England by the English Bowling Association, to which 2,620 clubs are affiliated. International, inter-county and national championship competitions are played.

Boxing

Boxing probably originated in England in Saxon times; its modern form – now adopted in many countries overseas – dates from 1865 when the Marquess of Queensberry drew up rules to eliminate much of the brutality that had characterised prize fighting.

Amateur boxing is governed by the Amateur Boxing Association and is pursued in many boys' schools, boys' clubs, universities and the three Services. Professional boxing is regulated by the British Boxing Board of Control, founded in 1929, with strict enforcement of medical examinations before, and control of contests to guard against over-matching and exploitation.

Since the presentation of Championship Challenge Belts by the late Lord Lonsdale in 1909, championships are organised by the ABA in ten weights – flyweight, bantamweight, featherweight, lightweight, light welterweight, welterweight, light middleweight, middleweight, light heavyweight and heavyweight. Light welterweight and light middleweight categories are absent in professional boxing.

Cricket

Often referred to as England's national game, cricket is known to have been played at Guildford Grammar School in 1550. The Marylebone Cricket Club (founded in 1787) became the governing body, its headquarters being in turn at Dorset Square, Regent's Park and St. John's Wood, all three grounds being named after the Yorkshireman, Thomas Lord. The game is now governed in Britain by the Cricket Council, although the MCC retains worldwide responsibility for the laws of the game.

While most towns and villages support teams, each of which usually play at least one game a week between late April and September, the main national interest in the game is focussed on the First Class County Championship between 17 counties, and a single-innings knock-out competition for the Gilette Cricket Cup, instituted in 1963. It was also in 1963 that the distinction between professional and amateur players was abolished.

The principal international competition lies in the "Test" series played in Britain during the summer months against a touring Commonwealth team. These Tests are played at Lords, the Kennington Oval, Old Trafford (Manchester), Trent Bridge (Nottingham), Headingley (Leeds), and Edgbaston (Birmingham).

Croquet

Originating in Britain about one hundred years ago, croquet is played by people of all ages. About 70 clubs are registered with the Croquet Association which was formed in 1896 to develop the game in Britain and maintain ties with similar associations overseas.

Cycling

Cycle racing in the United Kingdom is governed by the British Cycling Federation, an internationally recognised body to which 736 cycling clubs are affiliated. Cycle touring is catered for by the British Cycling Federation and the Cyclists' Touring Club – the latter, with a membership of about 20,000, is the world's oldest touring club.

Fencing

The Amateur Fencing Association was founded in 1902 and today ministers to about 700 clubs in Great Britain. Considerable strides have been made in this country since the last War and, frequently financed by local authorities, fencing is now practised in many schools, with National Championships for boys and girls.

Fishing

Of the three main country sports in Britain, fishing commands by far the largest number of adherents, some 450,000 being members of the National Federation of Anglers. Trout streams abound in most parts of the country and provide good sport, but the best salmon fishing is enjoyed in Scotland. Most fishing in England and Wales is for coarse fish such as bream, carp, chub, dace, perch, pike, roach and tench. An annual national angling championship is organised by the NFA which also enters a team in the International Angling Competition.

Coastal fishing has also recently gained popularity while deep-sea sport fishing for tuna and shark has also attracted many adherents.

Game Shooting

Organised game shooting in Britain dates from the early eighteen-hundreds, and today is largely confined to grouse, partridge, pheasant, snipe and woodcock. There is scarcely any free shooting in Britain and strict laws exist to license game killing and control the use of firearms. Most game birds are "preserved" by the legal enforcement of "close seasons".

Deer stalking is mainly confined to the Scottish Highlands, where deer are similarly safeguarded in the privately-owned forests during close seasons.

Golf

Golf originated in Scotland where, for many centuries, it has carried the title of the Royal and Ancient Game. The headquarters of the Royal and Ancient Golf Club is St. Andrews, Scotland.

The main events of the golfing year are the British Open Golf Championships (first played in 1860), the Walker Cup (for amateurs), the Ryder Cup (for professionals), the Amateur Championship, the World Amateur Team Championship and the Ladies' Championship.

Highland Games

The Highland Games are traditional gatherings in the Scottish Highlands at which sports, dancing and piping competitions are held. Famous among these unique spectacles, which attract crowds from all over the world, are the Braemar Gathering on Deeside (traditionally attended by the Royal Family) and the Argyllshire Gathering at Oban.

Hockey

Modern hockey dates from 1886, the year of formation of the Hockey Association of England. Today there are some 2,000 men's hockey clubs with at least 30,000 adult male players. The All England Women's Hockey Association (founded in 1895), to which are affiliated about 900 clubs and 2,200 schools, represents about 72,000 adults and 1·1 million schoolgirls.

Variations of hockey are still played extensively in Scotland (shinty) and Ireland (hurley).

Horse Racing

Horse racing in England dates from before Tudor times. The Jockey Club (founded in about 1750 to control flat racing) and the National Hunt Committee (founded in 1866 to control steeplechasing) amalgamated as the Jockey Club in 1968 to exercise control over all horse racing in England – and indirectly in numerous other countries – and two years later was granted a Royal Charter.

Classic flat races include the Newmarket Two Thousand Guineas for colts and fillies, and One Thousand Guineas for fillies only; the Epsom Derby for colts and fillies, and Oaks for fillies only; and the Doncaster St. Leger for colts and fillies. Most fashionable meeting of the season is Royal Ascot in mid-June, traditionally attended by the Sovereign.

The Cheltenham National Hunt Festival Meeting, held in March, is the most important steeplechase meeting, and the foremost single steeplechase race is the Aintree Grand National which has been run annually since 1839.

There are 58 race courses in England and Wales (excluding point-to-point courses), and some 11,000 race-horses are under training – at an average weekly cost of over £20 each – in Great Britain.

Lacrosse

Adapted from the game played by the Iroquois Indians of North America, lacrosse is now mainly played by women – in schools, universities and in lacrosse clubs – under the auspices of the All England Women's Lacrosse Association.

The man's game is played at ten universities and a number of colleges and clubs mainly in the London, Leeds, Manchester, Nottingham and Sheffield areas.

Lawn Tennis

The forerunner of present day lawn tennis was introduced into England from France in the fifteenth century, and Henry VIII's "tennis court" is still in use at Hampton Court. The British controlling body, the Lawn Tennis Association, was founded in 1888. The main event of the season in Britain – indeed in the world – is the Wimbledon Championships at the All England Club.

Other important tournaments are the British Hardcourt Championships, the British Junior Championships and the County Championships. The Davis Cup is the most important international contest (for men), as well as the Federation Cup (for women).

Motor Racing

More racing and sports racing cars have been built in Britain than any other country in the world, and motoring competition is one of the most popular spectator sports in the country, while British men and women drivers enjoy an unsurpassed reputation throughout the world. Apart from the classic international races, the Grand Prix and the Tourist Trophy, there are countless other races, rallies, trials, hill climbs and endurance tests arranged by various clubs, of which there are more than 1,100 in Great Britain.

The principal motor racing circuits are those at Brands Hatch, Kent; Silverstone, Northamptonshire; Crystal Palace, London (closing at the end of 1972); Snetterton, Norfolk; Mallory Park, Leicestershire; Oulton Park, Cheshire; and Thruxton, Hampshire.

The controlling body in Britain, founded in 1897, is the Royal Automobile Club.

Mountaineering

Mountaineering has fast grown in popularity in recent years. Clubs affiliated to the British Mountaineering Council and the Mountaineering Council for Scotland number over 190 and range from the Alpine Club (the oldest mountaineering club in the world, founded in 1857) to small regional clubs with a few dozen members.

Mountaineering centres and courses have been established by such bodies as the Central Council for Physical Recreation, the Outward Bound Trust, Youth Hostels Association and local education authorities.

British climbers have taken a leading part in conquering most of the world's great ranges and peaks, including the Matterhorn in 1865, Everest in 1953 and Kangchenjunga in 1955.

Netball
Controlled by the All England Netball Association, netball is popular among girls and women. There are county and Service teams; home international matches are regularly played and periodic Commonwealth tours arranged.

Polo
Polo was first played by the British in India and was introduced into England in 1869. Owing to the high cost of maintaining polo ponies, polo players represent a tiny section of the community, about 470 players being handicapped by the Hurlingham Polo Association, the governing body of British polo, although many other less expert players are locally handicapped.

Riding and Show Jumping
The British Horse Society, as the National Equestrian Federation of Great Britain, is the authority on all matters relating to horses and ponies, and is responsible for preparing teams for all international events, including the Olympic Games. Membership is about 17,000 (with 100,000 affiliated members). It is also the parent body of the Pony Club (open to young people up to the age of 21) which has 288 branches in Britain.

The outstanding equestrian events of the year include the three-day trials at Badminton, Gloucestershire in April, at Tidworth, Hampshire in May, and at Burghley House, Lincolnshire in September.

Rifle Shooting
The Joint Shooting Committee for Great Britain was founded in 1955 to represent its member associations, the National Rifle Association, the National Small-Bore Rifle Association and the Clay Pigeon Shooting Association, in the International Shooting Union and the British Olympic Association.

The National Rifle Association, founded in 1860, organises the annual Imperial Meeting at Bisley Camp in Surrey, the premier award of which is the Queen's Prize; this competition attracts some 1,000 entries.

Small-bore rifle and pistol shooting is practised by about 4,000 clubs affiliated to the National Small-Bore Rifle Association, which also organises a National Bisley Meeting.

Rowing
Rowing is taught in many schools, universities and rowing clubs throughout Britain. The Amateur Rowing Association governs the sport in England and Wales, and the Scottish Amateur Rowing Association in Scotland.

While many riverside resorts throughout the country arrange summer regattas, the most famous rowing events are the Henley Regatta, founded in 1839 and rowed in July; the Oxford and Cambridge Boat Race which originated in 1820 and which is rowed in the early spring on the Thames between Putney and Mortlake; and the Head of the River Race from Mortlake to Putney in March.

Rugby League
This 13-a-side professional version of rugby is governed by the Rugby Football League (instituted in 1895 with headquarters at Leeds), and is mostly played in the north of England. Touring teams frequently visit Australia and New Zealand, and the season's major match, the Rugby League Challenge Cup Final, often attracts crowds of 100,000 to London's Wembley Stadium.

Motor Racing, a sport in which British cars and drivers have dominated the world events for more than a dozen years. Shown here is a Lotus-Ford 72, winner of the 1972 Brands Hatch Race of Champions

Rugby Union

Governed by the Rugby Football Union, established in 1871, rugby football was first played at Rugby School during the first half of the nineteenth century, having been lifted out of the medieval "mob football" by the Rev. William Webb Ellis (c. 1807–1872). Headquarters of the R.F.U. is at Twickenham, near London, and membership – scrupulously confined to amateur clubs – amounts to over 1,600 clubs, with about 1,000 schools.

Important annual matches are the county championship competitions, the matches between Oxford and Cambridge universities, the Hospitals' Cup Final and the Inter-Services tournament. There are also the international matches between England, Scotland, Wales, Ireland and France, as well as frequent tours to South Africa, Australia and New Zealand.

Sailing

There are few sports in Britain whose popularity has increased in recent years as much as sailing – although it has always been a popular leisure time activity on inland and coastal waters. The Royal Yachting Association governs both sail and power yachting and has over 1,550 clubs and 32,000 individual members; it also administers sailing schools and a National Sailing Centre, as well as selecting Britain's Olympic team.

Major sailing events are held at such sailing centres as Burnham on Crouch, Falmouth, Harwich, Lowestoft, Poole and Plymouth, but undoubtedly the premier event, which carries substantial world prestige, is the Cowes regatta – known as Cowes Week, sailed annually during the first week in August.

Ski-ing

With the comparatively recent development of winter sports centres in the Cairngorms, Deeside, Glencoe and Glenshee, where ski-runs and instruction courses exist equal to those elsewhere in Europe, ski-ing in Scotland has become very popular, while 24 artificial ski-slopes have been developed elsewhere in Britain.

Swimming

As shown in Chapter Four, swimming commands the greatest following as a leisure sport in Britain. Most children in the country are taught to swim at school, and the provision in most towns of public indoor swimming baths renders all-year swimming possible. The sporting body which governs the formal rules of swimming competition is the Amateur Swimming Association, which also certificates coaching instructors. The ASA maintains the rules governing amateur swimming, diving and water polo championships and competition in England.

Wrestling

One of the oldest sports in the world, wrestling in Britain is principally confined to the "all-in" or free style, evolved from the Catch-as-Catch-Can or Lancashire style, although Cumberland, Westmorland and Cornish styles persist locally. Amateur wrestling in Britain is governed by the British Amateur Wrestling Association.

SOME GREAT BRITISH SPORTSMEN AND SPORTSWOMEN

ABRAHAMS, Harold, C.B.E. (*Athlete*). Born 15th December 1899 at Bedford. Not only has Harold Abrahams distinguished himself as an athlete, but also as a broadcaster, administrator and statistician. He was the first European and only Briton to win the Olympic 100-metres title, which he did in 1924 in 10·52 seconds; a month before this he had long-jumped 24 feet 2½ inches, establishing an English native record which stood for 32 years. His active career was cut short in 1925 when he broke his leg long-jumping.

ARCHER, Fred. (*Jockey*). Born at Cheltenham, 1857–1886. To many, Fred Archer was the greatest jockey of all time; certainly his record was not matched in the nineteenth century. Tall for a jockey at 5 feet 10 inches, Fred Archer rode his first winner in 1870 and won the 1872 Cesarewitch. During the remaining sixteen years of his life he was Leading Jockey for thirteen of them, 1874–1886 inclusive. He won the Derby five times, the St. Leger six times, the Oaks four times, the Two Thousand Guineas four times, and the One Thousand Guineas twice. He rode in 8,084 races and won 2,471 of them – a record only beaten during Gordon Richards' much longer career. Fred Archer contracted typhoid in 1886 and in a moment of terrible depression (for he had recently lost his wife) shot himself.

BAILEY, Trevor. (*Cricketer*). One particular innings in the 1953 Test series against the Australians, when he and Willie Watson batted for over a day to stave off defeat, earned Bailey the nickname "Barnacle". His main asset as a batsman was patience and unwavering concentration, and he was never a prolific run-scorer. His worth to the England team was as an all-rounder and he was only the second Englishman both to score 2,000 runs and take 100 wickets in Test Cricket. He was also a footballer, winning an F.A. Amateur Cup winners' medal with Walthamstow Avenue.

BALL, Alan. (*Footballer*). Now with his third club, Arsenal, Ball has also played for Blackpool and Everton, with whom he won a League Championship medal in 1970. It was while he was with Blackpool that Ball played in the England side of 1966. His skill and non-stop running during the 120-minute final of the World Cup "destroyed" Karl-Heinz Schnellinger, one of the world's top defenders, and was one of the main reasons for England's famous victory. Six years later, Ball is still a regular in the England team.

BANKS, Gordon. (*Footballer*). Described by many of the world's experts as the best goalkeeper in the world, Gordon Banks has played consistently as the last line of England's defence since 1965. During the 1966 World Cup tournament in Britain, Banks allowed only three goals to be scored against him in 9½ hours of football. He has played for three clubs, Chesterfield, Leicester and Stoke, with whom he won his first domestic honour, a League Cup winners' medal in March 1972.

BANNISTER, Roger. (*Athlete*). Born 23rd March 1929 at Harrow. Though he never achieved an Olympic medal, Roger Bannister must rank as one of the world's great athletes, running as he did on 6th May 1954 at Iffley Road, Oxford, the world's first "four-minute mile" – in 3 minutes 59·4 seconds. Ever since 1949, when he achieved a time of 4 minutes 11·1 seconds, he had shown all the signs of world athletic status, and two years later improved his time to 4 minutes 7·8 seconds. Unfortunately at the 1952 Olympics the inclusion of semi-finals in the 1500-metres proved too much for record-breaking stamina and Bannister finished fourth.

BEST, George. (*Footballer*). Potentially one of the greatest footballers the world has ever seen, Belfast-born Best is also something of an enigma. Probably the first British footballer with the charisma and wealth to become a "superstar", George Best's football career with Manchester United and Northern Ireland has undoubtedly suffered from his off-field interests. Publicity surrounds everything he does – sporting, social and business – to his own obviously increasing distress and the detriment of his play. He has won League Championship medals with United and was also a member of the only English team to become European champions since the inception of the championship when the Manchester team won in 1968.

BIRKIN, Sir Henry, Bt. (*Motor racing driver*). One of the famous "Bentley Boys", Captain "Tim" Birkin twice won the classic Le Mans 24-hour race, in 1929 in a Bentley with Woolf Barnato, and with Earl Howe in an Alfa Romeo in 1931. His greatest race was the 1930 French Grand Prix in which, against pure racing cars, he won second place in his supercharged 4½-litre Bentley sports car.

BOYCOTT, Geoff. (*Cricketer*). Now a wearer of contact lenses, Boycott was one of the few bespectacled batsmen to make himself a reputation as a world-class opener. In the summer of 1971 he became the first Englishman ever to record an average of over 100 runs in an English season. The captain of Yorkshire, Boycott is an automatic choice for England. He has scored 1,000 runs on each of tours to South Africa, Australia and the West Indies.

BLACK, Ian M. (*Swimmer*). Born 27th June 1941. Ian

Black's prime swimming career was short, from 1958 to 1960. At one time holder of nine of Britain's 18 swimming records, he swam to fame at the age of 17 in 1958 when he won three Gold medals at Budapest, taking the 400-metres free-style, the 200-metres butterfly and the 1500-metres. At the 1958 Empire Games at Cardiff he won the 220-yards butterfly Gold medal, and Silver medals in the 440-yards free-style and 4 × 220-yards relay. By the end of his career he had also held 18 Scottish titles.

BLANCHFLOWER, Danny. (*Footballer*). The first team to win the Football League Championship and the F.A. Cup in one season this century was Tottenham Hotspur, who achieved this remarkable double in 1960–61. Captain and master strategist in this side was Danny Blanchflower, an intelligent and voluble Irishman who also led the Northern Ireland team to its best-ever performance in the 1958 World Cup in Sweden. Asked for the secret of Irish success, he replied that it was simply a matter of "equalising before the other team scores". His other League clubs were Aston Villa and Barnsley. He is now a successful and respected sports journalist.

BONALLACK, Michael Francis, O.B.E. (*Golfer*). Born 31st December 1934 at Chigwell. Certainly Britain's leading amateur golfer, Michael Bonallack captained the British Walker Cup team to victory in 1971 – for the first time in 33 years – and was awarded his O.B.E. for his services to British golf. His huge number of personal triumphs include the Amateur Championship four times, the English Amateur Championship five times, English Stroke-Play Championship four times (and runner-up three times), and Leading Amateur Open Championship twice. He has played for England in home internationals every year since 1957, and with the British Walker Cup Team each year of the competition over the same period, and as captain in 1969 and 1971.

BRASHER, Chris. (*Athlete*). Born 21st August 1928 at Georgetown, Guyana. Among Chris Brasher's skills was his mountaineering ability (he was shortlisted for an Everest expedition), but his track achievements as a steeplechaser were supreme. Winning his place in the 1952 British Olympic team at Helsinki – where he failed to win a medal – he went on to become well-known during the next two years as Roger Bannister's pacemaker. He returned to steeplechasing in 1955 and ran in the 1956 Melbourne Olympic final of the 3,000-metres, winning the Gold medal to establish an Olympic and U.K. record of 8 minutes 41·2 seconds.

BURGHLEY, Lord, 6th Marquess of Exeter. (*Athlete*). Born 9th February 1905 at Stamford. Qualifying at the age of 19 as a 110-metre hurdler in the 1924 Olympic team, he won the Olympic Gold medal for 400-metres hurdles in 1928, was triple Gold medalist (120-yards hurdles, 440-yards hurdles, and 4 × 440-yards relay) at the 1930 Commonwealth Games, and Silver medallist in the 1932 Olympic 4 × 400-metre relay. The Marquess was president of the A.A.A. from 1936.

BUSBY, Sir Matt. (Footballer). Under the leadership of Sir Matt, now semi-retired into the general managership of the club, Manchester United have achieved a post-war record of consistent ascendancy that is without parallel in the history of football. They have been at the forefront of domestic competitions, winning the League in 1952, 1956, 1957, 1965 and 1967, and the Cup in 1948 and 1963. They were the first British club to achieve any sort of success in European competition, and in 1968 became the first English club to win the European Cup. By beating Benfica 4–1 at Wembley, the team achieved for Sir Matt the last ambition he professed to have. It was a victory made more poignant by memories of the tragic air crash ten years earlier in which eight United players lost their lives. They were returning from a successful European Cup tie in Belgrade; a player himself with Manchester City and Liverpool, as well as Scotland, Busby survived and recovered from grievous injuries.

CHAMBERS, Mrs. Dorothea Lambert. (Tennis player). Born at Ealing, died 1960. Probably the most successful British woman tennis player of all time, Mrs. Chambers played for Great Britain in the 1926 Wightman Cup twenty-three years after gaining her first Wimbledon singles title in 1903. She was Wimbledon champion seven times, in 1903, 1904, 1906, 1910, 1911, 1913 and 1914.

CHARLTON, Bobby. (Footballer). A creative mid-field player with one of the hardest shots in football, Bobby Charlton was outstanding even amongst the star-studded Manchester United and England teams of the late 'sixties and early 'seventies. He has World Cup, European Cup, League Championship and F.A. Cup medals to his credit, as well as a host of popularity poll votes. A survivor of the Munich air crash that decimated his club in 1958, Charlton would be a safe bet for anyone's "team of the century". He has played for England 106 times – a record as yet unbroken.

CHARLTON, Jack. (Footballer). This year the older of the two footballing Charltons joined his brother Bobby and ex-Liverpool star Roger Hunt in becoming the only three men in the world to have won World Cup, F.A. Cup and League Championship medals. A Leeds United player for the whole of his professional career, Jack Charlton has also suffered his fair share of disappointments

with the team that many call the best club side in the world. On his 37th birthday at the end of last season, Leeds failed by one goal to complete the Cup and League double, having won at Wembley 48 hours earlier.

CHICHESTER, Sir Francis, K.B.E. (Sailor). Born 17th September 1901. There is probably no greater name in sailing today than that of Sir Francis Chichester, whose first-time solo circumnavigation of the world in 1966–67 in Gypsy Moth IV via Capes Good Hope, Leeuwin and Horn (29,600 miles in 226 days), earned him fame and knighthood. Yet his record-breaking feats date back over forty years. He was the second pilot to fly solo from England to Australia (1929); the first to fly solo from New Zealand to Australia across the Tasman Sea, and was the first to fly solo from New Zealand to Japan in 1931. His last long distance solo sailing record was 1,017¾ miles in 5 days, sailing his Gypsy Moth V in 1971, at the age of 70.

CLARK, Jim. (Motor racing driver). 1936–1968. Certainly ranking among the great drivers of all time, Jim Clark – the "wee Scot" from Duns – graduated to GP racing from Porsche, Jaguar, Lister and Lotus sports cars. His first Grand Prix win was the 1961 Pau GP. He was World Champion Driver in 1963 with Grand Prix victories in Belgium, Britain, France, Holland, Italy, Mexico and South Africa with a Lotus Climax. He was World Champion again in 1965, the year he won the Indianapolis 500-Miles – the first time in forty-five years a European had done so. He died in an inexplicable crash in a German Formula 2 race in 1968.

COLLINS, Peter. (Motor racing driver). 1931–1958. Graduating to Grand Prix racing from 500-cc. cars, Peter Collins was also a great sports car driver, winning the Goodwood Nine Hours and 1953 Tourist Trophy. In 1956, driving Ferraris, he won the Belgian and French GPs, the Syracuse and Naples GPs of 1957, and the 1958 British GP. When fighting for the lead in the 1958 German GP at the Nurburgring, his car left the road and the "Gay Cavalier" was killed.

COMPTON, Denis. (Cricketer). Despite the intervention of the War years and the handicap of a bad knee injury in the 'fifties, Denis Compton appeared for England 78 times. His first Test was in 1938, and he scored a total of 5,807 runs for England, with 17 centuries. His best season for Middlesex and England was 1947, an idyllic summer during which Compton scored a record 3,816 runs, including a further record of 18 centuries, six of them against the South African touring team.

COOPER, Henry, O.B.E. (Boxer.) Uniquely popular with the English crowd, Londoner Henry Cooper became the first man to win three Lonsdale Belts. He took the British and Empire Heavyweight titles from Brian London in January 1959, and the European title from Karl Mildenberger. He held his crowns a record ten years five months, and was one of the few men ever to put Cassius Clay on the canvas. He was plagued by easily cut eyes; his Sunday punch was a terrible left, known to fans as "'Enery's 'Ammer".

COTTON, Thomas Henry, M.B.E. (*Golfer*). Born 26th January 1907 at Holmes Chapel, Cheshire. Henry Cotton was undoubtedly the greatest British professional golfer between the World Wars, and was still winning top class championships after the Second. He turned professional at the age of 17 and opened his title-winning career with the Kent Professional Championships every year from 1926 to 1930. He won the Belgian Open in 1930, 1934 and 1938, and the British Open in 1934 (the first British win in eleven years), 1937 and 1948. Other Open wins include the Italian (1936), the German (1937, 1938 and 1939), the Czechoslovak (1937 and 1938) and French (1946 and 1947). He was also the Ryder Cup Team Captain in 1947 and 1953.

COWDREY, Colin. (*Cricketer*). With the initials M.C.C. (his first name is Michael), it seems to have been destiny that brought Cowdrey to first-class cricket. In fact no player in the world has taken part in more Test matches or scored as many runs as Cowdrey. An elegant batsman, Cowdrey has captained Kent for 15 years and led England on 27 occasions.

DAVIES, Lynn. (*Athlete*). Born 20th May 1942 at Nantymoel, Glamorgan. Lynn Davies became the first Welshman ever to win an Olympic field event when, on 18th October 1964 at Tokyo, he defeated Ralph Boston (USA) and Igor Ter-Ovanesyan (USSR) – both previous 27-foot jumpers – by long-jumping 26 feet $5\frac{3}{4}$ inches in soggy, windy conditions. He went on to complete a trio of Gold medals, the Commonwealth title at 26 feet $2\frac{3}{4}$ inches, and European at 26 feet $2\frac{1}{4}$ inches.

DOCHERTY, Tommy. (*Footballer*). Docherty, currently emerging as one of the most successful national managers Scotland has ever had, had a solid hard-tackling reputation as a player with Preston North End, Arsenal, Scotland and, briefly, Chelsea before becoming manager in the early 'sixties. He took the West London club away from their long-time "joke" reputation to a position of prominence in the domestic soccer scene. His mercurial temperament led him away from Chelsea and through a succession of short-term managerships, including one in Portugal, before returning to Scotland in 1971.

DONOGHUE, Stephen. (*Jockey*). Born at Warrington, 1884–1945. Never once during his 33 years as a jockey was Steve Donoghue up before the stewards for an infringement of the rules. He was first and foremost a superb horseman who genuinely loved horses and whose beautiful style may never be matched. Perhaps his most memorable meeting was that of the 1920 Derby when he suffered a brutal fall on very hard ground in the classic race and lay prone in the path of the oncoming field, but picked himself up and walked back to the weighing-in room to ride two more winners that day. Steve Donoghue was Leading Jockey for ten years from 1914 until 1923; he won the Derby three times running in 1921, 1922 and 1923, and again in 1925. He also won the Irish Derby four times, the Grand Prix de Paris twice, and the Queen Alexandra Stakes at Royal Ascot six years running. He won the 1915 and 1917 St. Leger (run during the First World War at Newmarket) and as late as 1937 he rode Exhibitionist to win the Oaks.

DOUGAN, Derek. (*Footballer*). An Ulsterman who has played for Blackburn, Aston Villa, Portsmouth and Peterborough, and is a natural selection in his national side, Derek Dougan in the last few years has settled with Wolverhampton Wanderers and has laid to rest his earlier reputation as a hell-raiser. He is current chairman of the Professional Footballers Association, and it is difficult to associate the softly-spoken regular on TV soccer panels and local radio programmes with the man who once sported a totally-shaven head as a gimmick.

EDRICH, John. (*Cricketer*). One of the steadiest and least flashy of run-getters for England over the past few years, John Edrich started last season needing just 21 centuries to top the hundred in first-class cricket. A member of a famous cricketing family, he is also one of the few English batsmen to score a treble century in an innings in a Test match, with 310 against New Zealand in 1965. He is vice-captain of Surrey.

FARR, Tommy. (*Boxer*). One of three men ever to go the distance with Joe Louis, Welsh-born Tommy Farr enjoyed an unbroken run of eighteen victories which brought him the British Heavyweight crown, and a memorable win over Max Baer, both in March 1937.

FINNEY, Tom. (*Footballer*). Professional football occasionally throws up players whose names become legend and whose reputations will last as long as the game. Tom Finney, who played for Preston North End throughout the whole of his career, is one of these. He played for England 76 times in a career that began during the Second World War and lasted through the bleak 'fifties when English football was overtaken and eventually forced into revitalisation by the Hungarians and Brazilians. He and Bobby Charlton share an image of good sportsmanship on and off the field, while Finney – nicknamed "the ghost" in his heyday on the wing – never achieved the actual successes. The nearest he got to domestic honours was a loser's medal in the 1954 F.A. Cup Final.

FORDHAM, George. (Jockey). Born at Cambridge, 1837–1887. Probably second only to the great Fred Archer among nineteenth century riders, George Fordham was only 14 when he rode his first winner at Brighton in 1851, and weighed only 3 stone 12 pounds when he won the Cambridgeshire the following year. For years the Epsom Derby eluded him, but eventually he rode Sir Bevys to victory in 1879. George Fordham was Leading Jockey for a total of fourteen years, 1855–1863, 1865, 1867–1869, sharing top place with C. Maidment in 1871.

GODFREE, Mrs. Leslie (née Kitty McKane). (Tennis player). Although she never ranked as World No. 1 player, Kitty McKane nevertheless had the unique distinction of being the only player to beat the American Helen Wills (ranked No. 1 from 1927 to 1929) at Wimbledon. She was Wimbledon singles champion in 1924 and 1926, Wimbledon mixed doubles champion in the same years; American doubles champion in 1923 and 1927, and American mixed doubles champion in 1925; German doubles champion in 1930 and 1931; British covered court singles champion in 1928 and American indoor doubles champion in 1922 and 1923.

GRACE, Dr. William G. (Cricketer). 1848–1915. There can be few personalities whose names are more synonymous with their sport than W. G. Grace with cricket; this Grand Old Man of English Cricket did more to popularise the game than any of his day or since. Born at Downend, Bristol in 1848, he was only nine when he first played for West Gloucestershire, and captained the Gloucestershire side from 1871 until 1898. Although four men have scored more than his 54,896 runs in first-class cricket, the imperfect pitches of the last century emphasise the measure of his achievement. Added to this achievement was his aggregate of 2,876 wickets at an average cost of 17·92 runs, bowling slow-medium leg breaks. He captained England in 13 Tests, all against Australia, and was on the losing side only three times. He scored three triple centuries (344 v. Kent in 1876, 318 v. Yorkshire in 1876, and 301 v. Sussex in 1896), double centuries on ten other occasions, and 126 centuries. He played his last innings in first-class cricket in 1908 when he was 60.

GREAVES, Jimmy. (Footballer). Few players score goals in their first-class debuts. Jimmy Greaves did for Chelsea in 1957, and then went on to score the first time he played for the England youth team, the Under-23s, the full international side, for A.C. Milan on his transfer in 1961, a hat-trick for Spurs on his return a year later, and two for West Ham when he went to them in 1969. One of the greatest goal-scorers in the history of English football, Greaves loved the game and grew increasingly distressed at the way it became a hard, tactical business during his career. Eventually, last year, he retired but still plays park football. He played for England over 50 times and scored well over 350 goals in his career. Twice he scored five in a match (both times with Chelsea), hit a few fours and innumerable hat-tricks. Greaves was always elusive, and at his best untouchable. One soaking wet November Saturday in Lancashire he scored all Chelsea's goals in a 5–4 win over Preston; at the end of the match Greaves was the only one of the 22 players still with clean shorts – he hadn't been down once on the slippery, muddy pitch.

GRINHAM, Judith Brenda. (Swimmer). Born 5th March 1939. Judy Grinham, 17 at the time, was the first Briton to win an Olympic Gold medal for 32 years with her 100-metres back-stroke victory at Melbourne in 1956, a feat which earned her the vote as Britain's sportswoman of that year. Her legendary swimming career, from which she retired at the age of 20, included Gold medals for back-stroke in the 1958 Commonwealth Games and European Championship, Bronze for the 100-metres free-style at the Budapest European Championships, and A.S.A. back-stroke titles in 1955, 1956 and 1958.

HAWTHORN, John Michael. (Motor racing driver). 1929–1959. After a phenomenal rise to international fame in 1951–52, Mike Hawthorn joined the Italian Ferrari team in 1953, winning the French Grand Prix from the great Fangio, then the 1954 Spanish GP and the 1958 French GP. He also won the 1955 Le Mans 24-Hour sports car race for Jaguar, and was World Champion Driver in 1958. He retired from motor racing at the age of 29 after winning this Championship, only to be killed in a road accident at Guildford three months later.

HEMERY, David. (Athlete). Winner of the Gold Medal for the 120 yards hurdles at the 1966 Commonwealth Games, Hemery won Britain's only athletics gold medal in the 1968 Mexico Olympics for his win in the 400 metres in a World record time of 48·1 seconds, beating the West German silver medallist by almost a second – having trained in America for sixty consecutive weeks.

HILL, Albert. (Athlete). Born 24th March 1889. Now

frequently forgotten are the extraordinary feats of Albert Hill who won Gold medals for both the 800 and 1500-metres at the 1920 Olympic Games – ten years after he had won his first A.A.A. title at *4 miles*. Later he turned coach and trained the great Sydney Wooderson.

HILL, Graham. (*Motor racing driver*). Born in 1929 and the popular personification of the dashing, handsome driver, Londoner Graham Hill was World Champion in 1962 driving for B.R.M. and in 1968 for Lotus. His tremendous record of wins includes five Monaco GPs – a unique achievement – three American GPs, and the Dutch, German, Italian, Mexican, South African and Spanish GPs. He broke both legs in a crash during the 1969 American GP but displayed magnificent determination in his return to GP racing in 1971, and a popular win with a Matra in the 1972 Le Mans 24-Hour race.

HOBBS, Jack. (*Cricketer*). In his career the legendary Jack Hobbs totalled 61,237 runs, including 197 centuries. Over a 29-year period Hobbs dominated batting records for Surrey and England, playing 41 times for England.

HURST, Geoff. (*Footballer*). Although he now appears to be at the end of his seven-year England international career, Geoff Hurst can be sure of one soccer record that will never be broken, and that will always be a subject of English nostalgia. He was the first man ever to score three goals in a World Cup Final, and his feat enabled England to win the 1966 World Cup against West Germany by 4–2. For years he was one of the most feared strikers in the world game and in League football, where he once scored six in a match for his only club, West Ham. He was one of three West Ham players to be successful three years running in Wembley finals – in the F.A. Cup in 1964, the European Cup-Winners' Cup in 1965, and the World Cup of 1966.

HUTTON, Sir Leonard. (*Cricketer*). Up to the start of this summer's series against Australia, Yorkshire's Len Hutton, later knighted for his services to the game, was holder of the record for highest innings during matches between the two countries. His 364 at the Oval in 1938, when he was 22, was only beaten comparatively recently – and then by the great Garfield Sobers. Sir Len was the first professional cricketer to captain England when appointed in 1953, and although he never led a Yorkshire side, he was successful enough at the job to win the Ashes for England for the first time since the War. He retired in 1955.

ILLINGWORTH, Ray. (*Cricketer*). England's current captain, Ray Illingworth – a Yorkshireman now leading Leicestershire – had a Test career of only 30 games in eleven years before he was given the

leadership in 1969. Since then he had had the distinction of being the first captain in 38 years to regain the Ashes in Australia, which he did in 1971. Basically an off-spin bowler, Illingworth is now also a patient and very dependable middle-order batsman. He has now been with Leicestershire for three years and previously spent 18 seasons with Yorkshire.

JACKLIN, Anthony, O.B.E. (*Golfer*). Born 7th July 1944. Awarded the O.B.E. in 1970 for his services to golf, professional Tony Jacklin won his first important championship in 1965, and in 1967 won both the Pringle and Dunlop Masters. In 1968 he won the American Greater Jacksonville Open, and the British Open Championship the following year. His greatest success to date was winning the American Open Championship in 1970. Tony Jacklin is Life Vice-President of the Professional Golfers' Association.

JAMES, Alex. (*Footballer*). A short, stocky Scotsman who scored so few goals that they were to be commented upon, Alex James was an inside-forward who made the Arsenal team of the 'thirties the great team they were. He played for Raith Rovers and Preston North End as well, but it was with the London team that he reached the height of his fame. His gimmick – if such it can be called – was the bagginess of his shorts in days when footballer's knees were almost covered. He saved his best goals for Wembley, scoring for Arsenal in the Cup Final of 1930, and the year before, two for Scotland when the team that legend has called the "Wembley Wizards" thrashed England 5–1.

JONES, Mrs. Ann (*Ann Haydon*). (*Tennis player*). Ann Jones delighted the Wimbledon crowds by winning the Ladies' Singles title in 1970, the crowning achievement in a career marked by persistence, courage and good humour. Since the days when, as Ann Haydon, she had first transferred her attention from international table tennis to the lawn game, she had played careful and consistently strong tennis, but was always overshadowed by the American and Australian players who dominated the game in the late 1960s. Having achieved her great ambition with her victory over Mrs. Billie-Jean King in 1971, Ann Jones retired to have a baby.

LAKER, Jim. (*Cricketer*). Now a respected TV commentator, Jim Laker's greatest and best-remembered feat was to take 19 Australian wickets in a Test at Old Trafford in 1956. After taking 9 for 37 in the first innings – Surrey team-mate Tony Lock took the other wicket – Laker's off-spin baffled all the Australians into giving him their wickets in the second innings, when he returned figures of 10 for 53. He took 46 wickets in that summer's series, and went on to a total of 193

Tony Jacklin, O.B.E.

in his 46 Test appearances.

LAW, Denis. (Footballer). A fiercely competitive Scotsman, Denis Law has been in first-class football since he was 16, making his debut with Huddersfield and moving on to Manchester City before a spell with the Italian Torino club. Since the early 'sixties he has been one of the stars of Old Trafford, sharing in Manchester United's successes in the Cup, the League and the European championship. He is first and foremost a goal-scorer, with lightning reflexes and the ability to leap almost his own height. He set up one of football's most unusual records, scoring six goals for Manchester City in a Cup-tie at Luton – yet finishing on the losing side. City were 5-1 up – all scored by Law – when the game was abandoned because of a waterlogged pitch; when it was played again, Law scored another but City lost 3-1.

LEE, Francis. (Footballer). Manchester City's leading goal-scorer last season and a current regular in the England team, Francis Lee has spent the summer recovering from nervous exhaustion – a direct result of the intense emotional and physical pressure forced on the top footballers of today. Lee joined Manchester from another Lancashire club, Bolton, and is one of several City players who have become world class stars under the

club's management team of Joe Mercer and Malcolm Allison.

LIDDELL, Eric. (Athlete). Born 16th January 1902 at Tientsin, China, a Scot. A lifetime which included missionary work in China and international rugby for Scotland ended when Eric Liddell died in Japanese captivity in 1945. It was crowned by his achievements at the 1924 Olympics (when Harold Abrahams won the 100-metres), taking the Gold medal in the 400-metres in 47·6 seconds – although he had never bettered 49 seconds previously – and the Bronze in the 200-metres. He had withdrawn from the 100-metres because the heats were run on a Sunday.

LONSBROUGH, Anita. (Swimmer). Born 10th August 1941. At her home town of Huddersfield Anita Lonsbrough had to train almost on her own, but went on to establish an unparalleled swimming record representing Great Britain for seven years between 1958 and 1964. This record included seven Gold medals, three Silver and two Bronze in major Games. Her greatest performance was the win in the 200-metres breaststroke at the 1960 Rome Olympics in a world record time of 2 minutes 49·5 seconds, and in all broke four breaststroke records. Having established a British 440-yards medley record (at 5 minutes 36·8 seconds) and been twice voted Sportswoman of the Year – in 1960 and 1962 – she retired with an M.B.E., and married British Olympic cyclist Hugh Porter.

LOWE, Douglas. (Athlete). Born 7th August 1902 at Manchester. The remarkable feature of Douglas Lowe's athletic career was that he won his first Olympic Gold medal (for the 800-metres in 1924) before ever he managed to achieve an A.A.A. title. Moreover he went on in the 1928 Olympics to win a second Gold medal and improved his record to 1 minute 51·8 seconds.

MACKAY, Dave. (Footballer). Courage being an essential part of football, the value of a man like Dave Mackay to a team is probably incalculable. Mackay, the fiery heart of the double-winning Spurs side of 1961, broke a leg in two places in a game at Manchester in 1963; it was set and plastered and Mackay came home to London the same night, refusing a stretcher in favour of crutches. Ten months later, after all the pain and frustration of a fight back to full fitness, Mackay played in Spurs' reserves as a trial before returning to the first team, and broke his other leg. He was out of football effectively for two seasons, but returned with none of his old qualities lost to lead Spurs to an F.A. Cup victory in 1967. That was his third Cup medal and was added to Championship medals, a European Cup-winners' Cup medal and numerous Scottish caps. At what appeared to be the end of his career, he went to Derby County, then in the Second Division, and proceeded to lead them into the First. He was the rock upon which Derby built this year's championship success, although Mackay himself had moved on to Swindon Town in 1971 where he is now manager.

McCLINTOCK, Frank. (*Footballer*). Frank McClintock was sick with frustration and despair last May after Arsenal had lost to Leeds in the F.A. Cup Final at Wembley. Despite the glory of the season before, when Arsenal became only the second team this century to win both League and the Cup in one season, McClintock's reaction proved that in sport one is only as good as the last performance. The season of 1970–71 gave McClintock everything a footballer could wish for; he captained a double-winning team, he gained further caps for Scotland and he was voted Footballer of the Year by the British Press. In a career that has spanned more than a decade, playing for Leicester City and losing twice with them at Wembley, then with Arsenal and losing twice more before the 1970 victory, this tough, inspiring defender can be forgiven for his despondency at his fifth failure, this year.

McGREGOR, Robert Bilsland. (*Swimmer*). Born 3rd April 1944. Coached by his father David (a former Olympic water polo player), Bobby McGregor came to fame in the astonishing 100-metres freestyle race at Utrecht in 1966 when he was left at the start, believing that another swimmer had false-started and that the race would be called back. Nevertheless he was ahead at the turn and won in 53·7 seconds to become European 100-metres champion. Although he never won an Olympic Gold medal, he won Silvers in the 1964 Olympics, and 1962 and 1966 Commonwealth Games, all in the sprint races. He won the A.S.A. 110-yards title six times, was second in the World Student Games 100-metres, broke the world 110-yards record five times in three years, and received the M.B.E. for his swimming achievements.

MATTHEWS, Sir Stanley. (*Footballer*). When he retired at the age of 50 in 1964, Sir Stanley had played over 700 League games for his clubs, Stoke, Blackpool and Stoke again. He had played for England in 57 internationals plus a good number of wartime matches. He was knighted while he still played, and many experts who have seen sixty years of first-class football rate him as the greatest footballer of all time. Matthews was a winger with a devastating body swerve and an incredibly sharp turn of speed. Despite the fact that all opponents knew he liked to push the ball down the touch-line before centring, he was consistently able to do just that, week-in week-out, for goal after goal after goal, over a period of 33 years in football. His greatest triumph was the 1953 Cup Final when, with Blackpool, he reached Wembley for the third time in six seasons. The two previous attempts had ended in failure; but against Bolton in Coronation year Matthews won for his team and himself a Cup that seemed out of reach when Bolton led 3–1 with 20 minutes to go. It's known as the Matthews Final – he turned Bolton inside out, made two goals and to the delight of all except their opponents, Matthews and Blackpool won 4–3.

MAY, Peter. (*Cricketer*). Peter May, now one of the England selectors, probably suffered during the best part of his career from the weaknesses of many of his contemporaries. The strain of captaining England during a lean period in the late 'fifties led to a premature retirement at the age of 31 in 1961. He captained England a record 41 times, making 66 Test appearances in all. Despite the pressures of captaincy and of often having to support collapsing innings, May was arguably among the world's best middle-order batsmen of his time. He captained Surrey during the final two seasons of the record seven consecutive championships. At the start of this summer he held with Colin Cowdrey a Test record fourth-wicket partnership of 411, made in 1957 against the West Indies, when he totalled 285 not out.

MOORE, Bobby. (*Footballer*). It should not be long before England's current captain, Bobby Moore, reaches and passes the appearance record set by his team-mate Bobby Charlton. If Moore goes on to play in the 1974 World Cup Finals in West Germany he will have played in four such series, starting in Chile ten years ago, lifting the Jules Rimet trophy itself in 1966, and helping to defend it in 1970. It was before the last tournament, while the English side was acclimatising itself to South American conditions, that Moore was accused of theft in Bologna; he strongly denied the charge and it was never brought to court by the embarrassed authorities, but Moore remained a virtual prisoner for some days while the affair was sorted out, losing pounds in the pervading tension while his team tried to settle down to training in Mexico. When he eventually reached the field he still managed to lead the England side with the calm authority that has come to be expected of him. A West Ham player for the whole of his career, he captained them to success in the 1964 F.A. Cup, and the 1965 European Cup Winners' Cup, completing an incredible personal treble with the World Cup the following year.

MORTIMER, Angela. (*Tennis Player*). Born 21st April 1932 at Plymouth. The most successful British woman player since the Second World War, Angela Mortimer was ranked World No. 1 in 1961 and was Wimbledon singles champion that year. She also was singles champion in France (1955) and Australia (1958), and doubles champion at Wimbledon (1955) and Germany (1957). She was Scandinavian covered court singles champion six times, British covered court singles champion six times, British hard court singles champion four times, and gained numerous titles in doubles and mixed doubles championships throughout the world.

MORTON, Lucy. (*Swimmer*). Born 23rd February 1898. Lucy Morton was Britain's first woman swimmer to win an individual Olympic Gold Medal, achieving a surprise win in the 1924 200-metres breaststroke, setting a Games record at 3 minutes 33·2 seconds. She never held a world record for this distance although she twice set 200-yards records. She also set the world's first record for the 150-yards back-stroke in 1916.

MOSS, Stirling Craufurd, O.B.E. (*Motor racing driver*). Despite enjoying an unsurpassed career at the top of his profession, Stirling Moss never achieved the World Championship. During the nineteen-fifties he drove for Jaguar, Mercedes, Maserati, Vanwall and Aston Martin. His victory in the 1957 British GP driving a Vanwall was the first GP victory by a British driver in a British car since Segrave's Sunbeam win in the 1923 French GP. His impressive list of victories included seven R.A.C. TTs, four Nurburgring 1000-km races, three Monaco GPs, three Italian GPs, a German, Dutch and Argentine GP, the Targa Florio, the Mille Miglia and five Oulton Park Gold Cups. A crash at Goodwood decided this brilliant young driver to retire in 1962.

PACKER, Ann. (*Athlete*). Born 8th March 1942 at Moulsford, Berkshire. Starting her career as a sprinter, hurdler and jumper, Ann Packer found fame in the 800-metre event. She had won the 100-yards in the 1959 English Schools Championships, and the A.A.A. long-jump title in 1960. She moved up to the quarter-mile in 1963 with a world-class 53·4 seconds for 400-metres. When she went to Tokyo in 1964 her aim was to win the 400-metres but, despite returning a European record at 52·2 seconds, she had to settle for the Silver medal. Three days later however she went on to win the 800-metres Gold medal in a world record time of 2 minutes 1·1 seconds. She then, at the age of 22, decided to retire and later married Robbie Brightwell, Britain's Olympic team captain.

PERRY, Frederick John. (*Tennis player*). Born 18th May 1909 at Stockport. Fred Perry was Britain's outstanding tennis player of all time. His aggressive forehand stroke, taken running into the ball, was

David Colin Bedford, Britain's great 5,000 and 10,000 metres runner

the devastating strength of his skill. Ranked as World No. 1 in 1934, 1935 and 1936, he was Wimbledon singles champion in these three years, and mixed doubles champion in 1934 and 1936. He was U.S. singles champion in 1933, 1934 and 1936, French singles champion in 1935, Australian singles champion in 1934, and gained countless other doubles and mixed doubles championship titles besides. He played for Great Britain in the Davis Cup from 1931 to 1936 and was largely instrumental for the team's success from 1933 to 1936. He turned professional in 1936 and later became an American citizen.

PETERS, Martin. (*Footballer*). Shortly before the 1970 World Cup, Sir Alf Ramsey described Martin Peters as a player ten years ahead of his time. To his natural ability as a mid-field player, Peters has added the ability to appear in goal-scoring positions unmarked and unnoticed. A regular in the England side during and since the 1966 World Cup, Peters won an F.A. Cup medal and a European Cup Winners' Trophy medal with West Ham. He scored in the World Cup Final against West Germany, and in 1969 figured in the first British £200,000 transfer deal. A move across London to Tottenham Hotspur brought West Ham £146,000 plus Jimmy Greaves – valued towards the end of his career at £54,000.

PHELPS, Brian. (*Diver*). Born 21st April 1944. At the age of 14, Brian Phelps was the youngest man to win a European diving championship – for highboard in 1958. He won four Gold medals (more than any other, man or woman) in Commonwealth Games, for the springboard and high-board diving in 1962 and 1966; he was the first British man for 36 years – and only the second ever – to win an Olympic medal for diving, when he took the Bronze on the highboard at Rome in 1960. He was British high-board diving champion every year between 1958 and 1966 (except 1963 when injury kept him from competition), and springboard champion from 1960 to 1962, and at plain diving in 1957, 1960 and 1961.

PIGGOTT, Lester Keith. (*Jockey*). Born 5th November 1935. Grandson of Ernest Piggott, who rode two Grand National winners, Lester is the outstanding British jockey of today, having been Leading Jockey nine times (1960 and 1964–1971). Up to 1971 he had won the Derby five times, the St. Leger six times, and won the Washington, D.C. International on Sir Ivor (the first time since 1922 that an English Derby winner had raced in the U.S.A.), and again in 1969 on Karabas.

RAMSEY, Sir Alfred. (*Footballer*). When the great Hungarian side became the first Continental team ever to defeat England at Wembley in 1953, the England right back and penalty scorer of one of their three goals was Alf Ramsey, approaching the end of his playing career as a stylish, tactically-advanced defender with Tottenham and Southampton. That 6–3 defeat, followed a year later by England's largest-ever deficit – 7–1 in Budapest – made a deep impression on Ramsey. Some time after he had seen his England team win the World Cup in 1966, he remembered that 1953 match: "I have had one great ambition hanging over me for years, to replace the image of the great Hungarian side by the image of an even greater England team." His managerial career started with Ipswich Town, then a Third Division team, and he brought them to the top, culminating in the League Championship in 1961–62. After the next World Cup in 1962 he was appointed England team manager and given complete discretion with regard to selection and tactics – a revolutionary step for English football. The result was victory in 1966, a knighthood for Sir Alf and the respect of every soccer nation in the world.

RAND, Mary (*Mary Bignal*). (*Athlete*). Born 10th February 1940 at Wells, Somerset. A glance at Mary Rand's all-round achievements will indicate the astonishing quality of this superb sportswoman: 10·6 seconds for 100-yards; 11·7 seconds for 100-metres; 24·2 seconds for 200-yards; 10·8 seconds for 80-metres hurdles; 13·4 seconds for 100-metres hurdles; 5 feet 7¾ inches, high jump; 37 feet 8¾ inches, shot; 101 feet 5 inches, discus; and 94 feet 9 inches, javelin. It only remains to add that it was at the 1964 Tokyo Olympics that she won the long jump Gold medal (the first

Olympic Gold medal to be won by a British woman athlete) with a world record jump of 22 feet 2¼ inches, the Pentathlon Silver medal, and contributed to the British team's Bronze medal in the 4 × 100-metres relay.

REES, David James, C.B.E. (*Golfer*). Dai Rees is probably Wales' greatest professional golfer and represented the Principality in eight Canada Cups. He won the Dunlop Masters tournament in 1950 and 1962, and was the top money prize winner in British tournaments in 1950. He was a member of the British Ryder Cup team in 1937, 1947, 1949, 1951 and 1953, and team captain in 1955, 1957, 1959, 1961 and 1967. He also won countless other tournaments from 1935 to 1970.

RICHARDS, Sir Gordon. (*Jockey*). Born 1904 in Shropshire. The great Gordon Richards rode his first winner in 1921, and his last in 1954; from first to last he rode 4,870 winners – a total unapproached by any other jockey. He was moreover Leading Jockey for 26 years between 1925 and 1953, winning the Two Thousand Guineas three times, the One Thousand Guineas three times, the St. Leger five times and the Oaks twice. In full drama characteristic of the Coronation year, Gordon Richards was knighted for his services to racing, and then went on to win the Derby on Pinza – the one great classic which had hitherto eluded him. He retired in 1954 after a bad fall at Sandown, having established world and national records for winners, both as outright and annual totals.

ROUND, Dorothy (*Mrs. Leigh Little*). (*Tennis player*). Born 13th July 1909 at Dudley, Worcestershire. Ranked as World No. 1 ladies singles player in 1934, Dorothy Round was one of only two British women to win the Wimbledon singles between the Wars (the other was Kitty McKane); she was Wimbledon singles champion in 1934 and 1937, and mixed doubles champion from 1934 to 1936. She was Australian champion in 1935, British hard court singles champion in 1933 and 1934, hard court doubles champion in 1933, and mixed doubles champion in 1934 and 1936.

SANGSTER, Michael (*Tennis player*). Born 11th September 1940 at Torquay. Mike Sangster was the most successful British player for many years and was the only Briton to reach the top ten ranking World men since the 1939–45 War, being ranked No. 9 in 1963. His main strength lay in his very fast service (timed at 154 m.p.h. in 1963). He reached the Wimbledon singles semi-finals in 1961, won 43 of his 65 Davis Cup rubbers for Britain between 1960 and 1968, and was British covered court singles champion in 1964.

SEAMAN, Richard. (*Motor racing driver*). 1913–1939. At a time when Britain was racing voiturettes against the huge state-sponsored Grand Prix formula racing cars of Germany in the late 'thirties, Dick Seaman was invited to drive for the supreme Mercedes-Benz team in 1937. He won the 1938 German Grand Prix and finished second in the Swiss Grand Prix that year. He was leading the 1939 Belgian Grand Prix when his Mercedes crashed in heavy rain, and he died in the fire.

SEGRAVE, Sir Henry. (Motor racing driver). 1896–1930. The great British driver of the 1920s, Segrave drove a Sunbeam to victory in the 1923 French Grand Prix and many other minor races afterwards. He three times broke the World Land Speed Record in Sunbeams, in 1926 at 152·33 m.p.h., in 1927 at 203·79 m.p.h., and in 1929 at 231·44 m.p.h. (he was knighted for the last feat). He was killed in 1930 on Lake Windermere after setting a World Water Speed Record of 98·76 m.p.h.

SMYTHE, Pat, O.B.E. (Mrs. Patricia Rosemary Koechlin). (Show jumper). Born 22nd September 1928. Pat Smythe first went abroad with the British Show Jumping team in 1947, and thereafter became one of the world's leading lady riders. Her extraordinary list of successes include Leading Show Jumper of the Year in 1949, 1958 and 1962; European Ladies Champion in 1957, 1961, 1962 and 1963. She was a member of the British Olympic team in 1956 and 1960 (gaining a Bronze medal at Stockholm). She was winner of show jumping championships all over the world, and has been made a Freeman of the City of London and honorary Freeman of the Worshipful Companies of Farriers, Loriners and Saddlers. Her O.B.E. was awarded in 1956.

SNOW, John. (Cricketer). Although there have obviously been men of wild character among batsmen, it is traditionally the fast bowler who shows himself to be independent of authority. John Snow, who can perhaps claim to be the most intimidating fast bowler in the world today – and certainly the only one to find relaxation in writing poetry – is certainly of this ilk. He was instrumental in regaining the Ashes during the M.C.C. tour of Australia in 1970–71, taking 31 Australian wickets. In the English season following this triumph, Snow was dropped by his county (Sussex) "for lack of effort", and was left out of the England side for one Test after a "collision" with an Indian batsman. He is also a better-than-average tail-end batsman.

STATHAM, Brian. (Cricketer). For long overshadowed by his mercurial fast bowling partner, Fred Trueman, Brian Statham took 252 Test wickets in a 70-match career. He served 19 years with Lancashire, three of them as captain, and took 2,260 wickets in his career. He was also a very fine fieldsman, possessing one of the most accurate

and fast throws English cricket has ever seen.

STEWART, Jackie. (Motor racing driver). Born in 1939. Jackie Stewart came into Formula One racing in 1965 with B.R.M. Several Grand Prix victories followed for this young Scotsman, but it was not until 1969 that he took the World Championship with wins in the British, Dutch, French, Italian, South African and Spanish GPs. Driving the new Tyrrell-Ford, he was again World Champion in 1971 and is unquestionably the greatest living racing driver today.

SURTEES, John. (Motor cyclist and motor racing driver). Born 1934. With no less than seven world motor cycling championships behind him, John Surtees entered motor racing in 1960 in Formula Junior. He joined Ferrari in 1963, and won the World Championship in 1964 with wins in the German and Italian GPs, as well as other good placings. Disappointing seasons with Honda and B.R.M. decided John Surtees to launch out as a manufacturer, and since 1969 he has achieved several outstanding successes in cars bearing his own name.

SWIFT, Frank. (Footballer). One of the greatest of English goalkeepers, Frank Swift's career spanned most of the 'thirties through to the late 'forties. He won many caps, a Cup medal and a First Division championship medal, and is the only man to have captained England from goal since the War. Always a colourful personality he was once accused of showmanship; his reply, "Football's only a game after all", was not a reflection of his attitude during his appearance at Wembley in the 1934 Cup Final for his only club, Manchester City. An early mistake by Swift gave Portsmouth the lead, but City won by two late goals, and the youthful Swift fainted under his crossbar at the final whistle! He retired early to make a career as a sports journalist – and became very successful – until he was killed with members of the Manchester United team in the air crash at Munich in 1958.

THOMPSON, Donald. (Athlete). Born 20th January 1930 at Hillingdon, Middlesex. Hero of the 1960 British Olympic team was 5 foot 6¼ inches Don Thompson who took the 50,000-metres road-walk Gold medal in an Olympic record time of 4 hours 25 minutes 30 seconds. His first major success came in 1955 when he won the London to Brighton 52-mile walk, and went on to take the national 50,000-metre title for seven consecutive years, and set up United Kingdom records on the track at 20-miles, 30-miles and 50,000 metres.

TRUEMAN, Fred. (Cricketer). A true son of Yorkshire, Fred Trueman came back to first-class cricket last summer with some appearances for Derbyshire in one-day matches. He has taken more wickets in a legendary career than any other Test bowler, with 307 victims to his credit in 67 Tests. Also his record, of 8 for 31 against the Indians in 1952, is the best return ever by a Test fast bowler. Trueman retired from regular cricket in 1968 to become a professional night-club performer.

WHITLOCK, Harold H. (Athlete). Born 16th December 1903 at Hendon, Middlesex. By trade a motor racing mechanic at Brooklands, Harold Whitlock came to prominence as a road walker in 1931 when he was placed second in the national 50,000-metre championship, gaining the title two years later. In the 1936 Berlin Olympics he won the Gold medal for the event, and in 1938 completed the double by carrying off the European title. As late as 1952, at the age of 48, he came 11th in the Olympic event.

WOODERSON, Sydney C. (Athlete). Born 30th August 1914 in London. Small, bespectacled Sydney Wooderson ran his way into British hearts over a period of thirteen years between 1936 and 1948. Yet he never won an Olympic title since he cracked a bone in his ankle at the time of the 1936 Berlin Olympics, and the War intervened at the height of his running life. Nevertheless he won the 1938 1500-metres European Championships and set a seal on a remarkable career by winning the 1948 English cross-country title.

WOODROFFE, Martyn John. (Swimmer). Born 8th September 1950. The only Briton to win a swim-ming medal at the 1968 Mexican Olympics, Martyn Woodroffe, a Welshman from Cardiff, won the 200-metres butterfly Silver medal. The following year he established a British record for the 400-metres free-style and won the international invitation 200-metre butterfly at Santa Clara, California, in a European record time of 2 minutes 7·8 seconds. He retired from swimming five days after his 20th birthday.

WRIGHT, Billy. (Footballer). The first man ever to play 100 times for his country, Billy Wright, England's captain for most of the 'fifties, was the epitome of "the British sportsman". A master of every foot-ball skill, Wright was the forerunner of the modern "jack of all trades" player. For his only club, Wolves, he played in four defensive positions and was talented enough to have been able to do the same thing in attack. Throughout a period when England reached both the heights and depths – from a superb 4–0 victory against a crack Italian side at Turin in 1948, to the 1–7 defeat by the Hungarians six years later – Wright developed his talent for captaincy to the point at which he became an automatic selection. Part of his total 105 caps, 90 of them as captain, comprised an unbroken run of 70 appearances. He also played for Wolves 490 times, captaining them during their dominating period in the first half of the 'fifties when he won both Cup and League medals.

CHAPTER 8

ᨠ Defence and the Armed Forces ᨠ

The three fighting Services are manned exclusively by regular personnel – that is, by volunteers who enlist for fixed terms of service. Conscription, in the form of the National Service system by which all males were required to serve for two years, generally between the age of 18 and 20 (subject to a variety of grounds for deferment or remittance of service altogether) was abandoned some ten years ago. The reduction in numerical strength consequent upon this decision has been tolerable, thus far, because of Britain's steadily declining world-wide military rôle. It has, on the credit side, led to the attainment of very high standards of professional skill and reliability throughout the armed forces, standards which are generally conceded to be almost impossible to achieve among conscript forces whose motivation is, inevitably, weaker than that of career volunteers.

Throughout the past ten years Britain's military rôle has centred more and more firmly on the continent of Europe. Subject to the requirements of a series of "post colonial" campaigns which accompanied the gradual achievement of national independence by a large number of ex-Imperial possessions overseas, large permanent garrisons outside Europe have been run down. The point has now been reached where very few major sovereign bases are maintained outside Europe. The nation's main military function, apart from simple national self-defence, is the committment to the North Atlantic Treaty Organisation. The Royal Navy's fighting strength is almost wholly committed to operations connected with the co-ordinated Western defence structure. The major operational commands of the other two Services are BAOR – British Army of the Rhine, a corps of three divisions with supporting corps units – and RAF Germany. Forces deployed in the United Kingdom are largely earmarked for service on the northern flank of the NATO front line in time of emergency. The Royal Navy *Polaris* submarine force is engaged upon continuous deterrent patrol, and

The armed forces of the British Crown comprise the Royal Navy and Royal Marines, the British Army, and the Royal Air Force. Each of the Services consists of regular and reserve forces. The strengths of the three services consists of regular and reserve forces. The strengths of the three services in regular uniformed manpower as at 1st April 1972 were as follows:

Royal Navy and Royal Marines	81,900 men and women, all ranks
British Army	172,400 men and women, all ranks
Royal Air Force	110,300 men and women, all ranks

As the three women's Services – the Women's Royal Naval Service, the Women's Royal Army Corps, and the Women's Royal Air Force – are integral parts of the three main Services, with detachments serving at home and abroad alongside male personnel in all types of Service establishment, their strengths have been included in these figures. The figures do not, however, include personnel recruited outside the United Kingdom. These personnel – certain local auxiliary forces, and the Brigade of Gurkhas (which is described below) – add a further 9,900 uniformed male personnel of all ranks.

The total defence expenditure (published in the February 1972 *Statement on the Defence Estimates*) for the year 1972–73 is £2,854,000,000; this total represents approximately 5·5 per cent of the gross national product.

a system of dual, alternating crews for each vessel allows a high degree of combat readiness at all times.

Certain forces are still maintained outside the continent of Europe in accordance with Britain's other military committments, which may be described briefly as the defence of the country's remaining overseas dependencies, and guaranteeing the continued stability and independence of various Commonwealth countries which have concluded defence agreements with Britain on achieving nationhood. The current policy calls for the replacement of large and costly overseas bases by "skeleton" facilities with small specialist garrisons, which can be reinforced by sea and air in times of crisis. Speedy and substantial reinforcement of these areas by quick-response forces based in the United Kingdom is a major element of British policy, and operational techniques in this field have been perfected.

Such overseas bases as remain are increasingly commanded by officers of any one of the three Services supported by inter-Service staffs and combat units trained in close inter-Service co-operation.

"Caretaker" garrisons of specialist troops are maintained in the Persian Gulf, British Honduras, Cyprus, Malta, Gibraltar, the Falkland Islands, and various staging posts across the world. Major garrisons remain in the Far East, to fulfil Britain's traditional defence responsibilities for certain areas of South-East Asia. Army, naval and air elements are based – in rotation – in Malaysia as part of the five-nation ANZUK force; Britain's partners in this area are Australia, New Zealand, Malaysia and Singapore. A strong garrison remains in the Crown colony of Hong Kong. Prominent among British units in the Far East is the Brigade of Gurkhas; the Brigade is based on Hong Kong and deployed in the colony, in Malaysia and in Brunei, with one battalion usually posted to the United Kingdom at any one time. Training facilities in Malaysia, the Persian Gulf and the continent of Europe are in constant use, ensuring that British forces are fully trained in combat techniques relevant to operations in all types of terrain and climate, from the Arctic Circle to arid desert and dense jungle.

Britain also maintains an infantry battalion and an air-portable armoured reconnaissance squadron with the United Nations Peacekeeping Force in Cyprus, the British contingent representing about one-third of the total force.

Supreme responsibility for national defence, under the Queen as titular commander-in-chief of the armed forces, lies with the Prime Minister and Cabinet, responsible to Parliament. In descending order of responsibility, the organs of defence policy and execution are as follows: The Prime Minister chairs the Committee on Defence and Overseas Policy, on which sits the Secretary of State for Defence. The Secretary of State for Defence chairs the Defence Council, consisting of the Minister of State for Defence (a unified Ministry of Defence replaced the old Admiralty, War Office and Air Ministry in 1964); the three Parliamentary Under-Secretaries for the Navy, the Army and the Air Force; the Chief of the Defence Staff (Britain's senior military appointment); the three Service Chiefs of Staff; the Chief Adviser (Projects and Research); and the Chief of Personnel and Logistics. Professional advice on strategy, the military implications of government policy, and the execution of operations is provided by the Chiefs of Staff Committee, comprising the three Service Chiefs under the chairmanship of the Chief of the Defence Staff. The management of the three Services on a daily basis is the responsibility of the Admiralty, Army and Air Force Boards of the Defence Council.

COMBAT FORCES: THE ROYAL NAVY AND ROYAL MARINES

The "Senior Service" and the Corps of Royal Marines are integral parts of the country's maritime forces and are traditionally treated under a single heading.

The recent simplification of the naval command structure, and the closing of permanent shore establishments and headquarters overseas, have produced a structure of only two main headquarters. These are Commander-in-Chief, Naval Home Command, covering all shore estab-

An impression of the new Through-Deck Cruiser being developed for the Royal Navy

lishments in the United Kingdom; and Commander-in-Chief, Fleet, covering all seagoing commands anywhere in the world.

The government decision to run down the carrier strength of the Royal Navy has left the Service with only one carrier (at the time of writing) operating fixed-wing combat aircraft. The fixed-wing rôle of the Fleet Air Arm is coming to an end; a new generation of warships capable of carrying, launching and supporting vertical take-off fixed-wing combat aircraft is planned, under the designation "Through-deck Cruisers", but the aircraft carried on these vessels will be flown by detached Royal Air Force personnel.

The Corps of Royal Marines fulfil several functions. Detachments are carried on various classes of naval vessels, and form a division of the working ship's company; they provide landing parties where necessary. (In the last century the traditional secondary rôle of the R.M. detachment – the protection of the officers against disaffected elements of the ship's company – has, happily, ceased to be significant!) The Corps also represents the nation's foremost source of experts in all the special skills connected with amphibious warfare, and such specialist detachments may be called upon to serve anywhere in the world alongside the other fighting Services. Finally, the Commando forces – 3rd Royal Marine Commando Brigade – play a leading part in the nation's capability for quick-response operations anywhere in the world where British or allied interests or territorial integrity are threatened. The brigade consists of four Commandos – Nos. 40, 41, 42 and 45; these are formations roughly comparable to infantry battalions, with attached artillery and other supporting arms. They may be deployed as conventional infantry formations, or embarked on one of the Commando Carriers. These are converted aircraft carriers specially refitted for the troop-carrying rôle; each can accommodate a full Commando with its heavy weapons and vehicles, and each carries a large force of troop-carrying helicopters. The entire force can be air-lifted to land, supported, directed and re-embarked on the carrier by the employment of the carrier's own resources. They thus represent an extremely potent weapon, and a versatile unit in any naval task force.

The major fighting vessels of the Fleet are listed below. It should be emphasised that only those vessels whose function involves operations in the presence of the enemy are included. Warships launched but not, at the time of writing, commissioned are omitted, as are new vessels currently under construction. The very brief details accompanying each class of vessel consist of the full load displacement, the usual size of the ship's complement, and the main armament. Relatively light anti-aircraft weapons are not listed; in the case of small warships such as inshore minesweepers this may give the impression that the vessels are unarmed, but all the surface ships listed below in fact mount at least one 40-mm anti-aircraft weapon.

FIXED-WING AIRCRAFT CARRIER

H.M.S. *Ark Royal*	(50,786 tons; 260 Officers, 2,380 ratings; 30 jet fighter/ground attack aircraft)

COMMANDO CARRIERS

H.M.S. *Bulwark*	(27,705 tons; 1,035 crew + 900
H.M.S. *Albion*	Royal Marines; 20 troop-carrying helicopters)

(H.M.S. *Hermes*, 28,700 tons, is under conversion from fixed-wing to Commando carrier rôle, and is scheduled to enter service during 1973.)

NUCLEAR-POWERED BALLISTIC MISSILE SUBMARINES

H.M.S. *Renown*	(8,400 tons submerged; 13 offi-
H.M.S. *Repulse*	cers, 128 ratings; 16 Polaris mis-
H.M.S. *Resolution*	siles; six 21-inch torpedo tubes)
H.M.S. *Revenge*	

NUCLEAR-POWERED FLEET SUBMARINES

H.M.S. *Churchill*	(4,500 tons submerged; 13 offi-
H.M.S. *Conqueror*	cers, 90 ratings; six 21-inch tor-
H.M.S. *Valiant*	pedo tubes)
H.M.S. *Warspite*	
H.M.S. *Courageous*	

(H.M.S. *Swiftsure*, H.M.S. *Sovereign* and H.M.S. *Superb* have been launched, but at the time of writing are not yet in commission.)

PROTOTYPE NUCLEAR-POWERED FLEET SUBMARINE

H.M.S. *Dreadnought*	(4,000 tons submerged; 11 offi- cers, 77 ratings; six 21-inch tor- pedo tubes)

DIESEL-POWERED PATROL SUBMARINES

"Oberon" Class	(2,410 tons submerged; 6 officers, 62 ratings; six 21-inch torpedo tubes)

H.M.S. *Oberon*	H.M.S. *Opportune*
H.M.S. *Ocelot*	H.M.S. *Oracle*
H.M.S. *Odin*	H.M.S. *Orpheus*
H.M.S. *Olympus*	H.M.S. *Osiris*
H.M.S. *Onslaught*	H.M.S. *Otter*
H.M.S. *Onyx*	H.M.S. *Otus*
H.M.S. *Opossum*	

"Porpoise" Class	(2,405 tons submerged; 6 officers, 65 ratings; eight 21-inch torpedo tubes)

H.M.S. *Cachalot*	H.M.S. *Porpoise*
H.M.S. *Finwhale*	H.M.S. *Rorqual*
H.M.S. *Grampus*	H.M.S. *Sealion*
H.M.S. *Narwhal*	H.M.S. *Walrus*

"A" Class (1,620 tons submerged; 5 officers, 63 ratings; six 21-inch torpedo tubes)

H.M.S. *Aeneas* H.M.S. *Artemis*
H.M.S. *Alliance* H.M.S. *Auriga*
  H.M.S. *Andrew*

ASSAULT SHIPS (AMPHIBIOUS CRUISER TYPE)

H.M.S. *Fearless* (12,120 tons; 36 officers, 520
H.M.S. *Intrepid* ratings; 111 Army or Royal Marines personnel)
(These vessels are equipped to land, support and direct amphibious forces. They carry six helicopters, and a typical hardware load would comprise 15 tanks and about 30 trucks or other vehicles. They have gun and missile anti-aircraft defences, and sophisticated communications equipment including a satellite link.)

HELICOPTER CRUISERS

H.M.S. *Blake* (12,080 tons; 85 officers, 800
H.M.S. *Tiger* ratings; two 6-inch guns, two 3-inch guns and two quadruple Seacat missile-launchers; four Sea King helicopters)
(H.M.S. *Lion*, of the same class, is in the process of converting to this standard. Original armament included four 6-inch and six 3-inch guns.)

GUIDED MISSILE-ARMED DESTROYERS

(6,200 tons; 33 officers, 438 ratings; four 4·5-inch guns, one twin Seaslug missile-launcher and two quadruple Seacat missile-launchers; one Wessex helicopter)
H.M.S. *Antrim* H.M.S. *Hampshire*
H.M.S. *Devonshire* H.M.S. *Kent*
H.M.S. *Fife* H.M.S. *London*
H.M.S. *Glamorgan* H.M.S. *Norfolk*
(H.M.S. *Bristol*, launched in 1969 but not yet in commission at the time of writing, will be the first of the new Type 82 vessels. She will have a displacement of 6,750 tons, a complement of 33 officers and 400 ratings, and be armed with a single 4·5-inch gun, and multiple Seadart and Ikara missile-launchers.)

DESTROYERS (*De-commissioned June 1972*)

(2,749 tons; 10 officers, 176 ratings; three 4·5-inch guns and one quadruple Seacat missile-launcher)
H.M.S. *Caprice* H.M.S. *Cavalier*

GENERAL PURPOSE FRIGATES (ANTI-SUBMARINE VERSATILE TYPE)

(2,860 tons; 17 officers, 246 ratings; two 4·5-inch guns, two quadruple Seacat missile-launchers, two sextuple 3-inch Mk. 4 rocket-launchers and one triple depth-charge

mortar; one Wasp helicopter with homing torpedo capability)
H.M.S. *Ajax* H.M.S. *Danae*
H.M.S. *Dido* H.M.S. *Juno*
H.M.S. *Leander* H.M.S. *Argonaut*
H.M.S. *Penelope* H.M.S. *Andromeda*
H.M.S. *Aurora* H.M.S. *Jupiter*
H.M.S. *Euryalus* H.M.S. *Hermione*
H.M.S. *Galatea* H.M.S. *Bacchante*
H.M.S. *Arethusa* H.M.S. *Scylla*
H.M.S. *Naiad* H.M.S. *Charybdis*
H.M.S. *Cleopatra* H.M.S. *Achilles*
H.M.S. *Sirius* H.M.S. *Diomede*
H.M.S. *Minerva* H.M.S. *Apollo*
H.M.S. *Phoebe* H.M.S. *Ariadne*

ANTI-SUBMARINE FRIGATES

"Rothesay" Class (2,800 tons; 15 officers, 220 ratings; one quadruple Seacat missile-launcher, one sextuple 3-inch Mk. 4 rocket-launcher, two 4·5-inch guns and one triple Limbo depth-charge mortar; one Wasp helicopter with homing torpedo capability)
H.M.S. *Berwick* H.M.S. *Plymouth*
H.M.S. *Brighton* H.M.S. *Rhyl*
H.M.S. *Falmouth* H.M.S. *Rothesay*
H.M.S. *Londonderry* H.M.S. *Yarmouth*
H.M.S. *Lowestoft*

"Whitby" Class (2,560 tons; 12 officers, 213 ratings; two 4·5-inch guns and two triple Limbo depth-charge mortars)
H.M.S. *Blackpool* H.M.S. *Tenby*
H.M.S. *Eastbourne* H.M.S. *Torquay*
H.M.S. *Scarborough* H.M.S. *Whitby*

"Blackwood" Class, (1,456 tons; 8 officers, 132 ratings;
Type 14 two triple Limbo depth-charge launchers)
H.M.S. *Duncan* H.M.S. *Keppel*
H.M.S. *Dundas* H.M.S. *Malcolm*
H.M.S. *Exmouth* H.M.S. *Palliser*
H.M.S. *Hardy* H.M.S. *Russell*

GENERAL PURPOSE FRIGATES

"Tribal" Class, (2,700 tons; 13 officers, 240 rat-
Type 81 ings; two 4·5-inch guns, two quadruple Seacat missile-launchers, two sextuple 3-inch Mk 4. rocket-launchers (in some ships) and one triple Limbo depth-charge mortar; one Wasp helicopter)

H.M.S. *Ashanti*   H.M.S. *Nubian*
H.M.S. *Eskimo*   H.M.S. *Tartar*
H.M.S. *Gurkha*   H.M.S. *Zulu*
H.M.S. *Mohawk*

AIRCRAFT DIRECTION FRIGATES

"*Salisbury*" Class, Type 61	(2,408 tons; 14 officers, 223 ratings; two 4·5-inch guns, one quadruple Seacat and two sextuple 3-inch Mk 4 rocket-launchers (in *Lincoln* and *Salisbury*) and one triple Squid depth-charge mortar
H.M.S. *Chester*	H.M.S. *Llandaff*
H.M.S. *Lincoln*	H.M.S. *Salisbury*

FAST ANTI-SUBMARINE FRIGATES

Type 15, 1st Rate	(2,880 tons; 15 officers, 180 ratings; two 4-inch guns and two triple Limbo depth-charge mortars in *Ulster* and *Undaunted*)
H.M.S. *Grenville*	H.M.S. *Ulster*
H.M.S. *Rapid*	H.M.S. *Undaunted*

ANTI-AIRCRAFT FRIGATES

"*Leopard*" Class, Type 41	(2,520 tons; 15 officers, 220 ratings; four 4·5-inch guns and one triple Squid depth-charge mortar)
H.M.S. *Jaguar*	H.M.S. *Lynx*
H.M.S. *Leopard*	H.M.S. *Puma*

LOGISTIC LANDING SHIPS

(5,550–5,674 tons; 18 officers, 50 ratings; 340 military personnel; two helicopter pads)

H.M.S. *Sir Lancelot*	H.M.S. *Sir Bedivere*
H.M.S. *Sir Galahad*	H.M.S. *Sir Tristram*
H.M.S. *Sir Geraint*	H.M.S. *Sir Percival*

COASTAL MINESWEEPERS

(425 tons; 5 officers, 31 ratings)

H.M.S. *Ashton*	H.M.S. *Maxton*
H.M.S. *Beachampton*	H.M.S. *Mersey*
H.M.S. *Belton*	H.M.S. *Monckton*
H.M.S. *Bildeston*	H.M.S. *Montrose*
H.M.S. *Bossington*	H.M.S. *Northumbria*
H.M.S. *Brereton*	H.M.S. *Nurton*
H.M.S. *Brinton*	H.M.S. *Puncheston*
H.M.S. *Bronington*	H.M.S. *St. David*
H.M.S. *Chawton*	H.M.S. *Shavington*
H.M.S. *Clyde*	H.M.S. *Sheraton*
H.M.S. *Curzon*	H.M.S. *Shoulton*
H.M.S. *Cuxton*	H.M.S. *Soberton*
H.M.S. *Gavinton*	H.M.S. *Solent*
H.M.S. *Glasserton*	H.M.S. *Stubbington*
H.M.S. *Highburton*	H.M.S. *Thames*
H.M.S. *Hubberston*	H.M.S. *Upton*
H.M.S. *Iveston*	H.M.S. *Venturer*
H.M.S. *Keddleston*	H.M.S. *Walkerton*
H.M.S. *Kellington*	H.M.S. *Wasperton*
H.M.S. *Killiecrankie*	H.M.S. *Wilkieston*
H.M.S. *Kilmorey*	H.M.S. *Wiston*
H.M.S. *Kirkliston*	H.M.S. *Wolverton*
H.M.S. *Laleston*	H.M.S. *Wotton*
H.M.S. *Lewiston*	H.M.S. *Yarnton*
H.M.S. *Maddiston*	

The Westland Sea King anti-submarine helicopter

INSHORE MINESWEEPERS

"Ham" Class   (159 tons; 2 officers, 13 ratings)

H.M.S. *Arlingham*	H.M.S. *Haversham*
H.M.S. *Birdham*	H.M.S. *Lasham*
H.M.S. *Bottisham*	H.M.S. *Odiham*
H.M.S. *Bucklesham*	H.M.S. *Pagham*
H.M.S. *Chelsham*	H.M.S. *Portisham*
H.M.S. *Dittisham*	H.M.S. *Puttenham*
H.M.S. *Downham*	H.M.S. *Shipham*
H.M.S. *Everingham*	H.M.S. *Thakeham*
H.M.S. *Flintham*	H.M.S. *Thatcham*
H.M.S. *Fordham*	H.M.S. *Tongham*
H.M.S. *Fritham*	H.M.S. *Warmingham*

"Ley" Class   (164 tons; 2 officers, 13 ratings)

H.M.S. *Aveley*	H.M.S. *Isis*

In addition to the 206 fighting vessels listed above, the Royal Navy operates just over 400 other vessels. These include maintenance, survey, diving, cable, depot, hospital, repair and support ships, a wide variety of tenders, tugs, oilers and landing craft, mining and countermeasures ships, and fast lightly-armed patrol boats.

RESERVE FORCES

The Royal Navy Regular Reserve consists of certain categories of former career personnel, both commissioned and ratings, who are liable for recall in times of emergency. The Volunteer Reserves, comprising the Royal Naval Reserve, the Woman's Royal Naval Reserve and the Royal Marine Reserve, carry out regular part-time training and provide, in the former case, the complements for a number of operational light vessels such as inshore minesweepers.

NAVAL AIRCRAFT

When the fixed-wing rôle of the Fleet Air Arm is phased out in the mid-1970s some of the combat aircraft currently operated from H.M.S. *Ark Royal* and from shore establishments will be handed over to the Royal Air Force; rotary-winged aircraft will continue to play an important, indeed an increasing part in naval operations.

The current air strength of the Fleet is as follows:

24 McDonnell Douglas F-4K Phantom II fighter/ground attack aircraft

64 (approx.) Hawker Siddeley Buccaneer S.2 low-level strike aircraft

36 Hawker Siddeley Sea Vixen interceptor aircraft organised in a total of nine squadrons. Fairey Gannet airborne early-warning aircraft and Supermarine Scimitar tanker aircraft are operated by several independent flights. Helicopters include 60 Westland Sea King anti-submarine aircraft; 150 Westland Wessex of various marks, both anti-submarine and assault; ninety Westland Wasp general purpose aircraft (due to be replaced over the next three years by 100 Westland WG.13); and a number of miscellaneous types.

COMBAT FORCES: THE BRITISH ARMY

In common with the other two Services the army has recently simplified its command structure. All land forces in the United Kingdom now come under a single command, HQ United Kingdom Land Forces, and are organised in ten military districts (North-West, North-East, Wales, Midlands, Eastern, South-West, South-East, London, Scotland and Northern Ireland). The other major commands are the land element of United Kingdom Mobile Force, the British element of Allied Command Europe (Land), and British Army of the Rhine; in time of crisis both the former are earmarked for NATO service. (A detailed list of the deployment of the main land combat forces, as at 1st April 1972, is given below, after the list of combat units.)

The British Army is organised in a large number of arms and services, of which the most prominent are the Household Cavalry and Royal Armoured Corps, the Foot Guards and Infantry of the Line, the Royal Regiment of Artillery, the Corps of Royal Engineers, the Royal Corps of Signals, the Army Air Corps, the Royal Corps of Transport, the Royal Army Ordnance Corps, the Royal Army Medical Corps and the Royal Electrical and Mechanical Engineers. The Parachute Regiment, and the Special Air Service Regiment, are not organisationally part of the Infantry of the Line.

In the main combat arms – that is, the infantry and the mechanised cavalry – the rapid changes in the techniques and technology of warfare over the past half-century have led to a situation which is not easy to describe succinctly. Briefly, the old numbered infantry regiments of the line used to be exactly that – permanent units which fought side-by-side in the physical line of battle, being grouped into divisions for tactical purposes during any given campaign. In most of the world's armies the philosophy of the mixed-arms formation – the armoured division, for instance, which comprises tank and light armoured units, armoured or lorry-borne infantry, divisional artillery and numerous divisional units of specialists – has spelt the end of the ancient regiments within each combat arm. Centuries-old regional or titular associations have been discarded, and logical sequences of numbered units have taken their place.

In Britain's land forces this has not been so. The very real value, in terms of morale and battlefield performance, of maintaining the identity, traditions and spirit of regiments, which in some cases have colourful and inspiring records reaching back to the 17th century, have been recognised. There have been, necessarily, many amalgamations and some disbandments, in order to make military sense of the available manpower in these days of reduced military forces; but by and large the army has preserved the essential identity of the ancient regiments, their uniform distinctions and rolls of battle-honours, their traditional customs and privileges, and conse-

The new British armoured fighting vehicle, the Scorpion Reconnaissance Tank

quently, and most important of all, their unique *esprit de corps*. The price has been a system of military nomenclature and organisation which most foreigners and many British civilians find bewildering, and which many soldiers would be hard-pressed to describe in logical terms – it is simply there, and it works, and any further understanding seems to be absorbed instinctively rather than academically!

The British infantry "regiment" consists of a base depot, a number of uniform peculiarities, a jealously-guarded record of slaughter and suffering over some two or three hundred years – and nothing else. The infantry "regiment" has no tactical reality. The basic tactical formation is the battalion, comprising perhaps 500 men, bearing a number and the name of the old regiment. There may be one, two or more battalions bearing the name of any regiment at any one time; all follow the uniform distinctions of the regiment, honour its traditions and boast of its record. They are very seldom posted to serve together. They have no common command level. They are assigned to numbered brigades entirely according to the tactical requirements of the situation. Often Territorial (volunteer reserve) battalions are affiliated to a regiment, bearing some title such as "3rd (Volunteer) Bn., The Royal ***shire Regiment". These are mobilised in wartime and assigned to brigades and divisions according to tactical requirements.

If conscription is introduced wholly-new battalions are raised, perhaps around a small cadre of officers and

NCOs detached from a regular battalion of the same regiment, and in the bloodbath of the Western Front during the First World War there were units bearing battalion numbers in the twenties and thirties. When the tactical unit, the actual flesh and blood battalion, is wiped out to a man, the regimental identity is unaffected; another chapter is added to the cherished record, and a new battalion is formed. This is the central idea: that a British regiment can never be destroyed; that the accumulated tradition of centuries is unkillable.

The list of combat units currently operational with the British Army which is given below includes many which have been formed in the past twenty years by the amalgamation of older units. Where this is the case, a footnote gives details.

The Royal Armoured Corps and the Household Cavalry, listed first as is the ancient privilege of the cavalry, are organised in tactical units known as regiments. These are of a size and internal structure roughly comparable to an infantry battalion. The Royal Regiment of Artillery is, tactically, a corps, consisting of a number of numbered regiments, each of which is roughly comparable in size and basic structure to an infantry battalion. The Parachute Regiment is organised into three battalions of parachute infantry, comparable in size and structure to conventional infantry battalions.

The "Divisions" in which the infantry are listed here are not tactical divisions.

Finally, a word of explanation about the Brigade of

Gurkhas, a unique formation in the British or any other army. In the days of the British Raj, the regiments of native troops in the old Indian Army raised among the hill tribes of Nepal and the surrounding areas of the northern Indian sub-continent forged a tradition of toughness, reliability and unswerving loyalty second to none throughout the Empire. A great mutual affection and respect sprang up between the Gurkhas and their British officers, in one of the happiest chapters of the Imperial story, and this mutual regard has never been shaken. So strong was it that it survived the tides of nationalism which swept across India in the 1940s; and after India and Nepal had both become totally independent sovereign states, and the Indian Army had been disbanded, the Nepalese pressed for a continuation of the traditional link. Although much reduced in strength – the four infantry battalions of the Brigade, and their supporting services, now total between 6,000 and 8,000 men – the Gurkhas still serve, as paid regulars in their own special corps, within the British Army. The batallions are officered by a mixture of British and Nepalese. The Brigade is normally based in Hong Kong, with battalions detached to Brunei or other parts of Malaysia, and one battalion is currently based in the United Kingdom.

In the Second World War, the Malayan Emergency of the 1950s and the Malaysian/Indonesian "confrontation" on the 1960s, the Gurkhas proved to be masterly jungle fighters. They are equipped by Britain, and wear British uniform. The unique nature of the Gurkha soldiers' link with the British Crown is paralleled by the unique affection and admiration in which they are held by the rest of the army and by the British public at large.

*　　*　　*　　*

THE HOUSEHOLD CAVALRY

The Life Guards
The Blues and Royals (The Royal Horse
Guards and 1st Dragoons)
(The Royal Horse Guards (The Blues) and The Royal Dragoons (1st Dragoons) were amalgamated in 1969.)

THE ROYAL ARMOURED CORPS

1st The Queen's Dragoon Guards
The Royal Scots Dragoon Guards (Carabiniers
and Greys)[1]
4th/7th Royal Dragoon Guards
5th Royal Inniskilling Dragoon Guards
The Queen's Own Hussars[2]
The Queen's Royal Irish Hussars[3]
9th/12th Royal Lancers (Prince of Wales's)[4]
The Royal Hussars[5]
13th/18th Royal Hussars (Queen Mary's Own)
14th/20th King's Hussars
15th/19th The King's Royal Hussars
16th/5th The Queen's Royal Lancers
17th/21st Lancers
1st, 2nd, 3rd and 4th Royal Tank Regiment

[1] Formed 1971 by amalgamation of The 3rd Carabiniers (Prince of Wales's Dragoon Guards), and The Royal Scots Greys (2nd Dragoons).
[2] Formed 1958 by amalgamation of 3rd The King's Own Hussars, and 7th Queen's Own Hussars.
[3] Formed 1958 by amalgamation of 4th Queen's Own Hussars, and 8th King's Royal Irish Hussars.
[4] Formed 1960 by amalgamation of 9th Queen's Royal Lancers, and 12th Royal Lancers (Prince of Wales's).
[5] Formed 1969 by amalgamation of The 10th Royal Hussars (Prince of Wales's Own) and 11th Hussars (Prince Albert's Own).

A Saladin armoured car of A Squadron,
The Queen's Own Hussars

FOOT GUARDS AND INFANTRY OF THE LINE

The infantry and Foot Guards are listed in Divisions, as follows. The Guards units are equipped in every respect as combat infantry, and fulfil normal infantry duties everywhere in the world; a single battalion is based in the London area, in rotation, to provide ceremonial guards in addition to their normal duties.

GUARDS DIVISION

1st and 2nd Bns., Grenadier Guards
1st and 2nd Bns., Coldstream Guards
1st and 2nd Bns., Scots Guards
1st Bn., Irish Guards
1st Bn., Welsh Guards

THE SCOTTISH DIVISION

1st Bn., The Royal Scots (The Royal Regiment)
1st Bn., The Royal Highland Fusiliers (Princess Margaret's Own Glasgow and Ayrshire Regiment)[6]
1st Bn., The King's Own Scottish Borderers
1st Bn., The Black Watch (Royal Highland Regiment)
1st Bn., The Queen's Own Highlanders (Seaforth and Camerons)[7]
1st Bn., The Gordon Highlanders
1st Bn., The Argyll and Sutherland Highlanders (Princess Louise's)

[6] Formed 1959 by amalgamation of The Royal Scots Fusiliers, and The Highland Light Infantry.
[7] Formed 1961 by amalgamation of The Seaforth Highlanders, and The Queen's Own Cameron Highlanders.

THE QUEEN'S DIVISION

1st, 2nd, 3rd and 4th Bns., The Queen's Regiment[8]
1st, 2nd and 3rd Bns., The Royal Regiment of Fusiliers[9]
1st, 2nd, 3rd and 4th Bns., The Royal Anglian Regiment[10]

[8] "Large regiment" formed 1966 from Home Counties Brigade. *1st Bn.*, formerly The Queen's Royal Surrey Regiment, itself an amalgamation of The Queen's Royal Regiment (West Surrey) and The East Surrey Regiment. *2nd Bn.*, formerly The Queen's Own Buffs, itself an amalgamation of The Buffs (Royal East Kent Regiment) and The Queen's Own Royal West Kent Regiment. *3rd Bn.*, formerly The Royal Sussex Regiment. *4th Bn.*, formerly The Middlesex Regiment, is currently a residual unit of company size, the "Albuera Company", maintaining the existence and traditions of the regiment until such time as the battalion is expanded again to meet defence needs.
[9] "Large regiment" formed 1968 from the Fusilier Brigade. *1st Bn.*, formerly The Royal Northumberland Fusiliers. *2nd Bn.*, formerly The Royal Warwickshire Fusiliers. *3rd Bn.*, formerly The Royal Fusiliers (City of London Regiment).
[10] "Large regiment" formed 1964 from several progressive amalgamations. Original titles of component units: The Royal Norfolk Regiment, The Suffolk Regiment, The Royal Lincolnshire Regiment, The Northamptonshire Regiment, The Bedfordshire and Hertfordshire Regiment, The Essex Regiment, The Royal Leicestershire Regiment.

THE KING'S DIVISION

1st Bn., The King's Own Border Regiment[11]
1st Bn., The King's Regiment (Manchester and Liverpool)[12]
1st Bn., The Prince of Wales's Own Regiment of Yorkshire[13]
1st Bn., The Green Howards (Alexandra, Princess of Wales's Own Yorkshire Regiment)
1st and 2nd Bns., The Royal Irish Rangers[14]
1st Bn., The Duke of Wellington's Regiment (West Riding)

[11] Formed 1959 by amalgamation of The King's Own Royal Regiment (Lancaster), and The Border Regiment.
[12] Formed 1958 by amalgamation of The King's Regiment (Liverpool), and The Manchester Regiment.
[13] Formed 1958 by amalgamation of The West Yorkshire Regiment (The Prince of Wales's Own), and The East Yorkshire Regiment (Duke of York's Own).
[14] Formed 1968 by amalgamation of The Royal Inniskilling Fusiliers, and The Royal Ulster Rifles.

THE PRINCE OF WALES'S DIVISION

1st Bn., The Devonshire and Dorset Regiment[15]
1st Bn., The Cheshire Regiment
1st Bn., The Royal Welsh Fusiliers
1st Bn., The Royal Regiment of Wales[16]
1st Bn., The Gloucestershire Regiment
1st Bn., The Worcestershire and Sherwood Foresters Regiment[17]
1st Bn., The Royal Hampshire Regiment
1st Bn., The Staffordshire Regiment (Prince of Wales's)
1st Bn., The Duke of Edinburgh's Royal Regiment (Berkshire and Wiltshire)[18]

[15] Formed 1958 by amalgamation of The Devonshire Regiment, and The Dorset Regiment.
[16] Formed 1969 by amalgamation of The South Wales Borderers, and The Welsh Regiment.
[17] Formed 1970 by amalgamation of The Worcestershire Regiment, and The Sherwood Foresters (Nottinghamshire and Derbyshire Regiment).
[18] Formed 1959 by amalgamation of The Royal Berkshire Regiment, and The Wiltshire Regiment.

THE LIGHT DIVISION

1st, 2nd, and 3rd Bns., The Light Infantry[19]
1st, 2nd, and 3rd Bns., The Royal Green Jackets[20]

[19] "Large regiment" formed 1968 from the Light Infantry Brigade. *1st Bn.*, formerly The Somerset and Cornwall Light Infantry, an amalgamation of The Somerset Light Infantry (Prince Albert's), and The Duke of Cornwall's Light Infantry. *2nd Bn.*, formerly The King's Own Yorkshire Light Infantry. *3rd Bn.*, formerly The King's Shropshire Light Infantry. *4th Bn.*, formerly The Durham Light Infantry, disbanded 1969.
[20] "Large regiment" formed 1966 from The Green Jackets Brigade. *1st Bn.*, formerly The Oxfordshire and Buckinghamshire Light Infantry. *2nd Bn.*, formerly The King's Royal Rifle Corps. *3rd Bn.*, formerly The Rifle Brigade (Prince Consort's Own).

THE BRIGADE OF GURKHAS

1st Bn., 2nd King Edward VII's Own Goorkhas
1st Bn., 6th Queen Elizabeth's Own Gurkha Rifles
1st Bn., 7th Duke of Edinburgh's Own Gurkha Rifles
1st Bn., 10th Princess Mary's Own Gurkha Rifles

THE ROYAL REGIMENT OF ARTILLERY

A corps of twenty-four numbered Field, Medium, Heavy, Light Air Defence and Heavy Air Defence Regiments, including 1st, 2nd and 3rd Royal Horse Artillery.

THE PARACHUTE REGIMENT

1st, 2nd and 3rd Bns., The Parachute Regiment. Tactically these units are brigaded with parachute artillery, engineer, signals, medical and other service units.

THE SPECIAL AIR SERVICE REGIMENT

Currently one active battalion, *22nd Special Air Service Regiment.* This is a "special forces" unit whose rôle and present operations are classified. In the event of a European war the unit is earmarked for NATO service.
(It is emphasised that for reasons of space, only those units whose primary rôle is offensive have been listed here. There are of course many other specialist units in the Corps of Royal Engineers, the Royal Corps of Signals, and other arms whose rôle involves functioning in the presence of the enemy.)

DEPLOYMENT

Brief details of the deployment of British land forces, as at 1st April 1972, have been published: an extraction is as follows:

Great Britain	United Kingdom Mobile Force, comprising one division, three brigades and one parachute brigade. United Kingdom element of Allied Command Europe Mobile Force (Land). Special Air Service Regiment.
Northern Ireland	Two armoured reconnaissance regiments, fifteen battalion or equivalent units in infantry rôle, three engineer squadrons, one Royal Air Force Regiment squadron.
West Germany	British Army of the Rhine, comprising a corps of three divisions, five armoured brigades, one mechanised brigade and two artillery brigades. Two Royal Air Force Regiment squadrons.
Berlin	One independent infantry brigade.
Hong Kong	Two British infantry battalions, two Gurkha infantry battalions and additional Gurkha units, and one artillery regiment.
Singapore	Infantry battalion group.
Brunei	One Gurkha infantry battalion.
Cyprus	Two infantry battalions, two armoured reconnaissance squadrons, one of each being assigned to the United Nations force and one of each to British sovereign bases.
Gibraltar	One infantry battalion and one independent company.
British Honduras	One infantry battalion.

(One Royal Marine Commando is currently based in Northern Ireland, and one in Malta; smaller detachments are based in the Falkland Islands and in Gibraltar.)

EQUIPMENT

The basic infantry weapons currently issued to the British Army and the Royal Marines consist of the self-loading rifle, the sub-machine-gun, the general purpose machine-gun, and the automatic pistol. The issue sidearm for officers and vehicle crews, etc., is the 9-mm FN-Browning automatic pistol of the type commercially known as the Hi-Power; this has a total capacity of fourteen rounds. The sub-machine-gun, firing the same round as the automatic pistol, is the Sterling; the latest model in service is the L2A3. The rifle is the L1A1 7·62-mm self-loading model, popularly known as the "SLR", a British-made version of the standard NATO weapon. The SLR replaced the manual bolt action 0·303-inch Lee-Enfield Mk 4 rifle in 1958, but numbers of the older rifle are retained for certain special uses, such as sniping, in which its heavy weight and long range accuracy are preferable to the greater volume of fire of the SLR. The magazine capacities of the Sterling and the SLR are thirty and twenty rounds respectively. Stocks of the lightweight American M-16 rifle are held for issue to troops under certain conditions, such as jungle operations. The standard machine-gun, both for infantry and vehicle-mounted use, is the belt-fed 7·62-mm L7A1; stocks of the older magazine-fed Bren LMG, rebarrelled to 7·62-mm calibre, are held for issue to troops in the Far East. In addition to these main weapons, the infantry also have available a wide variety of small projectiles and hand grenades of different types. At platoon and section level anti-tank protection is provided by the 84-mm *Carl Gustav* shoulder-fired weapon; the basic support weapons at battalion level are the 81-mm mortar and the 120-mm recoilless anti-tank gun.

The Royal Armoured Corps is divided into tank and armoured reconnaissance regiments. At the time of writing all but one of the tank regiments had completed replacement of the *Centurion* by the *Chieftain 2* main battle tank, a fifty-one ton vehicle mounting the L11A2 gun of 120-mm calibre. The Leyland L60 diesel engine, developing 650 b.h.p., gives a top speed of around 25 m.p.h. The tank has a range of some 250 miles, carries a crew of four, and has internal stowage for fifty-three rounds of ammunition for the main armament; the main types of projectile carried are the HESH (High Explosive

The Wombat 120 mm recoilless anti-tank weapon

Squash Head) and APDS (Armour Piercing Discarding Sabot) rounds.

Armoured reconnaissance units employ two types of vehicle within the armoured car troop. These are the *Saladin 2* armoured car and the *Ferret* scout car. The *Saladin 2* is a ten-ton six-wheeled vehicle mounting the L5A1 76-mm gun in a fully-revolving turret; with a crew of three, its 160-b.h.p. eight-cylinder Rolls-Royce engine gives a top speed in excess of 45 m.p.h. *Ferret* is a small lightly-armoured scout car mounting a single machine-gun, sometimes supplemented by externally-mounted *Vigilant* or *Swingfire* anti-tank guided missiles; it has a crew of two or three, and a top speed of about 58 m.p.h. Apart from their primary reconnaissance mission both these vehicles have been, and are still widely used in a variety of security rôles.

Since the 1950s the basic armoured personnel carrier (APC) has been the *Saracen*, a six-wheeled vehicle bearing a close similarity in the fundamentals of design to *Saladin*. It carries a driver, commander, radio operator and infantry section of nine men. *Saracen* has now been replaced as the primary transport of the infantry battalion within an armoured brigade by *FV432*, a fully-enclosed, fully-tracked vehicle of roughly similar load carrying capacity. *Saracen* remains in service in a wide variety of general purpose and security rôles.

A new and remarkable series of fully-tracked armoured fighting vehicles is currently in production for the Army, and the first armoured reconnaissance regiment is due to be re-equipped with them in 1972–73, in place of *Saladin* and various other light armoured vehicles of a specialised nature. The basic vehicle is *Scorpion* CVR(T), an eight-ton, three-man reconnaissance tank mounting a 76-mm gun in a fully-revolving turret. A modified 4·2-litre Jaguar XK engine gives it a top speed in the region of 50–60 m.p.h. Due to its very light weight, achieved by the use of aluminium alloy armour with a superior strength/weight ratio and of new construction techniques, the tank is fully air-portable. A "family" of specialised vehicles based on this design will include the *Spartan* light-armoured personnel carrier, the *Striker* anti-tank guided missile vehicle, the *Samaritan* ambulance vehicle, the *Sultan* armoured command vehicle, the *Samson* armoured recovery vehicle, and the *Scimitar* reconnaissance tank – this latter being similar to *Scorpion* but mounting the 30-mm Rarden high-velocity cannon in place of the 76-mm main armament. This extremely powerful weapon, with very high penetrative power at long range, is also the main armament of the *Fox* four-wheeled armoured car, soon to replace *Ferret*.

The Royal Artillery and Royal Horse Artillery are equipped according to posting and function; artillery elements of BAOR are self-propelled, in keeping with their mission as integral parts of the armoured and mechanised group. The main equipment of the artillery consists of the 105-mm pack howitzer and the *Abbot* SP gun of similar calibre (Field Regiments); the 5·5-inch gun (Medium Regiments); and the 155-mm, 8-inch and 175-mm SP guns (Heavy Regiments). Several different types of missile are held by the artillery, including the *Honest John*; together with the 8-inch howitzer, this provides a tactical nuclear capability. Air defence elements operate the mobile *Thunderbird* and *Rapier* guided missile systems.

ARMY AIRCRAFT

The Army Air Corps operates in a series of rôles, primarily reconnaissance, communications, liaison and light transport, although there is a light fire-support capability. Squadrons are attached according to tactical requirements to land forces, usually at brigade level. Current equipment includes some 150 Westland Scout helicopters, due for replacement by 250 Westland WG.13 helicopters during the early 1970s; 175 Westland 47G Sioux helicopters, likewise due for replacement by 300 Westland-Sud SA.340 Gazelles; and a number of Sud Alouette II and Bell G4 helicopters. Some 40 de Havilland Canada DHC-2 Beaver light utility transport aircraft are also in service. The Corps has only a small permanent establishment, and most personnel are on secondment from other corps and regiments.

RESERVE FORCES

Personnel who have completed the Colour term of their enlistment with the regular forces are retained on the Regular Army Reserve for an additional term, according to the type of enlistment they originally chose, and for that period are liable for recall to the Colours. Thereafter they transfer to the Long Term Reserve until they reach the age of 45, and are liable to recall in an emergency. The Territorial and Army Volunteer Reserve consists of independent units raised on a regional basis and affiliated to regular units; personnel train regularly in their spare time, and receive certain bounties. In time of emergency these forces would be mobilised to reinforce the regular forces. The current strength of the T & AVR is approximately 56,300.

COMBAT FORCES:
THE ROYAL AIR FORCE

The recent re-alignments and re-deployments of British military formations have seen an end of two major R.A.F. overseas commands – Air Forces Gulf and Far East Air Force. The basic structure of the R.A.F. now consists of four main divisions: Strike Command, Air Support Command, Maintenance Command and Training Command. The picture will shortly be simplified further by the amalgamation of Strike and Air Support Commands, bringing the R.A.F.'s general purpose combat forces all over the world into a single operational framework.

Strike Command is responsible for the air defence of the United Kingdom, and consists of the main strike, attack, interceptor, reconnaissance, maritime patrol and anti-submarine warfare forces based in the United Kingdom. *Air Support Command* comprises the bulk of the transport and tanker fleet, with some integral fighter, ground attack and tactical reconnaissance units; it is based in the United Kingdom, and is responsible for the air mobility of the forces as a whole, and for the rapid deployment of

its combat element overseas according to tactical requirements. *RAF Germany* is the major overseas command, and is assigned to NATO as part of the allied tactical air forces. *Near East Air Force*, based in Cyprus, is predominantly a reconnaissance, maritime patrol and anti-submarine warfare command fulfilling British commitments to the southern flank of the NATO defences and to CENTO. A maritime patrol element operates from Singapore as part of the five-nation defence force in the Far East, and combat units make frequent temporary visits to Hong Kong, Singapore and other Far East locations.

Due to the recent reorganisations, the temporary nature of certain postings, and the requirements of security, it has not been thought desirable to give a full list of R.A.F. deployments at the time of writing, although full details – accurate as of August 1971 – have been published elsewhere. The four main operational commands dispose of a total of some eighty numbered squadrons. In 1971–72 their comparative strength was a follows:

AIR SUPPORT COMMAND	Twelve transport squadrons Three fighter/strike squadrons One fixed-wing *plus* three helicopter communications/general duties squadrons
STRIKE COMMAND	Five heavy bomber squadrons One strike bomber squadron Five fighter/strike squadrons Six reconnaissance squadrons Five maritime patrol/anti-submarine squadrons One transport squadron One fixed-wing *plus* one helicopter communications/general duties squadron
RAF GERMANY	Eight fighter/strike squadrons One strike bomber squadron Two reconnaissance squadrons One fixed-wing *plus* one helicopter communications/general duties squadron
NEAR EAST AIR FORCE	One mixed fighter/strike, reconnaissance squadron Two heavy bomber squadrons One reconnaissance squadron One maritime patrol/anti-submarine squadron One transport squadron

The forces withdrawn from the Persian Gulf and Far East areas during 1971–72, and since redeployed under the other four commands, are believed to total:

Three fighter/strike squadrons
Three helicopter communications/ general duties squadrons
One transport squadron

The Hawker Siddeley Harrier GR.1, the world's first, and so far only operational vertical take-off close-support strike fighter

EQUIPMENT

The following list of the main aircraft types operated by each operational R.A.F. squadron is believed to be accurate at the time of writing, but by the time these words are published certain changes are inevitable. At least one additional squadron of Hawker Siddeley Harrier vertical/short take-off fighter/ground attack/reconnaissance aircraft, and one further squadron of Hawker Siddeley Buccaneer S.2B low-level strike bombers will be added to **RAF GERMANY** in 1972.

No.	*1 Squadron*	*Hawker Siddeley Harrier*
No.	*2 Squadron*	*McDonnell Douglas Phantom*
No.	*3 Squadron*	*Hawker Siddeley Harrier*
No.	*4 Squadron*	*Hawker Siddeley Harrier*
No.	*5 Squadron*	*B.A.C. Lightning*
No.	*6 Squadron*	*McDonnell Douglas Phantom*
No.	*7 Squadron*	*B.A.C. Canberra*
No.	*8 Squadron*	*Hawker Siddeley Shackleton*
No.	*9 Squadron*	*Hawker Siddeley Vulcan*
No.	*10 Squadron*	*B.A.C. VC-10*
No.	*11 Squadron*	*B.A.C. Lightning*
No.	*12 Squadron*	*Hawker Siddeley Buccaneer*
No.	*13 Squadron*	*B.A.C. Canberra*
No.	*14 Squadron*	*McDonnell Douglas Phantom*
No.	*15 Squadron*	*Hawker Siddeley Buccaneer*
No.	*16 Squadron*	*Hawker Siddeley Buccaneer*
No.	*17 Squadron*	*McDonnell Douglas Phantom*
No.	*18 Squadron*	*Westland Wessex*
No.	*19 Squadron*	*B.A.C. Lightning*
No.	*20 Squadron*	*Hawker Siddeley Harrier*

No.	*21 Squadron*	{*Hawker Siddeley Devon* / *Hunting Pembroke*
No.	*22 Squadron*	*Westland Whirlwind*
No.	*23 Squadron*	*B.A.C. Lightning*
No.	*24 Squadron*	*Lockheed Hercules*
No.	*26 Squadron*	{*Beagle Basset* / *Hawker Siddeley Devon*
No.	*27 Squadron*	*Hawker Siddeley Vulcan*
No.	*28 Squadron*	*Westland Whirlwind*
No.	*29 Squadron*	*B.A.C. Lightning*
No.	*30 Squadron*	*Lockheed Hercules*
No.	*31 Squadron*	*McDonnell Douglas Phantom*
No.	*32 Squadron*	*Various general-duty aircraft*
No.	*33 Squadron*	*Sud-Westland Puma*
No.	*35 Squadron*	*Hawker Siddeley Vulcan*
No.	*36 Squadron*	*Lockheed Hercules*
No.	*37 Squadron*	*Hawker Siddeley Nimrod*
No.	*39 Squadron*	*B.A.C. Lightning*
No.	*41 Squadron*	*McDonnell Douglas Phantom*
No.	*42 Squadron*	*Hawker Siddeley Nimrod*
No.	*43 Squadron*	*McDonnell Douglas Phantom*
No.	*44 Squadron*	*Hawker Siddeley Vulcan*
No.	*46 Squadron*	*Hawker Siddeley Andover*
No.	*47 Squadron*	*Lockheed Hercules*
No.	*48 Squadron*	{*Lockheed Hercules* / *Hawker Siddeley Andover*
No.	*50 Squadron*	*Hawker Siddeley Vulcan*
No.	*51 Squadron*	*Hawker Siddeley Nimrod*
No.	*53 Squadron*	*Short Belfast*
No.	*54 Squadron*	*McDonnell Douglas Phantom*
No.	*55 Squadron*	*Handley-Page Victor*

No. 56 Squadron	*B.A.C. Lightning, B.A.C. Canberra*
No. 57 Squadron	*Handley-Page Victor*
No. 60 Squadron	*Various general-duty aircraft*
No. 63 Squadron	*Hawker Siddeley Hunter*
No. 64 Squadron	*McDonnell Douglas Phantom*
No. 65 Squadron	*B.A.C. Lightning*
No. 70 Squadron	*Lockheed Hercules*
No. 72 Squadron	*Westland Wessex*
No. 74 Squadron	*B.A.C. Lightning*
No. 78 Squadron	*Westland Wessex*
No. 79 Squadron	*Hawker Siddeley Hunter*
No. 84 Squadron	*Hawker Siddeley Andover*
No. 85 Squadron	*B.A.C. Canberra*
No. 92 Squadron	*B.A.C. Lightning*
No. 98 Squadron	*B.A.C. Canberra*
No. 99 Squadron	*B.A.C. Britannia*
No. 101 Squadron	*Hawker Siddeley Vulcan*
No. 103 Squadron	*Westland Whirlwind*
No. 111 Squadron	*B.A.C. Lightning*
No. 114 Squadron	*Lockheed Hercules*
No. 115 Squadron	*Lockheed Hercules*
No. 120 Squadron	*Hawker Siddeley Nimrod*
No. 145 Squadron	*B.A.C. Lightning*
No. 201 Squadron	*Hawker Siddeley Nimrod*
No. 202 Squadron	*Westland Whirlwind*
No. 203 Squadron	*Hawker Siddeley Nimrod*
No. 204 Squadron	*Hawker Siddeley Shackleton*
No. 206 Squadron	*Hawker Siddeley Nimrod*
No. 207 Squadron	*Various general-duty aircraft*
No. 208 Squadron	*Hawker Siddeley Hunter*
No. 210 Squadron	*Hawker Siddeley Shackleton*
No. 214 Squadron	*Handley-Page Victor*
No. 216 Squadron	*Hawker Siddeley Comet*
No. 230 Squadron	*Sud-Westland Puma*

No. 234 Squadron	*Hawker Siddeley Hunter*
No. 360 Squadron	*B.A.C. Canberra*
No. 511 Squadron	*B.A.C. Britannia*
No. 543 Squadron	*Handley-Page Victor*
No. 617 Squadron	*Hawker Siddeley Vulcan*

BRIEF DETAILS OF AIRCRAFT IN SERVICE

Hawker Siddeley Harrier GR Mark 1. Single-seat, vertical/short take-off and landing, close-support and tactical reconnaissance aircraft – the only operational V/STOL aircraft in the world (other than helicopters). Powered by one Rolls-Royce-Bristol Pegasus Mk. 101 vectored-thrust turbofan, 19,000 lb.s.l.s.t. Five armament points under fuselage and wings, plus two optional attachment points under fuselage for 30-mm Aden cannon packs. Wide variety of offensive stores, reconnaissance equipment and fuel pods can be carried; typical load, two Aden guns and one 1,000-lb. bomb under fuselage, two 1,000-lb. bombs on inboard wing pylons, and two Matra rocket launchers each carrying nineteen 68-mm SNEB projectiles on outboard wing pylons. Fuselage and inboard pylons stressed to 2,000 lb. each, outboard pylons to 650 lb. each. Maximum diving speed, approx. Mach 1·3; maximum low altitude level speed, approx. 740 m.p.h. Ceiling, in excess of 50,000 feet; unrefuelled range, 2,300 miles; some one hundred aircraft in service (including some two-seat trainers, the T.Mk. 2), plus approx. twenty more on order at the time of writing.

The supersonic Jaguar strike fighter, designed and built by the British Aircraft Corporation and Breguet Aviation. Capable of carrying a very wide range of weapons and equipped with comprehensive navigation/attack equipment, it will represent Europe's most advanced military aircraft when it enters service with the Royal Air Force in 1973–74

McDonnell Douglas Phantom FGR Mark 2. (British version of the F-4M.) Two-seat all-weather fighter and strike aircraft powered by two Rolls-Royce Spey turbofans, each of 12,500 lb.s.l.s.t. Wide variety of bombs, gun packs, rocket packs, missiles and reconnaissance equipment can be carried on under-fuselage and wing pylons, to a total of about 16,000 lb. Typical loads include eighteen 750-lb. bombs; eleven 1,000-lb. bombs; or eleven 150-gallon napalm tanks, etc. Nuclear stores can be carried. Maximum level speed with warload, in excess of Mach 2. Combat ceiling, 71,000 feet. Some 140 aircraft in service, plus 24 Royal Navy machines (due to be handed over when Fleet Air Arm runs down fixed-wing rôle).

B.A.C. Lightning F Mark 1 – F Mark 7. Single-seat all-weather interceptor, strike and reconnaissance aircraft powered by two Rolls-Royce Avon turbojets each of 16,300 lb.s.l.s.t. Wide variety of offensive stores, reconnaissance equipment and fuel pods may be carried on under- and over-wing pylons and in under-fuselage packs. Pairs of Red Top or Firestreak air-to-air infra-red seeking missiles, or multi-rocket launchers, or 30-mm Aden gun packs may be carried under the fuselage; the two underwing pylons can accommodate two 1,000-lb. bombs each, a variety of missiles, or twin machine-gun packs. The two overwing pylons, from which stores can be released upwards by an ejector system at very low level, can each accommodate one 1,000-lb. store, missile launchers or fuel pods. Maximum level speed at operational altitude, in excess of Mach 2. Operational ceiling, in excess of 70,000 feet. Time to operational altitude, 2·5 minutes. Some 100 aircraft in service.

B.A.C. Canberra B Mark 2, B I Mark 8, B Mark 15, B Mark 16, P.R. Mark 16, T Mark 4 etc. Many versions of this venerable and much-developed twin-jet bomber are retained in service in many secondary rôles.

Hawker Siddeley Hunter FGA Mark 9. Single-seat, single-jet fighter which has formed the mainstay of fighter/ground-attack force for sixteen years; small numbers still in squadron service awaiting early replacement by *B.A.C.-Breguet Jaguar* strike aircraft within next two years (164 *Jaguars* are on order for the R.A.F.).

Hawker Siddeley Vulcan B Mark 2. Heavy nuclear and tactical bomber, powered by four Rolls-Royce Olympus 301 turbojets, each of 20,000 lb.s.l.s.t. Usual warload, Blue Steel nuclear stand-off bomb. Maximum speed, approx. 645 m.p.h. (Mach 0·98); cruising speed at 55,000 feet, 620 m.p.h. Combat radius, unrefuelled, approx. 2,300 miles. Fifty aircraft in service.

B.A.C. VC-10 C Mark 1. Royal Air Force version of the civil airliner, in service with Air Support Command. Powered by four Rolls-Royce Conway turbofans, the military *VC-10* can carry some 150 passengers. Maximum payload is 57,400 lb. Range with maximum payload, cruising at 425 m.p.h. at 30,000 feet, is 3,900 miles. Fourteen aircraft in service.

Hawker Siddeley Buccaneer S Mark 2. Two-seat strike bomber, designed for sustained near-sonic flight at sea level, powered by two Rolls-Royce Spey turbofans each of 11,100 lb.s.l.s.t. Rotating bomb-bay can carry extra fuel, a variety of camera equipment, or weapons. Additional wing pylons can each accommodate: one 1,000-lb. bomb; two 500-lb. bombs; one 18 × 68-mm rocket pod; one 36 × 2-inch rocket pod; one HSD-Matra Martel air-to-surface missile, etc. Maximum design level speed at 200 feet, 645 m.p.h. Strike range, 2,300 miles. Between 35 and 50 aircraft in service (more on order), plus 64 Royal Navy aircraft due for handover to R.A.F. when F.A.A. runs down fixed-wing rôle.

Westland Wessex HC Mark 2 and 10; Westland Whirlwind HC Mark 10; Sud-Westland SA. 330 Puma HC Mark 1 general duties helicopters. Some 70 Wessex and more than 40 Puma in service (plus further Puma on order). Last Whirlwinds are due for replacement by Wessex during 1972–73.

Lockheed Hercules C Mark 1. British service version of C-130H and K. Transport aircraft powered by four Allison T56-A-15 turboprops, each of 4,910 e.s.h.p. Maximum payload, 45,000 lb. Hold volume, 4,500 cubic feet; can carry 92 troops or 64 paratroopers. Maximum speed at maximum take-off weight, 384 m.p.h. Range at maximum payload, 2,450 miles. Sixty-six aircraft in service.

Hawker Siddeley Nimrod MR Mark 1. Maritime patrol, anti-submarine and reconnaissance aircraft derived from the *Comet 4C* airliner. Powered by four Rolls-Royce Spey Mark 250 turbofans each of 11,500 lb.s.l.s.t., the *Nimrod* has a maximum speed of 575 m.p.h. and a range in excess of 5,000 miles. Normal crew is twelve, but forty-five can be carried. A wide range of weapons can be carried, including Martel missiles; there are two wing attachment points in addition to the 50-foot-long internal bomb-bay. Some 40 aircraft in service.

Hawker Siddeley Andover CC Mark 2. Military transport version of *HS 748* short-medium range twin-turboprop airliner. Powered by two Rolls-Royce Dart engines, the *Andover* has accommodation for 58 passengers and a maximum payload of 11,800 lb. Range with maximum payload, 530 miles; take-off run at maximum weight, 2,710 feet. Cruising speed, 278 m.p.h. Ceiling, 25,000 feet. Some 30 aircraft in service.

Short Belfast C Mark 1. Heavy transport aircraft powered by four Rolls-Royce Tyne turboprops, each of 5,730 e.s.h.p. Maximum payload, 78,000 lb. Hold volume, 11,000 cubic feet. Range, 5,300 miles. Ceiling, 30,000 feet. Cruising speed at 24,000 feet, 350 m.p.h. Ten aircraft in service.

Other equipment includes twenty *B.A.C. Britannia* and six *Hawker Siddeley Comet 4* transports, and numbers of communications and general duty types such as the *B.A.C. Pembroke* and *Varsity*, the *Hawker Siddeley Dove, Heron* and *Dominie*; and training types such as the *B.A.C. Jet Provost* and *Hawker Siddeley Gnat.*

RESERVE FORCES

The Regular Reserve is made up of former career officers and men, some detailed for specific tasks in an emergency, and all liable for recall. The Royal Auxiliary Air Force comprises three maritime HQ units which would, in an emergency, reinforce Strike Command; the Royal Air Force Volunteer Reserve includes sixteen University Air Squadrons who are required to take regular training. Both are subject to call-up in an emergency.

The anti-submarine frigate, H.M.S. Rothesay, *2,800 tons, refuelling a Westland Wessex 3 helicopter*

Index